BODY COUNT: GLOBAL AVOIDABLE MORTALITY SINCE 1950

KP

First edition (2007). ISBN: 1921377051.

Second edition (2021). ISBN: 978-87-93987-83-8.

Book cover & editing by Søren Roest Korsgaard.

CONTENTS

DETAILED CONTENTS

"Over the expanse of five continents throughout the coming years an endless struggle is going to be pursued between violence and friendly persuasion, a struggle in which, granted, the former has a thousand times the chances of success than that of the latter. But I have always held that, if he who bases his hopes on human nature is a fool, he who gives up in the face of circumstances is a coward. And henceforth, the only honorable course will be to stake everything on a formidable gamble: that words are more powerful than munitions."

Albert Camus in *Neither Victims nor Executioners* (1946).[1]

"Article 55. To the fullest extent of the means available to it, the Occupying Power has the duty of ensuring the food and medical supplies of the population; it should, in particular, bring in the necessary foodstuffs, medical stores and other articles if the resources of the occupied territory are inadequate ...

Article 56. To the fullest extent of the means available to it, the Occupying Power has the duty of ensuring and maintaining, with the cooperation of the national and local authorities, the medical and hospital establishments and services, public health and hygiene in the occupied territory, with particular reference to the adoption and application of the prophylactic and preventive measures necessary to combat the spread of contagious diseases and epidemics. Medical personnel of all categories shall be allowed to carry out their duties...".

Geneva Convention relative to the Protection of Civilian Persons in Time of War (1950).[2]

"We hold these truths to be self-evident, that all men are created equal, that they are endowed by their Creator with certain unalienable Rights, that among these are Life, Liberty, and the pursuit of Happiness."

American Declaration of Independence (1776).[3]

"... consider the dreadful nature of the suspicions you have entertained. What have you been judging from? Remember the country and the age in which we live. Remember that we are English, that we are Christians. Consult your own understanding, your own sense of the probable, your own observation of what is passing around you. Does our education prepare us for such atrocities? Do our laws connive at them? Could they be perpetrated without being known, in a country like this, where social and literary intercourse is on such a footing, where every man is surrounded by a neighborhood of voluntary spies, and where roads and newspapers lay everything open?"

Henry Tilney to Catherine Morland in *Northanger Abbey* by Jane Austen.[4]

"We have come into this world to accept it, not merely to know it. We may become powerful through knowledge, but we attain fullness through sympathy."

Rabindranath Tagore quoted in *Moloch* by Henry Miller.[5]

8.16 APPENDIX – State of the World (2003) in relation to population, mortality, excess mortality, under-5 infant mortality and HIV/AIDS
Tables 8.1-8.12

9. Progress by 2020 but urgent action needed on global avoidable mortality and key existential threats

9.1 Insufficient action on the existential threats from climate change and nuclear weapons
9.2 Carbon Price, Cabon Debt, and costing air pollution deaths and avoidable deaths
 9.3 Infant mortality has halved in 17 years but 96% of avoidable mortality occurs in non-European countries
9.4 Poverty kills as revealed by comparing regional wealth and avoidable mortality
9.5 Entitlement of everyone in the World to a modest survival in a decent life
9.6 Solutions – sustainable social humanism (eco-socialism) not neoliberalism, global annual wealth tax, aid, debt relief, and a one-person-one-vote World Parliament
9.7 APPENDIX – State of the World (2020) in relation to population, under-5 infant mortality and avoidable mortality
Tables 9.1-9.12

TABLES

PREFACE (2007)

All human life is precious. Decent humans endeavor to preserve human life, albeit with a declining sense of urgency (or increasing *disregard*) as we progress from the immediate family, to the state and thence to the world as a whole.

Avoiding mortality is clearly a primary goal of humanity and this book is about how and why the world has performed very badly in this quest over the last half century. Fundamentally, avoiding mortality requires sensible risk management, this involving the successive processes of reportage, scientific analysis and systemic change. Unfortunately, in most areas of human activity this "World's Best Practice" protocol is replaced by its counterproductive obverse, namely (a) lack of reportage through censorship, self-censorship and intimidation); (b) politicized, corrupted and self-serving analysis; and (c) vengeful or cynical punishment of suitable culprits (rather than useful, risk-minimizing changes to flawed human systems). In the final analysis, we have to make sensible judgments about *risks* to human life and the *proportionality* and *effectiveness* of our responses.

This book exposes the horrendous extent of global avoidable mortality that has totaled 1.3 billion since 1950, a figure consonant with an independent estimate of post-1950 under-5 infant mortality totaling about 0.9 billion. A broad attempt is made to rationalize this catastrophe. A major determinant is clearly war, foreign occupation and consequent increased *disregard* of rulers for their subjects. The last few pages of this book list positive suggestions for addressing the global avoidable mortality holocaust. The contents of this book are systematically organized as outlined in Detailed Contents with countries in the major regions dealt with in alphabetical order. Accordingly there is no subject index provided.

I would urge the readers of this book to personally humanize the avoidable mortality statistics with reference to their own experience of immediate family, the wider community and of people around the world. Further, Edmund Burke famously stated that evil occurs because of good men doing nothing. We can *all* do something *immediately* by *informing others* and through *ethical dealings* with people, corporations and countries contributing to the horrendous global avoidable mortality holocaust - a holocaust which is fundamentally due to violence, deprivation, disease and *lying*.

Peace is the only way but silence kills and silence is complicity. We cannot walk by on the other side.

Dr Gideon Polya

Melbourne, May, 2007

PREFACE (2021)

This second, revised and updated edition of "Body Count: Global Avoidable Mortality Since 1950" has come about due to urging over several years by humanitarian activist and publisher Søren Roest Korsgaard. This revised edition involves some important additions to the first edition that are set out below.

A new final Chapter 9 includes 12 Tables that record estimations (from pre-Covid -19 Pandemic, 2019 UN projections for 2020) of population, "under-5 infant mortality" and "avoidable mortality" ("excess mortality') for 2020 in the absence of the Covid-19 Pandemic. It thus represents an important comparative benchmark for post-Covid-19 demographic changes, as well as comparing how each country and region has performed in these areas over the last 17 years.

Every section, including each of the succinct, avoidable mortality-related "short histories" of about 200 countries, concludes with a "2021 update" that updates the latest key events and provides key relevant statistics for 2020 that indicate how each country has performed in relation to the 2003 data set of the first edition.[6]

For each country the "2021 update" compares the pre-Covid-19 projected 2020 "under-5 infant mortality as a percentage of total population" (a) with that for Japan (the best performing country), and (b) with that in 2003 (to see how things have improved in the last 17 years).

The good news is that global annual "under-5 infant mortality as a percentage of total population" has roughly halved since 2003, but the bad news is that an appalling 5.3 million under-5 year old infants still die each year, and mostly avoidably.

It should be noted that the updating Tables in the new Chapter 9 report "avoidable mortality as a percentage of total global population" that was crudely estimated for 2020 as 1.4 times the exactly determined "under-5 infant mortality as a percentage of total population" for each country. This simplifying common factor of 1.4 was chosen because in 2003 the global avoidable mortality (laboriously estimated for each country by an exacting process)[6] was about 1.4 times the under-5 infant mortality.

Humanity and the Biosphere are existentially threatened by (a) man-made climate change (unless requisite action is taken 10 billion people will die in a worsening Climate Genocide en route to a sustainable human population in 2100 of only 1 billion),[7] and (b) by nuclear weapons (a post-nuclear exchange nuclear winter threatens to decimate Humanity and the Biosphere).[8]

Indeed one of Humanity's greatest minds, Stephen Hawking, has concluded "We see great peril if governments and societies do not take action now to render nuclear weapons obsolete and to prevent further climate change."[9]

Accordingly, the "2021 updates" include for each country (a) a "revised annual greenhouse gas (GHG) pollution in tonnes CO_2-equivalent per person per year" (taking land use into account and assuming a methane Global Warming Potential of 105 on a 20 year time frame and with aerosol impacts considered)[10] together a brief mention where pertinent of contributing factors (e.g. fossil fuel use, methanogenic livestock production, deforestation); and (b) ratification or otherwise of the 2021 UN Treaty on Prohibition of Nuclear Weapons (TPNW) that came into force for States Parties on 22 January 2021.[11]

Each national "2021 update" also includes the per capita GDP (nominal) in US dollars (UN, 2019)[12] for each country (because poverty kills), and "Covid-19 deaths per million of population"[13] as a mixed indicator of ability to act and of intra-national altruism.[14]

Finally I must record my deep gratitude to humanitarian activist and publisher Søren Roest Korsgaard for his enthusiasm, dedication and technical skill in driving this humanitarian project. Peace is the only way but silence kills and silence is complicity. We cannot walk by on the other side.

Dr Gideon Polya

Melbourne, March, 2021

CHAPTER 1: INTRODUCTION – GLOBAL AVOIDABLE MORTALITY

"What are a few hundred thousand to the Multitudians, whose myriads are countless?! A loss that goes unnoticed is no loss at all."

The Multitudians to the Great Constructor Trurl in *The Cyberiad* by Stanislaw Lem.[1]

"But the main thing he sees is that the whole system of the world is built on a lie."

Jake in *The Heart is a Lonely Hunter* by Carson McCullers.[2]

"In the standard of life they have nothing to spare. The slightest fall from the present standard of life in India means slow starvation, and the actual squeezing out of life, not only of millions but of scores of millions of people, who have come into the world at your invitation and under the shield and protection of British power."

Winston Churchill, speech to the House of Commons (1935).[3]

"But the agony of European Jewry was enacted in a separate moral arena, a grim twilight world where their conventional ethical moral code did not apply. And so they "came and looked, and passed by on the other side"".

Bernard Wasserstein on British Establishment moral perception of the Jewish Holocaust.[4]

"Le scandale du monde est ce que fait l'offence, Et ce n'est pas pécher que pécher en silence (It is public scandal that constitutes offence, and to sin in secret is not to sin at all)."

Molière (Jean-Baptiste Poquelin) in *Le Tartuffe.*[5]

1.1 Science & history – history ignored yields history repeated

Humanity has made immense strides over the last few millennia through rational investigation of the world. Scientific analysis of the world involves truth, reason, free communication and application of the scientific method involving generating and critically testing potentially falsifiable hypotheses.[6] Departure from this methodology de-rails the scientific process (although as analysed by Kuhn[7], Koestler[8] and others there are other ways of approaching reality and "right brain" mysticism, aesthetics and poetry have been important in the *genesis* of some radical new views of reality leading to major scientific breakthroughs).

Critically, lying by omission (ignoring, rubbing out, deleting or hiding the data) or lying by commission (falsifying the data) are fundamentally inimical to understanding reality. This is particularly true in scientific approaches to history and human affairs. "Rubbing out" data relating to mass human mortality greatly increases the probability of the recurrence of such events. Thus we are familiar with the adage "history ignored yields history repeated"[9] and the post-Jewish Holocaust (Shoah) resolution "Never again" of the Jewish people. Indeed in this same spirit, Germany, France, Austria, Switzerland and Israel have made holocaust denial illegal (albeit only in relation to the Jewish Holocaust).

While we are all aware of the horror and magnitude of the Jewish Holocaust (6 million victims) we shall see that other immense, man-made mass mortality events have been deleted from history even as they were happening.

1.2 Deleting history – the "forgotten", man-made, WW2 Bengal Famine

Even in the liberal Anglo-Celtic democracies, huge, man-made mass mortality events continue to be "rubbed out" of history books, media offerings and hence from general public perception. Thus during World War 2 (WW2) in British-ruled India there was an immense man-made, economic, "market forces" famine in the major province of Bengal that killed an estimated 4 million Hindu and Muslim victims in Bengal and killed 6-7 million Indians in Bengal and the adjoining provinces of Assam, Bihar and Orissa. In essence, a number of factors had led to an increase in the price of rice, the Bengali staple. Those who could not afford the ultimate 4-fold increase in the price of rice simply perished in the context of callous foreign rule.

Major factors contributing to the increase in the price of rice included a huge decrease in Indian grain imports, Japanese occupation of rice-producing areas of Burma, decreases in rice production due to storm and fungal pathogen infection, British strategic seizure of boats, British sequestration of some food stocks, a massive decrease in Indian Ocean Allied shipping (in turn due to the successive events of strategically erroneous Allied bombing of Germany, decreased protection of Atlantic convoys and big losses of Allied shipping), granting of provincial autonomy over their own grain reserves (a divide and rule policy), deliberate British ignoring of the Famine Codes for "political reasons", hoarding, and racist British administrative lethargy. Calcutta was a major industrial city undergoing a war-time boom and essentially sucked food out of a starving, food-producing countryside.[10]

Keeping the Indians half-starved was evidently a successful British control policy over 2 centuries. However it has been suggested that the real reason for the Bengal Famine was a cold-blooded, deliberate scorched earth policy so that any Japanese invasion of India from Burma would encounter a starving countryside[11] - rather akin to the highly successful British strategy by Sir Arthur Wellesley (later Lord Wellington) against the French under Masséna in the defence of Lisbon in 1811 during the Napoleonic Wars).[12]

Civilian and military sexual exploitation of starving women and girls involved some 30,000 victims in Calcutta alone, possibly hundreds of thousands throughout Bengal and was so large as to impact upon female survival statistics. The involvement of the British Military Labour Corps in this famine-enforced violation of women and girls demands comparison with the notorious WW2 "comfort women" abuses of the Japanese Imperial Army.[13]

Remarkably, this horrendous, man-made disaster that occurred at the same time as the Jewish Holocaust and killed a similar number of people has been largely "rubbed out" of British history books and from general public perception – it represents a major "forgotten holocaust" because "history is written by the victor". The reader can readily estimate the extent of this continuing British academic, politician and media holocaust-denial by scanning relevant texts in their personal, local, city or university libraries.

Bengal is well-watered, has rich soil, an energetic population and abundant sunshine. It is definitely one part of South Asia that should be famine-proof. However a dozen years after the conquest of Bengal by Robert Clive (at the Battle of Plassey, 1757), a man-made famine in 1769-1770, precipitated by food shortage and exacerbated by rapacious British taxation, killed 10 million Bengalis or one third of the population. Yet the Great Bengal Famine is substantially deleted from British history and when rarely mentioned is dismissed in a few words. During the subsequent 2 centuries, Bengal (as well as other parts of British-ruled India) was swept by repeated famines, with this culminating in the "forgotten" WW2 Bengal Famine.

In 1971 the US-armed and US-backed military regime in West Pakistan overturned the results of a democratic election and invaded East Pakistan (the future Bangladesh). 3 million Bengalis were killed and 0.3 million Bengali women and girls raped.[14] However an even worse disaster now faces Bengal due to the consequences of First World industrial profligacy, namely inundation of this substantially deltaic country from the successive consequences of global warming, sea level rises, increases in cyclonic intensity and storm surges (a fate threatening other tropical delta regions including southern Thailand, parts of China and the Gulf states of the USA).

Thus in both 1988 and 1998 over half of Bangladesh was under water (from excess monsoon run-off) and 2005 saw the devastating inundation of New Orleans after Hurricane Katrina. Humanity is being seriously endangered by First World greed and unacceptable disregard of history and physical reality. However a holocaust has been happening over the last 70 years that dwarfs the Jewish Holocaust and the "forgotten" Bengal Famine by a factor of about 100 – a largely unreported Global Avoidable Mortality Holocaust that has taken the lives of about 1.5 billion human beings since 1950.

1.3 Avoidable mortality (excess mortality), under-5 infant mortality and foreign occupation

Europeans are aware from daily news reports that the human condition can be dreadful in the non-European world. This awfulness can be quantitatively assessed by dispassionately measuring human mortality over the last 70 years using publicly-available United Nations (UN) data.

The United Nations Population Division provides periodically updated demographic estimates and projections for every country and region of the World since 1950. When this project commenced in 2003, the latest data was the "2002 Revision" (later supplanted in 2005 by the "2004 Revision").[15] The data tabulated in the 2007 first edition of this book were laboriously calculated over 18 months using the "2002 Revision" data and projections.

Avoidable mortality (technically, excess mortality) is the difference between the ACTUAL mortality in a country and the mortality EXPECTED in a peaceful, decently-run country with the same demographics.

By 1950 ALL the World potentially had access to the requisites for the very low avoidable mortality obtaining in European countries, namely clean water, sanitation, proper nutrition, literacy (especially female literacy), primary health care, antibiotics and major preventive medicine programs including public health education, prophylactics (such as insecticides, antiseptics, mosquito netting, soap and condoms) and major vaccinations.

However such benefits took decades to arrive in many countries and are still variously lacking in African countries. Nevertheless, in most countries outside Africa the annual mortality rate (expressed as deaths per 1,000 people per year) typically declined to a minimum and in the best countries (typically European and East Asian countries) eventually began to rise, with this reflecting aging populations.

In the present analysis the baseline *expected* mortality rates for all countries were estimated graphically for countries grouped demographically in relation to birth rate, a key demographic parameter. This methodology (detailed in Chapter 2) has a fundamental assumption, namely that from 1950 *all* the World could and should have had access to the basic requisites for human survival outlined above.

In reality, in the preceding decade most of the non-European World was under First World hegemony (Central and South America) or First World occupation (most of Asia, Africa and the Pacific). Despite the Geneva Conventions (1949) that unambiguously specified that occupying powers were obliged to do everything possible to preserve the lives of their conquered subjects,[16] the subject non-European World did not receive such life-sustaining requisites from their colonial and neo-colonial masters.

As outlined above, using Web-accessible UN Population Division demographic data, avoidable mortality (excess mortality) was calculated for every country in the World for 1950-2005. The results are horrendous as outlined below.

1.4 Global avoidable mortality (excess mortality)

The 1950-2005 avoidable mortality (excess mortality) has been 1.3 billion for the World, 1.2 billion for the non-European World and about 0.6 billion for the Muslim World - a Muslim Holocaust about 100 times greater than the World War 2 Jewish Holocaust (5-6 million victims) and the "forgotten" World War 2 Bengal Famine (WW2 Bengali Holocaust, WW2 Indian Holocaust) in British-ruled India (6-7 million Hindu and Muslim victims).

By way of corroboration, using UN data it is possible to calculate the under-5 infant mortality for every country in the World for the period 1950-2005. The under-5 infant mortality has been 0.88 billion for the World, 0.85 billion for the non-European World and about 0.4 billion for the Muslim World.

Whether a person dies *violently* or dies *non-violently* from deprivation or malnourishment-exacerbated disease, the end result is the same and the culpability the same. Further, the Ruler is responsible for the Ruled and (as clearly specified by the Geneva Conventions) an Occupying Power is clearly responsible for avoidable mortality in a conquered country. However avoidable mortality consequent on callous foreign control does not typically cease when foreign soldiers depart. Thus "occupation" can include economic and political hegemony by a foreign power.

First World countries (notably the US, UK, France, Portugal and Russia) variously have a major responsibility for the horrendous post-1950 avoidable mortality in the non-European World through impositions such as colonial occupation, neo-colonial control, corrupt client régimes, militarization, debt, economic exclusion, economic constraint, malignant interference, international war and civil war.

War and foreign occupation have had a major impact on avoidable mortality. This is simply illustrated by geo-political grouping of the countries of the World and expressing their post-1950 avoidable mortality and under-5 infant mortality as percentages of the present (2005) population (indicative of how many post-1950 avoidable deaths or under-5 year old deaths, respectively, for every 100 people alive today for the country or region in question).

The 1950-2005 avoidable mortality as a percentage of the 2005 population has been 2.7% (Overseas Europe, comprising North America, Australasia and Israel), 5.0% (Western Europe), 7.5% (Eastern Europe), 9.4% (Latin America and Caribbean), 10.9% (East Asia), 20.7% (Central Asia), 23.0% (Arab North Africa and Middle East), 25.1% (South East Asia), 27.3% (the Pacific), 31.9% (South Asia) and 43.2% (non-Arab Africa).

The 1950-2005 under-5 infant mortality as a percentage of the 2005 population has been 1.5% (Overseas Europe), 1.7% (Western Europe), 3.8% (Eastern Europe), 9.7% (Latin America and Caribbean), 10.7% (East Asia), 12.8% (South East Asia), 13.0% (the Pacific), 17.0% (Central Asia), 15.4% (Arab North Africa and Middle East), 19.5% (South Asia) and 27.3% (non-Arab Africa).

It can be clearly seen from the above data that elevated post-1950 avoidable mortality and under-5 infant mortality is generally associated with First World occupation and hegemony.

1.5 Non-reportage of global avoidable mortality ensures its continuance

As outlined above, non-reportage of man-made mass mortality events helps ensure their future repetition. Denial of the Jewish Holocaust is regarded as utterly repugnant and indeed is a criminal offence in a number of countries historically linked to that catastrophe. Nevertheless, First World-dominated global mainstream media in general utterly refuse to report the greatest crime in human history, namely the First World-complicit global avoidable mortality holocaust. Academics, politicians and public figures are also complicit in this almost comprehensive, holocaust-denying lying by omission.

Holocaust-ignoring has deadly consequences. Thus the World largely ignored a dozen years of Nazi anti-Jewish anti-Semitism and it was only 30 months before the end of WW2 that the Allied Governments formally acknowledged the reality of the Jewish Holocaust. On 17 December 1942 in the House of Commons, Anthony Eden formally read out a joint statement on behalf of 11 Allied Governments: "numerous reports from Europe [indicate] that the German authorities, not content with denying to persons of Jewish race in all the territories over which their barbarous rule has been extended the elementary rights, are now carrying into effect Hitler's oft-repeated intention to exterminate the Jewish people of Europe. The number of victims of these bloody cruelties is reckoned in many hundreds of thousands of entirely innocent men, women and children…".[16]

75 years on from the end of WW2, the First World is gripped with a new kind of racism and indeed a new kind of anti-Semitism. If the academics, journalists, politicians, teachers and other public figures of a prosperous, selfish and right-wing First World country such as Australia were to resolutely ignore the Jewish Holocaust, the world would be quite reasonable in regarding them as racist and, specifically, anti-Jewish anti-Semitic. Yet the US-led Anglo-Celtic Coalition countries, including Australia, resolutely ignore the global excess mortality holocaust and First World complicity in

this avoidable carnage – and while ignoring horrendous continuing injustice to Muslims and Arabs, have demonized and violated these very people in the dishonestly-named, horrendously disproportionate and anti-Arab anti-Semitic War on Terror. The First World ignoring of the First World-complicit Global Avoidable Mortality Holocaust is dishonest, racist and deadly.

This book has been written because, while peace is the only way, silence kills and silence is complicity. We are obliged to inform everyone about ongoing, avoidable human mass mortality. We cannot walk by on the other side.[17]

1.6 Summary

Highly successful, rational, scientific approaches to reality involve truth, reason, free communication and the critical testing of potentially falsifiable hypotheses. Lying by omission and commission derails the scientific process. The victor writes history but history ignored yields history repeated. "Rubbing out" or ignoring mass mortality events increases the probability of their recurrence. While we are all aware of the WW2 Jewish Holocaust, the WW2 man-made Bengal Famine in British-ruled India has been largely deleted from history and from general perception. The World is also generally unaware of the horrendous extent of First World-complicit avoidable mortality (excess mortality) in non-European countries. Avoidable mortality (excess mortality) is defined as the difference between the actual mortality and the mortality expected in a peaceful, decently-run country with the same demographics. Publicly-available UN demographic data have enabled calculation of the post-1950 excess mortality for virtually every country in the World. The 1950-2005 excess mortality has been 1.3 billion for the World, 1.2 billion for the non-European World and 0.6 billion for the Muslim World, a Muslim Holocaust 100 times greater than the Jewish Holocaust or the "forgotten" Bengal Famine.

By way of corroboration, the 1950-2005 under-5 infant mortality has been 0.88 billion for the World, 0.85 billion for the non-European World and 0.4 billion for the Muslim World. About 90% of the under-5 infant mortality in the non-European world has been avoidable. The First World (principally the UK, the US, France,

Portugal and Russia) have had major complicity in post-1950 excess mortality, this variously involving colonial occupation, neo-colonial hegemony, corrupt client régimes, economic constraint, economic exclusion, militarization, debt, malignant interference, international war and civil war. Non-reportage by media, academics and politicians of the horrendous extent of global excess mortality and infant mortality ensures a continuing carnage of about 20,000 avoidable deaths every day (2020) (55,000 avoidable deaths every day in 2003). Peace is the only way but silence kills and silence is complicity. We cannot walk by on the other side.

CHAPTER 2: GLOBAL POST-1950 EXCESS MORTALITY AND UNDER-5 INFANT MORTALITY

"A single death is a tragedy, a million deaths is a statistic."

Joseph Stalin.[1]

"We are responsible not only for what we do but also for what we could have prevented... We should consider the consequences both of what we do and what we decide not to do."

Peter Singer in *Writings on an Ethical Life.*[2]

"Thou shalt not kill."

Ten Commandments of the Holy Bible, *Exodus*, 20:13.[3]

"Everyone has the right to life, liberty and security of person."

Article 3, UN Universal Declaration of Human Rights.[4]

"We hold these truths to be self-evident, that all Men are created equal, that they are endowed by their Creator with certain unalienable Rights, that among these are Life, Liberty and the pursuit of Happiness."

Thomas Jefferson, The American Declaration of Independence.[5]

2.1 Estimation of mortality and avoidable mortality (excess mortality)

Excess mortality for a given country for a given period is the difference between the ACTUAL mortality and the deaths EXPECTED for a decently run, peaceful country with the same demographics. The problem of assessing such "ideal", EXPECTED mortality rates has been approached here in an empirical, interpolative fashion. The United Nations Populations Division has provided detailed demographic data of population, crude birth rate and crude death rate for the period from 1950 onwards for essentially all countries in the world together with projections for beyond 2005. This enables simple calculation of mortality for all countries in the world for the period 1950-2005 (or, precisely, from mid-1950 to mid-2005). This detailed demographic data has also been used graphically to assess baseline "ideal" mortality rates for all countries to enable calculation of "excess mortality" over the period since 1950 as described below.

Typically, since 1950 the observed crude death rate for a "good" country starts out at a relatively very high value, progressively declines to a minimum value and then starts increasing slightly, this latter effect reflecting an increasingly older population. However there are a number of variations on this theme:

a. In the case of the Netherlands the mortality rate did not decrease since 1950 and in fact has steadily increased, albeit very slightly. This situation formally yields an excess mortality estimate of zero over this period.

b. A more typical result for "good" countries (notably most Western European countries but with numerous examples in the non-European world) involves a slight decrease in the death rate to a minimum value, this being followed by a very small but steady increase reflecting an increasingly aged population (in an ideal situation only the elderly would die). This minimum value has been taken as a "baseline" estimate of "ideal" mortality rate for the preceding period, excess mortality being taken as zero for the period after this minimum was achieved.

c. With some European countries, notably many in Eastern Europe (and Hungary in particular), the death rate from the 1960s onwards has been slightly but distinctly higher than that obtained in Western European countries. The causes of this small elevation in death rate are not clear (although smoking, excess alcohol consumption and socio-medical factors linked to authoritarian communist régimes can be speculatively invoked). This post-minimum "extra" mortality rate has been taken into account for these countries.

d. For "good" non-European countries with an initially high but subsequently declining birth rate (notably in East Asia and in many countries of South East Asia, South America, the Pacific and the Arab Persian Gulf), the values for the minimum post-1950 baseline annual mortality rate cluster around 4 per 1,000 of population. This has been taken as the "baseline" mortality rate value for a swathe of initially high birth rate countries in Africa, Asia, South America and the Pacific in which the mortality rate has not reached a minimum since 1950. It has also been used as a baseline for a swathe of countries in Africa in which the birth rate has remained very high, this being a conservative assumption that will actually *underestimate* the excess mortality because ideally mortality rate should be very low in countries with a very young population.

This empirical, interpolative approach has been applied to virtually all countries in the world (with the omission of some tiny states such as Andorra, Monaco, Liechtenstein and some island states of the Caribbean and Pacific). The total excess mortalities since 1950 were then calculated for all countries by simple addition. This then enabled calculation of the post-1950 excess mortalities for specific, geopolitically defined regions and the total excess mortality for the whole world.

No doubt much more exacting analyses can be performed using highly-tuned mathematical modelling employing baseline mortality estimates responding exquisitely to subtle changes in demographic patterns. Nevertheless, as outlined in the Introductory Chapter, my approach was dictated by resources, acceptable simplicity and the urgent need to get a reasonable figure before an unheeding and unresponsive world in order to minimize the carnage. Further, the quantitative validity of the present approach has been checked by applying a completely different approach, namely that of estimating post-1950 under-5 infant mortality.

In an ideal world, death would overwhelmingly involve the elderly. However in reality most "excess mortality" occurs in relatively high birth rate non-European countries with children being the major victims of avoidable death. Thus the total 1950-2005 excess mortality of the world is 1,302 million with 55 million (4.2%) of this deriving from relatively low birth rate European countries. In comparison, the total 1950-2005 under-5 infant mortality is 878 million of which 25 million (2.8%) derives from European countries. The under-5 infant mortality total is thus clearly consonant with the total excess mortality estimate. The calculation of under-5 infant mortality is outlined below.

2.2 Calculation of under-5 infant mortality

The United Nations Children's Fund (UNICEF) provides detailed statistics on under-5 infant mortality rates (annual under-5 year old deaths per 1,000 live births) for virtually all countries in the world since 1950. Under-5 mortality rates were plotted versus time; rates in the short intervals of 1950-1960 and 2002-2005 were obtained elsewhere or by extrapolation and rates between the major period of 1960-2005 by interpolation. In some cases (notably for several Pacific, Caribbean, African and Central Asian countries), estimates of under-5 infant mortality at particular times were obtained from data for demographically similar countries within the same geopolitical grouping.

The United Nations Population Division provides population and crude birth rate data back to 1950. Using this data, live births were calculated for all countries over this period. Using under-5 infant mortality rates per 1,000 live births, the under-5 infant mortality was thence calculated for all countries since 1950. The 2003 estimates of annual under-5 deaths are in agreement with UNICEF calculations (UNICEF, 2005) indicating the validity of the methodology used in this analysis. As indicated above, the total 1950-2005 under-5 infant mortality of 878 million for the world is consonant with the total global 1950-2005 excess mortality estimate of 1,302 million. These two parameters are compared further below.

2.3 Comparison of global and regional post-1950 total mortality and under-5 infant mortality

Table 2.1 and the following tables summarize regional and global data for 1950-2005 excess mortality and 1950-2005 under-5 infant mortality. In these tables the "1950-2005 excess mortality/2005 population ratio" is abbreviated as EM/POP and the "1950-2005 under-5 infant mortality/2005 population ratio" is represented as IM/POP.

We are all aware from electronic and print media that mortality, and infant mortality in particular, are "very bad" in the Third World but the actual numerical magnitudes of the total global 1950-2005 excess mortality (1.3 billion) and under-5 infant mortality (0.9 billion) are utterly appalling. It is accordingly important to examine the validity and consistency of these estimates.

As outlined above, the calculations of total mortality and under-5 infant mortality are straightforward and the 2003 results are in precise agreement with UNICEF calculations.

Thus the total mortality and under-5 infant mortality estimates are essentially unexceptional from a methodological point of view. On the other hand, the excess mortality calculations depend on assumptions of estimated baselines of "ideal" mortality expected for decently-run, peaceful countries with the same demographics (high birth rates for non-European countries). However the values used have involved conservative judgments and the methodology has been applied consistently to obtain estimates of "avoidable mortality" (excess mortality). Of course, the accuracy of the primary UN data could be sensibly questioned but for the present humanitarian exercise it is essentially all that is readily available.

Everyone has to die but the most vulnerable people are the very young and the very old. Thus plots of mortality versus age show marked elevation at either end of the age spectrum. The total mortality in a society will depend upon birth rate, death rate, age distribution and the social parameters influencing these factors. Thus in typically well-run, peaceful and prosperous societies such as those of European countries, children represent a lower proportion of society than in non-European countries, mortality is largely confined to the elderly and infant mortality is a very low proportion of total mortality (Table 2.1).[6]

Estimates of total mortality for various geopolitical groupings can be "normalized" for the purposes of comparison, for example by expressing 1950-2005 mortality as a percentage of the present population (Table 2.1). The values of "1950-2005 mortality/2005 population" range from about 30.6% (Latin America and the Caribbean) to 54.9% (non-Arab Africa), these values reflecting high birth rate/low death rate and high birth rate/high death rate combinations, respectively. However a sharper focus is obtained by examining mortality among specific age groups, such as infants under the age of 5.

1950-2005 under-5 infant mortality as a percentage of total mortality is 3.3-7.2% (European groupings) and 28.6-49.7% (non-European groupings) (Table 2.1). However these quotients depend upon factors influencing the numerator and the denominator - infant mortality will depend upon social conditions affecting the rate of infant mortality and the number of infants; the total mortality will depend upon factors influencing mortality in various age ranges and the proportions within those ranges. Thus in European countries there is a low infant proportion/low infant mortality rate combination but in most non-European countries there is a combination of a higher proportion of infants and high infant mortality. This is dramatized by the under-5 infant mortality/total mortality percentages of 3.3% for Western Europe and 49.7% for non-Arab Africa.

2.4 Estimation of avoidable under-5 infant mortality

From the under-5 infant mortality/total mortality ratios we can already see a marked divide between European and non-European groupings but the ratio *per se* does not tell us of the underlying contributing parameters of age distribution and age-specific mortality and the social factors giving rise to these. However, expressing post-1950 under-5 infant mortality as a percentage of the present population gets us much closer to an idea of what have been "good" and "bad" societies in terms of infant mortality - this ratio averages 2.2% for European societies, 15.9% for non-European countries and 13.6% for the world as a whole. However such differences must be assessed properly by taking demographic differences into account, specifically the proportion of under-5 year olds in the various groups; such an approach enables estimation of how much of the observed under-5 infant mortality is "avoidable" in relation to an appropriate baseline.

When the 1950-2005 under-5 mortality/2005 population percentage for every country is tabulated, the 4 best countries are revealed as Iceland (population 0.3 million), Norway (population 4.6 million), Netherlands (population 16.3 million) and Australia (population 20 million), each having a percentage "score" of 1.0%. Australia is ethnically diverse and more populous than the other countries and can accordingly be conveniently used for a baseline to indicate "world's best practice" in terms of achievement of low under-5 infant mortality over the period 1950-2005.

Assuming that the Australian total 1950-2005 under-5 infant mortality of 0.202 million is as good as any country could do over this period, we can further assume that this result represents the "unavoidable" under-5 infant mortality for any human population over this period with the same key demographic components, namely an average population of 14.162 million and an average under-5 infant percentage of the population of 8.65%. We can solve for the "intrinsic factor", F, that yields this result from the following equation:

Australian total 1950-2005 "unavoidable" under-5 infant mortality = F x 14.162 million x 0.0865 = 0.202 million. The value of F is 0.165. We can now apply this value of F to other situations in the post-1950 period as described below.

Afghanistan had an average post-1950 population of 14.550 million, a total under-5 infant mortality of 11.514 million and an under-5 age group representing an average of 17.75% of the population. Using our factor F from our analysis of the Australian result we can calculate that the Afghanistan total 1950-2005 "unavoidable" under-5 infant mortality = 0.165 x 14.550 million x 0.1775 = 0.424 million. The "avoidable" infant mortality is thus 11.514 – 0.424 = 11.090 million, this representing 96.3% of the total under-5 infant mortality.

Similar calculations involving UN data of under-5 percentage of population, 1950-2005 average population, 1950-2005 under-5 infant mortality and the same F value of 0.165 can be performed for other countries and groups of countries to estimate the "avoidable" under-5 infant mortality. Thus the "avoidable" 1950-2005 under-5 infant mortality for Iraq represents about 88% of the total for Iraq and that for the whole world represents about 90% of the total for the world.

This analysis indicates that about 90% of the post-1950 under-5 infant mortality in high death rate countries and in the world as a whole has been "avoidable" based on the Australian "world's best practice" standard as a baseline. Of course for prosperous countries the "avoidable" percentage of the under-5 infant mortality has been much lower e.g. about 20% for the US and, by definition, 0% for Australia.

2.5 Comparison of under-5 infant mortality and excess mortality

Measurements can be made of differences in mortality between countries (differential mortality) but for the purposes of valid comparison the mortality statistics have to be "normalized" e.g. by expressing them as a ratio with respect to the present population or the average population over a given period. We have seen that ratios such as total under-5 infant mortality/present population give pointers to differential mortality in different countries and groups of countries but that such parameters have to be corrected by taking into account the actual proportion of under-5 year olds. Calculation of such corrected and "normalized" "under-5 infant mortalities" (or indeed mortalities in other population segments) for every country in the world for the period from 1950 onwards is possible - but this would be an immense task.

As described in section 2.1, an all-encompassing approach to the problem of calculating differential mortality in the world is to estimate "excess mortality" (avoidable mortality), this being the difference between the ACTUAL mortality for a country in a given period and the mortality EXPECTED for a well-administered, peaceful country with the same demographics. The approach taken here for every country in the world for the period 1950-2005 has been to obtain estimates of what the "base-line" death rate should have been over this period, to then calculate the "excess mortality rate" and hence calculate the excess mortality. This approach takes into account differences in demography between countries and does not confine itself to only one age segment of each population.

More exquisitely massaged estimates of the "excess mortality rate" can be envisaged using sophisticated mathematical modelling and people can legitimately quibble about the methodology employed here. Nevertheless the methodology employed has been reasonable, well-defined and consistently applied. Further, the independently calculated total 1950-2005 under-5 infant mortality of 878 million is similar to the total excess mortality (1,302 million). However more exacting comparisons can be made as outlined below.

Empirically for the whole world, the total 1950-2005 infant mortality is 67.4% of the estimated total excess mortality. However it is clear that the world falls into 2 clear-cut sets in relation to total 1950-2005 under-5 infant mortality - thus the ratio of this parameter to total mortality is 4.8% for the European world and 38.4% for the non-European world, and the ratio to current population averages 2.2% for the Europeans and 15.9% for the non-Europeans. The ratio (as a percentage) of total 1950-2005 under-5 infant mortality to total post-1950 excess mortality is 45.7% for the European countries (value range 34.8-54.8% for regional subsets) and 68.4% for non-European countries (with values ranging from 47.5% to 103.3% for the various regional subsets).

It is apparent from the data presented in Tables 2.1-2.12 that there are big differences between countries and regions in the total mortality, under-5 infant mortality and excess mortality when these parameters are "normalized" by expressing these parameters as ratios of each other or as ratios with respect to the current relevant population. It is important to note that while under-5 infant mortality and excess mortality have been calculated by independent approaches, the ratios of these parameters to total mortality and current population all essentially follow a consistent pattern when the various geopolitical regions of the world are ranked. The calculation here of under-5 infant mortality involves unexceptional

and straightforward arithmetic employing UN- and UNICEF-
derived statistical data on population, birth rate per 1,000 of
population and under-5 infant deaths/per 1,000 births. While the
calculation of total mortality is similarly straightforward (simply
involving knowledge of population and deaths per 1,000 of
population), assessment of excess mortality involves more
complicated, interpolative assessments of graphical presentations
of mortality versus time, assessments of demographic similarities,
and estimations of what are "ideal" mortalities for particular
countries over time. Nevertheless, excess mortality is a useful
parameter in that it provides a measure of avoidable mortality for
all subsections of a population.

The consistency in the relative values of 1950-2005 excess
mortality and 1950-2005 under-5 infant mortality (Tables 2.1-2.12)
means that for particular countries and regions we can now very
simply (albeit crudely) estimate excess mortality from
unexceptional and straightforward calculations of under-5 infant
mortality from UN and UNICEF data.

2.6 "Humanizing" mortality

People inevitably die but ideally were expected do so in past
decades after "three score years and ten" (or perhaps "four score
years" in more recent years). The values of total 1950-2005
mortality expressed as a percentage of current population cover a
relatively narrow span from 30.6% (relatively poor Latin America
and the Caribbean) to 54.9% (for wretchedly poor, high birth rate
non-Arab Africa) (Table 2.1). The average values of this parameter
are 42.4% (for the world), 46.9% (for the European world) and
41.5% (for the non-European world). The similarity in these values
simply reflects the reality that we all have to die and nearly all do
so in the time span of the order of a century.

In an "ideal" world, mortality would be largely confined to the
elderly and accordingly the "1950-2005 mortality/2005 population"
ratio should ideally be much lower for the non-European world
which has a much higher proportion of children than European
societies - the numerator should be lower (because of the lower
mortality of children), the denominator should be higher (because
of the relatively higher population growth in high birth rate

societies) and accordingly the quotient should be lower. However the very similarity of the average 1950-2005 mortality/2005 population ratios for the European and non-European groupings and the much higher ratio for non-Arab Africa (54.9%) than for Overseas Europe (35.9%) both tell us that something is seriously wrong in the world, that there is a major departure from the "ideal".

Fundamental human expectations of "ideal" circumstances color our attitudes as exampled by the simple statement above that "something is seriously wrong in the world", that there is a major departure from the "ideal". Thomas Jefferson in the American Declaration of Independence provided a powerfully succinct statement of fundamental human expectations of the "ideal" in his enunciation of "self-evident" "truths":

"We hold these Truths to be self-evident, that all Men are created equal, that they are endowed by their Creator with certain unalienable Rights, that among these are Life, Liberty and the Pursuit of Happiness".

2.7 "Humanizing" excess mortality

We have all become familiar via the electronic and print mass media with the phenomena of poverty, disease, violence, mass mortality and mass infant mortality in the Third World. However the present analysis aims to quantitate global mortality by estimating the actual numbers involved - and hence instigate more resolute action to stop this immense crime against humanity in a globalized and highly militarized world. Thus we are all aware of the World War 2 Jewish Holocaust and most people are aware that some 6 million people died. The simple idea that "many" or "lots" of Jews died is insufficient - the quantitation of "6 million" really challenges our comprehension of that appalling crime. Further, the figure of "6 million" and its psychological consequences powerfully underscore the Jewish resolution of "Never again".[7]

However the numbers involved in global mass mortality are 2 orders of magnitude greater than the death toll of the Jewish Holocaust. Global 1950-2005 excess mortality and under-5 infant mortality total 1.3 billion and 0.9 billion, respectively, and about 90% of the non-European under-5 infant mortality of over 0.8

billion has been avoidable. The challenge is to come to grips with these immense numbers in human terms. Some approaches to "humanizing" excess mortality and under-5 infant mortality are outlined below.

Excess mortality can be expressed as a percentage of mortality, thus telling us what proportion of observed mortality has been avoidable. We are familiar with responses to particular kinds of death that have in an absolute or statistical sense been unavoidable. Thus the death of the very old will typically be described as death after "a good innings". Given that cancer and some other debilitating and painful diseases are major causes of premature death among the middle aged in the West, people might say in retrospect that "it was good that the suffering was not too prolonged". Deaths from accidents, adverse medical circumstances and even from smoking evoke sympathy, especially when the victims are very young or in the prime of life. However passion and anger only emerge when there has been clear-cut human avoidability – as in murder, manslaughter and social or individual negligence.

There is a marked divide in relation to the 1950-2005 excess mortality/ post-1950 mortality ratio between the European world (average 10.6%; range 3.3-26.3%) and the non-European world (average 56.2%; range 8.2-87.0%). The excess mortality (avoidable mortality)/total mortality ratio has been on average over 5 times greater in the non-European world than in European countries i.e. in a risk assessment sense, avoidable mortality has been much more likely for non-Europeans than for Europeans. Overall only 10.6% of mortality has been avoidable in the European world whereas the 56.6% proportion means avoidable death is much more likely than unavoidable death for non-Europeans.

However the excess mortality/mortality ratio still gives us a somewhat depersonalized, statistical view of avoidable mortality. We have some perception of the dangers of some relatively common human pursuits – thus there are 6 billion people in the world and yet each year 1 million (0.017%) die in car accidents and 5 million (0.083%) die from cigarette-smoking-related causes (2007 data). Nevertheless, in prosperous, risk-conscious European societies nearly everyone will travel by car and perhaps 10% of people smoke. A more personalized estimate of excess mortality is accordingly required.

Expressing 1950-2005 excess mortality as a percentage of the current (2005) population for given groupings is one way of "humanizing" these mortality statistics. Thus for Australia the excess mortality/present population ratio is 2.9% i.e. about 3 people died avoidably since 1950 for every 100 Australians alive today. Thus at a wedding or another such big gathering of happy people only several guests out of 100 would carry the weight of some tragic, avoidable loss over the preceding half century. Indeed, for my own immediate family in Australia (blood relatives, spouses and offspring), the definitely avoidable post-1950 mortality/current people ratio has been 1/31 i.e. 3.2%.

On the other hand, the post-1950 excess mortality/present population ratio for Timor-Leste (East Timor) is 81.0% i.e. for every 100 people alive in East Timor today, since 1950 there have been 81 avoidable deaths (from deprivation, malnourishment-related disease, lack of primary health care and outright genocidal violence). Again I can offer an "anecdotal" personal experience relating to this appalling statistic. Several years ago we attended a huge wedding reception in Melbourne for a lovely couple who had both been involved in help for East Timorese refugees. We sat at a table with many East Timorese, young and old. The adults spoke very little English but I solved my communication problem by ducking out of the feast, purchasing a ream of A4 paper and some black felt-tipped pens and then drawing rapid portraits of everyone. The children were delighted and happy. The adults were also happy but in the portraiture process I had to look deeply into their eyes – and saw, without exception, pain from their dreadful experiences and loss.

Of course the issue arises of how "avoidable" the estimated "avoidable" mortality has actually been. This analysis covers the period from 1950 onwards during which period the UN has provided the requisite demographic statistics for this study. However the post-1950 period is important for another reason. Since that time potentially everyone in the world could have had access to a whole range of survivability-linked social benefits -

including sanitation, clean drinking water, soap, antiseptics, major vaccinations, mosquito netting, anti-malarial drugs, antibiotics, universal literacy, preventative health education and primary health care. Indeed the "baselines" used in this study are not the products of space-age 21st century medical miracles but the empirical results actually achieved by demographically similar countries over this post-1950 period.

2.8 The human aspect of under-5 infant mortality

A common fundamental trait of human beings is affection for children. Human offspring are peculiar in their post-partum helplessness and long-term dependence on their mothers and indeed on other members of their social group. The size of the human brain requires birth at a stage permitting safe egress that is then followed by lengthy period of dependence. This lengthy rearing process involves a major social investment that is reflected in maternal love, paternal and sibling affection, the involvement of other family members (notably the "allomothering" or "aunt-behavior" of women) and the warm regard and conspicuous protection offered by society as a whole.[8]

Good treatment of infants is characteristic of orderly human societies but within populous societies under acute stress such decent human behaviors will be discarded. However, even in some conspicuously violent, male-dominated societies there are conventions prohibiting male violence against other men in the presence of women and children. Nevertheless, from child labour in the colonial era and the early days of the industrial revolution to present-day Third World child labour, child soldiers and child prostitution, economic pressure and greed have perverted "natural" human behaviour towards infants.

Historically, mass mortality of infants was associated with the genocidal European invasions of North America, South America, Australasia and the Pacific in which introduced disease was more important than conventional violence in decimating native populations. In the last century explicit, violent mass murder of infants (as well as of adults) occurred repeatedly, as for example during the genocides applied to the Hereros of Namibia, the Armenians of Anatolia, the Jews of Europe, the Cambodian civilian victims of the Khmer Rouge, the Tutsis of Rwanda and the East Timorese victims of the Anglo-American-backed Indonesian military.

Whether a child dies a violent death or dies of deprivation or malnourishment-exacerbated disease, the end result is the same. Accordingly, to this list of infanticidal horrors of the last century we should add the victims of enormous man-made famines in Russia (the early 1920s), Iran (circa 1920), the Ukraine (early 1930s), British-occupied Bengal (during World War 2), China (during the Great Leap Forward), and Ethiopia (1970s and 1980s). Major wars such as the Japanese invasion of China, World War 1 and World War 2 have been major killers of civilians through the accompanying social and economic dislocation. Notwithstanding the creation of the UN after World War 2, there has been immense avoidable infant mortality over the last half century that is closely linked to First World-imposed occupation, neo-colonial "occupation", economic exploitation, economic exclusion, militarization, debt, corrupt client régimes and war.

For decent human beings like ourselves, the mass abuse and mortality of infants is simply unacceptable. It nevertheless continues unabated – as evidenced by the 0.9 billion 1950-2005 under-5 infant mortality. One is almost reduced to impotent despair when one sees that the mainstream media of the First World countries with a massive responsibility for this carnage will not even *report* the magnitude of this holocaust. Politicians when very rarely cornered on this issue will obfuscate by solely addressing the issue of *violence*-associated infant death that is very difficult to quantitate (as in war-torn Iraq at the moment) while utterly ignoring the overwhelmingly much more important issue of overall avoidable infant mortality.

Avoidable mortality in non-European countries is regarded by politicians and media as somehow "normal" or "too hard" to deal with – but neither proposition is correct. Avoidable mass infant mortality is utterly abnormal, unacceptable and the outcome of obscene socio-political pathology. Assertions by Europeans that high mortality for non-Europeans is somehow a "normal state" are simply racist and implicitly genocidal. Further, a long list of "good outcome" countries detailed here show that this immense crime can be readily addressed. One way of addressing this evil is to identify the dimensions of the problem and to establish causality. Tables 2.1-2.12 document the extent of 1950-2005 excess mortality and under-5 infant mortality for all regions and essentially all countries in the world. Tables 2.2-2.12 also include circa 2003 data on life expectancy, *per capita* income and literacy for each country to enable ready correlative assessments.

The "post-1950 excess mortality/2005 population ratio" averages are as follows in *increasing* order for the major groupings: 2.7% (Overseas Europe) < 5.0% (Western Europe) < 7.5% (Eastern Europe) < 9.4% (Latin America and Caribbean) < 10.9% (East Asia) < 20.7% (Turkey, Iran and Central Asia) < 23.0% (Arab Middle East and North Africa) < 25.1% (South East Asia) < 27.3% (the Pacific) < 31.9% (South Asia) < 43.2% (non-Arab Africa). This pattern is substantially reflected in that for the "1950-2005 under-5 infant mortality/2005 population ratio", the order being: 1.5% (Overseas Europe) < 1.7% (Western Europe) < 7.2% (Eastern Europe) < 9.7% (Latin America and Caribbean) < 10.3% (East Asia) < 12.8% (South East Asia) < 13.0% (the Pacific) <15.4% (Arab Middle East and North Africa) < 17.0% (Turkey, Iran and Central Asia) < 19.5% (South Asia) < 27.3% (non-Arab Africa) (Table 2.1).

In general, 1950-2005 excess mortality increases with decreasing *per capita* income but excellent outcomes have been achieved in countries with relatively low annual *per capita* incomes of about $1,000, namely Cuba, Paraguay and Sri Lanka which have "post-1950 excess mortality/2005 population" ratios of 4.1-9.4% as compared to that of 2.8% for the US (annual *per capita* income about $38,000). Low excess mortality is associated with high adult literacy but appallingly high post-1950 excess mortality can still occur in countries with adult literacy in excess of 80% e.g. Congo (Brazzaville), Lesotho, Namibia, South Africa, Swaziland [Eswatini] and Zimbabwe. However, war and occupation imposed by First World countries generally correlate with excess mortality. The following chapters analyse the dimensions, correlates and causes of the continuing humanitarian disaster of global avoidable mortality.

Table 2.1 Post-1950 global excess mortality and under-5 infant mortality

Region	EM (m)	IM (m)	IM/EM (%)	POP (m)	MORT (m)	MORT/ POP (%)	EM/ POP (%)	EM/ MORT (%)	IM/ POP (%)	IM/ MORT (%)
Overseas Europe	9.750	5.344	55	366.747	131.795	36	2.7	7.4	1.5	4.1
Western Europe	19.680	6.857	35	394.384	205.574	52	5.0	9.6	1.7	3.3
Eastern Europe	25.578	12.781	51	338.752	178.344	53	7.6	14.3	3.8	7.2
Latin America & Caribbean	50.579	52.232	103	540.034	165.220	31	9.4	30.6	9.7	31.6
East Asia	168.585	165.795	98	1544.460	579.519	38	10.9	29.1	10.7	28.6
Central Asia, Iran & Turkey	49.147	40.459	82	237.356	88.216	37	20.7	55.7	17.0	45.9
Arab North Africa & Middle East	70.516	47.174	67	305.985	107.101	35	23.0	65.8	15.4	44.0
South East Asia	140.222	71.492	51	558.155	224.318	40	25.1	62.5	12.8	31.9
Pacific	2.347	1.114	47	8.595	3.503	41	27.3	67.0	13.0	31.8
South Asia	465.320	284.797	61	1459.046	669.115	46	31.9	69.5	19.5	42.6
Non-Arab Africa	300.834	189.834	63	696.515	382.116	55	43.2	78.7	27.3	49.7
EUROPE	55.008	24.982	46	1099.883	515.713	47	5.0	10.7	2.2	4.8
NON-EUROPE	1247.550	852.897	68	5350.146	2219.108	41	23.3	56.2	15.9	38.4
TOTAL	1302.558	877.879	67	6450.029	2734.821	42	20.2	47.6	13.6	32.1

Abbreviations: EM, total 1950-2005 (mid-1950-mid-2005) excess mortality; IM, total 1950-2005 under-5 infant mortality; LE, life expectancy at birth (UNICEF, 2003); MORT, total 1950-2005 mortality; POP, 2005 population; m, million.

Notes. Overseas Europe includes Australia, Canada, Israel, New Zealand, Puerto Rico, USA and US Virgin Islands. Armenia and

Georgia as Christian countries of the former Soviet Union are included conveniently in the Eastern Europe category. Population and mortality data have been conveniently rounded-off in Tables 2.1-2.12.

Table 2.2 Excess mortality and under-5 infant mortality in Overseas Europe

Country	EM (m)	IM (m)	POP (m)	MORT (m)	EM/ POP (%)	EM/ MORT (%)	IM/ POP (%)	IM/ MORT (%)	LE (yr)	PCI ($)	LIT (%)
Australia	0.587	0.202	20.092	6.084	2.9	9.6	1.0	3.3	79	21,650	~98
Canada	0.428	0.442	31.972	9.552	1.4	4.6	1.4	4.6	79	23,930	~98
Israel	0.095	0.091	6.685	1.305	1.4	7.3	1.4	7.0	79	16,030	~98
New Zealand	0.143	0.054	3.932	1.355	3.6	10.6	1.4	4.0	78	15,870	~98
Puerto Rico	0.039	0.080	3.915	1.195	1.0	3.3	2.0	6.7			
USA	8.455	4.473	300.038	112.281	2.8	7.5	1.5	4.0	79	37,610	~98
US Virgin Islands	0.003	0.002	0.113	0.023	2.4	11.7	1.5	7.4			
TOTAL	9.750	5.344	366.747	131.795	2.7	7.4	1.5	4.1			

Notes. LE, life expectancy at birth (UNICEF, 2003); LIT, adult literacy (% literate over 15 years old) (UNICEF, 2000); PCI, per capita income (gross national income per person) in US$ (UNICEF, 2003); other abbreviations are as for Table 2.1. Notwithstanding substantial non-European populations, Israel is conveniently grouped here and the US Virgin Islands and Puerto Rico are similarly conveniently included here with metropolitan USA.

Table 2.3 Excess mortality and under-5 infant mortality in Western Europe

Country	EM (m)	IM (m)	POP (m)	MORT (m)	EM/ POP (%)	EM/ MORT (%)	IM/ POP (%)	IM/ MORT (%)	LE (yr)	PCI $1000	LIT (%)
Austria	0.734	0.142	8.120	4.834	9.0	15.2	1.7	2.9	79	26.72	~98
Belgium	0.749	0.162	10.359	6.026	7.2	12.4	1.6	2.7	79	25.82	~98
Cyprus	0.054	0.017	0.813	0.315	6.6	17.1	2.1	5.4	78	12.32	~98
Denmark	0.203	0.059	5.386	2.878	3.8	7.1	1.1	2.1	77	33.75	~98
Finland	0.024	0.064	5.224	2.484	0.5	1.0	1.2	2.6	78	27.02	~98
France	3.275	0.857	60.711	29.850	5.4	11.0	1.4	2.9	79	24.77	~98
Germany	7.061	1.292	82.560	49.235	8.6	14.3	1.6	2.6	78	25.25	~98
Greece	0.027	0.273	10.978	4.551	0.2	0.6	2.5	6.0	78	13.72	97
Iceland	0.003	0.003	0.294	0.084	1.1	3.8	1.0	3.5	80	30.81	~98
Ireland	0.389	0.071	4.040	1.836	9.6	21.2	1.8	3.9	77	26.96	~98
Italy	0.846	1.227	57.273	29.546	1.5	2.9	2.1	4.2	79	21.56	~98
Luxembourg	0.050	0.006	0.465	0.211	10.8	23.7	1.2	2.7	78	43.94	~98
Malta	0.019	0.009	0.397	0.159	4.8	11.9	2.3	5.7	78	9.26	92
Netherlands	0.000	0.163	16.300	6.194	0.0	0.0	1.0	2.6	78	26.31	~98
Norway	0.032	0.047	4.570	2.155	0.7	1.5	1.0	2.2	79	43.35	~98
Portugal	0.429	0.577	10.080	5.485	4.3	7.8	5.7	10.5	76	12.13	92
Spain	1.049	0.964	41.184	17.132	2.5	6.1	2.3	5.6	80	28.84	~98
Sweden	0.249	0.070	8.895	4.698	2.8	5.3	0.8	1.5	79	16.99	98
Switzerland	0.076	0.077	7.157	3.234	1.1	2.4	1.1	2.4	79	39.88	~98
United Kingdom	4.411	0.777	59.598	34.667	7.4	12.7	1.3	2.2	78	28.35	~98
TOTAL	19.680	6.857	394.384	205.574	5.0	9.6	1.7	3.3			

Notes. Abbreviations are as for Table 2.1. Andorra, Lichtenstein and Monaco are not included.

Table 2.4 Excess mortality and under-5 infant mortality in Eastern Europe

COUNTRY	EM (m)	IM (m)	POP (m)	MORT (m)	EM/ POP (%)	EM/ MORT (%)	IM/ POP (%)	IM/ MORT (%)	LE (yr)	PCI $	LIT (%)
Albania	0.251	0.301	3.220	0.956	7.8	26.3	9.3	31.5	74	1,740	85
Armenia	0.091	0.289	3.043	1.002	3.0	9.1	9.5	28.8	72	950	98
Belarus	0.683	0.269	9.809	5.187	7.0	13.2	2.7	5.2	70	590	~98
Bosnia & Herzegovina	0.230	0.396	4.209	1.611	5.5	14.3	9.4	24.6	74	1,540	93
Bulgaria	0.769	0.275	7.763	5.063	9.9	15.2	3.5	5.4	71	2,130	98
Croatia	0.291	0.191	4.405	2.635	6.6	11.0	4.3	7.2	74	5,350	98
Czech Republic	1.087	0.142	10.216	6.062	10.6	17.9	1.4	2.3	76	6,740	~98
Estonia	0.166	0.032	1.294	0.918	12.8	18.1	2.5	3.5	72	4,960	~98
Georgia	0.281	0.231	5.026	2.490	5.6	11.3	4.6	9.3	74	830	~98
Hungary	1.363	0.288	9.784	6.986	13.9	19.5	2.9	4.1	72	6,330	~98
Latvia	0.288	0.053	2.265	1.582	12.7	18.2	2.3	3.4	71	4,070	~98
Lithuania	0.143	0.107	3.401	1.798	4.2	8.0	3.1	6.0	73	4,490	~98
Macedonia	0.145	0.221	2.076	0.842	7.0	17.2	10.6	26.2	74	1,980	96
Moldova	0.254	0.239	4.259	2.296	6.0	11.1	5.6	10.4	69	590	~98
Poland	0.677	1.368	38.516	17.549	1.8	3.9	3.6	7.8	74	5,270	~98
Romania	1.133	1.029	22.228	12.034	5.1	9.4	4.6	8.6	71	2,310	98
Russia	11.897	5.093	141.553	71.020	8.4	16.8	3.6	7.2	67	2,610	~98
Serbia & Montenegro	0.388	0.620	10.513	5.253	3.7	7.4	5.9	11.8	73	1,910	~98
Slovakia	0.130	0.119	5.411	2.579	2.4	5.0	2.2	4.6	74	4,920	~98
Slovenia	0.032	0.038	1.979	0.990	1.6	3.2	1.9	3.8	76	11,830	~98
Ukraine	5.279	1.480	47.782	29.491	11.0	17.9	3.1	5.0	70	970	~98
TOTAL	25.578	12.781	338.752	178.344	7.6	14.3	3.8	7.2			

Notes. Abbreviations are as for Tables 2.1 and 2.2. For convenience and consistency, Armenia and Georgia are included with the other Christian countries of the former Soviet Union and Soviet Empire.

Table 2.5 Excess mortality and under-5 infant mortality in Latin America and the Caribbean

COUNTRY	EM (m)	IM (m)	POP (m)	MORT (m)	EM/ POP (%)	EM/ MORT (%)	IM/ POP (%)	IM/ MORT (%)	LE (yr)	PCI ($)	LIT (%)
Argentina	1.310	1.501	39.311	12.777	3.3	10.3	3.8	11.7	74	3,650	97
Bahamas	0.007	0.011	0.321	0.077	2.3	9.5	3.4	14.3	67	14,290	95
Barbados	0.015	0.016	0.272	0.122	5.5	12.3	5.9	13.1	77	9,270	~98
Belize	0.014	0.020	0.266	0.055	5.3	25.5	7.5	36.4	71		93
Bolivia	3.004	1.880	9.138	4.130	32.9	72.7	20.6	45.5	64	890	85
Brazil	13.114	19.407	182.798	58.034	7.2	22.6	10.6	33.4	68	2,710	87
Chile	1.427	1.135	16.185	4.669	8.8	30.6	7.0	24.3	76	4,390	96
Colombia	3.722	3.367	45.600	11.923	8.2	31.2	7.4	28.2	72	1,810	92
Costa Rica	0.259	0.199	4.327	0.756	6.0	34.3	4.6	26.3	78	4,280	96
Cuba	0.469	0.349	11.353	3.691	4.1	12.7	3.1	9.5	77	~1,170	97
Dominican Republic	0.806	0.974	8.998	2.784	9.0	29.0	10.8	35.0	67	2,070	84
Ecuador	1.404	1.426	13.379	3.893	10.5	36.1	10.7	36.6	71	1,790	92
El Salvador	0.936	0.942	6.709	2.299	14.0	40.7	14.0	41.0	71	2,200	79

French Guiana	0.010	0.004	0.187	0.027	5.3	37.0	2.3	15.9			
Guadeloupe	0.025	0.022	0.446	0.138	5.6	18.1	4.9	15.9			
Guatemala	2.757	1.878	12.978	4.275	21.2	64.5	14.5	43.9	66	1,910	69
Guyana	0.086	0.121	0.768	0.397	11.2	21.7	15.8	30.5	63	900	~98
Haiti	4.098	2.142	8.549	5.313	47.9	77.1	25.1	40.3	50	380	50
Honduras	0.822	0.845	7.257	1.978	11.3	41.6	11.6	42.7	69	970	75
Jamaica	0.245	0.153	2.701	0.850	9.1	28.8	5.7	18.0	76	2,760	87
Martinique	0.022	0.022	0.397	0.134	5.5	16.4	5.5	16.4			
Mexico	8.850	9.095	106.385	26.815	8.3	33.0	8.5	33.9	74	6,230	91
Netherlands Antilles	0.009	0.010	0.224	0.066	3.9	13.2	4.5	15.2			
Nicaragua	0.934	0.725	5.727	1.580	16.3	59.1	12.7	45.9	70	730	64
Panama	0.172	0.162	3.235	0.693	5.3	24.8	5.0	23.4	75	4,250	92
Paraguay	0.577	0.339	6.160	1.282	9.4	45.0	5.5	26.4	71	1,100	93
Peru	4.094	4.132	27.968	9.552	14.6	42.9	14.8	43.3	70	2,150	90
Saint Lucia	0.012	0.009	0.152	0.050	7.9	24.0	6.1	18.4	73	4,050	~98
Saint Vincent & Grenadines	0.018	0.009	0.121	0.049	14.9	36.7	7.2	17.8	74	3,300	~~98
Suriname	0.039	0.043	0.442	0.151	8.8	25.8	9.7	28.5	71	~1,940	94
Trinidad & Tobago	0.052	0.071	1.311	0.425	4.0	12.2	5.4	16.7	71	7,260	98
Uruguay	0.138	0.125	3.463	1.546	4.0	8.9	3.6	8.1	75	3,820	98
Venezuela	1.132	1.099	26.640	4.759	4.2	23.8	4.1	23.1	74	3,490	93
TOTAL	50.579	52.232	540.034	165.220	9.4	30.6	9.7	31.6			

Notes. Abbreviations are as for Tables 2.1 and 2.2. The Falkland Islands (Malvinas) are not included.

Table 2.6 Excess mortality and under-5 infant mortality in East Asia

COUNTRY	EM (m)	IM (m)	POP (m)	MORT (m)	EM/ POP (%)	EM/ MORT (%)	IM/ POP (%)	IM/ MORT (%)	LE (yr)	PCI US$	LIT (%)
China	155.670	157.726	1322.273	504.199	11.8	30.9	11.9	31.3	71	1,100	85
Hong Kong	0.125	0.105	7.182	1.445	1.7	8.7	1.5	7.3			
Macao	0.036	0.007	0.472	0.107	7.6	33.6	1.4	6.3			
Taiwan	0.560	0.459	22.894	5.268	2.4	10.6	2.0	8.7			
Japan	3.596	2.452	127.914	43.718	2.8	8.2	1.9	5.6	82	34,510	~98
North Korea	2.945	1.559	22.876	8.225	12.9	35.8	6.8	19.0	63	~500	98
South Korea	5.013	3.085	48.182	15.568	10.4	32.2	6.4	19.8	76	12,030	98
Mongolia	0.640	0.402	2.667	0.989	24.0	64.7	15.0	40.6	64	480	98
TOTAL	168.585	165.795	1544.460	579.519	10.9	29.1	10.7	28.6			

Notes. Abbreviations for Tables 2.6 are as for Tables 2.1 and 2.2.

Table 2.7 Excess mortality and under-5 infant mortality in Turkey, Iran and Central Asia

COUNTRY	EM (m)	IM (m)	POP (m)	MORT (m)	EM/ POP (%)	EM/ MORT (%)	IM/ POP (%)	IM/ MORT (%)	LE (yr)	PCI ($)	LIT (%)
Afghanistan	16.609	11.514	25.971	19.739	64.0	84.1	44.3	58.3	43	~250	36
Azerbaijan	0.428	1.032	8.527	2.222	5.0	19.3	12.1	46.4	72	810	~97
Iran	14.272	10.875	70.675	21.710	20.2	65.7	15.4	50.1	70	2,000	76
Kazakhstan	0.983	1.661	15.364	7.147	6.4	13.8	10.8	23.2	67	1,780	~98
Kyrgyzstan	1.041	0.657	5.278	1.800	19.7	57.8	12.4	36.5	69	330	~98
Tajikistan	0.924	0.739	6.356	1.771	14.5	52.2	11.6	41.7	69	190	~98
Turkey	10.488	10.987	73.302	25.381	14.3	41.3	15.0	43.3	71	2,790	85
Turkmenistan	0.817	0.591	5.015	1.443	16.3	56.6	11.8	41.0	67	1,120	~98
Uzbekistan	3.585	2.403	26.868	7.003	13.3	51.2	8.9	34.3	70	420	~98
TOTAL	49.147	40.459	237.356	88.216	20.7	55.7	17.0	45.9			

Notes. Abbreviations for Tables 2.6 are as for Tables 2.1 and 2.2. Mongolia is conveniently included with East Asia (Table 2.6).

Table 2.8 Excess mortality and under-5 infant mortality in Arab North Africa and Middle East

COUNTRY	EM (m)	IM (m)	POP (m)	MORT (m)	EM/ POP (%)	EM/ MORT (%)	IM/ POP (%)	IM/ MORT (%)	LE (yr)	PCI ($)	LIT (%)
Algeria	7.167	5.812	32.877	11.302	21.8	63.4	17.7	51.4	70	1,890	67
Bahrain	0.054	0.033	0.754	0.111	7.2	48.6	4.4	29.7	74	~10,840	88
Egypt	19.818	14.143	74.878	29.533	26.5	67.1	18.9	47.9	69	1,390	55
Iraq	5.283	3.446	26.555	8.288	19.9	63.7	13.0	41.5	61	~2,170	39
Jordan	0.630	0.331	5.750	1.166	11.0	54.0	5.8	28.4	71	1,850	90
Kuwait	0.089	0.076	2.671	0.215	3.3	41.4	2.8	35.3	77	~16,340	82
Lebanon	0.535	0.236	3.761	1.285	14.2	41.6	6.3	18.4	74	4,040	86
Libya	0.785	0.626	5.768	1.478	13.6	53.1	10.9	42.4	73	~5,540	80
Morocco	8.202	5.098	31.564	12.401	26.0	66.1	16.2	41.1	69	1,320	49
Occupied Palestinian Territories	0.677	0.295	3.815	1.061	17.7	63.8	7.7	27.8	73	1,100	~98
Oman	0.359	0.288	3.020	0.589	11.9	61.0	9.5	48.9	73	~7,830	72
Qatar	0.029	0.013	0.628	0.080	4.6	36.3	2.1	16.3	72	~12,000	94
Saudi Arabia	2.752	2.085	25.626	4.974	10.7	55.3	8.1	41.9	72	~8,530	76
Sudan	13.471	6.225	35.040	17.754	38.4	75.9	17.8	35.1	56	460	58
Syria	2.198	1.718	18.650	4.202	11.8	52.3	9.2	40.9	72	1,160	74
Tunisia	1.582	1.568	10.042	3.530	15.8	44.8	15.6	44.4	73	2,240	71
United Arab Emirates	0.087	0.046	3.106	0.233	2.8	37.3	1.5	19.7	75	~18,060	76
Yemen	6.798	5.135	21.480	8.899	31.6	76.4	23.9	57.7	60	520	46
TOTAL	70.516	47.174	305.985	107.101	23.0	65.8	15.4	44.0			

Notes. Abbreviations are as for Tables 2.1 and 2.2. Notwithstanding a substantial Arab population and a substantial Jewish population deriving from Arab countries, Israel has been conveniently included with "Overseas" Europe in Table 2.2.

Table 2.9 Excess mortality and under-5 infant mortality in South East Asia

COUNTRY	EM (m)	IM (m)	POP (m)	MORT (m)	EM/ POP (%)	EM/ MORT (%)	IM/ POP (%)	IM/ MORT (%)	LE (yr)	PCI ($)	LIT (%)
Brunei	0.020	0.011	0.374	0.047	5.3	42.6	2.9	23.4	76	~24,100	92
Cambodia	5.852	3.180	14.825	7.634	39.5	76.7	21.5	41.7	57	310	68
Indonesia	71.521	34.516	225.313	103.580	31.7	69.0	15.3	33.3	67	610	87
Laos	2.653	1.383	5.918	3.394	44.8	78.2	23.4	40.7	55	320	65
Malaysia	2.344	1.176	25.325	5.891	9.3	39.8	4.6	20.0	73	3,780	87
Myanmar	20.174	9.992	50.696	27.362	39.8	73.7	19.7	36.5	57	220	85
Philippines	9.080	6.665	82.809	22.064	11.0	41.2	8.0	30.2	70	1,080	95
Singapore	0.113	0.061	4.372	0.781	2.6	14.5	1.4	7.8	78	21,230	92
Thailand	3.756	5.442	64.081	16.947	5.9	22.2	8.5	32.1	69	2,190	96
Timor-Leste	0.694	0.236	0.857	0.833	81.0	83.3	27.5	28.3	50	430	~70
Vietnam	24.015	8.830	83.585	35.785	28.7	67.1	10.6	24.7	69	480	93
TOTAL	140.222	71.492	558.155	224.318	25.1	62.5	12.8	31.9			

Notes. Abbreviations are as for Tables 2.1 and 2.2.

Table 2.10 Excess mortality and under-5 infant mortality in the Pacific

Country	EM (m)	IM (m)	POP (m)	MORT (m)	EM/ POP (%)	EM/ MORT (%)	IM/ POP (%)	IM/ MORT (%)	LE (yr)	PCI ($)	LIT (%)
Fiji	0.054	0.056	0.854	0.232	6.3	23.3	6.6	24.1	70	2,360	93
Guam	0.005	0.008	0.168	0.029	3.0	17.2	4.9	28.3			
Federated States of Micronesia	0.016	0.007	0.111	0.032	14.4	50.0	6.6	22.8	69	2,090	67
French Polynesia	0.018	0.003	0.252	0.057	7.1	31.6	1.5	6.5			
New Caledonia	0.017	0.003	0.237	0.054	7.2	31.5	1.3	5.6			
Papua New Guinea	2.091	0.918	5.959	2.823	35.1	74.1	15.4	32.5	58	510	64
Samoa	0.039	0.034	0.182	0.071	21.4	54.9	18.7	47.9	70	1,600	~98
Solomon Islands	0.050	0.036	0.504	0.103	9.9	48.5	7.1	35.0	69	600	
Tonga	0.020	0.020	0.106	0.039	18.9	51.3	18.9	51.3	69	1,490	~98
Vanuatu	0.037	0.029	0.222	0.063	16.7	58.7	13.1	46.0	69	1,180	~98
TOTAL	2.347	1.114	8.595	3.503	27.3	67.0	13.0	31.8			

Notes. Abbreviations are as for Tables 2.1 and 2.2. The tiny Pacific states of Tuvalu, Kiribati, Palau, American Samoa, Pitcairn Island, the Marshall Islands and Nauru are not included.

Table 2.11 Excess mortality and under-5 infant mortality in South Asia

Country	EM (m)	IM (m)	POP (m)	MORT (m)	EM/ POP (%)	EM/ MORT (%)	IM/ POP (%)	IM/ MORT (%)	LE (yr)	PCI ($)	LIT (%)
Bangladesh	51.196	32.908	152.593	72.853	33.6	70.3	21.6	45.2	62	400	40
Bhutan	0.908	0.597	2.392	1.204	38.0	75.4	25.0	49.6	63	660	47
India	351.900	214.260	1096.917	506.769	32.1	69.4	19.5	42.3	64	530	57
Maldives	0.015	0.012	0.338	0.023	4.4	65.2	3.6	52.2	68	2,300	97
Nepal	10.650	6.213	26.289	14.005	40.5	76.0	23.6	44.4	60	240	42
Pakistan	49.700	29.407	161.151	68.387	30.8	72.7	18.2	43.0	61	470	43
Sri Lanka	0.951	1.400	19.366	5.874	4.9	16.2	7.2	23.8	73	930	92
TOTAL	465.320	284.797	1459.046	669.115	31.9	69.5	19.5	42.6			

Notes. Abbreviations are as for Tables 2.1 and 2.2.

Table 2.12 Excess mortality and under-5 infant mortality in non-Arab Africa

Country	EM (m)	IM (m)	POP (m)	MORT (m)	EM/ POP (%)	EM/ MORT (%)	IM/ POP (%)	IM/ MORT (%)	LE (yr)	PCI US$	LIT (%)
Angola	9.207	6.002	14.533	10.648	63.4	86.5	41.3	56.4	40	740	~40
Benin	3.267	2.093	7.103	4.086	46.0	80.0	29.5	51.2	51	440	37
Botswana	0.443	0.236	1.801	0.664	24.6	66.7	13.1	35.5	39	3,430	77
Burkina Faso	6.810	4.793	13.798	8.399	49.4	81.1	34.7	57.1	46	300	24
Burundi	4.097	2.263	7.319	4.950	56.0	82.8	30.9	45.7	41	100	48
Cameroon	6.669	3.818	16.564	8.663	40.3	77.0	23.0	44.1	46	640	71
Cape Verde	0.099	0.061	0.482	0.162	20.5	61.1	12.7	37.7	70	1,490	74
Central African Republic	2.274	1.199	3.962	2.793	57.4	81.4	30.3	42.9	40	260	47
Chad	5.085	2.989	9.117	6.143	55.8	82.8	32.8	48.7	45	250	43
Comoros	0.204	0.149	0.812	0.293	25.1	69.6	18.3	50.9	61	450	56
Congo (Brazzaville)	1.085	0.619	3.921	1.506	27.7	72.0	15.8	41.1	48	640	81
Congo (Zaire)	26.677	17.425	56.079	33.200	47.6	80.4	31.1	52.5	42	100	61
Côte d'Ivoire	6.953	4.196	17.165	8.860	40.5	79.0	24.4	47.4	41	660	49
Djibouti	0.265	0.141	0.721	0.335	36.8	79.1	19.6	42.1	46	910	65

Country	EM (m)	IM (m)	POP (m)	MORT (m)	EM/ POP (%)	EM/ MORT (%)	IM/ POP (%)	IM/ MORT (%)	LE (yr)	PCI US$	LIT (%)
Equatorial Guinea	0.305	0.168	0.521	0.383	58.5	79.6	32.2	43.9	49	~930	83
Eritrea	1.757	1.036	4.456	2.284	39.4	76.9	23.2	45.4	53	190	56
Ethiopia	36.133	21.590	74.189	44.964	48.7	80.4	29.1	48.0	46	90	39
Gabon	0.504	0.186	1.375	0.671	36.7	75.1	13.5	27.7	57	3,580	71
Gambia	0.606	0.363	1.499	0.762	40.4	79.5	24.2	47.6	54	310	37
Ghana	6.089	3.972	21.833	8.667	27.9	70.3	18.2	45.8	58	320	72
Guinea	5.185	3.611	8.788	6.278	59.0	82.6	41.1	57.5	49	430	41
Guinea-Bissau	0.945	0.611	1.584	1.128	59.7	83.8	38.6	54.2	45	140	38
Kenya	10.015	5.358	32.849	13.732	30.5	72.9	16.3	39.0	38	390	44
Lesotho	0.951	0.386	1.797	1.225	52.9	77.6	21.5	31.5	35	590	83
Liberia	1.754	1.209	3.603	2.148	48.7	81.7	33.6	56.3	41	130	54
Madagascar	7.098	3.867	18.409	9.170	38.6	77.4	21.0	42.2	54	290	67
Malawi	6.976	4.794	12.572	8.425	55.5	82.8	38.1	56.9	38	170	60
Mali	6.808	6.438	13.829	8.407	49.2	81.0	46.6	76.6	49	290	26
Mauritania	1.294	0.848	3.069	1.655	42.2	78.2	27.6	51.2	53	430	40
Mauritius	0.064	0.078	1.244	0.377	5.1	17.0	6.3	20.7	72	4,090	85
Mozambique	12.462	7.200	19.495	15.034	63.9	82.9	36.9	47.9	38	210	44
Namibia	0.672	0.281	2.032	0.912	33.1	73.7	13.8	30.8	44	1,870	82
Niger	6.558	5.674	12.873	7.874	50.9	83.3	44.1	72.1	46	200	16

Country	EM (m)	IM (m)	POP (m)	MORT (m)	EM/ POP (%)	EM/ MORT (%)	IM/ POP (%)	IM/ MORT (%)	LE (yr)	PCI US$	LIT (%)
Niger	6.558	5.674	12.873	7.874	50.9	83.3	44.1	72.1	46	200	16
Nigeria	49.737	38.297	130.236	64.395	38.2	77.2	29.4	59.5	51	320	64
Réunion	0.047	0.041	0.777	0.194	6.0	24.2	5.3	21.1			
Rwanda	5.190	2.577	8.607	6.245	60.3	83.1	29.9	41.3	39	220	67
Sao Tome & Principe	0.039	0.033	0.169	0.060	23.1	65.0	19.5	55.0	70	320	
Senegal	4.457	2.770	9.393	5.699	47.5	78.2	29.5	48.6	53	550	37
Sierra Leone	4.548	2.846	5.340	5.279	85.2	86.2	53.3	53.9	34	150	36
Somalia	5.568	3.582	10.742	6.681	51.8	83.3	33.3	53.6	48	130	
South Africa	13.534	4.623	45.323	19.822	29.9	68.3	10.2	23.3	47	2,780	85
Swaziland	0.471	0.233	1.087	0.607	43.3	77.6	21.4	38.4	34	1,350	80
Tanzania	14.682	8.991	38.365	19.017	38.3	77.2	23.4	47.3	43	290	75
Togo	1.950	1.186	5.129	2.540	38.0	76.8	23.1	46.7	50	310	57
Uganda	11.121	6.301	27.623	14.032	40.3	79.3	22.8	44.9	47	240	67
Western Sahara	0.063	0.052	0.324	0.095	19.4	66.3	16.0	54.7			
Zambia	5.463	2.848	11.043	6.276	49.5	87.0	25.8	45.4	33	380	78
Zimbabwe	4.653	1.800	12.963	6.376	35.9	73.0	13.9	28.2	33	~480	89
TOTAL	300.834	189.834	696.515	382.116	43.2	78.7	27.3	49.7			

Notes. Abbreviations are as for Tables 2.1 and 2.2. Not included are Diego Garcia (largely depopulated by the UK and US for global warfare reasons) and the Seychelles.

2.9 Summary

Excess mortality (avoidable mortality) for a given country for a given period is the difference between the ACTUAL mortality and the deaths EXPECTED for a decently run, peaceful country with the same demographics. Using United Nations Population Division demographic data going back to 1950 (the 2002 Revision), it was possible to make base-line estimates of expected mortality for various demographically distinct groups. For many Third World countries the base-line mortality estimates clustered about 4 deaths per 1,000 of population. Excess mortality was calculated for all countries in the world in pentades (5 year periods) from 1950-2005 (actually from mid-1950-mid-2005) and the results were tabulated in various regional groupings together with corroborative and independent estimates of under-5 infant mortality and life expectancy, annual *per capita* income and adult literacy data. A useful comparative measure of excess mortality is obtained from the "1950-2005 excess mortality/2005 population ratio" which averages as follows in *increasing* order for the major groupings: 2.7% (Overseas Europe) < 5.0% (Western Europe) < 7.5% (Eastern Europe) < 9.4% (Latin America and Caribbean) < 10.9% (East Asia) < 20.7% (Turkey, Iran and Central Asia) < 23.0 (Arab Middle East and North Africa) < 25.1 (South East Asia) < 27.3% (the Pacific) < 31.9% (South Asia) < 43.2% (non-Arab Africa). 1950-2005 excess mortality increases with decreasing annual *per capita* income but excellent outcomes have been achieved in countries with relatively low *per capita* incomes of about $1,000-$2,000 (as compared to $38,000 for the US), namely Cuba, Fiji, the Maldives, Paraguay and Sri Lanka. Low excess mortality is associated with high adult literacy but very high post-1950 excess mortality can still occur in countries with adult literacy in excess of 80% e.g. Congo (Brazzaville), Lesotho, Namibia, South Africa, Swaziland and Zimbabwe. The post-1950 excess mortality correlates with war, occupation by First World countries and consequent increased disregard for the occupied by their rulers. The impact of foreign occupation is explored in subsequent Chapters.

CHAPTER 3: CORRELATES AND CAUSES OF POST-1950 AVOIDABLE GLOBAL MASS MORTALITY

"Cry "Havoc", and let slip the dogs of war."

Mark Antony in Shakespeare, *Julius Caesar.*[1]

"The American people will not relish the idea of any American citizen growing rich and fat in an emergency of blood and slaughter and human suffering."

Franklin Delano Roosevelt, radio broadcast, May 1940.[2]

"Ill fares the land, to hastening ills a prey, Where wealth accumulates, and men decay"

Oliver Goldsmith, *The Deserted Village.*[3]

"Ignorance is degrading only when found in company with riches."

Schopenhauer, Essays: *On Books and Reading.*[4]

"About morals, what is moral is what you feel good after and what is immoral is what you feel bad after."

Ernest Hemingway, *Death in the Afternoon.*[5]

3.1 "Big picture" regional analysis of global post-1950 under-5 infant mortality and excess mortality

Table 2.1 summarizes 1950-2005 excess mortality and under-5 infant mortality for the various regions of the world. The following Tables 2.2 -2.12 provide detailed country-by-country mortality data together with complementary current information on present life expectancy, annual *per capita* income and adult literacy. We can now briefly examine the major regional differences with a view to identifying some major correlates and causes of the excess mortality holocaust.

In a sense everyone knows that the Third World has suffered a major burden of "poverty, war and disease" but, as discussed in the previous chapters, it is important to *quantitate* the human cost. Having calculated 1950-2005 excess mortality and under-5 infant mortality for essentially every country in the world, it has been possible to sum, group and organize the data to permit sensible analysis of this immense catastrophe. The following sections deal with 1950-2005 mortality in various regions of the world in order of increasing values of average 1950-2005 excess mortality/current population.

The regions in Table 2.1 are also listed in order of increasing 1950-2005 excess mortality/current population. However it will become glaringly obvious that the best mortality outcomes correlate with high annual *per capita* income, high adult literacy, lack of invasion by foreign powers and, for many such countries, a post-1950 record of occupying and invading other countries. Conversely, low annual *per capita* income, low adult literacy and a burden of occupation and war (universally with major First World involvement) correlates with a poor mortality outcome.

3.2 Overseas Europe: domestic democracy, prosperity, peace and Anglo-American invasion of distant lands

The best outcome region is "Overseas Europe" which includes Australia, Canada, New Zealand, Israel and the US (plus associated territories such as the US Virgin Islands and Puerto Rico that we will here conveniently subsume under the aegis of the US) and Canada. Inspection of the detailed information for this region

(Table 2.2) reveals that these countries have the very high life expectancies (78-79 years), high annual *per capita* incomes ($15,870-$37,610) and the high adult literacy (~98%) found for the best-achieving countries in Western Europe. For the Western European countries the 1950-2005 excess mortality/2005 population ratio ranges from 1.0-3.6%% and the 1950-2005 under-5 infant mortality/2005 population ranges from 3.3-7.0%% (Table 2.2).

None of these "Overseas Europe" countries have been subject to invasion in the post-1950 period but have *all* been involved in invading and occupying *other* countries. There is an extraordinary and obscene contrast between the social profiles of these countries and the countries in which they have waged war in the post-1950 era: on the perpetrator side peace, democracy, prosperity and very low mortality – and, on the other side, horrendous mortality from which the victim countries are variously recovering.

3.3 Western Europe: domestic bliss and colonial and neo-colonial wars abroad

The Western Europe group of countries has high average mortality outcomes comparable to those of the Overseas Europe and these countries also exhibit high life expectancy (76-80 years) and high adult literacy (92-~98%) together with high annual *per capita* incomes ($9,260-$43,940). The 4 poorest countries are (in ascending order of wealth) Malta, Portugal, Cyprus and Greece; these countries have relatively low *per capita* incomes ($9,260-$13,720) but exhibit high adult literacy (92-~98%) and high life expectancies (76-78 years). As we will discuss later, some non-European countries, notably Cuba, Fiji, Mauritius, the Maldives, Paraguay, Sri Lanka and Thailand have very low annual *per capita* incomes in the range of about $1,000-$2,000 but also have excellent excess mortality and under-5 infant mortality outcomes (Tables 2.2-2.12). For the Western European countries the 1950-2005 excess mortality/2005 population ratio ranges from 0-10.8% and the 1950-2005 under-5 infant mortality/2005 population ranges from 0.8%-5.7% (Table 2.3).

None of the Western European countries have been invaded by foreign powers in the post-1950 period but many have been involved in the occupation and invasion of distant countries in this period, the list including Belgium, Denmark, France, Germany, Italy, the Netherlands, Norway, Portugal, Spain and the UK. Thus in the last 2 decades, Germany, the Netherlands and the UK were involved with the NATO involvement in Balkans; Belgium, Denmark, France, Germany, Italy the Netherlands, Norway, Portugal, Spain and the UK were involved in US-occupied Afghanistan; and Denmark, Iceland, Italy, the Netherlands, Norway, Portugal and Spain sent military or other personnel to join the UK-US occupation of Iraq. The complicity of these countries in horrendous post-1950 mortality in the victim countries will be explored later.

3.4 Eastern Europe: totalitarianism, Russian occupation, general peace and low mortality

The Eastern European group of countries are somewhat worse off than the other European countries in relation to post-1950 excess mortality and under-5 infant mortality but much better off than the better non-European groupings. In general, the Eastern European countries have lower life expectancies (67-76 years) and much lower annual *per capita* incomes ($590-$11,830) than the other European countries; however adult literacy (85-~98%) is very high for all countries (~98%) other than Albania (85%), Bosnia and Herzegovina (93%) and Macedonia (96%). Slovenia (life expectancy 76 years, annual *per capita* income $11,830 and adult literacy ~98%) is the only country of this group with a "Western" level for all these three parameters as well as for 1950-2005 excess mortality/2005 population (1.6%) and 1950-2005 under-5 infant mortality/2005 population (1.9%) (Table 2.4).

In the Eastern European group of countries the 1950-2005 excess mortality/2005 population ratio ranges from 1.6-13.9% and the 1950-2005 under-5 infant mortality/2005 population ranges from 1.4-10.6%; the countries with the highest 1950-2005 excess mortality/2005 population ratios include Hungary (13.9%), Estonia (12.8%), Latvia (12.7%), the Ukraine (11.0%), the Czech Republic (10.6%) and Bulgaria (9.3%). The countries with the worst 1950-2005 under-5 infant mortality/2005 population ratios include Macedonia (10.6%), Armenia (9.5%), Bosnia and Herzegovina (9.4%) and Albania (6.7%), with the rest having values in the range

1.4% (the Czech Republic) to 5.9% (Serbia and Montenegro) (Table 2.4).

The "best" Eastern European countries (Croatia, Georgia, Lithuania, Moldavia, Poland, Romania, Russia, Serbia and Montenegro, Slovakia and Slovenia) have 1950-2005 excess mortality/2005 population ratios ranging from 1.6-8.4% and 1950-2005 under-5 infant mortality/2005 population ratios ranging from 1.9-5.6%. The "worst" eastern European countries (Albania, Armenia, Belarus, Bosnia and Herzegovina, Bulgaria, the Czech Republic, Estonia, Hungary, Latvia and Macedonia) have 1950-2005 excess mortality/2005 population ratios ranging from 3.0-13.9% and 1950-2005 under-5 infant mortality/2005 population ratios ranging from 1.4-10.6% (Table 2.4).

All of the East European countries (except for the Balkan countries) were occupied by the Soviet Union for most of the post-1950 era since the end of WW2, and Hungary and the Czech Republic were further violently invaded by the Soviet Union in 1956 and 1968, respectively. For most of this era only the Soviet Union (Russia) was involved in invasion and occupation of other countries. However in recent years many Eastern European countries joined the US in the illegal occupation of Iraq, namely Albania, Bosnia and Herzegovina, Bulgaria, the Czech Republic, Estonia, Georgia, Hungary, Latvia, Lithuania, Macedonia, Moldova, Poland, Romania, Slovakia and the Ukraine. All European NATO members sent forces to Occupied Afghanistan.

3.5 Latin America and Caribbean: colonial and US hegemony – increased violence yields increased mortality

The Latin American plus Caribbean group (but excluding Haiti) has an overall profile resembling that of the Eastern European group but with lower life expectancy (64-~98 years), modest annual *per capita* income ($890-$14,290) and with generally much poorer adult literacy (64-~98%); Haiti stands out as the poorest performer with levels of these parameters (50 years, $380 and 50%, respectively) similar to those found in non-Arab Africa. The Latin American and Caribbean countries with the highest life expectancies are Cuba and Costa Rica (77 and 78 years, respectively); these countries have modest annual *per capita* incomes (~$1,170 and $4,280, respectively) but have adult literacy rates of 97% and 96%, respectively, and 1950-2005 excess mortality and infant mortality outcomes at a top Western European level (1950-2005 under-5 infant mortality/2005 population ratios of 3.1% and 4.6%, respectively) (Table 2.5).

For the Latin American and Caribbean countries the post-1950 excess mortality/2000 population ratio range from 2.3% (Bahamas) and 3.3% (Argentina) to 32.9% (Bolivia) and 47.9% (Haiti); the 1950-2005 under-5 infant mortality/2005 population ratios range from 2.1% (French Guiana) and 3.1% (Cuba) to 20.1% (Bolivia) and 25.1% (Haiti) (Table 2.5).

Apart from Cuban advisers helping the Angolan government forces against US- and South African-backed forces, Honduran involvement in US-backed terrorism in Central America, and token multinational participations in the US invasion of Grenada, none of the Latin American countries were involved in occupation of other countries until the Dominican Republic, El Salvador, Honduras and Nicaragua joined the illegal US occupation of Iraq. In contrast, most of the Latin American and Caribbean countries have experienced acute US or Western European impositions since 1950, including explicit colonial occupation, foreign-backed dictatorships, terrorism, civil conflicts and other malignant, violent and human rights-abusive interference. There was explicit US military invasion of Cuba, the Dominican Republic, Grenada, Haiti and Panama in the post-1950 era as well as major US involvement in the Honduras-based Contra actions against Nicaragua. The Dominican Republic, El Salvador, Honduras and Nicaragua (all having suffered violent US impositions) provided forces to support the US occupation of Iraq.

3.6 East Asia: remarkable resurgence from European wars and sanctions

The decline in mortality in the East Asian region is a tremendous success story in the light of the pre-1950 devastation of defeated imperial Japan and the devastation of China by Japan and in the US-backed civil war. The post-1950 era saw massive military threat to China from both the US and the Soviet Union, sanctions applied to China by the US and its allies, and the devastation of the

Korean War. The population of China is so large and energetic that traditional violent colonial occupation was not an option for the US, this then allowing for economic recovery by China despite acute US hostility and economic exclusion for half of the post-1950 era.

China sent forces to support North Korea against the US, militarily occupied its Tibetan region, transiently invaded its neighbor India (except for continuing occupation of Ladakh) and had short-lived military exchanges with its neighbor Vietnam. However, apart from South Korean involvement in Vietnam and Iraq and Japanese and Mongolian participation in Iraq, there has been no invasion of *distant* lands by these countries.

Japan, Hong Kong and Taiwan have achieved Western European outcomes in relation to excess mortality and under-5 infant mortality. North Korea, South Korea and China have overall achieved a Latin American standard in the 1950-2005 era but South Korea and China have now bounded ahead. Resource-poor Mongolia, sandwiched between two powers subject to sustained US hostility and economic blockade for much of the post-1950 era, has done very poorly. A major feature in all of these countries has been high adult literacy but the lower life expectancies in China, North Korea and Mongolia correlate with very low annual *per capita* incomes.

For the East Asian countries the 1950-2005 excess mortality/2005 population ratio range from 1.7% (Hong Kong), 2.4% (Taiwan) and 2.8% (Japan) to 10.4% (South Korea), 11.8% (China), 12.9% (North Korea) and 24.0% (Mongolia); the 1950-2005 under-5 infant mortality/2005 population ratios range from 1.4% (Macao), 1.5% (Hong Kong), 1.9% (Japan) and 2.0% (Taiwan) to 6.4% (South Korea), 6.8% (North Korea), 11.9% (China) and 15.0% (Mongolia) (Table 2.6).

3.7 Turkey, Iran and Central Asia: European occupation, intervention and war

In the Turkey, Iran and Central Asia group of countries, Afghanistan (adult literacy 36% and life expectancy 43 years) stands out for appalling outcomes in all mortality-related indices.

Turkey and Iran have somewhat better mortality indices but their adult literacy percentages are 85% and 76%, respectively, notwithstanding relatively high annual *per capita* incomes of $2,790 and $2,000, respectively. The former Soviet Union Central Asian republics have very high adult literacy (~98%) and have achieved the best under-5 infant mortalities in this group of countries, notwithstanding modest annual *per capita* incomes in the range of $190-$1,780 (Table 2.7).

For the Central Asian countries the 1950-2005 excess mortality/2005 population ratios range from 5.0% (Azerbaijan) and 6.4% (Kazakhstan) to 19.2% (Kyrgyzstan), 20.2% (Iran) and 64.0% (Afghanistan); the post-1950 under-5 infant mortality/2005 population ratios range from.8.9% (Uzbekistan) and 10.8% (Kazakhstan) to 15.0% (Turkey), 15.4% (Iran) and 44.3% (Afghanistan) (Table 2.7).

The Central Asian countries were occupied by the Russians until about 1990 and have generally been peaceful except for the Armenian-Azerbaijan conflict and civil conflict in Uzbekistan. US-backed Turkey has a very poor human rights record in the post-1950 era involving invasion of and occupation of part of Cyprus and horrendous, genocidal violence against Muslim Kurdish and Syriac Christian minorities; the prior, horrendous Armenian Genocide is officially denied and indeed it is now illegal to mention this matter in Turkey. Iran has had a heavy burden of violent US hostility and interference culminating in the bloody Iran-Iraq War. Afghanistan has had an appalling burden of civil war, Soviet invasion, further US-backed civil war and thence US invasion to oust the Taliban that is reflected in horrendous infant mortality and excess mortality statistics. Despite a long history of foreign invasion and occupation, some of the Central Asian countries have descended into the moral pit of invading non-contiguous, distant foreign lands, namely Azerbaijan and Kazakhstan through their contributions (albeit very modest) to the US Coalition of the Willing in Iraq, and Uzbekistan, which provided the US with air force base facilities.

3.8 Arab North Africa and the Middle East: decolonization, Anglo-American and Israeli wars and oil

The Arab countries of North Africa and the Middle East variously emerged from European colonial occupation or "protection" with pro-Western royal dictatorships that were thence transformed in some countries into more "representative" republican dictatorships. Independence was hard-won in the Algerian War of Independence from France that killed millions. Violent Western military intervention in these countries in the post-1950 era variously involved the highly-prosperous European-origin countries of the US, Canada, Australia, New Zealand and Israel and the prosperous Western European countries of Denmark, France, Iceland, Italy, the Netherlands, Norway, Spain and the UK. A variety of countries have provided forces for the US Coalition of the Willing in Iraq, namely: Australia, the US (Overseas Europe), the UK, Denmark, Iceland, Italy, the Netherlands, Norway, Portugal and Spain (Western Europe), Albania, Bosnia & Herzegovina, Bulgaria, Czech Republic, Estonia, Georgia, Hungary, Latvia, Lithuania, Macedonia, Moldova, Poland, Romania, Slovakia and the Ukraine (Eastern Europe), the Dominican Republic, El Salvador, Honduras and Nicaragua (Central America), Japan, South Korea and Mongolia (East Asia), Azerbaijan and Kazakhstan (Central Asia), Philippines, Singapore and South Korea (South East Asia) and Tonga (the Pacific).

The intrinsically European Israeli colonization of Palestine and associated conflicts have involved successive wars over half a century between indigenous Arab states and colonial Israel. Israel has been in conflict with all of its immediate neighbors (Egypt, Jordan, Palestine, Lebanon and Syria) as well as having been involved in violent attacks on Iraq (bombed), Libya (shooting down of a civilian airliner), Tunisia (bombing), Uganda (military raid), Sudan (bombing), Turkey (attacks on ships) and the US (attack on the USS Liberty). Inspection of the excess mortality and under-5 infant mortality in the Arab world reveals the horrendous cost of First World colonization, imperialism and militarism. Of course, Western hysteria notwithstanding, no Arab states have invaded, attacked or otherwise violently engaged *any* non-contiguous countries in the post-1950 period (excepting the continuing obscene invasion of starving Yemen by the Saudi-led Coalition).

An interesting exercise to delineate factors contributing to 1950-2005 avoidable mortality in the Arab world involves dissecting out (1) the oil-rich, high income Gulf State Western "protectorates" of Bahrain, Kuwait, Oman, Qatar, and the United Arab Emirates, (2) the "disaster areas" of Iraq, Syria, Sudan and Yemen and (3) the rest. For the Arab Gulf States (excluding US-afflicted Iraq) the 1950-2005 under-5 infant mortality/2005 population ratio ranges from 1.5-9.5% and the 1950-2005 excess mortality/population ratio ranges from 2.8-11.9%; for the "disaster areas" these ratios range from 13.0-23.9% and 19.9-38.4%, respectively; and for "the rest", these ratios range from 5.8-17.7% and 11.0-26.5%, respectively (Table 2.8).

However, when one inspects the average life expectancy, annual *per capita* income and adult literacy of these three regions we see that the Gulf States have range values of 72-77 years, $7,830-$18,060 and 76-94%, respectively; the "disaster areas" 56-61 years, $460-$2,170 and 39-58%, respectively; and "the rest" 69-74 years, $1,390-$5,540 and 49-~98%, respectively.

The mortality-related statistics for the horribly-abused and resource-poor Occupied Palestinian Territories are quite good in the given circumstances – 1950-2005 infant mortality/2005 population 7.7%, 1950-2005 excess mortality/2005 population 17.7%, life expectancy 73 years, annual *per capita* income $1,100 and adult literacy ~98%. Thus high literacy and a very modest income can still yield a reasonable life expectancy and an under-5 infant mortality of the same order as that found in the European Balkans. However the outcomes are inferior to what obtains in "good" non-European countries.

In contrast, the oil-rich states have done well in relation to mortality and annual *per capita* income if not in relation to adult literacy (this latter deficit reflecting entrenched sexism). The Gulf States mortality success associated with peace and wealth has not been translated into democracy, universal literacy and equal options for women. Indeed the Arab countries that made the greatest strides in relation to women's rights, namely Lebanon,

Iraq, Syria and Libya, have been violently crippled this century by the ostensibly liberal, egalitarian and feminist-tolerant Anglo-American democracies. The ultimate "right" of a woman, the survival of her offspring, has been lost in US-UK-occupied Iraq – what is potentially one of the richest countries in the world has been wrecked with a concomitant appalling under-5 infant mortality totalling 1.9 million since the West returned to Iraq with sanctions and total war in 1990 (2021 estimate).

3.9 South East Asia – European-imposed colonialism, occupation, war and militarism

South East Asia further illustrates the correlation of horrendous First World-imposed violence on excess mortality and infant mortality. In the post-1950 period all South East Asian countries except Thailand and the Philippines experienced the tail-end of extended periods of colonial occupation by European countries, namely the UK, France, the Netherlands and Portugal. All South East Asian countries except for Brunei, Thailand and Singapore have experienced substantial European-supplied military violence, this variously involving civil war, local insurgencies or horrendous foreign invasion, occupation and prolonged violence.

In relation to avoidable mortality, the South East Asian countries can be conveniently grouped into the Western European-like countries (Brunei and Singapore), Eastern European-like (Malaysia, Thailand and Philippines) and unambiguously Third World countries (the rest). These categories clearly illustrate the impact of war on mortality as outlined below.

The Western European-like countries of oil-rich Brunei and highly entrepreneurial, urban Singapore have annual *per capita* incomes of ~$24,100 and $21,230, respectively; life expectancies of 76 and 78, respectively; and adult literacy of 92%. These countries have adult literacy less than that in Western European countries and slightly lower life expectancies (circa 2003 data). Both Brunei and Singapore have escaped the Anglo-American-prosecuted post-1950 wars in the region and indeed have profited commercially from them. The 1950-2005 excess mortality/2005 population ratios for Brunei and Singapore are 5.3% and 2.6%, respectively, while the

post-1950 under-5 infant mortality/2005 population ratios are 2.9%
and 1.4%, respectively (Table 2.9).

The Eastern European-like group of countries have substantially
evaded war for most of the post-1950 period - thus Malaysia
suffered colonial rule, the Malaysian Emergency and Confrontation
with Indonesia; Thailand suffered repeated but relatively benign
military coups by US-armed and trained military; Philippines
suffered coups by US-armed and trained military and sustained,
albeit relatively localized, Muslim separatist insurgency. This is
reflected in a 1950-2005 under-5 infant mortality/2005 population
range of 4.6-8.5%, an annual *per capita* income range of $1,080-
$3,780, life expectancies of 69-73 years and adult literacies in the
range 87-96% (circa 2003 data). The 1950-2005 excess
mortality/2005 population ratios for Malaysia, the Philippines and
Thailand are 9.3%, 11.0% and 5.9%, respectively, while the 1950-
2005 under-5 infant mortality/2005 population ratios are 4.6%,
8.0% and 8.5%, respectively (Table 2.9).

The remainder of the South East Asian group are "typical" Third
World countries that have experienced the violence of European
colonialism and of post-colonial European-imposed and European-
supplied war - Myanmar (violent military dictatorship, civil war),
Laos (US Indochina War, continuing insurgency), Cambodia (US
Indochina War, genocide by the Khmer Rouge), Vietnam (war of
independence against the French, US Indochina War, post-war US
sanctions), Indonesia (US-backed military coup, 4 decades of
corrupt, violent, Anglo-American-supported military dictatorship)
and Timor-Leste (US-backed Indonesian invasion and horrendous
genocide of 0.2 million East Timorese). The mortality-related
statistics for this war-ravaged group of countries are appalling –
1950-2005 excess mortality/2005 population ratios of 28.7-81.0%;
1950-2005 under-5 infant mortality/2005 population ratios of 10.6-
27.5%; an annual *per capita* income range of $310-$610, life
expectancies of 50-69 years and adult literacy in the range 65-93%
(Table 2.9).

Vietnam provides a remarkable example of post-war resilience:
under-5 infant mortality/present population ratio 10.6%, an annual
per capita income of $480, life expectancy 69 years and an adult
literacy of 93%. The example of Vietnam again shows that war-

ravaged countries can achieve survival miracles in the face of long-term Western hostility with a combination of high adult literacy, modest annual *per capita* income and commitment to good primary health care and education.

3.10 The Pacific- mixed colonial occupation and post-colonial outcomes

With the exceptions of French New Caledonia, French Polynesia and various US-linked territories, the Pacific island states and New Guinea emerged from colonial occupation in the post-1950 era. The Pacific countries considered in this analysis can be put into 2 major categories in relation to excess mortality and under-5 infant mortality outcomes, namely the "good" and the "bad".

The good outcome countries include Fiji (a former UK colony), US-linked Guam and Micronesia and the French "overseas" territories of French Caledonia and French Polynesia. The mortality-related statistics for this "good" group are as follows: 1950-2005 under-5 infant mortality/2005 population ratios from 1.3-6.6%; annual *per capita* incomes of $2,090 and $2,360 for Micronesia and Fiji, respectively; life expectancies of 69-70 years; and adult literacy in the range 93-~98% (Table 2.10). Fiji has a substantial business- and professionally-oriented Indian population; the US-linked states have benefited economically from US military and other strategic expenditures; and the French dependencies have benefited economically from French military expenditure and French colonists. Inter-racial strife in Fiji and independence-related troubles in the French territories have ostensibly produced few casualties.

The bad outcome countries (former colonial masters into the post-1950 era in parenthesis) include the Melanesian states of the Solomon Islands (UK), Vanuatu (UK and France) and Papua New Guinea (Australia), and the Polynesian states of Tonga (UK) and Samoa (New Zealand). Taken together, these poor outcome countries have the following mortality-related statistics (circa 2003 estimations) – 1950-2005 excess mortality/2005 population ratios of 9.9-35.1%; 1950-2005 under-5 infant mortality/2005 population ratios of 7.1-18.9%; annual *per capita* incomes of $510-$1,600; life expectancies of 58-70 years; and adult literacy in the range 64-

~98% (Table 2.10). Civil strife has occurred in the Melanesian states, of which the most costly in human lives was the attempted secession of Bougainville from Papua New Guinea (about 10,000 deaths, mostly from disease and ultimately due to civil disruption and deprivation).

3.11 South Asia – crippled by the legacies from British imperialism

The South Asian countries were granted independence from Britain in the immediate post-war years. Bhutan and Nepal were left as impoverished feudal societies with this situation degenerating into sustained, continuing civil war in the case of Nepal. India and Pakistan were left as impoverished, mutually-hostile societies as the outcome of British divide-and-rule policies favoring Muslim separatism. Partition, Partition atrocities, repeated war over Kashmir and communal violence have contributed to hugely expensive, First World-supplied military hostility that has now become a nuclear stand-off. Post-Partition Hindu West Bengal and Muslim Bangladesh recovered demographically after the horrendous World War 2 Bengal Famine (4 million victims in Bengal; 6-7 million dead in Bengal, Assam, Bihar and Orissa) that the British have generally rubbed out of their history books. Bangladesh was borne out of the genocidal and anti-democratic intervention of the US-backed West Pakistan military in 1971.

The Maldives (tiny but strategically used by the UK) and Sri Lanka (democratic and well-administered but with sustained Tamil versus Sinhalese civil war) have had the best outcomes in South Asia with Eastern European mortality-related statistics – 1950-2005 excess mortality/2005 population ratios of 4.4% and 4.9%, respectively; 1950-2005 under-5 infant mortality/2005 population ratios of 3.6% and 7.2%, respectively; life expectancies of 68 and 73 years; annual *per capita* incomes of $2,300 and $930; and adult literacy of 97% and 92%, respectively (Table 2.11).

The poor outcome remainder of the South Asian nations have a surprisingly consistent set of mortality-related statistics - post-1950 excess mortality/2005 population ratios of 30.8-33.6%; post-1950 under-5 infant mortality/2005 population ratios from 18.2-25.0%; per capita incomes of $240-$660; life expectancies of 60-64 years;

and adult literacy in the range 40-57% (Table 2.11). These very poor mortality outcomes correlate with a combination of low annual *per capita* income and low adult literacy.

3.12 Non-Arab Africa – colonialism, neo-colonialism, corruption, militarism, war and HIV-1

The 1950-2005 excess mortality and under-5 infant mortality for non-Arab Africa totals about 0.3 billion and 0.2 billion, respectively. This worst mortality region in the world suffered centuries of brutal colonial occupation that ostensibly came to an end in the post-1950 era. However explicit colonial occupation was variously replaced (after bloody wars of independence in many cases) by corrupt and incompetent client régimes, militarization, debt, economic exclusion, malignant interference, inter-country wars and ethnically-, tribally- and Cold War-based civil wars. The First World had a major role in these post-colonial impositions with the major players being the UK, US, France, Belgium, Portugal, Spain, Russia and the White minority-ruled countries of South Africa and Southern Rhodesia.

The outstanding countries with Eastern European-style mortality-related statistics are the tiny, peaceful and prosperous Indian Ocean island countries of Réunion and Mauritius with 1950-2005 excess mortality/2005 population ratios of 5.1% and 6.0%, respectively, and 1950-2005 under-5 infant mortality/2005 population ratios of 5.3% and 6.3%, respectively. Mauritius has a life expectancy of 72 years, an annual *per capita* income of $4,090 and an adult literacy of 85% (Table 2.12).

A further set of countries with some glimmerings of hope include Botswana, Cape Verde, Comoros, Gabon, Ghana, Sao Tome and Principe and South Africa with 1950-2005 excess mortality/2005 population ratios of 20.5-36.7%, 1950-2005 under-5 infant mortality/2005 population ratios of 10.2-19.5%, life expectancies of 39-70 years, annual *per capita* incomes of $320-$3,580 and adult literacy of 56-85% (Table 2.12).

The remaining majority of non-Arab African countries have very poor mortality-related statistics - 1950-2005 excess mortality/2005 population ratios of 23.1-85.2%, 1950-2005 under-5 infant mortality/2005 population ratios of 13.8-53.3%, life expectancies of 33-54 years, *per capita* incomes of $90-$3,430 and adult literacy of 16-89% (Table 2.12). Some of these countries have been relatively peaceful but many have been ravaged by colonial wars or post-colonial civil wars. Such conflicts will be detailed in the country-by-country "short history" analysis in Chapter 7 that includes 2021 updates about 2020 under-5 infant mortality and avoidable mortality (Tables 9.1-9.12) in comparison with data for 2003 (Tables 8.1-8.12).

The scourge of HIV-1 infection in sub-Saharan Africa has massively perturbed the mortality outcomes and our ability to make sense of key mortality-inducing factors. In sub-Saharan Africa in 2005 there were 3 million newly-infected HIV-1 victims – 64% of the total number of new infections for the whole world. Thus badly impacted Botswana, Namibia, Swaziland and Zimbabwe have 1950-2005 excess mortality/2005 population ratios of 24.6-43.3%, 1950-2005 under-5 mortality/2005 population ratios of 13.1-21.4%, annual *per capita* incomes of ~$480-$3,430, adult literacy of 77-89% and life expectancies of only 33-44 years (Table 2.12).

3.13 To be or not to be - lowest mortality countries invading *distant* high mortality countries

As outlined above, a major difference between "good" and "bad" mortality outcome countries lies in the patterns of major, violent military involvement by these countries since 1950 with *distant* and *contiguous* combatants. The distinction between distant and contiguous countries is useful since it is difficult to avoid some conflict with immediate neighbors. These military involvements are summarized below for alphabetically-listed countries within the various regional groupings (arranged in order of 1950-2005 infant mortality/2005 population ratio). Involvements with contiguous countries are (marked below with an asterisk (*)). The countries are conveniently grouped into (a) European and (b) non-European countries.

(a) European countries

i. Overseas Europe

No countries in this lowest mortality group have *ever* been significantly invaded and all have been repeatedly involved during the post-1950 era in the invasion, occupation or attack on forces of distant lands.

Australia – Afghanistan, China (Korean War), Indochina (Vietnam, Laos, Cambodia), Indonesia (Confrontation), Iraq, Korea, Malaysia, Nauru, Papua New Guinea*, Solomon Islands, Somalia, Syria, Timor-Leste.

Canada - Afghanistan, China (Korean War), Iraq, Korea.

New Zealand – China (Korean War), Indochina (Vietnam, Laos, Cambodia), Indonesia (Confrontation), Iraq, Korea, Malaysia, Samoa, Timor-Leste, Tokelau.

Israel – Egypt*, Jordan*, Lebanon*, Libya, Occupied Palestinian Territories*, Sudan, Syria*, Tunisia, Turkey (attack on ships), Uganda, US (deliberate attack on USS Liberty).

US – Afghanistan, Bosnia-Herzegovina, China (Korean War), Colombia, Cuba, Diego Garcia, Dominican Republic, Germany, Grenada, Guam, Haiti, Indochina (Vietnam, Laos, Cambodia), Iraq, Iran, Japan, Korea, Kuwait, Liberia, Libya, Marshall Islands, Micronesia, Pakistan, Panama, Philippines, Somalia, Serbia-Montenegro, Syria, Yemen,Venezuela, *plus* world-wide involvement in other violence (e.g. civil wars and the Honduras-based Contra terrorism against Nicaragua) and about 700 military bases in about 70 countries throughout the world.

ii. Western Europe

Western European like Overseas European countries have very low infant mortalities and excess mortalities coupled with very high life expectancies, annual *per capita* incomes and adult literacy outcomes. However there is now a "mixed" result in relation to military action against combatants in *distant* countries.

Belgium – Afghanistan, Burundi, Congo (Zaire), Rwanda.

Denmark – Afghanistan, Greenland, Iraq.

France – Afghanistan, Algeria, Benin, Burkina Faso, Cambodia, Cameroon, Central African Republic, Chad, Comoros, Congo (Brazzaville), Cote d'Ivoire, Djibouti, Equatorial Guinea, French Guiana, French Polynesia, Gabon, Guadeloupe, Guinea, Haiti, Iraq, Laos, Libya, Madagascar, Mali, Martinique, Mauritania, Morocco, New Caledonia, Niger, Pondicherry, Réunion, Senegal, Somalia, Togo, Vanuatu, Vietnam.

Germany – Afghanistan, Serbia (Balkans).

Iceland – Afghanistan, Iraq.

Italy – Afghanistan, Iraq.

Netherlands – Afghanistan, Indonesia, Iraq, Aruba, Netherlands Antilles, Suriname, West New Guinea.

Norway - Afghanistan, Iraq.

Portugal – Afghanistan, Angola, Goa, Iraq, Macao, Mozambique, Cape Verde, Sao Tome and Principe, Timor-Leste.

Spain – Afghanistan, Equatorial Guinea, Iraq, Morocco, Western Sahara.

United Kingdom – Afghanistan, Argentina, Bahamas, Bahrain, Barbados, Belize, Botswana, Brunei, China (Korean War), Diego Garcia, Egypt, Fiji, Gambia, Ghana, Guyana, Hong Kong, Indonesia (Confrontation), Iraq, Jamaica, Kenya, Kiribati, Korea (North & South), Kuwait, Lesotho, Libya, Malaysia, Maldives, Malta, Mauritius, Nigeria, Oman, Saint Lucia, Saint Vincent and the Grenadines, Serbia, Seychelles, Sierra Leone, Singapore, Solomon Islands, Sudan, Syria, Tanzania, Trinidad & Tobago, Tonga, Tuvalu, United Arab Emirates, Vanuatu, Yemen.
To their immense credit, Austria, Finland, Greece, Ireland, Luxembourg, Malta, Sweden and Switzerland stayed home (although one could cast a jaundiced eye over Swiss banking of the ill-gotten gains of corrupt régimes around the world).

iii. Eastern Europe

The Eastern European countries were nearly all dominated by the former Soviet Union since the end of World War 2 (exceptions being Albania and the countries of the former Yugoslavia). Armenia and Georgia, formerly Soviet-ruled countries with a Christian tradition, have been conveniently included in this group. The Eastern European group does significantly worse than the other European groupings with respect to 1950-2005 excess mortality, 1950-2005 under-5 infant mortality, annual *per capita* income and life expectancy but nevertheless on average does much better than the best of the non-European group, namely Latin America and the Caribbean. Adult literacy in Eastern Europe is on a par with that in the West.

Notwithstanding their bad "press" in the West, these countries, apart from Russia, have a fairly mild record of imperialism and military adventurism compared to that of Overseas Europe and Western Europe. Indeed, apart from Russia's extensive record of occupation (Eastern Europe and Central Asia), invasion (Afghanistan) and re-invasion (Hungary, Czechoslovakia and Chechnya; annexation of Crimea), Armenia's spat with Azerbaijan, and the civil war in the former Yugoslavia (that Slovenia very sensibly bought its way out of), the only other Eastern European military adventures are the token involvements of all of these countries – except for Armenia, Byelorussia, Russia, Serbia and Slovenia - in the occupation of Iraq. In their various involvements in US-occupied Iraq and US-occupied Afghanistan the Czechs, Poles, Slovaks, and Ukrainians conveniently forgot their occupations by Nazi Germany and Communist Russia, and the Bulgarians, Estonians, Hungarians, Latvians, Lithuanians and Romanians equally shamefully emulated their earlier collaboration with Nazi German militarism.

Albania - Afghanistan, Iraq.

Armenia – Azerbaijan*.

Azerbaijan – Iraq, Armenia*.

Bosnia-Herzegovina – Iraq.

Bulgaria – Afghanistan, Iraq.

Croatia – Afghanistan.

Czech Republic – Afghanistan, Iraq.

Estonia - Afghanistan, Iraq.

Georgia – Iraq.

Hungary – Afghanistan, Iraq.

Latvia – Afghanistan, Iraq.

Lithuania - Afghanistan, Iraq.

Macedonia – Afghanistan, Iraq.

Moldova – Iraq.

Poland – Afghanistan Iraq.

Romania - Afghanistan, Iraq.

Russia – Afghanistan*, Armenia*, Azerbaijan*, Belarus*, Bulgaria*, Czech Republic*, Estonia*, Georgia*, Germany (East)*, Hungary*, Latvia*, Lithuania*, Moldova*, Mongolia*, Poland*, Romania*, Serbia-Bosnia-Herzegovina*, Slovakia*, Syria (invited by the Syrian Government), Ukraine* (plus extensive military aid to combatants in Africa and Asia).

Slovakia - Afghanistan, Iraq.

Slovenia – Afghanistan.

Ukraine – Afghanistan, Iraq.

Notable are the obscene involvements in *distant* Iraq of most newly independent Eastern European countries. Armenia fought over territory with its neighbor Azerbaijan. While the USSR provided arms for many Third World countries or liberation movements, Russia confined its direct military involvements or threats of such attacks to its *contiguous* post-war subjects and to Afghanistan (except for its Syrian Government-invited key role in the Syrian War).

Belarus, Croatia, Romania, Slovakia, Serbia & Montenegro and Slovenia did not even invade their neighbours (although Bosnia-Herzegovina, Croatia,and Serbia-Montenegro were involved in a complex civil war involving horrible war crimes).

(b) Non-European countries

We can now turn to countries in the non-European world to see what extent these typically very poor countries have emulated the active militarism of the European powers over the last half century. Many of these violent non-European countries have suffered civil wars (with major First World complicity) and have been ruled by violent dictators (of whom many were assisted in their rise to power by First World powers). Apart from the US-inspired Iraq involvements listed below, in most cases the international involvements of non-European countries have typically involved major military actions in immediately neighboring countries and variously involved some very short to longer term *occupations* of *contiguous* foreign lands (marked thus: *) as detailed below.

iv. Latin America and the Caribbean

Argentina – Falkland Islands* (UK).

Dominican Republic – Iraq.

El Salvador – Iraq.

Honduras – Iraq, Nicaragua* (via the Contras).

Nicaragua – Iraq.

In addition, a number of Caribbean states sent token forces to assist the US occupation of Grenada.

v. East Asia

China – India*, Korea*, Vietnam*.

Japan – Iraq.

South Korea – Iraq, Vietnam.

vi. Arab North Africa and Middle East

Iraq – Iran*, Kuwait*.

Libya – Chad*.

Morocco – Western Sahara*.

Saudi Arabia – Bahrain*, Yemen*.

Syria – Lebanon* (invited as peace-keepers).

The Gulf States are part of a Saudi Coalition making war on starving Yemen (Qatar withdrew).

vii. Turkey, Iran & Central Asia

Azerbaijan – Armenia*, Iraq.

Iran – Iraq*.

Kazakhstan – Iraq.

Turkey – Cyprus*, Korea, Syria*.

viii. South East Asia

Indonesia – Malaysia*, Timor-Leste*.

Philippines – Iraq, Vietnam.

ix. Pacific

Tonga – Iraq.

x. South Asia

India – Pakistan*.

Pakistan – Bangladesh (East Pakistan)*, India*.

xi. Non-Arab Africa

Eritrea – Ethiopia*.

Ethiopia – Eritrea*, Somalia*.

Kenya – Somalia*.

Mauritania – Western Sahara*.

Rwanda - Congo (Zaire)*.

South Africa –Angola, Botswana*, Lesotho*, Mozambique*, Namibia*, Zambia*, Zimbabwe*.

Southern Rhodesia –Mozambique*, Zambia*.

Tanzania – Uganda*.

Uganda – Congo (Zaire)*, Tanzania*.

Finally it must be noted that a number of cross-border military incursions have occurred involving *neighbouring* countries in non-Arab Africa, notably in West Africa and variously involving Angola, Congo (Zaire), Liberia, Rwanda, Sierra Leone and Zambia.

3.14 Quantitative assessment of the mortality consequences of occupation

Already we can see from the above analysis that major countries in the "best outcome" European group have variously been very busy since 1950 occupying, invading or otherwise fighting with combatants from a variety of distant countries around the world. Adding the excess mortality or infant mortality tolls of *victim countries* can give us a quantitative measure of the *complicity* of these countries in the global post-1950 excess mortality and under-5 infant mortality.

It is difficult to assess the degree of complicity and culpability. Thus a getaway driver may not be directly responsible for acts of violence in a bank robbery but is nevertheless complicit – and the greater the number of such occurrences and the greater the human cost the greater the degree of culpability. Further, the period of impact of invasion, war and occupation can extend to well after cessation of such impositions (as seen in the generally disastrous mortality statistics of the post-colonial Third World). The actual involvement of the First World in global mass mortality extends well beyond mere military violence against billions of unarmed civilians and poorly armed opponents, and also includes arms supply, militarization, malignant interference, threat, debt and economic exclusion. Indeed the period prior to invasion is likely to be dangerous for human survival as the victim country uses scarce resources to meet a building threat (an extreme example of this being the appalling suffering of the Iraqis under sanctions between 1990, when they commenced, and the final actual invasion in 2003).

The invasion and occupation of any country is typically associated with (1) prior coveting, threat and interference by the prospective Occupier, who is accordingly complicit in bad mortality outcomes in the pre-invasion period; (2) violent occupation involving explicit responsibility by the Occupier for any associated avoidable mortality (excess mortality) as clearly set out in the Geneva Conventions; and (3) a post-occupation period typically involving recovery of a shattered country with continuing malignant interference from the former Occupier. Massive evidence for the *continuing* post-occupation impact of occupation is provided by appalling avoidable mortality outcomes in a swathe of victim countries in the non-European world. Accordingly, in assessing *complicity in* and *responsibility for* avoidable mortality associated with violent occupation of countries we need to consider *all* three phases.

As detailed in Chapters 2-7, the 1950-2005 avoidable mortality has totalled 1.3 billion for the world, 1.2 billion for the non-European World and 0.6 billion for the Muslim world – and there has been major First World complicity in this catastrophe. Using our guide of considering *all three phases of occupation*, we can obtain quantitative, upper limit estimates of the *1950-2005 occupation-related avoidable mortality* associated with specific, substantial, non-transient, violent occupations in which particular countries were the *major* occupiers in the *post-WW2 era*. Occupations of the Falkland Islands (Malvinas), Germany, Japan, Kashmir, Kosovo and Ladakh are *ignored* for realistic simplicity as are many peace-keeping military involvements (including the recently-terminated Syrian presence in Lebanon), post-independence conflicts over the

Western Sahara, many massive covert and overt US military involvements around the world, notably in Latin America, Africa and Asia (e.g. the US-backed coup, military dictatorship and mass murder in Chile (1975-1989) and US bases in scores of countries).

This summary data provided below is of 1950-2005 excess mortality/ 2005 population (both in millions, m) and expressed as a percentage (%); this ratio is given for each major Occupier, for each country occupied and as a total for all the countries subject to a particular Occupier. The asterisk (*) below indicates a *major* occupation by *more than one country* in the post-WW2 era (thus I have listed only the UK and the US as major occupiers of Afghanistan, Iraq and Korea, leaving aside the many other minor participants in these conflicts) [the data are as for 2005 and do not include subsequent invasions and occupations].

Australia [0.587m/20.092m = 2.9%] - Papua New Guinea [2.091m/5.959m = 35.1%], Solomon Islands* [0.050m/0.504m = 9.9%], *total* = 2.141m/6.463m = 33.1%.

Belgium [0.749m/10.359m = 7.2%] - Burundi [4.097m/7.319m = 56.0%], Congo (Zaire) [26.677m/56.079m = 47.6%], Rwanda [5.190m/8.607m = 60.3%], *total* = 35.964m/72.005m = 49.9%.

Ethiopia [36.133m/74.189m = 48.7%] - Eritrea* [1.757m/4.456m = 39.4%], *total* = 1.757m/4.456m = 39.4%.

France [3.275m/60.711m = 5.4%] - Algeria [7.167m/32.877m =21.8%], Benin [3.267m/7.103m = 46.0%], Burkina Faso [6.810m/13.798m = 49.4%], Cambodia* [5.852m/14.825m = 39.5%], Cameroon* [6.669m/16.564m = 40.3%], Central African Republic [2.274m/3.962m =57.4%], Chad [5.085m/9.117m = 55.8%], Comoros [0.204m/0.812m =25.1%], Congo (Brazzaville) [1.085m/3.921m = 27.7%], Côte d'Ivoire [6.953m/17.165m = 40.5%], Djibouti [0.265m/0.721m = 36.8%], Egypt* [19.818m/74.878m = 26.5%], French Guiana [0.010m/0.187m = 5.3%], French Polynesia [0.018m/0.252m = 7.1%], Gabon [0.504m/1.375m = 36.7%], Guadeloupe [0.025m/0.446m = 5.6%], Guinea [5.185m/8.788m = 59.0%], Haiti* [4.089m/8.549m = 47.9%], Laos* [2.653m/5.918m = 44.8%], Madagascar [7.098m/18.409m = 38.6%], Mali [6.808m/13.829m = 49.2%],

Martinique [0.022m/0.397m = 5.5%], Mauritania [1.294m/3.069m = 42.2%], Mauritius [0.064m/1.244m = 5.18], Morocco* [8.202m/31.564m = 26.0%], New Caledonia [0.017m/0.237m = 7.2%], Niger [6.558m/12.873m = 50.9%], Réunion [0.047m/0.777m = 6.0%], Senegal [4.457m/9.393m = 47.5%], Syria* [2.198m/18.650m = 11.8%], Togo [1.950m/5.129m = 38.0%], Tunisia [1.582m/10.042m =15.8%], Vanuatu* [0.037m/0.222m = 16.7%], Vietnam* [24.015m/83.585m = 28.7%], *total* = 142.291m/430.678m = 33.0%.

Indonesia [71.521m/225.313 = 31.7%] - Timor Leste* [0.694m/0.857m = 81.0%] - *total* = 0.694m/0.857m = 81.0%.

Iraq [5.283m/26.555m = 19.9%] - Kuwait* [0.089m/2.671m = 3.3%], *total* = 0.089m/2.671m = 3.3%.

Israel [0.095m/6.685m =1.4%] - Egypt* [19.818m/74.878m = 26.5%], Jordan* [0.630m/5.750m = 11.0%], Lebanon* [0.535m/3.761m = 14.2%], Occupied Palestinian Territories *[0.677m/3.815m = 17.7%], Syria* [2.198m/18.650m = 11.8%], *total* = 23.858m/106.854 = 22.3%.

Netherlands [0.0m/16.300m = 0%] - Indonesia [71.521m/225.313m = 31.7%], Netherlands Antilles [0.009m/0.224m = 3.9%], Suriname [0.039m/0.442m = 8.8%], *total* = 71.569m/225.979 = 31.7%.

New Zealand [0.143m/3.932m = 3.6%] - Samoa [0.039m/0.182m = 21.4%], *total* = 0.039m/0.182m = 21.4%.

Pakistan [49.700m/161.151m = 30.8%] - Bangladesh*[51.196m/152.593m = 33.6%], *total* = 51.196m/152.593m = 33.6%.

Portugal [0.429m/10.080m = 4.3%] - Angola [9.207m/14.533m = 63.4%], Cape Verde [0.099m/0.482m = 20.5%], Guinea-Bissau [0.945m/1.584m = 59.7%], Macao [0.036m/0.472m = 7.6%], Mozambique [12.462m/19.495m = 63.9%], São Tome and Príncipe [0.039m/0.169m = 23.1%], Timor Leste*[0.694m/0.857m = 81.0%], *total* = 23.482m/37.592 = 62.5%.

Russia [11.897m/141.553m = 8.4%] - Afghanistan
[16.609m/25.971m = 64.0%], Armenia [0.091m/3.043m = 3.0%],
Azerbaijan [0.428m/8.527m = 5.0%], Belarus [0.375m/9.809m =
3.8%], Bulgaria [0.769m/7.763m = 9.9%], Czech Republic
[1.087m/10.216m = 10.6%], Estonia [0.166m/1.294m = 12.8%],
Georgia [0.281m/5.026m = 5.6%], Hungary [1.363m/9.784m =
13.9%], Kazakhstan [0.983m/15.364m = 6.4%], Kyrgyzstan
[1.041m/5.278m = 19.7%], Latvia [0.288m/2.265m = 12.7%],
Lithuania [0.143m/3.401m = 4.2%], Moldova [0.254m/4.259m =
6.0%], Mongolia [0.640m/2.667m = 24.0%], Poland
[0.677m/38.516m = 1.8%], Romania [1.133m/22.228m = 5.1%],
Slovakia [0.130m/5.411m = 2.4%], Tajikistan [0.924m/6.356m =
14.5%], Turkmenistan [0.817m/5.015m = 16.3%], Ukraine
[5.279m/47.782m = 11.0%], Uzbekistan [3.585m/26.868m =
13.3%], *total* = 37.063m/266.843m = 13.9%.

South Africa [13.534m/45.323m = 29.9%] - Namibia
[0.672m/2.032m = 33.1%], *total* = 0.672m/2.032m = 33.1%.

Spain [1.049m/41.184m = 2.5%] - Equatorial Guinea
[0.305m/0.521m = 58.5%], Morocco* [8.202m/31.564m = 26.0%],
Western Sahara [0.063m/0.324m = 19.4%], *total* =
8.570m/32.409m = 26.4%.

Turkey [10.488m/73.302m = 14.3%] – Cyprus [0.054m/0.813m =
6.6%], *total* = 0.054m/0.813m = 6.6%.

UK [4.411m/59.598m = 7.4%] - Afghanistan* [16.609m/25.971m
= 64.0%], Bahamas [0.007m/0.321m = 2.3%], Bahrain
[0.054m/0.754m = 7.2%], Bangladesh* [51.196m/152.593m =
33.6%], Barbados [0.015m/0.272m = 5.5%], Belize
[0.014m/0.266m = 5.3%], Bhutan [0.908m/2.392m = 38.0%],
Botswana [0.443m/1.801m = 24.6%], Brunei [0.020m/0.374m =
5.3%], Cameroon* [6.669m/16.564m = 40.3%], Cyprus
[0.054m/0.813m = 6.6%]; Egypt* [19.818m/74.878m = 26.5%],
Eritrea* [1.757m/4.456m = 39.4%], Ethiopia [36.133m/74.189m =
48.7%], Fiji [0.054m/0.854m = 6.3%], Gambia [0.606m/1.499m =
47.6%], Ghana [6.089m/21.833m = 27.9%], Greece*
[0.027m/10.978m = 0.2%], Grenada* [0.018m/0.121m = 14.9%],
Guyana [0.086m/0.768m = 11.2%], Hong Kong [0.125m/7.182m =
1.7%], India [351.900m/1096.917m = 32.1%], Iraq*

[5.283m/26.555m = 19.9%], Israel [0.095m/6.685 = 1.4%],
Jamaica [0.245m/2.701m =9.1%], Jordan* [0.630m/5.750m =
11.0%], Kenya [10.015m/32.849m = 30.5%], Korea*
[7.958m/71.058m = 11.2%], Kuwait* [0.089m/2.671m = 3.3%],
Lesotho [0.951m/1.797m =52.9%], Libya [0.785m/5.768m
=13.6%], Malawi [6.976m/12.572m = 55.5%], Malaysia
[2.344m/25.325m = 9.3%], Maldives [0.015m/0.338m = 4.4%],
Malta [0.019m/0.397m = 4.8%], Myanmar [20.174m/50.696 =
39.8%], Nepal [10.650m/26.289m = 40.5%], Nigeria
[49.737m/130.236m =38.2%], Occupied Palestinian Territories
[0.677m/3.815m = 17.7%], Oman [0.359m/3.020m =11.9%],
Pakistan [49.700m/161.151m = 30.8%], Qatar [0.029m/0.628m =
4.6%], Saint Lucia [0.012m/0.152m = 7.9%], Saint Vincent &
Grenadines [0.018m/0.121m =14.9%], Sierra Leone
[4.548m/5.340m = 85.2%], Singapore [0.113m/4.372m = 2.6%],
Solomon Islands* [0.050m/0.504m = 48.5%], Somalia*
[5.568m/10.742m =51.8%], Sri Lanka [0.951m/19.366m = 4.9%],
Sudan [13.471m/35.040m = 38.4%], Swaziland [0.471m/1.087m =
43.3%], Tanzania [14.682m/38.365m =38.3%], Tonga
[0.020m/0.106m = 18.9%], Trinidad & Tobago [0.052m/1.311m =
4.0%], Uganda [11.121m/27.623m = 40.3%], United Arab
Emirates [0.087m/3.106m =2.8%], Vanuatu [0.037m/0.222m =
16.7%], Yemen [6.798m/21.480m = 31.6%], Zambia
[5.463m/11.043m = 49.5%], Zimbabwe [4.653m/12.963m
=35.9%], *total* = 727.448m/2247.711m = 32.4%.

US [8.455m/300.038m = 2.8%] - Afghanistan* [16.609m/25.971m
= 64.0%], Cambodia* [5.852m/14.825m = 39.5%], Dominican
Republic [0.806m/8.998m = 9.0%], Federated States of Micronesia
[0.016m/0.111m = 14.4%], Greece* [0.027m/10.978m = 0.2%],
Grenada* [0.018m/0.121m = 14.9%], Guam [0.005m/0.168m =
3.0%], Haiti* [4.089m/8.549m = 47.9%], Iraq* [5.283m/26.555m =
19.9%], Korea* [7.958m/71.058m = 11.2%], Laos*
[2.653m/5.918m = 44.8%], Panama [0.172m/3.235m = 5.3%],
Philippines [9.080m/82.809m = 11.0%], Puerto Rico
[0.039m/3.915m = 1.0%], Somalia* [5.568m/10.742m = 51.8%],
US Virgin Islands [0.003m/0.113m = 2.4%], Vietnam*
[24.015m/83.585m = 28.7%], *total* = 82.193m/357.651m = 23.0%

This catalogue of post-1950 avoidable mortality due to violent occupation [as of 2007] can be roughly converted to post-1950 under-5 infant mortality by multiplying by a factor of about 0.7 (the ratio of post-1950 under-5 infant mortality to post-1950 avoidable mortality for the non-European world). This data can be used to provide a relative impact statement (noting, of course, that there are various ways in which this kind of assessment could be made e.g. by considering excess mortality for only the period of occupation).

In order of *descending* absolute 1950-2005 excess mortality in which they have been complicit we have the following order: UK (727.3m) > France (142.3m) > US (82.2m) > Netherlands (71.6m) > Pakistan (51.2m) > Russia (37.1m)> Belgium (36.0m) > Israel (23.9m) > Portugal (23.5m) > Spain (8.6m) (the Big League) followed by a Minor League of Australia (2.1m) > Ethiopia (1.8m) > Indonesia (0.7m) > South Africa (0.7m) > > > Iraq (0.09m) > Turkey (0.05m) > New Zealand (0.04m).

The above arrangement could be seen to be somewhat unfair on the Russians, (a) because it includes countries that were occupied by Russia for a century or more; (b) all the occupied countries have been contiguous with Russia and (c) the Russian hegemony over Eastern Europe is included while US hegemony over Latin America and the Caribbean (and indeed much of the Third World) is ignored. Accordingly, 2 further arrangements of the data are offered below.

In *descending order* of "1950-2005 excess mortality/2005 population ratio" from the summed data for *each* set of victim countries we have the following order: Indonesia (81.0%) > Portugal (62.5%) > Belgium (49.9%) > Ethiopia (39.4%) > Pakistan (33.6%) > South Africa (33.1%) = Australia (33.1%) > France (33.0%) > UK (32.5%) > Netherlands (31.7%) > Spain (26.4%) > US (23.0%) > Israel (22.3%) > New Zealand (21.4%) > Russia (13.9%) > Turkey (6.6%) > Iraq (3.3%). Seen in this light, the victims of Russian, Turkish and (transient) Iraqi occupation (of Kuwait) have done much better overall since 1950 than the other victims of occupation. However an even fairer way of arranging the data would be to normalize it relative to the present population of the *occupier* i.e. to give a measure of the *relative human impact* of these "occupier" societies.

In *descending order* of "total victim country 1950-2005 excess mortality/2005 occupier population" (expressed as a percentage) we have the following order: UK (1220.3%) > Netherlands (439.1%) > Israel (356.8%) > Belgium (347.2%) > Portugal (233.0%) > France (234.3%) > Pakistan (31.8%) > US (27.4%) > Russia (26.2%) > Spain (20.8%) > Australia (10.7%) (the Big League) > a Minor League of Ethiopia (2.4%) > South Africa (1.5%) > New Zealand (1.0%) > Indonesia (0.3%) = Iraq (0.3%) > Turkey (0.07%). Of course the magnitude of this parameter depends upon a mixture of *disregard* and *opportunity*. Thus (as shown below) the Australians had a high degree of disregard for their foreign subjects but had very few of them whereas the British had an apparent 2-fold better intrinsic regard but had vastly more victims in their Empire on which the Sun never set.

In order to delineate *disregard* of the occupiers for their victims a useful measure is obtained by dividing the "1950-2005 excess mortality/2005 population" ratio for each set of victim countries by the value of this parameter for the Occupier. This gives a good measure of the relative mortalities in the victim and occupier countries. Thus a ratio of 1.0 tells us that the victims were no worse off than the occupiers. A ratio under 1.0 tells us that the victims were actually better off in the post-1950 era than the occupiers. Values greater than 1.0 provide a measure of the *disregard* of occupiers for their victims i.e. of *entrenched racism*.

In descending order of "victim country"/ "occupier country" 1950-2005 excess mortality/2005 population ratios we have the following order: Netherlands (63.4) > Israel (15.9) > Portugal (14.5) > Australia (11.4) > Spain (10.6) > US (8.6) > Belgium (6.9) > France (6.1) > New Zealand (5.9) > UK (4.4) > Indonesia (2.6) > Russia (1.7) > South Africa (1.1) = Pakistan (1.1) > Ethiopia (0.8) > Turkey (0.5) > Iraq (0.2) (the 1950-2005 excess mortality/2005 population ratio for the Netherlands has been taken as about 1% i.e. the approximate value for the "best" Western European countries). This ordering arrangement provides a much better assessment of the post-1950 excess mortality of significantly occupied countries but each case has to be intelligently interpreted. Thus the ratios of much less than 1.0 for Turkey and Iraq reflect occupation of countries that were much wealthier than the Occupiers. The values of about 1 for Ethiopia, South Africa and Pakistan reflect the similar burden of excess mortality in occupier and victim countries.

Normal human nature explains the value for Russia (1.7) i.e. one expects the Occupier to be a bit better off than the occupied - an imperfect application (in a formally atheist empire) of "do unto others as you would have them do unto you". This analysis illustrates the phenomenon of increasing *disregard* for others as we go from the immediate family to local community and thence to distant societies. The value of 2.6 for Indonesia reflects egregious genocide in East Timor over a quarter century by a brutal, military régime that treated its *own* citizens badly for 4 decades. However the very high ratios for European countries (other than Russia) simply indicate *deep disregard* for their colonial and neo-colonial subjects i.e. profound *racism*. (notwithstanding their politically correct protestations otherwise that "We are not racists"). Foreign occupation simply imposes rulers who have less regard for their subjects than do indigenous rulers.

3.15 Summary

Regional analysis of post-1950 global avoidable mortality broadly reveals that low annual *per capita* income, low adult literacy and a burden of occupation and war correlate with poor mortality outcomes. However adult literacy can still be about 50% in the poorest countries of the world, and some well-run countries (notably Cuba and Sri Lanka) have annual *per capita* incomes 40 times lower than for the US but nevertheless have very good mortality outcomes.

War and occupation correlate best with poor mortality outcomes and this can be summarized [2007] in *ascending* order of "occupier country"/ "victim country" ratios of the "1950-2005 excess mortality/2005 population" ratio outcomes that are as follows: *Overseas Europe* (rich countries that have never been invaded but with post-war records of egregious invasion and occupation of distant lands) < *Western Europe* (a set of rich countries that have not been invaded since WW2 but including some countries associated with imposing colonial occupation, neo-colonial occupation and war on non-European countries across the globe in the post-war era) < *Eastern Europe* (post-war "welfare state" rule by the Soviet Union or other Communist dictatorships, generally peaceful - with the exception of 3 post-war Soviet invasions of contiguous countries and the civil wars in the Balkans, Moldova and Chechnya - and with no occupation of *distant* lands) < *South America* (moderate incomes, generally peaceful but variously with US hegemony, US-backed military dictatorships, coups, invasions and civil wars and generally no invasions of distant lands, with the exception of US Coalition involvements) < *East Asia* (remarkable social and economic recovery from WW2, the Korean War and US sanctions against China, some conflicts with contiguous countries but no invasions of distant lands with the exception of US-linked involvements) < *Turkey, Iran and Central Asia* (variously suffering from European occupation and malignant intervention with major First World-backed wars involving Iran and Afghanistan) < *Arab North Africa and the Middle East* (decolonization, British, French, US and Israeli wars, oil, excellent outcomes in the peaceful Gulf states and no invasions of distant lands (except for war on Yemen) < *South East Asia* (variously European-imposed colonialism, occupation, war, militarism and corruption) < *the Pacific* (mixed outcomes from colonial occupation and neo-colonial consequences) < *South Asia* (crippled by the consequences of 2 centuries of racist and exploitative British imperialism, namely communal hatreds, unresolved territorial and religious issues, militarism, war, nuclearization, corruption, poverty and acute economic and health issues)< *Non-Arab Africa* (colonialism, neo-colonialism, corruption, militarism, debt, malignant First World interference, economic exclusion, poverty, disease and the tragically avoidable HIV/AIDS epidemic).

As a measure of Occupier disregard for their Conquered Subjects, in descending order of the "victim country"/ "occupier country" ratios of the "1950-2005 excess mortality/2005 population" ratio outcomes we have the following order: the Netherlands (arguably infinity) > Spain (17.4) > Israel (15.9) > Portugal (14.5) > Australia (11.4) > US (8.5) > Belgium (6.9) > France (6.1) > New Zealand (5.9) > UK (4.4) > Indonesia (2.6) > Russia (1.7) > South Africa (1.1) = Pakistan (1.1) > Ethiopia (0.8) > Turkey (0.5) > Iraq (0.2). The very high ratios for occupier European countries (other than

Russia) simply indicate *deep disregard* for their colonial and neo-colonial subjects i.e. *profound racism*. Foreign occupation results in rulers with less intrinsic regard for the ruled than with indigenous rulers.

CHAPTER 4:
COUNTRY-BY-COUNTRY ANALYSIS OF AVOIDABLE MORTALITY IN EUROPEAN COUNTRIES

"Veni, vidi, vici" (*I came, I saw, I conquered"*)

Julius Caesar.[1]

"History is a set of lies agreed upon."

Napoleon Bonaparte.[2]

"If the public knew the truth, the war would end tomorrow. But they don't know and they can't know"

Lloyd George to *Manchester Guardian* editor C.P. Scott, 1914.[3]

"The quickest way of ending a war is to lose it."

George Orwell.[4]

"I do not know with what weapons World War 3 will be fought, but World War 4 will be fought with sticks and stones."

Albert Einstein.[5]

4.1 Introduction – matching excess mortality with foreign occupation

A huge historical work would be required to precisely match post-1950 events with changes in excess mortality and under-5 infant mortality for every country in the world. However it is useful to at least sketch some of the salient events (especially those involving violent foreign occupation of countries) in relation to changes in mortality. In doing so we will again go from the best region to the worst region in a systematic fashion. In Chapters 4-7 "short histories" are provided to simply and succinctly document the historical background to the glaringly obvious reality described in Chapter 3 of post-war avoidable mortality correlating with violent pre- and post-1950 First World impositions on victim countries. Readers are simply invited to inspect this succinctly presented historical record, assess the excess mortality statistics and then consider their own conclusions.

Of course post-1950 avoidable mortality does not only relate to concurrent foreign occupation of a country - thus prior colonial occupation and the violence of such occupation will have a big impact. By way of example, British occupation of Australia commenced in 1788 and by 1900 the indigenous population had dropped from about 1 million to 90,000 through dispossession, violence and introduced disease. Two centuries after the commencement of this genocide, the indigenous death rate is 3 times greater than in Australia as a whole and this yields an excess mortality of about 4,000 - 8,000 annually (2007 estimate) that is reflected in a life expectancy gap of about 10 years between Indigenous and non-Indigenous Australians.[6]

Accordingly, pre-1950 violent foreign occupations over the last half millennium or so are also briefly summarized at the end of each of the snapshot, "short history" accounts given below, together with (simplified) pre-1950 foreign military presence, post-1950 foreign military occupation, post-1950 foreign military presence and 1950-2005 excess mortality and 1950-2005 under-5 infant mortality in millions (m) and also expressed as percentages (%) of the 2005 population.

87

As you go through this sad testimonial in the following "short history" Chapters, think of the extreme situations that scientists call the "boundary conditions" i.e. consider the best and the worst outcome countries. Thus the "Overseas European" countries, which have the lowest avoidable mortality, have not been occupied by foreigners *ever*, let alone in the post-1950 era – and, conversely, have *all* invaded and occupied non-European countries during that era. At the other extreme, *nearly all* of the countries of non-Arab Africa have been subject to violent European occupation for a substantial part of the post-1950 era, *none* have invaded non-contiguous states and *nearly all* continue to suffer horrendous avoidable mortality.

Specifically, consider the assertedly democratic - but in horrible reality a democracy by genocide and Apartheid - state of Israel. Of Apartheid Israel's 7.2 million Indigenous Palestinian Subjects that represent 50% of its Subjects (as compared to the Jewish Israelis who represent 47%), 5.2 million Occupied Palestinians (72%) cannot vote for the government ruling them i.e. a system of egregious Apartheid. However Apartheid Israel has not ever been occupied by foreign forces since independence, but has militarily attacked 13 other countries, has violently occupied the territory of 5 of them for substantial periods, continues to occupy the territory of 4 of them, and has one of the best excess mortality outcomes. The entry below for Israel concludes thus (m = million): *foreign occupation:* none (pre-1950); none (post-1950); *post-1950 foreign military presence:* none; *1950-2005 excess mortality/2005 population* = 0.095m/6.685m = 1.4%; *1950-2005 under-5 infant mortality/2005 population* = 0.091m/6.685m = 1.4%. At the other extreme, Timor-Leste was occupied by brutal colonial powers both before and after 1950, has attacked no other country and has one of the very worst excess mortality outcomes: *foreign occupation:* Portugal, Japan (pre-1950); Portugal, Indonesia (post-1950); *post-1950 foreign military presence:* Portugal, Indonesia, UN peace-keeping forces (notably Australian); *1950-2005 excess mortality/2005 population* = 0.0.694m/0.857m = 81.0%; *1950-2005 under-5 infant mortality/2005 population* = 0.236m/0.857m = 27.5%.

2021 updates: The original 2007 first edition text has been largely unchanged except for corrections, amplification and updating. 2021 updates are added at the end of each "short history". In particular, because Humanity is existentially threatened by (a) climate change and (b) nuclear weapons, the 2021 updates include information on each country in relation to (a) climate change (notably revised annual greenhouse gas (GHG) pollution taking land use into account and expressed as tonnes CO_2-equivalent (CO_2-e) per person per year), and (b) ratification or otherwise of the UN Treaty on the Prohibition of Nuclear Weapons (TPNW) that came into effect in International Law on 22 January 2021 and which prohibits States Parties from both possession of nuclear weapons and support for such possession "in any way" (data from the Nobel Prize-winning International Campaign Against Nuclear Weapons (ICAN)). Thus all 9 nuclear weapons-possessing countries reject the TPNW. Further, non-nuclear weapons countries of the "US nuclear umbrella" that expect assistance and protection from nuclear-armed America (Japan, South Korea, NATO countries and Australia) also endorse the use of nuclear weapons and reject the TPNW. Only about 25% of the world's nations have ratified the TPNW.

The updated 2020 demographic data are from the pre-Covid-19 pandemic UN Population Division World Population Prospects 2019 projections for 2020 (Tables 9.1-9.12). These data provide a very useful comparison with the 2003 data (Tables 8.1-8.12), and also represent an important demographic benchmark for immediately prior to the start of the Covid-19 pandemic in 2020.

Most rich Western countries have performed very badly in the Covid-19 Pandemic in comparison to East Asia, Australia and New Zealand. Gross government inaction in the Covid-19 pandemic has been associated with huge "Covid-19 deaths per million of population", with such avoidable deaths being mainly of the elderly (Gerocide) (95% of US Covid-19 deaths have been of people 50 and older). The remorselessly accumulating mortality data is changing daily in 2021 but reference is made to this Covid-19-related avoidable mortality in the 2021 updates for all countries (except when unavailable in rare instances) as "Covid-19 deaths per million of population" (March 2021). Since 95% of the Covid-

19 deaths have been of 50 and over people this deliberately imposed avoidable mortality (most appallingly in the US and UK) is described here as Gerocide, a term introduced in relation to the Covid-19 Pandemic avoidable mortality by several front-line Italian physicians. In the 2021 update for each country the "Covid-19 deaths per million of population" is compared to that for the best-performing Taiwan (0.4). Thus, for comparison, the "Covid-19 deaths per million of population" was a gerocidal 1,687 (US) and a gerocidal 1,857 (UK) as compared to only 0.4 for best-performing Taiwan. This provides a topical and pertinent insight into the utter immorality of the Establishments of these imperialist states (already shockingly evident from the data discussed in Chapter 3) that have been prepared to deliberately sacrifice the lives of horrendous numbers of their own citizens (so far, over 561,000 in the US and over 127,000 in the UK as compared to only 26 Covid-19 deaths in decent New Zealand) (March 2021 data).

The 2021 updates compare the pre-Covid-19 projected 2020 "under-5 infant mortality as a percentage of total population" for each country (a) with that for Japan (the best performing country at 0.00145%), and (b) with that for each country in 2003 (the good news is that global annual "under-5 infant mortality as a percentage of total population" has roughly halved since 2003, noting that world population has increased from 6.3 billion to 7.8 billion over this period). **Thus compare Tables 8.1-8.12 (2003 data) with Tables 9.1-9.12 (2020 data).** Tables 9.1-9.12 also report "avoidable mortality as a percentage of total population" that is crudely estimated for 2020 as 1.4 times the "under-5 infant mortality as a percentage of total population" for each country. For simplicity this common factor was conservatively chosen for all countries because in 2003, the global avoidable mortality was about 1.4 times the under-5 infant deaths (Tables 8.1-8.12).

Poverty kills, and the per capita GDP (nominal) in US dollars (UN, 2019) is given for each country at the end of each national summary.

Humanity and the Biosphere are existentially threatened by (a) man-made climate change (unless requisite action is taken 10 billion people will die in a worsening Climate Genocide en route to a sustainable human population in 2100 of only1 billion), and (b) by nuclear weapons (a post-nuclear exchange nuclear winter threatens to decimate Humanity and the Biosphere). Accordingly a "revised annual greenhouse gas (GHG) pollution in tonnes CO_2-equivalent per person per year" (taking land use into account and assuming a methane Global Warming Potential of 105) is given for each country, together with a brief mention, where merited, of contributing factors (e.g. fossil fuel use, methanogenic livestock, and deforestation).

4.2 Overseas Europe – internal democracy, external violence

After the victory of the Allies over the Axis powers in World War 2 (WW2) there was a major shift of global power from Western Europe to the US (the American Empire) and the USSR (the Russian Empire). The Anglo-Celtic countries of Overseas Europe (Australia, New Zealand and Canada) continued their close military and intelligence association with the US, and the new colonization- and genocide-based state of Apartheid Israel has become the key US-backed satellite in the Middle East. All of these societies have a blind-spot in common with the people of their patron and ally, the US – an inability to see the immense world-wide carnage in which they have variously been complicit in the pre- and post-war eras. Briefly outlined below are the stories of some of the world's most prosperous, healthy and *aggressive* societies.

Australia: inhabited by indigenous people for some 65,000 years before European invasion (the oldest continuous cultures in the world); 17th century, Portuguese, Spanish, British and Dutch explorers (named New Holland); 1642, Tasman discovered Tasmania (Van Dieman's Land); 1770, Cook explored and claimed Australia; 1788, penal settlement at Port Jackson (Sydney); 1803, settlement of Tasmania; 19th century, agriculture initially using convict labour; Merino sheep introduced for wool; later pastoralists used aboriginal labour; Melanesian slaves (Kanakas) brought to Queensland sugar cane plantations; violent genocide and introduced disease reduced the indigenous Australian population from about 0.75 million to 0.1 million in 100 years; indigenous populations also declined catastrophically in New Zealand and the Pacific; mid-19th century, gold rushes opened up Victoria; other colonies were founded; 1901, Federation of the States as an independent Australia; commencement of the racist White Australian Policy; 19th-20th century, mostly Anglo-Celtic Australians actively participated in British wars, namely the Sudan Campaign, the Boer War, WW1 (notably in France, Palestine and Gallipoli in Turkey), WW2 (the fall of Singapore - with 8,000 out of 22,000 Australian prisoners of war dying in captivity – and the crucial US war effort led to victory over the Japanese and to ANZUS, the post-war Australian and New Zealand alliance with the US); post-war, mass immigration from Europe; participation in UK and/or US wars, namely the Malaya Emergency, Korean War, Confrontation with Indonesia, Indo-China War, Gulf War, Iraq Sanctions, Iraq War and Afghanistan War; 1967, "legitimation" of aborigines as citizens to be counted and covered by federal laws; late 1960s, cessation of an extensive genocidal policy of child-removal from aboriginal mothers (but still continuing at a record rate as "welfare"); 1973, White Australia Policy effectively revoked by anti-racism legislation; 1975, conservative, pro-US Governor-General dismissed the elected Labor Government; 1975, Papua New Guinea independence; assisted PNG forces in Bougainville; peacekeeping troops to East Timor; Australian military peace-keepers to the Solomon Islands; 21st century, continuing prosperity but one of the oldest continuing democracies brought in imprisonment without charge for boat-borne refugees (indefinite) and for terrorism-related suspects (2 week stretches). Australia is the world's biggest coal exporter and liquid natural gas (LNG) exporter, and is committed to fossil fuel exploitation.

2021 update: Australia joined the US in invasion of Afghanistan (2001) and of Iraq (2003); 2001 onwards, plethora of civil liberties-violating anti-terrorism laws; Australia has participated in all post-1950 US Asian wars (40 million Asian deaths from violence and deprivation); 2010-2018, intra-government coups meant 6 Labor or Coalition PMs in a decade; despite a national "Sorry" over the aboriginal child-removal "Stolen Generations" (2008), child removal from aboriginal (Indigenous) mothers continues at a record rate; 2013 onwards, boat-borne refugees imprisoned indefinitely without charge or trial; unnamed citizens subject to secret trials; 2020, Australia among world leaders in 16 areas of climate criminality and worst in the Developed World for climate action policies; greenhouse gas (GHG) pollution 52.9 tonnes CO_2-e per person per year (116 if including exports); Australia is tightly complicit in US nuclear terrorism via the Pine Gap base, hosting US nuclear-armed warships, and rejecting the 2021 UN Treaty on Prohibition of Nuclear Weapons (TPNW). "Covid-19 deaths per million of population" was 35 as compared to 0.4 for Taiwan but 1,857 for the UK and 5 for New Zealand (March 2021). In 2020 the "annual under-5 infant mortality as a percentage of total population" for Australia (0.0044%) was 3.0 times greater than for Japan (0.00145%), but 11.5 times greater than for Japan for Indigenous Australians; the 2020 "annual under-5 infant mortality as a percentage of total population" was 1.6 times lower than that in 2003 (0.0070%).

Foreign occupation: Britain (pre-1950); none (post-1950); *post-1950 foreign military presence:* US (ships, bases, nuclear defence, communications), UK (nuclear tests); 1950-2005 excess mortality/2005 population = 0.587m/20.092m = 2.9%; 1950-2005 under-5 infant mortality/2005 population = 0.202m/20.092m = 1.0%.* Per capita GDP (nominal) $54,763.

New Zealand: 1000AD, settled by Polynesian Maoris from Pacific Polynesia; 1642-1643, Dutch Tasman discovery of New Zealand; 1769-1770, Cook exploration; 1792-1849, European settlements for sealing and whaling; 1815-1840, tens of thousands died in intertribal wars; 1840, settlement of Wellington by Wakefield's New Zealand Company; separated from New South Wales (Australia); Treaty of Waitangi with Maoris; British settlement; 1860-1872, British-Maori Wars, indigenous defense (notably *pa* earth defenses); the Maori population dropped from 0.1-0.2 million in 1800 to 42,000 in 1893, mostly through disease, dispossession and war; 1852, self-government; 1907, independent as Dominion of New Zealand; 1947, final separation from UK by confirming the1931 Statute of Westminster; New Zealand participation in Anglo-American Wars including WW1, WW2, Korean War, Vietnam War and Gulf War and member of ANZUS treaty with Australia and the US; 1986, ANZUS suspended after New Zealand opposition to visits by US nuclear-armed ships; opposition to French nuclear tests (Greenpeace's ship *Rainbow Warrior* sunk by French agents); did not join the US invasion of Iraq. **2020 update:**

2001, New Zealand participated in the US Alliance occupation of Afghanistan; 2018, New Zealand ratified the TPNW; 2019, Christchurch Massacres of 51 Muslim worshippers in 2 mosques by an Australian far right extremist. Wealth and livestock production contribute to annual greenhouse gas (GHG) pollution of 53.2 tonnes CO_2-e per person per year; "Covid-19 deaths per million of population" was a European best of 5 as compared to 0.4 for Taiwan, 35 for cousin Australia and 1,857 for the UK, the Mother Country (March 2021). In 2020 "under-5 infant mortality as a percentage of total population" (0.0056%) was 3.9 times greater than for Japan (0.00145%), and 1.4 times lower than that in 2003 (0.0080%).

Foreign occupation: UK (pre-1950); none (post-1950); *post-1950 foreign military presence:* none; *1950-2005 excess mortality/2005 population* = 0.143m/3.932m = 3.6%; *1950-2005 under-5 infant mortality/2005 population* = 0.054m/3.932m = 1.4%. Per capita GDP (nominal) $43,264.

Canada: pre-colonial Inuit and Amerindians from about 15,000 BCE; about 1000 CE, Vikings settled transiently in Vinland (Eastern Canada); 1497, English Cabot landed; 1534, Cartier claimed Canada for France; 1605, French settlement at Port Royal (Annapolis Royal); 1608, French founded Québec; 1629, 1632 British captured and then lost Québec; 1670, British Hudson's Bay Company formed; 18th century, world-wide Anglo-French wars; 1759, 1760, Québec and Montréal fell to the British; 1763, Treaty of Paris, Louisiana went to Spain and East of the Mississippi to Britain; 1775, US invasion of Canada repulsed; 1784, New Brunswick created for loyalists; 1791, separation of Ontario (Upper Canada) and Québec (Lower Canada); 1789-1793, Mackenzie explored to the Arctic and Pacific regions; War of 1812, US invasion repulsed; 1846, Oregon boundary finalized; 1867, federation of the Canadian Provinces; Canadian participation in WW1, WW2 and the Korean, Gulf and Afghanistan Wars; Canadian offer of wheat for the Bengal Famine rejected by Churchill; 1949, joined NATO; 1960s onwards, increasing French separatism (provocative "Québec libre" call by Charles De Gaulle of France); maple leaf flag; bilingualism encouraged; 1992, Charlottetown Accord to pacify separatism; 1998, apology to

Indigenous people; 1999, large Inuit territory of Nunavut granted; 1994, North American Free Trade Agreement (NAFTA) between Canada, the US and Mexico; 2001, Canada in the Afghanistan War but not in the subsequently launched Iraq War. **2020 update:** Canada supports the Keystone XL pipeline for exploiting oil from Alberta tar sands ("game over for the planet"); greenhouse gas (GHG) pollution 50.1 tonnes CO_2-e per person per year; Canada belongs to nuclear-armed NATO, refuses to sign and ratify the TPNW, and is closely linked to US, UK and France nuclear terrorism; "Covid-19 deaths per million of population" was a bad 600 as compared to 0.4 for Taiwan (March 2021). In 2020 the "under-5 infant mortality as a percentage of total population" (0.0052%) was 3.6 times greater than for Japan (0.00145%), and 1.3 times lower than that in 2003 (0.0070%).

Foreign occupation: UK (pre-1950); none (post-1950); *post-1950 foreign military presence:* US (nuclear early warning); *1950-2005 excess mortality/2005 population* = 0.428m/31.972m = 1.4%; *1950-2005 under-5 infant mortality/2005 population* = 0.442m/31.972m = 1.4%. Per capita GDP (nominal) $46,550.

United States of America: 15,000 BCE, Mongoloid Amerindians; 1492, Columbus discoveries; 16th century, European invasion and settlement; 1565, Spanish settled in Florida and thence in the South West and California; French settlement in Québec, Montreal and Louisiana; 1607, English settlement at Jamestown, Virginia; 1620, Plymouth settlement by the Pilgrim Fathers; 17th-19th century, African slave trade and the plantation economy in the South; 1775-1783, American Revolution against Britain under Washington; Jefferson and the Declaration of Independence (equality of man and the right to life, liberty and the pursuit of happiness); American constitution, democracy and the rule of law; independence from Britain critically allowed genocidal invasion of Indian lands to the West; 1803, Louisiana Purchase from France; 1812, War with Britain; 1812, Monroe Doctrine opposing European interference in the Americas; 1819, Florida obtained from Spain; Westward spread with extermination of Indians through disease, dispossession and violence; 1836-1846, settlement of Texas and war with Mexico culminating in acquisition of Texas, the Southwest and California; Indians ethnically cleansed by federal law from East of the

Mississippi; 1853, Gadsden Purchase and acquisition of the Northwest; 1848, California gold rush; 1861-1865, Civil War between pro-slavery Southern Confederacy and the industrial, abolitionist North under Lincoln; defeat of the South but retention of *de facto* suppression of Afro-Americans for over a century (Jim Crow laws); late 19th century, Westward expansion and final dispossession of Indians; acquisition of Hawaii (1898) and American Samoa (1899); 1898, Spanish-American War with acquisition of Puerto Rico, Cuba, and the Philippines with US Latin American hegemony; early 20th century, US imperialism rampant: 1899-1902, Philippines War (1 million Filipinos died), Panama Canal, US-controlled Canal Zone and repeated military interventions in Panama (1864-1989), Cuba (1898-1920), Dominican Republic (1916-1934), Haiti (US occupation forces 1919-1934) and Nicaragua (1912-1915); WW1 (1917-1918); "acquired" the Virgin Islands from Denmark (1917); between-wars depression, prohibition, gangsterism, Roosevelt New Deal and a massive international arms race; WW2 (militarist Imperial Japan squeezed into war; UK and US pre-knowledge of Japanese attack realized at Pearl Harbor; industrial warfare; high-gear commencement of the highly profitable military-industrial complex, total air war against civilians e.g. Tokyo, Nagasaki and Hiroshima (both destroyed in an instant by atomic bombs), Hamburg, Berlin, Dresden, and Tokyo (66 Japanese cities substantially destroyed; 500,000 killed); post-war economic, cultural and military domination of world by an immensely rich, technologically-advanced USA; 1970s, improved Afro-American civil rights; 1990s, final victory over the USSR in the Star Wars segment of the post-war Cold War that had involved megaton hydrogen bombs, ICBMs, nuclear-armed submarines, nuclear "Mutually Assured Destruction" (MAD) and East- and West-supported armed conflicts throughout the world; major post-war invasions and occupations: Korean War (1950-1953), Vietnam War (1954-1975), Dominican Republic (1965), Cuba (1961 failed invasion; economic sanctions, 1964-present), El Salvador (US-backed coup, death squads and civil war, 1972-1992, 30,000 killed), Guatemala (via US-armed and backed military from Honduras, 1954-1990, 0.5 million refugees), Nicaragua (via US-armed and backed Contras from Honduras, 1982-1990), Panama (1989), Grenada (1983), Colombia (US military involvement in the civil war since 1964), Afghanistan (Soviet invasion and US-backed resistance and civil war, 6.3 million deaths), Afghanistan (2001-present), Iran (overthrow of democracy, 1953-1979; military raid, 1979; backing Iraq in the Iran-Iraq War, 1979-1988, 1.5 million dead), Iraq Gulf War and Sanctions war (1990-2003; 1.7 million deaths), Iraq War (2003- 2011, 1.5 million violent deaths, 1.2 million avoidable deaths from deprivation); 1994, North American Free Trade Agreement (NAFTA) between Mexico, US and Canada; 2001, 9/11 atrocity (3,000 killed) and subsequent post-Reichstag-style, open-ended "War on Terror"; 2001-March 2007, 2.4 million post-invasion excess deaths in Afghanistan War; 2003-March 2007, 1.0 million post-invasion excess deaths in Iraq War; 2005, Hurricane Katrina further exposed US establishment callousness to the massive underprivileged population; 2001-2005, 50,000 US opioid drug deaths linked to US restoration of the Taliban-destroyed opium industry in Afghanistan to 90% of world market share.

2021 update: 2011, France-UK-US (FUKUS) Coalition devastated Libya; US backed coups in Honduras (2009), Ukraine (2014), and Egypt (2014); 2012 onwards, US-, UK-, France-, Turkey-, Israel-, Saudi-, jihadi- and ISIS-involved but unsuccessful attempt to remove the Syrian Government but Syria devastated, and partially occupied with 0.5 million killed and 12 million refugees; continued US bombing of Libya, Somalia, Yemen, Syria, Iraq, Afghanistan and Pakistan; post-9/11, US-imposed Muslim Holocaust and Muslim Genocide with 32 million Muslims dying from violence, 5 million, or from imposed deprivation, 27 million, in 20 countries invaded by the US Alliance since the US Government's 9/11 false flag atrocity that killed 3,000 (2015 estimates); 2017-2021, Trump populism, isolationism, climate change inaction, and ramped up hostility and trade war against China; 2020, US ranked second worst for climate action policies after Australia and ranked worst in the world for overall climate action; unsuccessful Operation Gideon invasion of Venezuela led by US mercenaries; 2021, Republican Trump populism defeated by Democrats but remains very popular; newly elected Biden (30% Jewish Zionist Cabinet) reverses key Trump decisions and re-joins WHO, re-bans Keystone XL pipeline, re-joins Paris Climate Agreement, and bans oil and gas exploration on Federal lands, but disastrously rejects a Carbon

Tax and supports a disastrous coal-to-gas transition that locks in fossil fuel use long-term; revised greenhouse gas (GHG) pollution 41.0 tonnes CO_2-e per person per year; America possesses 5,800 nuclear weapons and rejects the UN Treaty on the Prohibition of Nuclear Weapons (TPNW) that came into effect in International Law on 22 January 2021; "Covid-19 deaths per million of population" was an appalling and gerocidal 1,687 as compared to 0.4 for Taiwan (March 2021). In 2020 the "under-5 infant mortality as a percentage of total population" (0.0084%) was 5.8 times greater than for Japan (0.00145%), and 1.4 times lower than that in 2003 (0.0120%).

Foreign occupation: none (pre-1950); none (post-1950); *post-1950 foreign military presence:* none; *1950-2005 excess mortality/2005 population* = 8.455m/300.038m = 2.8%; *1950-2005 under-5 infant mortality/2005 population* = 4.473m/300.038m = 1.5%. Per capita GDP (nominal) $65,134.

Israel: 3000-2000BCE, Arabian Semitic Canaanites settled Palestine and founded Jerusalem (Al Quds); Hebrew/Jewish co-occupation with Samaritans, Philistines and other groups from 1200BCE until Jewish rebel expulsion in 135CE; 135, Jews partly expelled; Palestine subsequently ruled successively by Romans and Byzantines; 611, Persian occupation; 634, Muslim Arab conquest (Jerusalem site of Mohammed's ascension into Heaven); 11th-13th century, periodic and partial Crusader occupation reversed by Saladin; 1516, Ottoman Turkish conquest; **1880, 500,000 Arabs and 25,000 Jews (half of the latter being immigrants);** 1917, Turks defeated by British-Arab coalition; WW1 Palestinian Famine (100,000 died); 1917, evil UK Balfour Declaration (Jewish Home provided no detriment to Arabs or Jews); 1922, League of Nations Mandate to Britain; 1900-1939, Jewish population from 50,000 to 300,000; 1936, Palestinian general strike; guerrilla war between Arabs and Jews; 1939, British White Paper constraining Jewish immigration; 1944, UK War Cabinet agreed on Partition; 1939-1945, illegal immigration of Jews fleeing Nazis; 1947, UN partition Plan; 1948, British left, UN recognized State of Israel, war between Israel and Arabs; Deir Yassin massacre; 0.8 million Palestinians fled in the Nakba (Catastrophe); 1956, Israeli war against Egypt in collusion with UK and France; 1964, Palestine Liberation

Organization (PLO) formed; 1967, Israel attacked neighbors (and USS *Liberty*) with occupation of the Sinai (Egypt), Gaza (Egypt), the West Bank (Jordan), Jerusalem (Jordan) and the Golan Heights (Syria); 0.4 million Arabs fled in the Naksa (Setback); Israeli acquisition of nuclear weapons and plan to use them; 1973, Yom Kippur War (Egypt-Israel); 1974, PLO leader Arafat addressed UN; 1979, peace with Egypt; 1982-2000, Israeli occupation of southern Lebanon; 1982, Sabra and Shatila refugee camp massacres (3,000 Palestinians murdered in Israeli-occupied Beirut by Christian Falangists); 1987, first Palestinian Intifada; 1988, Arafat eschewed militant action and recognized Israel; 1993, Oslo Agreement for Palestinian self-government permitted arming of Palestinians; continued seizure of Arab lands; 2000, renewed Intifada; 21st century, US-backed Israeli occupation, illegal settlements and violence with continuing violent responses from Palestinians; millions of displaced Palestinians in neighbouring countries and around the world (7 million Exiled Palestinians, 7 million refugees inside and outside of Palestine, 6 million registered with the UN in the Middle East); 2005, Israel pull-out from Gaza but strict border control, continued air attacks and retention of an increasingly diminished Palestinian West Bank; 1967-2007 excess mortality in the Occupied Palestinian Territories, 0.3 million.

2021 update: 2009 onwards, extreme right wing and violent Likud-dominated governments under Benjamin Netanyahu; repeated violent attacks on the Occupied Palestinians confined to the Gaza Concentration Camp (Gaza Massacres) with thousands killed, tens of thousands wounded, massive infrastructure and home destruction (2006, 2008-2009, 2014, 2018-2019, 2021), and imposition of blockade to deliberately achieve near-unlivable conditions; massive, illegal Jews-only settlements in the Occupied West Bank with 90% of Palestine now ethnically cleansed, this rendering the "two state solution" impossible, and underscoring the reality of Israeli Apartheid; 2017, Trump America recognized all of Occupied East Jerusalem and West Jerusalem as Israel's capital, this prompting weekly demonstrations by unarmed Occupied Palestinians in the Gaza Concentration Camp (over 180 killed, and 9,200 wounded in the weekly Great March of Return); 2018, the genocidally racist "Basic Law: Israel as the Nation-State of the

Jewish People" passed by the Knesset (62 for, 55 against, 2 abstentions) with Hebrew made the official language and the Indigenous Palestinian Arabic given a "special status"; Occupied Palestinians have zero human rights and Palestinian Israelis are subject to over 60 race-based laws; 2019, Trump America recognized Israeli annexation of the ethnically cleansed Syrian Golan Heights; Israel has invaded the territory of 13 countries, has occupied 5 countries, still occupies territory of 4 countries, and has backed genocidal atrocities with arms including the Guatemalan Maya Genocide, the Sri Lanka Tamil Genocide, the Myanmar Rohingya Genocide, the Lebanon civil war and the South Sudan civil war; Israel proposes formal massive annexation of the West Bank; Israel has launched attacks on Iran and routinely bombs Syria and Iraq; by bombing attacks and purchase of ISIS oil, Israel backed the US, UK, France, Turkey jihadi, ISIS and Saudi campaign to remove the Syrian Government and Balkanise Syria and Iraq; 2020, the International Criminal Court (ICC) to investigate Israeli war crimes; 2021, Israel leads the world in Covid-19 vaccination per capita but has violated the Fourth Geneva Convention by its disastrous Covid-19 policies and refusing to vaccinate Occupied Palestinians except for 5,000 medical workers (the 5.2 million Occupied Palestinians and 2 million Israeli Palestinians represent 50% of the Subjects of Apartheid Israel, Jewish Israelis 47%; the Occupied Palestinians cannot vote for the government ruling them i.e Apartheid); the ongoing Palestinian Genocide has been associated with 2.2 million Palestinian deaths from violence, 0.1 million, or from imposed deprivation, 2.1 million, since 1916 whereas 5,000 Zionist invaders/Israelis have been killed by Palestinians since 1920; UAE, Bahrain, Sudan and Morocco recognized Apartheid Israel; supports disastrous off-shore gas exploitation transition that locks in fossil fuel use long-term (gas can be worse than coal GHG-wise); greenhouse gas (GHG) pollution 20.2 tonnes CO_2-e per person per year; Israel has 90 nuclear weapons with some on 6 German-supplied submarines, rejects and refuses to sign or ratify the UN Treaty on the Prohibition of Nuclear Weapons (TPNW) that came into effect in International Law on 22 January 2021. "Covid-19 deaths per million of population" was a bad 670 (and a war criminal and Fourth Geneva Convention-violating 489 for its Occupied Palestinian Subjects refused Covid-19 vaccination by their war criminal Occupiers except for medical staff and those working for Israelis) as compared to 0.4 for Taiwan (March 2021). Apartheid Israel is the biggest recipient of economic and military aid from Zionist-subverted America and is thus disproportionately complicit in the Global Avoidable Mortality Holocaust in which 7.5 million people presently die annually from deprivation. In 2020 the "under-5 infant mortality as a percentage of total population" (0.0059%) was 4.1 times greater than for Japan (0.00145%), and 2.0 times lower than that in 2003 (0.0120%).

Foreign occupation: Turkey, Britain (pre-1950); none (post-1948); none (post-1950); *post-1950 foreign military presence:* none; *1950-2005 excess mortality/2005 population* = 0.095m/6.685m = 1.4%; *1950-2005 under-5 infant mortality/2005 population* = 0.091m/6.685m = 1.4%. Per capita GDP (nominal) $46,376 [Occupied Palestinian per capita GDP (nominal) $3,424].

2020 statistical update: Table 9.2 summarizes population, under-5 infant mortality (IM) and excess mortality (EM; avoidable mortality from deprivation) in Overseas Europe in 2020 (pre-Covid-19 projection in 2019 for 2020 by the UN Population Division). Table 9.1 compares Overseas Europe with other global regions. Presented in square brackets for each country is the "Relative EM Score" of EM/Pop (%) divided by that for the best-performing country, Japan (0.0020%), which accordingly has a "Relative EM Score" of 1.0.

In terms of "Relative EM Score" and "per capita GDP" the best performing country is Australia (3.0 and $54,763) with similar "Relative EM Scores" for similarly rich Canada (3.6), Apartheid Israel (4.1) and New Zealand (3.9). The more harshly neoliberal US (5.8 and $65,134) was the worst performer. The under-5 infant mortality, already low in these countries in 2003, declined 1.3-4-fold by 2020. The outcome for Apartheid Israel's 5.2 million Occupied Palestinian Subjects (37.7 and $3,424) is a dreadful 10-fold worse in comparison with that of Occupier Apartheid Israel (4.1 and $46,376), evidence of gross violation of the Fourth Geneva Convention by serial war criminal Apartheid Israel.

4.3 Western Europe – participation in colonial, neo-colonial and US-led "democratic imperialist" wars

Western Europe generally has essentially the same level of prosperity and survivability as the Overseas European countries. However while none of the Overseas European countries have ever been occupied, all Western European countries (with the exceptions of Ireland, Britain, Portugal, Spain and Sweden) have suffered from foreign occupation within the last 80 years i.e. within one Western human lifetime. However universal domestic peace and high technology have enabled auto-compounding prosperity. This prosperity has also been associated in many cases with past imperialism and colonialism that has variously spilled over into the post-1950 era. WW1 took some 16 million lives (9 million military and 7 million civilian). WW2 took some 35 million lives in Europe. Nazi racism, disregard and mass murder resulted in 6 million deaths in Poland and 24 million deaths in the Soviet Union. The Nazis deliberately exterminated about 0.5 million Gypsies (Roma) and 5-6 million Jews by violence and deprivation). Estimates by Gilbert (1969) of the numbers of Jews killed out of the Jewish population left in 1941 are included in the relevant entries below e.g. the murder of 60,000 out of 70,000 Austrian Jews is denoted as 60,000/70,000.[7]

Post-war, the Marshall Plan permitted reconstruction, NATO provided security and the rise and continuing extension of the European Union (EU) finally provided sanity in a continent that had seen 2 catastrophic world wars in one century. Major colonial powers surrendered their empires (while retaining neo-colonial economic hegemony in many cases). The hope that the world had seen the end of European colonial wars was dashed by Anglo-American interventions in Iraq and Afghanistan with the active (if often token) support of many Western European and Eastern European countries. Thus, as with the Overseas European countries, for most Western European countries (with the notable exceptions of Austria, Cyprus, Finland, Ireland, Malta, Sweden and Switzerland) *internal* decency was coupled with criminal support for military violence in a distant land.

Austria: pre-Roman Celtic and Suebi people; 15BCE-10CE, Roman conquest and Roman provinces of Rhaetia, Noricum and Upper Pannonia; 5th century, successive Hun, Ostrogoth and Lombard invasions; 6th century, Slav settlement of Styria, Lower Austria and Carinthia; 788, conquest by Charlemagne, Christianizing by the sword; 9th century, occupation by Moravians and Magyars; 955, conquered by Otto I, part of the Holy Roman Empire; 976, Leopold of Babenberg; 11th-12th century, feudalism and Danube commerce exploiting entrance to Europe from the Danubian plain and to Italy (via the Brenner Pass); 1251-1269, under Ottocar II of Bohemia; 1273, Rudolph I (Hapsburg); 14th century, expansion to Tyrol (1363) and Trieste (1382); 1438, Albert II (Hapsburg) Holy Roman Emperor; 1526, Austria, Bohemia and Hungary under Ferdinand I; 1524-1526, Peasants' War; 1526, Vienna besieged by Turks; 16th-17th century, Protestant Reformation and Catholic Counter Reformation; 1618-1648, Thirty Years War; 1620, Protestant Bohemia and Moravia taken by Catholic Austria after the Battle of the White Mountain; 1648, Peace of Westphalia, Hapsburg Empire; 1683, Turkish siege of Vienna relieved with Polish help and longer-range diplomatic consequences (e.g. accession to the English throne of Protestant William of Orange); 1687, Turks ceded Hungary to Austria; 18th century, conflict with Prussia: Charles VI (1711-1740) succeeded by Maria Theresa; War of the Austrian Succession, the Seven Years War, loss of Silesia to Prussia; Austrian gains from successive Polish Partitions (1772-1775); 1792-1815, Napoleonic Wars; Austria defeated at Austerlitz (1805) and Wagram (1809); 1806, Holy Roman Empire dissolved; 1814-1815, Congress of Vienna, Austria lost Netherlands and Baden possessions but gained Lombardy, Venetia, Istria and Dalmatia; 1809-1848, Metternich foreign minister, repression of subject nationalism; 1848, revolutionary period; Hungarian revolt suppressed; rebellions in Galicia, Italy and Bohemia; 1859, Italian war, Lombardy lost; 1856, defeated in Austro-Prussian war; Venetia ceded to Italy; 1867, Ausgleich (compromise) established Austro-Hungarian monarchy under Emperor Joseph; 1914-1918, WW1, precipitated by Sarajevo assassination of Franz Josef by a Serbian nationalist; Austria and Germany defeated; 1919, Treaty of Saint-Germain and the Versailles Treaty forbade any union with Germany; Austro-Hungarian Empire split up; inter-war poverty and conservative-socialist political dichotomy; 1934, socialist revolt put down by army; 1938, annexation by Germany (Anschloss); 1939-1945, WW2, alliance with Germany; 60,000/70,000 Jews killed; finally occupied by US and Soviet forces; 1955, full sovereignty, neutrality and UN membership; conservative-socialist democratic politics; President Waldheim linked to Nazi atrocities; 1999, EU sanctions over the involvement in government of the right-wing Freedom Party of Haider; did not join US occupation of Iraq.

2021 update: 2017-2109, progressive Sebastian Kurz chancellor; 2020, victory of the Austrian People's Party (ÖVP) which under Sebastian Kurz as chancellor formed a coalition-government with the Greens; greenhouse gas (GHG) pollution 13.0 tonnes CO_2-e per person per year; Austria is not a member of nuclear-armed NATO and has signed and ratified the UN Treaty on the Prohibition of Nuclear Weapons (TPNW) that came into effect in International Law on 22 January 2021; "Covid-19 deaths per million of population" was an appalling and gerocidal 1,017 as compared to 0.4 for Taiwan (March 2021). In 2020 the "under-5 infant mortality as a percentage of total population" (0.0035%) was 2.4 times greater than for Japan (0.00145%), and 1.2 times higher than that in 2003 (0.0030%).

Foreign occupation: Turkey, Germany (pre-1950); US, USSR (post-1950); *post-1950 foreign military presence:* US, USSR; *1950-2005 excess mortality/2005 population* = 0.734m/8.120m = 9.0%; *1950-2005 under-5 infant mortality/2005 population* = 0.142m/8.120m = 1.7 %. Per capita GDP (nominal) $49,701.

Belgium: 1st century BCE, Celtic Belgae tribe conquered by Romans; 3rd century, Franks invaded; 9th-12th century, part of Charlemagne's empire (Christian), Lotharingia and thence Lower Lorraine; 12th century, medieval Duchies of Brabant and Luxembourg and Bishopric of Liège; 15th century -18th century, Burgundian rule followed successively by Spanish and Austrian Hapsburg rule; 1797, French rule; 1815, Battle of Waterloo, Napoleon defeated by an Anglo-Prussian coalition; Belgium became part of the Netherlands through the Congress of Vienna; 1830, language and religious concerns led to Belgian rebellion; 1838-1839, London Conference finalized peace and Belgian independence under Leopold I (from Saxe-Coburg-Gotha); mid-19th century-early 20th century, industrialization; brutal exploitation of the Belgian Congo by Leopold II – 10 million Congolese died from Belgian rubber collection and related atrocities; 1914-1918, WW1, nearly all of Belgium occupied by the Germans; 1919, Belgian mandate over Rwanda and Burundi in former German East Africa; 1921, Belgium-Luxembourg economic association; 1939-1945, WW2, German occupation; Leopold III surrender; 28,000/85,000Jews killed; final German counter-offensive in the Battle of the Bulge; 1950, compromised Leopold III returned and abdicated in 1951; 1958, Benelux Union with Netherlands and Luxembourg; EU foundation; Brussels seat of EU bureaucracy and NATO headquarters; 1960, Congo independence but followed by 2 decades of French and Belgian military intervention; 1970s-1990s, ethnic tensions involving French, Flemish and German groups were resolved by autonomy arrangements; 1990s, corruption scandals.

2021 update: 2020, Belgian political parties found an agreement and formed a 7-party governing coalition (the "Vivaldi Government"). The Belgian Green Parties, Ecolo (French) and Groen (Flemish), joined the 7-party Coalition Government, this making Belgium the 6th EU member state with Greens in government; greenhouse gas (GHG) pollution 26.3 tonnes CO_2-e per person per year; Belgium is a member of nuclear-armed NATO, sent forces to US-occupied Afghanistan, and opposed the TPNW. However the new Coalition Government has made some preliminary noises in the face of 65% of Belgians supporting the TPNW. "Covid-19 deaths per million of population" was an appalling and gerocidal 1,962 as compared to 0.4 for Taiwan (March 2021). In 2020 the "under-5 infant mortality as a percentage of total population" (0.0032%) was 2.2 times greater than for Japan (0.00145%), but 2.2 times better than that in 2003 (0.0070%).

Foreign occupation: France, Netherlands, Germany (pre-1950); none (post-1950); *post-1950 foreign military presence:* none; *1950-2005 excess mortality/2005 population* = 0.749m/10.359m = 7.2%; *1950-2005 under-5 infant mortality/2005 population* = 0.162m/10.359m = 1.6%. Per capita GDP (nominal) $46,198.

Cyprus: 6000-3000BCE, Neolithic culture; 1500BCE onwards, Greek influences; 800BCE, Phoenician settlement; subsequent Assyrian, Egyptian and Persian rule; 333BCE, conquered by Alexander the Great; subsequent Ptolemaic Egyptian territory; cult of Aphrodite; 58BCE, Roman conquest; 395CE, Byzantine rule; 1191, British conquest under Richard I and then given to the French; 1489, Venetian rule; 1571, Turkish conquest; 1878, British rule; 1914, formal British annexation; 1955, Greek EOKA terrorist campaign launched; 1960, independence under Archbishop Makarios; subsequent Greek union, EOKA and Turkish minority tensions; 1974, Makarios overthrown; Turkey invaded; 200,000 Greeks displaced from the Turkish enclave; Cyprus joined EU.

2021 update: 2019, EU concerns over corruption involving Cyprus passports, banking, Russian oligarchs and other dubious foreign nationals leading to law changes; 2020, increasing dispute involving Cyprus, Greece, and Israel versus Turkey over exclusive economic zones and oil and gas exploitation in the Eastern Mediterranean (depending on the degree of gas leakage, burning gas is worse than burning coal greenhouse gas (GHG)-wise); greenhouse gas (GHG) pollution 21.4 tonnes CO_2-e per person per year; Cyprus is not a member of nuclear-armed NATO but hosts bases of nuclear-armed UK, and has not ratified the TPNW. "Covid-19 deaths per million of population" was 204 as compared to 0.4 for Taiwan (March 2021). In 2020 the "under-5 infant mortality as a percentage of total population" (0.0040%) was 2.8 times greater than for Japan (0.00145%), but 1.8 times better than that in 2003 (0.0070%).

Foreign occupation: Turkey, Britain (pre-1950); UK, Turkey (post-1950); *post-1950 foreign military presence:* UK, Turkey; *1950-2005 excess mortality/2005 population* = 0.054m/0.813m = 6.6%; *1950-2005 under-5 infant mortality/2005 population* = 0.017m/0.813m = 2.1%. Per capita GDP (nominal) $28,285.

Denmark: 9th century, significant conversion to Christianity; 9th-11th century, Viking (Norsemen) raids on Western Europe, notably France and Britain; 1018-1035, Denmark, England and Norway under King Canute (Knut); 1397-1523, union with Sweden; 1658, southern Sweden relinquished by treaty but retention of Iceland and

Greenland; 17th century, Danish Virgin islands acquired (sold to the US in 1917); 18th century, traders to India (Bengal); Greenland settled; 1814, defeated by British and Norway surrendered; 1849, democratic monarchy; 1848-1850, 1863-1864, wars with Prussia and final loss of Schleswig-Holstein; WW1, neutral; 1920, recovered northern Schleswig through plebiscite; 1940-1945, occupation by Germany; most of Danish Jews escaped to Sweden but 100/6,000 were killed; 1949, joined NATO; 1972, joined EU; 1944, Iceland independence; 1948, home rule to Faeroes; 1979, home rule to Greenland; 2003, joined US Iraq occupation.

2021 update: Major methanogenic livestock industry; greenhouse gas (GHG) pollution 27.8 tonnes CO_2-e per person per year; Denmark belongs to nuclear-armed NATO, sent forces to US-occupied Afghanistan, supports retention and use of nuclear weapons on its behalf, and rejects the TPNW. Trump America sought to buy Greenland. "Covid-19 deaths per million of population" was 415 as compared to 0.4 for Taiwan (March 2021). In 2020 the "under-5 infant mortality as a percentage of total population" (0.0038%) was 2.6 times greater than for Japan (0.00145%), but 1.1 times lower than that in 2003 (0.0040%).

Foreign occupation: Germany (pre-1950); none (post-1950); *post-1950 foreign military presence:* US (Greenland base); *1950-2005 excess mortality/2005 population* = 0.203m/5.386m = 3.8%; *1950-2005 under-5 infant mortality/2005 population* = 0.059m/5.386m = 1.1%. Per capita GDP (nominal) $60,657.

Finland: 8th century, Finns displaced Lapps to far north; 11th century, Christianized; 13th century, Swedish conquest; 16th century, Lutheranism; 1581, Grand Duchy; 16th-19th century, Russian-Swedish conflict; 1696, famine killed 1/3 of population; 1721, 1743, progressive Russian acquisitions; 1808-1809, final Russian conquest; 19th century, Finnish autonomy, democracy and nationalism; Russification opposed; 1917, independence declared; 1917-1920, civil war (Soviet-assisted Red Guards versus German-assisted White Guards) culminating in independence; 1939-1945, allied with Germany, war with USSR, loss of territory to USSR with 0.4 million Finns displaced, post-war reparations; 1956, Porkkala returned to Finland; post-war Communist, Social

Democrat and Conservative electoral contests; 1991, collapse of USSR had a big economic impact; subsequent excellent economic growth.

2021 update: Finland is top or near-top in many areas, namely economic performance (e.g. Nokia), child education, competitiveness, civil liberties, gender equality, happiness, human capital, human development, press freedom, quality of life and stability. Greenhouse gas (GHG) pollution 20.6 tonnes CO_2-e per person per year. 84% of Finns want Finland to sign and ratify the TPNW but the Finnish Government refuses to do so. "Covid-19 deaths per million of population" was 147 as compared to 0.4 for Taiwan (March 2021). In 2020 the "under-5 infant mortality as a percentage of total population" (0.0018%) was 1.2 times greater than for Japan (0.00145%), but 2.8 times lower than that in 2003 (0.0050%).

Foreign occupation: Sweden, Germany, Russia (pre-1950); Russia (partial) post-1950); *post-1950 foreign military presence:* Russia; *1950-2005 excess mortality/2005 population* = 0.024m/5.224m = 0.5%; *1950-2005 under-5 infant mortality/2005 population* = 0.064m/5.224m = 1.2%. Per capita GDP (nominal) $48,678.

France: pre-Roman Basques in southwest and Celtic Gauls; 7th century BCE, Phoenician and Greek Mediterranean settlements; 2nd century BCE, Roman settlement of Provence; 1st century BCE, genocidal Roman conquest; 1st century CE, Christianity introduced; Germanic invasions by Visigoths, Franks, Burgundii and Huns; 486, Frank Clovis defeated Roman Gaul; 6th-7th centuries, Merovingian kings; 800, Charlemagne crowned Emperor; spread his rule and enforced Christianity by the sword; 8th-10th century, Norse invasions; 911, Rollo, Duke of Normandy; 11th-15th century, Norman kings of England; 13th century Crusades; 1208-1226, Albigensian crusades; massacre of Béziers, destruction of the Cathars and establishment of the Inquisition to eliminate heresy, 1337-1453, Hundred Years War between England and France; 14th century, Black Death, bubonic plague epidemic; 1/3 of Europe population killed; 75-200 million died in Europe and North Africa; French defeated by the English at Crécy (1346), Poitiers (1356) and at Agincourt (1420); 16th century, Protestant

Reformation; 1572, Saint Bartholomew's Day Massacre of
Protestant Huguenots; 1594; Protestant Henry of Navarre
converted, became Henry IV, first Bourbon king; 1598, Edict of
Nantes for religious tolerance; 1610, Henry IV assassinated; 1643-
1715, Louis XIV; Richelieu and Mazarin advisers; stunning
Versailles Court; colonial expansion; Edict of Nantes revoked
(1685), persecution of Huguenots and loss through emigration of
skilled artisans; war of the Spanish Succession (1701-1714)
constrained French hegemony; 1715-1774, Louis XV, unsuccessful
wars, loss of Indian and Canadian possessions to British; 1774-
1792, Louis XVI, supported American revolution (1775-1783);
1789, French revolution; Louis XVI and Marie Antoinette
beheaded (1792) and reign of terror under Robespierre; 1799-1815,
Napoleon Bonaparte; sophisticated but imperialist administration;
conquered Europe; French Army devastated by winter in the
Russian campaign; key British victories at the Nile (Aboukir Bay,
1798), Trafalgar (1805), the Iberian Peninsular (1810) and
Waterloo (1815); 1814-1815, Congress of Vienna restored
monarchy under Louis XVIII; 1830-1838, Algeria conquered under
Louis Philippe; 1848, February Revolution; 1852, Napoleon
elected president of the Second Republic and thence became
Napoleon III by coup; Second Empire colonial expansion in Africa
and Asia; 1870-1871, Franco-Prussian war; 1870-1940, Third
Republic; brutal French colonial expansion into North Africa, West
Africa, and Indochina; Triple Entente of England, France and
Russia against Germany and Austria; 1914-1918, WW1; prolonged
trench warfare; millions died; Treaty of Versailles exacted
reparations, Alsace and Lorraine returned; 1923-1925, France
reoccupied the Ruhr; appeasement of Nazi Germany; 1939-1945,
WW2; German invasion; evacuation of 0.3 million mainly British
forces from Dunkirk; Petain headed collaborationist Vichy
Government; Free French government (de Gaulle) and resistance;
65,000/300,000 Jews were killed with Vichy complicity; 1944,
Allied Normandy landings and liberation; 1946, Fourth Republic;
1954, loss of Dien Bien Phu and thence of Indochina; 1956,
invasion of Egypt with the UK and Israel; 1960, became a military
nuclear power; massive dependence on nuclear power stations; war
in Algeria led to a right wing military coup in Algiers; 1958, Fifth
Republic established under Charles de Gaulle; Algerian
independence despite French OAS terrorism; France joined the EU;

1960s, African decolonization albeit with considerable neo-colonial control; 1985, French state terrorists sank Greenpeace's ship "Rainbow Warrior" in Auckland, New Zealand; 2002-2003, France opposed illegal UK-US invasion of Iraq; 2004, heat wave killed 11,000 mainly elderly people over one month; 2005, Muslim riots throughout France.

2021 update. France participated in the US Alliance Occupation of Afghanistan (2001 onwards), the France-UK-US (FUKUS) Alliance devastation of Libya (2011), the US Alliance destruction of Syria (2012 onwards) and numerous military operations in countries of former French Africa (Operation Barkhane). A number of awful terrorist atrocities by jihadis in France; rise of far right populism in France that now could conceivably win government; major French complicity in post-9/11, US-imposed Muslim Holocaust and Muslim Genocide with 32 million Muslims dying from violence, 5 million, or from imposed deprivation, 27 million, in 20 countries invaded by the US Alliance since the US Government's 9/11 false flag atrocity that killed 3,000 (2015 estimates). Greenhouse gas (GHG) pollution 17.7 tonnes CO_2-e per person per year. France has a major nuclear power industry, possesses 290 nuclear weapons, and assisted Israeli acquisition of nuclear weapons by 1967; France belongs to nuclear –armed NATO, sent forces to US-occupied Afghanistan, and opposes and rejects the TPNW. "Covid-19 deaths per million of population" was an appalling and gerocidal 1,442 as compared to 0.4 for Taiwan (March 2021). In 2020 the "under-5 infant mortality as a percentage of total population" (0.0039%) was 2.7 times greater than for Japan (0.0015%), but 1.5 times lower than that in 2003 (0.0060%).

Foreign occupation: England; Germany (pre-1950); none post-1950); *post-1950 foreign military presence:* none; *1950-2005 excess mortality/2005 population* = 3.275m/60.711m = 5.4%; *1950-2005 under-5 infant mortality/2005 population* = 0.857m/60.711m = 1.4%. Per capita GDP (nominal) $40,319.

Germany: Neolithic and thence Celtic tribes; 2nd century BCE, German tribes; 1st century BCE-1st century CE, partial Roman conquest; 4th-5th century, German tribes invaded Roman Empire;

6th century, Angles, Saxons and Jutes dominated England; Franks dominated France and South Germany; 751, Pepin deposed Merovingians and started the Carolingian line; 800, Charlemagne crowned Emperor; 9th-12th century, invasions by Norsemen (coastal), Slavs (Eastern) and Magyars (Danubian plain); 962, Holy Roman Empire under Otto I; 1152-1190, Frederick I (Barbarossa) split Saxony and Bavaria leading to decentralized rule until 19th century unification; 12th-13th century, wars against Slavs in the East led by the Teutonic Knights; 13th-15th century, Hanseatic League and Baltic commerce; 13th century, Mongols got as far as Germany; 16th century, Protestant Reformation; Martin Luther; 1524-1526, Peasants' War; 17th century, Counter Reformation; 1618-1648, Thirty Years War devastated Germany; 1648, Peace of Westphalia and administrative division; 18th-19th century, Prussian Empire; 1740-1786, Frederick II, Prussian power and anti-Jewish anti-Semitism; 1796-1815, Napoleonic dominance; 1806, end of Holy Roman Empire; 1815, Battle of Waterloo, British (Wellington) and Prussians (Blucher) defeated France; 1814-1815, Congress of Vienna, Prussia and Bavaria expanded and a German Confederation; 1848, revolutionary year; 1862-1890, Bismarck generated German Empire; Austro-Prussian war (1866); Franco-Prussian War (1870-1871); seizure of Schleswig-Holstein from Danes; French Alsace and Lorraine made part of Germany; William I crowned Emperor of Germany; 19th century, rise of liberalism and nationalism; German colonies in the Pacific, East Africa and South West Africa; 1900-1905, German genocide of 0.1 million Namibian Hereros; 1914-1918, WW1; prolonged trench warfare, tanks, gas and aircraft; 1917, Russian revolution and Treaty of Brest Litovsk with Russia; millions died; 1919, Treaty of Versailles, loss of territory and punitive reparations for defeated Germany; 1919-1933, Weimar republic; mass unemployment, recession, hyperinflation and rise of Nazism; 1933, Hitler exploited Reichstag fire and fear of Communism and gained a bare parliamentary majority; Enabling Act, Nazi dictatorship (Third Reich); 1933-1945, Nazi era; Hitler Youth, Gestapo, SS, repression, violence, anti-Jewish anti-Semitism and mass Jewish emigration; 1934, President and Chancellor positions combined as Fuhrer; 1935, Nuremberg Laws against Jews; concentration camps for Jews, homosexuals, socialists and dissidents; re-armament; economic prosperity; autobahns; 1936-1939, interference in the

Spanish Civil War (e.g. Guernica bombing immortalized by Pablo Picasso's anti-war painting); 1938, Austria annexed (Anschloss); Munich Pact with Britain and France ("peace in our time"); 1939, annexed Sudetenland and thence Czechoslovakia; nonaggression pact with USSR; blitzkrieg on Poland; 1939-1945, WW2: 1939, invasion of Europe 1940, British evacuation at Dunkirk and Battle of Britain; 1941, invasion of Russia, mass extermination by violence or imposed deprivation of 30 million Slavs (24 million in the Soviet Union), Jews (5-6 million), and Gypsies (1 million); 180,000/250,000 German Jews were killed; Japanese attack on Pearl Harbor and war with USA; 1942, defeated in North Africa, held at Stalingrad and Leningrad; 1942-1945, UK-US bombing of German cities (0.6 million died); 1943, surrender at Stalingrad; defeat at Kursk; Allies invaded Italy; 1944, Allied Normandy landings; France liberated; 1945, Berlin captured; Yalta Agreement and Potsdam Conference; post-war Allied Zones in East and West Germany, Berlin and Austria, loss of territory to France, Poland and USSR; Nuremberg war crimes trials; 1941-1950, 9 million German dead from violence or deprivation; US Marshall Plan for reconstruction; Allied airlift to Allied-occupied Berlin; Federal Republic of Germany, de-Nazification and liberal democracy with Christian Democrat and Social Democrat dichotomy, joined NATO (1955), joined EEC (EU) (1958) and post-WW2 economic resurgence; German Democratic Republic: Communist police state, Stasi secret police, the Berlin Wall prevented movement of people; 1989, popular dissent and New Forum, Honecker resigned and the Wall came down; 1990, formal reunification; 1993, all-Germany elections; 1994, last Russian soldiers left; 2002-2003, opposition to US invasion of Iraq.

2021 update: Germany participated in US Alliance invasion and Occupation of Afghanistan; steady rise of the far right; Chancellor Angela Merkel welcomed many refugees from Syria and elsewhere; growing anti-Muslim, anti-immigrant and far right populism; rise of the pro-planet Greens. Greenhouse gas (GHG) pollution 18.6 tonnes CO_2-e per person per year; massive adoption of clean energy policies countered by use of gas from Russia (opposed by the US). Germany supplied nuclear–armed Israel with 6 submarines to carry nuclear weapons; Germany is part of nuclear-armed NATO, helped NATO forces bomb Serbia in the Balkans

War, sent forces to US-occupied Afghanistan, has 20 nuclear weapons on its soil, refuses to sign or ratify the Treaty on the Prohibition of Nuclear Weapons (TPNW), and supports the retention and potential use of nuclear weapons on its behalf, despite 83% of Germans supporting the TPNW and nuclear weapons removal. "Covid-19 deaths per million of population" was a bad 909 as compared to 0.4 for Taiwan (March 2021). In 2020 the "under-5 infant mortality as a percentage of total population" (0.0033%) was 2.3 times greater than for Japan (0.0015%), but 1.8 times lower than that in 2003 (0.0060%).

Foreign occupation: Austria, France, Russia, Britain, US (pre-1950); France, Russia, Britain, US none (post-1950); *post-1950 foreign military presence:* France, Russia, UK, US; *1950-2005 excess mortality/2005 population* = 7.061m/82.560m = 8.6%; *1950-2005 under-5 infant mortality/2005 population* = 1.292m/82.560m = 1.6%. Per capita GDP (nominal) $46,232.

Greece: Neolithic cultures; 3rd-2nd millennia BCE, Bronze age Mycenaean and Minoan (Crete) civilizations; 14th-13th century BCE, Greek Achaeans into Peloponnesus; Aeolian, Dorian and Ionian groups; about 1000BCE, Ionian settlement of Aegean islands and Asia Minor; 8th-6th century, Greek colonies in Black Sea region, Bosphorus, Aegean, Sicily, Italy and Balearic Islands; formation of Greek city states (e.g. Athens and Sparta); 499-449BCE, Persian wars; 495-429BCE, era of Pericles in Athens; 5th-4th century BCE, Golden Age of Greece with huge impact on Western philosophy, science, literature, art, music, theatre, ethics and society; 431-404 BCE, Athens defeated in Peloponnesian War; 338BCE, Athens defeated by Macedonia under Phillip II; 336-323BCE, Alexander the Great, conquered Persians, Babylonians and Egyptians; Greek hegemony as far as India; Hellenic Empire divided e.g. Ptolemy dynasty ruled Egypt; 146BCE, Roman conquest; 395CE, Roman Empire divided into Western (based on Rome) and Eastern (Byzantine) Empires; 378, Visigoth victory; 867-1025, Macedonian dynasty of Byzantine emperors based on Constantinople; 11th century, mounting Seljuk Turk incursions; 12th-13th century, disruption by Crusaders; much of Greece under French and Italian rule; 1261-1453, restored Byzantine Empire; 15th century, Turkish invasion; 1453, fall of Constantinople to

Ottoman Turks (big impact on Western European Renaissance); 1821, Greek War of Independence; Western European and Russian support; 1832, Greek independence under Bavarian king; 1862, Danish king George I, constitutional reforms; 1912-1913, Balkan Wars with Albania; WW1, Greek neutrality until 1917; alliance with Allies yielded territorial gains; 1921, Greek invasion of Anatolia defeated; 1923, Treaty of Lausanne; 1923, 1.5 million Greeks left Asia Minor and 0.8 million Turks and 80,000 Bulgarians left Greek territory; massacres of Greeks in Asia Minor; 1936, Metaxas dictatorship; 1939-1945, WW2; 1939, Greece neutral; 1940, Italian invasion; 1941, German invasion, Allies defeated; 60,000/67,000 Jews killed; 1941-1944, guerrilla war against Germans by Communist EAM-ELAS; 1944-1945, Allied attacks on guerrillas; 1947-1949, British and US war against Communist guerrillas; 1967-1974, US-complicit coup followed by military rule and human rights abuses; 1974, democracy restored; continuing Greco-Turkish tensions over Cyprus and Greco-Macedonia tensions over the name "Macedonia".

2021 update: 1981, membership of European Community (EU); 2019, name change of Macedonia to "Republic of North Macedonia" settled a long-standing dispute with Greece; acute financial distress, associated unrest and reactions from EU Creditor nations, especially Germany (although "Conventional Debt plus Carbon Debt" is greater for Germany than for Greece). Deadly wildfires (2018) linked to global warming and 2018 European heat wave; greenhouse gas (GHG) pollution 18.6 tonnes CO_2-e per person per year. Member of nuclear-armed NATO, endorses nuclear weapons, opposes and rejects the TPNW. "Covid-19 deaths per million of population" was a bad 747 as compared to 0.4 for Taiwan (March 2021). In 2020 the "under-5 infant mortality as a percentage of total population" (0.0022%) was 1.5 times greater than for Japan (0.0015%), but 1.8 times lower than that in 2003 (0.0040%).

Foreign occupation: Turkey (pre-1950); none (post-1950); *post-1950 foreign military presence:* none; *1950-2005 excess mortality/2005 population* = 0.027m/10.978m = 0.2%; *1950-2005 under-5 infant mortality/2005 population* = 0.273m/10.978m = 2.5%. Per capita GDP (nominal) $19,604.

Iceland: 9th century, Norse settlers with mainly female Irish and Scottish slaves; 930, Althing assembly; 10th century, Christianized; 12th-14th century, civil conflict and increasing control by Norway; 1380, Danish rule; 1539-1551, Lutheranism imposed; 17th-18th century, English, Spanish and Algerian pirates; vulcanism; small ice age; 1602, Danish private trade monopoly; 1690s, "small Ice Age" and famine; 1771, Danish royal trade monopoly; 1786, trade open to Danes and Norwegians; 1800, Althing abolished; 1843, re-establishment of the Althing; 1874, home rule; 1918, sovereign state in union with Denmark; 1944, independence; 1946, NATO membership; 1951, US base; 1958-1961, 1972-1973, 1975-1976, "Cod Wars" with UK over fishing culminating in UK recognition of a 200 mile fishing limit; 1973, continuation of US airforce base; Helgafell volcanic eruption; 2003, joined US Coalition in Iraq.

2021 update: 2010 eruption of Eyjafjallajökull disrupted air travel in Europe; 2008-2009, Iceland famously responded to the Global Financial Crisis (GFC) by jailing complicit bankers (banksters). Greenhouse gas (GHG) pollution 14.2 tonnes CO_2-e per person per year. Member of nuclear-armed NATO, endorses nuclear weapons, and rejects the TPNW. "Covid-19 deaths per million of population" was 85 as compared to 0.4 for Taiwan (March 2021). In 2020 the "under-5 infant mortality as a percentage of total population" (0.0024%) was 1.7 times greater than for Japan (0.0015%), but 2.5 times lower than that in 2003 (0.0060%).

Foreign occupation: Norway, Denmark (pre-1950); none (post-1950); *post-1950 foreign military presence:* US; 1950-2005 *excess mortality/2005 population* = 0.003m/0.294m = 1.1%; 1950-2005 *under-5 infant mortality/2005 population* = 0.003m/0.294m = 1.0%. Per capita GDP (nominal) $71,345.

Ireland: Neolithic cultures; 3rd century BCE, Celtic invasions; 5th-6th century CE, Irish settlement in Scotland; 5th century, Christianizing, Saint Patrick, monasteries and missionaries; 8th century-12th century, Norse depredations; 1014, Brian Boru defeated Norsemen; 12th century-15th century, English conquest; 1537, Henry VIII confiscated monastic lands and introduced Protestantism but Ireland remained Catholic; rebellions cruelly suppressed under Elizabeth I; Ulster settlement with Protestants under James I; 1641-1650, rebellion suppressed by Cromwell (hundreds of thousands killed); 1649, Drogheda Massacre; 1690, Battle of the Boyne, victory of Protestant William I over Catholic James II; 1798, rebellion by Wolfe Tone suppressed; 1829, Daniel O'Connell activism led to Catholic Emancipation Act; 1845-1850, Potato Famine; mass starvation despite grain exports under the Corn Laws stopped; 1 million died; 1.5 million emigrated (many perishing *in transit* or in the first North American winter); 1905, Sinn Fein founded; Home Rule enacted in 1914 but WW1 intervened; 1916, Easter Sunday uprising; leaders hanged; 1918, Sinn Fein electoral victory; formed Dáil Éireann and declared independence; 1919-1921, war involving notorious British Black and Tans; 1922, Irish Free State; 1948, Irish Republic; 1970s-1990s, IRA war in Ulster; 2005, IRA disarmament; EU membership; Irish prosperity.

2021 update: 2015, same-sex marriage permitted; 2018, abortion permitted and regulated in this very Catholic country; 2020, UK departure from the EU (Brexit) has serious implication for Ireland, Northern Ireland and enduring peace. Livestock industry contributes to a greenhouse gas (GHG) pollution of 41.4 tonnes CO_2-e per person per year. Ireland is a nuclear weapons-free state, signed and ratified the TPNW. "Covid-19 deaths per million of population" was a bad 934 as compared to 0.4 for Taiwan (March 2021). In 2020 the "under-5 infant mortality as a percentage of total population" (0.0030%) was 2.1 times greater than for Japan (0.00145%), but 3.0 times lower than that in 2003 (0.0090%).

Foreign occupation: Britain (pre-1950); none (post-1950); *post-1950 foreign military presence:* US (in transit to Iraq); *1950-2005 excess mortality/2005 population* = 0.389m/4.050m = 9.6%; *1950-2005 under-5 infant mortality/2005 population* = 0.071m/4.050m = 1.8%. Per capita GDP (nominal) $81,637.

Italy: 9th-4th century BCE, Etruscans; 4th century BCE, Etruscans attacked by Gauls from the North and Samnites from the South; 5th century BCE, growth of Rome; Punic Wars eventually destroyed Carthage; Roman Empire at its peak stretched from Britain to Persia; 5th century CE, successive invasions by Visigoths, Huns, Heruli and Ostrogoths; 476, last Western Empire Emperor deposed;

493, Ostrogoth Theodoric took Ravenna; 593, Lombard rule; 800, Frank Charlemagne crowned in Rome; German Otto I invaded Italy; commencement of Holy Roman Empire; 11th century, Norman rule in South and Sicily; 12th -15th century, cultural and commercial flowering of the major medieval and Renaissance city states (notably Milan, Florence, Venice, Siena and the Papal states); Renaissance after fall of Constantinople to the Ottoman Turks; 16th-18th century, invasions by Spain, France and Austria; 1796-1815, Napoleonic conquests; 1814-1815, Congress of Vienna restored Austrian power; Risorgimento led by Cavour, Garibaldi and Victor Emmanuel triumphed in 1861 with constitutional monarchy under Victor Emmanuel; Italian colonial expansions in Somalia (1889) and Eritrea (1890); 1896, Ethiopians defeated Italians; Libya and Dodecanese conquered (1911-1912); 1914-1918, WW1; initially neutral, Italy entered the war on the Allied side and gained territories from Austria-Hungary; 1922, Mussolini made premier; 1935-1935, conquered Ethiopia; 1936-1939, intervened in Spanish Civil War; 1939, invaded Albania; 1940-1943, allied to Germany; 9,000/120,000 Jews killed; Allied victories in North Africa followed by invasion of Italy; 1943, Italy surrendered; 1944, Rome liberated from the Germans; 1945, Mussolini killed; post-war, Italy lost its colonial acquisitions in Europe and Africa; resumption of mass migration; joined NATO, 1949; joined EEC (now EU) in 1958; numerous Italian governments with Christian Democrats, Communists and Socialists as major parties; 2003, joined US in Iraq (withdrawal by the end of 2006).

2021 update: 2013 onwards, massive 0.7 million refugee intake from Africa; 2020 onwards, massive mainly elderly deaths from the Covid-19 pandemic due to deliberate government inaction and termed a Gerocide by front-line Italian physicians. "Covid-19 deaths per million of population" was an appalling and gerocidal 1,776 as compared to 0.4 for Taiwan (March 2021). Greenhouse gas (GHG) pollution 17.6 tonnes CO_2-e per person per year. Italy is a member of nuclear-armed NATO, sent forces to US-occupied Afghanistan, hosts 40 nuclear weapons, endorses nuclear weapons, and opposes and rejects the TPNW. In 2020 the "under-5 infant mortality as a percentage of total population" (0.0022%) was 1.5

times greater than for Japan (0.0015%), but 2.3 times lower than that in 2003 (0.0050%).

Foreign occupation: France, Austria, Germany, Britain, US (pre-1950); none (post-1950); post-1950 foreign military presence: none, US-backed Gladio terrorism; 1950-2005 excess mortality/2005 population = 0.846m/57.253m = 1.5%; 1950-2005 under-5 infant mortality/2005 population = 1.227m/57.235m = 2.1%. Per capita GDP (nominal) $33,090.

Luxembourg: major medieval and Holy Roman Empire duchy with rulers variously from Bohemia, Burgundy and the Hapsburgs of Austria and Spain; 1797, French occupation; 1814-1815, Congress of Vienna, grand duchy in union with Netherlands but simultaneously a member of the German Confederation with Prussian occupation; 1830-1839, joined Belgian revolt against the Netherlands; a large part became part of Belgium; 1866-1867, sale to France by Netherlands; William III provoked Franco-Prussian crisis; Prussians left; Luxembourg declared neutral; 1890, no male heir of William III; Grand Duke Adolph succeeded; WW1 and WW2, occupied by Germany; 1946, joined UN; 1949, joined NATO; 1958, joined with Belgium and Netherlands in Benelux Union; founding member of EEC (EU).

2021 update: Luxembourg is a major tax haven for corporations and others and thus is deeply complicit in the Global Avoidable Mortality Holocaust (pre-Covid-19 estimate of 7.4 million avoidable deaths from deprivation globally in 2020; Table 9.1). Greenhouse gas (GHG) pollution 23.6 tonnes CO_2-e per person per year. "Covid-19 deaths per million of population" was a gerocidal 1,165 as compared to 0.4 for Taiwan (March 2021). Luxembourg is a member of nuclear-armed NATO, endorses the retention and potential use of nuclear weapons, and rejects the TPNW. In 2020 the "under-5 infant mortality as a percentage of total population" (0.0037%) was 2.6 times greater than for Japan (0.00145%), but 1.6 times lower than that in 2003 (0.0060%).

Foreign occupation: Netherlands, Germany (pre-1950); none (post-1950); *post-1950 foreign military presence:* none; *1950-2005 excess mortality/2005 population* = 0.050m/0.465m = 10.8%;

1950-2005 under-5 infant mortality/2005 population =
0.006m/0.465m = 1.2%. Per capita GDP (nominal) $115,481.

Malta: prehistoric Neolithic cultures from 5900 BCE; rock-cut
tombs; successive Phoenician, Greek, Carthaginian and Roman rule
(Melita); 870CE, Arab rule; 1090, Sicilian Norman conquest; 1530,
Hapsburg Charles V granted Malta to the Knights Hospitalers;
1565, withstood Ottoman Turkish siege; 1798, Napoleonic French
conquest; 1800, British conquest; 1814, British crown colony;
19th-20th century, key shipping and naval port, especially after the
Suez Canal opening (1869); 1921-1936, some self-government;
1942, withstood huge Italian and German bombing; 1947-1959,
constitutional development; 1964, independence; 1974, republic;
1971-1987, Labour government; 2004, joined EU.

2021 update: Greenhouse gas (GHG) pollution 13.3 tonnes CO_2-e
per person per year. "Covid-19 deaths per million of population"
was a bad 863 as compared to 0.4 for Taiwan (March 2021). Malta
is not a member of nuclear-armed NATO, and has signed and
ratified the TPNW. In 2020 the "under-5 infant mortality as a
percentage of total population" (0.0054%) was 3.7 times greater
than for Japan (0.00145%), but 1.3 times lower than that in 2003
(0.0070%).

Foreign occupation: Spain, France, Britain (pre-1950); UK (post-
1950); *post-1950 foreign military presence:* UK; *1950-2005 excess
mortality/2005 population* = 0.019m/0.397m = 4.8%; *1950-2005
under-5 infant mortality/2005 population* = 0.009m/0.019m =
2.3%. Per capita GDP (nominal) $33,752.

Netherlands: 1st century BCE, Batavi and Northern Frisians;
Roman conquest of Lower Germany; 4th-8th century, Franks
invaded; 9th century, part of Holy Roman Empire; 14th-15th
century, Hanseatic League prosperity, rule by Dukes of Burgundy
and thence by Hapsburg Emperors Maximilian I, Charles V and
Philip II of Spain; 1562-1648, national and religious tensions led to
wars for independence from Spain; Thirty Years War (1618-1648);
1648, Treaty of Westphalia; independence of the United Provinces
(the Netherlands); 1602, Dutch East India Company formed and
thence often egregiously violent exploitation of East Indies; Dutch
West India Company (slavery, Caribbean possessions); Jews (from

Spain and Portugal) and Huguenots (from Catholic France)
promoted prosperity; Anglo-Dutch wars (1652-1654, 1664-1667);
17th-18th century wars against France; 1668, Triple Alliance with
England and Sweden against Louis XIV; 1672, dikes opened to halt
French invasion; War of the Grand Alliance (1688-1697); War of
the Spanish Succession involving England, Austria and the Dutch
versus France (1701-1714); 1794, revolutionary French conquest;
Congress of Vienna, independence of Low Countries under
William I; 1839, Belgian independence; WW1, Dutch neutrality;
inter-war polder development; 1940-1945, WW2, German
occupation; extermination of 104,000/140,000 Jews; 1945-1949,
conflict with Indonesians ending with Indonesian independence;
1953, North Sea storms and flooding; 1962, West Irian ceded to
Indonesia; 1975, Suriname independence; 1981-1982, US cruise
missile base controversy; 1991, Gulf War participation against
Iraq; 1995, Dutch UN peacekeepers stood by during Serbian
massacres of Bosnians in Srebrenica; 2003, participation in US
occupation of Iraq.

2021 update: Socially progressive but growing anti-Muslim, anti-
immigrant and far right populism; greenhouse gas (GHG) pollution
24.9 tonnes CO_2-e per person per year. "Covid-19 deaths per
million of population" was a bad 957 as compared to 0.4 for
Taiwan (March 2021). The Netherlands is a member of nuclear-
armed NATO, sent forces to US-occupied Afghanistan, hosts 20
nuclear weapons, endorses the retention and potential use of
nuclear weapons, and rejects the TPNW. In 2020 the "under-5
infant mortality as a percentage of total population" (0.0031%) was
2.1 times greater than for Japan (0.00145%), but 2.3 times lower
than that in 2003 (0.0070%).

Foreign occupation: Spain, France, Germany (pre-1950); none
(post-1950); *post-1950 foreign military presence:* US; *1950-2005
excess mortality/2005 population* = 0.000m/16.300m = 0.0%;
1950-2005 under-5 infant mortality/2005 population =
0.163m/16.300m = 1.0%. Per capita GDP (nominal) $53,053.

Norway: 9th–11th century, Norsemen raided Western Europe; the
Shetlands, Orkneys, Iceland, Greenland and coastal Britain and
France under Norse rule; 14th century-18th century, Norway ruled

by Denmark; 1814, British defeated the Danes, and Norway united with Sweden; 19th century, major migration to the US, shipping expansion and growing nationalism; 1905, overwhelming plebiscite vote and separation from Sweden as a democratic monarchy; WW1, neutral; the period between wars saw increased social welfare; 1940-1945, German conquest and rule by Quisling; 1992, international controversy over Norwegian whaling; 1972 and 1994, rejection of EU association; 2003, joined US Coalition in Iraq.

2021 update: 2011, 67 people killed in attacks by a right-wing extremist; massive income from North Sea oil and gas but aims to rapidly transition to electric vehicles (EVs); huge iron ore production; greenhouse gas (GHG) pollution 20.1 tonnes CO_2-e per person per year. "Covid-19 deaths per million of population" was a bad 120 as compared to 0.4 for Taiwan (March 2021). Norway is a member of nuclear-armed NATO, sent forces to US-occupied Afghanistan, endorses the retention and potential use of nuclear weapons, and rejects the TPNW. In 2020 the "under-5 infant mortality as a percentage of total population" (0.0022%) was 1.5 times greater than for Japan (0.00145%), but 2.3 times lower than that in 2003 (0.0050%).

Foreign occupation: Denmark, Sweden, Germany (pre-1950); none (post-1950); *post-1950 foreign military presence:* none; *1950-2005 excess mortality/2005 population* = 0.032m/4.570m = 0.7%; *1950-2005 under-5 infant mortality/2005 population* = 0.047m/4.570m = 1.0%. Per capita GDP (nominal) $74,986.

Portugal: 1000BCE, Celtic Lusitanians; 1st century BCE, Roman conquest; 5th century, Visigoth conquest of most of the Iberian Peninsular; 6th-7th century, Byzantine rule in south; 711, Moorish invasion; 8th-15th century, Christian conflict with Moors; 1143, Portuguese independence; 15th century, exploration and conquest: Diaz rounded the Cape of Good Hope (1488), Treaty of Tordesillas with Spain dividing New World (1494), Vasco da Gama sailed to India (1497-1498); Portuguese acquisition of Brazil (1500), Goa (1510), Malacca (1511) and Hormuz (1515); 15th-19th century, African slave trade; 17th-18th century, Portuguese involvement in Spanish, French and British Iberian wars; 1807, French occupied Portugal; 1811, French expelled by British under Wellington (use of food as a weapon of war); 1822, liberal revolution; Brazil declared independence under Emperor Pedro; 19th century, Portuguese conquest of Angola and Mozambique; WW1, Portugal neutral and then joined the Allies (1916); 1933-1968, Salazar dictatorship; WW2, pro-Allied neutrality; 1961, Goa seized by India; 1960s, rebellions in Angola, Mozambique and Portuguese Guinea; 1968, Salazar had a stroke; replaced by Caetano; 1974, Captain's Revolution and democracy; 1975, Angola, Mozambique, Sao Tome and Principe and Cape Verde independent; East Timor invaded by Indonesia; 1986, EU membership; 2003, joined US Coalition in Iraq.

2021 update: Portugal is socially progressive (e.g. decriminalizing of drugs). Greenhouse gas (GHG) pollution 15.0 tonnes CO_2-e per person per year. "Covid-19 deaths per million of population" was an appalling and gerocidal 1,653 as compared to 0.4 for Taiwan (March 2021). Portugal is a member of nuclear-armed NATO, sent forces to US-occupied Afghanistan, endorses the retention and potential use of nuclear weapons, and rejects the TPNW. The 2020 "under-5 infant mortality as a percentage of total population" (0.0023%) was 1.6 times greater than for Japan (0.00145%), but 3.0 times lower than that in 2003 (0.0070%).

Foreign occupation: France (pre-1950); none (post-1950); *post-1950 foreign military presence:* none; *1950-2005 excess mortality/2005 population = 0.429m/10.080m = 4.3%; 1950-2005 under-5 infant mortality/2005 population = 0.577m/10.080m =* 5.7%. Per capita GDP (nominal) $23,350.

Spain: prehistoric Neolithic people; early Basque settlement followed by Celtic invasion; 9th century BCE, Phoenician settlements; later Carthaginian settlements; Greek settlements in the Balearic Islands; 3rd century BCE, Carthaginian conquest; 218-201BCE, Romans defeated Carthaginians in 2nd Punic War; 1st century, Spain Roman; progressively Christianized; 409, Suevi and Vandal invasions; 419, Visigoth invasion; 507, Franks expelled Visigoths from Gaul (France); 6th century, Visigoth conquest of most of Spain; 6th-7th century, Byzantine rule in the South; 711, Muslim Berbers invaded; Moors dominated Spain except for northern Basque and Visigoth strongholds; 8th-11th century, flowering of Jewish and Moorish culture; 1212, Moors defeated by Castilians; 1478, Spanish Inquisition; 1492, Moor Granada captured by Ferdinand and Isabella and Moors and Jews expelled from Spain; 1492, Columbus discovered America; 1494, Treaty of Tordesillas divided the New World between Portugal and Spain; 16th century, conquest of Central and South America; 100 million indigenous people died from disease and deprivation in the Americas; 1494-1559, Italian Wars with France yielded Milan and Naples; 1516, Charles I (Holy Roman Emperor Charles V), first of Hapsburg rulers; 1556, Phillip II ruled Spain, parts of Italy and the Netherlands; 1588, failed Spanish Armada attack on England; 1609, final expulsion of Christian Moors; 1618-1648, Thirty Years War; 1701-1714, War of the Spanish Succession, Bourbon line established; 18th century, attempted reforms; 1808, French occupation; 1814, final British and Spanish victory over the French in the Peninsular War (scorched earth policy); 1825, most of Latin America had gained independence; 1833-1868, violent period under Isabella II; 1868, constitutional monarchy; 1898, Spanish American War, loss of the Philippines, Cuba, Puerto Rico; WW1, neutral; 1936-1939, Spanish Civil War; conservative insurgents (with Nazi German and Fascist Italian help) defeated socialist Loyalists; 1939-1975, Franco dictatorship; WW2 neutrality; 1953, US bases; decolonization of Spanish Morocco (1956), Spanish Equatorial Guinea (1968), Ifni (1969) and Spanish Sahara (1976); 1975, constitutional monarchy; 1970s-present, ETA Basque terrorism; 1982, joined NATO; 1986, joined EU; 2003, joined US Coalition in Iraq; 2004, Madrid terrorist bombing followed by withdrawal from Iraq by the newly elected government.

2021 update: Economic distress after the 2008-2009 Global Financial Crisis; 2017, Catalan referendum found for Catalan independence followed by Central Government repression. Greenhouse gas (GHG) pollution 20.9 tonnes CO_2-e per person per year. "Covid-19 deaths per million of population" was an appalling and gerocidal 1,604 as compared to 0.4 for Taiwan (March 2021). Spain is a member of nuclear-armed NATO, sent forces to US-occupied Afghanistan, endorses the retention and potential use of nuclear weapons, and rejects the TPNW. A political deal with Podemos involved future support for the TPNW but no action has resulted. In 2020 the "under-5 infant mortality as a percentage of total population" (0.0021%) was 1.4 times greater than for Japan (0.0015%), but 2.9 times lower than that in 2003 (0.0060%).

Foreign occupation: France (pre-1950); none (post-1950); *post-1950 foreign military presence:* US; *1950-2005 excess mortality/2005 population* = 1.049m/41.184m = 2.5%; *1950-2005 under-5 infant mortality/2005 population* = 0.964m/41.184m = 2.3%. Per capita GDP (nominal) $29,816.

Sweden: 1st century, the Sveare (Suiones) occupied Svearland; 6th century, conquered Götar; 9th-12th century, Christianized; 10th century, Varangians (Swedes, Norsemen and Vikings) spread through Russia to the Black Sea; 1319, Sweden and Norway united; 1397-1523, Sweden, Norway and Denmark united; 1520, Stockholm massacre of nobles; 1523, Gustavus I, founded the modern Swedish state, broke Hanseatic League Baltic control, established the Vasa dynasty and made Lutheranism the state religion; 1561, conquered Estonia; 1611-1632, Gustavus II (Gustavus Adolphus); major victories in Poland and Germany made Sweden a European power; 1648, Treaty of Westphalia ended the Thirty Years War with West Pomerania, Wismar and Bremen going to Sweden; 1660, southern provinces secured from Denmark; 1720-1721, Baltic conquests relinquished to Hanover, Prussia and Russia; 1809, Finland ceded to Russia; constitutional monarchy; 1813-1814, war against Napoleon; Congress of Vienna gave Norway to Sweden; 1905, Norway independent; WW1 and WW2, neutrality; post-war, continued prosperity as a democratic welfare state.

2021 update: Sweden is socially progressive and libertarian but played a rotten role in the ongoing US and UK persecution of the world's most famous journalist, Australian Julian Assange; greenhouse gas (GHG) pollution 15.0 tonnes CO_2-e per person per year. The Swedish Government notably refused to take tough measures in the Covid-19 Pandemic and "Covid-19 deaths per million of population" was an appalling and gerocidal 1,321 as compared to 0.4 for Taiwan (March 2021). Sweden is neutral and not a member of nuclear-armed NATO, but in 2019 it refused to support the TPNW. In 2020 the "under-5 infant mortality as a percentage of total population" (0.0024%) was 1.7 times greater

than for Japan (0.00145%), but 1.3 times lower than that in 2003 (0.0030%).

Foreign occupation: Denmark, (pre-1950); none (post-1950); *post-1950 foreign military presence:* none; *1950-2005 excess mortality/2005 population* = 0.249m/8.895m = 2.8%; *1950-2005 under-5 infant mortality/2005 population* = 0.070m/8.895m = 0.8%. Per capita GDP (nominal) $52,896.

Switzerland: 58BCE, Helvetii conquered by Romans; 5th century, invaded by the Alemanni and Burgundii; 6th century, Franks invaded; 9th century, dominated by Swabia and Southern Burgundy; 1033, part of Holy Roman Empire; 13th-14th century, successful coalition against Habsburg power; 15th century, victories against Burgundy and the Holy Roman Empire; 1499, effective independence; 1515-1516, defeated by French leading to "perpetual alliance" with France, neutrality and Swiss employment as mercenaries; 16th century, Protestant Reformation; 1618-1648, Swiss essentially uninvolved in the Thirty Years War; 1648, independence recognized by the Treaty of Westphalia; 1798-1803, Helvetic Republic formed by Napoleonic French invaders; 1815, Congress of Vienna and Pact of Restoration; 1815, Treaty of Paris guaranteed independence; economic recession, migration and moves for centralization; 1848, federal state constitution under the Radical Party; WW1 and WW2, armed neutrality; 1979, Jura became the 23rd canton of the Swiss Confederation; 1971, women's suffrage and candidature; 1986, rejected UN membership; 1990s, criticism over WW2 Nazi and Jewish Holocaust victim assets in Swiss Banks; 2000, closer links to EU; 2002, approved UN membership.

2021 update: Notwithstanding some OECD-demanded reform moves on tax avoidance, Switzerland remains a haven for morally or illicitly ill-gotten gains by One Percenters, criminals, dictators and greedy leaders world-wide; greenhouse gas (GHG) pollution 11.0 tonnes CO_2-e per person per year. "Covid-19 deaths per million of population" was an appalling and gerocidal 1,184 as compared to 0.4 for Taiwan (March 2021). Switzerland is neutral and is not a member of nuclear-armed NATO, but it has not signed or ratified the TPNW (however both houses of the Swiss

Parliament have demanded ratification of the TPNW). In 2020 the "under-5 infant mortality as a percentage of total population" (0.0036%) was 2.5 times greater than for Japan (0.00145%), but 1.4 times lower than that in 2003 (0.0030%).

Foreign occupation: France, (pre-1950); none (post-1950); *post-1950 foreign military presence:* none; *1950-2005 excess mortality/2005 population* = 0.076m/7.157m = 1.1%; *1950-2005 under-5 infant mortality/2005 population* = 0.077m/7.157m = 1.1%. Per capita GDP (nominal) $85,135.

United Kingdom: prehistoric Neolithic culture; 5th century BCE, Celtic metallurgical culture; 54BCE-2nd century CE, Roman conquest and foundation of Londinium (London); 410, Roman withdrawal; 5th century, Germanic Angles, Saxons and Jutes invaded; Christianizing; 8th–9th century, Norse Viking raids; Vikings notably opposed by King Alfred; 1016, King Canute (Knut) ruled both England and Denmark; 1066, Norman conquest under William the Conqueror followed by genocide of English peasantry ("harrying of the north"); 1171, Norman invasion of Ireland; 1215, nobles constrained arbitrary royal power by Magna Carta; 13th century, invasions of Wales and Scotland; 1237-1337, Hundred Years War with France; 1348, devastating Black Death (bubonic plague) killed 2 million or 40% of the population, and the labor shortage empowered skilled workers; 14th century, Wars of the Roses culminating in Tudor rule of Henry VII and administrative sharpening; Henry VIII confiscated Church lands and instituted Protestant Reformation; Elizabeth I, consolidation of Protestantism; defeat of Spanish Armada (1588); commencement of maritime exploration and American settlements; founding of British East India company (1600); 17th century, Stuart period; conflict with Parliament; English Civil War between Puritans and Royalists; Charles I beheaded; *habeus corpus* and increased Parliamentary power; Cromwell republic and atrocities in Ireland killed 600,000 or 40% of the population; restoration of Charles II but defeat of Catholic James II by Protestant William of Orange at the Battle of the Boyne (1689); 18th century, Britain emerged as a major world power; 1707, act of union with Scotland; Hanoverian succession; 1701-1714, War of the Spanish Succession against France; 1756-1763, Seven Years War against France left Britain the dominant colonial power in North America and India; African slave trade; 1746, Scots finally defeated at the Battle of Culloden – last battle on British soil; 1757, Bengal conquered and rapaciously taxed; 1769-1770, Great Bengal Famine killed 10 million; 1776, American independence allowing genocidal westward expansion; 1788, settlement of Australia and commencement of the Australian Aboriginal Genocide; 19th century, Napoleonic Wars with defeat of Napoleonic France at Trafalgar under Nelson (1805) and finally at Waterloo under Wellington (1815); industrialization fed by Empire; further conquest in India, Africa,the Americas, Asia, and the Pacific; 1845-1850, Irish famine (1 million dead; 1.5 million fled overseas), Indian cholera epidemics (25 million victims) and famines (tens of millions of victims); 19th century, Scottish Highland Clearances; Irish Famine; 1857 onwards, 10 million Indians killed in reprisals for the Indian Rebellion; 1854-1856, Crimean War with Russia; Queen Victoria and the British empire; late 19th century, conquest of Southern Africa and victory over the Dutch Afrikaaners in the Boer War (British use of concentration camps); 20th century, arms race; 1914-1918, WW1, horrendous casualties, Austro-Hungarian and Turkish Empires dismembered; post-war, Irish independence; women's suffrage; oil and British power in the Middle East; 1917 Balfour Declaration and UK-backed Zionist colonization and ethnic cleansing of Palestine; 1929, Wall Street collapse followed by depression and European re-armament; 1939-1945, WW2, Nazism eventually defeated, Europe temporarily wrecked; 1942-1945, WW2 Bengali Holocaust; Eastern Europe enslaved by Russia; post-war, British technological advance, welfare state, civil nuclear power and nuclear arms; UN and decolonization; colonial and neo-colonial Asian and African wars; 1982, Falklands Island War against Argentinian invaders; increasing political conservatism under Thatcher (Thatcherism) and then under right-wing Labor under Blair; decades of IRA terrorism in Ulster and England followed by political accommodation; UK-US democratic imperialism and criminal invasions of Iraq and Afghanistan; 2005, IRA disarmament; Muslim-origin London bombings followed by strengthened anti-terror laws.

2021 update: 2011, France-UK-US (FUKUS) Coalition devastatingly bombed Libya, formerly the richest country in Africa; 2012 onwards, UK involved with arms and military forces in US-backed attempts to remove the Syrian Government; 2015, UK involved in US-backed, Saudi-led Yemeni Genocide; continuing terrorist atrocities in the UK; as a key player in Carbon Price-ignoring global financial services the UK is deeply complicit in the worsening climate crisis, "the greatest market failure in history"; 2020, UK departed the EU (Brexit); greenhouse gas (GHG) pollution 21.5 tonnes CO_2-e per person per year. "Covid-19 deaths per million of population" was an appalling and gerocidal 1,857 as compared to 0.4 for Taiwan (March 2021). UK is a member of nuclear-armed NATO, has 215 nuclear warheads, has not signed or ratified the TPNW and rejects the TPNW that became International Law on 22 January 2021. The 2020 "under-5 infant mortality as a percentage of total population" (0.0046%) was 3.2 times greater than for Japan (0.00145%), but 2.0 times lower than that in 2003 (0.0090%).

Foreign occupation: none since Danes in 11th century (pre-1950); none (post-1950); *post-1950 foreign military presence:* US; *1950-2005 excess mortality/2005 population* = 4.411m/59.598m = 7.4%; *1950-2005 under-5 infant mortality/2005 population* = 0.777m/59.598m = 1.3%. Per capita GDP (nominal) $41,855.

2020 statistical update for Western Europe. Table 9.3 summarizes population, under-5 infant mortality (IM) and excess mortality (EM; avoidable mortality from deprivation) in Western Europe in 2020 (pre-Covid-19 projection in 2019 for 2020 by the UN Population Division). Table 9.1 compares Western Europe with other global regions. Presented in square brackets for each country is the "Relative EM Score" of EM/Pop (%) divided by that for the best-performing country, Japan (0.0020%), which accordingly has a "Relative EM Score" of 1.0.

 In terms of "Relative EM Score" and "per capita GDP", the outcomes range from Finland (1.2 and $48,678) to the UK (3.2 and $41,855) and Malta (3.8 and $33,752). While the average "Relative EM Score" is 2.2 for Western Europe it is a shocking 176.6 for non-Arab Africa (Table 9.1). Under-5 infant mortality, already very low in 2003, declined 1.1-3.0-fold in the various countries except in Austria where it increased slightly (1.2-fold).

4.4 Eastern Europe – Communism, foreign occupation and tyranny but peace and good social services

Aside from Muslim Albania and the major Muslim populations of Bosnia-Herzegovina, Macedonia, Bulgaria and the Kosovo region of Serbia-Montenegro, the formerly Communist-ruled Eastern European group countries (conveniently including Armenia and Georgia for the purposes of this analysis) have a Christian background. Eastern European nationalist desires that surged in the 19th century were largely thwarted by the Turkish, German, Austro-Hungarian and Russian Empires but realized in some cases (Albania, Bulgaria, Czechoslovakia, Estonia, Hungary, Latvia, Lithuania, Poland, Romania and Yugoslavia) between WW1 and WW2. 20 million died in the Soviet Union under Communism including, 5 million (1920s Russian Famine) and 7 million (1930s Ukrainian Famine). The cataclysm of WW2 destroyed the Jewish populations of Eastern Europe (5-6 million from violence and deprivation), and killed some 24 million Soviet citizens, 6 million Poles and 1 million Yugoslavs. Red Army victory over genocidal German Nazism delivered all these countries to Russian Communist control – with the exceptions of Albania and Yugoslavia, which nevertheless were ruled by Communist regimes. The collapse of Communism in 1989-1991 finally led to self-determination for the Eastern European peoples under relatively democratic systems but with perturbations ranging from electoral fraud to civil war in the Balkans, Moldova, Chechnya and the Ukraine. The post-war Communist systems provided good education, health and full employment coupled with repression and eventual economic decline and crisis from market failure. Actual Soviet military intervention occurred in Hungary (1956) and Czechoslovakia (1968). The welfare state circumstances produced avoidable mortality outcomes that were good by world standards but not as good as those obtaining in Western Europe. Indeed in some Eastern European countries (notably Bulgaria, Estonia, Hungary, Latvia, Russia and the Ukraine and also in Germany and Austria, countries which were subject to partial post-war Soviet occupation) there were small but marked elevations in excess mortality from about 1970 onwards that may possibly be linked to smoking, alcoholism, pollution, non-reported radiological contamination, impoverished minorities (notably Gypsies) and tensions of life in repressed societies.[8]

Albania: ancient Illyrian and Thracian peoples; Illyria and Epirus; 3rd century CE, independent kingdom; 395 CE, division of Roman Empire; 7th century, Serbia invaded the north; 9th century, south taken by Bulgaria; 1014, Byzantines retook south; 11th century, Venice founded coastal towns; 1272, Norman Charles I of Naples King of Albania; 14th century, Serb conquest; resistance to Turks under Scanderbeg supported by Venice and Naples; 1478, Ottoman Turkish rule; Islamic conversion; 1877, Treaty of San Stefano, Albanian territory handed to Serbia; 1912, First Balkan War, Albanian independence; loss of territory to Serbia, Montenegro and Greece; 1920, independence accepted; 1924-1928, machinations culminating in invasion and installation of King Zog; 1939, Italian invasion; partisan opposition lead by Hoxha; 1946, Communist government under Hoxha; 1961-1977, friendship with China, hostility to the US and the USSR; 1991, elections; 1997, rebellion in southern Albania; aid and security provided by international European forces; 1998-1999, refugees from Kosovo; impoverished country; 2003, joined the US Coalition in Iraq.

2021 update: Greenhouse gas (GHG) pollution 13.3 tonnes CO_2-e per person per year. "Covid-19 deaths per million of population" was a bad 766 as compared to 0.4 for Taiwan (March 2021). Albania is a member of nuclear-armed NATO, sent forces to US-occupied Afghanistan, and has not signed the TPNW. In 2020 the "under-5 infant mortality as a percentage of total population" (0.0120%) was 8.3 times greater than for Japan (0.00145%), but 4.1 times lower than that in 2003 (0.0490%).

Foreign occupation: Turkey, Serbia, Italy, Germany (pre-1950); none (post-1950); *post-1950 foreign military presence:* European peace-keeping force; *1950-2005 excess mortality/2005 population* = 0.251m/3.220m = 7.8%; *1950-2005 under-5 infant mortality/2005 population* = 0.301m/3.220m = 9.3%. Per capita GDP (nominal) $5,303.

Armenia: 8th century BCE, Armenian settlement; 6th-4th century BCE, Persian tributary; 330BCE, conquered by Alexander; subsequently part of Seleucid Syria; 190BCE, Roman conquest of

Syria; Armenian independence; 69-67BCE, Roman conquest; 1st
century, Christian conversion (the oldest Christian state); 3rd
century, conquered by Sassanid Persians; 387, partition between
Roman and Persian spheres; 4th century-9th century, successive
war and occupation by Byzantines, Huns, Khazars and Arabs; 886-
1046, independent; 1046, Byzantine conquest; 1071, Seljuk Turk
conquest; 1080-1375, Little Armenia; 1236-1243, Mongol
invasion; 1375, conquered by Mamluks; 1386-1394, Timur invaded
Greater Armenia and exterminated most of the population; 1405,
Ottoman Turks invaded; 16th century, under Turkish rule; 1828,
Russia took Eastern Armenia from Persia; 1894, Turkish
massacres; 1915, commencement of the Armenian Genocide,
coinciding with the Anglo-French Dardanelles invasion at
Gallipoli; 1.5 million Armenians were killed or died from
deportation (still denied by Turkey); 1921, Russo-Turkish Treaty;
Armenia part of USSR; 1988, devastating earthquake; 1988,
fighting in Nagorno-Karabakh Armenian region of Azerbaijan;
1991, Armenian independence; continuing Turkish and Azerbaijan
blockades.

2021 update: renewed war with Azerbaijan with Armenia agreeing
to withdrawal from some territory (2020); greenhouse gas (GHG)
pollution 2.3 tonnes CO_2-e per person per year. "Covid-19 deaths
per million of population" was an appalling and gerocidal 1,157 as
compared to 0.4 for Taiwan (March 2021). Armenia is a nuclear-
weapons-free state but has not signed and ratified the TPNW and
consistently abstains at the UNGA on this matter. In 2020 the
"under-5 infant mortality as a percentage of total population"
(0.0159%) was 11.0 times greater than for Japan (0.00145%), but
1.9 times lower than that in 2003 (0.0300%).

Foreign occupation: Persia, Turkey, Russia (pre-1950); Russia;
post-1950 foreign military presence: Russia; *1950-2005 excess
mortality/2005 population* = 0.091m/3.043m = 3.0%; *1950-2005
under-5 infant mortality/2005 population* = 0.289m/3.043m =
9.5%. Per capita GDP (nominal) $4,623.

Belarus: 5th-6th century CE, Slavic settlement; 9th century, part of
Kievan Rus; 13th century, Mongol invasion; 14th century,
Lithuanian conquest; significant Khazar-derived Ashkenazi Jewish

settlement; 1569, part of merged Polish-Lithuanian state; 1772, 1793 and 1795 partitions of Poland left Belarus part of the Russian Empire; 1812, devastated during the Napoleonic retreat from Moscow; 19th century, anti-Jewish anti-Semitic pogroms and Jewish emigration to the US; 1914-1917, WW1, major zone of Russo-German fighting; 1918, Belarussian republic declared in Minsk; 1919, Red Army occupied Minsk and Belarus; 1919-1920, Polish-Russian War; 1921, Treaty of Riga, Western Belarus to Poland; 1922, Byelorussian republic within the USSR; 1939, USSR occupied Western Belarus; 1941, German invasion; horrendous destruction and mass extermination of Jews; 1945, member of the UN; 1991, independence from Russia and joined the CIS; 1994, Lukashenko elected president and subsequently re-elected repeatedly in controversial elections; post-independence, close economic and other links with Russia but mounting protests over unfair elections and human rights abuses.

2021 update: massive continuing protests and mass arrests over unfair elections. Greenhouse gas (GHG) pollution 8.6 tonnes CO_2-e per person per year. "Covid-19 deaths per million of population" was 233 as compared to 0.4 for Taiwan (March 2021). Belarus is a nuclear-weapons endorser and has not signed and ratified the TPNW. In 2020 the "under-5 infant mortality as a percentage of total population" (0.0040%) was 2.8 times greater than for Japan (0.00145%), but 4.3 times lower than that in 2003 (0.0170%).

Foreign occupation: Lithuania, Poland, Russia, Germany (pre-1950); *post-1950 foreign military presence:* Russia; *1950-2005 excess mortality/2005 population* = 0.375m/9.809m = 3.8%; *1950-2005 under-5 infant mortality/2005 population* = 0.269m/9.809m = 2.7%. Per capita GDP (nominal) $6,674.

Bosnia & Herzegovina: 1st century CE, Roman Illyricum; 7th century, Slavic Serb settlement; 12th-15th century, an independent entity with Hungarian hegemony; 1148, Duchy of Hum autonomous as Herzegovina; 1463, Turkish conquest of Bosnia; 1482, Herzegovina conquered by Turks; major conversion to Islam; 15th-19th century, backward, isolated society; 1875, peasant uprising; 1877-1878, Russo-Turkish War; Congress of Vienna, under Austrian administration and occupation but with formal

Turkish sultan sovereignty; 1908, annexed to Austria-Hungary; increased Serbian nationalism; 1914, assassination of Archduke Francis Ferdinand by a Bosnian Serb in Sarajevo led to the catastrophic WW1 (total death toll about 16 million); 1918, part of Yugoslavia; 1941-1945, WW2, Italian and German occupation; gross human rights abuse and exterminations; anti-fascist partisan activity; 1 million Yugoslavs including 58,000 out of 70,000 Jews killed by the Germans; 1946, part of Yugoslavia; 1992, Croatians and Bosnians declared independence from Serbia; 1992-1995, horrendous civil war; isolation and shelling of multi-ethnic Sarajevo; immense war crimes and ethnic cleansing (e.g. 1995 Srebrenica massacre of 8,000 men and boys by Serbs); 200,000 dead; 1995, Dayton Accord, Croat-Bosnian and Serb autonomous regions; NATO forces supervised peace; 2003, joined US Coalition in Iraq; 2004, EU peace-keeping; continuing war crimes trials at The Hague, notably of Serb leader Milosevic and others.

2021 update: Greenhouse gas (GHG) pollution 7.2 tonnes CO_2-e per person per year. "Covid-19 deaths per million of population" was a gerocidal 1,905 as compared to 0.4 for Taiwan (March 2021). A candidate for NATO membership, it opposed and has not joined the TPNW. In 2020 the "under-5 infant mortality as a percentage of total population" (0.0051%) was 3.5 times greater than for Japan (0.00145%), but 3.5 times lower than that in 2003 (0.0180%).

Foreign occupation: Turkey, Austria, Hungary, Italy, Germany, multi-ethnic Yugoslavia (pre-1950); multi-ethnic Yugoslavia, Croatia, Serbia, NATO, EU (post-1950); *post-1950 foreign military presence:* multi-ethnic Yugoslavia, Croatia, Serbia, NATO, EU; *1950-2005 excess mortality/2005 population* = 0.230m/4.209m = 5.5%; *1950-2005 under-5 infant mortality/2005 population* = 0.275m/7.763m = 3.5%. Per capita GDP (nominal) $6,109.

Bulgaria: ancient Thrace and Moesia; 6th century, Slavic settlement; 679-680, Eastern Bulgars settled; Slavic culture continued; 8th-9th century, Bulgarian power; Bulgarian Orthodox Church; St Cyril and writing; 809, Khan Krum captured Sophia; 811, defeated Byzantines and besieged Constantinople; 865, adopted Christianity; 893-927, Czar Simeon; 1018, annexation by resurgent Byzantium; 10th century, Pecheneg and Cuman invasions; 1186-1396, second Bulgarian empire; 1218-1241, Czar Ivan extended Bulgarian power over all the Balkans except Greece; 1330, Macedonia conquered by Serbia; Turkish Balkan victories at Kosovo (1389) and Nikopol (1396); Turkish rule until 1908; repression of Bulgarian Church and culture; 1876, rebellion suppressed violently; Turkish responsibility for Bulgarian atrocities prompted further Russian Balkans involvement; 1877-1878, Russo-Turkish War; Eastern Rumelia autonomous; Macedonia under direct Turkish rule; 1885, Eastern Rumelia taken by Alexander (Battenberg, of Saxe-Coburg-Gotha, as with much of European royalty); defeated Serbia; 1908, Ferdinand declared independence; 1911-1912, First Balkan War, defeated Turkey; 1913, Second Balkan War, lost most of Macedonia to Serbia and Greece; 1915, supported Germany over the Macedonia issue; 1918, lost Aegean outlet; 1923, coup and subsequent authoritarian rule; 1940, WW2, supported Germany; 1944, USSR invaded; Bulgarian coup and declaration of war on Germany; 40,000/48,000 Jews killed; 1946, Communist republic; 1951-1952, 160,000 Turkish citizens deported to Turkey; mid-1980s, Bulgarization campaign against 0.8 million ethnic Turks; 1990, non-Communist Zhelev elected; 2003, part of US Coalition in Iraq; 2004, joined NATO.

2021 update: 2018, ranked as the most corrupt country in the EU. Greenhouse gas (GHG) pollution 10.1 tonnes CO_2-e per person per year. "Covid-19 deaths per million of population" was a gerocidal 1,811 as compared to 0.4 for Taiwan (March 2021). A member of nuclear-armed NATO, it is a nuclear weapons endorser, sent forces to US-occupied Afghanistan, and opposes the TPNW. In 2020 the "under-5 infant mortality as a percentage of total population" (0.0058%) was 4.0 times greater than for Japan (0.00145%), but 2.2 times lower than that in 2003 (0.0130%).

Foreign occupation: Turkey, Greece, Serbia, Germany (pre-1950); Russia (post-1950); *post-1950 foreign military presence:* Russia; *1950-2005 excess mortality/2005 population* = 0.769m/7.763m = 9.9%; *1950-2005 under-5 infant mortality/2005 population* = 0.275m/7.763m = 3.5%. Per capita GDP (nominal) $9,703.

Croatia: 1st century BCE, Roman Pannonia; 7th century CE, Slavic Croat settlement; 9th century, Christianized (Catholicism); 10th century, Dalmatia conquered; 11th century, conflict with Venice; 1091, conquest by Hungary; 1526, Battle of Mohács, much of Croatia under the Turks; 1527, alliance with Habsburgs against the Turks; 16th century onwards, Croatian mercenaries; 19th century, Magyarization; 1848-1849, Jellacic led Croatians against revolutionary Hungarians; 1867, Austro-Hungarian monarchy; Croatia and Slavonia linked to Hungary; Istria and Dalmatia linked to Austria; 1918, independence together with Serbia, Slovenia and Bosnia as Yugoslavia; 1939, autonomous Croatian state; 1941, German invasion; Croatian independence under Italian and German military control and led by fascist Ustaše under Pavelic; genocide against Serbs, Jews and Gypsies – Jasenovac was the 3rd biggest death camp in Nazi Europe (0.2 million victims murdered); Croatian Communist Tito led partisans against the Germans; 1945-1991, semi-autonomous part of Yugoslavia; post-war US- and Vatican- complicit Ustaše-sympathetic migration and thence international activism and terrorism; 1980, Tito died; 1991, Croatian independence under Tudjman; war against Serbs and Bosnian Muslims; huge war crimes including "ethnic cleansing"; 1998, final peace agreements.

2021 update: EU member. Greenhouse gas (GHG) pollution 7.4 tonnes CO_2-e per person per year. "Covid-19 deaths per million of population" was a gerocidal 1,432 as compared to 0.4 for Taiwan (March 2021). A member of nuclear-armed NATO, it is a nuclear weapons endorser, sent forces to US-occupied Afghanistan, and opposes the TPNW. In 2020 the "under-5 infant mortality as a percentage of total population" (0.0039%) was 2.7 times greater than for Japan (0.00145%), but 2.3 times lower than that in 2003 (0.0090%).

Foreign occupation: Turkey, Austria, Hungary, Italy, Germany (pre-1950); multi-ethnic Yugoslavia (post-1950); *post-1950 foreign military presence:* multi-ethnic Yugoslavia; *1950-2005 excess mortality/2005 population* = 0.291m/4.405m = 6.6%; *1950-2005 under-5 infant mortality/2005 population* = 0.191m/4.405m = 4.3%. Per capita GDP (nominal) $14,627.

Czechia (Czech Republic): Boli Celtic tribe in Bolohaemia of Roman times; 1st-5th century CE, Slavic Czech invasion; 7th century, overcame Avar occupation; 9th century, Christianized; part of Moravia; 920-929, Wenceslaus resisted the Germans; 950, autonomous part of Holy Roman Empire; 1253-1278, Ottocar II extended Bohemian domains to Adriatic; 1415, Jan Hus burnt at the stake; 1415-1439, Hussite Wars; 16th century, Reformation; 1526, Emperor Ferdinand I re-established Catholicism; Protestant opposition; 1609, Emperor Rudolph gave freedom of religion; 1618, countermanding of religious freedom by Emperor Matthias; Protestant defenestration of 2 imperial regents from Hradčany Castle in Prague - they survived but this precipitated the Thirty Years War and European devastation; 1618-1648, Thirty Years War involving major powers of Europe; 1620, Protestants crushed at the Battle of the White Mountain; 1648, Treaty of Westphalia, Germanization, taxation, absentee landlords; 18th-19th century, increasing industrialization; 19th century, increasing Czech nationalism; 1867, Austro-Hungarian Monarchy; 1914-1918, WW1; 1918, Czechoslovakian independence under T.G. Masaryk; 1938, Germany seized Sudetenland; 1939-1945, WW2; 1944, extermination of 60,000/81,000 Czechoslovakian Jews; Theresienstadt concentration camp (holding Jews prior to Auschwitz extermination); Churchill spared Prague from Allied bombing; 1945, fall of Prague to the Red Army; Potsdam Conference, 3 million Germans expelled; Ruthenia handed to the USSR; 1946, Communist political dominance; death of foreign minister Jan Masaryk (likely murder by defenestration); 1948, new constitution; Beneš resigned; Communist dictatorship and purge trials; 1953, riots followed by some liberalization; 1968, Prague Spring under Dubček; suppressed by USSR and Warsaw Pact invasion; severe repression; 1977, Charter 77, human rights declaration; 1989, massive demonstrations in Prague; Velvet Revolution, non-Communist government elected under Havel; 1991, last Russian troops left; 1993, separate Slovakia and Czechia republics; 2003, joined US Coalition in Iraq.

2021 update: EU member. Greenhouse gas (GHG) pollution 23.5 tonnes CO_2-e per person per year. "Covid-19 deaths per million of population" was a gerocidal and world-leading 2,391 as compared to 0.4 for Taiwan (March 2021). A member of nuclear-armed

NATO, it is a nuclear weapons endorser, sent forces to US-occupied Afghanistan, and opposes the TPNW. In 2020 the "under-5 infant mortality as a percentage of total population" (0.0025%) was 1.7 times greater than for Japan (0.00145%), but 1.6 times lower than that in 2003 (0.0040%).

Foreign occupation: Russia, Austria, Germany (pre-1950); Russia (post-1950); *post-1950 foreign military presence:* Russia; *1950-2005 excess mortality/2005 population* = 1.087m/10.216m = 10.6%; *1950-2005 under-5 infant mortality/2005 population* = 0.142m/10.216m = 1.4%. Per capita GDP (nominal) $23,452.

Estonia: 1st century BCE, occupied by Aesti; 13th century, conquered by Danes and German Livonian Brothers of the Sword (Teutonic Knights); 1219, Tallinn founded by Danes; 1346, Danes sold northern Estonia to the Knights; major Hanseatic commerce; 1561, Teutonic knights defeated; north to Sweden; south to Poland; 1629, Polish-Swedish war, all of Estonia ruled by Sweden; 1710, Peter the Great conquered Livonia; 1721, Russian rule confirmed by Treaty of Nystad; German aristocracy commercially dominant; 19th century, Russification and emigration; 1905, reprisals for Estonian participation in the Russian revolution; 1917, Russian revolution; puppet Communist regime; 1918, independence; German occupation; 1918, German collapse; Russian invasion repelled; 1920, Russian recognition; 1934, dictatorship installed; 1939-1940, Russian occupation; 60,000 Estonians killed or deported; 1941-1944, Estonian support for Germans; 1944, Russian victory; mass deportation and killing of Estonians; 1991, independence; 1994, last Russian troops left; 2003, joined US Coalition in Iraq; 2004, Estonia joined NATO and the EU.

2021 update: problems over language and citizenship rights for ethnic Russians (24% of the population). Greenhouse gas (GHG) pollution 25.4 tonnes CO_2-e per person per year. "Covid-19 deaths per million of population" was a bad 638 as compared to 0.4 for Taiwan (March 2021). A member of nuclear-armed NATO, it is a nuclear weapons endorser, sent forces to US-occupied Afghanistan, and opposes the TPNW. In 2020 the "under-5 infant mortality as a percentage of total population" (0.0025%) was 1.7 times greater

than for Japan (0.00145%), but 3.6 times lower than that in 2003 (0.0090%).

Foreign occupation: Denmark, Sweden, Poland, Russia, Germany (pre-1950); Russia (post-1950); *post-1950 foreign military presence:* Russia; *1950-2005 excess mortality/2005 population =* 0.166m/1.294m = 12.8%; *1950-2005 under-5 infant mortality/2005 population* = 0.032m/1.294m = 2.5%. Per capita GDP (nominal) $23,740.

Georgia: Colchis of Ancient Greeks (land of the Golden Fleece); 4th century BCE, kingdom; 3rd century, Persian Sassanid rule; 4th century, Christianity; 6th-13th century, Georgian independence except for a period of Seljuk Turk rule in the 11th century; 13th century, Mongol invasion; 1386-1403, invaded by Timur; 1555, divided between Persia and Turkey; 1773, accepted Russian protection; 1801, king abdicated and ceded to Russia for protection from Persians; 1803-1829, Russia seized Georgian territories from Turkey; 1918, independence; 1921, Soviet republic; Soviet Union dictator Joseph Stalin a Georgian; 1941-1943, part-occupied by Germans; 1945, Stalin deported hundreds of thousands as collaborators; 1991, independence; 1992, violence involving pro-Russian South Ossetia separatists and Abkhazia rebels wanting independence; 1993, Georgia joined CIS; Russian bases and concerns over Chechen rebel use of Georgian territory; 2003, joined US Coalition in Iraq.

2021 update: 2008, Russia recognised Abkhazia and South Ossetia as separate republics. Greenhouse gas (GHG) pollution 4.0 tonnes CO_2-e per person per year. "Covid-19 deaths per million of population" was a bad 938 as compared to 0.4 for Taiwan (March 2021). While not a member of nuclear-armed NATO, it has operated with NATO in Occupied Afghanistan, is a nuclear weapons endorser and has not joined the TPNW. In 2020 the "under-5 infant mortality as a percentage of total population" (0.0123%) was 8.5 times greater than for Japan (0.00145%), but 2.4 times lower than that in 2003 (0.0300%).

Foreign occupation: Turkey, Persia, Russia (pre-1950); Russia (post-1950); *post-1950 foreign military presence:* Russia; *1950-2005 excess mortality/2005 population* = 0.281m/5.026m = 5.6%;

1950-2005 under-5 infant mortality/2005 population =
0.166m/5.026m = 4.6%. Per capita GDP (nominal) $4,439.

Hungary: 1st century, Pannonia and Dacia Roman provinces;
successive invasions by Huns (4th century), Avars (6th century),
and by Magyars and Jewish-convert, Turkic Khazars (9th century);
1055, Magyar defeat by Holy Roman Empire at Lechfeld; 1001-
1038, Stephen Christianized Hungarians; 1172-1196, Bela
increased Western contacts; 1222, nobles demanded Golden Bull
constraining royal authority of King Andrew; 1241, Mongol
invasion; 14th century, Hungarian expansion met Turkish
expansion; Hungarian and allied losses to the Turks at Kosovo
(1389), Nikopol (1396) and Varna (1444); 1456, Hungarian victory
at Belgrade under John Hunyadi; 1458-1490, King Matthias; 1526,
critical defeat by Turks at the Battle of Mohács; Ferdinand of
Austria claimed Hungarian throne versus John Zapolya; Great Plain
under the Turks; 16th century, Protestant Reformation; 1557,
religious tolerance (largely Catholic, one fifth Presbyterian); 1683,
siege of Vienna marked furthest extent of Turkish power; 1686,
Budapest liberated from Turks; 1687, recognition of Austrian
Habsburg claim to the Hungarian throne; Peace of Kalowitz, Turks
ceded Hungary and Transylvania to Austria; 1711, defeat of
Francis II Rákóczy by Austrians; 1718, Austrians seized the Banat
from the Turks; 18th century; German and Slav immigration into
Hungary; 19th century, increasing Hungarian nationalist activism;
1848, Hungarian parliament passed laws for liberal monarchy;
1848, war on Hungary by Francis Joseph; 1849, Kossuth declared
an independent republic; Russians helped Austrians crush the
revolt; 1866, Austrians defeated by Prussia; 1867, Austro-
Hungarian Monarchy set up by the Ausgleich agreement; Emperor
Joseph crowned King of Hungary (incorporating Transylvania,
Slovakia, Ruthenia, Croatia, Slovenia and the Banat region of
south-east Hungary); 1914-1918, WW1; Hungary fought with
Austria and Germany; post-war loss of territory; 1919, Bela Kun
communist government removed by UK-backed invading
Romanians; 1920, Horthy made regent; 1920, Treaty of Trianon,
stripped Hungary of much territory; 1938-1944, Hungary
temporarily regained much territory; 1944, the Germans occupied
the country when Hungary sought to protect its Jewish population;
200,000/710,000 Jews killed; 1944-1945, liberation by the

Russians; 1948, Communist takeover engineered; collectivization and nationalization; 1955, Hungary joined Warsaw Pact and the UN; 1956, anti-communist revolution; Nagy appealed to the UN; Russians invaded, 0.2 million fled; as many as 0.1 million deported or killed; 1989, opened border with Austria; 1990, multi-party democracy; 1991, departure of last Russian troops; 2003, joined US Coalition in Iraq.

2021 update: 2018, over two thirds of the European Parliament voted that the authoritarian, anti-academic, anti-immigrant, populist and popular Hungarian Government under Viktor Orbán's Fidesz Party posed a "systemic threat" to democracy. Greenhouse gas (GHG) 15.5 tonnes CO_2-e per person per year. "Covid-19 deaths per million of population" was a gerocidal 2,022 as compared to 0.4 for Taiwan (March 2021). Hungary is a member of nuclear-armed NATO, is a nuclear weapons endorser, sent forces to US-occupied Afghanistan, opposed and has not joined the TPNW. In 2020 the "under-5 infant mortality as a percentage of total population" (0.0042%) was 2.9 times greater than for Japan (0.00145%), but 1.9 times lower than that in 2003 (0.0080%).

Foreign occupation: Turkey, Austria, Germany, Romania, Russia (pre-1950); Russia (post-1950); *post-1950 foreign military presence:* Russia; *1950-2005 excess mortality/2005 population =* 1.363m/9.784m = 13.9%; *1950-2005 under-5 infant mortality/2005 population* = 0.288m/9.784m = 2.9%. Per capita GDP (nominal) $16,879.

Latvia: 1st millennium CE, Letts occupied Baltic Lettland; 13th century, Christianized by Livonian Brothers of the Sword; 1629, Sweden conquered Livonia; 1721, Livonia conquered by Russia; 1817-1819, emancipation of the serfs; 1885, landowner and economic élite German replaced by Russian as the official language; 1905, Russian Revolution; subsequent punishment of Latvian participants; 1914-1918, WW1, massive destruction as zone of major Russo-German conflict; 1918, independence; 1920, peace with Russia; 1922, constitutional democracy; 1936, dictatorship; 1939, bases granted to the USSR and the German minority transferred to Germany; 1940, Russian occupation; 1941-1944, German invasion and occupation with Latvian support;

horrendous extermination of 70,000/100,000 Jews with Latvian participation; 1944, the Russians expelled the Germans; hundreds of thousands of Latvians were deported to suffering or death in Siberia; extensive Russian settlement followed in subsequent decades; 1990, independent; 1991, independence recognized by Russia; UN membership; 1994, last Russian soldiers left; mounting discrimination against the substantial Russian minority; 2003, joined the US Coalition in Iraq; 2004, member of NATO and EU.

2021 update: 27% of the population of Latvia are ethnic Russians of whom many are denied citizenship. Greenhouse gas (GHG) 11.4 tonnes CO_2-e per person per year. "Covid-19 deaths per million of population" was a bad 998 as compared to 0.4 for Taiwan (March 2021). Latvia is a member of nuclear-armed NATO, is a nuclear weapons endorser, sent forces to US-occupied Afghanistan, opposed and has not joined the TPNW. In 2020 the "under-5 infant mortality as a percentage of total population" (0.0052%) was 3.1 times greater than for Japan (0.00145%), but 3.1 times lower than that in 2003 (0.0160%).

Foreign occupation: Sweden, Russia, Germany (pre-1950); Russia (post-1950); *post-1950 foreign military presence:* Russia; *1950-2005 excess mortality/2005 population* = 0.288m/2.265m = 12.7%; *1950-2005 under-5 infant mortality/2005 population* = 0.053m/2.265m = 2.3%. Per capita GDP (nominal) $17,885.

Lithuania: 1500BCE, Liths settled Nemen River region; 13th-15th century, Lithuanians fought Germanic Knights (Livonian Brothers of the Sword and Teutonic Knights); Lithuania expanded to include Belarus and parts of Russia and Ukraine to the Black Sea; 1386, Jagiello became Ladislau II of Poland-Lithuania; 1410, Teutonic Knights defeated at Tannenberg; 1569, Lithuania joined with Poland and became Polonized; 1772, 1793 and 1795, successive Polish partitions between Prussia, Austria and Russia; 19th century, Catholic clergy-led cultural revival and nationalism; 1914-1918, WW1; 1918, Lithuanian independence; 1920-1927, war with Poland; dictatorships; 1939, Vilnius returned from conquered Poland; 1940, USSR occupation; 1941-1944, German invasion and occupation; extermination of 104,000/140,000 Jews; 1944, Russian return; anti-Communist guerrillas; huge deportations to Siberia;

1950s-1990s, severe repression; improved circumstances after 1956 with USSR under Krushchev; 1990, Lithuanian independence opposed militarily by Russia; 1991, independence recognized; 1993, last Russian troops left; 2003, joined NATO; joined US Coalition in Iraq; 2004, joined EU.

2021 update: Declining population as in much of Europe (and good for the planet). Greenhouse gas (GHG) 5.9 tonnes CO_2-e per person per year. "Covid-19 deaths per million of population" was a gerocidal 1,310 as compared to 0.4 for Taiwan (March 2021). Lithuania is a member of nuclear-armed NATO, is a nuclear weapons endorser, sent forces to US-occupied Afghanistan, opposed and has not joined the TPNW. In 2020 the "under-5 infant mortality as a percentage of total population" (0.0045%) was 3.1 times greater than for Japan (0.00145%), but 2.0 times lower than that in 2003 (0.0090%).

Foreign occupation: Russia, Poland, Germany (pre-1950); Russia (post-1950); *post-1950 foreign military presence:* Russia; *1950-2005 excess mortality/2005 population* = 0.143m/3.401m = 4.2%; *1950-2005 under-5 infant mortality/2005 population* = 0.107m/3.401m = 3.1%. Per capita GDP (nominal) $19,795.

Macedonia (North Macedonia): Classical Macedonia, Thrace and Epirus encompassed present-day southern Serbia, Macedonia, southern Bulgaria and northern Greece; 8th century BCE, first Macedonians; 5th century BCE, adopted Greek language; 359-336BCE, Philip expanded Macedonia; 336-323 BCE, Alexander the Great expanded his empire to the Indus River, encompassing Greece, Asia Minor, Egypt, Syria and Persia; post-Alexander Hellenic era; 2nd century CE, Roman province; 395, Division of Roman Empire; Macedonia under Byzantium; 9th century, conquered by Bulgarians; 12th century, re-conquest by Byzantium; 1204, invasion by the Fourth Crusade and period of contestation; 1261, Byzantine control re-established; 14th century, Serbian conquest; late 14th century, Ottoman Turkish rule until the late 19th century; 1877-1878, Russo-Turkish War, most of Macedonia went to Bulgaria; 1912-1913, Balkans Wars, Greece and Serbia dispossessed Bulgaria of most of Macedonia; thousands of Macedonians fled to Bulgaria; 1914-1918, WW1; 1923, population exchanges between Turkey, Greece and Bulgaria; Slavic and Turkish people in Greek Macedonia were replaced by Greek refugees from Asia Minor; 1925-1926, hostilities between Bulgaria and Greece; 1939-1945, WW2; Axis-linked Bulgaria occupied Macedonia; 1945-1947, restoration of pre-war status; 1946, Macedonian autonomous region in Yugoslavia; 1945-1949, Greek Civil War, Yugoslav-Greek tensions and Hellenization in Northern Greece; 1990, Slavic Macedonian independence; Greek hostility and insistence on "Former Yugoslav Republic of Macedonia" nomenclature; Kosovo ethnic cleansing, huge influx of Muslim Kosovo refugees and subsequent Albanian agitation and guerrilla action in Macedonia; ethnic Albanian and Macedonian accommodation; 2003, joined US Coalition in Iraq.

2021 update: 2018, ongoing dispute with Greece over naming (Macedonia is also the name of part of northern Greece) was finally resolved by a naming change to Republic of North Macedonia. Greenhouse gas (GHG) 8.5 tonnes CO_2-e per person per year. "Covid-19 deaths per million of population" was a gerocidal 1,731 as compared to 0.4 for Taiwan (March 2021). Macedonia is a member of nuclear-armed NATO, sent forces to US-occupied Afghanistan, opposed and has not joined the TPNW. In 2020 the "under-5 infant mortality as a percentage of total population" (0.0115%) was 7.9 times greater than for Japan (0.00145%), but 3.3 times lower than that in 2003 (0.0380%).

Foreign occupation: Turkey, Serbia, Bulgaria, Greece, Germany, multi-ethnic Yugoslavia (pre-1950); multi-ethnic Yugoslavia (post-1950); *post-1950 foreign military presence:* multi-ethnic Yugoslavia; *1950-2005 excess mortality/2005 population =* 0.145m/2.076m = 7.0%; *1950-2005 under-5 infant mortality/2005 population* = 0.221m/2.076m = 10.6%. Per capita GDP (nominal) $6,903.

Moldova: 14th century CE, Moldavia independent; 16th century, Ottoman Turkish conquest; 1791-1793, East Moldavia conquered by Russia; 1812, Russian occupation of Bessarabia; 1914-1918, WW1; 1918, Romanian acquisition of Turkish Moldavia and Bessarabia; 1924, USSR established a constituent Moldova republic; 1939-1945, WW2; 1941, annexed by Romania; 1944, reconquest by Russia; 1991, Moldova independence; joined the CIS; rebellion of the heavily Russian Trans-Dniester region east of the Dniester River; 1997, peace with more autonomy and safeguards for ethnic Russian and Turkish regions; 1999, most Russian troops left but with some remaining in the Trans-Dniester region; continuing Communist support in post-independence democratic elections; 2003, joined US Coalition in Iraq.

2021 update: One of the poorest European countries. Greenhouse gas (GHG) 4.0 tonnes CO_2-e per person per year. "Covid-19 deaths per million of population" was a gerocidal 1,178 as compared to 0.4 for Taiwan (March 2021). Moldova has not joined the TPNW. In 2020 the "under-5 infant mortality as a percentage of total population" (0.0127%) was 8.8 times greater than for Japan (0.00145%), but 2.9 times lower than that in 2003 (0.0370%).

Foreign occupation: Turkey, Romania, Germany, Russia (pre-1950); Russia (post-1950); *post-1950 foreign military presence:* Russia; *1950-2005 excess mortality/2005 population =* 0.254m/4.259m = 6.0%; *1950-2005 under-5 infant mortality/2005 population* = 0.239m/4.259m = 5.6%. Per capita GDP (nominal) $2,957.

[**Montenegro:** Early Medieval period, 3 Slavic principalities Duklja, Travunia and Raska; 1042, Duklja independence from Byzantine Empire; 13th century, Zeta principality in south; 1421, annexed by Serbia; 1496-1878, part of Ottoman Empire but with some autonomy and conflict; 1877-1878, Russian victory in Russo-Turkish War resulting in Montenegro independence; 1910, Kingdom of Montenegro; 1916-1918, Austro-Hungarian occupation; 1922, part of Serbia; 1941-1944, German and Italian occupation with Partisan resistance; 1945-1992, part of Yugoslavia; 1992, part of Serbia-Montenegro; 1999, bombed by NATO in the Balkans War; **2006, independence by referendum from Serbia;** member of NATO.

2021 update: Greenhouse gas (GHG) pollution 10.4 tonnes CO_2-e per person per year. Member of nuclear-armed NATO, endorses nuclear weapons, opposes and hence violates the TPNW. "Covid-19 deaths per million of population" was a gerocidal 1,965 as compared to 0.4 for Taiwan (March 2021). The 2020 "under-5 infant mortality as a percentage of total population" (0.0035%) was 2.4 times greater than for Japan (0.00145%), but 6.3 times lower than that in 2003 (0.0220%).

Pre-2006 statistics as for Serbia and Montenegro in Table 8.4. *Foreign occupation:* Turkey, Austria, Hungary, Bulgaria, Germany (pre-1950); multi-ethnic Yugoslavia (post-1950); *post-1950 foreign military presence:* multi-ethnic Yugoslavia, NATO, US, UK and German air forces; *1950-2005 excess mortality/2005 population* = 0.388m/10.513m = 3.7%; *1950-2005 under-5 infant mortality/2005 population* = 0.620m/10.513m = 5.9%. Per capita GDP (nominal) $8,825.]

Poland: 9th-10th century CE, Slavic Polians dominant, Wend communities; 1410, Polish-Lithuanian army defeated Teutonic Knights at Tannenberg; 1386-1572, Polish-Lithuanian Jagiello dynasty founded by Ladislaus II; 1462, Teutonic Knights crushed; 1569, union of Lithuania and Poland; 16th-17th century, wars against Turks, Sweden and Russia; 1655, Swedish victories; North Livonia lost; 1677, Ukraine lost to Russia; 1683, John Sobiewski defended Vienna from the Turks; 18th century, increasing Russian domination; successive 1772, 1793 and 1795 partitions distributed Poland between Prussia, Russia and Austria; 1794, revolt by Tadeusz Kosciuszko; mass emigration; 1807, Napoleonic Treaty of Tilsit, Grand Duchy of Warsaw; 1815, Congress of Vienna, "Congress Poland" linked to Russia, Western Poland to Prussians, Galicia to Austria and Krakow independent; 1830 November Revolution, eventually defeated by Russians; 1848, Galician revolt suppressed and Krakow annexed; 1848, rebellions in Prussian and Austrian Poland; 1863, January Revolution in Russian Poland; subsequent Prussian area Germanification and Russian area Russification; WW1, Poland under Piludski initially against the Russians; 1917, Germans imprisoned Piludski; 1918, Poland independent; 1919, Treaty of Versaille, return of Silesia and a Polish Corridor to the Baltic; 1920-1921, war with Russia; 1926, coup; increasing anti-Jewish anti-Semitism; 1939, German-USSR non-aggression treaty; September 1 1939, German Blitzkrieg on Poland; WW2 commenced; Russians later invaded from East; 1941, Germany attacked Russia; Jewish Warsaw Ghetto revolt (13,000 died); 6 million Poles died including 2.6 million/3.0

million Jews; industrial killing at Auschwitz killed 1 million people; 1943, Germans revealed Russian Katyn Massacre of 10,000 Polish officers (admitted by the Russians in 1990); 1944, the Russians waited for reinforcements and permitted the Germans to crush the Warsaw uprising (0.2 million killed); 1945, liberation of death camps; Potsdam Conference, Prussia East of the Oder and Neisse Rivers to Poland and Germans expelled; 1947, "elected" Communist government; 1949, joined COMECON; 1955, Warsaw Treaty Organization; 1956, Poznan riots; 1960, Gomulka denounced Stalinist excesses and freed Cardinal Wyszynski but revived anti-Jewish anti-Semitism and practised repression; 1968, Poland assisted in the invasion of Czechoslovakia; 1978, Bishop of Krakow, Karol Wojtyla became Pope John Paul II (Pope from 1978-2005); 1980, economic privation; Gdansk strikes, Solidarity Movement led by Lech Walesa; 1989, Solidarity legalized, won elections; 1990, Walesa president; 2003, Poland joined US Coalition in Iraq.

2021 update: Social conservatism of the ruling Law and Justice Party causing friction with the rest of the EU. Greenhouse gas (GHG) pollution 12.9 tonnes CO_2-e per person per year. Member of nuclear-armed NATO, endorses nuclear weapons, sent forces to US-occupied Afghanistan, opposes the TPNW. "Covid-19 deaths per million of population" was a gerocidal 1,357 as compared to 0.4 for Taiwan (March 2021). The 2020 "under-5 infant mortality as a percentage of total population" (0.0034%) was 2.4 times greater than for Japan (0.00145%), but 2.4 times lower than that in 2003 (0.0080%).

Foreign occupation: Turkey, Sweden, Austria, Prussia, Russia, Germany (pre-1950); Russia (post-1950); *post-1950 foreign military presence:* Russia; *1950-2005 excess mortality/2005 population* = 0.677m/38.516m = 7.8%; *1950-2005 under-5 infant mortality/2005 population* = 1.368m/38.516m = 3.6%. Per capita GDP (nominal) $15,727.

Romania: 2nd-3rd century CE, Roman Dacia; Roman language and Christianization; successive invasions by Goths, Huns, Avars, Bulgars and Magyars; 13th century, Mongol invasion and occupation; 1417, Wallachia submitted to Ottoman Turkish hegemony; 16th century, Moldavia taken by Turks; Transylvanian Hungarian hegemony; 1601, Michael the Brave of Wallachia ruled most of Romania; 1711, Turkish domination; Constantinople Greek (Phanariot) governors; 1774, increased Russian influence by treaty in Wallachia and Moldavia; 1821, Romanian and Turkish expulsion of Greeks from Moldavia; 1822, Turkish concession of Romanian governors; 1828-1829, Russo-Turkish War; 1848, Romanian rebellion suppressed by Turks and Russians; Moldavia and Wallachia under Turkish hegemony, South Bessarabia to Moldavia; 1859-1866, Cuza ruled Wallachia and Moldavia, relieved peasantry; 1866, constitution; 1877, joined Russia against the Turks; 1878, Congress of Berlin, Romanian independence; 1881, constitutional monarchy; 1914-1918, WW1; 1916-1918, defeated by Austria-Germany; 1918, annexed Bessarabia (from Russia), Bukovina (from Austria) and Transylvania (from Hungary); 1919, put down Bela Kun communist régime and installed Admiral Horthy in Hungary; 1920s, anti-Jewish anti-Semitism and persecution and massacres of Hungarians; 1930s, rise of fascist politics and the Iron Guard; 1939-1945, WW2; 1940, Russia seized territories; 1941-1944, Romania allied with Germany; 750,000/1 million Jews killed and the survivors largely went to Israel post-war; 1945, Communist government; 1947-1965, Gheorgiu-Dej Communist dictator; 1965-1989, Ceauşescu Communist dictatorship increasingly independent of the Soviet line; 1980s, increasing poverty; 1989, Ceauşescu and his wife captured and executed; 1990, constitutional democracy; 2003, joined US Coalition in Iraq; 2004, joined NATO.

2021 update: Economic prosperity and significant Romanian emigration to the Western EU and elsewhere. Greenhouse gas (GHG) pollution 10.9 tonnes CO_2-e per person per year. Member of nuclear-armed NATO, endorses nuclear weapons, opposes and hence violates the TPNW. "Covid-19 deaths per million of population" was a gerocidal 1,193 as compared to 0.4 for Taiwan (March 2021). The 2020 "under-5 infant mortality as a percentage of total population" (0.0072%) was 5.0 times greater than for Japan (0.00145%), but 2.9 times lower than that in 2003 (0.0210%).

Foreign occupation: Turkey, Hungary, Austria, Germany, Russia (pre-1950); Russia (post-1950); *post-1950 foreign military presence:* Russia; *1950-2005 excess mortality/2005 population =* 1.133m/22.228m = 5.1%; *1950-2005 under-5 infant mortality/2005 population* = 1.029m/22.228m = 4.6%. Per capita GDP (nominal) $12,914.

Russia: 7th century BCE, Celtic Scythians; 3rd century, Sarmatians; successive invasions by Goths (3rd century), Huns (4th century), Avars (6th century), Khazars (7th century) and Eastern Bulgars (8th century); 9th century, extensive Slav settlement; Varangians (Norse Viking traders and soldiers from Scandinavia) founded Novgorod and Kiev; 10th century, Orthodox Christianity; Kievan Rus destroyed Jewish convert Khazar capital Atil on the Volga delta; 10th -13th century, Kievan Rus empire; 13th century, devastating Mongol (Tatar) invasion (40-60 million died in Eurasia due to the Mongol invasion); 1237-1480, Tatar Empire of the Golden Horde; 14th century, Belarus, Ukraine and part of Russia ruled by Lithuania-Poland; 14th-16th century, rise of Moscow-based Russian state; progressive defeat of Tatars; 1533-1584, Ivan the Terrible, defeated Tatar Khanates, began colonization of Siberia and broke the power of the nobles (boyars); 17th century, defeat of Polish invaders; commencement of the Romanov dynasty; establishment of peasant serfdom; 1689-1725, Peter the Great Westernized; conquered Ingria, Livonia, Estonia, Karelia and Finland; controlled the Church; 1762-1796, Catherine the Great defeated Poles; Russia occupied Belarus, Ukraine, Crimea, Eastern Poland and Lithuania; 1812, the Napoleonic invasion army was virtually destroyed by the Russian winter; 19th century, massive Russian expansion into Finland, Siberia, the Far East, the Caucasus, the Balkans and Central Asia; industrialization; emergence as a dominant European power; expansion of liberal views; anti-Jewish anti-Semitic pogroms led to mass Jewish migration to America; 1854-1856, Crimean War against Britain and Turkey; 1861, liberation of the serfs; 1860, Vladivostok founded; 1892, Triple Entente of Britain, France and Russia; 1904-1905, defeated by the Japanese; 1905, Revolution suppressed; continuation of anti-Jewish anti-Semitic pogroms; 1914-1918, WW1, Russia fought the German-Austrian alliance; 1917, Russian Revolution, 1918, Treaty of Brest-Litovsk, loss of Baltic states and Eastern Poland (the 1917 UK Balfour Declaration initiating colonization of Palestine was to get Russian Zionists to try to keep

Russia in the war); 1917-1922, civil war between Red and White Armies (US and UK unsuccessfully invaded); Russian famine (5 million died); 1920s-1930s, Lenin; Stalin; massive industrialization and collectivisation; Ukrainian deportations, killings and famine (7 million dead); Stalinist purges (up to 20 million killed in purges and famine); 1939, non-aggression pact with Germany; 1939-1945, WW2; 1941, German invasion; siege of Leningrad (St Petersburg) (1941-1944); Battle of Stalingrad (1942-1943); Battle of Kursk (1943); Battle for Berlin (1945); 24 million Soviet war dead; 13 million military deaths; 750,000/2.5 million Soviet Jews killed; 1945, Yalta Conference of Allies; Potsdam Conference of Allies; 1945-1990, USSR control over Eastern Europe; installed communist regimes; Cold War with support notably for Cuba, Egypt, Vietnam; 1956, de-Stalinization under Kruschev; 1963, Cuban missile crisis; 1960s, Sputnik-led lead in Space Race; 1956, invasion of Hungary (0.1 million Hungarians killed or deported); 1968, invasion of Czechoslovakia; 1979-1990, invasion of Afghanistan (15,000 Russian deaths; Afghan excess mortality 2.7 million); 1986, Chernobyl nuclear power station disaster; 1980s, USSR lost the Star Wars race; 1991, Yeltsin, democratic Russian leader; Gorbachev resigned; break-up of the USSR, independence for various republics, formation of the CIS (Commonwealth of Independent States); 1990s, continued rapprochement with the West, immense, corrupt privatization of Russian assets and rise of the Russian oligarchs and Russian Mafia; 1999, under Putin Russian forces invaded Chechnya (the war killed 0.2 million); 2004, Beslan massacre atrocity; agreements with China.

2021 update: 1999 onwards, Putin era with Vladimir Putin variously Prime Minister or President; declining birthrate (as with other European countries); massive oil and gas exports; 2014, in response to the US-backed Ukrainian Revolution, Russia backed Russian separatists in East Ukraine and annexed Crimea; 2015, Russian airpower successfully supported the Assad Syrian Government against attempts by the US Alliance, Turkey, Israel, Saudi Arabia and ISIS to remove it; harsh treatment of dissidents and increasingly authoritarian government; 2020-2021, severe poisoning and thence imprisonment of opposition leader Alexei Navalny with mass imprisonment of demonstrators. Greenhouse gas (GHG) pollution 16.2 tonnes CO_2-e per person per year.

Possesses 6,375 nuclear weapons, opposes and rejects the TPNW. "Covid-19 deaths per million of population" was a bad 665 as compared to 0.4 for Taiwan (March 2021). 2021, Apartheid Israel refused to vaccinate all but 0.1 million of its Occupied Palestinian Subjects and blocked Russian Sputnik V vaccine entering the Gaza Concentration Camp. The 2020 "under-5 infant mortality as a percentage of total population" (0.0078%) was 5.4 times greater than for Japan (0.00145%), but 2.3 times lower than that in 2003 (0.0180%).

Foreign occupation: Germany (pre-1950); none (post-1950); *post-1950 foreign military presence:* none; 1950-2005 *excess mortality/2005 population* = 11.897m/141.553m = 8.4%; 1950-2005 *under-5 infant mortality/2005 population* = 5.093m/141.553m = 3.6%. Per capita GDP (nominal) $11,606.

Serbia: 6th-7th century CE, settlement by Slav Serbs; 9th century, Christianization (Orthodox); Rascia; conflict with Hungarians and Bulgarians; 1159, Stephen Nemanja founded Serbian dynasty; 1219, Serbian Orthodox Church; 1371, Maritsa River defeat by the Turks; 1389, defeat by the Turks at the Battle of Kosovo Field; subsequent tribute to the Turks; 1459, annexation by the Turks; 1521, Hungarian-held areas captured by the Turks; 16th-19th century, Serbia under oppressive Turkish rule, disarmament and nobles eliminated; 1804, Karageorge (Karadjordjević; Dorde Petrovic) led rebellion; Belgrade liberated; 1812, Treaty of Bucharest, temporary Serbian autonomy agreed; 1812, Milos Obrenović rebellion; 1817, Karageorge assassinated; 1842-1858, Alexander Karadjordjević took power as Prince of Serbia; Congress of Paris, Serbia under European protection but Turkish hegemony; Milos Obrenović returned; 1867, Turks left; liberal constitution under Milan Obrenović; 1876, war on Turkey, Serbs defeated and Russian involvement; 1878, Congress of Berlin, Serbian independence recognized; 1882, Milan Obrenović made king; 1903, assassinations of the last Obrenović rulers; Peter Karadjordjević (grandson of Karageorge) as king; 1880, Austria-Hungary annexed Bosnia-Herzegovina; Serbian instigated Balkan league (Serbia, Montenegro, Bulgaria and Greece) to counter Austro-Hungarians and Turks; 1912, defeated Turkey; 1914, Serbia defeated Bulgaria and acquired Macedonia; 1914, Austria-Hungary declared war on Serbia after assassination of Austrian Archduke Franz Ferdinand, precipitating Russian involvement and WW1; 1914-1918, WW1; 1915, Bulgaria joined Austria-Hungary and Germany and Serbia was defeated; 1918, Yugoslavia formed; 1940, Germany invaded; Mihajlovic nationalists and Tito Communists fought the Nazis; 58,000/70,000 Yugoslav Jews killed; 1 million Yugoslavs died; 1946, Yugoslavia with 6 constituent republics under Tito; 1980, Tito died; 1986, Milosevic Serbian leader; 1989, Kosovo autonomy ended; 1992-1995, Balkans war; 200,000 dead; war crimes and ethnic cleansing; 1995, Dayton Accord; NATO peacekeepers; 1999, Serbian and Kosovo Liberation Front violence in Kosovo, NATO bombing of Serbia and Kosovo; hundreds of thousands of Muslim Kosovans were deported or fled to Macedonia or Albania; 2002, Milosevic handed over to war crimes commission; assassination of Djindjic.

2021 update: 2006, independence of Montenegro from Serbia by referendum; 2008, unilateral declaration of independence of Kosovo from Serbia recognized by the US and some other countries. Greenhouse gas (GHG) pollution 10.4 tonnes CO_2-e per person per year. Has not joined the TPNW. "Covid-19 deaths per million of population" was a bad 587 as compared to 0.4 for Taiwan (March 2021). The 2020 "under-5 infant mortality as a percentage of total population" (0.0051%) was 3.5 times greater than for Japan (0.00145%), but 4.3 times lower than that in 2003 (0.0220%).

Foreign occupation: Turkey, Austria, Hungary, Bulgaria, Germany (pre-1950); multi-ethnic Yugoslavia (post-1950); *post-1950 foreign military presence:* multi-ethnic Yugoslavia, NATO, US, UK and German air forces; 1950-2005 *excess mortality/2005 population* = 0.388m/10.513m = 3.7%; 1950-2005 *under-5 infant mortality/2005 population* = 0.620m/10.513m = 5.9%. Per capita GDP (nominal) $7,359.

Slovakia: 5th-6th century CE, Slavic settlement; 9th century, part of Moravia and Christianized; 10th century, Magyar (Hungarian) conquest; 10th century-1918, major Hungarian domination; 1526, Turkish victory over the Hungarians at Mohács; Slovakia came under greater Hungarian and Austrian Habsburg control; 19th century, increasing Magyarization and increased Slovak nationalism; 1920-1938, Slovakia (with a big Hungarian minority) was a province of Czechoslovakia; 1938-1944, largely Catholic Slovakia was an autonomous state of Czechoslovakia under Catholic Father Tiso during German occupation; extermination of Jews and Gypsies; 1944, liberated by USSR; 1945, again a province of Czechoslovakia; 1948, Communist government in Soviet-dominated Czechoslovakia; 1968, Soviet invasion to crush the Dubček-led "Prague Spring"; 1969, increased autonomy; 1989, fall of Communism; 1993, independent Slovakia; 2003, joined US Coalition in Iraq; 2004, became a member of NATO and of the EU.

2021 update: Socially progressive but the world's largest annual car producer per capita. Greenhouse gas (GHG) pollution 15.9 tonnes CO_2-e per person per year. Member of nuclear-armed NATO, endorses nuclear weapons, sent forces to US-occupied Afghanistan, opposes and rejects the TPNW. "Covid-19 deaths per million of population" was a gerocidal 1,716 as compared to 0.4 for Taiwan (March 2021). The 2020 "under-5 infant mortality as a percentage of total population" (0.0056%) was 3.9 times greater than for Japan (0.00145%), but 1.6 times lower than that in 2003 (0.0092%).

Foreign occupation: Austria, Hungary, Germany, Russia (pre-1950); Russia (post-1950); *post-1950 foreign military presence:* Russia; 1950-2005 *excess mortality/2005 population =* 0.130m/5.411m = 2.4%; 1950-2005 *under-5 infant mortality/2005 population =* 0.119m/5.411m = 2.2%. Per capita GDP (nominal) $19,256.

Slovenia: Illyrian and Celtic tribes; 1st century BCE, Roman Pannonia and Panicum; 6th century CE Slav Sarno society; 788, conquered by Franks; Christianized under Charlemagne; 843, under Bavaria; 1335-1918, Carinthia, Carniola and Styria regions part of Austria; 1918, part of Yugoslavia; 1939-1945, WW2; 1941, divided between Italy, Germany and Hungary; 1945, part of Yugoslavia; 1990, elected non-Communist government under Kučan; 1991, declared independence; Yugoslav forces entered for several weeks and then withdrew; "money for blood" Yugoslav debt reconciliation deal brokered by Austria; 2004, member of NATO and the EU.

2021 update: Greenhouse gas (GHG) pollution 16.5 tonnes CO_2-e per person per year. Member of nuclear-armed NATO, endorses nuclear weapons, sent forces to US-occupied Afghanistan, opposes and rejects the TPNW. "Covid-19 deaths per million of population" was a gerocidal 1,928 as compared to 0.4 for Taiwan (March 2021). The 2020 "under-5 infant mortality as a percentage of total population" (0.0019%) was 1.3 times greater than for Japan (0.00145%), but 2.1 times lower than that in 2003 (0.0040%).

Foreign occupation: Austria, Austria-Hungary, multi-ethnic Yugoslavia, Italy, Germany (pre-1950); multi-ethnic Yugoslavia (post-1950); *post-1950 foreign military presence:* multi-ethnic Yugoslavia; 1950-2005 *excess mortality/2005 population* = 0.032m/1.979m = 1.6%; 1950-2005 *under-5 infant mortality/2005 population* = 0.038m/1.979m = 1.9%. Per capita GDP (nominal) $26,062.

Ukraine: pre-Christian era Celtic Scythians and then Sarmatians; 1st-4th century CE, successive Goth, Hun and Avar invasions; 4th-7th century, Slavic consolidations; 7th century, part of Khazar Empire; 10th century, Varangians (Norse Vikings from Sweden and Scandinavia) defeated the Jewish convert Khazars and established the Kievan Rus; 1019-1054, Yaroslav lead Kiev-based empire; 13th century, genocidal conquest by Mongols; 14th century, Lithuanian and Polish expansion into Ukraine; 1478, Tatar Khanates of Crimea became part of the Ottoman Turkish Empire; 1596, Catholic persecution of Orthodox Christianity led to Uniate (Greek Catholic) Church recognizing Papal authority; 16th-17th century, Cossack rebellions against Polish rule; 1654, Cossack Chmielnicki reached accommodation with Moscow-based Russians; 1667, Russo-Polish War, Ukraine split around the Dnieper River, west to Poland, east to Russia; 1709, Mazepa in alliance with Swedes was defeated by Russians under Peter the Great; 18th century, Catherine the Great consolidated Russian control over the Ukraine; 1783, Crimea annexed; 1772-1795, partitions of Poland re-joined western and eastern Ukraine under Russian rule; 19th century, industrialization and increased nationalism, especially in Galicia; 1918, Ukraine independence under Symon Petliura; 1922, final Soviet victory; 1920s and 1930s, state terror, forced collectivization, deportation and murder of Ukrainians; 1930-1933, Stalin-made Ukrainian Famine (Holodomor), 7 million perished; 1941-1944, German invasion; extermination of Jews (e.g. the Babi Yar atrocity near Kiev); slave labour of Ukrainians; killing of prisoners of war; USSR war dead about 24 million; extensive Ukrainian collaboration as well as opposition by partisans; post-war payback: killing of Ukrainian collaborating soldiers returned by Allies; Crimean Tatars exiled to Siberia; Russification resisted by Ukrainians; 1986, Chernobyl nuclear disaster contaminated huge areas of Ukraine and Byelorussia; 1990, declaration of sovereignty; 1991, independence; member of CIS; 1994, signed Nuclear Non-proliferation Treaty; 1996, completed nuclear arsenal transfer to Russia; tensions over the Crimea Black Sea fleet; 2003, Azov Sea agreement with Russia; 2004, "Orange Revolution" over pro-Russian Eastern Ukraine political corruption; new election gave victory to pro-Western Yushchenko (non-fatally poisoned by secret agents before the election); Ukrainian forces joined the US Coalition in Iraq.

2021 update: 2014, US-backed Ukrainian Revolution overthrew pro-Russian Yanukovich; Russia annexed Crimea and supported ethnic Russian rebels in the eastern Donbass region. The Ukraine is the poorest country in Europe, and suffers from corruption. Major wheat producer and transit country for Russian gas to Western Europe. Greenhouse gas (GHG) pollution 19.1 tonnes CO_2-e per person per year. Ukraine is not a member of NATO but sent forces to US-occupied Afghanistan, and has not joined the TPNW. "Covid-19 deaths per million of population" was a bad 688 as compared to 0.4 for Taiwan (March 2021). The 2020 "under-5 infant mortality as a percentage of total population" (0.0073%) was 5.0 times greater than for Japan (0.00145%), but 2.3 times lower than that in 2003 (0.0170%).

Foreign occupation: Lithuania, Poland, Russia, Germany (pre-1950); Russia (post-1950); *post-1950 foreign military presence:* Russia; 1950-2005 *excess mortality/2005 population* = 5.279m/47.782m = 11.0%; 1950-2005 *under-5 infant mortality/2005 population* = 1.480m/47.782m = 3.1%. Per capita GDP (nominal) $3,496.

2020 statistical update for Eastern Europe. Table 9.4 summarizes population, under-5 infant mortality (IM) and excess mortality (EM; avoidable mortality from deprivation) in Eastern Europe in 2020 (pre-Covid-19 projection in 2019 for 2020 by the UN Population Division). Table 9.1 compares Eastern Europe with other global regions. Presented in square brackets for each country is the "Relative EM Score" of EM/Pop (%) divided by that for the best-performing country, Japan (0.0020%), which accordingly has a "Relative EM Score" of 1.0.

In terms of "Relative EM Score" and "per capita GDP" the outcomes range from Slovenia (1.3 and $26,062) to Armenia (11.2 and ($4,623). While the average "Relative EM Score" is 2.2 for Western Europe and 6.7 for significantly poorer Eastern Europe, it is a shocking 176.6 for non-Arab Africa (Table 9.1). The "under-5 infant mortality as a percentage of total population" in 2020 decreased 1.6-4.3-fold from that in 2003 for Eastern European countries.

2020 statistical update for European countries. Tables 9.1 and 9.4 summarize population, under-5 infant mortality (IM) and excess mortality (EM; avoidable mortality from deprivation) for Overseas Europe, Western Europe and Eastern Europe in 2020 (pre-Covid-19 projection in 2019 for 2020 by the UN Population Division). Table 9.1 compares Overseas Europe, Western Europe and Eastern Europe with other global regions. Presented in square brackets for each region is the "Relative EM Score" of EM/Pop (%) divided by that for the best-performing country, Japan (0.0020%), which accordingly has a "Relative EM Score" of 1.0.

The "Relative EM Score" outcomes in 2020 are as follows for the various regions: 2.2 (Western Europe), 5.4 (Overseas Europe), 6.7 (Eastern Europe), and 4.4 (Europe as a whole) as compared to 54.4 (the non-European world) and a shocking 176.6 for non-Arab Africa (Table 9.1).

The good news is that the global "under-5 infant mortality as a percentage of total population" in 2020 (0.0689%) had decreased from that in 2003 (0.1680%) by a factor of 2.4. Indeed for European countries the decrease in "under-5 infant mortality as a percentage of total population" in this 17 year period ranged from 1.1-fold (Australia) to 4.3-fold (Serbia).

In 2020 avoidable deaths from deprivation totaled about 92,000 for the European World (population 1,062 million) as compared to 3.8 million in the non-European World (population 6,625 million) and 7.4 million in the whole World (population 7,687 million).

4.5 Summary for European countries

Europe was successively settled by Celtic, Germanic, Slavic, Finno-Ugric (e.g. Finns, Magyars), Turkic and other groups (e.g. the Turkic Khazar convert-derived Ashkenazi Jews[9] and the India-derived Gypsies or Roma). Early sophisticated urban civilizations flourished in Mediterranean Italy, Spain and Greece. Western and Southern Europe were incorporated into the Roman Empire which finally succumbed to Germanic invaders. Slavic invaders occupied most of Eastern Europe with particular areas dominated by Letts, Wends, Estonians, Finns and Hungarians (Magyars). Muslim Moorish civilization flowered in Spain. Charlemagne forcibly spread Christianity to Central Europe. Norse invaders from Scandinavia impacted on Britain, Ireland, France, Italy and Russia. The so-called Dark Ages led to a prosperous Medieval period that was temporarily crushed by the 14th century bubonic plague, the Black Death involving 75-200 million deaths in Eurasia and North Africa, and about 25 million deaths in Europe or about 1/3 of the population). The 13th century Mongol invasion killed 40-60 million people in Eurasia. Constantinople and the Balkans fell to the Ottoman Turks with the consequent cultural Renaissance in the West and ultimately the Protestant Reformation and Catholic Counter-Reformation. Major Medieval and Renaissance states included England, France, Spain, the Holy Roman Empire (variously including Spain, the Netherlands, German states, Bohemia, Austria and Hungary), the Italian city states, the Hanseatic League, Denmark-Sweden, Poland-Lithuania and Russia.

After the expulsion of the Moors, Spain and Portugal variously invaded the Americas, Africa and South East Asia. Britain and France consolidated and colonized North America. The decimation of indigenous Indian populations in the Americas (100 million dying from disease and deprivation) was followed by importation of African slaves (20 million perished in the Atlantic slave trade). Holland seized the East Indies, Britain defeated the French and took India (1,800 million Indians died avoidably from deprivation in 2 centuries of British rule),[10] with Genocide of indigenous people by Canada and Australia (the Australian Aboriginal Genocide involved 2 million indigenous deaths from violence, deprivation and disease over 2 centuries).[11] The independent United States seized the American West and incorporated French and Spanish North American possessions. The 19th century saw the final carve up of Africa, Asia and the Pacific, Russian expansion into Central Asia, Latin American independence, and ultimately US hegemony over South and Central America and the Caribbean. The 16th century onwards Enlightenment and the 18th century Industrial Revolution were followed by increasing liberal and nationalist sentiment in the 19th century.

The catastrophe of WW1 led to the Russian revolution and transient independence for Eastern European countries. In WW2 the German Nazis conquered most of Europe, killed 5-6 million Jews, 6 million Poles, 1 million Yugoslavs, 1 million Gypsies and 24 million Soviet citizens but were finally defeated after the industrially-dominant US entered the war after the Japanese attack on Pearl Harbor. Post-war, Western Europe re-built and finally consolidated peacefully and rationally into the European Economic Community (EEC) and thence the European Union (EU). Eastern Europe had nearly half a century under Communism with all but Albania and Yugoslavia under Soviet hegemony behind the Iron Curtain. Western European countries formally surrendered their colonial empires after a short era of colonial wars. However post-WW2 the US exercised military power globally with major Asian wars and occupations, Latin American invasions, surrogate violence, and Cold War African conflicts. Other Overseas European countries variously participated in the Asian wars of the US Empire, and US-backed Apartheid Israeli colonialism in Palestine involved repeated wars with its neighbors. US victory over Russia in the Arms Race and the incipient Star Wars led to the collapse of Communism, freedom for Eastern European and Central Asian republics, and increased domination of the world by an increasingly violent and unilateralist US. Violent world domination by the "democratic imperialism" of the US Empire is in marked contrast to the immediately post-WW2 era of UN oversight of a peaceful and decolonizing world.[12]

2021 update for European countries: Most Western European and Eastern European countries ended up as members of both the EU but the UK bizarrely left the EU for nationalist and populist reasons in 2020, this having serious implications for the UK and Ireland with which it shares a border that was formerly non-policed. Different political system values and populist trends will continue to put strains on the economy- and peace-promoting EU.

The world is existentially threatened by (a) man-made climate change (unless requisite action is taken, 10 billion people will die en route to a sustainable human population in 2100 of merely 1 billion)[13] and (b) nuclear weapons (a post-nuclear holocaust nuclear winter will wipe out most of Humanity and the Biosphere). Indeed one of humanity's greatest minds, Stephen Hawking has stated "We see great peril if governments and societies do not take action now to render nuclear weapons obsolete and to prevent further climate change".[14]

Increasing renewable energy (notably wind and solar), decreased birth rate and decreasing population in Europe are positive trends for the survival of Humanity and the Biosphere. However there is no adoption of a requisite and properly accounted Carbon Price and Carbon Tax (about $200 per tonne CO_2-equivalent as compared to the present world average of $2 per tonne CO_2-equivalent), and the overall Carbon Debt of the generally prosperous Europeans continues to rise relentlessly, notwithstanding the 2015 Paris Agreement for a less than 2C temperature rise (plus 1.5C will be reached in the coming decade and a catastrophic 2C appears unavoidable).

Further, most Western European and Eastern European countries ended up as members of a nuclear-armed NATO that borders on Russia. Unfortunately most European countries endorse nuclear weapons and oppose the Treaty for the Prohibition of Nuclear Weapons (TPNW).

The good news from this updated analysis is the big decrease globally in under-5 infant mortality (and hence in avoidable mortality from deprivation) in the period 2003-2020 (Tables 8.1-8.12 and 9.1-9.12). Thus for the World "annual under-5 infant deaths" fell 2.0-fold from 10.6 million (2003) to 5.3 million (2020), and "under-5 infant deaths as a percentage of population" fell 2.4-fold from 0.1680% (2003) to 0.0689% (2020).

The global 5.3 million under-5 deaths in 2020 correspond to 7.4 million avoidable deaths from deprivation in 2020, an appalling figure that is similar to the 5-6 million Jews killed from violence and deprivation in the Germany-imposed 1939-1945 WW2 Jewish Holocaust and the 6-7 million Indians killed in the British-imposed and Australia-complicit 1942-1945 WW2 Bengali Holocaust (WW2 Bengal Famine, WW2 Indian Holocaust).

CHAPTER 5:
LATIN AMERICA AND THE CARIBBEAN – FROM EUROPEAN INVASION, GENOCIDE AND SLAVERY TO US HEGEMONY

"As for the newly born, they died early because their mothers, overworked and famished, had no milk to nurse them with, and for this reason, while I was in Cuba, 7,000 children died in three months."

Bartolomé de las Casas on Spanish enslavement of Indians in Cuba.[1]

"The bodies of these Indians and of the slaves who died in the mines produced such a stench that it caused a pestilence ... the flocks of birds and crows that came to feed on the corpses were so numerous that they darkened the sun, so that many villages along the road and in the district were deserted."

Fray Toribio de Benavente (Motolinia) on Indian slaves of the Spanish.[2]

"This is a dark picture, but how much more shocking is the undeniable fact that all the women who appear above twenty years old are massacred in cold blood! When I exclaimed that this appeared rather inhuman, he answered "Why what can be done? They breed so!"

Charles Darwin recounting a Spanish commander's view of genocide in Argentina.[3]

"When Darwin published The Descent of Man in 1871, the hunting down of Indians was still going on in Argentina, financed by a bond loan. When the land was cleared of Indians, it was shared among the bondholders, each bond giving a right to twenty-five hundred hectares."

Sven Lindqvist.[4]

"I spent thirty-three years and four months in active military service as a member of this country's most agile military force, the Marine Corps ... And during that period, I spent most of my time being a high class muscle-man for Big Business, for Wall Street

and for the Bankers. In short, I was a racketeer, a gangster for capitalism ...I helped make Honduras "right" for American fruit companies in 1903...I helped in the raping of half a dozen Central American republics for the benefit of Wall Street ... Looking back on it I feel that I could have given Al Capone a few hints. The best he could do was to operate his racket in three districts. I operated on three continents."

Major General Smedley Butler (1888-1940), one of America's greatest generals.[5]

5.1 Overview

Christopher Columbus arrived in the Caribbean in 1492 and the decimation of indigenous peoples commenced. The general pattern in the Caribbean involved Spanish invasion, enslavement of Carib and residual Arawak Indians and importation of African slaves to work sugar and cotton plantations after Indian populations crashed due to disease, deprivation and violence.[6] British, French, Dutch and Danish colonial involvements were followed by major US interventions in the 19th century. Haiti and the Dominican Republic achieved independence in the 19th century but US hegemony was reinforced by post-WW2 military invasions. Similarly, Cuba achieved independence from Spain but was immediately seized, together with Puerto Rico, by the US. Since the 1960s Cuban independence has been associated with sustained US economic blockade and threat. Most of the very small Caribbean islands variously gained independence in the post-1950 era with continuing neo-colonial arrangements and general US hegemony involving commercial domination, threat and invasion in the case of Grenada.

In Central America the pre-colonial Aztec and Maya civilizations were remarkable for their social organization and public architecture. Spanish invasion in the 16th century led immediately to decimation of indigenous populations by disease and colonial violence. The subsequent Spanish colonies achieved independence in the early 19th century with politics involving liberal/conservative and military/civilian dichotomies. However there was major repeated commercial and military intervention by Britain, France and the US in the 19th century. Thus the US successively removed huge swathes of Mexican territory and excised Panama from Colombia, the British excised Belize and the French installed an Emperor in Mexico. US hegemony expanded further in the 20th century with direct and indirect military involvements and long-term physical occupation in the case of Panama. Honduras-based US military backing of rightists against the left was variously associated with prolonged civil wars and huge civilian deaths in Nicaragua, Guatemala and El Salvador in the post-1950 era. [7]

Papal intervention determined general Portuguese confinement (with minor perturbations) to Brazil with Spanish conquest of the rest of South America. Portuguese invasion was associated with decimation of indigenous populations and the consequent need for African slaves to work sugar, cotton and coffee plantations. Decimation of indigenous Arawak, Chibcha and Carib peoples through disease and violence led to African slavery in the Atlantic countries of the Caribbean islands, Colombia, Venezuela and French, Dutch and British Guiana. Spanish exploration of the Amazon caused utter devastation of a sophisticated Amazon basin agrarian civilization. Spanish conquest of Ecuador, Bolivia, Peru and Chile destroyed the sophisticated Inca civilization through disease and enslavement. Indigenous societies in Argentina, Paraguay and Uruguay were variously destroyed by disease, dispossession, war and ultimately by explicit, merciless genocide in the 19th century. Brazil achieved independence associated with Anglo-French war in Europe. Revolution against Spanish rule variously succeeded under Simon Bolivar in the early 19th century. Subsequent social development in the Spanish and Portuguese countries involved liberal/conservative and civilian/military political tensions, European immigration and malignant external intervention (primarily from the US, Britain and France). In the 20th century, US hegemony was reinforced by explicit military invasions, commercial dominance, backing of military régimes against socialists and malignant interference, most clearly seen in the US-backed overthrow of democracy and associated mass murder in Chile.

5.2 Latin American and Caribbean histories

The following succinct historical summaries ("short histories") deal with pre-colonial times up to the present and conclude with a summary of pre- and post-1950 foreign occupation, post-1950 foreign military presence, and 1950-2005 excess mortality/2005 population and 1950-2005 under-5 infant mortality/2005 population (in millions, m) and expressed as percentages (%) (Tables 2.1-2.12). These histories summarize major foreign occupation events and major mortality catastrophes, and provide background information relating to foreign hegemony or occupation as significant contributors to post-1950 excess mortality.

2021 updates: The original edition text has been largely unchanged except for some corrections, added details and amplifications. 2021 updates are added at the end of each short history. In particular, because Humanity is existentially threatened by (a) climate change and (b) nuclear weapons, the 2021 updates include information on each country in relation to (a) climate change (notably revised annual greenhouse gas pollution taking land use into account and expressed as tonnes CO_2-equivalent (CO_2-e) per person per year),[8] and (b) ratification or otherwise of the UN Treaty on the Prohibition of Nuclear Weapons (TPNW) that came into effect in International Law on 22 January 2021 and which prohibits State Parties from both possession of nuclear weapons and support for such possession "in any way" (data from the Nobel Prize-winning International Campaign Against Nuclear Weapons (ICAN).[9] Poverty kills, and included at the end of each national history is per capita GDP (nominal) (UN, 2019, in US dollars).[10] "Covid-19 deaths per million of population" are presented compared to that for the world's best 0.4 for Taiwan (Worldometer, March 2021) as an indicator of intra-national altruism.[11] The 2020 "under-5 infant mortality as a percentage of total population" is compared (a) to that of the world's best, Japan (Tables 9.1 and 9.5), and (b) to that in 2003 (Tables 8.1 and 8.5) for a measure of improvement over 17 years in under-5 infant mortality, and in avoidable mortality (excess mortality) from deprivation (crudely assessed for all countries as 1.4 times the under-5 infant mortality).

American Virgin Islands: Pre-colonial Arawak and Carib people; 1493, Columbus arrived; 16th-17th century, Spanish extermination of indigenous Indians; 18th century Danish settlement, sugar plantations, cotton and African slaves; 1848, abolition of slavery; 1917, Denmark sold its Virgin Islands possessions to the US but retained Greenland.

2021 update: Tourism is the primary industry. 2020, Denmark rejected Trump America's request for purchase of Greenland.

Greenhouse gas (GHG) pollution roughly estimated as of the order of about 10 tonnes CO_2-e per person per year; it belongs to nuclear-armed America that has 5,800 nuclear weapons and rejects the TPNW. "Covid-19 deaths per million of population" was a bad 239 as compared to 0.4 for Taiwan (March 2021). In 2020 the "under-5 infant mortality as a percentage of total population" (0.0133%) was 9.2 times greater than for Japan (0.00145%), but 1.1 times greater than that in 2003 (0.0120%).

Foreign occupation: Spain, Denmark, US (pre-1950); US (post-1950); *post-1950 foreign military presence:* US; 1950-2005 *excess mortality/2005 population* = 0.003m/0.113m = 2.4%; 1950-2005 *under-5 infant mortality/2005 population* = 0.002m/0.113m = 1.5%.

Argentina: Pre-colonial Patagonian and Andean people; 16th century, Spanish exploration; 17th-18th century, Araucans fled Spanish Chile; 1536, initial settlement of Buenos Aires; mid-18th century, Chile, Paraguay, Argentina and Bolivia ruled from Buenos Aires; 1806-1807, British invaders expelled; 1816, independence from Spain; 1829, conflict with Britain and France under De Rosas; 1833, Britain occupied Malvinas (Falkland Islands) with US backing; 1839-1852, Great War in Uruguay involving Britain, France, Argentina, Uruguay and Brazil; 1865-1870, War of the Triple Alliance (Argentina, Brazil and Uruguay) against Paraguay killed 1 million Paraguayan Indians; 19th century, outright genocide of Patagonia and Chaco Indians witnessed and protested by Charles Darwin; 1919, workers machine-gunned; 1929, impact of depression in Britain-connected economy; WW2, while India starved, due to a coal shortage Argentina burned 2 million tonnes of wheat in its railways; 1946, Peron leader; 1955, US-backed military coup followed by further coups, right/left violence and urban guerrilla warfare; 1973, Peron restored followed by wife Isobel; 1976, Isobel Peron removed by US-backed military coup; further military coups and era of 30,000 "missing persons"; 1981, Galtieri accession; 1982, war with Britain over Argentinian invasion of the Falkland Islands (Malvinas); 1983, democracy restored; major, continuing economic difficulties.

2021 update: continuing economic and corruption problems. Livestock production contributes to a greenhouse gas (GHG) pollution of 23.7 tonnes CO_2-e per person per year; it has not signed or ratified the TPNW. "Covid-19 deaths per million of population" was a gerocidal 1,211 as compared to 0.4 for Taiwan (March 2021). In 2020 the "under-5 infant mortality as a percentage of total population" (0.0183%) was 12.6 times greater than for Japan (0.00145%), but 1.7 times lower than that in 2003 (0.0320%).

Foreign occupation: Spain, (pre-1950); none (post-1950); *post-1950 foreign military presence:* none; 1950-2005 *excess mortality/2005 population* = 1.310m/39.311m = 3.3%; 1950-2005 *under-5 infant mortality/2005 population* = 1.501m/39.311m = 3.8%. Per capita GDP (nominal) $10,041.

Bahamas: Pre-colonial Arawak people; 1492, Columbus landed on San Salvador; 16th-18th century, Indian depopulation through slavery and disease; base for pirates; 1647, British settlement; 1783, British colony; 1873, British sovereignty established by Treaty of Madrid; 1973, independence; post-independence income from tourism, banking and tax haven status; involvement in drugs and people smuggling into the US.

2021 update: 2019, devastation by Hurricane Dorian (50 killed, 1,300 missing). Greenhouse gas (GHG) pollution 12.1 tonnes CO_2-e per person per year; it has not joined the TPNW. "Covid-19 deaths per million of population" was a bad 475 as compared to 0.4 for Taiwan (March 2021). In 2020 the "under-5 infant mortality as a percentage of total population" (0.0084%) was 5.8 times greater than for Japan (0.00145%), but 3.5 times lower than that in 2003 (0.0290%).

Foreign occupation: Spain, Britain (pre-1950); UK (post-1950); *post-1950 foreign military presence:* UK; 1950-2005 *excess mortality/2005 population* = 0.007m/0.321m = 2.3%; 1950-2005 *under-5 infant mortality/2005 population* = 0.011m/0.321m = 3.4%. Per capita GDP (nominal) $34,864.

Barbados: Pre-colonial Arawak people; 16th century, Spanish arrival and subsequent depopulation through slavery and disease; 1627, British settlement of the now-uninhabited islands; tobacco, cotton and thence sugar cane plantations worked by African slaves; 1816, slave revolt; 1834, slavery formally abolished but there was a captive labour market; 1958-1962, member of British West Indies Federation; 1961, internal autonomy; 1966, independence with democracy; 1981, Barbados associated with US invasion of Grenada; stable democracy economically dependent on sugar, tourism and manufacturing.

2021 update: 2021, to become a republic within the British Commonwealth. Greenhouse gas (GHG) pollution 9.1 tonnes CO_2-e per person per year; it has not joined the TPNW. "Covid-19 deaths per million of population" was 139 as compared to 0.4 for Taiwan (March 2021). In 2020 the "under-5 infant mortality as a percentage of total population" (0.0123%) was 8.5 times greater than for Japan (0.00145%), but 1.4 times lower than that in 2003 (0.0170%).

Foreign occupation: Spain, Britain (pre-1950); UK (post-1950); *post-1950 foreign military presence:* UK; 1950-2005 *excess mortality/2005 population* = 0.015m/0.272m = 5.5%; 1950-2005 *under-5 infant mortality/2005 population* = 0.016m/0.272m = 5.9%.

Belize: Pre-colonial history as part of Mayan empire 1500BCE-1200CE; 1502, Columbus sailed along coast; 16th century, indigenous opposition repelled Spanish; 1638, British settlement by shipwrecked sailors; 17th-19th century, British exploitation of lumber with slaves; 18th century, Spanish attempts to seize territory; 1798, British defeated the Spanish; 1859, borders defined with independent Guatemala; 1964, internal autonomy; 1981, independence and Guatemalan hostility requiring British military presence; 1991, Guatemala recognized Belize while retaining claims; current high unemployment, dependence on tourism and increased drug trade involvement.

2021 update: World-leading greenhouse gas (GHG) pollution of 366.9 tonnes CO_2-e per person per year due to deforestation; it has signed and ratified the TPNW. "Covid-19 deaths per million of population" was a bad 787 as compared to 0.4 for Taiwan (March 2021). In 2020 the "under-5 infant mortality as a percentage of total population" (0.0284%) was 19.6 times greater than for Japan (0.00145%), but 3.7 times lower than that in 2003 (0.1060%).

Foreign occupation: Spain, Britain (pre-1950); UK (post-1950); *post-1950 foreign military presence:* UK; 1950-2005 *excess mortality/2005 population* = 0.014m/0.266m = 5.3%; 1950-2005 *under-5 infant mortality/2005 population* = 0.020m/0.266m = 7.5%. Per capita GDP (nominal) $4,884.

Bermuda: 1503, sighted by Spaniard Bermudez (uninhabited); 1609, colonized by shipwrecked British (first British colony); 1612, given to Virginia Company; about 1684, reverted to the Crown; first parliament in the Americas, second parliament in the World; 17th-19th century, plantations and African slaves; current tax-haven and tourism economy; 1995, referendum for independence defeated. Remains a British Overseas Territory.

2021 update: Located in Hurricane Alley and subject to more intense tropical hurricanes. Greenhouse gas (GHG) pollution estimated of the order of 10 tonnes CO_2-e per person per year. The ruling UK is a member of nuclear-armed NATO, has 215 nuclear warheads, has not signed or ratified the TPNW and rejects the TPNW that became International Law on 22 January 2021. "Covid-19 deaths per million of population" was 193 as compared to 0.4 for Taiwan (March 2021). Under-5 infant mortality data not available.

Foreign occupation: Britain (pre-1950); UK (post-1950); *post-1950 foreign military presence:* Canada, UK, US. Per capita GDP (nominal) $117,768.

Bolivia: Pre-colonial agriculture 2000BCE; 9th-16th century, Inca empire; 16th century, Spanish arrival and conquest; silver mines with Indian slave labour; 18th century, continued Indian resistance; 1825, independence and named Bolivia after "The Liberator" Simon Bolivar; 1879-1884, Pacific War against Chile, lost sea outlet; 1903, rubber-rich region ceded to Brazil; 1932-1935, lost huge territory in Chaco War against Paraguay; post-WW2 coups, right-left violence and US-backed military dictatorships; 1967, revolutionary guerrilla Che Guevara captured and killed by US-trained military; 1982, restoration of civilian rule; continuing poverty, mining, illegal cocaine trade and corruption; 2005, socialist Evo Morales became Bolivia's first indigenous Indian president.

2021 update: 2005-2019, Evo Morales presidency; 2006, Morales nationalized huge gas industry; 2019 Morales removed in an effective coup d'état; Morales and associates flew to Mexico; 2020, Morales' party won in a landslide. Greenhouse gas (GHG) pollution of 27.3 tonnes CO_2-e per person per year; massive gas production; it has signed and ratified the TPNW. "Covid-19 deaths per million of population" was a gerocidal 1,029 as compared to 0.4 for Taiwan (March 2021). In 2020 the "under-5 infant mortality as a percentage of total population" (0.0967%) was 66.7 times greater than for Japan (0.00145%), but 2.2 times lower than that in 2003 (0.2082%).

Foreign occupation: Spanish (pre-1950); none (post-1950); *post-1950 foreign military presence:* US (hegemony and military involvement); 1950-2005 *excess mortality/2005 population =* 3.004m/9.138m = 32.9%; 1950-2005 *under-5 infant mortality/2005 population* = 1.880m/9.138m = 20.6%. Per capita GDP (nominal) $3,552.

Brazil: Pre-colonial: Tupi, Guarani, Carib and Arawak people; major agrarian Amazon civilization (destroyed by disease after exposure to Spanish explorers from the West); 1494, Tordesilla Treaty assigned the Brazil region to Portugal; 1500, Portuguese arrival; 1532, Portuguese colonization commenced; 16th-19th century, huge slave trade from Africa for Brazilian plantations; 1822, independence from Portugal under Pedro I; 1888, abolition of slavery; 1889, republic under military dictatorship; 19th -20th century, major immigration from Europe; 1930s-1950s, Vargas dominated political life; 1964, US-backed military coup, subsequent military régimes and repression via US-trained death squads; 1985, restoration of democracy; huge population and resources, huge inequalities, destruction of the Amazon rainforest for agriculture, ethanol from sugar cane for fuel (a food for fuel obscenity), set to be a major world economic power; 2002, leftist Lula da Silva elected president.

2021 update: Massive corruption in Brazil; 2010, Dilma Rousseff succeeded Lula but was impeached in 2016; 2019, Trumpist fascoid and effective climate change denier Jair Bolsonaro elected president; massive Amazon rain forest burning outrages the world. Greenhouse gas (GHG) pollution of 43.4 tonnes CO_2-e per person per year; 2019, Lula released from prison; 2021, Lula's convictions nullified. Brazil has signed but not yet ratified the TPNW. "Covid-19 deaths per million of population" was a gerocidal 1,437 as compared to 0.4 for Taiwan` (March 2021). In 2020 the "under-5 infant mortality as a percentage of total population" (0.0188%) was 13.0 times greater than for Japan (0.00145%), but 3.6 times lower than that in 2003 (0.0670%).

Foreign occupation: Portugal (pre-1950); none (post-1950); *post-1950 foreign military presence:* US (hegemony, militarization and military involvement); 1950-2005 *excess mortality/2005 population* = 13.114m/182.798m = 7.2%; 1950-2005 *under-5 infant mortality/2005 population* = 19.407m/182.798m = 10.6 %. Per capita GDP (nominal) $8,755.

British Virgin Islands: Pre-colonial Arawak and Carib people; 1493, Columbus arrived; 16th century, Spanish exterminated indigenous Indians; 1648, Dutch settlement; 1672, British annexation; 17th-19th century, British control, cotton, indigo and sugar plantations, African slaves; 1967, first elections; 1977, self-rule under British control; economically closely linked to adjacent US Virgin Islands. A British Overseas Territory.

2021 update: susceptible to tropical hurricanes that are increasing in energy due to global warming; 2017, devastation by Hurricane Irma. The ruling country Britain is a member of nuclear-armed NATO, has 215 nuclear warheads, opposes the TPNW, and rejects the TPNW that became International Law on 22 January 2021. "Covid-19 deaths per million of population" was a good 33 as compared to 0.4 for Taiwan (March 2021). No "under-5 infant mortality as a percentage of total population" data.

Foreign occupation: Spain, Britain (pre-1950); UK (post-1950); *post-1950 foreign military presence:* UK. Per capita GDP (nominal) $48,511.

Chile: Pre-colonial, Inca empire in northern Chile, Araucanos in south; 16th-19th century, Spanish conquest; 1514, Valdivio founded Santiago; 1810, declared independence from Spain; 1818, independence from Spain under O'Higgins and San Martin; 1879-1884, British-backed war against Peru and Bolivia; 1925, constitution followed by removal of the military from politics; 1970, socialist Allende elected; 1973, US-backed Pinochet military coup against Allende, thousands murdered, Allende died; 1990, restoration of democracy (1973-1990 excess mortality 0.3 million); Pinochet subsequently lost immunity from prosecution; currently increasing prosperity under democratic government; 2004, free trade agreement with the US.

2021 update: 2010, deadly earthquake; rescue of 33 trapped miners followed globally; 2019-2020, unrest over subway fare increases, inequity and living costs; creation of a new constitution to be put to referendum. Greenhouse gas (GHG) pollution of 8.7 tonnes CO_2-e per person per year; it has signed but not ratified the TPNW. "Covid-19 deaths per million of population" was a gerocidal 1,174 as compared to 0.4 for Taiwan (March 2021). In 2020 the "under-5 infant mortality as a percentage of total population" (0.0091%) was 6.3 times greater than for Japan (0.00145%), but 2.4 times lower than that in 2003 (0.0220%).

Foreign occupation: Spain (pre-1950); none (post-1950); *post-1950 foreign military presence:* US (hegemony, militarization and military coup involvement); 1950-2005 *excess mortality/2005 population* = 1.427m/16.185m = 8.8%; 1950-2005 *under-5 infant mortality/2005 population* = 1.135m/16.185m = 7.0%. Per capita GDP (nominal) $14,896.

Colombia: Pre-colonial Chibcha (Muisca) people; 16th-17th century, Spanish conquest, plantations, decimation of indigenous people by disease and violence, African slavery for plantations; 1510, Darien first European settlement on mainland; 1538, New Granada established; 1819, Simon Bolivar defeated the Spanish and founded the Republic of Greater Colombia (including Colombia, Ecuador, Panama and Venezuela); 1830, Colombia separated from Gran Colombia; 19th century, repeated wars and coups; 1861, United States of New Granada; 1863, United States of Colombia; 1899-1902, civil war; 1903, US-engineered Panama independence with subsequent US invasion and occupation of the Canal Zone; 20th century, violent politics, civil war, military juntas and elected governments, left/right dichotomies; 1964-present, guerrilla war by FARC opposed by US-backed régimes involving US Special Forces and anti-insurgent paramilitary forces seeking control of the major cocaine trade run by drug cartels.

2021 update: 2016, Colombian Government-FARC peace deal; 2019-2020 protests over inequity, human rights violations and peace. Massive deforestation; greenhouse gas (GHG) pollution of 19.8 tonnes CO_2-e per person per year; it has signed but not ratified the TPNW. "Covid-19 deaths per million of population" was a gerocidal 1,219 as compared to 0.4 for Taiwan (March 2021). In 2020 the "under-5 infant mortality as a percentage of total population" (0.0202%) was 13.9 times greater than for Japan (0.00145%), but 2.3 times lower than that in 2003 (0.0470%).

Foreign occupation: Spanish, US (Panama) (pre-1950); none (post-1950); *post-1950 foreign military presence:* US (hegemony, militarization and military involvement); 1950-2005 *excess mortality/2005 population* = 3.722m/45.600m = 8.2%; 1950-2005 *under-5 infant mortality/2005 population* = 3.367m/45.600m = 7.4%. Per capita GDP (nominal) $6,432.

Costa Rica: Pre-colonial Chibcha people; 1502, Columbus landed; 16th century, Spanish conquest, settlement and extermination of Indians; 1553, Spanish conquest; initial Indian population 400,000; Indians largely exterminated; 1821-1840, part of independent United Provinces of Central America; 2 years as part of Iturbide's Mexican empire; 1848, formed independent state; defeated US banditry; 1870-1882, Guardia military dictatorship followed by over a century of peaceful, civilian rule; mid-19th-20th century, peaceful society; 1948, brief civil war prompted by rigged elections; 1949, Figueres in first of several presidencies; post-1950 era, peaceful, conservative, democratic society; famously without an army but pro-US and permitted US-backed anti-Nicaragua incursions; agriculture, tourism and technology sectors; National Biodiversity Institute deals for commercial exploitation of rain forest plant-derived bioactive compounds.

2021 update: Greenhouse gas (GHG) pollution of 17.1 tonnes CO_2-e per person per year; it has signed and ratified the TPNW. "Covid-19 deaths per million of population" was a bad 572 as compared to 0.4 for Taiwan (March 2021). In 2020 the "under-5 infant mortality as a percentage of total population" (0.0114%) was 7.9 times greater than for Japan (0.00145%), but 1.5 times lower than that in 2003 (0.0170%).

Foreign occupation: Spanish (pre-1950); none (post-1950); *post-1950 foreign military presence:* US (hegemony, Contra support); 1950-2005 *excess mortality/2005 population* = 0.259m/4.327m = 6.0%; 1950-2005 *under-5 infant mortality/2005 population* = 0.199m/4.327m = 4.6%. Per capita GDP (nominal) $12, 238.

Cuba: Pre-colonial Arawak, Taino and Ciboney people; 1492, Columbus arrived; 16th century, indigenous people decimated by disease, violence and slavery; 16th-19th century, sugar plantations worked by African slaves; 1511, settlements founded by Velasquez; 1876-1886, Ten Years War led to abolition of slavery in 1886; 1895-1898, war of independence against Spain; 1898, defeat of Spanish forces by Cubans followed by US declaration of war against Spain and invasion; 1899-1902, US occupied Cuba and subsequently retained Guantanamo Bay; 1902-1920, repeated US military intervention; 1933, military coup; 1940-1958, Batista dictatorship; 1958, Batista overthrown by Che Guevara and Fidel Castro; 1961, US Bay of Pigs invasion defeated; 1962, Cuban missile crisis involving US and USSR; 1964, continuing) US economic blockade against Cuba and its Communist régime; post-1958 era Cuban involvement in Latin America, Ethiopia and Angola; Cuban refugees to the US; 21st century, continued excellent medical outcomes; Cuban medical personnel aid to

Venezuela (and also offered to post-Hurricane Katrina New Orleans) – it can be calculated that possession of Cuban-style medical-related systems would have saved 36 million under-5 infant lives in "free" Latin America and the Caribbean.

2021 update: US sanctions partly lifted by Obama America but re-imposed by Trump; Greenhouse gas (GHG) pollution of 3.5 tonnes CO_2-e per person per year; it has signed and ratified the TPNW. "Covid-19 deaths per million of population" was 36 as compared to 0.4 for Taiwan (March 2021). In 2020 the "under-5 infant mortality as a percentage of total population" (0.0054%) was 3.7 times greater than for Japan (0.00145%), but 1.9 times lower than that in 2003 (0.0100%).

Foreign occupation: Spain, US (pre-1950); none (post-1950); *post-1950 foreign military presence:* US (unsuccessful invasion, Guantanamo Bay), USSR (advisers, missiles); 1950-2005 *excess mortality/2005 population* = 0.469m/11.353m = 4.1%; 1950-2005 *under-5 infant mortality/2005 population* = 0.349m/11.353m = 3.1%. Per capita GDP (nominal) $9,296.

Dominica: Pre-colonial Carib people; 15th century, Spanish conquest, decimation of indigenous people through disease and exploitation, introduction of African slaves to work plantations; 17th century, French takeover, coffee and cotton plantations; 18th century, British/French conflict; 1763, ceded to Britain; 1805, British colony; 1967, internal autonomy with free association with other British West Indian Associated States; 1978, independence; 1980-1995, Mary Charles Prime Minister; 1981, coup plot; currently, still a remnant 3,000 Carib Indian population.

2021 update: Greenhouse gas pollution of 4.2 tonnes CO_2-e per person per year. No data available on "under-5 infant mortality as a percentage of total population".

Foreign occupation: Spain, France, Britain (pre-1950); UK (post-1950); *post-1950 foreign military presence:* UK. Per capita GDP (nominal) $8,111.

Dominican Republic: Pre-colonial Carib people; 1492, Columbus arrived; 1496 Santo Domingo oldest New World European settlement; subsequent enslavement and decimation of Caribs; 16th -18th century, African slavery to replace exterminated Caribs; sugar plantations and cattle; 1697, French occupied Haiti portion and thence all of Hispaniola; 1795, ceded to France; 1801, Toussaint L'Ouvertue revolt; 1808, revolution; 1814, Dominican portion returned to Spanish rule; 1822, Haitian Afro-American régime seized the whole island; 1844, Haitians expelled; 1861, return to the Spanish Empire; 1863, revolt against Spain; 1865, final independence; 1907, major US hegemony commenced with a protectorate arrangement; 1916-1934, US invasion and occupation; 1924, US-backed Trujillo regime; 1961, US-complicit assassination of Trujillo; 1962, democratic election; 1963, US-backed military coup and popular resistance; 1965, US invasion and eventual restoration of US-compatible "democracy"; 1966, Balaguer elected; Balaguer famously preserved the forests to please his sisters; 1996, Balaguer stepped down due protests about flawed elections; continued poverty, flawed democracy, corruption and centre-left/conservative political dichotomy; 2003, military support for US occupation of Iraq.

2021 update: year-round golf courses attractive to Americans and Canadians; very fast growing economy. Greenhouse gas (GHG) pollution of 7.1 tonnes CO_2-e per person per year; it has signed but not ratified the TPNW. "Covid-19 deaths per million of population" was a bad 302 as compared to 0.4 for Taiwan (March 2021). In 2020 the "under-5 infant mortality as a percentage of total population" (0.0518%) was 35.7 times greater than for Japan (0.00145% and 1.9 times greater than that in 2003 (0.1000%).

Foreign occupation: Spain, France, US (pre-1950); US (post-1950); *post-1950 foreign military presence:* US (hegemony, militarization, invasion and occupation); *1950-2005 excess mortality/2005 population* = 0.806m/8.998m = 9.0%; *1950-2005 under-5 infant mortality/2005 population* = 0.974m/8.998m = 10.8%. Per capita GDP (nominal) $8,282.

Ecuador: Pre-colonial sophisticated Inca empire; 1532, invasion by Spanish conquistador Pizarro; 1594, conquests by Spanish conquistador Benalcazar; 16th -18th century, brutal enslavement and decimation of Indians; 1822, Spain defeated and Ecuador became part of Bolivar's Greater Colombia; 1830, Ecuador seceded and became an independent entity; 1895, liberal revolution; 1944, further revolution; 1941, 1981 and 1995 border wars with Peru; 1950s and 1960s, increasing US-backed repression and malignant US involvement (hegemony, militarization, "running" leaders as "US assets", secretly bombing churches to excite anti-communist sentiment; this was revealed by Philip Agee for the CIA in Ecuador in his book "Inside the Company: CIA Diary" and one supposes such CIA subversion and terrorism could be general world-wide); 1970s, oil industry commenced with subsequent massive environmental and social damage; 1981, 1995 Ecuador-Peru wars; 1999, Ecuador-Peru peace; 2000, military coup involving Guiterrez; democracy restored; 2003, Guiterrez elected (6th president in 10 years).

2021 update: 2008, Correa defaulted on debt; 2012-2019, Australian Julian Assange, world hero and the world's most famous journalist, given sanctuary from the UK and US in the Ecuadorean Embassy in London but then handed over to UK police; 2019, protests over austerity policies of Moreno. Oil and deforestation contribute to GHG pollution of 26.2 tonnes CO_2-e per person per year; it has signed and ratified the TPNW. "Covid-19 deaths per million of population" was a bad 932 as compared to 0.4 for Taiwan (March 2021). In 2020 the "under-5 infant mortality as a percentage of total population" (0.0288%) was 19.9 times greater than for Japan (0.00145% and 2.2 times less than that in 2003 (0.0640%).

Foreign occupation: Spain (pre-1950); none (post-1950); *post-1950 foreign military presence:* US (hegemony and military training); *1950-2005 excess mortality/2005 population =* 1.404m/13.379m = 10.5%; *1950-2005 under-5 infant mortality/2005 population =* 1.426m/13.379m = 10.7%. Per capita GDP (nominal) $6,184.

El Salvador: Pre-colonial Pipil, Chibcha and Maya people; 1525, Spanish invasion under Alvarado; 1532, conquest by Spanish under conquistador Pizarro; 1821, independence from Spain as part of Central American Federation; 1839, the Central American Federation collapsed associated with British interference and British naval blockade; late 19th century, increasing US interference; 1880, Liberal Revolution and expansion of estates at the expense of peasant farmers; 1932, popular rebellion crushed with 30,000 victims by General Martinez to be followed by a half century of military dictatorships; 1969, Honduras-El Salvador "football war"; 1970s-1992, civil war with the US backing the rightists;1972, electoral fraud established US-backed rightist Duarte regime and prompted insurgency; 1979, US-backed military coup; 1979-1981, 30,000 killed by US-backed death squads;1980, rightist assassination of Archbishop Romero; 1980s-1990s, bloody civil war; 1992, end of civil war (75,000 killed; 1972-1992 excess mortality, 0.4 million); elections; 2003, military support for US occupation of Iraq.

2021 update: country still beset by poverty, inequity and gang-related violent crime. GHG pollution of 6.0 tonnes CO_2-e per person per year; it has signed and ratified the TPNW. "Covid-19 deaths per million of population" was 307 as compared to 0.4 for Taiwan (March 2021). In 2020 the "under-5 infant mortality as a percentage of total population" (0.0276%) was 19.0 times greater than for Japan (0.00145%) and 3.4 times less than that in 2003 (0.0930%).

Foreign occupation: Spain (pre-1950); none (post-1950); *post-1950 foreign military presence:* US (hegemony, militarization and military training); *1950-2005 excess mortality/2005 population =* 0.936m/6.709m = 14.0%; *1950-2005 under-5 infant mortality/2005 population* = 0.942m/6.709m = 14.0%. Per capita GDP (nominal) $4,187.

French Guiana: Pre-colonial Arawak people displaced by Caribs; about 1500, Spanish arrival and Carib resistance; 1604, French arrival in addition to Spanish, English, Dutch and Portuguese involvements; 1676, French rule; famous for Devil's Island prison in which, notably, Dreyfus was falsely imprisoned (19th century); 1946, became a French Overseas Department; 1951, penal settlements ceased; Kourou site of French space launches for the European Space Agency.

2021 update: the Guiana Amazonia Park is the biggest national park in the EU. GHG pollution of 25 tonnes CO_2-e per person per year for neighboring Suriname; the ruler France has 293 nuclear weapons, opposes and rejects the TPNW. "Covid-19 deaths per million of population" was 292 as compared to 0.4 for Taiwan (March 2021). In 2020 the "under-5 infant mortality as a percentage of total population" (0.0234%) was 16.1 times greater than for Japan (0.00145%) and 2.1 times less than that in 2003 (0.0490%).

Foreign occupation: Spain, France (pre-1950); France (post-1950); *post-1950 foreign military presence:* France; *1950-2005 excess mortality/2005 population* = 0.010m/0.187m = 5.3%; *1950-2005 under-5 infant mortality/2005 population* = 0.004m/0.187m = 2.3%.

Grenada: Pre-colonial Carib people; 1498, Columbus arrived; 1674, French rule; 17th-18th century, French overcame Carib resistance, indigenous people exterminated by violence and disease, African slaves imported to work plantations; late 18th century, British takeover; 1958-1962, joined Federation of British West Indies; 1967, associate state of the British Antilles; 1974, independence under Gairy with anti-independence violence; 1979, bloodless leftist coup installed Bishop as PM; 1981, Bishop killed and replaced as PM; 1983, US invasion together with 300 police from 6 pro-US Caribbean countries; 1984, new elections.

2021 update: 2004, Hurricane Ivan damaged or destroyed 90% of homes; GHG pollution of 6.4 tonnes CO_2-e per person per year; it has signed but not ratified the TPNW. "Covid-19 deaths per million of population" was 9 as compared to 0.4 for Taiwan (March 2021). Data not available for "under-5 infant mortality as a percentage of total population".

Foreign occupation: France, UK (pre-1950); UK, US (post-1950); *post-1950 foreign military presence:* UK, US.

Guadeloupe: Pre-colonial Carib people; 1493, Spanish arrived; 16th–17th century, French sugar plantations with African slaves, extermination of the Caribs by disease and violence; 1635, French possession; 1815, abolition of the slave trade; 1946, Overseas Department of France; 1980s onwards, increasing inter-racial tension and pro-independence activism.

2021 update: 2009, 44 day labor union strike. GHG pollution of 4.7 tonnes CO_2-e per person per year; the ruler, France, has 293 nuclear weapons, opposes and rejects the TPNW. "Covid-19 deaths per million of population" was a bad 412 as compared to 0.4 for Taiwan (March 2021). In 2020 the "under-5 infant mortality as a percentage of total population" (0.0052%) was 3.6 times greater than for Japan (0.00145%) and 6.2 times less than that in 2003 (0.0320%).

Foreign occupation: France (pre-1950); France (post-1950); *post-1950 foreign military presence:* France; *1950-2005 excess mortality/2005 population* = 0.025m/0.446m = 5.6%; *1950-2005 under-5 infant mortality/2005 population* = 0.022m/0.446m = 4.9%.

Guatemala: Pre-colonial sophisticated Mayan civilization (great pyramids, high societal organization); 1524, Spanish invasion under Alvaredo; 1821, independence from Spain in Federation of Central American States; 1831, British Honduras (Belize) ceded to Britain for lumber; 1839, Federation dissolved under British pressure; mid-19th century-20th century, liberal-conservative political dichotomy, German immigration, increasing US corporate involvement; 1944, popular revolution leading to election of reformist Arévalo; 1951, leftist Arbenz Guzmán elected, expropriated estates, angered the United Fruit Company and the US; 1954, US-backed invasion from Honduras resulting in military rule, repression and guerrilla insurgency; 1960-1996, extreme repression by US-backed and Israeli-armed government, guerrilla resistance and civil war, 0.1 million killed and 1.0 million refugees in the Guatemalan Mayan Indian Genocide (1960-1996 excess mortality 1.9 million); 1996, reconciliation; 1999, presidential elections; subsequent irregularities; 2002, draft settlement with Belize; 2004, end of UN supervision of the peace process.

2021 update: country still beset by poverty, inequity and gang- and drugs-related violent crime; 2021, refugee marchers from Honduras beaten and tear gassed. Deforestation and GHG pollution of 26.9 tonnes CO_2-e per person per year; it has signed but not ratified the TPNW. "Covid-19 deaths per million of population" was a bad 373 as compared to 0.4 for Taiwan (March 2021). In 2020 the "under-5 infant mortality as a percentage of total population" (0.0574%) was 39.6 times greater than for Japan (0.00145%) and 3.1 times less than that in 2003 (0.1780%).

Foreign occupation: Spain, Britain (Belize) (pre-1950); none (post-1950); *post-1950 foreign military presence:* US (hegemony and military training); *1950-2005 excess mortality/2005 population =* 2.757m/12.978m = 21.2%; *1950-2005 under-5 infant mortality/2005 population =* 1.878m/12.978m = 14.5%. Per capita GDP (nominal) $4,363.

Guyana: Pre-colonial Arawak people displaced by Caribs; late 15th century, Spanish exploration; 1616, Dutch fort built; 17th-18th century, British settlement, plantations with African slaves; 1815, British possession; 1763, British brutally suppressed slave revolt led by Cuffy; 1796, formal British rule; 19th century, abolition of slavery and indentured labour introduced from India, China and the East Indies; 1966, independence under conservative left Burnham; post-independence, US hostility to Guyana social democracy, Guyana-Venezuela territorial dispute; 1978, Jonestown sect mass murder/suicide atrocity (909 died); 1992-1997, Cheddi Jagan president; 1997-1999, widow Janet Jagan president. 2001, Bharrat Jagdeo re-elected president.

2021 update: Deforestation and GHG pollution of 203.1 tonnes CO_2-e per person per year; it has signed and ratified the TPNW. "Covid-19 deaths per million of population" was a bad 285 as compared to 0.4 for Taiwan (March 2021). In 2020 the "under-5 infant mortality as a percentage of total population" (0.0603%) was 41.6 times greater than for Japan (0.00145%) but 2.5 times less than that in 2003 (0.1510%).

Foreign occupation: Netherlands, Britain (pre-1950); UK (post-1950); *post-1950 foreign military presence:* none; *1950-2005 excess mortality/2005 population* = 0.086m/0.768m = 11.2%; *1950-2005 under-5 infant mortality/2005 population* = 0.121m/0.768m = 15.8%. Per capita GDP (nominal) $6,610.

Haiti: Pre-colonial Arawak people; 1492, Spanish discovery of Hispaniola by Columbus followed by brutal invasion and decimation of indigenous people; 1697, French acquisition of Haiti (Western half of Hispaniola) from Spain; 18th century, huge African slave importation for coffee and sugar plantations; 1789, French revolution led to African revolt; 1793, British invasion; 1795, Spain ceded Eastern half to France; 1801, Toussaint L'Ouverture conquered the whole island; 1804, French defeated and a black African republic proclaimed; 19th - 20th century, increasing US interference and repeated invasion and occupation; 1915-1934, US invasion and occupation; subsequent US-compliant, surrogate oligarchic administrations; 1960s-1980s, "Papa Doc" Duvalier and thence "Baby Doc" Duvalier dictatorships with Tonton Macoute state terror; 1986, uprising, "Baby Doc" evacuated by US military, followed by successive coups; 1991, restoration of democracy, Aristide elected; 2004, military revolt, Aristide "kidnapped" and removed to Africa by US, US invasion and US-French military presence with Canadians and Chileans; 2004, UN peace keeping force led by Brazil began replacing US and other forces.

2021 update: 2004-2008, succession of devastating hurricanes Fay, Gustav, Hanna and Ike (over 3,000 killed altogether by storms, flooding or deforestation-linked landslides); 2010, devastating earthquake (0.3 million dead, 1.3 million homeless); GHG pollution 5.0 tonnes CO_2-e per person per year; it has not signed the TPNW. "Covid-19 deaths per million of population" was 22 as compared to 0.4 for Taiwan (March 2021). In 2020 the "under-5 infant mortality as a percentage of total population" (0.1805%) was 124.5 times greater than for Japan (0.00145%) but 2.0 times less than that in 2003 (0.3640%).

Foreign occupation: Spain, France, US (pre-1950); US (post-1950); *post-1950 foreign military presence:* US, France; *1950-2005*

excess mortality/2005 population = 4.098m/8.549m = 47.9%;
1950-2005 under-5 infant mortality/2005 population =
2.142m/8.549m = 25.1%. Per capita GDP (nominal) $715.

Honduras: Pre-colonial Chibcha, Lenca and Maya people; 1498,
Florentine in Spanish service, Amerigo Vespucci, landed (hence
"America"); 16th century, Alvarado conquered region; 1821,
independence as part of Central American Federation; 19th
century, major interference by British (excision of British
Honduras) and US (notably by the United Fruit Company); 1924,
US invaded; 1933-1949, US-backed rightist dictatorship followed
by various military juntas; continuing major base of US economic,
political and military hegemony in Central America; 1954, US-
backed invasion of Guatemala from Honduras; 1969 "Soccer War"
with El Salvador; 1980s, major US military presence and
involvement with US-backed Nicaragua Contras; Honduran
assistance to rightist El Salvador government in the civil war; 1982,
"democratic" US-backed government elected; continued elections;
1998, Hurricane Mitch devastated Honduras killing 5,000; 2003,
military support for US occupation of Iraq.

2021 update: 2009, military coup backed by elements of the US
government; subsequent "elections"; poverty, inequity, gangs and
violent crime; 2020, flood of refugees marching north to Mexico
and the US from Honduras. GHG pollution 15.8 tonnes CO_2-e per
person per year; 2020, Honduras was the key 50th ratifier of the
Treaty on the Prohibition of Nuclear Weapons (TPNW) that meant
that it subsequently became International Law on 22 January 2021.
"Covid-19 deaths per million of population" was a bad 452 as
compared to 0.4 for Taiwan (March 2021). In 2020 the "under-5
infant mortality as a percentage of total population" (0.0421%) was
29.0 times greater than for Japan (0.00145%) but 2.6 times lower
than that in 2003 (0.1110%).

Foreign occupation: Spain, US (pre-1950); none (post-1950); *post-
1950 foreign military presence:* US (hegemony and military
training); *1950-2005 excess mortality/2005 population* =
0.822m/7.257m = 11.3%; *1950-2005 under-5 infant mortality/2005*

population = 0.845m/7.257m = 11.6%. Per capita GDP (nominal) $2,575.

Jamaica: Pre-colonial Arawak people; 1494, Columbus arrived; 1509, Spanish invaded Jamaica; 16th century, Spanish settlement; Arawaks exterminated by 1545 from a pre-colonial population of 60,000; plantations, African slaves, sugar, cotton and cattle; 1655, British finally displaced the Spanish; 1760, 1795 successive slave rebellions put down ferociously; 1833-1838, slavery abolished; 1865, revolt by freedmen suppressed by the British; late 19th century, Indian indentured labour; 1938, African riots; 1942, bauxite exploitation commenced and increased US interest; 1962, independence; 1974, Manley elected; 1980, US-backed rightist elected; 1983, Jamaica sent forces to support US invasion of Grenada; 1989, leftist return under Manley; 1992, leftist Patterson replaced Manley and was subsequently re-elected in 1997 and 2002.

2021 update: big international impact in sports and music; GHG pollution 12.8 tonnes CO_2-e per person per year; it has signed and ratified the TPNW. "Covid-19 deaths per million of population" was 188 as compared to 0.4 for Taiwan (March 2021). In 2020 the "under-5 infant mortality as a percentage of total population" (0.0227%) was 29.0 times greater than for Japan (0.00145%) but 2.6 times less than that in 2003 (0.0410%).

Foreign occupation: Spain, Britain (pre-1950); UK (post-1950); *post-1950 foreign military presence:* US hegemony; *1950-2005 excess mortality/2005 population* = 0.245m/2.701m = 9.1%; *1950-2005 under-5 infant mortality/2005 population* = 0.153m/2.701m = 5.7%. Per capita GDP (nominal) $5,369.

Martinique: Pre-colonial Carib people; 1635, French invasion; Caribs were promised half the island but were eventually exterminated; 17th-19th century, sugar plantations worked by African slaves; 19th century, repeated slave rebellions; 1848, slavery abolished; 1902, Mount Pelée eruption destroyed St. Pierre; 1943, US displacement of Vichy authority; 1948, made an Overseas Department of France; post-war, increased pro-independence activism.

2021 update: 2009, strikes and protests over poverty, inequity and internal French dominance; GHG pollution 4.8 tonnes CO_2-e per person per year; ruler France has 293 nuclear weapons, opposes and rejects the TPNW. "Covid-19 deaths per million of population" was 131 as compared to 0.4 for Taiwan (March 2021). In 2020 the "under-5 infant mortality as a percentage of total population" (0.0059%) was 4.1 times greater than for Japan (0.00145%) but times 4.6 times lower than that in 2003 (0.0%).

Foreign occupation: France (pre-1950); France (post-1950); *post-1950 foreign military presence:* France; *1950-2005 excess mortality/2005 population* = 0.022m/0.397m = 5.5%; *1950-2005 under-5 infant mortality/2005 population* = 0.022m/0.397m = 5.5%.

Mexico: Pre-colonial Olmeca, Teotihuaca, Maya, Mexica and Aztec people; successive Olmec (1200-400BCE), Maya (300-900CE), Toltec (900-1200) and Aztec (1200-1519) civilizations; 1519, Spanish invasion under Cortes; 1521, Aztecs under Montezuma defeated by Spanish conquistador Cortes associated with decimation of Indian population by disease; 16th-17th century, extensive Spanish settlement; 1810, independence movement commenced; 1821, General Iturbide as Emperor; 1823, republic set up by Santa Anna and Gudalupe Victoria; 19th century, major Spanish, French, British and US aggression; liberal versus conservative political dichotomies; 1836, US settled eastern Texas; 1846-1848, US invaded and annexed California, Nevada, Arizona, New Mexico and the rest of Texas; 1861, liberal electoral victory followed by clerical and conservative reaction and the Reform War; Spanish, French and British invasion; French-imposed monarchy; 1867, republican restoration under Juarez; 1876-1911, Diaz dictatorship; 1910, Mexican Revolution launched; 1911, Madero president; 1913, US-backed opposition and assassination of Madero followed by armed struggle under Zapata and Villa; 1917, new constitution under Caranza; 1929, National Revolutionary Party under Calles, thence rule under same group (renamed Institutional Revolutionary Party in 1946) until 2000 with the Fox electoral victory; 1994, North American Free Trade Agreement (NAFTA) between Mexico, US and Canada, exploitation of Mexican labour, violence against women workers and major immigration to the US; 2006, disputed Conservative electoral victory.

2021 update: entrenched problems of corruption, drug trafficking and horrendous gang-related crime, violence and horrendous murders; 2017-2021, Trump America hostility to Mexicans and Latin American refugees; NAFTA renegotiated in favor of the US; GHG pollution 13.9 tonnes CO_2-e per person per year; it has signed and ratified the TPNW. "Covid-19 deaths per million of population" was a gerocidal 1,541 as compared to 0.4 for Taiwan (March 2021). In 2020 the "under-5 infant mortality as a percentage of total population" (0.0255%) was 17.6 times greater than for Japan (0.00145%) and 2.4 times lower than that in 2003 (0.0610%).

Foreign occupation: Spain, France, Britain, US (massive annexation of territory) (pre-1950); none (post-1950); *post-1950 foreign military presence:* US hegemony; *1950-2005 excess mortality/2005 population* = 8.850m/106.385m = 8.3%; *1950-2005 under-5 infant mortality/2005 population* = 9.095m/106.385m = 8.5%. Per capita GDP (nominal) $9,849.

Monserrat: Pre-colonial Carib people; 1493, Columbus visited; 16th–19th century, Caribs exterminated, British/French conflict over possession, African slaves for sugar plantations, major Irish Catholic settlement (1632); post-war membership of various British Caribbean federations; still a British Overseas Territory.

2021 update: 1995-2010, volcanic activity meant all but 1,200 left and over half the island became an exclusion zone; present population about 5,000; greenhouse gas (GHG) pollution not available; the ruler, Britain, is a member of nuclear-armed NATO, has 215 nuclear warheads, opposes and rejects the TPNW. Data not available for "under-5 infant mortality as a percentage of total population".

Foreign occupation: France, Britain (pre-1950); UK (post-1950); *post-1950 foreign military presence:* UK. Per capita GDP (nominal) $13,487.

Netherlands Antilles: Pre-colonial Caiqueti, Carib and Arawak people; 1499, Spanish removed inhabitants to Hispaniola; 16th century, Dutch salt mining and formation of West Indies Company; 1634, Dutch occupied Curacao; 1648, further islands added by the Dutch; 17th-19th century, Dutch plantations, African slaves and violently suppressed slave rebellions; intermittent British occupation during the Napoleonic era; 1863, slavery abolished; 20th century, major oil industry; post-war, increased independence activism; 1986, Aruba was separated administratively in the Dutch Caribbean.

2021 update: 2010, dissolution of the Netherlands Antilles as a unified political entity; Curaçao, Sint Maarten and Aruba are all autonomous constituent countries within the Kingdom of the Netherlands with Bonaire, Sint Eustatius, and Saba becoming special municipalities of the Netherlands proper. The ruler, the Netherlands, is a member of nuclear-armed NATO, opposes and rejects the TPNW. "Covid-19 deaths per million of population" was 706 (Aruba), 625 (Sint Maarten) and 170 (Curacao) as compared to 0.4 for Taiwan (March 2021). No data available for "under-5 infant mortality as a percentage of total population".

Foreign occupation: Spain, Netherlands, Britain (pre-1950); Netherlands (post-1950); *post-1950 foreign military presence:* Netherlands; *1950-2005 excess mortality/2005 population* = 0.009m/0.224m = 3.9%; *1950-2005 under-5 infant mortality/2005 population* = 0.010m/0.224m = 4.5%. Per capita GDP (nominal) $18,980 (Curacao), and $30,975 (Aruba).

Nicaragua: Pre-colonial Chibcha and Maya people with Caribbean coastal Miskito Indians; 1502, Columbus arrived; 16th-18th century, Spanish conquest and settlement; 1821, independence from Spain, briefly part of Iturbide's Mexican Empire and then a member of the Central American Federation; 1839, independence; 1850, US-British accord over their interests; 1851, trans-isthmus route for California gold-rush participants; 1856, US-backed adventurer Walker invaded but was defeated in 1857; 1875 and 1895, ports occupied by British and German forces; 1912-1915, US invaded and occupied; 1925, US re-invasion resisted by Sandino for 6 years; 1933, US Marines left; 1936, US-backed dictator Somoza installed; 1956, Somoza was killed and was successively replaced by his sons; 1960s, Sandanista insurgency against US-backed Somoza dictatorship; 1979, Somoza overthrown by Sandanistas; extensive social reform; US hostility 1982, Pastora led US-backed Contras from Costa Rica and US-dominated Honduras; 1984, US mined Nicaraguan ports; 1990, US-backed civil war (with the illegal Irangate funding of the Contras) ended with elections (1979-1992 excess mortality 0.2 million; 30,000 killed violently); conservative Violeta Chamorro defeated Sandanista Ortega; 2003, military support for US occupation of Iraq.

2021 update: 2006 onwards, Sandanista Ortega elected and re-elected in subsequent elections; 2018, deadly anti-Sandanista mass demonstrations. Deforestation (only 25% tree cover left by 2018) and GHG pollution of 51.2 tonnes CO_2-e per person per year; it has signed and ratified the TPNW. "Covid-19 deaths per million of population" was 26 as compared to 0.4 for Taiwan (March 2021). In 2020 the "under-5 infant mortality as a percentage of total population" (0.0366%) was 25.2 times greater than for Japan (0.00145%) and 3.6 times less than that in 2003 (0.1330%).

Foreign occupation: Spain, Britain (ports), Germany (ports), US (pre-1950); US (post-1950); *post-1950 foreign military presence:* US (hegemony, military training and civil war); *1950-2005 excess mortality/2005 population* = 0.934m/5.727m = 16.3%; *1950-2005 under-5 infant mortality/2005 population* = 0.725m/5.727m = 12.7%. Per capita GDP (nominal) $1,913.

Panama: Pre-colonial Chibcha people; 1502, Columbus; 1508, Spanish invasion; 1513, Balboa saw the Pacific; 16th century, Spanish colonization, destruction of Indian population by disease and violence, British piracy; 17th century, Scottish Darién settlement scheme failed; 1821, independence from Spain as part of New Granada; 1831, Panama seceded from New Granada and then re-incorporated; 1848-1855, US-built railway; 1855, Panama a state in the Federation of New Granada; 1864, treaty with the US; late 19th century-1914, French and finally US construction of Panama Canal; 1903, US-backed Panama independence from Colombia followed by US invasion and treaty giving the US the

Canal Zone; 1908, 1912, 1918, US military invasions; 1940, Arias was elected, subsequently removed by the US, seized power (1949) but was ousted (1951); 1977, treaty for eventual Panamanian control of the Canal Zone; 1968, Arias removed in a coup by Torrijos (Noriega was his military intelligence chief). After Torrijos' death in a plane crash (!) in 1981, in 1983-1989, CIA-linked Noriega was the de facto ruler of Panama but failed to sufficiently please his US masters; US sanctions imposed; 1989, US invaded, up to 10,000 Panamanians killed; Noriega was tried and imprisoned in the US on drugs charges.

2021 update: Noriega was accused by the US (!) of involvement in drug smuggling – but the US itself was successively illicitly involved in opiates in Turkey, thence Vietnam and South East Asia, and from 2001 onwards rapidly restored the Afghan opiate industry from 6% world share (under the Taliban in 2001) to 90% of world share by 2007. US protected Occupied Afghanistan opiates dominate the world market. Illicit drugs kill 600,000 people annually, mostly via opiates and opioids. US-sanctioned Iran leads the world in interdiction of opiates. GHG pollution of 68.0 tonnes CO_2-e per person per year; 2016, release of the Panama Papers revealing massive tax avoidance by the global wealthy (One Percenters); 2019, Panama the first Latin American country to sign up to China's Belt and Road with consequent US hostility. Deforestation and GHG pollution of 68.0 tonnes CO_2-e per person per year; Panama has signed and ratified the TPNW. "Covid-19 deaths per million of population" was a gerocidal 1,392 as compared to 0.4 for Taiwan (March 2021). In 2020 the "under-5 infant mortality as a percentage of total population" (0.0333%) was 23.0 times greater than for Japan (0.00145%) and 1.7 times lower than that in 2003 (0.0550%).

Foreign occupation: Spain, US (pre-1950); US (post-1950); *post-1950 foreign military presence:* US (hegemony, military training, invasion and occupation); *1950-2005 excess mortality/2005 population* = 0.172m/3.235m = 5.3%; *1950-2005 under-5 infant mortality/2005 population* = 0.162m/3.235m = 5.0%. Per capita GDP (nominal) $15,728.

Paraguay: Pre-colonial agrarian central Guarani people and nomadic Guaycuru and Payagua people in the southern Chaco region; 16th-18th century, Spanish conquest, settlement and cattle; Jesuits formed Paraguayan communes; 1767, Jesuits expelled and Paraguayans enslaved; 1811, Spanish rule defeated; subsequent rule by a succession of military dictators; 1865-1870, British-backed Triple Alliance of Argentina, Brazil and Uruguay invaded and 1 million Paraguayans died (about half the population); 1932-1935, Chaco War with Bolivia and 50,000 Paraguayan war dead; 20th century, political instability and numerous coups and juntas; 1954-1989, US-backed General Stroessner dictatorship with rigged elections; 1989, coup and turbulent democracy restored. 1992, democratic constitution.

2021 update: 2008, Fernando Lugo, a former Roman Catholic Bishop and an adherent of liberation theology, elected president; 2012, Lugo removed by impeachment in an effective coup d'état by rightists. Massive deforestation for methanogenic cattle and GHG pollution of 37.2 tonnes CO_2-e per person per year; it has signed and ratified the TPNW. "Covid-19 deaths per million of population" was a bad 543 as compared to 0.4 for Taiwan (March 2021). In 2020 the "under-5 infant mortality as a percentage of total population" (0.0411%) was 28.3 times greater than for Japan (0.00145%) and 2.2 times lower than that in 2003 (0.0890%).

Foreign occupation: Spain, [Brazil, Argentina, Uruguay, Bolivia invasions] (pre-1950); none (post-1950); *post-1950 foreign military presence:* US (hegemony and militarization); *1950-2005 excess mortality/2005 population* = 0.577m/6.160m = 9.4%; *1950-2005 under-5 infant mortality/2005 population* = 0.339m/6.160m = 5.5%. Per capita GDP (nominal) \$5,406.

Peru: Pre-colonial Inca civilization; 1524, Spanish invasion led by conquistador Pizarro; 1532-1533, Inca Empire conquered, Inca Emperor Atahualpa tricked and murdered; 16th-18th century, indigenous resistance and huge population decline from disease, dispossession and violence; 1780-1783, defeat of Tupac Amaru rebellion; 1818-1824, San Martin and Bolivar fought and eventually defeated the Spanish; 1827, war with Colombia; 1835, unification with Brazil unsuccessful; 1845-1862, abolition of slavery and institution of constitutional rule under Castilla; 1866, final defeat of Spanish fleet; 1879, British-backed Chile defeated Peru and Bolivia (War of the Pacific); 19th-20th century, silver, guano and thence copper mining; horrendous brutality towards Amazonian Indian rubber collectors (cf the Belgian Congolese Genocide under King Leopold); 1960s, successive military coups; 1980, elections but declining economic circumstances stimulated Shining Light insurgency; 1990, Fujimori elected but was subsequently defeated after corrupt administration and fled to Japan (2000); currently democratic; ongoing corruption; massive environmental damage from US oil industry.

2021 update: ongoing corruption scandals. Deforestation and oil contribute to a GHG pollution of 34.8 tonnes CO_2-e per person per year; it has signed but not ratified the TPNW. "Covid-19 deaths per million of population" was a gerocidal 1,526 as compared to 0.4 for Taiwan (March 2021). In 2020 the "under-5 infant mortality as a percentage of total population" (0.0262%) was 18.1 times greater than for Japan (0.00145%) and 2.9 times lower than that in 2003 (0.0770%).

Foreign occupation: Spain [Chile invasion] (pre-1950); US (post-1950); *post-1950 foreign military presence:* US (hegemony and military training); *1950-2005 excess mortality/2005 population =* 4.094m/27.968m = 14.6%; *1950-2005 under-5 infant mortality/2005 population* = 4.132m/27.968m = 14.8%. Per capita GDP (nominal) $6,978.

Puerto Rico: Pre-colonial Arawak Taino people; 1493, Columbus; 1508, Spanish invasion under Ponce de Léon; 16th-18th century, plantations, extermination of indigenous people, African slaves (first introduced in 1513), piracy and naval activity by English, French and Dutch; 1820s, some rebellions; 1873, slavery abolished; 1868-1898, armed struggle for independence; 1897, some autonomy granted by Spain; 1898, US-confected Spanish-American war ("remember the Maine", the US warship blown up in Havana harbor in 1898) and the US invaded and occupied; 1900, direct US military rule ceased; 1917, Puerto Ricans could be US citizens; 1946, local autonomy; 1959, Commonwealth association with US; post-WW2, massive Puerto Rican emigration to US;1967-1998, repeated plebiscites confirming continued commonwealth association with the US.

2021 update: Puerto Ricans still cannot vote in Federal elections; 2016, a majority still supported statehood; 2017, devastated by Hurricane Maria but limited Federal response; like other tropical island states it is subject to worsening threat from high energy hurricanes due to man-made global warming; the ruling America has 5,800 nuclear weapons, and rejects the TPNW. Covid-19 deaths per million of population" was a bad 692 as compared to 0.4 for Taiwan (March 2021). In 2020 the "under-5 infant mortality as a percentage of total population" (0.0038%) was 2.6 times greater than for Japan (0.00145%) and 3.2 times lower than that in 2003 (0.0120%).

Foreign occupation: Spain, US (pre-1950); US (post-1950); *post-1950 foreign military presence:* US; *1950-2005 excess mortality/2005 population* = 0.039m/3.915m = 1.0%; *1950-2005 under-5 infant mortality/2005 population* = 0.080m/3.915m = 2.0%. Per capita GDP (nominal) $35,791.

Saint Kitts and Nevis: Pre-colonial Carib people; 1493, Columbus arrived; 1623, Walker set up the first English settlement in the Caribbean; 17th-19th century, extermination of Caribs; sugar plantations and African slaves; 1983, independence within the British Commonwealth.

2021 update: GHG pollution of the order of 10 tonnes CO_2-e per person per year; it has signed and ratified the TPNW. Data not available for "Covid-19 deaths per million of population" and "under-5 infant mortality as a percentage of total population".

Foreign occupation: Britain (pre-1950); UK (post-1950); *post-1950 foreign military presence:* UK. Per capita GDP (nominal) $19,896.

Saint Lucia: Pre-colonial Arawaks, superseded by Caribs; 1502, Columbus arrived; 1660, French treaty with the indigenous Caribs; 17th-19th century British and French conflict with Caribs and

Anglo-French conflict; sugar plantations and African slaves; 1803, final British control; 1814, Treaty of Paris and formal British possession; 20th century, bananas; 1959-1962, British West Indies Federation membership; 1967, one of 6 members of the West Indies Associated States; 1978, independence; 1979, together with Jamaica, Guyana and Grenada denounced US militarism in the region; 1982-1996, conservative rule; 1997, Labour government.

2021 update: continuing democracy with a moderate right-left dichotomy; GHG pollution of 2.9 tonnes CO_2-e per person per year; it has signed and ratified the TPNW. "Covid-19 deaths per million of population" was 315 as compared to 0.4 for Taiwan (March 2021). In 2020 the "under-5 infant mortality as a percentage of total population" (0.0180%) was 12.4 times greater than for Japan (0.00145%) but 2.3 times lower than that in 2003 (0.0410%).

Foreign occupation: France, Britain (pre-1950); UK (post-1950); *post-1950 foreign military presence:* US (regional hegemony); *1950-2005 excess mortality/2005 population* = 0.012m/0.152m = 7.9%; *1950-2005 under-5 infant mortality/2005 population* = 0.009m/0.152m = 6.1%. Per capita GDP (nominal) $11,611.

Saint Vincent and the Grenadines: Pre-colonial Arawaks superseded by Carib people; 1498, Columbus arrived; 16th -18th century, conflict between indigenous Caribs, escaped slaves and Europeans; 1783, British colony; 1795-1796, brutal suppression of rebellion by the Black Caribs (deriving from African slave and Carib unions); 5,000 Black Caribs removed to Roatan Island off Honduras;16th-20th century, sugar, cotton, cocoa, cotton; 1834, slavery abolished followed by Portuguese immigrants (1840s) and Indian indentured labour (1860s); 1902, La Soufriere volcanic eruption; 1979, last of Windward Islands to achieve independence.

2021 update: subject to worsening hurricanes; 1999, Hurricane Lenny caused extensive damage to the west coast; 2001 onwards, Gonsalves of the Unity Labour Party repeatedly elected and demanded European reparations for the Atlantic slave trade; GHG pollution of 2.4 tonnes CO_2-e per person per year; it has signed and ratified the TPNW. "Covid-19 deaths per million of population" was 90 as compared to 0.4 for Taiwan (March 2021). In 2020 the "under-5 infant mortality as a percentage of total population" (0.0209%) was 14.4 times greater than for Japan (0.00145%) but 1.9 times lower than that in 2003 (0.0%).

Foreign occupation: Spain, Britain (pre-1950); UK (post-1950); *post-1950 foreign military presence:* US (regional hegemony); *1950-2005 excess mortality/2005 population* = 0.018m/0.121m = 14.9%; *1950-2005 under-5 infant mortality/2005 population* = 0.009m/0.121m = 7.2%. Per capita GDP (nominal) $7,464.

Suriname: Pre-colonial Arawak and thence Carib people; 1630, British colony failed; 1651, British Willoughbyland; 1667, Dutch invaded; British ceded Suriname in exchange for New Amsterdam (New York); 17th century, settled by Dutch expelled from Brazil; plantations and African slaves; 1799-1816, British rule (Napoleonic Wars); 1816, resumption of Dutch rule; Maroons (Bush Negroes), escaped slaves in the interior; 1863, slavery abolished; Indian and East Indies (Javanese) indentured labour; post-WW2, independence activism; bauxite; 1975, independence; 1980, Bouterse military coup followed by flawed restored democracy, military murder of opposition politicians (1982), elections and a further coup; Dutch and US opposition; 1986, rightist Maroon rebellion and mercenary terrorism from French Guyana; 1992, peace settlement with Maroon rebels; 2000-2010, Venetiaan president. Coalition.

2021 update: 2010 and 2015, Bouterse elected in successive elections; 2019, Bouterse convicted in absentia for 1982 killings; 2020, Santokhi president after winning elections. Deforestation and GHG pollution of 25.1 tonnes CO_2-e per person per year; it has not joined the TPNW. "Covid-19 deaths per million of population" was 300 as compared to 0.4 for Taiwan (March 2021). In 2020 the "under-5 infant mortality as a percentage of total population" (0.0335%) was 23.1times greater than for Japan (0.00145%) but 2.1 times lower than that in 2003 (0.0770%).

Foreign occupation: Netherlands (pre-1950); Netherlands (post-1950); *post-1950 foreign military presence:* US regional hegemony; *1950-2005 excess mortality/2005 population* =

0.039m/0.442m = 8.8%; *1950-2005 under-5 infant mortality/2005 population* = 0.043m/0.442m = 9.7%. Per capita GDP (nominal) $6,360.

Trinidad and Tobago: Pre-colonial Arawak and Carib people; 1498, Columbus arrived; 15th century, Spanish territory; 16th-18th century, Spanish, Dutch, English, French and Courlander (Baltic German) involvements, sugar plantations and African slaves; 1802, Trinidad British colony; 1814, Tobago British colony; 1834, abolition of slavery and importation of Indian, Chinese, Portuguese and African indentured labour; 20th century, oil industry and increased political activism; 1950, internal autonomy; 1958-1962, part of British West Indies Federation; 1962, independence; 1976, republic; 1983, opposed US Grenada invasion; US hostility; 1990, coup attempt; liberal democracy; prosperity from agriculture, tourism and oil.

2021 update: V.S. Naipaul Literature Nobel Prize (2001). GHG pollution of 29.8 tonnes CO_2-e per person per year; it has not joined the TPNW. "Covid-19 deaths per million of population" was 101 as compared to 0.4 for Taiwan (March 2021). In 2020 the "under-5 infant mortality as a percentage of total population" (0.0301%) was 29.8 times greater than for Japan (0.00145%) and slightly greater than that in 2003 (0.0290%).

Foreign occupation: Spain, Britain (pre-1950); UK (post-1950); *post-1950 foreign military presence:* US regional hegemony; *1950-2005 excess mortality/2005 population* = 0.052m/1.311m = 4.0%; *1950-2005 under-5 infant mortality/2005 population* = 0.071m/1.311m = 5.4%. Per capita GDP (nominal) $16,637.

Turks and Caicos: Pre-colonial Arawak people; 1492, the first place Columbus landed in the New World; 1512, Spaniard Ponce de Léon; population of the archipelago subsequently completely destroyed by disease and slavery; 1678, British settlement; salt; 17th century, French, Spanish and British involvements; 1764, French displaced British settlers; 1787, British colonization, cotton plantations, African slaves; 1874, annexed to Jamaica; WW2, US airstrip; 1951, US naval base; 1962, crown colony; 1970s, pro-independence left versus pro-US right politics; 1973, own governor when Bahamas gained independence; 1988, self-government; tourism and Canadian links; British Overseas Territory.

2021 update: Estimated GHG pollution of the order of 10 tonnes CO_2-e per person per year. The ruling power, the UK, has 215 nuclear weapons, opposes and rejects the TPNW. "Covid-19 deaths per million of population" was a bad 435 as compared to 0.4 for Taiwan (March 2021). No data available for "under-5 infant mortality as a percentage of total population".

Foreign occupation: Spain, France, Britain (pre-1950); UK (post-1950); *post-1950 foreign military presence:* UK, US. Per capita GDP (nominal) $31,353.

Uruguay: Pre-colonial nomadic Charrua and agrarian Chanae and Guarani people; 1502, Spanish under Italian Amerigo Vespucci landed in America (hence "America"); 1527, Spanish settlement; 1611, cattle introduced; 17th-19th century, displacement and genocidal extermination of indigenous Indians; 1860, Portuguese settlement of Colonia; 1724, Spanish fort at Montevideo; 1816, Portuguese invasion followed by conflict involving Argentina, Brazil and Portugal; 1828, independence established via Argentina, Brazil and Britain; 1830 Constitution with subsequent Red and White parties; 1831, massacre of the last Charrua Indians by General Fructuoso Rivera (first President); 1833, some surviving Charrua Indians "exhibited" in Paris; late 19th century, fencing of territory (and hence final Indian dispossession) completed; Spanish and Italian immigration; 1904, brief civil war followed by liberal democracy; 1960s, 1970s, increasing economic problems, rise of Tupamaros guerrillas with corresponding government repression; 1973, military coup; 1984, restoration of "democracy".

2021 update: socially progressive (same sex marriage, abortion, cannabis legal, gay rights); 95% electrical energy from renewables; deforestation and methanogenic cattle industry contribute to GHG pollution of 23.7 tonnes CO_2-e per person per year; it has signed and ratified the TPNW. "Covid-19 deaths per million of population" was 246 as compared to 0.4 for Taiwan (March 2021). In 2020 the "under-5 infant mortality as a percentage of total population" (0.0129%) was 8.9 times greater than for Japan (0.00145%) and 1.9 times less than that in 2003 (0.0165%).

Foreign occupation: Spain, Portugal (pre-1950); none (post-1950); *post-1950 foreign military presence:* US (hegemony and military training); *post-1950 excess mortality/2005 population =* 0.138m/3.463m = 4.0%; *post-1950 under-5 infant mortality/2005 population* = 0.125m/3.463m = 3.6%. Per capita GDP (nominal) $16,190.

Venezuela: Pre-colonial Arawak, Chibcha and Carib people; 1498, Columbus arrived; 16th-18th century, Spanish settlement, Venezuela a Captaincy General of New Granada; 1810, revolt against Spain; 1811, independence leader Miranda defeated by Spanish; 1813, Bolivar captured Caracas; 1814, Bolivar defeated by Spanish; 1819, Bolivar defeated Spanish and established Gran Colombia (Colombia, Ecuador, Panama and Venezuela); 1830, Paez succeeded Bolivar; Venezuela independent of Gran Colombia; 19th-20th century, succession of military dictatorships notably that of Gomez in the period 1908-1935; 1930s, oil industry started; 1947, elections followed by coup; 1948-1958, Jimenez dictatorship; post-WW2, major oil industry, left-right political dichotomy, US involvement; 1958, restoration of democracy; 1998, leftist Hugo Chavez elected with subsequent constitutional change; 2000, Chavez re-elected; massive US interference and threat; 2001, massive US-backed, right-wing opposition strikes and demonstrations; 2002, massive opposition demonstration and killing by shooting of 18 demonstrators by the military; 2004, the opposition obtained 2 million signatures for a referendum on Chavez's continuance; Chavez won the referendum with 60% of the internationally-inspected vote; medical support from Cuba; continued threat from the US.

2021 update: 2013 Hugo Chavez died; presidential election returned Nicolás Maduro but disputed by the US and the US-backed opposition; 2019, US imposition of crippling sanctions; 4 million refugees; 2020, unsuccessful US-backed Operation Gideon invasion involving Venezuelans and US mercenaries. Oil industry and deforestation contribute to a GHG pollution of 45.2 tonnes

CO_2-e per person per year; it has signed and ratified the TPNW. "Covid-19 deaths per million of population" was 54 as compared to 0.4 for Taiwan (March 2021). In 2020 the "under-5 infant mortality as a percentage of total population" (0.0531%) was 36.6 times greater than for Japan (0.00145%) and 1.2 times greater than that in 2003 (0.0%) [US Sanctions kill children].

Foreign occupation: Spain (pre-1950); none (post-1950); *post-1950 foreign military presence:* US (hegemony, militarization and acute threat); *1950-2005 excess mortality/2005 population =* 1.132m/26.640m = 4.2%; *1950-2005 under-5 infant mortality/2005 population* = 1.099m/26.640m = 4.1%. Per capita GDP (nominal) $4,733.

2020 statistical update for Latin America and the Caribbean. Table 9.5 summarizes population, under-5 infant mortality (IM) and excess mortality (EM; avoidable mortality from deprivation) in Latin America and the Caribbean in 2020 (pre-Covid-19 projection in 2019 for 2020 by the UN Population Division). Table 9.1 compares Latin America and the Caribbean with other global regions. Presented in square brackets for each country is the "Relative EM Score" of EM/Pop (%) divided by that for the best-performing country, Japan (0.0020%), which accordingly has a "Relative EM Score" of 1.0.

In terms of "Relative EM Score" and "per capita GDP" the outcomes fall into 3 groups, (1) good outcome countries ranging from Puerto Rico (2.6 and $35,791) to the American Virgin Islands (9.2) and Uruguay (8.9 and $16,190); (2) worse outcomes from Saint Lucia (12.4 and $11,611) to Guyana (41.6 and $6,610); and (3) impoverished and devastated Haiti (124.5 and $715).

While the 2020 average "Relative EM Score" is 4.4 for European countries and 19.9 for Latin America and the Caribbean, it is a shocking 176.6 for non-Arab Africa (Table 9.1). "Under-5 infant mortality as a percentage of total population" decreased 1.2-3.6-fold in Latin America and the Caribbean countries with the exception of Trinidad and Tobago (no change) and American Virgin Islands (a slight 1.1-fold increase).

5.3 Summary

Human settlement of the Americas dates back to about 15,000BCE. Populous civilizations along the Mississippi and the Amazon and in Mexico, Central America and Peru were destroyed by European invasion in the 15th-16th centuries that was accompanied by deadly disease and brutal slavery. African slavery was introduced to man plantations because of the decimation of indigenous people. Papal interventions delineated Brazil (Portuguese) and Spanish-dominated Latin America. British, Dutch, Danish, French and Courland (Baltic German) colonialism, largely in and around the Caribbean. The 19th century saw independence from Spanish and Portuguese rule, followed by increasing Anglo-American interference and horrendous "commercial" genocide of Indians in Peru, Brazil, Paraguay, Uruguay and Argentina.

The Spanish-American War at the end of the 19th century established US hegemony in Latin America and the Caribbean that was repeatedly backed up with egregious force. Repeated violent US invasions and interventions and US backing of violent military dictatorships and right-wing terrorism have dominated the latter half of the 20th century. The 21st century sees very general democratization but with increasing competition for finite global resources Latin America is under serious threat from a violent, powerful and unilateralist US Empire. However massive popular support for leftists Fidel Castro and Raúl Castro (Cuba), Hugo Chavez and Nicolás Maduro (Venezuela), Lula da Silva (Brazil) and Evo Morales (Bolivia) indicated that the US administration had compromised its "traditional" US Western Hemisphere hegemony through its oil-driven obsession with violent "democratic imperialism" in Africa, the Middle East and Central Asia.

CHAPTER 6: NORTH AFRICA, ASIA & PACIFIC – THE IMPACT OF COLONIALISM, NEO-COLONIALISM AND WAR

"Several of the factors mentioned above suggest a British "scorched earth" policy designed to deny assets in Bengal to the Japanese, at monstrous cost, should they successfully invade India. Those consequences severely indict British policy makers of the time, and the failure to investigate and acknowledge them is to the discredit of all subsequent British governments."

Colin Mason (2000) on the "forgotten", man-made 1942-1945 Bengal Famine (4 million Bengali victims and 6-7 million Indian victims in Bengal and adjacent provinces).[1]

"All or nearly all of the whole Korean peninsular is a terrible mess. Everything has been destroyed, there's nothing left standing."

General Emmett O'Donnell, Chief of Bomber Command (1951).[2]

"In the councils of government we must guard against the acquisition of unwarranted influence, whether sought of unsought, by the military-industrial complex. The potential for the disastrous rise of misplaced power exists and will persist."

Dwight Eisenhower, farewell speech, 17 January 1961.[3]

"Well, we had to destroy the town in order to save it."

US major in Ben Tre, Vietnam (1968), reported by Peter Arnett.[4]

"The price was worth it."

Madeleine Albright, former US Secretary of State and UN Ambassador, when asked by Leslie Stahl in 1996 about the death of half a million Iraqi children due to UN-imposed, and US-enforced sanctions.[5]

6.1 Overview

As seen in Chapter 5, many Latin American countries escaped violent invasion and occupation by First World armies (or their local surrogates) in the post-1950 era. Thus the list of Central and South American countries that experienced direct invasion by US forces in this period includes the Dominican Republic, Panama, Grenada, Haiti, and Cuba; those experiencing violent surrogate invasions from US-trained armies include Guatemala, Nicaragua, El Salvador and Venezuela. However most of the countries merely suffered the consequences of US hegemony through US-backed military dictatorships, mass murder of political dissidents and elevated mortality due to excesses of the US-backed élites. The colonial regimes in Belize, Suriname, French Guiana, Guyana and the Caribbean islands were relatively benign. [6]

In contrast, nearly all the countries of the global East-West axis reaching from North Africa through Asia to the Pacific have experienced partial or complete First World military occupation or protectorate status in the post-war era. Indeed it is simplest to list the *three exceptions* to this, namely Turkey, Thailand and Saudi Arabia, of which all have nevertheless experienced US-based militarization and a major US military presence at various times, namely air force and missile bases (US NATO and CENTO partner Turkey), air force bases and Vietnam War R&R sex industry (Thailand) and huge all-service military presence (Saudi Arabia). As discussed by Diamond (1997),[7] the East-West axis Eurasian land mass countries have benefited historically from the rapid East-West movement of agricultural and technological advances. However, in the end colonialism funded the industrial revolution, Europe won the global arms race, and as Mao Tse-Tung famously put it: "Political power grows out of the barrel of a gun".[8] The process is still continuing with the rampant militarism of the US Empire evidenced by 700 US military bases located across the world in 70 countries, horrendous US and/or Israeli occupation of the territory of 7 Asian countries (Lebanon, Syria, Palestine, Egypt, Jordan, Iraq and Afghanistan), acute threat to other Asian countries (notably North Korea, China, and Iran) and on-going, high technology, civilian-butchering war against lightly-armed, indigenous insurgents in Afghanistan, Iraq, Syria, Yemen, Somalia, the Sahel and the Occupied Palestinian Territories. The post-invasion excess mortality in the Occupied Palestinian, Iraqi and Afghan territories totals 0.3, 0.5 and 1.6 million, respectively; the post-invasion under-5 infant mortality in the Occupied Palestinian, Iraqi and Afghan territories totals 0.2, 0.3 and 1.4 million, respectively (2007 estimates). Peace is the only way but silence kills and silence is complicity. America's "enemies" meriting high technology extermination were primarily "Communists" in the 1950s to the 1970s, but since the 1990s the US "enemies" meriting such deadly violence have been "Muslims". The new US "enemy" is China but, unlike the lightly-armed indigenous Asian "Communists" and "Muslims" that the US slaughtered in their millions, China has a huge economy and a huge and technologically sophisticated defence industry, air force, navy, army and nuclear arsenal.

The following "short histories" concentrate on major events impacting on human mortality. It becomes quite clear that a variety of First World impositions have impacted on avoidable mass mortality in North Africa, Asia and the Pacific in the post-war era. Such First World impositions have included economic hegemony, colonial occupation, corrupt client régimes, wars, civil wars, genocide, man-made famine, militarization, debt and malignant interference. The UN demographic data yielding the avoidable mortality estimates analysed in this book constitute a "smoking gun" pointing to the sheer magnitude of the human consequences of violence in particular periods of the post-1950 era.

The primary mortality data that was summed and collated in Chapter 2 has been used to provide estimates of the excess mortality *immediately* associated with *particular* post-1950 events such as the Algerian War of Independence against the French (Algeria 1954-1962 excess mortality 1.241 million) and the US Indo-China War (Vietnam 1955-1975 excess mortality 11.939 million). Note, however, that such cataclysms were associated with mortality effects *before* the actual armed conflict and *after* the formal cessation of particular hostilities. Accordingly, each entry also concludes with a summary of pre- and post-war foreign military presence and estimates (in millions, m) of "1950-2005 excess mortality/2005 population" and "1950-2005 under-5 infant mortality/2005 population", with every ratio value being expressed as a percentage (%).

2021 updates: The original edition text has been largely unchanged except for some useful insertions, updates, amplifications and corrections. 2021 updates are added at the end of each short history. In particular, because Humanity is existentially threatened by (a) climate change and (b) nuclear weapons, the 2021 updates include information on each country in relation to (a) climate change (notably revised annual greenhouse gas pollution taking land use into account and expressed as tonnes CO_2-equivalent (CO_2-e) per person per year), and (b) ratification or otherwise of the UN Treaty on the Prohibition of Nuclear Weapons (TPNW) that came into effect in International Law on 22 January 2021 and which prohibits State Parties from both possession of nuclear weapons and support for such possession "in any way" (data from the Nobel Prize-winning International Campaign Against Nuclear Weapons (ICAN)). Poverty kills, and included at the end of each national history is "per capita GDP (nominal)" (UN, 2019, in US dollars). "Covid-19 deaths per million of population" is included as an indicator of intra-national altruism. Finally, the 2020 "under-5 infant mortality as a percentage of population" for each country is compared to that for Japan (the best performing country) and with that in 2003 (to provide a measure of improvement over the last 17 years).

6.2 East Asia – recovery from First World-imposed war and sanctions

The East Asian countries of China, Korea and Japan have sophisticated civilizations dating back millennia. Isolated Mongolia had an immense historical impact through the Mongolian conquests of the 13th and 14th centuries that devastated Eurasia and killed 40-60 million people. The continuous Eurasian land mass and its East-West axis also permitted rapid spread of the bubonic plague that killed 75-200 million people. European and Japanese imperialism had a devastating impact on China over the last 2 centuries. Russian imperialism was constrained by Japan which then violently imposed its will on China, Korea and thence on South East Asia during WW2. After the carnage of WW2 (associated with an estimated 35-40 million deaths in China alone since the Japanese invasion in 1937), China went through the civil war, participation in the Korean War, 3 decades of US sanctions and threat, and huge mortality associated with the Great Leap Forward. Mongolia suffered from being caught between 2 mutually hostile empires with both being subject to decades of acute US Cold War hostility. Korea suffered devastation from the Korean War (US bombing destroyed every building on the Korean Peninsular and killed 28% of the North Korean population). Nevertheless East Asia (excluding Mongolia and North Korea) has recovered remarkably from these relatively recent events. China, Japan and South Korea are major industrial countries and the overall average post-1950 excess mortality outcome for East Asia is now similar to that for the mostly peaceful Latin American and Caribbean grouping. The outstandingly good outcome countries in this group are Macau, Hong Kong, Japan and Taiwan with 1950-2005 excess mortality/2005 population ratios of 1.4%, 1.5%, 1.9% and 2.0%, respectively, that are similar to those for Western Europe – all these countries having essentially had peace, prosperity and good governance for all of the post-1950 era. In 2019 China has the second biggest economy in the world, followed by Japan (3rd) and South Korea (10th).

China: 3,000BCE, agrarian civilization around Yellow River; 1027-256BCE, Chou dynasty, Confucius, Lao Tzu, Mencius, writing; 221-206BCE, Emperor Ch'in, territorial consolidation, Great Wall commenced; 202BCE-220CE, Han dynasty, great imperial age; 22-265, Three Kingdoms period, warfare and Hun invasions; 265-420, Tsin dynasty, central government weak; 618-907, T'ang dynasty, unification and good administration; 960-1279, Sung dynasty, high culture; 1276-1368, China invaded by Genghis Khan, subsequent rule by grandson Kublai Khan, Yuan dynasty, failed naval invasion of Japan; 1368-1644, Ming dynasty; 1644-1911, Chi'ing (Manchu) dynasty; 1557, Portugal acquired Macau; 1757, British conquered Bengal and thence set up the opium trade to China (Bengali opium for silver and tea); 1839-1842, British defeated China in the First Opium War, opened ports and acquired Hong Kong island; 1850-1864, anti-Western Taiping Rebellion put down with help of European forces (20-100 million victims of associated famine and violence); 1856-1860, Anglo-French forces defeated China and captured Beijing; 1895, Japan invaded Korea and Taiwan; 1898, anti-Western Boxer Rebellion subdued by British, Russian, German, French, Japanese and US forces and zones of influence established (e.g. Shanghai); 1911, republic under Sun Yat Sen; 1921, Chinese Communist Party formed and involvement in labor unions; 1926, Communist alliance with Chiang Kai-shek's Kuomintang (KMT); 1927, KMT forces massacred 40,000 Communist labor organizers; 1934, "Long March" of Communists under Mao Zedong to evade KMT attacks; 1937-1945, Japanese invasion and occupation; appalling atrocities (e.g. rape of Nanjing, 300,000 victims); Chinese losses from violence and deprivation 35-40 million; fragile Communist-KMT alliance (violated by KMT attacks on Communists); 1945-1949, civil war culminating in Communist victory; KMT fled to Taiwan under US protection; subsequent US protection of Taiwan, non-recognition of "Communist China" by the US and US economic boycott; Mao Zedong (Chairman Mao) founded the People's Republic of China (PRC), chairman of the Chinese Communist Party (1949-1976); 1950-1953, limited Chinese involvement in the Korean War (a potential trigger for US nuclear destruction of China); 1957, "let 100 flowers bloom" followed by crackdown on dissent; 1958-1961, Great Leap Forward to speed industrialization and agricultural collectivisation; 20-30 million died in the associated famine compounded by exclusion by the US Alliance; 1962, Liu Shaoqi chairman of the PRC; 1963, severe rift with USSR, departure of Soviet advisors; 1964, first atomic bomb; 1966-1976, Cultural Revolution lead by Red Guards, severe persecution of intellectuals; 1970s, major Chinese diplomacy towards Third World by Zhou Enlai; 1971, China replaced Taiwan at UN; 1976, Zhou and Mao died; Deng Xiaoping removed and then restored; trial of Gang of Four, including Mao's widow Jiang Qing; Beijing Spring and opinions on the "Democracy Wall" but subsequent repression of dissent; US-China diplomatic relations restored; 1979, short China war with Vietnam over Vietnamese defeat of Cambodian Khmer Rouge; 1978, Deng formally rehabilitated; 1980s, increasing economic decentralization, liberalization, consumerism and reform; 1984, Special Economic Zones created near Hong Kong and Macau; 1986, pro-democracy students arrested in Shanghai; 1989, shooting and arrest of Tibet protestors and separatist revolt in western China; 1989, death of reformist Hu Yaobang; Tienanmen Square massacre of hundreds of students; Li Peng as prime minister; 1990s, huge economic growth; "one child per family" population control (1980-2015); 1997, Hong Kong re-incorporated as Special Administrative Region of China with special "Basic Law" and civil rights protections; 1998, huge floods; 21st century, continuing massive economic growth with 800 million Chinese taken out of poverty and major Chinese involvement in the US economy and trade.

2021 update: continuing economic growth making China's economy second only to that of the US. Increasing US Alliance hostility over Chinese trade, diplomacy and "island making" on disputed uninhabited reefs in the South China Sea. 2012 onwards, rule by Xi Jinping; 2013 onwards, anti-corruption program and Belt and Road initiative with massive Chinese investment world-wide. Mass detention and re-education of 1 million Uighurs in Xinjiang (population half Han and half Uighur). International concerns over harsh treatment of dissidents and growing Social Credit surveillance state (neither unique to China, cf revelations and harsh treatment of Julian Assange, Chelsea Manning and Edward Snowden by the serial war criminal US). 2019, massive pro-democracy demonstrations in Hong Kong over new security laws; 2020, Covid-19 Pandemic apparently started in Wuhan with the SARS-Cov-2 virus possibly deriving from bats via another animal vector (as of March 2021, globally 127 million infected, 2.8 million deaths, overwhelmingly elderly e.g. 95% of deaths over 50 years old in the US). China performed brilliantly with "Covid-19 deaths per million of population" of 3 as compared to 0.4 for Taiwan, 1,687 for the US and 1,857 for the UK (March 2021). China leads the world in renewable energy; revised greenhouse gas (GHG) pollution 7.4 tonnes CO_2-e per person per year. China has 323 nuclear weapons and has not signed or ratified the TPNW. In 2020 the "under-5 infant mortality as a percentage of total population" (0.0124%) was 8.7 times greater than for Japan (0.00145%), but 4.6 times lower than that in 2003 (0.0570%).

Foreign occupation: Mongols, Manchurians, Britain, Portugal, Japan (pre-1950); none (post-1950); *post-1950 foreign military presence:* none; *1950-2005 excess mortality/2005 population* = 155.670m/1322.273m = 11.8%; *1950-2005 under-5 infant mortality/2005 population* = 157.226m/1,322.273m = 11.9%. Per capita GDP (nominal) $10,004.

Hong Kong: 1842, Hong Kong Island ceded to Britain by China after the First Opium War (UK forcing opium on China in exchange for silver and tea); 1860, Kowloon Peninsula secured by Britain; 1898, British 99 year lease on New Territories; 1941-1945, Japanese occupation and atrocities; 1950s-1970s, after Mao-led Communist victory, US imposed a trade boycott on China; Hong Kong developed light industry, textiles, commerce and international trading; mid-1970s onwards, Chinese economic liberalization and US recognition of China made Hong Kong a major conduit for China trade; 1980s, negotiations finalized handover of Hong Kong in 1997; millions of Hong Kong residents lost British citizenship; 1989, Tienanmen Square Massacre and 1.5 million Hong Kong citizens marched for democracy; 1997, handover to China; Special Administrative region of China with special "Basic Law" and civil rights protections.

2021 update: 2019, massive pro-democracy demonstrations in Hong Kong over new Beijing-dictated security laws; 2020 onwards, Covid-19 Pandemic with "Covid-19 deaths per million of population" of 27 for Hong Kong as compared to 3 for China, 0.4 for Taiwan, 1,687 for the US and 1,857 for the UK (March 2021). Revised greenhouse gas (GHG) pollution estimated as of the order of 10 tonnes CO_2-e per person per year. The ruling State China has 323 nuclear weapons and has not signed or ratified the TPNW. In 2020 the "under-5 infant mortality as a percentage of total population" (0.0022%) was 1.6 times greater than for Japan (0.00145%), but 1.4 times lower than that in 2003 (0.0030%).

Foreign occupation: Britain, Japan (pre-1950); UK (post-1950); *post-1950 foreign military presence:* UK; *1950-2005 excess mortality/2005 population* = 0.125m/7.182m = 1.7%; *1950-2005 under-5 infant mortality/2005 population* = 0.105m/7.182m = 1.5%. Per capita GDP (nominal) $49,180.

Macau (Macao): 1557, Portuguese acquired Macau as a key East Asian port; 1849, Portugal ceased rental payments and declared Macau independent of China; 1887, China agreed to Portuguese rule of Macau; 1941-1945, Japanese control but ostensible non-occupation; 1951, Overseas Province of Portugal; post-war, tourist and gambling venue; 1974, Salazar regime fell in Portugal; Portugal offered to hand Macau back but China declined; 1985, Hong Kong return finalized; China negotiated Macau return in 1999; Macau residents retained Portuguese citizenship; 1999, Macau returned to China; most densely populated territory on earth; huge gambling revenue.

2021 update: 2016, Chinese employees of Australian gambling company Crown arrested for violating China's anti-gambling laws; continuing Crown scandals in Australia. Revised greenhouse gas (GHG) pollution estimated as of the order of 10 tonnes CO_2-e per person per year. The ruling State China has 323 nuclear weapons and has not signed or ratified the TPNW. In 2020 the "under-5 infant mortality as a percentage of total population" (0.0037%) was 2.6 times greater than for Japan (0.00145%), but 1.1 times lower than that in 2003 (0.0040%).

Foreign occupation: Portugal, Japan (pre-1950); Portugal (post-1950); *post-1950 foreign military presence:* Portugal; *1950-2005 excess mortality/2005 population* = 0.036m/0.472m = 7.6%; *1950-2005 under-5 infant mortality/2005 population* = 0.007m/0.472m = 1.4%. Per capita GDP (nominal) $84,097.

Taiwan: prehistoric, aboriginal Malay settlement; 7th century, first Chinese settlement; 1590, Portuguese arrived; 1620s, Dutch and Spanish forts established; 1641, Dutch displaced the Spanish; 1662, Taiwan conquered by Ming dynasty General Koxinga; 1683, Manchu conquest; 1887, separate province of China; 1895, Japanese colony after China was defeated in Sino-Japanese War; 1945, returned to China; 1947, indigenous Taiwanese demonstrations against Chinese Nationalist Kuomintang (KMT);

KMT forces massacred thousands; 1949, after Communist victory on mainland China, Taiwan became a US-protected bastion of Chiang Kai-shek's Kuomintang (KMT) and was recognized as the "official" China by the US and most of its allies (the "Two China Policy"); 1950-1953, Korean War and increased US militarization and support for the KMT regime; 1950s, US-backed conflict with China in the Taiwan Strait; 1960s onwards, US-backed industrialization and remarkable economic growth; 1971, US permitted the People's Republic of China to take Taiwan's place at the UN; 1980s, increasing democratization; 1986, the Democratic Progress Party challenged the KMT; 1989, KMT won elections; 1990s, increasing democracy and accommodation with China; increasing international diplomatic isolation as China exerted increased diplomatic and economic influence; 21st century, mounting tensions with China over the pro-independence issue.

2021 update: continuing political tensions over independence or eventual reunification with China; increasing wealth and diplomacy of China has meant Taiwan losing support from some Pacific Island nations; 2020 onwards, Covid-19 pandemic with a world's best "Covid-19 deaths per million of population" of 0.4 as compared to 3 for China, 1,687 for the US and 1,857 for the UK (March 2021). Revised greenhouse gas (GHG) pollution estimated as of the order of 10 tonnes CO_2-e per person per year. As a party to the US "nuclear umbrella" Taiwan rejects the TPNW. In 2020 the "under-5 infant mortality as a percentage of total population" (0.0038%) was 2.7 times greater than for Japan (0.00145%), but 4.2 times lower than that in 2003 (0.0160%).

Foreign occupation: Japan (pre-1950); none (post-1950); *post-1950 foreign military presence:* none (but major US-armed surrogate); *1950-2005 excess mortality/2005 population =* 0.560m/22.894m = 2.4%; *1950-2005 under-5 infant mortality/2005 population* = 0.459m/22.894m = 2.0%. Per capita GDP (nominal) about $27,000.

Japan: 30,000BCE, earliest human presence; 4th-5th century BCE, early Neolithic cultures; 250BCE, Neolithic Jomon replaced by Yayoi; 3rd century BCE, advanced culture on Kyushu; 1st century

CE, bronze and iron working from Korea; 4th century, Japan united under the Yamato clan; 7th century, Prince Shotoku centralized administration; 9th-12th century, Fujiwara clan dominated imperial court; increased feudal military aristocracy at the expense of central power; Buddhism established; 1159, Taira clan seized power; 1189, Minamoto clan took over; Shogun Yoritomo; 1274, 1281, unsuccessful attempts at invasion by Mongols; 1333, Emperor Daigo II re-established direct imperial rule; 1338, Ashikaga clan restored military government (*bukufu*) and increased the power of regional military governors; 1542, Portuguese contact; 1549, St Francis Xavier introduced Christianity; 1573, Ashikaga overthrown; 1600, Tokugawa ascendancy; 1603, re-establishment of *bukufu*; 1854, US Commodore Perry forced opening of trade with the West; 1868, Meiji Restoration restored direct imperial rule, abolished feudal privileges and centralized power; imperial administration shifted from Kyoto to Tokyo; 1871, feudalism abolished; 1895, First Sino-Japanese War; Taiwan colonized; 1889, constitution; 1904-1905, Russo-Japanese War and Japanese expansion in Korea; 1910, Korea formally annexed; WW1, Japan allied with Allies; 1937, Japan invaded China (Second Sino-Japanese War); immense atrocities and 35-40 million Chinese war dead; 1941, Japan was progressively cornered by the US, attacked Pearl Harbor and subsequently conquered South East Asia and much of the Pacific; 60 Japanese cities bombed by the US; 1945, atomic bombs destroyed Hiroshima and Nagasaki killing 200,000; USSR entered the war and occupied the Kuril Islands; Japan surrendered; post-war, democratic constitution with anti-militarism provisions, huge economic growth and peace yielded one of the richest societies in the world; 2003, joined the US Coalition in Iraq.

2021 update: continued tension with China over the Senkaku Islands and WW2 Japanese atrocities; 2011, nuclear accident at the Fukushima Daiichi Nuclear Power Plant caused by the 2011 Tōhoku earthquake and tsunami that killed 15,900; massive evacuation and continuing massive clean-up. 2020 onwards, Covid-19 pandemic with "Covid-19 deaths per million of population" of 71 as compared to 0.4 for Taiwan, 3 for China, 1,687 for the US and 1,857 for the UK (March 2021). Revised greenhouse gas (GHG) pollution 10.7 tonnes CO_2-e per person per year. Although the only country to have suffered nuclear bombing of cities, Japan is a nuclear weapons endorser, and has not signed or ratified the TPNW. In 2020 the "under-5 infant mortality as a percentage of total population" (0.00145%) was the lowest in the world and 2.7 times lower than that in 2003 (0.0040%).

Foreign occupation: US (pre-1950); US (post-1950); *post-1950 foreign military presence:* US; *1950-2005 excess mortality/2005 population* = 155.670m/1322.273m = 11.8%; *1950-2005 under-5 infant mortality/2005 population* = 2.452m/127.914m = 1.9%. Per capita GDP (nominal) $40,063.

Korea: settled by Tungusic people; 2333BCE, precursor Old Choson founded; 1st century BCE-7th century CE, Koguryo kingdom in the North; resistance to Chinese invasions; 1st century BCE-7th century CE, Paekche and Silla Kingdoms in the South; 667CE, Silla tribe unified Korea; 10th century, Koryo family took power; 1392, Choson (Yi) dynasty (which ruled until 1910); 13th century, Mongol invasions and subsequent Manchurian domination; 1592, Japanese invasion defeated by Choson and Ming forces; 1637, tributary of the Manchus; 18th century, cultural renaissance and Korea became isolated as the "hermit kingdom"; 1905, Russia was defeated by Japan and Korea was colonized by Japan; 1910, Korea annexed by Japan; 1930s, industrialization of northern Korea by Japan; 1945, Japan defeated; Soviet armies entered but halted north of the 38th parallel (US forces to the south); 1948, Rhee installed by the US in the South; the Communist regime under Kim Il Sung in the North; 1948, Soviet forces withdrew but US forces remained; 1950-1953, Korean War – US driven to Pusan, US counter-attack, Chinese entry, MacArthur sacked by Truman over China policy; final armistice with 1 million dead and "nothing left standing" (Korean 1950-1953 excess mortality 1.0 million; 28% of the North Korean population was killed by US bombing, and no buildings were left standing).

North Korea: communist dictatorship under Kim Il Sung and thence his son Kim Jong-il; cult of personality; 1990s-present, catastrophic famine and shortages; 2004-2005, threat of North Korea nuclear weapons and missiles.

2021 update: 2011, Kim Jong-il died and was succeeded by his youngest son Kim Jong–un. Crippling US and US Alliance Sanctions in response to nuclear testing and missile testing notwithstanding person-to-person diplomatic breakthroughs with the US and South Korea. 2020 onwards, Covid-19 pandemic with "Covid-19 deaths per million of population" not known. Revised greenhouse gas (GHG) pollution 12.1 tonnes CO_2-e per person per year. North Korea has 30-40 nuclear weapons and has not signed or ratified the TPNW. In 2020 the "under-5 infant mortality as a percentage of total population" (0.0226%) was 15.8 times greater than for Japan (0.00145%), but 4.0 times lower than that in 2003 (0.0900%).

Foreign occupation: Japan, USSR (pre-1950); US (post-1950); *post-1950 foreign military presence:* China, US; *1950-2005 excess mortality/2005 population* = 2.945m/22.876m = 12.9%; *1950-2005 under-5 infant mortality/2005 population* = 1.559m/22.876m = 6.8%. Per capita GDP (nominal) $640.

South Korea: 1948-1961, US-backed Rhee regime; 1958, National Security Laws and repression; 1961, General Park coup; 1963, Park won election and thence 3 further rigged elections; 1979, Park assassinated; martial law; opposition leader Kim Jae Dung arrested; Kwanju uprising put down with massacres; repression under Chun; 1987, strikes for unions and democracy; Roh succeeded Chun; 1987, opposition split in elections and conservatives retained power; 1988, Seoul Olympic Games; 1990s, renewed government action over trade unions; continued economic growth; moves to rapprochement with the North; 1992, Kim elected; first civilian president since the Korean War; 1996, trials of people involved in the 1979 coup and subsequent massacre; 21st century, issues of reunification, North Korean famine and North Korean nuclear and missile program.

2021 update: continuing major industrial economy; welcome diplomatic advances with North Korea notwithstanding continuing North Korean nuclear and long-range missile tests. 2020 onwards, Covid-19 pandemic with "Covid-19 deaths per million of population" of 33 as compared to 3 for China, 0.4 for Taiwan,

1,687 for the US and 1,857 for the UK (March 2021). Revised greenhouse gas (GHG) pollution 12.7 tonnes CO_2-e per person per year. South Korea agrees to a US "nuclear umbrella" and opposes the TPNW. In 2020 the "under-5 infant mortality as a percentage of total population" (0.0018%) was 1.3 times greater than for Japan (0.00145%), but 2.8 times lower than that in 2003 (0.0050%).

Foreign occupation: Japan, US (pre-1950); US (post-1950); *post-1950 foreign military presence:* US; *1950-2005 excess mortality/2005 population* = 5.013m/48.182m = 10.4%; *1950-2005 under-5 infant mortality/2005 population* = 3.085m/48.182m = 6.4%. Per capita GDP (nominal) $32,143.

Mongolia: the Mongolian steppes were originally inhabited over 2 millennia by nomadic horsemen including the Hsiung-nu (Huns), Orkhun Turks, Mongol Jou-jans and Uighurs (impelling construction of the Great Wall of China); 13th century, Mongols under Genghis Khan conquered northern China and Central Asia; 1277, Genghis Khan died; his sons extended Mongol rule over Russia through to Eastern Europe, over northern China and over Central Asia through to Iran and Iraq (accompanied by horrendous genocide and urban destruction; 40-60 million people killed); 1260, Kublai Khan established Yuan dynasty in Beijing (Venetian trader Marco Polo visited); 1368, end of Yuan dynasty; 1691-1911, Manchu Chinese control; 1911, Mongol princes took over; 1918-1921, during the Russian Civil war the Chinese annexed Outer Mongolia; 1921, White Russians expelled the Chinese but were thence removed by the Soviet Red Army; 1924, Soviet rapprochement with China but *de facto* Soviet-dominated, Communist Mongolian People's Republic; 1932, Lama Rebellion, priests led refugees into Inner Mongolia; 1936, mutual aid pact with the USSR; 1945, war in Manchuria against Japan at the end of WW2; plebiscite for continued independence; 1961, joined the UN; 1992, democratic constitution followed by non-Communist victory and transition to a market economy; 1996, huge forest fires; 1997, Communist electoral victories; 21st century, an impoverished and isolated country.

2021 update: 2020 onwards, Covid-19 pandemic with "Covid-19 deaths per million of population" of 2 as compared to 3 for China, 0.4 for Taiwan, 1,687 for the US and 1,857 for the UK (March 2021). Livestock and revised greenhouse gas (GHG) pollution 32.2 tonnes CO_2-e per person per year. Mongolia has not signed or ratified the TPNW. In 2020 the "under-5 infant mortality as a percentage of total population" (0.0451%) was 31.6 times greater than for Japan (0.00145%), but 4.5 times lower than that in 2003 (0.2040%).

Foreign occupation: China, Russia (pre-1950); none (post-1950); *post-1950 foreign military presence:* none; *1950-2005 excess mortality/2005 population* = 0.640m/2.667m = 24.0%; *1950-2005 under-5 infant mortality/2005 population* = 0.402m/2.667m = 15.0%. Per capita GDP (nominal) $4,295.

2020 statistical update for East Asia: Table 9.6 summarizes population, under-5 infant mortality (IM) and excess mortality (EM; avoidable mortality from deprivation) in East Asia in 2020 (pre-Covid-19 projection in 2019 for 2020 by the UN Population Division). Table 9.1 compares East Asia with other global regions. Presented in square brackets for each country is the "Relative EM Score" of EM/Pop (%) divided by that for the best-performing country, Japan (0.0020%), which accordingly has a "Relative EM Score" of 1.0.

In terms of "Relative EM Score" and "per capita GDP" the best performing countries have outcomes ranging from Japan (1.0 and $40,063) to Taiwan (2.7 and $26,910). China (8.7 and $10,000) performs very well as a top Developing Country. Mongolia (31.6 and $4,295) has the poorest outcome. While the average "Relative EM Score" is 2.2 for Western Europe and 7.9 for East Asia it is a shocking 176.6 for non-Arab Africa (Table 9.1). "Under-5 infant mortality as a percentage of total population" in 2020 had decreased 1.1-4.6-fold from that in 2003.

6.3 Turkey, Iran and Central Asia - Russian occupation, US interference, war and peace

Central Asia has been a major conduit for the East-West movement of peoples, armies, disease (notably the bubonic plague) and trade (notably the Great Silk Road from China to Europe). Access to oil-rich Middle East regions, India and the Indian Ocean dominated the "Great Game" involving Russia, Turkey, Persia (Iran) and Britain in the 19th and 20th centuries - and now crucially involves the US, China and Pakistan as well as the independent Central Asian republics. Conflicting Big Power interests and geographical remoteness protected these countries to some extent but post-war global extension of US military violence has had a major impact on this region.

Westernized Iran has suffered significantly from Russian, British and US imposts (notably from US overthrow of democracy and installation of the pro-US Shah, post-Shah sustained US hostility, the US-supplied Iran-Iraq War that killed 1.5 million, and deadly US sanctions), and Afghanistan has endured about 40 years of US subversion, Russian invasion, US-backed resistance and civil war, and now the continuing US occupation and war. These harsh realities are reflected in "1950-2005 excess mortality/2005 population percentages" of 20.2% and 64.0% for Iran and Afghanistan, respectively; with the exception of oil-rich Azerbaijan (5.0%) and partly Russified Kazakhstan (6.4%), this parameter is in the range 13.3-19.7% for the remaining countries (cf the Central American countries of El Salvador, Nicaragua and Guatemala subject to sustained US-backed terrorism and with 1950-2005 excess mortality/2005 population "scores" in the range 11.3-21.2%)

Afghanistan: prehistoric cultures; *ca* 500BCE, conquered by Persian Darius I; 329-327BCE, conquered by Alexander the Great; 4th century BCE, Seleucid empire; 2nd century BCE, northern Bactria conquered by the Parthians; Buddhism introduced by the Kushan dynasty based at Peshawar; 3rd century CE, successive, Sassanid, Ephthalite and Turkish rule; 7th century, Muslim conversion; 11th century, Mahmud of Ghazna ruled from Khorasan

(Iran) to the Punjab (India); 13th century, Mongol conquest under Genghis Khan; 14th century, conquest by Timur; 16th century, Babur ruled from Kabul and conquered Northern India, establishing the Mughal Empire; 18th century, the Persian ruler Nadir Shah conquered much of northern Afghanistan; 1747, Ahmed Shah unified Afghanistan and established the Durrani dynasty (1747-1818); 1760, Hindu Marathas were defeated at the immense Battle of Panipot by the Muslim-Afghan confederacy under Ahmed Shah (who thence returned to Kabul); 19th -20th century, British, Russian and Persian conflict with Afghans; 1826-1863, Dost Muhammed; 1838-1842, First Afghan War, British unsuccessfully deposed Dost Muhammed; 1857, alliance with British; 1863, Sher Ali succeeded but fell out with the British; 1878-1879, Second Afghan War; Khyber Pass ceded; British occupied Kabul; British agreements with Russia and Persia over Afghanistan; 1907, Anglo-Russian Agreement; British control of Afghan foreign affairs; WW1, neutral; 1919, Third Afghan War, Afghanistan invaded India; Afghanistan recovered control of foreign affairs; WW2, neutral; 1973, military coup; enlightened republic; 1978, coup installed a communist government; communist leader Taraki killed and US-backed Amin installed; USSR invaded; 1979-1989, Afghanistan War, Russians versus US-backed mujaheddin; 50,000 Russians died and millions of Afghans (1979-1989 Afghanistan excess mortality 2.9 million); 1992, Kabul captured; 1994-1999, Pashtun Islamic fundamentalist religious student militia, the Taliban, conquered all but the Northerm Alliance areas, notably those held by Massoud; 1996, Kabul captured by the Taliban; 1997, Taliban banned smoking by civil servants and soldiers (the further deadly evils of alcohol and illicit drugs were of course banned as un-Islamic) ; 1998, US cruise missile attacks over Afghan refusal to hand over Al Qaeda leader Osama bin Laden (accused of the 1998 Kenya and Tanzania US embassy bombings); 1999, UN-brokered peace between the Taliban and Massoud; 1 million dead, 3 million refugees (1989-1999 excess mortality 3.3 million); 2000, Taliban banned opium poppy growing (a major financial source for Afghan farmers); 2001, 94% reduction in opium production in Afghanistan; September 11, World Trade Centre attacks; October, US invasion after massive bombing (although no Afghans were implicated in the atrocity by the US "official version of 9/11"); 2002, Taliban largely defeated; Kabul area protected by NATO forces; most of country reverted to war lords; opium poppy production back to "normal" by mid-2002 (76% of world opium production); 2005, Taliban resurgence; continuing war; still 3 million Afghan refugees despite 2.4 million repatriated; opium production nearly 90% of the world total (2001-2005 Afghanistan excess mortality 1.7 million; 2001-2005, global opioid drug deaths about 0.4 million).

2021 update: 2011, Osama bin Laden allegedly killed by the US and the body rapidly disposed of at sea; 2015, former US-installed President Karzai denies Al Qaeda present in Afghanistan and declines to endorse the "official US version of 9/11" (the excuses used by the US for invasion); 2020, substantial reductions in US military; 2020 onwards, Covid-19 pandemic with "Covid-19 deaths per million of population" of 62 as compared to 3 for China and 0.4 for Taiwan (March 2021). Revised greenhouse gas (GHG) pollution 3.6 tonnes CO_2-e per person per year. Occupied Afghanistan has not signed or ratified the TPNW. In 2020 the "under-5 infant mortality as a percentage of total population" (0.1950%) was a shocking 118.5 times greater than for Japan (0.00145%) (evidence of gross violation of the Fourth Geneva Convention by the occupying US Alliance countries), but 6.2 times lower than that in 2003 (1.2180%).

Foreign occupation: Britain (pre-1950); Russia, US (post-1950); *post-1950 foreign military presence:* Russia, US, Australia, UK and Canadian, German and other NATO forces; *1950-2005 excess mortality/2005 population* = 16.609m/25.971m = 64.0%; *1950-2005 infant mortality/2005 population* = 11.514m/25.971m = 44.3%. Per capita GDP (nominal) a deadly $470.

Azerbaijan: ancient Albania (Arran); 4th century, conquered by Shapur II (the Great) of Persia; 7th century, conversion to Islam; 13th century, invaded by the Mongols; 15th century, splintered after the reign of Timur; 19th century, Russian acquisition through war and Treaties of Gulistan (1813) and Turkamanchai (1828). 1917, anti-Bolshevik Transcaucasian Federation with Georgia and Armenia; 1920, re-conquest by the Soviet forces; 1936, separate republic within the USSR; post-war, communist base for independence for Azeris in Iran; 1991, independent from Russia and joined the CIS; 1992, Elchibey elected president; 1992-2003, Communist Heydar Aliyev successively re-elected as leader in flawed elections; 1992-1994, Armenian inhabitants took over much of the Nagorno-Karabakh region; 1 million Azeris were refugees from the consequent conflict; 2003, Heydar's son Iham Aliyev elected; continuing tensions with Armenia (Azeri rights), Russia (security) and Iran (oil rights and Azeri Islamic groups within Azerbaijan).

2021 update: 2020, renewed conflict with Armenia surrendering some territory in the disputed Nagorno-Karabakh region; democracy but increasing repression; 2020 onwards, Covid-19 pandemic with "Covid-19 deaths per million of population" of 338 as compared to 0.4 for Taiwan (March 2021). Oil rich; revised greenhouse gas (GHG) pollution 16.4 tonnes CO_2-e per person per year. Has not signed or ratified the TPNW. In 2020 the "under-5 infant mortality as a percentage of total population" (0.0372%) was 26.0 times greater than for Japan (0.00145%), but 5.0 times lower than that in 2003 (0.1870%).

Foreign occupation: Russia (pre-1950); Russia, Armenia (post-1950); *post-1950 foreign military presence:* Russia, Armenia; *1950-2005 excess mortality/2005 population* = 0.428m/8.527m = 5.0%; *1950-2005 under-5 infant mortality/2005 population* = 1.032m/8.527m = 12.1%. Per capita GDP (nominal) $4,782.

Iran: 4000BCE, early settlements; 1800-800BCE, occupied by the Aryan Medes and Persians; *circa* 1500BCE, Zarathushtra (Zoroaster) and Zoroastrianism; 6th century BCE, Cyrus the Great conquered the Medes; 525BCE, Persian Empire from the Nile to the Indus; 331-330BCE, conquered by Alexander the Great; 312-302BCE Seleucid rule; 247BCE-226CE, rule by Greek-speaking Parthians; 3rd-7th century, Sassanian rule; 641, Arab Muslim conquest; 7th-13th century, major cultural centre; 1258, destructive conquest by Mongols under Genghis Khan and his sons; subsequent rule by their successors e.g. Timur; 1501-1722, Safavid dynasty founded by Shah Ismail; Shi'ite dominance; 1587-1629, Shah Abbas; Portuguese defeated in the Persian Gulf; 1722,

Russians seized Georgia, Baku and thence Central Asia; Afghan
dominance; 1736, Afshar dynasty under Nadir Shah; 1794-1925,
Qajar dynasty; Anglo-Russian "Great Game" over influence;
Russian acquisition of Iranian Caucasus territories through war and
the Treaties of Gulistan (1813) and Turkamanchai (1828); early
19th century, oil discovered; 1906, constitution and parliament;
WW1, Iran neutral but Anglo-Russian involvements; 1917-1919,
WW1-related Iranian Famine, 2-10 million deaths; 1921, USSR
withdrew forces and recognized Iran sovereignty; coup by Reza
Khan; 1925-1941, Reza Shah Pahlevi (Reza Khan), modernization,
pro-Axis; 1941, Anglo-Russian occupation; installation of Shah's
son; 1941-1979, Mohammed Shah Pahlevi; 1946, withdrawal of
USSR forces; 1949, constitution curtailed Shah; Prime Minister
Mossadegh attempted nationalization of Anglo-Iranian oil; 1953,
economic blockade and UK MI6- and US CIA-backed coup,
thousands killed (the CIA secretly invoked Queen Elizabeth II to
stop a nervous and ambivalent Shah from quitting before the
foreign-instigated coup); US-backed authoritarian Shah régime;
Anglo-American, French and Dutch oil interests dominant; 1978,
martial law against Islamist opponents; 1979, Shah fled; Islamic
theocracy under Ayatollah Khomeini; US hostage crisis and
unsuccessful US military raid; 1980-1988, Iran-Iraq War initiated
by US-backed Iraq invasion and employing war gas; 1.5 million
dead (1980-1988 excess mortality 2.1 million); 1981, US hostages
released, Irangate Contra arms deal scandal; 1989, Ayatollah
Khomeini died and Ayatollah Khamenei succeeded; 1997,
moderate Khatami elected president; 21st century, US hostility and
threats over Iran nuclear program and hostility to Apartheid Israel;
2004, conservative victory in elections.

2021 update: 2005-2013, articulate engineer Mahmoud
Ahmadinejad president; 2012 onwards, support for Syria and Iraq
against Islamic State in Iraq and Syria (ISIS); 2015, the Iran
nuclear agreement, the Joint Comprehensive Plan of Action
(JCPOA), adopted by Iran and major states; 2018, fervently pro-
Zionist Trump US withdrew and re-imposed crippling sanctions;
2020, Qasem Soleimani (Iranian hero and head of the Islamic
Revolutionary Guard Corps (IRGC) Quds Force, 1998-2020)
assassinated at Baghdad Airport by US drone strike ordered by

Trump. US and Apartheid Israel routinely bombing Iranian forces in Syria and Iraq. Ukrainian airliner accidentally downed by nervous Iranian air defense fearing a US attack. 2021, Zionist-subverted Biden US (30% of his cabinet are Jewish Zionists, the remainder being Christian Zionists) negotiating to rejoin the JCPOA; 2020 onwards, Covid-19 pandemic with "Covid-19 deaths per million of population" of 734 as compared to 0.4 for Taiwan (March 2021). Oil exploitation and revised greenhouse gas (GHG) pollution 14.5 tonnes CO_2-e per person per year. Iran does not have or seek nuclear weapons, and voted for the TPNW but has not signed or ratified the TPNW. Iran leads the world in interdiction of opiate drugs (from US-occupied Afghanistan); 600,000 people die globally each year from illicit drugs (mostly opiates and opioids). In 2020 the "under-5 infant mortality as a percentage of total population" (0.0239%) was 16.8 times greater than for Japan (0.00145%), but 3.3 times lower than that in 2003 (0.0790%).

Foreign occupation: UK, USSR (pre-1950); none (post-1950); *post-1950 foreign military presence:* US, Iraq (incursions); *1950-2005 excess mortality/2005 population* = 14.272m/70.675m = 20.2%; *1950-2005 under-5 infant mortality/2005 population* = 10.875m/70.675m = 15.4%. Per capita GDP (nominal) $7,282.

Kazakhstan: nomadic Turkic peoples; 13th century, conquered by Mongols under Genghis Khan; subsequent rule by various khanates; 1730-1840, Russian conquest; 1916, rebellion against Russian rule; 1917, Russian revolution; 1920, Red Army control; 1936, constituent republic of the Soviet Union; major collectivisation, resettlement in the South, agricultural development and oil; 1991, independence and membership of the CIS under Nazarbayev; flawed democracy and repeated re-election of Nazarbayev; 2003, economic agreement between Belarus, Kazakhstan, Russia and the Ukraine.

2021 update: Nazarbayev resigned and succeeded by Tokayev in elections. Population 68% Kazakh, 20% Russian; secular democracy and one of the more progressive Muslim majority nations. 2020 onwards, Covid-19 pandemic with "Covid-19 deaths per million of population" of 156 as compared to 0.4 for Taiwan

(March 2021). Revised greenhouse gas (GHG) pollution 15.4 tonnes CO_2-e per person per year. 1949-1989, 456 Soviet nuclear tests (116 atmospheric tests) at the Semipalatinsk test site; 1991, Kazakhstan relinquished 1,400 Soviet nuclear warheads. Kazakhstan has signed and ratified the TPNW. In 2020 the "under-5 infant mortality as a percentage of total population" (0.0159%) was 11.2 times greater than for Japan (0.00145%), but 7.9 times lower than that in 2003 (0.1250%).

Foreign occupation: Russia (pre-1950); Russia (post-1950); *post-1950 foreign military presence:* Russia; *1950-2005 excess mortality/2005 population* = 0.983m/15.364m = 6.4%; *1950-2005 under-5 infant mortality/2005 population* = 1.661m/15.364m = 10.8%. Per capita GDP (nominal) $9,793.

Kyrgyzstan: 7th-17th century, nomadic Kyrgyz (Kara Kyrgyz) roamed upper Yenisei region and thence came to the present Kyrgyzstan region; 8th century, Muslim conversion; 9th century, rule by Kokand khanate; 1855-1876, annexation by Russia; 1916, opposed conscription and suffered consequent violent suppression; 1917-1921, opposed communists; 1921-1922, war and famine, 0.5 million died and many fled to China; 1926, autonomous republic of Russian Republic; 1936, constituent republic of the USSR; 1926-1959, major Russian and Ukrainian migration; 1990, non-communist Akayev made president; 1991, coup suppressed and independence from Soviet Union declared; Kyrgyzstan membership of the post-USSR CIS; post-independence economic, security, insurrection and political corruption problems.

2021 update: 1991-2005, Akayev president but was deposed in the "Tulip Revolution"; 2005-2010, Bakiyev president but resigned after deadly protests with allegations of Russian instigation; 2010-2011, Roza Otunbayeva, female president; continuing disturbances relating to politics and the Uzbek minority; 2020 onwards, Covid-19 pandemic with "Covid-19 deaths per million of population" of 226 as compared 0.4 for Taiwan (March 2010). Revised greenhouse gas (GHG) pollution 3.4 tonnes CO_2-e per person per year. Kyrgyzstan has not signed or ratified the TPNW. In 2020 the "under-5 infant mortality as a percentage of total population"

(0.0394%) was 27.6 times greater than for Japan (0.00145%), but 3.3 times lower than that in 2003 (0.1310%).

Foreign occupation: Russia (pre-1950); Russia (post-1950); *post-1950 foreign military presence:* Russia; *1950-2005 excess mortality/2005 population* = 1.041m/5.278m = 19.7%; *1950-2005 under-5 infant mortality/2005 population* = 0.657m/5.278m = 12.4%. Per capita GDP (nominal) $1,318.

Tajikistan: ancient Sogdiana; 7th century, Muslim conversion; 13th century, Mongol invasion; 16th century, ruled by the Bokhara khanate; 1880s, extension of Russian control; 1917, Tajik independence ; 1921, defeated by Soviet Russia; 1924, autonomous republic within Uzbekhistan; 1929, constituent republic of the Soviet Union; Soviet period, major expansion of irrigation and cotton; 1978, anti-Russian riots; 1990, independence declared;1991, part of the CIS; former Communist boss Nabiyev president; 1992, armed deposition of Nabiyev; government recapture of the capital; pro-Russian Rahmon (born Emomali Rakhmonov) elected president; 1992-1997, civil war between Russian-backed government and Afghanistan-based Islamic opposition; 30,000-100,000 died and massive destruction (1992-1997 excess mortality 0.9 million); 400,000 Russians left; 1994, elections boycotted by the opposition; Russian-backed Rahmon elected; 1996, short-lived Uzbek revolt; 1997, peace accord permitting Islamic political participation; 2005, flawed elections returned the government.

2021 update: 2006, presidential election boycotted by opposition and Islamists; Rahmon returned; 2019, UN Ambassadors of Tajikistan and 36 other countries signed a letter defending Chinese treatment of Uighurs in Xinjiang; restrictions on press reportage. 2020 onwards, Covid-19 pandemic with "Covid-19 deaths per million of population" of 9 as compared to 3 for China, 0.4 for Taiwan (March 2010). Revised greenhouse gas (GHG) pollution 3.7 tonnes CO_2-e per person per year. Tajikistan has not signed or ratified the TPNW. In 2020 the "under-5 infant mortality as a percentage of total population" (0.0858%) was 60.1 times greater

than for Japan (0.00145%), but 2.1 times lower than that in 2003 (0.1760%).

Foreign occupation: Russia (pre-1950); Russia (post-1950); *post-1950 foreign military presence:* Russia; *1950-2005 excess mortality/2005 population* = 0.924m/6.356m = 14.5%; *1950-2005 under-5 infant mortality/2005 population* = 0.739m/6.356m = 11.6%. Per capita GDP (nominal) $894.

Turkey: from 1800BCE, Hittite Empire in Anatolia (Asia Minor), cities, armies, trade and writing; from 8th century BCE, coastal Greek settlements; ancient Anatolian kingdoms of Phrygia, Lydia and Troy; the sacking of Troy by the Greeks recorded in Homer's *Iliad*; 6th century BCE, Persian conquest; 4th century BCE, conquest by Alexander the Great followed by administrative splintering; 2nd century BCE, Roman conquest; 1st century CE, Christian conversion starting with Saint Paul; 395, Western and Eastern Roman Empires divided and thence Anatolia and Balkans part of Byzantine Empire; 616-626, Persian invasion; 668, Muslim Arab invasion and conversion; 1061, Seljuk Turk invasion; 1243, Mongol invasion; 14th-15th century, Ottoman Turk expansion into Byzantine Empire lands of Anatolia and the Balkans; 14th century-20th century, Ottoman Turkish Empire; 1326, capture of Bursa; 1361, Adrianople (Edirne) captured; 1389, Battle of Kosovo; 1396, Battle of Nikopol; 1402, Turks defeated by Timur at Beyazid; 1444, victory at Varna over Poles; 1451-1481, Muhammed II established Ottoman Turk superiority; 1453, capture of Constantinople (Istanbul); Mameluks defeated in Egypt and Syria and Cairo captured (1517); Algiers captured (1518); Suleyman the Magnificent (1520-1566), administration, diplomacy, culture, janissary army, much-feared Mediterranean navy under Barbarossa; successive Ottoman victories over Hungarians at Mohács (1536) and Buda (1541); 1571, Turks defeated by the Venetians at the naval Battle of Lepanto; 1683, siege of Vienna relieved by Poles; 1699, Treaty of Karlowitz, Hungary lost; 18th century, Russo-Turkish wars, Napoleon transiently took Egypt; 19th century, "Sick Man of Europe", progressive loss of Greece, Egypt, Moldavia and Wallachia (Romania), Serbia and Montenegro; Allied with Britain against Russia in the Crimean War

(1854-1856); late 19th century, massacres of Armenians; 1908, rise of the Young Turks; Balkans Wars, loss of most remaining European territory to Bulgaria, Serbia, Albania and Greece; WW1, pressure by the British forced alliance with Germany; 1915, Gallipoli invasion repulsed; 1915-1919, Armenian Genocide (1.5 million murdered or killed by savage deportations); Arabs revolted and Arab possessions lost; 1922, Sultan overthrown; 1923, secular republic under Mustafa Kemal Ataturk; Treaty of Sèvres defined modern boundaries; 1.5 million Greeks to Greece, 0.8 million Turks from Greece and Bulgaria to Turkey; genocidal persecution of Greeks, Kurds and Syriac Christians (Assyrians); WW2, neutral; post-war, US bases and nuclear missile bases in Turkey; tensions with Greece over Cyprus; Kurdish autonomy and human rights demands; left-right political dichotomy and violence; from 1970s, horrendous violence and abuses associated with Kurdish separatism (30,000 deaths) and maltreatment of Syriac Christians; 1974, invasion and occupation of part of Cyprus; 1984 onwards, violent actions against Kurds and US Alliance-backed designation of the Kurdish PKK as "terrorists"; 1989, 0.3 million Bulgarian Turkish refugees fled to Turkey to escape Bulgarization; 1991, US bases used in the Gulf War; 2003, parliament refused US use of its Turkish bases to attack Iraq; 1999 PKK founder Abdullah Öcalan was arrested and sentenced for terrorism and treason; 2003-2014, Recep Tayyip Erdogan prime minister and president from 2014 onwards; 2005, continued negotiations with the EU still clouded by objections to Turkish human rights abuses.

2021 update: 2012 onwards, Turkey joined US Alliance against ISIS and against the anti-ISIS Syrian Government; Turkey permitted ISIS oil sales to EU and Apartheid Israel; 2013, widespread protests over plan to demolish Gezi Park; 2016, unsuccessful coup attempt tried to oust the government, this being followed by extensive purges of Erdogan opponents and Kurds; Erdogan blamed US-located Fethullah Gülen and his supporters; 2019, Turkey occupied part of northern Syria and attacked Kurds in Syria and Iraq; Libyan involvement; increasing departure from the post-WW1 secular state; 2020 onwards, Covid-19 pandemic with "Covid-19 deaths per million of population" of 362 as compared to 0.4 for Taiwan (March 2021). Revised greenhouse gas (GHG) pollution 9.2 tonnes CO_2-e per person per year. Turkey is a member of nuclear-armed NATO, hosts 50 nuclear weapons, endorses nuclear weapons and opposes and rejects the TPNW. In 2020 the "under-5 infant mortality as a percentage of total population" (0.0187%) was 13.1 times greater than for Japan (0.00145%), but 4.5 times lower than that in 2003 (0.0840%). Per capita GDP (nominal) $9,127.

Foreign occupation: none (pre-1950); none (post-1950); *post-1950 foreign military presence:* US; *1950-2005 excess mortality/2005 population* = 10.488m/73.302m = 14.3%; *1950-2005 under-5 infant mortality/2005 population* = 10.987m/73.302m = 15.0%. Per capita GDP (nominal) $9,127.

Turkmenistan: northern part of ancient Persia; 8th century, Arab conquest and Muslim conversion; 11th century, Seljuk Turks; 13th century, conquered by Mongols under Genghis Khan; 14th -15th century, conquest and rule by Timur and his successors; 16th-17th century, ruled by Uzbeks; early 19th century, Khiva khanate; 1869-1881, Russian conquest; subsequent periodic revolts; 1919-1920, conquest by Red Army; 1925, constituent Soviet republic; Turkmen populations in Iraq, Iran and Afghanistan; 1991, independence from Russia and joined the CIS under Niyazov; 1990s and 2000s, continuing rule by Niyazov, suppression of opposition and associated cult of personality.

2021 update: 2006, death of Niyazov, succeeded by Gurbanguly Berdimuhamedow who was re-elected in subsequent elections (an implausible 97% support in 2012); 2020 onwards, Covid-19 pandemic with "Covid-19 deaths per million of population" unknown as of March 2021 (Turkmenistan insists that there are no cases). Revised greenhouse gas (GHG) pollution 23.5 tonnes CO_2-e per person per year; exploitation of massive gas reserves. Turkmenistan has not signed or ratified the TPNW. In 2020 the "under-5 infant mortality as a percentage of total population" (0.1098%) was 76.9 times greater than for Japan (0.00145%), but 2.0 times lower than that in 2003 (0.2200%).

Foreign occupation: Mongols, Uzbeks, Russia (pre-1950); Russia (post-1950); *post-1950 foreign military presence:* none; *1950-2005 excess mortality/2005 population* = 0.817m/5.015m = 16.3%; *1950-2005 under-5 infant mortality/2005 population =* 0.591m/5.015m = 11.8%. Per capita GDP (nominal) $8,124.

Uzbekistan: ancient Persian Sogdiana; 4th century BCE, conquered by Alexander; 6th century, Turkic nomad entry; 8th century, Arab conquest and conversion to Islam; 12th century, ruled by Seljuk Turks; 13th century, conquered by Mongols under Genghis Khan; 14th-15th century, ruled from Samarkand by Timur and his successors; great era of the fabled cities of Tashkent, Samarkand and Bukhara; 16th century, Uzbek invasion followed by the split of an extensive Uzbek empire into the Khiva, Kokand and Bukhara khanates; 19th century, Russian invasion; 1924, Uzbek republic; 1929; separate Tajikistan republic; 1991, Uzbekistan independent but member of the CIS under Karimov; controls on devout Muslims, human rights abuses, guerrillas and terrorism; 2001, US bases for Afghanistan campaign; 2005, Andijan massacre of 700 demonstrators and international disapproval; Uzbekistan asked US to leave bases.

2021 update: 2016, death of Islam Karimov, succeeded by Shavkat Mirziyoyev; huge cotton production (the Aral Sea has almost disappeared) and huge gas exploitation. Revised greenhouse gas (GHG) pollution 17.5 tonnes CO_2-e per person per year. 2020 onwards, Covid-19 pandemic with "Covid-19 deaths per million of population" of 18 as compared to 0.4 for Taiwan (March 2019). Uzbekistan has not signed or ratified the TPNW. In 2020 the "under-5 infant mortality as a percentage of total population" (0.0495%) was 34.7 times greater than for Japan (0.00145%), but 3.0 times lower than that in 2003 (0.1480%).

Foreign occupation: Mongols, Russia (pre-1950); Russia (post-1950); *post-1950 foreign military presence:* Russia, US; *1950-2005 excess mortality/2005 population* = 3.585m/26.868m = 13.3%; *1950-2005 under-5 infant mortality/2005 population =* 2.403m/26.868m = 8.9%. Per capita GDP (nominal) $1,756.

2020 statistical update for Turkey, Iran and Central Asia:
Table 9.7 summarizes population, under-5 infant mortality (IM) and excess mortality (EM; avoidable mortality from deprivation) in Central Asia, Turkey and Iran in 2020 (pre-Covid-19 projection in 2019 for 2020 by the UN Population Division). Table 9.1 compares Central Asia, Turkey and Iran with other global regions. Presented in square brackets for each country is the "Relative EM Score" of EM/Pop (%) divided by that for the best-performing country, Japan (0.0020%), which accordingly has a "Relative EM Score" of 1.0.

In terms of "Relative EM Score" and "per capita GDP" the best performing countries are Kazakhstan (11.2 and $9,793, Turkey (13.1 and $9,127) and Iran (16.8 and $7,282). The standout bad outcome is US-occupied Afghanistan (118.5 and $470), this being striking evidence of gross violation of the Fourth Geneva Convention by the war criminal occupying US Alliance (the US, NATO and Australia). The other outcomes range from Azerbaijan (26.0 and $4,782) to Turkmenistan (76.9 and $8,124). While the average "Relative EM Score" is 2.2 for Western Europe it is 36.6 for Central Asia, Turkey and Iran, and a shocking 176.6 for non-Arab Africa (Table 9.1). The "under-5 infant mortality as a percentage of total population" in 2020 for countries in this group had decreased from that in 2003 by a factor of 2.0-7.9.

6.4 Arab North Africa and Middle East – Anglo-American, French and Israeli war and occupation

This general region yielded the earliest civilizations of Egypt, Phoenicia and Sumeria (the Fertile Crescent). The Phoenician civilization spread to Carthage in North Africa and thence to Spain. After the Roman Empire era, Arab conquest led to a new cultural flowering from Mesopotamia, through Egypt and thence to Spain. Invasions of Syria and Palestine by European crusaders occurred in the 11th-13th centuries. In the 13th and 14th centuries the Mongols and their Timurid successors devastated Mesopotamia and Syria, their incursions reaching as far as Egypt. After the expulsion of the Moors and Jews from Spain and Ottoman Turkish conquest of much of the Arab North Africa and the Middle East, this region was relatively subdued in international affairs. European colonialism in the 19th and 20th centuries was ultimately unsuccessful with European powers variously departing in the post-WW2 era. Arab hopes for independence were temporarily dashed through British and French duplicity after WW1 and the West led by the US continues to exert a deadly and malignant influence on the region.

Jewish Zionist colonization of Palestine has remorselessly continued, backed by the US and its allies. The economic and human cost of sophisticated, democratic and nuclear-armed Apartheid Israel (current population of Israel proper, excluding the 5.2 million Occupied Palestinian Subjects, is 9.2 million) has been enormous – an estimated $3 trillion in direct economic costs to the US, 6 decades of war and occupation in the region, a 1950-2005 excess mortality in countries attacked by Israel totaling 43 million and post-invasion excess mortality and under-5 infant mortality in the Occupied Palestinian Territories now totaling 0.3 million and 0.2 million, respectively. US policy in the region has devastated Palestine, Syria, Lebanon, Iran, Yemen and Iraq, and there is a major, continuing US occupation of Iraq, continuing Israeli occupation of all of Palestine and part of Syria in defiance of repeated UN resolutions, and major US military presence in Persian Gulf States. The excess mortality and under-5 infant mortality in Iraq have totaled 1.7 million and 1.2 million, respectively for the 1990-2003 Gulf War and Sanctions Era and total 0.5 million and 0.3 million, respectively, for the post-invasion period (2003-2005) (1.2 million and 0.8 million, respectively, in the period 2003-2011). In contrast, the outstandingly good outcome countries in this group are the United Arab Emirates, Qatar, Kuwait and Bahrain with "1950-2005 excess mortality/2005 population" ratios of 1.5%, 2.1%, 2.8% and 4.4%, respectively – these countries having had peace, prosperity and good (albeit authoritarian) governance as common attributes for all or nearly all of the post-1950 era.

2021 update: The US determination for hegemony and control of oil has meant devastation of Libya, Yemen, Palestine, Lebanon, Syria, Iraq, Iran (through deadly sanctions as well as war), South Sudan, Sudan and Western Sahara. The UK and Apartheid Israel were variously involved in this anti-Arab anti-Semitic and

Islamophobic carnage. The US has found clients and allies in the rich Gulf States and recently the United Arab Emirates (UAE), Bahrain, Sudan and Morocco betrayed their fellow Arabs and Muslims by giving diplomatic recognition to anti-Arab anti-Semitic and Islamophobic Apartheid Israel (Egypt and Jordan having already been forced to do so as neighbours of this serial war criminal, genocidally racist and nuclear terrorist Apartheid rogue state).

Algeria: 2nd millennium BCE, Berber culture; 9th century BCE, Numidia under Carthaginian (Tunisia) hegemony; 146BCE, Romans destroyed Carthage; 106BCE, Romans conquered coastal Numidia; eventually Roman rule over Numidia and Mauritania Caesariensis; major food source for the Roman Empire; Christian era, spread of Christianity; 4th century, St Augustine bishop of Hippo (Annaba); 430-431, Vandal invasion; 6th century, Byzantine rule; 7th-8th century, Arab invasion, conversion to Islam and Arab culture; East and West regions under Tunisian and Moroccan influence, respectively; 1492, expulsion of Muslims and Jews from Spain; 16th century, Spanish rule over coastal areas; Turkish Barbarossa naval power liberated the Algerians from the Spanish; Ottoman Turkish rule; from 17th century, quasi-independence from Constantinople; piracy and slaves; 1816, British bombarded Algiers over piracy; 1820s, commencement of French hostilities; 1830, French invasion; 1840s, French settlement began with subsequent seizure of the best agricultural land; 1910, end of armed resistance to French rule; post-WW1, increasing indigenous activism for independence or for assimilation with France; WW2, initial Vichy rule; 1942, Algiers Allied HQ for North Africa and seat of Free French under Charles de Gaulle; 1945, uprising, 90 Europeans killed, up to 10,000 Algerians killed in the French response; 1954-1962, war of independence; 1954, National Liberation Front (FLN) formed; 1959, FLN Provisional Government at Tunis; 1962, French referendum for Algerian independence; French Secret Army Organization (OAS) terrorism; most of the 1 million colonists left; independence under Ben Khedda and thence Ben Bella; 10,000 French and 100,000 Algerian military deaths (1954-1962 excess mortality 1.2 million); 1992, rise of violent Islamic fundamentalism, terrorism, violent counter-terrorism; 2000, amnesty for Islamic guerrillas; 2001, demonstrations by Berbers over Arabic as the sole national language; the Berber language subsequently acknowledged.

2021 update: 1999-2019, successive elections of Abdelaziz Bouteflika; greatly decreased Islamist violence; 2020 onwards, Covid-19 pandemic with "Covid-19 deaths per million of population" of 69 as compared to 0.4 for Taiwan (March 2021). Algeria is a major oil and gas producer. Revised greenhouse gas (GHG) pollution 6.6 tonnes CO_2-e per person per year. 1961-1967, France conducted 17 nuclear test explosions in Algeria; Algeria has signed but not ratified the TPNW. In 2020 the "under-5 infant mortality as a percentage of total population" (0.0520%) was 36.4 times greater than for Japan (0.00145%), but 2.2 times lower than that in 2003 (0.1140%).

Foreign occupation: France, UK (pre-1950); France (post-1950); *post-1950 foreign military presence:* France; *1950-2005 excess mortality/2005 population* = 7.167m/32.877m = 21.8%; *1950-2005 under-5 infant mortality/2005 population* = 5.812m/32.877m = 17.7%. Per capita GDP (nominal) $3,976.

Bahrain: 3rd millennium BCE, major trading centre (Dilmun) between Middle East and India; Tylos to ancient Greeks; 16th century, Portuguese rule; 17th-18th century, Persian domination and rule; 1783, al-Khalifa tribe defeated Persians; 1861, British protectorate; from 1950s onwards, demonstrations against British rule; 1970, Iranian claim; 1971, independent with a national assembly; 1975, Sheikh dissolved the assembly; 1981, founding member of the Gulf Cooperation Council; member of the Arab League; from 1980s onwards, dispute with Qatar over natural gas resources; continued tensions due to Shi'ite majority but effective exclusion from government; 1991, used by US-Coalition forces; 1996, alleged Iranian-backed Shi'ite coup plot; 2001, new liberalized constitutional monarchy arrangements but flawed elections and Shi'ite boycotts.

2021 update: 2001, naval support for US in Afghanistan but opposed US war on Iraq; 2011-2013, Arab Spring-inspired protests by Bahrain's Shia majority against its Sunni ruler; Saudi military entered Bahrain; subsequent human rights abuses. Home to U.S. Naval Forces Central Command and nuclear-armed United States Fifth Fleet. 2020 onwards, Bahrain betrayed Arabs and recognized Apartheid Israel; Covid-19 pandemic with "Covid-19 deaths per million of population" of 294 as compared to 0.4 for Taiwan (March 2021). Major oil and gas producer. Revised greenhouse gas (GHG) pollution 30.5 tonnes CO_2-e per person per year. US-linked Bahrain has not signed or ratified the TPNW. In 2020 the "under-5 infant mortality as a percentage of total population" (0.0100%) was 7.0 times greater than for Japan (0.00145%), but 3.2 times lower than that in 2003 (0.0320%).

Foreign occupation: Britain (pre-1950); UK (post-1950); *post-1950 foreign military presence:* UK, US, Coalition, Saudi Arabia; *1950-2005 excess mortality/2005 population* = 0.054m/0.754m = 7.2%; *1950-2005 under-5 infant mortality/2005 population* = 0.033m/0.754m = 4.4%. Per capita GDP (nominal) $23,504.

Egypt: 3200-2134BCE, Old Kingdom, Egypt united under Menes; Khufu (ruled 2589-2566 BCE) built the Great Pyramid of Giza; 2134BCE-16th century BCE, Middle Kingdom; major civilization; 17th century BCE, brief period of Syrian Hyksos dominance; 16th century BCE-1st century CE, New Kingdom; Akhenaten ruled 1351–1334 BCE (transiently introduced monotheism); Tutankhamun ruled 1333-1323 BCE; 1274 BCE, Ramses II lost the Battle of Kadesh in Syria to the Hittites but his publicists said the reverse; successive threats from Hittites, Assyrians, Babylon and Persia; 1,000 BCE, no non-Biblical evidence for the Hebrew Exodus from Egypt celebrated in the Passover Seder of Judaism; 673-650BCE, Assyrian rule; 332BCE, conquered by Greeks under Alexander leading to Alexandria Hellenic flowering and Ptolemy I – Ptolemy XIV (Cleopatra's son); 58BCE, Roman accession; Coptic Christian advance; 616, Persian conquest; 639-642, Arab conquest, Muslim conversion and Christian decline; Umayyad, Abbasid and Fatimid caliphates; 1219-1250, limited Crusader incursions; 1250-1517, slave soldier Mamluks ruled; 1517, Ottoman Turk conquest; 1768-1773, Ali Bey; 1798-1801, French conquest under Napoleon; 1805, Muhammed Ali appointed as

Pasha by the Ottoman Sultan; massacred the Mamluk leadership, westernized, eliminated the plague; 1854, De Lesseps commenced the Suez Canal; 1882, British conquest; 1923, independence but with British retention of troops; 1948, war with Israel; 1953, Farouk monarchy abolished; 1954, Gamal Abdel Nasser came to power; major Arab and non-aligned figure; Soviet-funded arms and Aswan Dam project ; 1956, Israel, UK and France attacked Egypt while Russia was invading Hungary; 1958-1961, merger with Syria as the United Arab Republic; 1967 war with Israel; Israel attacked and occupied Gaza and Sinai; 1967-1974, diplomatic rift with US; 1970, Nasser died, replaced by Sadat; 1973, Yom Kippur War; Egypt again defeated; 1979, peace with Israel; 1981, Sadat assassinated by Muslim extremists and replaced by pro-US Mubarak; major fundamentalist Muslim and Muslim Brotherhood unrest, persecution of Coptic Christians by fanatics and political repression (especially of Muslim activists); 2005, cosmetic moves towards democracy by Mubarak.

2021 update: 2011 Arab Spring Egyptian Revolution; mass protests centred on Cairo's Tahrir Square; Mubarak fled; elections; 2012-2013, Mohamed Morsi's Muslim Brotherhood government the first democratically-elected government in Egyptian history; 2013, General El-Sisi removed the Morsi government, tens of thousands imprisoned; 2020, escalation of dispute with Ethiopia over the Grand Ethiopian Renaissance Dam on the upper Nile; 2020 onwards, Covid-19 pandemic with "Covid-19 deaths per million of population" of 113 as compared to 0.4 for Taiwan (March 2021). Revised greenhouse gas (GHG) pollution 2.6 tonnes CO_2-e per person per year. The US-backed military dictatorship has not signed or ratified the TPNW. "Under -5 infant mortality as a percentage of total population" (0.0463%) was 32.4 times greater than for Japan (0.00145%), but 2.0 times lower than that in 2003 (0.0910%).

Foreign occupation: France, Britain (pre-1950); France, Israel, UK (post-1950); *post-1950 foreign military presence:* France, UK, Israel; *1950-2005 excess mortality/2005 population =* 19.818m/74.878m = 26.5%; *1950-2005 under-5 infant mortality/2005 population* = 14.143m/74.878m = 18.9%. Per capita GDP (nominal) $3,161.

Iraq: Mesopotamia a region of earliest civilizations involved in the development of agriculture, plant breeding, writing, astronomy, philosophies and cities, namely Sumer, Chaldea, Akkad, Assyria and Babylon; 6th century BCE, Persian conquest; 4th century BCE, Greek conquest under Alexander the Great; 1st century CE, Roman occupation; major food source for Roman Empire; 2nd-6th century, Persian rule; 7th century, Arab Muslim conquest; conversion to Islam; 8th century, Abbasid caliphate at Baghdad, a great cultural centre; 13th century, Mongol invasion and devastation; 16th century, Ottoman Turk subjugation; 19th century, Turkish provinces of Mosul, Baghdad and Basra; 1914-1918, WW1, dismemberment of the Turkish Empire; British invasion in 1914; 1920, Kurdish and Arab revolts suppressed (use of the Royal Air Force, RAF); Treaty of Sèvres made Iraq a British League of Nations Mandate; 1921, Kingdom under Faisal I; 1924, Iraq Assembly reluctantly agreed to British bases and British legislative veto; 1925, first oil concession; 1926, Iraqi government; 1930, 25-year alliance with Britain; 1932, British mandate terminated; Iraq joined League of Nations; 1933, Christian Assyrian revolt suppressed; Faisal I died; 1934, oil exports began; 1941, al-Gaylani ousted pro-British regent for infant Faisal II; defeated by the British; 1943, Iraq declared war on Axis countries; 1948, British demand for extension of the 1930 alliance was rejected by the Iraqi parliament; 1948, member of the Arab League; involved in Israel-Arab war; 1955, Iran, Turkey, Pakistan and Iraq formed pro-US Baghdad Pact; 1958, Kassem military coup, Faisal II killed; mid-1950s onwards, major Kurdish demands for autonomy; 1962, Kurds seized much of northern Iraq; 1963, coup dominated by socialist, pan-Arabist Ba'ath party; 1968, coup installed Bakr, followed by purges; 1979, accession of Saddam Hussein followed by purges; extremely repressive but secular régime; 1980-1988, Iran-Iraq War; US Alliance complicit in poison gas use by Iraq against Iran; huge death toll; 1988, poison gas used on Kurdish Halabja; 1990, Iran-Iraq diplomatic relations; 1990, US greenlighted Iraq invasion of Kuwait; sanctions imposed killing 1.7 million Iraqis; deadly US, UK and Israeli bombing of Iraqi infrastructure; 1991, US-led Gulf War; 200,000 Iraqi killed; hundreds of thousands of Iraqi refugees; Kurdish *de facto* independence protected by UK-US airpower; 1991, renewed threat to Kuwait; weapons inspection; 2001, 9/11 atrocity prompted US threats (1990-2003 excess mortality and under-5 infant mortality 1.7 million and 1.2 million, respectively); 2003, after extensive UK-US propaganda build-up involving major lies about actually non-existent Iraqi "weapons of mass destruction" (WMD), Iraq was invaded by US-led Coalition (initially the US, UK and Australia) and occupied; no "weapons of mass destruction" were found; continuing Sunni and Shia resistance; Sunnis excluded from Kurdish- and Shi'ite- dominated indigenous political process; massive death toll (post-invasion excess mortality and under-5 infant mortality 0.5 million and 0.4 million, respectively, in 2003-2006, and 1.2 million and 0.8 million, respectively, in 2003-2011).

2021 update: Iraqi deaths from Western-imposed violence and deprivation 9 million (1914-2011), 4.6 million (1990-2011), 2.7 million (2003-2011); 2012, rise of the barbaric Islamic State in Iraq and Syria (ISIS; IS, ISIL, Daesh) countered by US-led Coalition that variously wanted to remove the Syrian Government and variously collaborated with Sunni ISIS through oil purchases; Fallujah (the ancient "City of Mosques") destroyed by the US for the second time; Mosul (population 2 million) substantially destroyed with 40,000 inhabitants killed by US and allied bombing; Shia Iran supportive of largely Shia Iraq; 2020 onwards; continued US and Israeli bombing of Iraq-supporting Iranian forces in Iraq and Syria; 2020, US killed Iranian General Qassem Soleimani and Iranian and Iraqi associates at Baghdad Airport; US, UK, Germany and Australia rejected the demand from the Iraqi Parliament that they leave with Trump threatening to seize Iraqi banked assets and destroy the Iraqi economy; mass protests over economics and politics with many demonstrators killed. 2020 onwards, Covid-19 pandemic with "Covid-19 deaths per million of population" of 346 as compared to 0.4 for Taiwan (March 2021). Oil rich (the reason for repeated Western invasions and occupations from 1914 onwards). Revised greenhouse gas (GHG) pollution 5.5 tonnes CO_2-e per person per year. Still US-occupied, Iraq has not signed or ratified the TPNW. In 2020 the "under-5 infant mortality as a percentage of total population" (0.0747%) was 52.3 times greater than for Japan (0.00145%), but 6.2 times lower than that in 2003 (0.4600%).

Foreign occupation: Turkey, Britain (pre-1950); UK, US, Coalition countries (post-1950); *post-1950 foreign military presence:* UK, US, Coalition countries; *1950-2005 excess mortality/2005 population* = 5.283m/26.555m = 19.9%; *1950-2005 under-5 infant mortality/2005 population* = 3.446m/26.555m = 13.0%. Per capita GDP (nominal) $5,730.

Jordan: pre-Christian era lands of Ammon, Bashan, Edom and Moab; 4th century BCE-1st century, CE, Nabataean Kingdom around Petra; 1st century, Roman conquest; 6th-7th century CE, Byzantine-Persian conflict; 7th century, Muslim Arab invasion, conversion to Islam; 1099, Crusaders captured Jerusalem and nearby region; 1516-1918, part of Ottoman Empire; 1919, ruled by Faisal I from Damascus after cooperation with Lawrence and British against Turks during WW1; 1920, Faisal I removed by the French; Transjordan part of the British League of Nations Mandate; 1921, Abdullah (son of Faisal) made Emir; British trained the army; 1928, to be a constitutional monarchy; 1946, independent Hashemite Kingdom of Transjordan; 1948, defeated in Arab-Israeli war; 1949, changed name to Jordan to include West Bank incorporation; 1950, annexed West Bank; 1951, King Hussein succeeded his grandfather; 1958, Jordan and Iraq formed the Arab Federation; British troops sent to Jordan; 1961, Syria withdrew from UAR; 1963, Jordanian government-in-exile prompted US and UK military positioning; 1967, mutual defence pact with Egypt; 1967 War, Israel took the West Bank; 1968-1971, army action against Palestinians; 1972, West Bank-Jordan peace plan rejected by Israel and Arabs; 1979, moral support for Iraq in Iraq-Iran war; 1991, moral support for Iraq in the Gulf War; loss of US, Saudi and Kuwaiti aid; 0.7 million Jordanians lost employment in Kuwait; 1994, peace agreement with murderously and genocidally anti-Arab anti-Semitic Apartheid Israel; 1999, pro-Western Abdullah II; Palestinian, Islamist and Royalist political factions.

2021 update: Jordan was largely free from Arab Spring protests; 2.1 million Palestinian and 1.4 million Syrian refugees are hosted by Jordan; Jordan has an elected parliament but no parliamentary government; 2020 onwards, Covid-19 pandemic with "Covid-19 deaths per million of population" of 620 as compared to 0.4 for Taiwan (March 2021). Revised greenhouse gas (GHG) pollution 9.1 tonnes CO_2-e per person per year. Pro-Western Jordan has not signed or ratified the TPNW. In 2020 the "under-5 infant mortality as a percentage of total population" (0.0342%) was 23.9 times greater than for Japan (0.00145%), but 2.6 times lower than that in 2003 (0.0900%).

Foreign occupation: Turkey, Britain, Israel (pre-1950); Israel (post-1950); *post-1950 foreign military presence:* UK, Israel; *1950-2005 excess mortality/2005 population* = 0.630m/5.750m = 11.0%; *1950-2005 under-5 infant mortality/2005 population* = 0.331m/5.750m = 5.8%. Per capita GDP (nominal) $4,405.

Kuwait: 14th century-19th century, Ottoman province; 18th century, Arab Sabah sheikdom; 19th century, Wahhabi threat; 1897, British protectorate; 1961, independent sheikdom; British troops and thence Arab League troops remained because of Iraqi claims; founding member of OPEC; 1963, Iraq recognized Kuwait; founding member of OPEC; 1963, diplomatic relations with USSR; 1979, supported Iraq in Iran-Iraq War; 1981, Gulf Cooperation Council; 1987-1988, obtained US naval protection for Gulf oil tankers after Iranian attacks; 1990, greenlighted by the US, Iraq annexed Kuwait over oil dispute; 1991, US Gulf War freed Kuwait; 80% of oil wells destroyed; huge expulsion of Palestinian inhabitants; 1994, new crisis with Iraq; 2003, major Islamist representation in parliament; Kuwait was the launching site for the US invasion of Iraq; 2005, female suffrage.

2021 update: continuing semi-democratic rule. 2020 onwards, Covid-19 pandemic with "Covid-19 deaths per million of population" of 294 as compared to 0.4 for Taiwan (March 2021). Oil-rich country and a revised greenhouse gas (GHG) pollution 37.3 tonnes CO_2-e per person per year. Kuwait has not signed or ratified the TPNW. In 2020 the "under-5 infant mortality as a percentage of total population" (0.0096%) was 6.8 times greater than for Japan (0.00145%), but 2.1 times lower than that in 2003 (0.0200%).

Foreign occupation: Turkey, Britain (pre-1950); UK, Iraq, US (post-1950); *post-1950 foreign military presence:* UK, Iraq, US; *1950-2005 excess mortality/2005 population* = 0.089m/2.671m = 3.3%; *1950-2005 under-5 infant mortality/2005 population* = 0.076m/2.671m = 2.8%. Per capita GDP (nominal) $31,999.

Lebanon: early Canaanites; 12th century BCE, Phoenician cities (Tyre and Sidon); 5th century BCE, Persian hegemony; 4th century BCE, conquest by Alexander the Great and thence Hellenic rule; 64BCE, Roman conquest; 1st century, Christian conversion commenced; 7th century, Arab Muslim conquest; 11th century, Druze settlement in southern Lebanon; 11th-13th century, European Crusaders; 13th century, rule by Egyptian Mamluks; devastating Mongol invasion of Syria; 15th century, Ottoman Turkish rule; 1860, massacre of Maronite Christians by Druze; 1861, French intervention; 1914-1918, WW1; 1916, Sykes-Picot Agreement carving up the Arab world between the UK and France; 1919, French League of Nations mandate over Syria; 1926, French separated Lebanon from Syria; 1941, Free French and British defeated Vichy French; 1944, Lebanon independent; 1945, member of the UN; 1948, Arab-Israeli War; little participation but huge Palestinian refugee burden; major Christian and Shi'a Muslim populations and politics together with Palestinians, Sunni Muslims and Druze; 1952, pro-Western Christian Chamoun elected; 1958, riots, US forces called in; 1960s onwards, Israeli reprisals for Palestinian attacks; Lebanese Army-Palestinian conflicts; 1975, mounting civil war involving Christians, Muslims and Palestinians; 1976, Lebanese president invited Syrian forces in; 1978, Israeli invasion; replaced by UN peacekeepers; 1982, Israel invaded; 7,000 Palestinians forced to leave; Israel-allied Christian Falangist forces killed 3,000 unprotected civilian Palestinian refugees in Israeli-controlled areas (Sabra and Shatila massacres); 1983, terrorist bombings destroyed the US Embassy and thence many US and French soldiers; 1985, Israel withdrew to Southern Lebanon; 1990s, Israeli conflict with Shi'ite Muslim Hezbollah; 2000, Israel

finally departed but illegally retained the Shebaa Farms area and
left a surrogate Christian Army in Southern Lebanon which
subsequently collapsed; 2005, former PM Hariri blown up and UN
Security Council forced withdrawal of the (originally invited)
Syrian forces; 2006, Israeli War, Lebanon devastated, 1,000 killed,
1.0 million homeless.

2021 update: 2012, Syrian civil war led to 1.5 million Syrian
refugees and clashes between Sunnis and Alawites in Tripoli;
2019-2021, economic crisis compounded by the 2020 huge
explosion of stored ammonium nitrate that devastated the port of
Beirut and adjoining areas; 2020 onwards, Covid-19 pandemic with
"Covid-19 deaths per million of population" of a bad 884 as
compared to 0.4 for Taiwan (March 2021). Revised greenhouse gas
(GHG) pollution 9.8 tonnes CO_2-e per person per year. Lebanon
has not signed or ratified the TPNW. In 2020 the "under-5 infant
mortality as a percentage of total population" (0.0179%) was 12.3
times greater than for Japan (0.00145%), but 3.3 times lower than
that in 2003 (0.0590%).

Foreign occupation: Turkey, France, UK (pre-1950); France, Israel
(post-1950); *post-1950 foreign military presence:* US, France,
Israel, Syria; *1950-2005 excess mortality/2005 population =*
0.535m/3.761m = 14.2%; *1950-2005 under-5 infant mortality/2005*
population = 0.236m/3.761m = 6.3%. Per capita GDP (nominal)
$7,784.

Libya: North African Carthage destroyed by Rome in 2nd century
BCE; Tripolitania and Cyrenaica; 7th century CE, Arab invasion
and conversion to Islam; 16th century, Ottoman rule; Janissary
military power similar to that of the Egyptian Mamluks; 1711-
1835, Dey position held by Karamanli family; 1801-1805,
Tripolitan War with the US over protection money for Tripoli
pirates; 1815, Britain, France and the Sicilian Kingdom suppressed
pirates; 1835-1912, restored direct Ottoman rule; 1911-1912,
Turko-Italian war, the Turks were defeated but the Libyan Sanusi
continued resistance against the Italians; 1914, much of Libya
occupied by the genocidal Italians; 1934, Tripolitania and
Cyrenaica united; 1939, united with Italy; 1940-1943, WW2,

British and allies eventually prevailed over German and Italian forces; Anglo-French Government; 1949, UN jurisdiction; 1951, independent as a monarchy under King Idris (head of the Sanusi Brotherhood); 1953, Anglo-Libyan treaty permitted British forces until 1956; 1958, oil discovered; 1966, most British forces left; 1969, military coup by Qaddafi; 1970, forced UK and US to remove bases; 1973, Israel shot down Libyan airliner over the Sinai; 1982, US sanctions (after military air incident); 1986, US air strikes (after terrorist incident); 1988, US passenger plane destroyed over Lockerbie, Scotland; 1989, French passenger plane destroyed over Niger; 1992, UN sanctions; 1994, withdrew from disputed Chad territory; 1995, Islamist-military clashes; 1999, Libyan dissociation from terrorism; 2003-2004, admission of chemical weapons, compensation for plane victim families, renounced chemical, biological and nuclear weapons; US resumed diplomatic relations.

2021 update: 2011 onwards, France-UK-US (FUKUS) Coalition devastated Libya in UNSC-permitted intervention in the Libyan Civil War, 0.1 million killed, 1 million refugees, devastation of formerly the richest country in Africa; 2021, continuing civil war between UN- and Turkey-backed, Fayez Al-Sarraj-led Tripoli Government of National Accord (GNA) and the Tobruk-based, Khalifa Haftar-led, Egypt -, UAE-, Saudi- and Russia-backed Libyan National Army (LNA). 700,000 African refugees to Italy via Libya. 2020, Turkish Parliament-approved Turkish military intervention with advisers, air force, navy and Syrian mercenaries to support the Tripoli GNA; Libya–Turkey maritime deal to counter Greece, Cyprus and Apartheid Israel Mediterranean gas deal. Covid-19 pandemic with "Covid-19 deaths per million of population" of 375 as compared to 0.4 for Taiwan (March 2021). Major oil and gas industry. Revised greenhouse gas (GHG) pollution 24.9 tonnes CO_2-e per person per year. Libya has signed but not ratified the TPNW. In 2020 the "under-5 infant mortality as a percentage of total population" (0.0214%) was 14.8 times greater than for Japan (0.00145%), but 1.4 times lower than that in 2003 (0.0300%).

Foreign occupation: Turkey, Italy, France, Britain (pre-1950); UK (post-1950); *post-1950 foreign military presence:* France, UK, US; *1950-2005 excess mortality/2005 population* = 0.785m/5.768m = 13.6%; *1950-2005 under-5 infant mortality/2005 population* = 0.626m/5.768m = 10.9%. Per capita GDP (nominal) $4,810.

Morocco: 2nd millennium BCE, Berber occupation; Roman era Mauretania Tingitania; 5th century, Vandal invasion; 685, Muslim Arab invasion; conversion to Islam; Christianity declined; Judaism continued; 8th century, Berber and Arab Moroccan (Moor) invasion of Spain with consequent high Moorish civilization; subsequent Moroccan independence but Berber-Arab tensions; 1062, Almoravids conquered Morocco and ruled from Spain to Senegal; 1174, Almohads succeeded; 13th-16th century, Merinid dynasty largely ruled only Morocco; 1492, expulsion of Moors and Berber Jews from Spain; 1415, Portugal captured Ceuta and subsequently captured major ports; Melilla and Larache taken by Spain; 1554, Saadian (first Sherifian) dynasty; 1578, Battle of Ksar el Kebir, Moroccans defeated Portugal; 1660, Alawite (second Sherifian) dynasty; recapture of European holdings; 17th-18th century, pirate base (the Barbary Coast); 19th century, conquest by Spain and France; 1844, defeated by France; 1860, Spanish invasion; 1880, Madrid conference involving European powers and the US allowing everyone access to Morocco; 1905-1912, diplomatic conflict between France, Germany, Spain and Britain; 1912, Franco-Spanish division of Morocco into French Morocco, Spanish Morocco, a Spanish Protectorate (ruled as part of Spanish Sahara) and the international zone of Tangier; 1921-1926, Rif War revolt of Abd el-Krim; 1937, France suppressed nationalist revolt; 1936, Franco's Spanish fascist revolt began in Morocco; WW2, Vichy regime deposed in 1942; 1943, Casablanca conference of Allied leaders; Istiqlal independence movement commenced; 1950s, most of the Jewish population moved to Israel; 1952, Istiqlal banned; 1953, Sultan Sidi Muhammed deposed and exiled but finally restored (1955); 1956, French left; Spanish left Spanish Moroccco; Tangier restored to Morocco; 1957, King Muhammed V (Sidi Muhammed); 1958, Spanish ceded Southern Protectorate to Morocco; 1961, Hassan II; 1963, border conflict with Algeria; 1970, border settlement with Algeria; 1965, King Hassan declared a state of emergency (ameliorated in 1970); 1974-1991, Moroccan claims on Spanish Sahara; 1975, Hassan led the "Green March" of 0.3 million Moroccans into the Spanish Sahara region; 1976, Spanish cession of Spanish Sahara to Morocco and Mauritania; Western Sahara Polisario Front guerrilla opposition; 1991, ceasefire; 1999, Muhammed VI, reform; 2002, Moroccan-Spanish tension after Spanish reversal of Moroccan occupation of the uninhabited island of Perejil near Ceuta.

2021 update: 2011–2012, Moroccan protests over political reform and curbing the power of the king; 2020, Morocco betrayed Arabs and Muslims and recognized Apartheid Israel for US support over Western Sahara; 2020 onwards, Covid-19 pandemic with "Covid-19 deaths per million of population" of 236 as compared to 0.4 for Taiwan (March 2021). Revised greenhouse gas (GHG) pollution 2.5 tonnes CO_2-e per person per year. Morocco has not signed or ratified the TPNW. In 2020 the "under-5 infant mortality as a percentage of total population" (0.0381%) was 26.7 times greater than for Japan (0.00145%), but 2.5 times lower than that in 2003 (0.0950%).

Foreign occupation: France, UK, US (pre-1950); France (post-1950); *post-1950 foreign military presence:* France; *1950-2005 excess mortality/2005 population* = 8.202m/31.564m = 26.0%; *1950-2005 under-5 infant mortality/2005 population* = 5.098m/31.564m = 16.2%. Per capita GDP (nominal) $3,282.

Occupied Palestine: 3000-2000BCE, Arabian Semitic Canaanites settled and founded Jerusalem; 3200-1200 BCE, partial Egyptian hegemony; 1200 BCE, Hebrews, Canaanites and coastal Philistines; 721 BCE, Israel fell to Assyrians; 587 BCE, Judah fell to Babylonians; Jerusalem Temple destroyed by Nebuchadnezzar; about 560BC, Jews returned from Babylon under Persian Cyrus; 332 BCE, conquered by Greeks under Alexander the Great and subsequently ruled by the Ptolemy dynasty (Egypt) and the Seleucids (Syria); 67BCE, Maccabee revolt restored Jewish state under Ptolemaic hegemony; 63BCE, Roman occupation; Jesus (about 4BCE – 30 CE); 66CE, Jewish revolt; 70, Jerusalem Temple destroyed; 135, Jewish rebels expelled; Palestine subsequently

ruled successively by Romans and Byzantines (no non-Biblical
evidence for the Exodus from Egypt, the asserted Kingdom of
David and Solomon or indeed for mass expulsion (Exile) by the
Romans); 614, Persian occupation; 634, Arab conquest (Jerusalem,
Al Quds, site of Mohammed's ascension into Heaven); 640, Caliph
Umar; 691, Dome of the Rock and Al Aqsa mosque; 750, Abbasid
caliphate; 9th century, Fatimid rule; 11th -13th century, periodic
and partial Crusader occupation, 1099, conquest by Crusaders;
1187, Saladin defeated the Crusaders at the Battle of Hittin; 1291,
Mamluks defeated Crusaders; 1516, Ottoman Turkish conquest;
1916, secret Anglo-French Sykes-Picot Agreement to divide the
Middle East between France and Britain (notwithstanding
Lawrence-promoted Arab revolt on promise of Arab
independence); 1917, Turks defeated by British-Arab coalition;
1917, UK Balfour Declaration (Jewish Home provided no
detriment to Arabs and Jews); 1922, League of Nations Mandate to
Britain; 1900-1939, Jewish population from 50,000 to 300,000;
1936, Palestinian general strike; guerrilla war between Arabs and
Jews; 1939, British White Paper constrained Jewish immigration;
1939-1945, illegal Jewish immigration of Jews fleeing Nazis; 1944,
British War cabinet approved post-war Partition of Palestine; 1947,
UN Partition Plan; 1948, British left, UN recognized State of Israel,
war between Israel and Arabs; Deir Yassin massacre; 0.8 million
Arabs fled; 1956, Israeli war against Egypt with UK and France;
1964, Palestine Liberation Organization (PLO) formed; 1967,
Israel attacked neighbors (and USS Liberty) with occupation of
Sinai (Egypt), Gaza (Egypt), West Bank (Jordan), Jerusalem
(Jordan), Sheba Farms (Lebanon), and Golan Heights (Syria);
Israeli acquisition of nuclear weapons with US and French help;
1973, Yom Kippur War (Egypt-Israel); 1974, PLO leader Yasser
Arafat addressed UN; 1976, 6 Palestinians killed, 100 wounded and
hundreds arrested in Palestinian protest in Israel over land seizure
(subsequent annual 30 March Land Day protests); 1979, peace with
Egypt; 1982-2000, Israeli occupation of southern Lebanon, Sabra
and Shatila refugee camp massacres (3,000 Palestinians murdered
in Israeli-occupied Beirut by Christian Falangist Israeli allies);
1987, first Palestinian Intifada; 1988, Arafat eschewed violence and
recognized Israel; 1993, Oslo Agreement for Palestinian self-
government permitted arming of Palestinians; continued Zionist
settler seizure of Arab lands; 2000, renewed Intifada; 2004, Arafat

died (unexpectedly high levels of polonium found on his clothes); 2005, Israel pull-out from Gaza but strict border control, continued air attacks and retention of increasingly diminished West Bank; 21st century, US-backed Israeli occupation, illegal settlements and violence with continuing but ineffective responses from Palestinians; the dividing and encroaching Apartheid Wall; 6 million Palestinian refugees in the Middle East (post-1967 excess mortality 0.3 million; post-1967 under-5 infant mortality 0.2 million); 2006, Israeli War, Gaza devastated.

2021 update: repeated violent attacks on the Occupied Palestinians confined to the Gaza Concentration Camp (Gaza Massacres) with thousands killed, tens of thousands wounded, massive infrastructure and home destruction (2006, 2008-2009, 2014, 2018-2019, 2021), and imposition of deadly blockade to deliberately achieve near-unlivable conditions (only 40 Israelis have been killed in rocket attacks from Gaza since 2004; Israelis have murdered over 2,600 Israelis in the last 20 years); massive, illegal Jews-only settlements and Jews-only roads in the Occupied West Bank with 90% of Palestine now ethnically cleansed, this rendering the "two state solution" impossible, and underscoring the reality of Israeli Apartheid; 2017, Trump America recognized all of Occupied East Jerusalem and West Jerusalem as Israel's capital, this prompting weekly Friday demonstrations by unarmed Occupied Palestinians in the Gaza Concentration Camp (over 180 killed, and 9,200 wounded in the Great March on Return).The 5.2 million Occupied Palestinians (zero human rights) and 2 million Israeli Palestinians (subject to 60 race-based laws) represent 50% of the Subjects of Apartheid Israel, and Jewish Israelis 47%; the Occupied Palestinians have zero human rights, live under military rule, are confined to small parts of their own country, and cannot vote for the government ruling them (egregious Apartheid); the ongoing, 100 year Palestinian Genocide has been associated with 2.2 million Palestinian deaths from violence, 0.1 million, or from imposed deprivation, 2.1 million, since 1916 whereas 5,000 Zionist invaders/Israelis have been killed by Palestinians since 1920. Greenhouse gas (GHG) pollution about 9 tonnes CO_2-e per person per year; Occupier Apartheid Israel has 90 nuclear weapons with some on 6 German-supplied submarines, rejects the UN Treaty on the Prohibition of Nuclear Weapons (TPNW) that came into effect in International Law on 22 January 2021; 2012. UN recognition of State of Palestine but no voting rights; 2020, UAE, Bahrain, Sudan and Morocco betrayed Arabs and Muslims by recognizing anti-Arab anti-Semitic and Islamophobic Apartheid Israel. 2020, the International Criminal Court (ICC) to investigate Israeli war crimes; Palestine excluded from fishing and off-shore gas exploitation; Greece-Cyprus-Apartheid Israel plan for Mediterranean gas exploitation (gas leaks and is dirtier than coal GHG-wise). 2021, Israel leads the world in Covid-19 vaccination per capita but has violated the Fourth Geneva Convention by its disastrous Covid-19 policies and refusing to vaccinate Occupied Palestinians except for 5,000 medical workers and barring Russian Sputnik V vaccine from the Gaza Concentration Camp. 2020 onwards, Covid-19 pandemic with "Covid-19 deaths per million of population" of 489 as compared to 0.4 for Taiwan (March 2021). 8 million Exiled Palestinians excluded from Return by Apartheid Israel. Palestine excluded by Apartheid Israel from Mediterranean fish and gas exploitation and recreation. Revised greenhouse gas (GHG) pollution an estimated 9 tonnes CO_2-e per person per year. Palestine has signed and ratified the TPNW. In 2020 the "under-5 infant mortality as a percentage of total population" (0.0538%) was 37.7 times greater than for Japan (0.00145%), but 1.7 times lower than that in 2003 (0.0890%).

Foreign occupation: Egypt, Israel, Jordan, Turkey, UK (pre-1950); Egypt, Israel, Jordan (post-1950); *post-1950 foreign military presence:* Egypt, Israel, Jordan; *1950-2005 excess mortality/2005 population* = 0.0.677m/3.815m = 17.7%; *1950-2005 under-5 infant mortality/2005 population* = 0.295m/3.815m = 7.7%. Per capita GDP (nominal) $3,424.

Oman: 1508-1659, Portuguese control of the Persian Gulf; 1659, Ottoman Empire control; 1741, Turks ousted by Yemenis; ruling Said dynasty founded; late 18th century, British influence commenced; 18th-19th century, extensive Omani influence in coastal areas of East Africa (notably Zanzibar), Iran and Baluchistan (India); 1856, Zanzibar lost; 1958, Gwadar in Baluchistan ceded to Pakistan; 1957, interior revolt suppressed by

British forces; 1965, UN demanded British departure; 1970, some royal concessions but rebellion continued in Dhofar; 1971, joined UN and Arab League; 1981, joined Gulf Cooperation Council; 1991, bases given to US and Coalition forces; 1996, further royal liberalization; 2001, bases used by US in attacks on Afghanistan.

2021 update: continuing human rights abuse of dissidents by an authoritarian sultanate. 2020 onwards, Covid-19 pandemic with "Covid-19 deaths per million of population" of 317 as compared to 0.4 for Taiwan (March 2021). Major oil and gas exploitation. Revised greenhouse gas (GHG) pollution 13.8 tonnes CO_2-e per person per year. Oman has not signed or ratified the TPNW. In 2020 the "under-5 infant mortality as a percentage of total population" (0.0133%) was 9.3 times greater than for Japan (0.00145%), but 5.9 times lower than that in 2003 (0.0790%).

Foreign occupation: Britain (pre-1950); UK (post-1950); *post-1950 foreign military presence:* UK, US; *1950-2005 excess mortality/2005 population* = 0.359m/3.020m = 11.9%; *1950-2005 under-5 infant mortality/2005 population* = 0.288m/3.020m = 9.5%. Per capita GDP (nominal) $15,343.

Qatar: 1076, conquered by Emir of Bahrain; 16th century Portuguese occupation followed by largely nominal Ottoman rule; 1783, Persian invasion defeated; Wahhabi rule; 1815, moves for independence from Bahrain; 1867, Bahrain-Abu Dhabi coalition routed Qatar; 1868, British installed Al-Thani clan and controlled foreign policy; 1872-1913, formal Ottoman rule; 1916, formal British protectorate; 1939, oil discovered in Qatar; 1949, first oil to Europe; 1971, British left Trucial Coast leaving 7 emirates as United Arab Emirates; Bahrain and Qatar remained separate; 1972-1977, expropriation of all foreign oil installations; used as base during 1991 Gulf War; 1992, territorial dispute with Saudi Arabia resolved but dispute with Bahrain unresolved; 1994, defense pact with US; 1995, King deposed by his son with subsequent liberal reforms and municipal elections with women suffrage; 21st century, US domination; 2001, US base for regional war; 2003, HQ for US attack on Iraq; 2005, revelation of US plans to bomb Al Jazeera TV network HQ.

2021 update: 2017, Qatar withdrew from Yemen War; Egypt, Saudi Arabia, United Arab Emirates, and Bahrain cut off diplomatic relations with Qatar; increased Qatari economic and military ties with Turkey and Iran. 2020 onwards, Covid-19 pandemic with "Covid-19 deaths per million of population" of 100 as compared to 0.4 for Taiwan (March 2021). Massive oil and gas exploitation with revised greenhouse gas (GHG) pollution of 101.8 tonnes CO_2-e per person per year. Qatar seeks greater US military and naval presence and has not signed or ratified the TPNW. In 2020 the "under-5 infant mortality as a percentage of total population" (0.0069%) was 4.9 times greater than for Japan (0.00145%), but 3.8 times lower than that in 2003 (0.0260%).

Foreign occupation: UK (pre-1950); UK, US (post-1950); *post-1950 foreign military presence:* UK, US; *1950-2005 excess mortality/2005 population* = 0.029m/0.628m = 4.6%; *1950-2005 under-5 infant mortality/2005 population* = 0.013m/0.628m = 2.1%. Per capita GDP (nominal) $64,782.

Saudi Arabia: about 1000BCE, Ma'in, Himyar and Sheba (frankincense and myrrh, writing, Queen of Sheba); 6th century BCE, Darius conquered Northern Arabia; 24BCE, Romans invaded Northern Arabia; 330-378 CE, Ethiopian control of South West Arabia; 525-570, further Ethiopian rule of South West Arabia; 570, Persian Sassanians expelled the Ethiopians; 7th century, foundation of Islam by Prophet Muhammed; unification of Arabian Peninsular; 7th-8th century, Arab conquest of Syria, Mesopotamia, Persia, South West Asia, Egypt, North Africa and Spain; 732, Frank Charles Martel defeated the Arab invasion of France; caliphate transferred from Medina to Damascus; 1508-1659, Portuguese occupied Oman until expelled by the Ottoman Turks; 1799, Britain occupied Perim Island; 1839, Britain took Aden from the Turks; 1853, Trucial States of the Gulf recognized British dominance; 18th century, growth of Islamic Wahhabi sect ; 1811-1816, Wahhabis defeated by Egyptian forces; mid-19th century Wahhabi revival; 1891, Wahhabis crushed by Rashid tribe; 1902, Ibn Saud promoted Wahhabism, captured Rijyadh; 1906, conquered Nejd; 1914, took Al-Hasa region; 1924-1925, conquered Hejaz; 1932, Kingdom of Saudi Arabia under Ibn Saud; 1936 oil discovered by

US Arabian Standard Oil Company (became ARAMCO); 1938, commercial oil production; 1945, joined UN and Arab League; mainly financial support for "front-line" states against Israel; 1951-1962, US airforce base at Dhahran; 1956, split with Nasser's Egypt and allied with pro-Western Hashemite kingdoms of Jordan and Iraq (although past Saudi enemies); 1962, aided royalists against Egyptian-backed republicans; Faisal replaced Saud; 1970s, rapprochement with Egypt; encouraged UAE and good relations with pro-Western Iran; Saudi troops sent against leftist rebels in Yemen and Oman;1972-1974, increased control of oil industry to 60%; helped anti-Israel oil embargo in 1973; 1975, assassinated Faisal replaced by Khalid; Islamic orthodoxy and opposition to Egypt-Israel peace deal; 1979, Shah of Iran deposed, rise of Shi'ite fundamentalism; 1979, Islamist seizure of Mecca suppressed, hundreds killed; 1980, Shi'ite riots; financial support for Iraq in the Iran-Iraq war; full control of ARAMCO; 1981, Gulf Cooperation Council; 1982, King Fahd; 1987, Shi'ite Iranians rioted at Mecca during the Haj, 400 killed, Iran-Saudi relations severed; 1990, Iraq invaded Kuwait; US troops stationed in Saudi Arabia, 0.4 million Kuwaiti refugees came to Saudi Arabia; 1990s, bombings related to continuing US presence; 2001, 9/11 atrocity; leading Saudis flown out of the US; Saudi Al Qaeda led by Osama bin Laden accused over 9/11; US invaded Afghanistan; 2003, US invaded Iraq; Saudi constraints on US bases; more bombings in Saudi Arabia.

2021 update: continuing human rights abuses, suppression of women, massive arms purchases and US-backed hostility to Iran; 2015, backed by the US Alliance, a Saudi Arabian Coalition of Gulf and African states intervened in the Yemeni Civil War after Houthis removed pro-Saudi president of Yemen Abdrabbuh Mansur Hadi; horrendous Saudi bombing war crimes and horrendous famine; 2018, Saudi journalist Jamal Khashoggi, a Saudi dissident and US-based journalist, was shockingly murdered and dismembered in the Saudi consulate in Istanbul by agents of Mohammed bin Salman (MBS), the crown prince of Saudi Arabia; 2019, death of Sheik Ahmed Zaki Yamani, Minister of Petroleum and Mineral Resources from 1962 to 1986 and a leading figure in the Organization of the Petroleum Exporting Countries (OPEC) for 25 years (he latterly proposed increased oil production to avoid oil as a future "stranded asset"). 2020 onwards, Covid-19 pandemic with "Covid-19 deaths per million of population" of 189 as compared to 0.4 for Taiwan (March 2021). Massive oil and gas exploitation; revised greenhouse gas (GHG) pollution 16.6 tonnes CO_2-e per person per year. Saudi Arabia has not signed or ratified the TPNW. In 2020 the "under-5 infant mortality as a percentage of total population" (0.0110%) was 7.7 times greater than for Japan (0.00145%), but 7.5 times lower than that in 2003 (0.0820%).

Foreign occupation: Turkey (pre-1950); none (post-1950); *post-1950 foreign military presence:* US; *1950-2005 excess mortality/2005 population* = 2.752m/25.626m = 10.7%; *1950-2005 under-5 infant mortality/2005 population* = 2.085m/25.626m = 8.1%. Per capita GDP (nominal) $23,140.

South Sudan: South Sudan became independent from Sudan in 2011 (for prior details see Sudan).

2021 update: Sudan was occupied by Egypt under the Muhammad Ali dynasty and thence by the British after the Battle of Obdurman; 1958, Sudan independent; 1958-1972, First Sudanese Civil War; 1972-1983, Southern Sudan Autonomous Region formed; 1983-2005, Second Sudan Civil War; 2005, Comprehensive Peace Agreement and Autonomous Government of Southern Sudan; 2011, South Sudan became an independent state; 2013-2020, horrendous inter-ethnic violence and civil war with huge numbers of refugees (over 4 million refugees, 1.8 million internally displaced, 2.5 million in neighboring countries); malignant Israeli involvement with arms in support of the government; 2020, opposing leaders Salva Kiir Mayardit (Dinka ethnicity) and Riek Machar (Nuer Bentiu ethnicity) formed a coalition government. 2020, Covid-19 pandemic with "Covid-19 deaths per million of population" of a claimed 10 as compared to 0.4 for Taiwan (March 2021). Oil and gas resources being developed by China. Revised greenhouse gas (GHG) pollution about 17 tonnes CO_2-e per person per year. South Sudan has not signed or ratified the TPNW. In 2020 the "under-5 infant mortality as a percentage of total population" (0.3241%) was a shocking 226.9 times greater than for Japan

(0.00145%), and 1.1 times higher than that for Sudan as a whole in 2003 (0.3070%). Per capita GDP (nominal) $448.

Foreign occupation of Sudan: Egypt, Britain (pre-1950); UK (post-1950); *post-1950 foreign military presence:* UK; *1950-2005 excess mortality/2005 population* = 13.471m/35.040m = 38.4%; *1950-2005 under-5 infant mortality/2005 population* = 6.225m/35.040m = 17.8%. Per capita GDP (nominal) for South Sudan $448.

Sudan: ancient Nubia; about 2000BCE, conquered by Egypt; 8th century BCE-4th century CE, ruled by Kingdom of Cush; 6th century, conversion to Coptic Christianity; 7th century, Egypt subject to Muslim Arab invasion but Nubia resisted; 13th-14th century, Nubia became Muslim; the South remained animist; 16th century-1821, northern Funj state; 1821, conquered by Egypt under Muhammed Ali; slave and ivory trade; 1863-1879, Egyptian expansion south; 1881, revolt by the Mahdi (Muhammed Ahmed); 1885, General Gordon killed at Khartoum; the Mahdi died; 1896-1898, British Herbert (thence Lord Kitchener) defeated Mahdi followers at Obdurman with great ferocity (the British executed the Sudanese wounded); 1889, Anglo-Egyptian condominium over Sudan; 1924, South and North separated administratively; 1948, joint legislative council; 1952, Egyptian revolution; moves for independence; 1955, southern revolt; 1958, independence; 1958, military coup; 1964, civilian rule restored; 1958-1972, First Sudan Civil War; 1972, truce with the South; 1973, new constitution and rule under Nimeiry; 1980s, unrest increased in the South; 1985, Sharia law, increased opposition to Muslim North and famine in the Christian-animist South; 1985, coup; 1986, civilian rule; 1989, military coup by General Bashir; 1990s, continued civil war, increased power of the Muslim Brotherhood and US hostility; US halted famine relief; 1991, Sudan supported Iraq; 1996, Bashir elected in opposition-boycotted election; 1999, multiparty rule restored; 1998, US cruise missiles destroyed a pharmaceutical plant (no evidence for claimed "chemical warfare use"; Noam Chomsky estimated 10,000 consequent nation-wide deaths); 1998, cease-fire to permit humanitarian aid to the South; 2003-2004, agreements for peace in the civil war with withdrawal of government forces and joint government; millions had died; 2003, Western Darfur rebellion, horrendous raping, killing and village burning by government-linked militias; by 2005, 2 million displaced in Darfur, hundreds of thousands dead; 2005, final government-South peace agreement; Southern leader became Vice-President (1955-2005 excess mortality 12.4 million).

2021 update: 2011, South Sudan became independent; 2019, massive demonstrations leading to departure of Bashir and a military-civilian administration; 2020, Sudan betrayed Arabs and recognized Apartheid Israel in return for US favors; 2020 onwards, Covid-19 pandemic with "Covid-19 deaths per million of population" of 45 as compared to 0.4 for Taiwan (March 2021). Oil and gas production. Revised greenhouse gas (GHG) pollution 16.8 tonnes CO_2-e per person per year. Sudan has signed but not ratified the TPNW. In 2020 the "under-5 infant mortality as a percentage of total population" (0.1909%) was 133.7 times greater than for Japan (0.00145%), but 1.6 times lower than that in 2003 (0.3070%).

Foreign occupation: Egypt, Britain (pre-1950); UK (post-1950); *post-1950 foreign military presence:* UK; *1950-2005 excess mortality/2005 population* = 13.471m/35.040m = 38.4%; *post-1950 1950-2005 infant mortality/2005 population* = 6.225m/35.040m = 17.8%. Per capita GDP (nominal) $815.

Syria: 4,000BCE, beginnings of agriculture; 2100BCE, Semitic Amorite settlement; 15th-13th century BCE, Hittites dominated but came in conflict with Egypt; 13th century BCE, rise of Mediterranean Phoenician trading culture; 11th-6th century BCE, Assyrian and Babylonian invasions; 6th – 4th century BCE, Persian conquest; 333-331BCE, Greek conquest under Alexander the Great; 4th-1st century BCE, Seleucid dynasty and Hellenic culture; 1st century BCE, Armenian and Parthian invasions; 63BCE, Roman conquest; 1st century CE, Christianizing; 4th century, after division of Roman Empire; rule by Byzantium; 633-640, Arab Muslim conquest and conversion to Islam but with retention of a variety of Christian traditions (most notably the Greek Orthodox, Syriac Orthodox, Maronite and Nestorian); 11th-13th century Crusades; 12th century, Saladin defeated Crusaders; 1260, Mongol invasion and ravaging of Damascus and Aleppo (50,000 citizens slain); Mongols defeated by Egyptian Mamluks; 1410, Timur ravaged Damascus and Aleppo; 1516, conquest by Ottoman Turks; 1789-1799, coastal depredations by Napoleonic French forces; 1832-1833, Egyptians annexed Syria; 1840, British forced return to Ottoman rule; 1860, Lebanon autonomy; 1914-1918, Arab participation in the British defeat of the Turks but secret deception by the Allies (1916 Anglo-French Sykes-Picot Agreement dividing the Middle East between Britain and France); 1920, League of Nations mandate to France; 1925, Druze rebellion; French bombarded Damascus; 1926, Lebanon separated from Syria by France; 1936, Syria autonomy; 1939-1945, WW2; 1940, Vichy French control; 1941, British and Free French invaded; 1944, Syria independent; 1945, founding member of the UN; 1946, last French forces left; 1948, defeated in Arab-Israeli war; 1949, 3 coups; 1958-1961, joined with Egypt in the United Arab Republic; 1963, coup yielded joint Ba'ath Party and military government; 1967, Israel invaded and occupied the Golan Heights; 1970, Alawite Assad came to power; 1973, Yom Kippur war; fighting with Israel; UN-supervised cease-fire; 1970s, rise in Sunni Islamic fundamentalism influenced by Egyptian Muslim Brotherhood; 1982, Hama uprising quelled and thousands killed; 1982, Israel illegally annexed the Golan Heights; 1982-2000, Israeli occupation of southern Lebanon; 1982-2005, Syrian forces remained in Lebanon; 2000, Assad died and his son took over; opposition to the US Iraq War led to acute continuing threats from the US; 2005, assassination of former Lebanese PM Hariri forced Syrian withdrawal from Lebanon; continued US threats.

2021 update: 2012, mass demonstrations associated with the Arab Spring; Free Syrian Army, jihadis and ISIS seeking to overthrow the Syrian Government; US failed to get UN approval for bombing Syria; US-led Coalition of US, UK, France, Apartheid Israel, Saudi Arabia and Turkey versus Russia, Iran and Hezbollah support for the Assad Government; 2017, ISIS defeated, ISIS-held city of Raqqa destroyed (like the ISIS-held cities of Mosul and Fallujah), 0.5 million Syrians killed, war and massive human rights abuse led to 11 million refugees, US allegations of war gas and cluster bomb use; Apartheid Israel-sought Syria Balkanising with US-backed Kurdish enclave, Turkish-occupied enclave, Aleppo and other cities devastated; residual jihadi control of Idlib; 2019, Trump US recognized illegal Israeli annexation of the Israeli ethnically cleansed Syrian Golan Heights; 2021, US under Biden (30% Jewish Zionist Cabinet) resumed bombing anti-ISIS Syrian, Iraqi and Iranian forces in Syria; Apartheid Israel continues to bomb Syria; 2020 onwards, Covid-19 pandemic with "Covid-19 deaths per million of population" of 68 as compared to 0.4 for Taiwan (March 2021). Revised greenhouse gas (GHG) pollution 9.4 tonnes CO_2-e per person per year. Syria has not signed or ratified the TPNW. In 2020 the "under-5 infant mortality as a percentage of total population" (0.0351%) was 24.6 times greater than for Japan (0.00145%), but 2.1 times lower than that in 2003 (0.0750%).

Foreign occupation: Turkey, Britain, France (pre-1950); Israel (post-1950); *post-1950 foreign military presence:* Israel, Russia (invited), US Alliance (not invited); *1950-2005 excess mortality/2005 population* = 2.198m/18.650m = 11.8%; *1950-2005 under-5 infant mortality/2005 population* = 1.718m/18.650m = 9.2%. Per capita GDP (nominal) $1,194.

Tunisia: 10th century BCE, Phoenician coastal settlement; 6th century BCE, rise of Carthage; 2nd century BCE, Carthage totally destroyed by the Romans; major food source for Rome; 5th century, Vandal conquest; 6th century, Byzantine rule; 7th century, "Ifriqiya" conquered by Muslim Arabs; Berber conversion to Islam; Arab-Berber tensions; 9th century-10th century, Aghlabid rule; 10th century-11th century, Zirid rule; 1050, Fatimid Egypt invaded; 12th century, coastal rule by Norman Sicily; 1159, conquered by Almohad Moroccco; 1230-1574, rule by Berber Hafsids; 16th century, Spanish seizures of coastal cities were reversed by Ottoman sea power; nominal Ottoman Turkish authority; rule by Berber beys; piracy dominant (part of the Barbary Coast); 1705-1957, Hussein bey dynasty; 19th century, increasing European intervention; 1869, Italy controlled finances; 1881-1883, French invasion and occupation; 1920s and 1930s, increased independence activism, Bourguiba leadership for independence; WW2, Vichy French rule defeated by the Allies (1942); post-war agitation for independence; 1952, imprisonment of Bourguiba led to violence; 1956, independence; 1957, the Bey was removed; 1957-1963, tensions over continued French military presence that ended with French withdrawal; 1970, settlement of border with Algeria; 1985, Apartheid Israel bombed Tunisia; 1987, General Ben Ali coup removed Bourguiba; peace and cooperation with neighboring countries; 1989, Islamist advances in elections led to repression and effective one-party rule.

2021 update: 2011, start of the Arab Spring with mass demonstrations in Tunisia, removal of the Ben Ali regime and adoption of a pro-female rights democracy; continuing protests about economic circumstances; 2020 onwards, Covid-19 pandemic with "Covid-19 deaths per million of population" of a bad 729 as compared to 0.4 for Taiwan (March 2021). Revised greenhouse gas (GHG) pollution 7.0 tonnes CO_2-e per person per year. Tunisia has not signed or ratified the TPNW. In 2020 the "under-5 infant mortality as a percentage of total population" (0.0199%) was 13.9 times greater than for Japan (0.00145%), but 2.4 times lower than that in 2003 (0.0480%).

Foreign occupation: Turkey, France, Britain (pre-1950); France (post-1950); *post-1950 foreign military presence:* France; *1950-2005 excess mortality/2005 population* = 1.582m/10.042m = 15.8%; *1950-2005 under-5 infant mortality/2005 population* = 1.568m/10.042m = 15.6%. Per capita GDP (nominal) $3,398.

United Arab Emirates: pre-colonial trade with Persia and India; from 16th century, Portuguese incursions; Pirate Coast piracy; 1820, British agreements with Gulf sheiks; 1892, British protectorates established (Trucial States, Trucial Coast or Trucial Oman); 1968, confederation mooted but Bahrain and Qatar preferred independence; 1971, British withdrawal; Abu Dhabi Sheik al-Nahayan as leader; 1973, oil crisis, increased oil price and UAE wealth; 1981, joined Gulf Cooperation Council; 1979, overthrow of Iran Shah and growth of Islamic fundamentalism; 1990, Iraq hostility to Kuwait and UAE over overproduction of oil; Iraq invasion of Kuwait; 1991, UAE used by US-Coalition forces in the Gulf War; 21st century, great wealth; excellent health services; relatively benign autocratic rule by sheiks; exploitation of South Asian workers; cooperation with the US-Coalition forces attacking Iraq and Afghanistan; 2004, presidential succession by Sheik al-Nahayan's son.

2021 update: UAE involved in the Saudi-led, US Alliance-backed war on starving Yemen; 2020, UAE betrayed Arabs and recognized Apartheid Israel; continuing human rights abuse of women and of South Asian workers; 2021, UAE achieved a satellite orbiting Mars. 2020 onwards, Covid-19 pandemic with "Covid-19 deaths per million of population" of 148 as compared to 0.4 for Taiwan (March 2021). Massive oil and gas production. Revised greenhouse gas (GHG) pollution 82.4 tonnes CO_2-e per person per year. The UAE has not signed or ratified the TPNW. In 2020 the "under-5 infant mortality as a percentage of total population" (0.0061%) was 4.3 times greater than for Japan (0.00145%), but 2.5 times lower than that in 2003 (0.0150%).

Foreign occupation: Britain (pre-1950); UK (post-1950); *post-1950 foreign military presence:* UK, US; *1950-2005 excess mortality/2005 population* = 0.087m/3.106m = 2.8%; *1950-2005 under-5 infant mortality/2005 population* = 0.046m/3.106m = 1.5%. Per capita GDP (nominal) $43,103.

Yemen: 1st millennium BCE, Minaean and Sabaean civilizations; 750BCE-115BCE, Sabaean kingdom (writing, aqueducts, dams, irrigation, frankincense and myrrh trade; celebrated Queen of Sheba); 2nd-1st century BCE, Himyarites; 1st century BCE, Roman conquest; 340-378CE, Ethiopian conquest; rise of Christianity and Judaism; 378-525, second Himyarite Kingdom; 525, Ethiopian conquest; 575-628, Persian rule; 7th century, Muslim conquest and conversion; 8th century-1962, Northern Yemen ruled by theocratic Rassite dynasty involving imams of the Zaidi sect; about 1000-1175, Egyptian rule under Fatamid caliphs; 1175-1250, rule by Ayyubids; 16th century, rule by Ottoman Empire; early 19th century, puritanical Wahhabi sect displaced Zaidi imams; 1818, Egyptians defeated Wahhabis; 1840-1918, Ottoman rule; 1839, British East India Company took Aden; 1854, 1857, Kuria Muria and Perim Islands to Britain; 1886-1914, British protectorate agreements; 1937, Southern Yemen as the British Aden Protectorate thence administered as the East and West Aden protectorates; 1934, (North) Yemen hostilities with Saudi Arabia and Britain (protectorate of Aden) and subsequent border disturbances; WW2 neutrality; 1945, (North) Yemen joined the Arab League; 1947, (North) Yemen joined the UN; 1948, Imam assassinated and replaced; 1958-1961, (North) Yemen joined UAR with Egypt and Syria; 1959, British-ruled West Aden Protectorates formed the Federation of the Emirates of the South; 1963, British-ruled Aden became part of an enlarged Federation of South Arabia; (North) Yemen gained the region about the port of Hodeida; 1961-1970, Saudi- and Jordan-backed royalist versus pro-Egyptian republican civil war; 1967, independence from Britain of Marxist South Yemen; 1967-1972, 1979, fighting between North and South Yemen; 1989, Yemen unified; 1994, fighting between North and South army units; 1999, Saleh president after elections; 2000, USS Cole and British Embassy bombings in Aden; 2001, Yemen supported the US "War on Terror"; 21st century, Islamist versus government fighting.

2021 update: 2012, Arab Spring discontent, Ali Abdullah Saleh resigned as president and replaced by Abdrabbuh Mansur Hadi. Houthis seized the capital Sanaa and norther Yemen. 2012 onwards, US- and UK-backed intervention by Saudi Arabian Coalition of Gulf States and some African countries. About 60,000 killed violently and horrendous famine affecting 17 million people as the richest European and Arab nations make high technology war on a starving Yemeni population - an horrendous, ongoing crime of Yemeni Genocide grossly violating Natural Law, International Law and Islamic Law and variously involving Saudi Arabia, Egypt, Morocco, Jordan, Sudan, the United Arab Emirates, Kuwait, Qatar (now withdrawn), Bahrain, Academi (formerly called Blackwater) US mercenaries, Djibouti, Eritrea, Occupied Somalia, the US, the UK and US lackey Australia (remote targeting of US drone strikes). 2020 onwards, Covid-19 pandemic with "Covid-19 deaths per million of population" of a claimed 27 as compared to 0.4 for Taiwan (March 2021). Revised greenhouse gas (GHG) pollution 3.7 tonnes CO_2-e per person per year. Yemen has not signed or ratified the TPNW. In 2020 the "under-5 infant mortality as a percentage of total population" (0.1582%) was 110.8 times greater than for Japan (0.00145%), but 3.2 times lower than that in 2003 (0.5080%). 66,000 annual avoidable deaths from deprivation (2020).

Foreign occupation: Britain, Egypt (pre-1950); UK (post-1950); *post-1950 foreign military presence:* UK, , Saudi-led Coalition; *1950-2005 excess mortality/2005 population* = 6.798m/21.480m = 31.6%; *1950-2005 under-5 infant mortality/2005 population* = 5.135m/21.480m = 23.9%. Per capita GDP (nominal) $855.

2020 statistical update for Arab North Africa and Middle East. Table 9.8 summarizes population, under-5 infant mortality (IM) and excess mortality (EM; avoidable mortality from deprivation) in the Arab North Africa and Middle East in 2020 (pre-Covid-19 projection in 2019 for 2020 by the UN Population Division). Table 9.1 compares the Arab North Africa and Middle East with other global regions. Presented in square brackets for each country is the "Relative EM Score" of EM/Pop (%) divided by that for the best-performing country, Japan (0.0020%), which accordingly has a "Relative EM Score" of 1.0.

In terms of "Relative EM Score" and "per capita GDP" the best performing countries are clearly the Gulf States with outcomes ranging from the United Arab Emirates (4.3 and $43,103) to Oman (9.3 and $15,343). The oil-poor democracies Lebanon (12.3 and $7,784) and Tunisia (13.9 and $3,398) do worse than the oil-rich but authoritarian Gulf States. The war ravaged countries of Yemen (110.8 and $855), Sudan (133.7 and $815), and South Sudan (226.9 and $448) are testaments to the evil of war. The remaining countries have outcomes ranging from Jordan (23.9 and $4,405) to Occupied Palestine (37.7 and $3,424). The outcome for Occupied Palestine is evidence of gross violation of the Fourth Geneva Convention by the Occupier, serial war criminal Apartheid Israel.

While the average "Relative EM Score" is 2.2 for Western Europe, 36.6 for Central Asia, Turkey and Iran, and 50.5 for Arab North Africa and Middle East, it is a shocking 176.6 for non-Arab Africa (Table 9.1). The "under-5 infant mortality as a percentage of total population" in 2020 had decreased from that in 2003 by a factor ranging from 1.4 to 7.5., and increased slightly (1.1fold) in South Sudan

6.5 South East Asia – colonialism, colonial wars, US-driven war and militarization

Ancient Buddhism-inspired Burmese, Thai and Khmer civilizations defended themselves from each other and from China. The Hindu civilization of Java was eventually supplanted as Islam spread to Aceh and thence to Malaya, Indonesia and the Philippines. However British and French imperialism overtook Burma and Indo-China, respectively, in the 19th century. Spanish, Portuguese, Dutch and British imperialism took the Philippines, Timor, Indonesia and Malaya, respectively. There were inevitable revisions such as successive Portuguese, Dutch and British rule over Sri Lanka, the Portuguese and Dutch division of Timor, British and Dutch division of Borneo, and eventual US acquisition of the Philippines after the Spanish-American War of 1898.

Independence movements burgeoning in the 20th century were ultimately successful after Japanese occupation during WW2. However the US moved to fill a post-colonial vacuum with major influence in the Philippines, Thailand and Indonesia. The post-war Indo-China War of the French was continued with devastating impacts by the US until 1975 and then supplanted by economic sanctions. The US-backed military coup in Indonesia in 1965 led to the immediate death of about 0.75 million Indonesian Chinese and socialists through brutal massacres but over the next 4 decades was associated with an excess mortality from deprivation of 40.7 million Indonesians and the genocide of 0.2 million in East Timor. The outstandingly good outcome countries in this group are Singapore, Brunei and Malaysia with 1950-2005 excess mortality/2005 population ratios of 1.4%, 2.9% and 4.6%, respectively, these countries having had peace, prosperity and good governance as common attributes for most of the post-1950 era.

Brunei: early immigration from southern China; 13th century, Islamic empire in Borneo; 16th century, Portuguese, Dutch and Spanish presence; 19th century, Dutch occupation of the southern

part of Borneo (Kalimantan); 1841, sultan gave Sarawak to James
Brooke (the British "white rajah" of Sarawak); British annexed the
island of Labuan; British protectorate over Sarawak, Sabah and
Brunei; 1929, oil discovered; 1942-1945, Japanese occupation;
Sarawak and Sabah became British colonies, Kalimantan became
part of the new, self-declared independent Indonesia; 1962, part of
the Federation of Malaysia but with opposition from the Brunei
People' Party – their rebellion was defeated but Brunei withdrew
from the Federation and remained a British protectorate; 1959,
constitution; 1962, anti-monarchist electoral victory followed by
state of emergency and disbandment of the legislative council;
1970, sultan appointed; 1977, Brunei accepted delayed
independence from Britain, deferred until 1984; 1984, independent
but sultan abolished the legislative council, the 1962 declaration of
emergency remaining in force; 1987, financial support for US-
backed Contras in Nicaragua was revealed; 1988, large-scale
British military exercises; 2004, renewed appointed legislative
council.

2021 update: 2020 onwards, Covid-19 pandemic with "Covid-19
deaths per million of population" of 7 as compared to 0.4 for
Taiwan (March 2021). Oil, gas and timber industries. Revised
greenhouse gas (GHG) pollution 27.4 tonnes CO_2-e per person per
year. Brunei has signed but not ratified the TPNW. In 2020 the
"under-5 infant mortality as a percentage of total population"
(0.0134%) was 9.4 times greater than for Japan (0.00145%), but
1.04 times lower than that in 2003 (00.0140%).

Foreign occupation: UK (pre-1950); UK (post-1950); *post-1950
foreign military presence:* UK; *1950-2005 excess mortality/2005
population* = 0.020m/0.374m = 5.3%; *1950-2005 under-5 infant
mortality/2005 population* = 0.011m/0.374m = 2.9%. Per capita
GDP (nominal) $31,086.

Cambodia: 1st-6th century CE, Funan Empire; 4th century, Indian
culture and religion introduced; 6th century, Khmers conquered
Funan; 9th-13th century, peak of Khmer civilization and the marvel
of Angkor Wat; 15th century, decline of Khmer Empire under
pressure from Thailand; 17th century, pressure from Annam; 18th

century, major territorial losses to the Thais and Annamese; 1854, French protectorate; 1863-1887, French invasion and Khmer resistance; 1941-1945, Japanese occupation; 1945, King Norodom Sihanouk declared independence, France re-invaded; eventual rapprochement with autonomy; 1949, independence within the French Union (French military and control over foreign affairs); 1953, French withdrew; 1954, Geneva Agreement, all foreign forces had to leave; 1955, full independence; 1955, Prince Sihanouk abdicated to participate in democracy; 1960, Sihanouk head of state; 1965, broke relations with US; 1969, huge bombing by US; 1970, US-backed coup installed Lon Nol; US invaded against the Khmer Rouge; 1975, Pnom Penh captured; 1976, Sihanouk was head of state but was thence exiled and the Khmer Rouge took over; 1976-1979, genocide, 1.5 million murdered; 1979, Vietnam invaded, ousted the Khmer Rouge and installed the Heng Samrin regime; 1990s, final defeat of Khmer Rouge; country crippled by legacy of US bombing, war, genocide, civil war and landmines; 1998, Pol Pot died and the Khmer Rouge resistance collapsed (1975-1980 excess mortality 1.2 million;1965-1998 excess mortality 3.9 million); 1999, joined ASEAN; liberal, royalist and socialist politics.

2021 update: 1997 onwards, rule by authoritarian Hun Sen government; continuing problem of unexploded mines and bombs. 2020 onwards, Covid-19 pandemic but "Covid-19 deaths per million of population" not known. Timber a major industry. Revised greenhouse gas (GHG) pollution 40.5 tonnes CO_2-e per person per year. Cambodia has signed and ratified the TPNW. In 2020 the "under-5 infant mortality as a percentage of total population" (0.0539%) was 37.7 times greater than for Japan (0.00145%), but 9.0 times lower than that in 2003 (0.4850%).

Foreign occupation: France (pre-1950); France, US, Vietnam (post-1950); *post-1950 foreign military presence:* France, US, Vietnam; *1950-2005 excess mortality/2005 population =* 5.852m/14.825m = 39.5%; *1950-2005 under-5 infant mortality/2005 population* = 3.180m/14.825m = 21.5%. Per capita GDP (nominal) $1,644.

Indonesia: early immigration from southern China; 400BCE, ancient Hindu and Buddhist Indonesian states in Sumatra and Java; 7th-13th century, Buddhist Sri Vijaya Kingdom of Sumatra; 15th century peak of Indo-Indonesian civilization (presently evidenced by continuing Balinese Hindu culture and the giant 800 CE Javanese Borobudur stupa); 13th century, major conversion to Islam; 1511, Portuguese captured Melaka; 1521, Spanish occupation of Moluccas; 1595, first Dutch exploration; 1602, British East Indies Company ships reached Aceh (the matriarchal Acinese were impressed by the rule of England by Queen Elizabeth I), and Dutch East Indies Company ships arrived seeking spices; 17th-18th century, Spanish, Portuguese, Dutch and British conflict over the Spice Islands (e.g. the 1623 Ambon Massacre of English by the Dutch) and genocide of Indonesians by the Dutch; 1798, Dutch government rule over the Dutch East Indies; 1811-1815, British rule; 1815, formal resumption of Dutch control – huge wealth from spices, peanuts, timber and palm oil; 1825, Javanese resistance; 1906-1908, Balinese resistance; 20th century, almost continuous Acinese resistance to the Dutch and thence the Javanese; 1916, Volksraad of Indonesian nationalists; 1939, nationalist coalition formed; 1942-1945, Japanese occupation; 1945, Indonesia declared independence under Soekarno; 1945-1949, war of independence against UK-backed Dutch; 1949, independence under Dutch-Indonesian Union; 1954, full independence declared; 1955, Indonesia hosted important Bandung Conference of non-aligned nations; 1960s, confrontation between Indonesia and UK over Malaysia; 1963, Indonesia occupied West Irian (Western New Guinea); mid-60s, 3 million-strong Communist Party supported Soekarno, Royal Dutch Shell nationalized and PERTAMINO oil organization set up; 1965, US-backed coup by military under General Suharto on pretext of opposing a "communist coup" – 750,000 murdered (including many Chinese) and 200,000 imprisoned; 1967, Suharto formally made head of state; 1971, student riots; 1975, UK-, US- and Australia-approved invasion and occupation of Portuguese East Timor hours after US President Ford's visit – genocide killed 200,000 out of 600,000 population; 1999 US-backed Suharto military dictatorship replaced by democratically elected government under Abdur Raman Wahid (Gus Dur) (1965-1999 excess mortality 33.3 million); 1999-2002, UN-supervised East Timorese independence; 2004, tsunami tragedy (200,000 dead in Aceh); 2005, peace accord ended over 4 decades of Acinese armed resistance (the Australia-influenced US had supported Islamic insurgencies in circa 1960).

2021 update: secular democracy but increasing politician exploitation of strict Islam; continuing West Papuan secessionist activity in West Irian; 2020 onwards, Covid-19 pandemic with "Covid-19 deaths per million of population" of 146 as compared to 0.4 for Taiwan (March 2021). Timber, oil and palm oil involving massive deforestation and fires, with smoke impacting neighboring countries. Revised greenhouse gas (GHG) pollution 53.6 tonnes CO_2-e per person per year. Indonesia has signed but not ratified the TPNW. In 2020 the "under-5 infant mortality as a percentage of total population" (0.0403%) was 28.2 times greater than for Japan (0.00145%), but 2.2 times lower than that in 2003 (0.0870%).

Foreign occupation: Portugal, Netherlands, Japan, UK (pre-1950); Netherlands (West Irian) (post-1950); *post-1950 foreign military presence:* Netherlands (West Irian); *post-1950 excess mortality/2005 population* = 71.521m/225.313m = 31.7%; *post-1950 under-5 infant mortality/2005 population* = 34.516m/225.313m = 15.3 %. Per capita GDP (nominal) $4,136.

Laos: 13th century, Thai tribes spread into the region from Southern China; 14th century, Fa Ngoun unified North East Thailand and Laos as Lan Xang (Land of a Million Elephants); introduction of high culture and Theravada Buddhism; 14th-17th century, Lang Xang domination of the region; 18th century, Lan Xang split into the Luang Prabang, Champassac and Vientiane regions; 1827, revolt of Vientiane against the Thais was suppressed; 1893, French protectorate over Luang Prabang with the rest subsumed into Indo-China; 1942-1945, Japanese occupation; Sufanuvong proclaimed independence; French re-occupation and Communist Pathet Lao revolt; 1949, independence as part of French Union; 1953, final independence; 1958, leftist election victory but US hostility led to US-backed military government under Nosavang; 1960, Vientiane fell to pro-US forces after heavy bombing; 1962, tripartite agreement on government of national unity; 1964-1975, huge US bombing, especially of the Ho Chi

Minh Trail (more bombs than on all Europe in WW2); 1973, Pathet
Lao forced US advisers and Thai mercenaries to leave; 1975, free
of foreigners under Sufanuvong; Communist Pathet Lao
government (1955-1975 excess mortality 1.1 million); 1990s,
increasing economic pluralism; 1997, joined ASEAN.

2021 update: 200,000 Hmong fled to Thailand after defeat of the
US and punishment of collaborators; 2003, US accepted 15,000
Hmong refugees; 2020 onwards, continuing Laos problem of
unexploded bombs; close relations with similarly Communist-ruled
Vietnam complicating relations with China; problem of upstream
damming of the Mekong River. Covid-19 pandemic but no data on
"Covid-19 deaths per million of population". Forest exploitation
and revised greenhouse gas (GHG) pollution 25.3 tonnes CO_2-e per
person per year. Laos has signed and ratified the TPNW. In 2020
the "under-5 infant mortality as a percentage of total population"
(0.0994%) was 69.6 times greater than for Japan (0.00145%), but
3.5 times lower than that in 2003 (0.3490%).

Foreign occupation: Thailand, France, Japan (pre-1950); France,
Thailand, US (post-1950); *post-1950 foreign military presence:*
France, Thailand, US; *1950-2005 excess mortality/2005 population*
= 2.653m/5.918m = 44.8%; *1950-2005 under-5 infant
mortality/2005 population* = 1.383m/5.918m = 23.4%. Per capita
GDP (nominal) $2,625.

Malaysia: before 1,000 BCE, Malay people from southern China;
1st millennium CE, rice farming, fishing and trade with major
Indian cultural influence; 5th century, Mekong Buddhist Funan
kingdom spread to the Eastern coast of the peninsular; 15th
century, Melaka (Malacca) founded, Islamic conversion,
independence from tribute to Thailand; 1509, first Portuguese;
1511, Portuguese under de Alberquerque seized Melaka to secure
transit of spices from the Moluccas; 16th century, Johor, Aceh and
Brunei sultanates; 17th century, Dutch-Johor alliance removed
Portugal from Melaka; 1786, British founded Georgetown on
Penang; trade involved Chinese, Indians, Sumatrans and Malays;
1819, British under sympathetic colonialist and slavery Abolitionist
Stamford Raffles founded Singapore; 1824, British-Dutch treaty –

Malaya and North Borneo British and South Borneo (Kalimantan) and the rest of Indonesia Dutch; 1816-1841, conflict with Thailand over northern states; 19th century, Chinese labor for tin mines, Tamil labor for rubber plantations (*Hevea* seeds smuggled from Brazil); 1870s onwards, British protectorate agreements with sultanates; 1896, federation of Malay Peninsula sultanates under British protection and similar protectorates over Brunei, Sarawak and Sabah; 20th century political movements of Chinese (Sun Yat Sen, Communism), Indians (Congress and Gandhi) and Malays (Islamic reform) – British divide-and-rule political and economic arrangements; 1942-1945, Japanese occupation, Communist resistance and end of British invincibility; 1948-1960, Communist revolt suppressed by British and Commonwealth allies (Malaya Emergency) (1950-1960 excess mortality 1.0 million; 0.5 million Chinese resettled); 1957, independence under Tunku Abdul Rahman; special laws for advancement of Malays (Bumiputera); 1963, Singapore, Sarawak and Sabah joined Federation; 1963-1965, Confrontation with Indonesia; 1965, Chinese-dominated Singapore left the Malaysian Federation; 1967, joined ASEAN; 1969, loss of governing UMNO seats to Islamic and Chinese parties; serious anti-Chinese race riots and 2 year suspension of parliament; 1981, Dr Mahathir bin Mohamad elected; retention of Internal Security Act (detention without trial), support for Third World and Muslim countries, criticism of First World impositions, economic independence, deforestation; 1998-1999, recession associated with the Asian Financial Crisis; Malaysia adopted a successful non-IMF strategy of controlling capital markets and suspending trade in its currency; 1998-2004, false charging and imprisonment of deputy PM Anwar Ibrahim; 2003, progressive and anti-imperialist Mahatir stepped down and was replaced by Bedawi.

2021 update: 2015, PM Najib Razak accused of stealing $700 million; Pakatan Harapan victory in general election; Anwar Ibrahim pardoned, released and re-elected in a by-election, with his wife Wan Azizah Wan Ismail, serving as Deputy Prime Minister during Mahathir Mohammed's second period as Prime Minister; 2020, Razak jailed for massive corruption; 2020 onwards, Covid-19 pandemic with "Covid-19 deaths per million of population" of

38 as compared to 0.4 for Taiwan (March 2021). Massive timber industry destroying tropical rain forest. Revised greenhouse gas (GHG) pollution 126.0 tonnes CO_2-e per person per year. Malaysia has signed and ratified the TPNW. In 2020 the "under-5 infant mortality as a percentage of total population" (0.0106%) was 7.4 times greater than for Japan (0.00145%), but 1.5 times lower than that in 2003 (0.0160%).

Foreign occupation: Portugal, Britain, Japan (pre-1950); UK (post-1950); *post-1950 foreign military presence:* UK and allies; *1950-2005 excess mortality/2005 population* = 2.344m/25.325m = 9.3%; *1950-2005 under-5 infant mortality/2005 population* = 1.176m/25.325m = 4.6%. Per capita GDP (nominal) $11,414.

Myanmar: 11th century, Burmese conquered Hmongs and Kadus and formed Pagan state based on the rich rice-growing areas around the Irrawaddy River; 11th-13th century, major era of Burmese civilization; 1283-1301, Mongol invasion and occupation; Pagan state destroyed; 14th-16th century, small, ethnic-based states - Shan in the north and Hmong to the south; 16th century, Burmese Toungoo dynasty subjugated the Shans and reunited the region including parts of Laos and Thailand with subsequent high prosperity and culture; 18th century, increasing contact with Portuguese, Dutch, French and British traders; 1820-1826, 1852-1853 and 1885-1886 Anglo-Burmese wars; 1886, Burma became part of British India; 1930s, recession, increasing independence agitation and increased xenophobia against British, Chinese and Indians; 1937, administrative separation from British India; 1942-1945, Japanese occupation; lack of rice exports to Bengal exacerbated the price-driven Bengal Famine (4 million deaths in Bengal and 6-7 million deaths in Bengal, Assam, Bihar and Orissa); 1943, Burma made "independent" with Burmese National Army under General Ne Win; 1945, army declared war on Japan; 1947, Aung San led the independence movement, organized the transition government and drafted a constitution but was then assassinated; 1948, independence under U Nu (Buddhist socialism); US-backed, defeated Chinese Kuomintang forces involved in heroin trade and major ethnic separatism; 1960, U Nu re-elected; 1962, General Ne Win overthrew U Nu; subsequent military rule for over 4 decades associated with gross human rights abuses, ethnic rebellions (notably the Karen), US-involved opium trade and extreme poverty; 1979, Burma withdrew from the non-aligned movement; 1988, Ne Win retired and was replaced by other generals; name changed to Myanmar; 1990, Aung San Suu Kyi (daughter of nationalist hero Aung San) won landslide victory (80% of vote, 400 out of 485 seats) while in detention; 21st century, continuing gross civil rights abuses; 2005, Aung San Suu Kyi (1991 Nobel Peace Prize) still in detention and the military still in power (1962-2005 excess mortality 15.5 million).

2021 update: 2010, elections; 2011, a nominally civilian but military-controlled government, Aung San Suu Kyi and political prisoners released [she was inspired by "Seven Years Solitary" by political prisoner Dr Edith Bone, cousin of my Hungarian grandmother; my grandfather Jeno Polya, a world-famous surgeon, was arrested and killed by Hungarian fascists]; 2015, Aung San Suu Kyi's party won a majority in both houses but still major military control; 1970s onwards, severe persecution of the Muslim Rohingya minority; 2016, increased military anti-Rohingya violence; 2017, over 700,000 Rohingyas fled to Bangladesh, tens of thousands killed and large-scale rape and village burning; Aung San Suu Kyi disgraced herself internationally by silence, lying and supporting the military over the Rohingya genocide; 2021, military again seized power in a coup d'état, Aung San Suu Kyi and others imprisoned, mass demonstrations with military shooting hundreds of demonstrators, and some international sanctions. 2020 onwards, Covid-19 pandemic with "Covid-19 deaths per million of population" of 59 as compared to 0.4 for Taiwan (March 2021). Massive legal and illegal logging. Revised greenhouse gas (GHG) pollution 41.9 tonnes CO_2-e per person per year. Myanmar has signed but not ratified the TPNW. In 2020 the "under-5 infant mortality as a percentage of total population" (0.0776%) was 53.5 times greater than for Japan (0.00145%), but 3.3 times lower than that in 2003 (0.2560%).

Foreign occupation: Britain, Japan (pre-1950); none (post-1950); *post-1950 foreign military presence:* US-backed defeated Chinese Kuomintang army; *1950-2005 excess mortality/2005 population =*

20.174m/50.696m = 39.8%; *1950-2005 under-5 infant mortality/2005 population* = 9.992m/50.696m = 19.7%. Per capita GDP (nominal) $1,421.

Philippines: 900 BCE Neolithic culture; early migration from southern China; 2nd-15th century, migration from Indonesia; 15th century, Islam spread to southern regions; 1521, Magellan arrived (and died there); 1564, Spanish rule established but continuing Muslim resistance; 19th century, independence movement suppressed; 1898, independence declared but Spain ceded the Philippines to the US (Spanish-American War Paris Armistice); 1899-1913, Philippines-US War, 1 million Filipinos died in this war of national liberation against US forces under General MacArthur I; 1942-1945, Japanese occupation and immense atrocities; 1945, US General Douglas MacArthur II famously "returned"; 1946, independence but immense poverty due to landless peasantry, urban poor, entrenched elites, corruption and US bases; 1966, Marcos elected, increasing repression by a US-backed régime increasingly opposed by the Catholic Church; huge US bases of Clark Air Force Base and Subic Bay Naval Base; 1983, Benito Aquino assassinated on his return at Manila Airport; 1986, electoral fraud blocked widowed Corazon Aquino; Marcos was finally exiled by popular, military-backed consensus; 1986-1992, Corazon Aquino president; subsequent democracy – although there have been unsuccessful military insurrections and continuing Muslim insurrection in the South; 21st century, continuing political corruption, poverty and Muslim rebellion problems; 2003, troops in Iraq; 2004, troops withdrawn from Iraq over a Filipino hostage.

2021 update: continued abusive employment of Filipino workers in the Gulf States; 2016 onwards, Rodrigo Duterte populist president who espouses deadly anti-drug policies (5,000-20,000 killed in extrajudicial killings); 2017, massive bombing damage to Marawi in removal of Muslim insurgents; 2020 onwards, Covid-19 pandemic with "Covid-19 deaths per million of population" of 119 as compared to 0.4 for Taiwan (March 2021). With 7,641 islands the tropical Philippines is seriously threatened by climate change and is already subject to frequent and devastating high-intensity hurricanes (in 2013 Typhoon Haiyan left 8,000 dead or missing).

Revised greenhouse gas (GHG) pollution 9.0 tonnes CO_2-e per person per year. Philippines has signed and ratified the TPNW. In 2020 the "under-5 infant mortality as a percentage of total population" (0.0533%) was 37.3 times greater than for Japan (0.00145%), but 4.8 times lower than that in 2003 (0.2560%).

Foreign occupation: Spain, US, Japan (pre-1950); none (post-1950); *post-1950 foreign military presence:* US; *1950-2005 excess mortality/2005 population* = 9.080m/82.089m = 11.0%; *1950-2005 under-5 infant mortality/2005 population* = 6.665m/82.809m = 8.0%. Per capita GDP (nominal) $3,324.

Singapore: 13th century, originally Temasek inhabitants (people of the sea) and thence Singapura (city of the lion); 1819, British East Indies base under anti-racist and slavery Abolitionist Sir Stamford Raffles; 1824, Singapore Island and adjacent islands purchased by Raffles; key part of British Straits Settlements; 1942, "impregnable" Singapore fell to the Japanese with surrender of about 100,000 Allied soldiers (Australian, British and Indian) who were subsequently starved and severely maltreated; 1945, Allied victory; 1946, Singapore Labor Union general strike; 1948, anti-colonial uprising suppressed; Communists declared illegal and took to the jungle; 1949, municipal elections for English speakers; 1954, Socialist People's Action Party (PAP); 1957, Malaysian independence; 1959, PAP victory and Lee Kuan Yew prime minister of independent Singapore in Federation with Malaysia; PAP split into conservative mainstream and leftist Barisan Socialists favouring Malaysian federation; 1965, Singapore withdrew as an independent republic from the Federation in the context of Chinese-Malay differences; 1965-1975, Singapore economic benefit from Vietnam War; 1967, ASEAN membership; access of US warships to the Singapore naval base; 1974, oil crisis and increasing political conservatism to accommodate international corporate involvements; 1984, PAP re-elected with only 2 opposition members out of 79 members; 1987, opposition politician Jayaratnam removed from office; 1988, only 1 opposition member; 1980s onwards, great economic growth and wealth with diminished dissent; 1990 Lee Kuan Yew retired and replaced by

Goh Chock Tong; 2004, Lee Hsien Loong (son of Lee Kuan Yew) replaced Goh.

2021 update: 1965 onwards, the People's Action Party (PAP) has ruled continuously since independence in a wealth for effective one party rule trade-off; 2020 elections, the PAP dropped to 61% of the vote, and Workers' Party gained 10 of the 93 seats; 2020 onwards, Covid-19 pandemic with "Covid-19 deaths per million of population" of 5 as compared to 3 for China, 0.4 for Taiwan, 1,687 for the US and 1,857 for the UK (March 2021). Revised greenhouse gas (GHG) pollution for extremely prosperous Singapore of 31.2 tonnes CO_2-e per person per year. Singapore has not signed or ratified the TPNW. In 2020 the "under-5 infant mortality as a percentage of total population" (0.0017%) was 1.2 times greater than for Japan (0.00145%), but 2.4 times lower than that in 2003 (0.0040%).

Foreign occupation: Britain, Japan (pre-1950); UK (post-1950); *post-1950 foreign military presence:* UK, US; *1950-2005 excess mortality/2005 population* = 0.113m/4.372m = 2.6%; *1950-2005 under-5 infant mortality/2005 population* = 0.061m/4.372m = 1.4%. Per capita GDP (nominal) $64,103.

Thailand: Shan and Lao peoples in Northern Thailand; 7th century CE, Thai kingdom of Nanchao in Yunnan; 11th century, Nanchao a tributary of China; 1253, Mongol conquest; 13th century, Thais captured Khmer Sukhothai and founded Siam; 13th-18th century, conflict with Khmers (East) and Burmese (North West); 1260, Rama I founded the present dynasty; adoption of Khmer alphabet; 19th century, increasing European influence; British and French conflict over hegemony; 1896, Anglo-French accord, Thais preserved independence; WW1, Siam with Allies; 1932, coup limited powers of monarchy; 1941, accommodation under Pibul with Japan, occupation of part of North Malaya; 1946, relinquished North Malaya territory; 1946, Rama VIII assassinated, pro-US Rama IX installed, subsequent post-war pro-US stance; 1947-1957, Pibul dictatorship; Thai forces to the Korean War; 1954, US-allied South East Asia Treaty Organization (SEATO) based in Bangkok; 1961-1975, large US military presence, increased militarization, drug trade and prostitution; 1974, restored civilian rule; 1975, elections, anti-US Prince Pramoj; 1976, pro-US coup and student demonstrations; 1977, 2nd coup, more liberal military, assistance to anti-Vietnamese Khmer Rouge; 1981, failed military coup with Establishment complicity, General Prem prime minister; 1983, elections and continued democracy but with entrenched corruption, drug trade, prostitution and HIV/AIDS; 1985, 1991, further unsuccessful coups; 21st century, increasing insurrection in southern Muslim areas; 2004, tsunami disaster.

2021 update: 2001-2006, Thaksin Shinawatra Prime Minister; 2006, military coup, Thaksin Shinawatra exiled; 2011-2014, his sister Yingluck Shinawatra prime minister; 2014, military coup; United Front for Democracy Against Dictatorship or "Red Shirt" movement versus "Yellow Shirt" demonstrations; 2020 onwards, continuing massive Red Shirt demonstrations for restoration of democracy. 2020 onwards, Covid-19 pandemic with "Covid-19 deaths per million of population" of 1 as compared to 0.4 for Taiwan (March 2021). Revised greenhouse gas (GHG) pollution 8.7 tonnes CO_2-e per person per year. Thailand has signed and ratified the TPNW. In 2020 the "under-5 infant mortality as a percentage of total population" (0.0017%) was 1.2 times greater than for Japan (0.00145%), but 27.6 times lower than that in 2003 (0.0470%).

Foreign occupation: WW2 Japanese hegemony (pre-1950); none (post-1950); *post-1950 foreign military presence:* US (bases, hegemony, military training and involvement); *1950-2005 excess mortality/2005 population* = 3.756m/64.081m = 5.9%; *post-1950 under-5 infant mortality/2005 population* = 5.442m/64.081m = 8.5%. Per capita GDP (nominal) $7,785.

Timor-Leste: pre-colonial source of sandalwood for Chinese; 16th century, Portuguese occupation; 1719, rebellion suppressed; 1859, Portugal and the Netherlands divided the island; 1895, rebellion suppressed; 1904, Portuguese-Netherlands agreement ratified; 1942-1945, Japanese occupation; 1959, rebellion suppressed; 1974, metropolitan Portuguese Salazar dictatorship removed, pro-independence Fretilin and pro-Indonesian conflict and Portuguese withdrawal; 1975, independence declared by Fretilin followed by UK-, US- and Australia-backed invasion and occupation by Indonesia; 1975-1999, genocide of 200,000 East Timorese out of a population of about 600,000; 1999, UN-supervised plebiscite overwhelmingly for independence but followed by horrendous mass murder and destruction by Indonesian military and militias; UN peace keeping intervention (1975-2000 excess mortality 0.3 million); 2001, elections; 2002, Xanana Gusmao elected president; independence; continuing dispute with Australia over Timor Gap oil reserves (previously appropriated by Australia in agreement with Indonesia); 2006, renewed instability and renewed Australian and UN presence.

2021 update: 2012, UN ceased peacekeeping; 2014, Australian spies spied on Timor-Leste Cabinet for oil and gas interests and in 2018 Australian whistle-blower Witness K and his eminent lawyer, former Australian Capital Territory (ACT) Attorney General Bernard Collaery, charged in pre-police state Australia. 2020 onwards, Covid-19 pandemic but "Covid-19 deaths per million of population" not available (March 2021). Agreement with Australia over oil and gas exploitation boundary. Revised greenhouse gas (GHG) pollution data not available. Timor-Leste has signed but not ratified the TPNW. In 2020 the "under-5 infant mortality as a percentage of total population" (0.1253%) was 87.7 times greater than for Japan (0.00145%), but 2.1 times lower than that in 2003 (0.2590%). Per capita GDP (nominal) $1,561.

Foreign occupation: Portugal, Japan (pre-1950); Portugal, Indonesia, UN (post-1950); *post-1950 foreign military presence:* Portugal, Indonesia, UN; *post-1950 excess mortality/2005 population* = 0.694m/0.857m = 81.0%; *post-1950 under-5 infant mortality/2005 population* = 0.236m/0.857m = 27.5%.

Vietnam: 9th century, defeated Chinese invasion; 13th century, defeated Mongol invasion; 15th-19th century, continuing conflict with China; 1860, French commenced occupation; 1920, pro-independence movements; WW2, resistance to Japanese by Viet Minh founded by Ho Chi Minh; 1945, war against French; 1954, French disaster with Vietnamese capture of Dien Bien Phu; Geneva

Agreement for North and South regions and elections; US violated the agreement by setting up the South Vietnam régime; 1960, National Liberation Front war against US-backed South Vietnamese régime; escalation of the Vietnam War led to involvement of Cambodia and Laos, 580,000 US troops in 1969, greater tonnage of US bombs dropped on Vietnam than in all of WW2 massive defoliant use (with massive birth defect consequences), about 50,000 US dead, 5 million Vietnamese deaths; 1975, liberation of Saigon (Ho Chi Minh City) and US withdrawal (1955-1975 excess mortality 11.9 million); 1979, overthrow of genocidal Khmer Rouge Pol Pot regime; border war with China; 1995, Vietnam-US rapprochement and cessation of US economic sanctions; 21st century, improving economy; major concerns over avian flu infection of humans.

2021 update: pluralist economy under one-party Communist Government; dispute with China over uninhabited South China Sea reefs and upstream dams on the Mekong River; continuing health consequences of massive and war criminal US use of auxin herbicide defoliants with a teratogenic dioxin contaminant (a policy of denial of forest cover and of food) led to 3 million Vietnamese with health problems, 1 million birth defects and 24% of the land being defoliated. 2020 onwards, Covid-19 pandemic with "Covid-19 deaths per million of population" of 0.4 as compared to 0.4 also for Taiwan (March 2019). Revised greenhouse gas (GHG) pollution 1.9 tonnes CO_2-e per person per year. Vietnam has signed and ratified the TPNW. In 2020 the "under-5 infant mortality as a percentage of total population" (0.0320%) was 22.4 times greater than for Japan (0.00145%), but 2.2 times lower than that in 2003 (0.0690%).

Foreign occupation: France (pre-1950); France, US & US allies (post-1950); *post-1950 foreign military presence:* US and US allies (Australia, New Zealand, South Korea and Philippines); *1950-2005 excess mortality/2005 population* = 24.015m/83.585m = 28.7%; *1950-2005 under-5 infant mortality/2005 population* = 8.830m/83.585m = 10.6%. Per capita GDP (nominal) $2,715.

2020 statistical update for South East Asia: Table 9.9
summarizes population, under-5 infant mortality (IM) and excess
mortality (EM; avoidable mortality from deprivation) in South East
Asia in 2020 (pre-Covid-19 projection in 2019 for 2020 by the UN
Population Division). Table 9.1 compares non-Arab Africa with
other global regions. Presented in square brackets for each country
is the "Relative EM Score" of EM/Pop (%) divided by that for the
best-performing country, Japan (0.0020%), which accordingly has
a "Relative EM Score" of 1.0.

In terms of "Relative EM Score" and "per capita GDP" the best
performing countries are democratic Singapore (1.2 and $64,103),
intermittently democratic Thailand (1.2 and $7,785), democratic
Malaysia (7.4 and $11,414) and oil-rich sultanate Brunei (9.4 and
$31,086) (of which all have avoided war for the last half century).
The outcomes for the other countries range from Vietnam (22.4 and
$2,715) to Timor-Leste (87.7 and $1,561).

While the average "Relative EM Score" is 2.2 for Western Europe
and 27.4 for South East Asia it is a shocking 176.6 for non-Arab
Africa (Table 9.1). The "under-5 infant mortality as a percentage of
total population" in 2020 had decreased from that in 2003 by
factors ranging from 1.2 (Singapore) to 27.6 (Thailand).

6.6 The Pacific – colonialism, disease, war and maladministration

The Pacific Islands were variously settled from South East Asian-
derived Micronesians (e.g. Guam and Micronesia), Melanesians
(Papua New Guinea, New Caledonia, Vanuatu, the Solomons and
Fiji) and Polynesians (Samoa, Tonga, Hawaii, Tahiti and New
Zealand). While the Spanish had brutally seized Micronesian
islands in the 17th century, European imperialism involving
Britain, France, Germany and the US commenced in earnest in the
18th and 19th centuries. However Western intrusion into the South
Pacific brought devastation due to introduced disease with possibly
a million dying. Thus in 1875 about 40,000 Fijians died from
introduced measles out of a population of about 150,000. Malaria
in Papua New Guinea (PNG) and the Solomons restricted European

settlement there and consequent avoidance of genocidal dispossession of indigenous peoples as occurred in Australia, New Zealand and New Caledonia. With a mixture of independence and continuing European rule or association, there have been mixed mortality outcomes in the Pacific. Notwithstanding economic difficulties, racial tensions, and 4 essentially bloodless coups, Fiji (with an annual per capita income of only about $2,300) ($6,185 in 2020) has produced good post-1950 mortality outcomes through peace, the rule of law, education and good governance. Island isolation, border closures and cessation of tourism largely saved the South Pacific from Covid-19 but a huge public funeral in 2021 for Sir Michael Somare (first PNG PM) appears to have been a Covid-19 super-spreader event.

Federated States of Micronesia: pre-colonial Micronesian fishing and agrarian culture; 1521, Spaniard Magellan reached Marianas; 17th century Spanish colonization and conversion; 1885, attempted German protectorate but Spanish retention with Vatican intervention; 1898, Treaty of Paris, Guam handed to US; 1898, Marianas, Carolinas and Marshall Islands sold to Germany; 1914, WW1, Japanese occupation; 1918, US-Japanese demilitarization agreement; 1935, US-Japanese accord broken; 1941, Japanese attack on Pearl Harbor (under acute US pressure and with UK and US foreknowledge by code breakage) followed by war in Micronesia and US conquest; 1947, US trust territory under a UN mandate; 1947-1948, Bikini atoll atomic bomb tests; 1954, Eniwetok hydrogen bomb tests; 1968, Bikini and dozens of other sites declared safe but were still radioactive in 1977; continued military use and Johnson Island used for war gas storage; 1979, self-governing; 1982, voted for US Compact of Free Association with US involving US control over foreign affairs; 1986, independence with US control over external affairs; 1991, joined UN; 2002, Compact with the US renewed for 20 years; US occupies Wake Island with its air force but the island is claimed by Micronesia. 21st century, mounting concerns over global warming, sea level rise, more intense cyclones, and storm surges (concerns shared by the Maldives, Kiribati, Tuvalu, Fiji and other Island States world-wide together with deltaic regions such as Bengal and Louisiana).

2021 update: Micronesia votes with the US at the UN; 2019, 5 nations of the Micronesian region withdrew from the Pacific Islands Forum, thereby weakening its international position of strong action on climate change; 2020 onwards, Covid-19 pandemic but "Covid-19 deaths per million of population" not available Revised greenhouse gas (GHG) pollution not available. US-beholden but highly radioactively contaminated Micronesia has not signed or ratified the TPNW and has consistently opposed the TPNW. In 2020 the "under-5 infant mortality as a percentage of total population" (0.0689%) was 47.5 times greater than for Japan (0.00145%), and 1.2 times higher than that in 2003 (0.0560%).

Foreign occupation: Spain, Germany, Japan, US (pre-1950); US (post-1950); *post-1950 foreign military presence:* US; *1950-2005 excess mortality/2005 population* = 0.016m/0.111m = 14.4%; *1950-2005 under-5 infant mortality/2005 population* = 0.007m/0.111m = 6.6%. Per capita GDP (nominal) $3,640.

Fiji: 3000BCE, first settlement, Lapita pottery; 1500BCE, Melanesian settlement; 1643, Dutch explorer Tasman; 1774, British Captain James Cook reached the Polynesian Lau Islands; 1789, British Captain Bligh reached Fiji in an open boat after the mutiny on the *Bounty* ; 1808, Kasavu village massacre by musket-armed, ship-wrecked British sailor Charlie Savage; 1806, epidemic from shipwrecked *Argo* sailors; 1830, first Christian missionaries; 1840, US Commodore Wilkes visited but was subsequently tried and acquitted over abuses; 1871, chiefly federation based on Levuka, Ovalau; 1874, cession to Britain requested by Fijians concerned over US threat (Queen Victoria was amused); 1875, party of Chief Cakobau returned from Sydney with measles; 40,000 died out of a 150,000 population; 1879, first Indian indentured labour (5 year slaves) on the ship *Leonidas*; male to female ratio about 2; 1916, "Girmit" ("Agreement") indentured labor system ceased; 1920, last "5 year slaves" released; flu epidemic killed about 5,000; 1970, independence under Fijian-dominated Alliance led by Ratu Sir Kamisese Mara; 1982, Alliance rule continued; 1987, multi-racial Fijian-Indian Labour government under Dr Timoci Bavadra who upset the US by demanding a nuclear-free South Pacific, rapidly followed by 2 military coups by Sitiveni

Rabuka and republic status – but the so-called "bloodless coup" led to a subsequent increased excess mortality of about 4,500; evidence for US, Australian and Apartheid Israel involvement in the 1987 coup; about 100,000 Indo-Fijians migrated (mainly to North America, New Zealand and Australia); 1998, new constitution; 1999, first Indian prime minister Mahendra Chaudhry heading the multiracial Fiji Labour Party; 2000 Fijian coup led by Anglo-Fijian Australian George Speight with major Fijian political complicity, clear involvement of Apartheid Israel through supply of weapons to the plotters, and followed by military rule and military-installed ethnically indigenous Fijian interim government under Qarase; 2001, new elections won by Fijian United Party (SDL, ethnically indigenous Fijian); 2003, Supreme Court ruled exclusion of Indians from government illegal; 2005, major tourist resort expansion on track, major income from soldiers serving overseas in peace-keeping, devastating EU sugar price decrease foreshadowed; threat of military coup if corruption did not cease and if 2000 coup participants were released from prison.

2021 update: 2006, coup by the overwhelmingly indigenous Fijian Fiji Army led by Frank Bainimarama against corruption and to protect the mercantile Indian minority; 2014, democracy restored; 2014 onwards, Bainimarama Prime Minister; Fiji outspoken over the threat of climate change to Pacific Islands; 2016, Category 5 Cyclone Winston devastated Fiji; Fiji encounters roughly 1 cyclone annually but the intensity of tropical cyclones is increasing with global warming; 2020 onwards, Covid-19 pandemic with "Covid-19 deaths per million of population" of 2 as compared to 0.4 for Taiwan (March 2021). Revised greenhouse gas (GHG) pollution 8.7 tonnes CO_2-e per person per year. Fiji has signed and ratified the TPNW. In 2020 the "under-5 infant mortality as a percentage of total population" (0.0484%) was 33.4 times greater than for Japan (0.00145%), and 1.2 times higher than that in 2003 (0.0470%).

Foreign occupation: Britain (pre-1950); UK (post-1950); *post-1950 foreign military presence:* UK, New Zealand; *1950-2005 excess mortality/2005 population* = 0.054m/0.854m = 6.3%; *1950-2005 under-5 infant mortality/2005 population* = 0.056m/0.854m = 6.6%. Per capita GDP (nominal) $4,295.

French Polynesia: first millennium CE, Austronesian expansion to Tahiti and the Marquesas; 1606, de Quiros "discovered" Tahiti; 1767, Wallis arrived; 1768, Bougainville arrived; 1769, Cook arrived; 1774, Spanish exploration; 1791, Bligh arrived; 1797, London Missionary Society; 1820, Bellinghausen (Russia); 18th-19th century, French missionaries; 1840, French invasion; 1843, French annexation; 1770-1843, population collapse from 40,000 to 6,000 due to French-introduced disease; 1880, official French colony; 1958, "French Overseas Territory"; 1966, atomic tests on Muraroa atoll; 1975, underground tests on Fangataufa atoll; 1960s onwards, international and local opposition to nuclear tests, pressures for decolonization and heavy military presence; 1984, constitution with limited autonomy; 1985, anti-nuclear Greenpeace ship *Rainbow Warrior* sunk in New Zealand by French agents; 1989, European Parliament rejected inquiry into nuclear-related health matters; 21st century, continuing pro-independence movement.

2021 update: 2020 onwards, Covid-19 pandemic with "Covid-19 deaths per million of population" of 500 as compared to 0.4 for Taiwan (March 2021). Threatened by climate change via more energetic hurricanes, sea level rise and storm surges. Revised greenhouse gas (GHG) pollution not available. Occupier France rejects the TPNW, has 290 nuclear weapons and in 1966-1996, conducted 193 atmospheric and underground tests at Mururoa and Fangataufa atolls. In 2020 the "under-5 infant mortality as a percentage of total population" (0.0092%) was 6.3 times greater than for Japan (0.00145%), but 2.4 times lower than that in 2003 (0.0220%).

Foreign occupation: France (pre-1950); France (post-1950); *post-1950 foreign military presence:* France; *1950-2005 excess mortality/2005 population* = 0.018m/0.252m = 7.1%; *1950-2005 under-5 infant mortality/2005 population* = 0.004m/0.252m = 1.5%. Per capita GDP (nominal) $21,567.

Guam: 3000BCE, settlement from China and Formosa (Taiwan); 1521, Spanish Magellan "discovered" Micronesia; 1565, claimed by Spain and conversion to Catholicism; 1668-1695, genocidal invasion by the Spanish – massive decline of Chamorro people from 100,000 (1700) to 5,000 (1741); 1700-1898, stop-over *en route* from Philippines to Spain via Mexico; 1898, Treaty of Paris concluded the Spanish-American War with transfer of Guam, Philippines, Puerto Rica and Cuba to the US; 1941, Japanese invasion; 1944, re-conquest by US; 1950, US citizenship; 1973, UN urging for independence; 1982, 75% plebiscite vote for US-Guam association scheme; 1987, new association with US; 1988, catastrophic typhoon; 21st century, US citizens, elected governor, no Congressman and 1/3 of the island devoted to a major US air base and naval base threatening China and North Korea.

2021 update: continuing upset over US military and US historical military use of herbicides with teratogenic dioxin contaminants; 2020 onwards, Covid-19 pandemic with "Covid-19 deaths per million of population" not available. Threatened by global warming, sea level rise and high intensity tropical hurricanes. Revised greenhouse gas (GHG) pollution not available. The Occupier US has 5,800 nuclear weapons (some no doubt on Guam), opposes the TPNW and has made Guam (like the key US-Australian Pine Gap base near Alice Springs in Central Australia) a prime nuclear target for total thermonuclear destruction. In 2020 the "under-5 infant mortality as a percentage of total population" (0.0155%) was 10.7 times greater than for Japan (0.00145%), but 2.6 times lower than that in 2003 (0.0410%).

Foreign occupation: Japan, Spain, US (pre-1950); US (post-1950); *post-1950 foreign military presence:* US; *1950-2005 excess mortality/2005 population* = 0.0.005m/0.168m = 3.0%; *1950-2005 under-5 infant mortality/2005 population* = 0.008m/0.168m = 4.9%. Per capita GDP (nominal) about $30,000.

Kiribati; 2021 update: Kiribati, mainly the former 6 Gilbert Islands, inhabited by Austronesian peoples; Polynesian and Melanesian inputs; 1300 CE, significant Polynesian Samoan entry; 1892, UK protectorate with the Ellis Islands; exploitation of labour ("blackbirding" of "kanakas" by Australians and others); 1900, exploitation of Ocean Island (Banaba) phosphate; 1941-1943, Japanese occupation ended by US; 1945, Banabans relocated to

Rabi Island in Fiji; late 1950s and early 1960, Christmas Island was used by the US and UK for nuclear weapons testing including hydrogen bombs; 1979, independence; 1982, first elections; 1999, UN member; 2020 onwards, Covid-19 pandemic with "Covid-19 deaths per million of population" not available. Existentially threatened by climate change via more energetic hurricanes, rising sea level, storm surges and salinization; only 1.8 metres above sea level at highest, Kiribati (population 120,000) may disappear this century and speaks out at the UN, the Pacific Islands Forum and the South Pacific Forum. Revised greenhouse gas (GHG) pollution 1.2 tonnes CO_2-e per person per year. Kiribati has signed and ratified the TPNW. In 2020 the "under-5 infant mortality as a percentage of total population" (0.1361%) was 93.9 times greater than for Japan (0.00145%).

Foreign occupation: UK, US (pre-1950); UK (post-1950); *post-1950 foreign military presence:* UK. Per capita GDP (nominal) $1,655.

Nauru; 2021 update: 1000 BCE, settled by Micronesian and Polynesian people; 1888, annexed by Germany; 1906, exploitation of phosphate deposits; 1919, captured by Australian forces; 1920, influenza epidemic killed 18% of the Indigenous population; 1942-1945, Japanese occupation of Nauru ended by Australian forces; 1968, independence; disputation with Australia over phosphate mining compensation payments and possible re-location to Curtis Island off Queensland; 1999, UN member; 2012, onwards, boat-borne refugees indefinitely and highly abusively imprisoned on Nauru without charge or trial in Australian concentration camps; 2016, US agreed to take some of the refugees; many remain as a continuing human rights blot on Nauru and Australia. 2020 onwards, Covid-19 pandemic with "Covid-19 deaths per million of population" not available. Existentially threatened by climate change via more energetic hurricanes, rising sea level, and storm surges. Revised greenhouse gas (GHG) pollution 11.7 tonnes CO_2-e per person per year. Nauru has signed and ratified the TPNW.

Foreign occupation: Germany, Australia (pre-1950); Australia (post-1950); *post-1950 foreign military presence:* Australia. Per capita GDP (nominal) $9,459.

Tuvalu; 2021 update: settled by brilliant Polynesian ocean navigators; 1892, British protectorate as part of the Gilbert and Ellis Islands; 1941-1943, Japanese occupation of Kiribati ended by US operating from the Ellis Islands; 1975-1976, separation from the Gilbert Islands (Kiribati); 1978, independence; 2000, UN member. 2020 onwards, Covid-19 pandemic with "Covid-19 deaths per million of population" not available. Existentially threatened by climate change via more energetic hurricanes, rising sea level, storm surges and salinization; only 4.6 metres above sea level at highest, Tuvalu (population 12,000) may disappear this century and speaks out at the UN, the Pacific Islands Forum and the South Pacific Forum. Revised greenhouse gas (GHG) pollution 1.2 tonnes CO_2-e per person per year. Tuvalu has signed and ratified the TPNW.

Foreign occupation: UK, US (pre-1950); UK (post-1950); *post-1950 foreign military presence:* UK. Per capita GDP (nominal) $4,059.

New Caledonia: 1000BCE Austronesian settlement; 1774, "discovered" by Captain James Cook; 1853, indigenous Kanak population about 27,000; French annexation and subsequent settlement with convicts; 1860, Kanak resistance defeated and Kanaks relocated to reserves; 1860, measles introduced and 25% of indigenous population died; 1867-1897, penal settlement; 1878, further rebellion and destruction of French settlements; 1900s, further removal of Kanak land; 1917, further Kanak rebellion; 1921, Kanak population 18,600; 1946, French overseas territory; 1960s-1980s, nickel boom; 1990s, continuing Kanak drive for land rights; 1998, Noumea Accords postponed independence discussions until 2013; 2000, Kanaks 54,000 out of total population of 145,000.

2021 update: 2018 and 2020, successive referenda rejected independence. 2020 onwards, Covid-19 pandemic with "Covid-19 deaths per million of population" not available. Occupier France rejects the TPNW, has 290 nuclear weapons and in 1966-1996, conducted 193 atmospheric and underground tests at Mururoa and Fangataufa atolls in the Pacific. In 2020 the "under-5 infant mortality as a percentage of total population" (0.0174%) was 12.0 times greater than for Japan (0.00145%), but 1.2 times lower than that in 2003 (0.0210%).

Foreign occupation: France (pre-1950); France (post-1950); *post-1950 foreign military presence:* France; *1950-2005 excess mortality/2005 population* = 0.017m/0.237m = 7.2%; *1950-2005 under-5 infant mortality/2005 population* = 0.003m/0.237m = 1.3%. Per capita GDP (nominal) $34,942.

Papua New Guinea: 40,000BCE, first human settlement; 10000-7000BC, first agriculture; 7000-3000BCE, sophisticated highland valley agriculture among the world's earliest; 1511, "discovered" by Portuguese d'Abreu; 1828, Netherlands claimed the western half (now Indonesian West Irian); 1885; north eastern New Guinea under Germany and south eastern Papua under Britain; 1905, Papua under Australian administration; 1914, WW1, Australia captured German New Guinea; 1919, Papua-New Guinea an Australian League of Nations mandate; 1942, Japanese invasion halted; 1945, Australian UN Trusteeship; 1951, limited home rule; 1963, West New Guinea transferred to Indonesia (with subsequent, continuing indigenous opposition); 1969, Bougainville protests over copper mine environmental damage; 1972, mine established; 1975, independence under PM Michael Somare with post-independence aid from Australia; 1989, copper mine shut down by Bougainville revolutionary army; 1975-1991, PNG military operations in Bougainville backed by Australia; thousands died (mostly from disruption and lack of medicine); a markedly *increased* PNG excess mortality totalling 35,000 in the period 1985-2000 correlates with the Bougainville conflict; 1998, earthquake-triggered tsunami, 1,500 died; 21st century, mining- and forestry-related abuses, lawlessness, corruption, and HIV/AIDs epidemic.

2021 update: 2009, anti-Chinese rioting; 2011 constitutional crisis involving Michael Somare and parliament-elected PM Peter

O'Neill; 2012, army mutiny resolved; 2012-2019, Peter O'Neill PM; 2019, James Marape PM; continuing corruption, environmental problems and West Papua independence activity in Indonesian West Irian; 2012 the relocation of adult male boat-borne asylum-seekers to the Australian Manus Island Concentration Camp; 2016, refugee imprisonment deemed illegal by the PNG Supreme Court; 2013-2017, imprisoned Kurdish Iranian refugee Behrouz Boochani famously wrote his prize-winning book *"No Friend But the Mountains"* by mobile phone from the Australian Manus Island prison; 2017, remaining refugees moved to Port Moresby; 2019, Bougainville referendum, 98.31% were in favour of full Independence for the island; 2021, a huge public funeral for Sir Michael Somare (first PNG PM) appears to have been a Covid-19 super-spreader event. 2020 onwards, Covid-19 pandemic with "Covid-19 deaths per million of population" of 2 as compared to 0.4 for Taiwan (March 2021). Major forestry exploitation. Revised greenhouse gas (GHG) pollution 114.7 tonnes CO_2-e per person per year. The low-lying PNG Carteret Islands became uninhabitable due to sea level rise and the population had to be completely evacuated as "environmental refugees". PNG has not signed or ratified the TPNW. In 2020 the "under-5 infant mortality as a percentage of total population" (0.1314%) was 90.6 times greater than for Japan (0.00145%), but 2.2 times lower than that in 2003 (0.2940%). Per capita GDP (nominal) $2,845.

Foreign occupation: Germany, Britain, Australia (pre-1950); Australia (post-1950); *post-1950 foreign military presence:* Australia; *1950-2005 excess mortality/2005 population =* 0.2.091m/5.959m = 35.1%; *1950-2005 under-5 infant mortality/2005 population* = 0.918m/5.959m = 15.4%.

Samoa (Western): 1200BCE, Austronesian advance and Polynesian settlement; 1722, Dutch "discovery" (Roggeveen) followed by French traders; 19th century, UK, US and German interests; 1830, first missionaries; 1878, treaty with the US; 1885, German settlement and copra industry; 1889, territory divided by Treaty of Berlin – Germany (West) and US (East, now part of the US); 1900, agreement on German "ownership" with Britain "owning" Solomons and Tonga; 1914, WW1, New Zealand occupied Western Samoa and thence ruled it as a League of Nations Trust (from 1920); 1920, influenza epidemic, 21% of population died; 1920s, start of Mau independence movement; 1929, New Zealand troops fired on peaceful Mau demonstrators, killing 10 and wounding 50 on this Black Saturday massacre; 1946, UN trust territory of New Zealand; 1961, UN decolonization pressure led to plebiscite; 1962, independence as a constitutional monarchy; 1990, women's suffrage; 2002, apology by the prime minister of New Zealand to Samoa for past wrongs.

2021 update: 2009, shifted to driving on the left (like Australia and New Zealand); 2011, shifted time zone position (21 hours behind Sydney before, but 3 hours ahead after the change; good for business with Australia). 2016, 5th term as Prime Minister for Tuilaepa (first elected in 1998); 2017, Christianity made the state religion; 2019, measles epidemic due to anti-vaxxer-induced mere 31% of vaccination; ultimately 413 "measles deaths per million of population"; emergency actions (flags on houses, hygiene, curfew, anti-vaxxer prosecution) resulted in 94% vaccination, "herd immunity" and an end of the epidemic, 2020 onwards, Covid-19 pandemic with "Covid-19 deaths per million of population" not available. Revised greenhouse gas (GHG) pollution 6.2 tonnes CO_2-e per person per year. Samoa has signed and ratified the TPNW. In 2020 the "under-5 infant mortality as a percentage of total population" (0.0056%) was 3.9 times greater than for Japan (0.00145%), but 12.3 times lower than that in 2003 (0.0690%).

Foreign occupation: Germany, New Zealand, US (pre-1950); New Zealand (post-1950); *post-1950 foreign military presence:* New Zealand; *1950-2005 excess mortality/2005 population* = 0.039m/0.182m = 21.4%; *1950-2005 under-5 infant mortality/2005 population* = 0.034m/0.182m = 18.7%. Per capita GDP (nominal) $4,285.

Solomon Islands: 1600BCE, Austronesian expansion from South Eastern Asia reached Solomons; 1568, Spanish de Mendena de Neira "discovered" the Solomons; 18th-19th century, slavery ("Kanaka" blackbirding) to Fiji and Australian sugar plantations;

missionaries, slavery and trade associated with catastrophic epidemics; 1886, Britain and Germany agreed on Pacific holdings; Britain secured much of the Solomons; 1900, Germany transferred its holdings (except for Bougainville and Buka) to Britain; WW1, Bougainville and Buka occupied by Australia; 1942, Japanese invasion; 1943-1944, huge US-Japanese battles on Guadalcanal; war devastation; 1945, UK back; 1976, internal autonomy; 1978, independent; 1987-1988, US ship detained; 1988, republic within British Commonwealth; 1990s, problems associated with war on adjacent Bougainville; 1999, indigenous Guadalcanal Isatabus expelled 20,000 Malaitans; Malaitan Eagle Force seized Honiara; armed lawlessness; 2003, Australian peace keeping force intervened and disarmed militias.

2021 update: 2006, anti-Chinese riots; Manasseh Sogavare (hostile to Australian presence) elected PM by Parliament; fierce politics with allegations of corruption; 2019, Sogavare won elections and switched recognition from Taiwan to China; 2020 onwards, Covid-19 pandemic with "Covid-19 deaths per million of population" not available. Revised greenhouse gas (GHG) pollution 1.4 tonnes CO_2-e per person per year. Solomon Islands has not signed or ratified the TPNW. In 2020 the "under-5 infant mortality as a percentage of total population" (0.0597%) was 41.2 times greater than for Japan (0.00145%), but 1.3 times lower than that in 2003 (0.0800%).

Foreign occupation: Britain, Japan, US (pre-1950); UK, Australia (post-1950); *post-1950 foreign military presence:* UK, Australia; *1950-2005 excess mortality/2005 population* = 0.05m/0.504m = 9.9%; *1950-2005 under-5 infant mortality/2005 population* = 0.036m/0.504m = 7.1%. Per capita GDP (nominal) $1,945.

Tonga: 1200BCE, Austronesians arrived; 1616, first Dutch explorers; 1643, Dutch Tasman; 1773, 1777, British Captain James Cook visited the "Friendly Islands"; 18th–19th century, tribal wars; 1845-1893, King George Tupou I (a Christian) expanded the Tongan empire and saved Tonga from colonization; 1862, constitution and legal system; 1893-1918, King George Tupou II; 1889, Anglo-German agreement over Pacific areas of influence;

1890, British protectorate; 1918-1965, Queen Salote Tupou III; 1965, King Taufa'ahau Tupou IV; 1970, independence; authoritarian government dominated by an hereditary ruler; late 1980s, agitation for democratization; 21st century, constraints on freedom of speech.

2021 update: 2020 onwards, Covid-19 pandemic with "Covid-19 deaths per million of population" not available. Threatened by climate change via more energetic hurricanes, sea level rise and storm surges. Revised greenhouse gas (GHG) pollution 7.4 tonnes CO_2-e per person per year. Tonga has not signed or ratified the TPNW. In 2020 the "under-5 infant mortality as a percentage of total population" (0.0359%) was 24.8 times greater than for Japan (0.00145%), but 1.5 times lower than that in 2003 (0.0530%).

Foreign occupation: Britain (pre-1950); UK (post-1950); *post-1950 foreign military presence:* UK; *1950-2005 excess mortality/2005 population* = 0.020m/0.106m = 18.9%; *1950-2005 under-5 infant mortality/2005 population* = 0.020m/0.106m = 18.9%. Per capita GDP (nominal) $4,865.

Vanuatu: 1500-1600BCE, Austronesian expansion reached the Bismark and Solomons archipelagos; 1605, Portuguese de Quiros named Tierra del Espiritu Santo; 1750, de Bougainville circumnavigated; 1774, Cook named the New Hebrides; 19th century, traders, sandalwood exploitation, semi-slavery on plantations, slavery (blackbirding), importation of Vietnamese labour by the French, missionary activity; 1860, epidemic of measles introduced by Europeans killed 25% of the population; 1864, first New Hebrides and Solomons slave labor ("Kanaka" blackbirding) arrived in Fiji; 1887, joint Anglo-French naval Commission; 1906, Anglo-French Condominium; 1942-1945, major US war-time base; post war pro-independence activity; 1975, Melanesian voting for Legislative Assembly; 1979, pro-independence Vanuatu Party won 2/3 of vote over pro-French and pro-colonial interests; 1979-1980, French settlers and US interests behind Espiritu Santo rebellion; suppressed by Britain and France with Papua New Guinea assistance; 1980, independence; post-independence democracy and political corruption.

2021 update: continuing political corruption; 2015, devastated by Cyclone Pan; 2020, devastation by Category 5 Cyclone Harold; 2020 onwards, Covid-19 pandemic; "Covid-19 deaths per million of population" not available; Vanuatu, like other Pacific Islands, protected from Covid-19 by isolation and border control. Like other tropical Island Nations, threatened by climate change via more energetic hurricanes, sea level rise and storm surges. Revised greenhouse gas (GHG) pollution 11.1 tonnes CO_2-e per person per year. Vanuatu has signed and ratified the TPNW. In 2020 the "under-5 infant mortality as a percentage of total population" (0.0720%) was 49.7 times greater than for Japan (0.00145%), but 1.7 times lower than that in 2003 (0.1190%).

Foreign occupation: France, Britain, US (pre-1950); France, UK (post-1950); *post-1950 foreign military presence:* France, PNG, UK; *1950-2005 excess mortality/2005 population =* 0.037m/0.222m = 16.7%; *1950-2005 under-5 infant mortality/2005 population* = 0.029m/0.222m = 13.1%. Per capita GDP (nominal) $3,023.

2020 statistical update for the Pacific: Table 9.10 summarizes population, under-5 infant mortality (IM) and excess mortality (EM; avoidable mortality from deprivation) in the Pacific in 2020 (pre-Covid-19 projection in 2019 for 2020 by the UN Population Division). Table 9.1 compares the Pacific nations with other global regions. Presented in square brackets for each country is the "Relative EM Score" of EM/Pop (%) divided by that for the best-performing country, Japan (0.0020%), which accordingly has a "Relative EM Score" of 1.0.

 In terms of "Relative EM Score" and "per capita GDP" the best performing countries are Samoa (3.9 and $4,285), French Polynesia (6.3 and $21,567), Guam (10.7 and $30,500) and New Caledonia (12,0 and $34,942). The other countries have outcomes ranging from Tonga (24.8 and $4,865) to Papua New Guinea (90.6 and $2,845). While the average "Relative EM Score" is 2.2 for Western Europe and 76.4 for the Pacific it is a shocking 176.6 for non-Arab Africa (Table 9.1). The "under-5 infant mortality as a percentage of total population" in 2020 had decreased from that in 2003 by a factor of 1.2 to 2.6, excepting a 1.2-fold increase in Micronesia and staying roughly the same in Fiji.

6.7 South Asia – the disastrous legacy of rapacious British imperialism

The Indus valley was the site of one of the earliest civilizations. The original Dravidian peoples were forced south by subsequent Indo-European invaders. Hindu civilization (and thence Buddhism) still has a major impact in South Asia and South East Asia. The Mughal Empire brought a tolerant Islamic régime and central administration to South Asia. The huge defeat of the Hindu Marathas by an Afghan-Mughal coalition in the mid-18th century (the Battle of Panipot, 1760) occurred at a time of major expansion of British power in India at the expense of the French.

British exploitation of India was rapacious and highly destructive to human life and to a sophisticated civilization. Thus rapacious taxation and callous British disregard led to destruction of Indian industry, commerce and institutions, and a succession of immense famines from the Great Bengal Famine (1769-1770, 10 million victims) to the man-made WW2 Bengal Famine (1943-1945, 4 million victims in Bengal, and 6-7 million in Bengal and the adjoining provinces of Assam, Bihar and Orissa). Despite a very high birth rate, the Indian population did not increase between 1860 (292 million) and 1934 (292 million). The excess mortality in British-ruled India, calculated for the 8 decades since 1870 using published population and mortality data,[9] was 0.7 billion (the population increasing from 290 million in 1875 to 337 million in 1945 and the annual death rate decreasing over the same period from 48/1000 to 35/1000). Avoidable deaths from deprivation in India (including the native states) in the period 1757-1947 totalled 1,800 million[10]. British departure left a bitterly divided sub-continent and a legacy of communal violence, militarization and war leading to the obscenity of military nuclearization. A legacy of corruption, militarization, poverty and illiteracy have led to massive population growth associated with horrendous excess mortality. However the examples of Sri Lanka and the Maldives (Table 2.11) demonstrate that good mortality outcomes are achievable in this region with modest annual *per capita* income, good literacy, peace and good governance.

2021 update: The really great news is that under-5 infant mortality and avoidable death from deprivation as a percentage of population have decreased 2.9-fold in South Asia since 2003. The bad news is that for South Asia under-5 infant mortality and avoidable death from deprivation as a percentage of population in 2020 are an appalling 53 times greater than for Japan (Tables 9.1-9.12). Thus in 2003 South Asian avoidable deaths from deprivation totalled 5.3 million (Table 8.11) but in 2020 still totalled an appalling 2.0 million (Table 9.11).

Bangladesh: neolithic culture; 1st millennium BCE, ancient Bangla, written history; 800BCE, Aryan Hindu culture dominant in Bihar, Jharkhand and Bengal; 1576-1757, part of the Mughal Empire; 1576, conquered by Akbar; good administrations; taxes to zamindars, the Nawab and thence to the Mughal Emperor; 16th-18th century, Portuguese, Dutch, Danish, French and British traders; 1756, Siraj-ud-daulah captured British Fort William (Calcutta); genesis of the alleged "Black Hole" demonization of Indians (allegedly 146 prisoners went in and only 23 survived the overnight packed imprisonment); 1757, Clive victory at Plassey; 1757-1857, domination by British East India Company; rapacious taxation, famine, destruction of the important indigenous textile industry and genesis of the opium trade to China; 1769-1770, Great Bengal Famine, 10 million over-taxed victims (1/3 of the population); 1775-1785, Warren Hastings first governor-general of India; subsequently impeached by the British Parliament for his crimes in India (e.g. violation of the Begums of Oudh) but was acquitted; 19th century, cholera epidemics and famines; 1857, Indian "Mutiny", Indian rebellion and 10 million Indians killed in reprisals; 1905, administrative separation of West and East Bengal; 1919, influenza epidemic (17 million died in India); 1942-1945 man-made, UK-imposed and Australia-complicit Bengal Famine, 4 million deaths in Bengal (6-7 million deaths in Bengal, Assam, Bihar and Orissa); 1940s, famine- and Partition-influenced demographic deficit of 10 million in Bengal; 1947, independence associated with Hindu West Bengal, Muslim East Pakistan

Partition; millions displaced, 100,000 killed; 1970, Awami League victorious in Pakistan elections; 1971, US-backed West Pakistan military discarded the election results, invaded East Pakistan (East Bengal); 3 million killed (mostly men and boys in a "male gendercide"), 0.3 million women and girls raped, 10 million refugees; India forced to intervene; 1972, Bangladesh founded; 1974, famine; 1975, US-backed coup and assassination of Sheik Mujibur Rahman; 1990s, restoration of democracy; 1991, Bangladesh Nationalist Party elected; 1996, Awami League elected with Sheikh Hasina as PM; 21st century, huge population, groundwater arsenic, poverty, global warming and inundation concerns; continuing but challenged democracy.

2021 update: substantial concrete and steel Indian-Bangladesh Barrier (much of the planned 3,400 kilometres wall completed, 3 metres high, some parts electronic detection-based, ostensibly to stop smuggling but probably to block climate refugees from inundation of Bangladesh); 2004-2008, political turmoil, Islamist terrorism and emergency rule; 2008 onwards, rule by Awami League under Sheikh Hasina; 2018, Sheikh Hasina re-elected as the longest serving Bangladesh PM; road safety protests and student protests; eminent Bangladeshi photojournalist, teacher and social activist, Shahidul Alam, arrested but released after over 100 days after international protests. Major continuing issues of climate change, inundation, sustainability, and globalization-based labour exploitation. 2020, floods left one third of Bangladesh under water, displacing more than 1.5 million people. 2020 onwards, Covid-19 pandemic with "Covid-19 deaths per million of population" of 53 as compared to 0.4 for Taiwan, 3 for China, 1,687 for the US and 1,857 for the UK (March 2021). Bangladesh is already acutely impacted by devastating flooding from major rivers and from coastal inundation due to global warmimg, more energetic hurricanes, sea level rise and storm surges. Revised greenhouse gas (GHG) pollution 2.7 tonnes CO_2-e per person per year. Bangladesh has signed and ratified the TPNW. In 2020 the "under-5 infant mortality as a percentage of total population" (0.0509%) was 35.1 times greater than for Japan (0.00145%), but 4.1 times lower than that in 2003 (0.2110%).

Foreign occupation: Britain (pre-1950); West Pakistan (post-1950); *post-1950 foreign military presence:* West Pakistan (expelled by India); *1950-2005 excess mortality/2005 population =* 51.196m/152.593m = 33.6%; *1950-2005 under-5 infant mortality/2005 population* = 32.908m/152.593m = 21.6%. Per capita GDP (nominal) $1,846.

Bhutan: 7th century, Doukpa Buddhist culture; from 16th century, joint temporal (Deb Raja) and spiritual (Dharma Raja) leadership; 1774, first British contact; 1865, British occupation; 1774, 1865, successive accommodations with the British; 1907, Ugen Wangchuch established an hereditary monarchy; 1910, Treaty of Punalka, British protection but non-interference internally; 1949, treaty with India for protectorate without internal interference; 1960s, source of China-India tensions; 1971, joined UN; 21st century, continuing rule by monarchy; 1970s onwards, progressive democratization; 1989, expulsion of many Nepalese; 1990s onwards, Bhutan a base for Assamese and Bengali guerrillas.; 2006, UK study famously found Bhutan to be very "happy" despite great poverty.

2021 update: 1999, royalty-dominated Bhutan lifted a ban on television and the Internet. 2020 onwards, Covid-19 pandemic with "Covid-19 deaths per million of population" of 1 as compared to 3 for China and 0.4 for Taiwan (March 2021). Revised greenhouse gas (GHG) pollution 4.1 tonnes CO_2-e per person per year. Bhutan has not signed or ratified the TPNW. In 2020 the "under-5 infant mortality as a percentage of total population" (0.0450%) was 31.0 times greater than for Japan (0.00145%), but 7.0 times lower than that in 2003 (0.3170%).

Foreign occupation: British protection (pre-1950); British, Indian protection (post-1950); *post-1950 foreign military presence:* none; *1950-2005 excess mortality/2005 population* = 0.908m/2.392m = 38.0%; *1950-2005 under-5 infant mortality/2005 population* = 0.597m/2.392m = 25.0%. Per capita GDP (nominal) $3,361.

India: 3000-1700BCE, Harappa and Mohenjo Daro civilizations in the Indus Valley; about 16th century BCE, Aryan Indo-European invasion of the Punjab and the Gangetic plain; Brahmanic culture; 800BCE, Aryan Hindu culture dominant in Bihar, Jharkhand and Bengal; Magadha (based at Patna, encompassing Bihar and Jharkand) and Kosala (based at Ayodha, the birthplace of Lord Rama; encompassing Oudh or modern Uttar Pradesh); 540-490BCE, Magadha King Bimbisara, Jainism and Buddhism; 563-483BCE, Buddha; subsequent dominant Hindu-Buddhist culture; 327-325 BCE, transient Greek invasion of NW India under Alexander the Great; Chandragupta of Magadha ousted the Greek invaders and founded the Mauryan Empire; 274-232BCE, Ashoka extended the Mauryan Empire over nearly all India; 185BCE, Mauryan collapse; 2nd century BCE, South Indian prosperity, Tamil Pandya and Chola states; 4th century-1st century BCE, Indo-Greek Bactrian state (Afghanistan) supplanted through Scythian, Parthian, Afghan and Kushan invasions; 2nd century CE, Kushan state of Gandhara under King Kanishka in NW India; 4th and 5th century, Gupta dynasty dominated North India; 8th–13th century, major kingdoms included Palas (Bihar and Bengal), Chola (Tanjore), Chalukya (Deccan), Rajput (North India); 10th-11th century, Muslim incursions and Rajput resistance; Mahmud of Ghazna; 1192, Muslim Ghor defeated Hindus; sultanate of Delhi established; 13th century, Mongol incursions; 14th-16th century, Central Asian Muslim incursions by Timur and his successors; Vijayanagar Hindu Kingdom dominated South India; 1398, Delhi captured by Timur; 16th century, Barbur (1483-1530) founded the Muslim Mughal Empire; 1526, First Battle of Panipat, Muslims under Barbur victorious over Hindus; 16th-18th century, Mughal Empire, administrative efficiency, cultural flowering; Akbar (ruled 1556-1605); Jahangir (ruled 1605-1627); *circa* 1650, Taj Mahal built by Shah Jehan (ruled 1628-1658); Aurangzeb (ruled 1658-1707); 16th-18th century, Dutch, Portuguese, Danish, French and British incursions; 1600, British East India Company (EIC) formed; 1640, British Fort George, Madras (Chennai); 1687, British Bombay (Mumbai); 1698, British Fort William in Calicut (Calcutta, Kolkata); 18th century, major British victories over the French in South India; 1756, Bengal Nawab Siruj-ud-daulah captured Fort William (with the demonizing alleged Black Hole of Calcutta incident of "146 British prisoners in and only 23 out"); 1757, Clive victory at Plassey through bribery; 1760, Hindu Marathas defeated by Muslim-Afghan confederacy under Ahmed

Shah at the Third Battle of Panipat; EIC taxation of Bengal; 1769-1770, famine killed over-taxed Bengalis; 10 million (1/3 of population) perished; 1775-1785, Warren Hastings, 1st Governor-General of India (and adulterous, out-of-wedlock father of Jane Austen's cousin Eliza); extended British control to Oudh (Uttar Pradesh); further British victories over the French, the Mughal Empire, the Marathas, and the South Indian rulers of Mysore Haidar Ali and Tipu Ali; 1786-1795, Hastings impeached for crimes in India but was eventually acquitted; early 19th century, British conquests in India under Wellington and others; 1843, Sind conquered; 1849, Punjab, Kashmir and Peshawar annexed; 18th – 20th century, British rule associated with, massive taxation, destruction of indigenous textile industry, spread of cholera through railways and shipping (25 million deaths) and massive famines (tens of millions of deaths), notably: 1769-1770, Bengal (10 million deaths); 1782-1784, Gangetic plain; 1866-1874, Orissa (Odisha) and Bengal; Rajasthan (recurrently); 1899-1902, huge famine in northern India; 1942-1945, Bengal Famine (6-7 million victims in Bengal and adjoining provinces); 1919-1921, influenza killed 17 million; despite a high birth rate population static from 1860s to mid-1930s (due to deprivation, plague, famine and influenza); 1935-1947, excess mortality 50 million; 1857, Indian Rebellion (Indian Mutiny) suppressed with ferocity (estimates of reprisal deaths range up to 10 million); British government took over control from EIC; 1877, Queen Victoria, Empress of India; 1914-1918, WW1, major Indian military involvement; 1919, Amritsar massacre (380-1,000 killed); 1920s and 1930s, Congress agitation for self-rule led by Nehru and Gandhi; 1935, Government of India Act, provincial self-government, Congress and Muslim League participation in elections; 1939-1945, WW2, 2.4 million Indians in the army; huge decrease in grain imports; imprisonment of leading independence advocates; Bengal Famine (6-7 million deaths; 1940s, Bengal demographic deficit about 10 million); 1947, Independence and India-Pakistan partition associated with 18 million refugees (8 million Muslims and 10 million Hindus) and 0.5-1 million deaths; avoidable mortality in 2 centuries of British rule totalled about 1.5 billion (1.8 billion including the native states); 1948, Gandhi assassinated; post-independence, longstanding armed conflict with Pakistan over Jammu and Kashmir (wars in 1948, 1965 and 1971); India a major figure in the non-aligned movement; major projects (such as the Narmada Dam) have displaced 50 million Indians ("internal refugees"); 1962, China transiently invaded mountain regions and then largely withdrew; 1971, India forced because of 10 million refugees to help Bangladesh from US-backed West Pakistan military; 1975-1977, state of emergency under Indira Gandhi; 1980s and 1990s, communal violence associated with Sikh terrorism, Hindu nationalism and Hindu-Muslim antagonism; 1984, Indira Gandhi assassinated; 1987, tensions with Sri Lanka over Tamil separatists; 1990, Rajiv Gandhi assassinated; Kashmir and Punjab violence; India (1998) and subsequently Pakistan became military nuclear powers; 1990s, decline of Congress and rise of Hindu nationalist party, the Bharatiya Janata Party (BJP); anti-Muslim and anti-Sikh communal riots; 2001-2014, Narendra Modi Chief Minister of Gujarat; 2002, Gujarat riots, over 1,000 Muslims killed with the Modi administration held complicit; 2004, Congress re-elected; 21st century, major IT industry in India; HIV/AIDS threat; continuing poverty and high birth rate; increasing linkage with the US after the collapse of Russian Communism; 2004, tsunami hit the East coast; 2005, some rapprochement with Pakistan after the Kashmir earthquake; 2006, Mumbai 7/11 train bombing atrocity.

2021 update: 2014 onwards, Bharatiya Janata Party (BJP) majority in parliament under PM Modi (first major party majority since 1984); under Modi administration increased foreign investment, decreased healthcare and social welfare, more centralized administration, sanitation campaign, demonetisation of high denomination banknotes that impacted the poor, increased neoliberalism with weakening or abolition of environmental and labour laws, and increased links with Apartheid Israel (under Congress India had formerly led the world against Apartheid in South Africa); 2019, BJP victory under Modi; 2019 onwards, increased authoritarianism, revocation of the special status of Jammu and Kashmir, widespread protests over the anti-Muslim Citizenship Amendment Act; 2020, onwards, huge farmer protests of law changes that would promote big business control of agriculture; 2020, Himalaya border clashes with China with dozens killed; 2021, India, Japan, Australia and US "Quad" togetherness in an unspoken anti-China move. 2020 onwards, Covid-19 pandemic with "Covid-19 deaths per million of population" of 116 as compared to 3 for China, 0.4 for Taiwan, 1,687 for the US and 1,857 for the UK (March 2021). India under increasing impact and threat from climate change through monsoon changes, more intense cyclones, sea level rise, drought, aquifer depletion and deadly urban temperatures. Huge and deadly air pollution in cities with over 1 million deaths annually from ambient (outside) air pollution and a comparable number from indoor pollution; an estimated 1.4 million Indian air pollution deaths from the life-time operation of the "full plan" of the Adani coal mine in Australia. Revised greenhouse gas (GHG) pollution 2.1 tonnes CO_2-e per person per year. India has not signed or ratified the TPNW and with 150 nuclear weapons rejects the TPNW as a nuclear-armed state. In 2020 the "under-5 infant mortality as a percentage of total population" (0.0628%) was 43.3 times greater than for Japan (0.00145%), but 3.5 times lower than that in 2003 (0.2190%). Per capita GDP (nominal) $2,116.

Foreign occupation: Portugal, Britain, France (pre-1950); none (post-1950); *post-1950 foreign military presence:* China (invasion); *1950-2005 excess mortality/2005 population =* 351.900m/1096.917m = 32.1%; *1950-2005 under-5 infant mortality/2005 population* = 214.260m/1,096.917m = 19.5%.

Maldives: South Indian inhabitants; 12th century, Arabs converted islanders to Islam; 15th–16th century, resistance to Portuguese encroachment; 1887, Sultan accepted British protection; 19th-20th century, British naval base on Gan; 1952, republican insurrection against Sultan put down by British; 1957, UK demanded enlargement of Gan base; 1959, further rebellion; 1960, rebellion suppressed by British; 1965, Maldives independent and joined UN; 1968, republic established by plebiscite; 1975, British withdrew from the Gan base; 1980, 1988, successive coup attempts thwarted; 1990s-2000s, concerns over global warming and potential inundation; 2004, tsunami hit but with minimal losses.

2021 update: 2009, famous under-water Maldives cabinet meeting to protest sea level rise due to global warming; 2016 withdrew from the British Commonwealth over criticisms of its assertedly flawed democracy; re-joined in 2020; 2020 onwards, Covid-19 pandemic with "Covid-19 deaths per million of population" of 121 as compared to 0.4 for Taiwan (March 2021). Existentially threatened by global warming with an average ground-level elevation of 1.5 metres above sea level and the highest point 5.1 metres above sea level. Revised greenhouse gas (GHG) pollution 2.1 tonnes CO_2-e per person per year. Maldives signed and ratified the TPNW. In 2020 the "under-5 infant mortality as a percentage of total population" (0.0093%) was 6.4 times greater than for Japan (0.00145%), but 5.8 times lower than that in 2003 (0.0540%).

Foreign occupation: Britain (pre-1950); UK (post-1950); *post-1950 foreign military presence:* UK; *1950-2005 excess mortality/2005 population* = 0.015/0.338m = 4.4%; *1950-2005 under-5 infant mortality/2005 population* = 0.012m/0.338m = 3.6%. Per capita GDP (nominal) $10,626.

Nepal: 4th century CE, Newar Hindu-Buddhist culture of the Katmandu Valley; 8th-11th century, Buddhists from India; Hindu Rajputs established the Gurkha kingdom; 14th –18th century, Newar domination; 1769, Nepal unified by Gurkha King Prithur Narayan Shah; 1792, Gurkha invasion of Tibet stopped by the Chinese; 1814-1816, Gurkha invasion of North India and conflict with the British; Treaty of Sugauli gave British control over foreign affairs; 1846, Kot Massacre; Jang Bahadur Rana as prime minister; 1854, Nepal invaded Tibet (a tributary until 1953); 19th-20th century, international isolation; Gurkha volunteers for the British Army; 1923, British treaty confirmed Nepalese independence; 1950, Congress-led revolt and democratization; 1951, removal of Rana prime ministerial hereditary rule; 1957, the last Nepalese forces left Tibet; 1959, democratic elections; Congress victory; 1960, King Mahendra dissolved parliament; 1961, Sino-Nepalese Treaty; 1989, India closed its border; 1990, civil protest lead to restoration of democracy; 1990s, Congress electoral victories; mid-1990s, Maoist insurgency started; 2001, murder of royal family members by a disaffected prince; 2005, government dismissed and King assumed authority; continuing insurgency.

2021 update: 2008, secular republic ending the world's last Hindu monarchy; 2015 Constitution for a secular, democratic federal state; elected communist government. 2015, massive earthquake killed 9,000 people. 2020 onwards, Covid-19 pandemic with "Covid-19 deaths per million of population" of 102 as compared to 0.4 for Taiwan (March 2021). Revised greenhouse gas (GHG) pollution 24.6 tonnes CO_2-e per person per year. Nepal has signed but not ratified the TPNW. In 2020 the "under-5 infant mortality as a percentage of total population" (0.0593%) was 40.9 times greater than for Japan (0.00145%), but 3.1 times lower than that in 2003 (0.1810%).

Foreign occupation: Britain (pre-1950); none (post-1950); *post-1950 foreign military presence:* none; *1950-2005 excess mortality/2005 population* = 10.650m/26.289m = 40.5%; *1950-2005 under-5 infant mortality/2005 population* = 6.213m/26.289m = 23.6%. Per capita GDP (nominal) $1,074.

Pakistan: for pre-colonial and 18th-19th century history see the India entry; 1757, British defeat of Nawab Siraj-ud-daulah and conquest of Bengal; 19th century, British conquest of NW India; 1839-1842, First Afghan War; 1843, British conquered Sind; 1849, British conquered the Punjab; 1857, Indian Rebellion (Indian Mutiny) suppressed by the British; 1876, British took Quetta; 1878-1880, Second Afghan War of the British versus Baluchis and Pathans; 1906, All India Muslim League founded in Dhaka; 1909, British recognized representative authority of the Muslim league; 1930s-1940s, poet Muhammad Iqbal and lawyer Muhammad Ali Jinnah campaigned for separate Pakistan; 1942-1945, Bengal Famine (6-7 million deaths); 1947, Partition finally accepted by both Muslim League and Indian national congress; Independence and Partition (0.5-1 million dead from communal violence, 18 million refugees – 8 million Muslims, 10 million Hindus); 1954, SEATO member; 1956, CENTO member; US-backed military dictators: 1958, Ayub Khan; 1969, Yahya Khan; 1970, Awami League victory in East Pakistan; Sheik Mujibur Rahman arrested, West Pakistan invasion, 3 million killed (gendercide of males), 0.3 million women raped and 10 million refugees (India forced to intervene despite US threat), Bangladesh independent; 1972, Zulfikar Ali Bhutto formed Pakistan Peoples Party (PPP) government; 1977, Bhutto re-elected, deposed by General Zia ul-Haq and eventually hung after trial; Zia increased Islamic influence; 1985, pro-Zia government elected; 1988, Zia killed in an air crash; 1988, Benazir Bhutto and PPP elected; increase in women's rights; 1996, Bhutto deposed and exiled; 1998, nuclear power status achieved by both India and Pakistan; 1999, Musharraf military dictatorship; 2001, alliance with US against the Afghan Taliban, notwithstanding major Pakistan security and military links with the Taliban; 2005, horrendous earthquake in Kashmir prompted some rapprochement with India; continuing liberal versus strictly orthodox Muslim dichotomies.

2021 update: 1999, Kargil War with India; 1999-2001, General Pervez Musharraf coup d'état; 2001-2008, Musharraf as President from 2001 to 2008; 2007, assassination of Benazir Bhutto in 2007 (2 months before her death and in an interview with Sir David Frost censored by the BBC she had referred to "the man who murdered Osama bin Laden", the jihadi leader the US claimed to have killed in 2011); 2008, PPP victory, PM Gillani, Musharraf resigned; 2010, huge floods affecting 20% of Pakistan; 2012, Gillani disqualified from the Parliament; Pakistan's involvement in the US "War on Terror had cost $118 billion, 60,000 casualties and more than 1.8 million civilians displaced; 2013, Nawaz Sharif PM; 2018, Imran Khan PM; continuing progress to modernity but continuing poverty, corruption, violent extremism against minorities, and Kashmir dispute with India. 2020 onwards, Covid-19 pandemic with "Covid-19 deaths per million of population" of 63 as compared to 116 for India, 3 for China, and 0.4 for Taiwan (March 2021). Pakistan threatened by global warming, and consequent sea level rise, deadly urban temperatures, drought, aquifer depletion and desertification. Revised greenhouse gas (GHG) pollution 2.5 tonnes CO_2-e per person per year. Pakistan has 160 nuclear weapons, has not signed or ratified the TPNW and indeed opposes and rejects the TPNW. In 2020 the "under-5 infant mortality as a percentage of total population" (0.0451%) was 31.1 times greater than for Japan (0.00145%), but 4.5 times lower than that in 2003 (0.2040%).

Foreign occupation: Britain (pre-1950); none (post-1950); *post-1950 foreign military presence:* none; *1950-2005 excess mortality/2005 population* = 49.700/161.151m = 30.8%; *1950-2005 under-5 infant mortality/2005 population* = 29.407m/161.151m = 18.2%. Per capita GDP (nominal) $1,187.

Sri Lanka: early Vedda aboriginal inhabitants (still surviving in remote areas); 6th century, Sinhalese invasion from North India; 483BCE, Vijaya, first Sinhalese king; 3rd century BCE, Buddhism introduced; major Buddhist culture; 11th century, Tamil Chola invasions, Sinhalese resistance; 12th century, Tamil power in the North, Sinhalese power in the South West; 12th-13th century, limited Muslim conversion; 1505, first Portuguese contact; 16th century, Portuguese displaced by the Dutch; 1798, British defeated the Dutch; 1815, final defeat of indigenous resistance by the British; 19th century, introduction of tea, coffee and rubber cash crops; 20th century, independence movements; 1948, independence under S.W. Bandaranaike; 1959, S. Bandaranaike succeeded her assassinated husband; 1960s, growing conflict between Tamils and Sinhalese exacerbated by discriminations against Tamils; 1971, Marxist rebellion suppressed with international help; 1982, J. Jayawardene president; 1980s, worsening ethnic conflict; involvements with Apartheid Israel and the US against the Tamil Tigers; 1987, peace process involving Indian forces; 1990, Indian forces left; 2002, Norway-brokered peace agreement; 2004, Indian Ocean tsunami tragedy (38,000 died and 800,000 were displaced); 2005, peace prospects.

2021 update: 2009, critically supported by Apartheid Israel-supplied planes and bombs, Sri Lankan military defeated the Tamils; the war involved horrendous human rights abuses, 100,000 killed in the Tamil Genocide, 800,000 Tamils left Sri Lanka; 2019, jihadi bombing atrocity killed 267people in churches and tourist hotels; 2020 onwards; human rights abuses continuing; Covid-19 pandemic with "Covid-19 deaths per million of population" of 26 as compared to 0.4 for Taiwan (March 2021). As a large tropical Island Nation Sri Lanka is threatened by climate change. Revised greenhouse gas (GHG) pollution 8.5 tonnes CO_2-e per person per year. Sri Lanka has not signed or ratified the TPNW. In 2020 the "under-5 infant mortality as a percentage of total population" (0.0281%) was 15.0 times greater than for Japan (0.00145%), but 1.4 times lower than that in 2003 (0.0310%).

Foreign occupation: Portugal, Netherlands, Britain (pre-1950); none (post-1950); *post-1950 foreign military presence:* India; *1950-2005 excess mortality/2005 population* = 0.951m/19.366m = 4.9%; *1950-2005 under-5 infant mortality/2005 population* = 1.400m/19,366m = 7.2%. Per capita GDP (nominal) $3,940.

2020 statistical update for South Asia: Table 9.11 summarizes population, under-5 infant mortality (IM) and excess mortality (EM; avoidable mortality from deprivation) in South Asia in 2020 (pre-Covid-19 projection in 2019 for 2020 by the UN Population Division). Table 9.1 compares South Asia with other global regions. Presented in square brackets for each country is the "Relative EM Score" of EM/Pop (%) divided by that for the best-performing country, Japan (0.0020%), which accordingly has a "Relative EM Score" of 1.0.

In terms of "Relative EM Score" and "per capita GDP" the best performing countries are the Maldives (6.4 and $10,626) and Sri Lanka (15.0 and $3,924). The outcomes for the remaining countries range from Bhutan (31.0 and $3,361) to India (43.3 and $2,116) and Pakistan (134.3 and $1,187). While the average "Relative EM Score" is 2.2 for Western Europe and 54.5 for South Asia, it is a shocking 176.6 for non-Arab Africa (Table 9.1).

The good news is that the global "under-5 infant mortality as a percentage of total population" in 2020 (0.0689%) had decreased from that in 2003 (0.1680%) by a factor of 2.4. Indeed for South Asian countries the decrease in "under-5 infant mortality as a percentage of total population" in this 17 year period ranged from 1.4-fold (Sri Lanka) to 7.0-fold (Bhutan).

"2020 avoidable deaths from deprivation" in South Asia (population 1,817 million) totalled 2.0 million or 27% of the total of 7.4 million for the whole world (population 7,687 million), and in non-Arab Africa (population 1,083 million) totalled 3.8 million or 51% of the world's total.

2020 statistical update for North Africa, Asia and Pacific. Tables 9.1 and 9.6-9.11 summarize population, under-5 infant mortality (IM) and excess mortality (EM; avoidable mortality from deprivation) for North Africa, Asia and the Pacific in 2020 (pre-Covid-19 projection in 2019 for 2020 by the UN Population Division). Table 9.1 compares North Africa, Asia and the Pacific with other global regions. Presented in square brackets for each region is the "Relative EM Score" of EM/Pop (%) divided by that for the best-performing country, Japan (0.0020%), which accordingly has a "Relative EM Score" of 1.0.

 The "Relative EM Score" outcomes in 2020 are as follows for the various regions: 7.9 (East Asia), 27.4 (South East Asia), 36.6 (Central Asia, Turkey and Iran), 50.5 (Arab North Africa and the Middle East), 54.5 (South Asia), and 76.4 (Pacific) as compared to 4.4 (Europe as a whole), 54.4 (the non-European world) and a shocking 176.6 for non-Arab Africa (Table 9.1).

The good news is that the global "under-5 infant mortality as a percentage of total population" in 2020 (0.0689%) had decreased from that in 2003 (0.1680%) by a factor of 2.4. For North Africa, Asia and Pacific countries the decrease in "under-5 infant mortality as a percentage of total population" in this 17 year period ranged from 1.1-fold (Macao) to 7.9-fold (Kazakhstan).

In 2020 avoidable deaths from deprivation totalled 265,000 (East Asia, population 1,678 million), 370,000 (South East Asia, population 669 million million), 213,000 (Central Asia, Turkey and Iran, population 292 million), 427,000 (North Africa and Middle East, population 423 million), 1,979,000 (South Asia, population 1,817 million) and 18,500 (the Pacific, population 12 million) as compared to 92,000 for Europe (population 1,062 million), 3.8 million in the non-European World (population 6, 625 million) and 7.4 million in the whole World (population 7,687 million).

6.8 Summary

The World's oldest civilizations came from China, Egypt, Phoenicia, Sumeria and the Indus Valley. The Persian, Assyrian, Egyptian, Hittite and Phoenician empires were ultimately subsumed by the Greek Empire of Alexander with subsequent Hellenization from Afghanistan to Spain. The subsequent Roman

Empire expanded to include territories from Persia to Britain. The Arab conquests of the 7th and 8th centuries brought a flowering of Islamic culture from Persia to Spain that was damaged by the Mongol invasions of the 13th century and the expulsion of the Moors from Spain in the 15th century. Islamic culture variously continued within the Ottoman Empire, in Persia and Central Asia and with the Mughal Empire in India. The early Chinese civilization influenced early civilizations in Korea and Japan. The Hindu Dravidian and thence Indo-European cultures of India variously spread Hinduism and Buddhism to Sri Lanka and to the South East Asian civilizations in Burma, Thailand, Cambodia, Vietnam and Indonesia. Islam eventually variously spread through India, Sri Lanka, Aceh, Malaya, Indonesia and the southern Philippines.

Immensely destructive and violent Western European colonialism began in Asia and Africa in the 15th century and only formally ceased in the post-WW2 era, variously after bloody colonial and post-colonial wars. Russian occupation of the Muslim lands of Central Asia ceased in about 1990. Supplanting indigenous or Ottoman Turkish rule from North Africa to Arabia took the European powers 2 centuries. However Apartheid Israel still occupies Palestinian, Lebanese and Syrian territory and the US, in addition to major influence with Arab dictatorships and military bases in Central Asia and the Gulf States, has military variously occupying Iraq, Syria and Afghanistan. The post-1950 excess mortality associated with Asian wars directly involving US combat forces in the Middle East, Central Asia, East Asia and South East Asia has been horrendous, specifically: 0.8 million (Korea), 13.1 million (Cambodia, Laos and Vietnam), 2.3 million (Iraq) and 1.6 million (Afghanistan) (2007 estimates). Over the last half century the East Asian countries have recovered remarkably from the consequences of total war. A scattering of relatively poor but good mortality outcome countries, namely Malaysia, the Maldives, Sri Lanka and Thailand, illustrate what peace, literacy, modest prosperity and good governance can achieve in the way of eliminating avoidable mortality. The excess mortality in British India for the 9 decades since 1870 totalled 0.7 billion and represents an immense crime against humanity that is largely resolutely ignored by both academia and media. History ignored has meant history repeated in the post-1950 era including the 21st century. Bangladesh and West Bengal that have suffered enormously from European colonialism are now facing the acute danger of inundation from First World industrial profligacy, global warming and increases in sea level and high-energy tropical storms.

CHAPTER 7:
NON-ARAB AFRICA — COLONIALISM, NEO-COLONIALISM, MILITARISM, DEBT, ECONOMIC CONSTRAINT AND INCOMPETENCE

"Exterminate all the brutes."

Kurtz in *Heart of Darkness* by Joseph Conrad[1] and title of a key book on colonial racism by Sven Lindqvist.[2]

"I know enough tribes in Africa. They all have the same mentality insofar as they yield only to force. It was and remains my policy to apply this force by unmitigated terrorism and even cruelty. I shall destroy the rebellious tribes by shedding rivers of blood and money. Only thus will it be possible to sow the seeds of something new that will endure."

General von Trotha, responsible for the German genocide of the Hereros of South West Africa.[3]

"The Herero people will have to leave the country. Otherwise I shall force them to do so by means of guns. Within the German boundaries, every Herero, whether found armed or unarmed, with or without cattle, will be shot. I shall not accept any more women and children. I shall drive them back to their people – otherwise I shall order shots to be fired at them."

The "Extermination Order" by General von Trotha, 2 October 1904, that forced scores of thousands of Hereros to die in the desert.[4]

"The Nazis gave the Jews a star on their coats and crowded them into "reserves" – just as the Indians, the Hereros, the Bushmen, the Amandabele, and all the other children of the stars had been crowded together. They died on their own when the food supply was cut off ... Auschwitz was the modern industrial application of a policy of extermination on which European world domination had long since rested."

Sven Lindqvist in *Exterminate all the Brutes.*[5]

"Why is it that in this courtroom I am facing a white magistrate, confronted by a white prosecutor, escorted by white orderlies? Can

anybody honestly and seriously suggest that in this type of atmosphere the scales of justice are evenly balanced? Why is it that no African in the history of this country has ever had the honour of being tried by his own kith and kin? ... Your Worship, I hate racial discrimination most intensely and in all its manifestations. I have fought it all my life. I fight it now, and will do so until the end of my days. I detest most intensely the set-up that surrounds me here. It makes me feel that I am a black man in a white man's court. This should not be."

Nelson Mandela, defending himself in court, October 1962.[6]

7.1 Overview of the continuing African tragedy

The awful history of colonial and post-colonial non-Arab Africa is sketched below with key dates as points of relativity. The countries are dealt with in alphabetical order for simplicity and ease of reference in relation to the core mortality data presented in Tables 2.12, 8.12 and 9.12. Foreign countries explicitly involved by military participation in the pre- and post-1950 eras are listed at the end of each "history" together with the 1950-2005 excess mortality and 1950-2005 under-5 infant mortality (in millions, m) expressed as a ratio with respect to the 2005 population (in millions, m), each ratio being presented as a percentage (%). The 1950-2005 excess mortality/2005 population ratio is at a typical Western European level for the Indian Ocean island states of Mauritius and Réunion (5.1% and 6.0%, respectively), demonstrating that peace, humane administration, literacy and a modest annual *per capita* income can yield excellent mortality outcomes.

For the rest of non-Arab Africa the 1950-2005 excess mortality/2005 population ratio is appallingly high and ranges from 19.4% (Western Sahara) to 85.2% (Sierra Leone), the highest value for any country in the World. The colonial history of non-Arab Africa involves European invasion, occupation, indigenous dispossession, exploitation (through slavery, forced labour, dispossession and global economics) and crude destruction for commercial gain of sophisticated indigenous societies and economies that had evolved intelligently over centuries to maximize nutrition and minimize disease (notably malaria).

All of the countries of non-Arab Africa were occupied by First World countries in the post-war era but eventually secured indigenous rule. However the period after colonial or minority White rule typically involved neo-colonial First World impositions that variously included neo-colonial control; corrupt and incompetent rule by First World-installed client régimes or successor governments dominated by the military and/or privileged elites; economic exclusion, economic constraint and crippling debt; militarization, consequent debt, civil war and international war; and sustained malignant interference by First World powers, notably Britain, France, Portugal, White South Africa and the US.[7]

The sheer incompetence of the post-European régimes is illustrated by the spread of HIV/AIDS. Since AIDS was recognized in 1981, serological testing was rapidly developed and generally available since 1985. Prevention campaigns should have been a major priority for *all* countries and certainly worked extraordinarily well in the First World. While African régimes were able to spread the word on desired political allegiance throughout semi-literate populations they failed to prevent the spread of HIV infection. Sub-Saharan Africa with about 10% of the World's population has about 2/3 of the World's HIV-infected people. In 2005 in sub-Saharan Africa there were 25.8 million HIV positive people, 7% of adults were HIV positive, 3.2 million people were newly infected with HIV and 2.4 million died of AIDS.

The HIV/AIDS epidemic is particularly acute in Southern Africa, Central Africa and East Africa. Thus the percentage the population that is HIV positive (2003) (listed in descending order for the worst non-Arab African countries) is: 20.6% (Swaziland), 19.9% (Botswana), 17.9% (Lesotho), 14.1% (Zimbabwe), 11.9% (South Africa), 10.7% (Namibia), 8.6% (Zambia), 7.0% (Mozambique), 7.5% (Malawi), 6.8% (Central African Republic), 4.4% (Tanzania), 3.8% (Kenya), 3.7% (Burundi), 3.6% (Gabon), 3.5% (Côte d'Ivoire), 3.1% (Rwanda), 3.1% (Liberia), 2.9% (Nigeria), 2.4% (Congo, Brazzaville), 2.4% (Ethiopia), 2.4% (Chad), 2.3% (Togo), 2.1% (Congo, Zaire) and 2.1% (Uganda). Muslim countries and French West African countries have fared much better than the rest.[8]

7.2 Short histories of the countries of Non-Arab Africa

The following short histories of the countries of Non-Arab Africa provide evidentiary background to the proposition that the current appalling excess mortality in these states is linked to their colonial experience. These impoverished and colonially enslaved countries were the products of arbitrary European colonial activity (of which the most absurd was British sequestration of territory immediately adjacent to the Gambia River and French seizure of wider territories around this key fresh water and transport resource). Typically impoverished and with major internal disagreements relating to settlers, European hegemony, indigenous élites, tribal differences, religion and socialism/capitalism, these countries variously gained nominal independence in the 1960s and 1970s in the context of the Cold War and in many cases after protracted political and armed struggle.[9] However, independence was typically replaced by neo-colonial economic and indeed military involvements. Accordingly, each entry contains a summary including pre- and post-1950 foreign occupation, post-1950 foreign military presence and the "1950-2005 excess mortality/2005 population" and "1950-2005 under-5 infant mortality/2005 population" ratios. Because of the devastating impact of HIV/AIDS, the percentage of the population infected with HIV is also presented at the end of each entry.

2021 updates. The original edition text has been largely unchanged except for pertinent additions, amplifications and corrections. 2021 updates are added at the end of each short history. In particular, because Humanity is existentially threatened by (a) climate change and (b) nuclear weapons, the 2021 updates include information on each country in relation to (a) climate change (notably threats from man-made climate change and revised annual greenhouse gas (GHG) pollution taking land use into account and expressed as tonnes CO_2-equivalent (CO_2-e) per person per year),[10] and (b) ratification or otherwise of the UN Treaty on the Prohibition of Nuclear Weapons (TPNW) that came into effect in International Law on 22 January 2021 and which prohibits State Parties from possession of nuclear weapons and support for such possession "in any way" (data from the Nobel Prize-winning International Campaign Against Nuclear Weapons (ICAN)).[11] Poverty kills, and included at the end of each national history is per capita GDP (nominal) (UN, 2019, in US dollars).[12] "Covid-19 deaths per million of population" (Worldometer, March 2021)[13] are given as indicators of multivariable-determined intra-national altruism and ability to deal with the Covid-19 Pandemic.

Angola: pre-historical Khoisan hunter-gatherers; 13th century CE, Bantu invasion from the North; Portuguese fleet arrived; 1482-1902, resistance to Portuguese invasion and occupation, especially by the Mbundu Kingdom in Central Angola; 1482; 1641-1648, brief coastal Dutch occupation; 1575, Luanda established; rich source of slaves for Brazil; 1850, population only 8 million (reduced from 18 million in 1450 by slavery and war); 1884, Berlin Conference dividing up Africa; 1890-1902, continuing pacification and Portuguese colonization; 1902, Mbundu Kingdom crushed after capture of the Bié Plateau; 20th century, construction of the Benguela Railway and major Portuguese colonization of the highlands; 1956-1974, major armed resistance by the socialist Angolan MPLA against the Portuguese army (50,000 soldiers) and 500,000 Portuguese settlers; 1961, revolt suppressed; 1962, FNLA formed in the Congo; 1974, overthrow of the metropolitan Portuguese dictator Salazar by army; 1975, independence declared by the socialist MPLA (People's Movement for the Liberation of Angola, Movimento Popular de Libertação de Angola); 1975-2002, protracted civil war between MPLA government forces (Soviet-supported and eventually with Cuban forces) against US- and Zaire-backed FNLA (with invading Zairean forces) and South Africa- and colonist-backed UNITA (with invading South African forces); 1989, Cuban forces left; 1993, the fall of Apartheid in South Africa lessened UNITA support; 2001, international diamond certification restricted UNITA funding; 2002, fragile ceasefire after the UNITA leader Savimbi died and 1 million had been killed in the civil war (1955-2005 excess mortality 8.5 million); 21st century, poverty and HIV epidemic.

2021 update: 2008 and 2012, elections; 2016, new constitution adopted; continuing problems of poverty, minefields, pro-independence violence in the Cabinda enclave, refugees, human rights abuse and corruption. 2016 drought caused the worst food crisis in Southern Africa in 25 years, severely affecting 1.4 million people in 7 of 18 Angola provinces; 2017, José Eduardo dos Santos resigned and stepped down as president after 38 years, peacefully succeeded by João Lourenço. 2020 onwards, Covid-19 pandemic with "Covid-19 deaths per million of population" of 16 as compared to 0.4 for Taiwan (March 2021). Major forestry and fossil fuels industries. Revised greenhouse gas (GHG) pollution

23.8 tonnes CO_2-e per person per year. Angola has signed and but not yet ratified the TPNW. In 2020 the "under-5 infant mortality as a percentage of total population" (0.3012%) was 207.7 times greater than for Japan (0.00145%), but 4.5 times lower than that in 2003 (1.360%). Per capita GDP (nominal) $2,671.

Foreign occupation: Portugal (pre-1950); Portugal (post-1950); *post-1950 foreign military presence:* Cuba, Portugal, South Africa, Zaire; *1950-2005 excess mortality/2005 population =* 9.207m/14.533m = 63.4%; *1950-2005 under-5 infant mortality/2005 population* = 6.002m/14.533m = 41.3%; HIV positive (2003) 1.8%.

Benin: 12th -13th century CE, Aja people founded Allada; 16th-17th century, height of sophisticated Greater Ardra society based on Allada; 1602, foundation of Abomey by Aja people and development of Dahomey society; 17th-19th century, slavery by Dahomey supplying the British, French and Portuguese; 1818-1856, notwithstanding a British ban, slavery continued by circumvention; 1863, French protectorate over capital Porto-Novo; 1891-1894, French invasion and conquest; 1904, Benin part of French West Africa; 20th century, French economic exploitation of "Dahomey"; post-war resistance to brutal and exploitative French rule; 1946, a French overseas territory; 1958, member of the French Community; 1960, formal independence for an economically crippled country; 1963, military coup; 1972, military coup and long-term Kérékou socialist dictatorship; 1977, unsuccessful invasion by French mercenary, Morocco and Gabon forces; 1989-1991, economic crisis; 1991, first democratic elections won by opposition leader Soglo; 1996-2004, Kérékou was "democratically" elected in 1996 and again in 2001.

2021 update: 1999, Kérékou gave a national apology for African complicity in the Atlantic slave trade; 2006 and 2011, Yayi Boni elected president; 2016, businessman Patrice Talon elected president. 2020 onwards, Covid-19 pandemic with "Covid-19 deaths per million of population" of 7 as compared to 0.4 for Taiwan (March 2021). Lumber industry, deforestation and 2-fold "biocapacity deficit". Revised greenhouse gas (GHG) pollution

24.5 tonnes CO_2-e per person per year. Benin has signed and ratified the TPNW. In 2020 the "under-5 infant mortality as a percentage of total population" (0.3213%) was 221.6 times greater than for Japan (0.00145%), and 2.0 times lower than that in 2003 (0.6400%).

Foreign occupation: Britain, France, Portugal (pre-1950); Spain (post-1950); *post-1950 foreign military presence:* Gabon, France, Morocco; *1950-2005 excess mortality/2005 population* = 3.267m/7.103m = 46.0%; *1950-2005 under-5 infant mortality/2005 population* = 2.093m/7.103m = 29.5%; HIV positive (2003) 1.0%. Per capita GDP (nominal) $1,220.

Botswana: original San (Bushmen) hunter-gatherer inhabitants; 17th century CE, Tswana occupation; 19th century, increasing incursion by Dutch Boers and by Zulus displaced by Boers; 1820, Khama II successfully resisted the Zulu-derived Ndebele; 1867, gold discovered; late 19th century, increasing Boer intrusions and German depredations in South West Africa (Namibia); 1884-1885, Khama III secured British protectorate over Bechuanaland; 1948, rise of Afrikaaner National Party Apartheid; Britain unwilling to hand over Bechuanaland to South Africa; 1966, independent Botswana; democracy under Seretse Khama (ruled 1965-1980) who had famously married English woman Ruth Williams (this upsetting racist Apartheid South Africa and tribal conservatives); 1980s, notwithstanding close economic relations including major migrant labour to South Africa, increasing conflict with White-ruled South Africa over African National Congress (ANC) refuge in Botswana; 1985, South African military attack on capital Gaborone; 1993, end of Apartheid in South Africa followed by immense increases in HIV-1 infection in both countries (Botswana, Lesotho and Swaziland lead the world in HIV infection). Botswana National Front (BNF) (labour-oriented) and Botswana Democratic Party (BDP) political dichotomy; BDP in power since 1989.

2021 update: 1984, 1989 and 1994, Seretse Khama's former vice president Quett Masire successively elected president; 1999, dispute with Namibia over part of the Caprivi Strip resolved by the International Court of Justice; 1999 and 2004, Festus Mogae elected president; 2008, Ian Khama (son of the first President Seretse Khama) elected president; 2018 Mokgweetsi Eric Keabetswe Masisi president (all presidents elected since independence belonged to the Botswana Democratic Party). 2014, 20% of population HIV-1 positive, this being associated with employment in neighbouring South Africa; 2020 onwards, Covid-19 pandemic with "Covid-19 deaths per million of population" of 212 as compared to 0.4 for Taiwan (March 2021). Major methanogenic livestock industry. Revised greenhouse gas (GHG) pollution 64.9 tonnes CO_2-e per person per year. Botswana has signed and ratified the TPNW. In 2020 the "under-5 infant mortality as a percentage of total population" (0.0853%) was 58.8 times greater than for Japan (0.00145%), but 4.3 times lower than that in 2003 (0.3700%).

Foreign occupation: Britain, Dutch Boers (pre-1950); UK (post-1950); *post-1950 foreign military presence:* South Africa, UK; *1950-2005 excess mortality/2005 population* = 0.443m/1.801m = 24.6%; *1950-2005 under-5 infant mortality/2005 population* = 0.236m/1.801m = 13.1%; HIV positive (2003) 19.9%. Per capita GDP (nominal) $7,961.

Burkina Faso: 12th century CE, Bobo, Lobi and Gurunsi people (West), Mossi states (Central Ouagadougou, Yatenga and Tengkodogo states) and Gourma (East); 14th-16th centuries, sophisticated Mossi states defeated Mali and Songhai Empire invasions; the Burkinabes were fiercely independent but no match for heavily armed and brutal French invaders; 1885-1904, genocidal French invasion generated last ditch resistance that simply intensified French ferocity with millions fleeing to neighbouring countries; about 1900-1919, administered as part of French Soudan (Upper Senegal, now Mali); the major resource of the country was man-power for French plantations and war; 1919, Upper Volta; 1932, divided administratively between Cote d'Ivoire, Soudan and Niger; 1947, Upper Volta part of the French Union; 1958, autonomy within the French Community; 1960, nominal independence from France under Yaméogo; post-independence, short periods of elected governments interrupted by military coups;1965, Yaméogo re-elected; 1966, military coup under Lamizana; 1960s and 1970s, drought and major French aid; 1978, Lamizana elected under a new constitution; 1980, military coup; 1983, Sankara to power in a violent coup; non-alignment; 1987, further coup and Sankara killed.

2021 update: 1987, Blaise Compaoré became president; 1989 coup attempt; 1991, new constitution followed by successive flawed elections; 1991, 1998, and 2005, Blaise Compaoré was re-elected in elections boycotted by the opposition; post-independence French military presence and French forces boosted in 2013 as part of Operation Barkhane directed against Muslim rebels in the Sahel; 2014, Blaise Compaoré was ousted from power by popular revolt and exiled to the Ivory Coast; 2014, Michel Kafando transitional president; 2015, a military coup d'état against the Kafando government was carried out by the former presidential guard of Compaoré; 2015, after pressure from the African Union, the Economic Union of West African States and the armed forces, the military junta restored Kafando as acting president; 2015, Roch Marc Christian Kaboré elected president. 2020 onwards, Covid-19 pandemic with "Covid-19 deaths per million of population" of 7 as compared to 0.4 for Taiwan (March 2021). Subsistence agriculture and livestock economy threatened by climate change and drought. Revised greenhouse gas (GHG) pollution 7.3 tonnes CO_2-e per person per year. Burkina Faso has not signed or ratified the TPNW. In 2020 the "under-5 infant mortality as a percentage of total population" (0.2853%) was 196.8 times greater than for Japan (0.00145%), but 3.4 times lower than that in 2003 (0.9600%).

Foreign occupation: France (pre-1950); France (post-1950); *post-1950 foreign military presence:* France; *1950-2005 excess mortality/2005 population* = 6.810m/13.798m = 49.4%; *1950-2005 under-5 infant mortality/2005 population* = 4.793m/13.798m = 34.7%%; HIV positive (2003) 2.3%. Per capita GDP (nominal) $787.

Burundi: Original Twa inhabitants; 11th century CE, Hutu invasion; 15th century, Tutsi invasion; cattle-herding Tutsi dominance over agrarian Hutus; pre-colonial times with major strife between the two groups; 1890, German colonization and

ivory trade; part of German East Africa; 1899, Rwanda and
Burundi merged; 1918, Belgium took over the colony and
separated the 2 states; 1962, nominal independence under neo-
colonial puppet régime followed by a succession of coup-installed
governments; 1965, Hutu revolt suppressed with Hutu refugees
fleeing to Tanzania; 1967-1988, 1976-1987, 1988, further inter-
racial strife and massacres of Hutus; 1972, massive genocide of 0.3
million Hutus under the Tutsi-dominated government of Michel
Micombero; 1976, coup by Tutsi Colonel Jean-Baptiste Bagaza;
1984, Bagaza was elected head of state under a new constitution;
political repression; 1987, coup by Tutsi Major Pierre Buyoya
(Tutsi) who re-instated military rule; 1988, anti-Tutsi pogroms by
Hutus in northern Burundi killed 5,000; amnesty, "culture of
impunity" and increased Hutu ministerial representation; 1993, first
free elections won by Hutu Melchior Ndadaye who was murdered
in a subsequent coup by the Tutsi-dominated army; subsequent
Hutu rebellion, civil strife, neighbour and African Union
intervention with African Union and UN peace keepers.

2021 update: 1993–2005, Burundian Civil War between Hutu
rebels and the Tutsi army, with 300,000 people (mostly civilians)
killed; 1994, the parliament elected Hutu Cyprien Ntaryamira as
president; Cyprien Ntaryamira and Juvénal Habyarimana, the
president of Rwanda, both Hutus, killed when plane shot down;
more Hutu refugees fled to Rwanda; Hutu Sylvestre
Ntibantunganya made president; in neighbouring Rwanda, spurred
on by the government, Hutu soldiers and gangs killed 0.5-1.0
million Tutsis and connected Hutus (Rwanda Genocide); 1996,
Tutsi Pierre Buyoya took power through coup d'état; massive
internal refugee problem; peace talks initiated mediated by South
Africa; 2001, peace plan adopted; 2003, ceasefire between Tutsi-
dominated government and the largest Hutu rebel group; Hutu
Domitien Ndayizeye elected president; 2005, Hutu Pierre
Nkurunziza and former rebel group leader was elected president;
2020 onwards, Covid-19 pandemic with "Covid-19 deaths per
million of population" of an asserted 0.5 as compared to 0.4 for
Taiwan (March 2021). Subsistence agricultural and livestock
grazing leading to deforestation, soil erosion and massive
ecosystem loss; by 2005 less than 6% tree cover and half of that
commercial plantations. Revised greenhouse gas (GHG) pollution

5.5 tonnes CO_2-e per person per year. Burundi has not signed and ratified the TPNW. In 2020 the "under-5 infant mortality as a percentage of total population" (0.2211%) was 152.5 times greater than for Japan (0.00145%), but 3.8 times lower than that in 2003 (0.8400%).

Foreign occupation: Germany, Belgium (pre-1950); Belgium (post-1950); *post-1950 foreign military presence:* Belgium, UN; *1950-2005 excess mortality/2005 population* = 4.097m/7.319m = 38.3%; *1950-2005 under-5 infant mortality/2005 population* = 2.263m/7.319m = 30.9%; HIV positive (2003) 3.7%. Per capita GDP (nominal) $260.

Cameroon: Original homeland of Bantus who thence migrated south and east over the last 2 millennia; Fulani, Fang, Hausa, Kanuri people; Sao civilization around Lake Chad and Baka hunter-gatherers in southeastern rainforest; 1472, Portuguese contact; 15th-19th century, British, Dutch, French, Portuguese and Spanish slave trade; 19th century, Fulani soldiers founded Adamawa Emirate in the north; known as "Africa in miniature" because of its geographical and cultural diversity; 250 native languages spoken by 25 million people; 1850s, British missionary and trading; 1884, German protectorate of the coastal Doualas; 1894, northern Fulahs under German rule; 1897-1901, revolt of Doualas; 1911, additional territory acquired from France; 1916, brutal German administration removed by the British and French; formerly ceded territory re-joined French Equatorial Africa; 1919, British and French zones established in a League of Nations Mandate; post-war independence movements especially directed against French rule; 1946, joint Anglo-French UN Mandate; 1950s to 1971, insurrection in the French region by Union des Populations du Cameroun (UPC) in the Bamileke War; 1957, self-government granted by France; 1960, independence of the French region; 1961, UN plebiscite and integration as a federation under Ahmadou Ahidjo; 1972, unitary state established; one-party rule; 1982, Ahidjo appointed Paul Biya (PM 1975-1982) as his replacement; 1984, coup attempt failed; 1990, restoration of multi-party "democracy"; 1992, 1997, 2004, 2011 and 2018 Biya re-elected president; dominant Cameroon National Union (CNU) renamed Cameroon People's Democratic Movement in 1985; 1990s, clashes with Nigeria over the oil-rich Bakassi Peninsular; 2002, ICJ decision favoured the Bakassi Peninsular going to Cameroon; 2003, territorial adjustments.

2021 update: 2018, Biya re-elected; second-longest-ruling president in Africa (after Teodoro Obiang of Equatorial Guinea), and the oldest head-of-state in Africa; poverty, freedom of speech and human rights issues; 2020 onwards, Covid-19 pandemic with "Covid-19 deaths per million of population" of 22 as compared to 0.4 for Taiwan (March 2021). Major timber industry and significant deforestation for farming and palm oil; 64% tree cover and biodiversity hot spot; large decrease in shallow Lake Chad; climate change threat. Revised greenhouse gas (GHG) pollution 29.5 tonnes CO_2-e per person per year. Cameroon has not signed or ratified the TPNW. In 2020 the "under-5 infant mortality as a percentage of total population" (0.2864%) was 197.5 times greater than for Japan (0.00145%), but 2.1 times lower than that in 2003 (0.6100%).

Foreign occupation: Germany, Britain, France (pre-1950); UK, France (post-1950); *post-1950 foreign military presence:* France, UK; *1950-2005 excess mortality/2005 population =* 6.669m/16.564m = 40.3%; *1950-2005 under-5 infant mortality/2005 population* = 3.818m/16.564m = 23.0%; HIV positive (2003) 3.5%. Per capita GDP (nominal) $1,534.

Cape Verde: 15th century Portuguese discovery and invasion; 1456, discovery by da Cadamosto; 1460, Gomes landed on uninhabited islands; 1462, first Portuguese colonists; 15th-16th century Portuguese settlement; trans-shipment centre for the slave trade; subsequent penal colony; 1876, end of slave trade; 1879, cessation of Portuguese Guinea (Guinea-Bissau) administration with Cape Verde; 1951, overseas province of Portugal; 1956, African Party for the Independence of Guinea and Cape Verde (PAIGC) for independence of Portuguese West African Portuguese colonies; 1960s, 1970s, armed struggle in Guinea-Bissau, Angola and Mozambique; 1974, Portugal Salazar dictatorship overthrown by the military; 1975, Cape Verde independence and the revolutionary party PAIGC took power in both Cape Verde and Guinea-Bissau; 1980, coup in Guinea-Bissau, unity plans terminated and Cape Verde versus Guinea-Bissau tensions; 1981, PAIGC renamed African Party for the Independence of Cape Verde (PAICV), new constitution, Pereira elected; late 1970s and 1980s, Cape Verde broke African nation sanctions against Apartheid South Africa and permitted South African Airways overflights; 1983, relations re-established with Guinea Bissau; 1986, Pereira re-elected; 1990, Opposition groups formed the Movement for Democracy (MpD); 1991, Movement for Democracy Party (MpD) elected; António Mascarenhas Monteiro president; 1996, Monteiro elected unopposed; 2001, PAICV legislature control and the presidency under Pedro Pires; 2006, Pires re-elected; 21st century, poverty and food importation problems.

2021 update: 2011, Jorge Carlos Fonseca elected backed by MpD; 2016, Fonseca re-elected and MpD parliamentary majority. 2020 onwards, Covid-19 pandemic with "Covid-19 deaths per million of population" of 294 as compared to 0.4 for Taiwan (March 2021). Revised greenhouse gas (GHG) pollution 3.5 tonnes CO_2-e per person per year. Cape Verde has not signed or ratified the TPNW. In 2020 the "under-5 infant mortality as a percentage of total population" (0.0345%) was 23.8 times greater than for Japan (0.00145%), but 3.2 times lower than that in 2003 (0.1100%).

Foreign occupation: Portugal (pre-1950); Portugal (post-1950); *post-1950 foreign military presence:* Portugal; *1950-2005 excess mortality/2005 population* = 0.099m/0.482m = 20.5%; *1950-2005 under-5 infant mortality/2005 population* = 0.061m/0.482m = 12.7%. Per capita GDP (nominal) $3,604.

Central African Republic: 16th-19th century, European slave trade;19th century, Baya people fled North Cameroon Falani; Banda people fleeing from Muslim Sudan slavers; 1887, French invasion; late 19th-20th century, and exceptionally brutal French slavery conditions on concessions for exploitation of timber, ivory and rubber and thence of rubber, cotton, diamonds, cobalt and uranium; 1894, colony of Ubangi-Shari; 1906, governed with Chad; 1910, governed as part of French Equatorial Africa; 1928,

1935 and 1946, revolts against brutal conditions; 1946, own assembly and representation in the French Assembly; 1958, membership of the French Community; Boganda founded resistance movement MESAN (Social Evolution Movement for Black Africa); 1959, Boganda died in an air crash (possibly murdered by the French); 1960, independence with corrupt, neo-colonial regime of Dacko; 1965, Emperor Bokassa deposed Dacko by military coup; 1977, Emperor Bokassa restored; 1978, Bokassa diamond deal with the Apartheid Israeli Army; 1978, Bokassa sent troops to Zaire to assist pro-US Mobutu; 1979, coup and French army intervention to restore Dacko, subsequent political repression and French granted key military base; 1981, Dacko "re-elected" but deposed in a further military coup by General Kolingba; 1991, restoration of democracy; 1993, Ange-Félix Patassé won the first ever multi-party elections; 1996, army mutinies and coalition government under Patassé; 1997, French army intervention; 1999, French Army left, replaced by an African peacekeeping force; 1999, Patassé re-elected; 2001, 2002, insurrections put down with help from Libyan forces; 2003, General François Bozizé seized power while Patassé abroad; 2004, new constitution.

2021 update: Central African Republic Bush War between Muslims and Christians began in 2004; 2007 and 2011, attempts at peace; 2012, war continued; 2011, Bozizé was elected in a fraudulent election; 2012, Séléka, a coalition of Muslim rebel groups, seized towns in the northern and central regions of the country; 2013, Séléka seized capital and Bozizé fled; Michel Djotodia (Muslim) president; violence from Séléka (Muslim) and Christian "anti-balaka" Christian militias called "anti-balaka"; atrocities with over 200,000 internally displaced persons; 2013, Djotodia officially disbanded Séléka, but many rebels continued as ex- Séléka; forced displacement of Muslim civilians by anti-Balaka from Bangui and western region; 2014, president Michael Djotodia and PM Nicolas Tiengaye resigned; Catherine Samba-Panza was elected as interim president by the National Transitional Council; Séléka and anti-Balaka ceasefire; de facto partition between anti-Balaka (southwest) and ex- Séléka (northeast); most Muslims fled Bangui; 417 of 436 mosques in the country destroyed; 6,000 African Union soldiers and 2,000 French troops trying to prevent war and massacres; 2015, Séléka rebel leaders declared an independent Republic of Logone; 2016, former Prime Minister Faustin-Archange Touadéra elected president; no Séléka or "anti-Balaka" people in the government; 2020, new presidential elections (Bozizé excluded for his crimes) despite massive insecurity in the countryside (14% of 800 polling stations had to close). 2020 onwards, Covid-19 pandemic with "Covid-19 deaths per million of population" of 13 as compared to 0.4 for Taiwan (March 2021). Uranium, oil and major logging industry. Revised greenhouse gas (GHG) pollution 35.7 tonnes CO_2-e per person per year. The Central African Republic has signed but not yet ratified the TPNW. In 2020 the "under-5 infant mortality as a percentage of total population" (0.4002%) was 276.0 times greater than for Japan (0.00145%), but 1.7 times lower than that in 2003 (0.6800%).

Foreign occupation: France (pre-1950), France, Libya (post-1950); *post-1950 foreign military presence:* France, Libya; *1950-2005 excess mortality/2005 population* = 2.274m/3.962m = 57.4%; *1950-2005 under-5 infant mortality/2005 population* = 1.199m/3.962m = 30.3%; HIV positive (2003) 6.8%. Per capita GDP (nominal) $468.

Chad: trans-Saharan trade through Chad; 7th century CE, Arab contact and Islam; 8th –13th century, north African Kanem state; 14th-18th century, Bornu state; 16th –18th century, Wadai and Bagirmi states; pre-colonial nomadic Muslim north dominated the hunting and agrarian Sara south; 18th century Sara conversion to Christianity; late 19th century, Sudanese conquest under Rabah; 1890, first French incursions; 1894, Berlin Conference "awarded" Chad to France; 1900, Rabah defeated by the French; 1913, French control; variously administered with French Equatorial Africa and thence with Ubangi-Shari; 1920, separate colony; 1930s, cotton farming at the expense of food crops; 1946, local legislature; 1958, autonomy within the French Community; 1960, nominal independence under François Tombalbaye with southern support and with the French Army present; 1960s and 1970s, severe drought; 1965, effective one-party rule; 1966, revolt by the northern Muslim Chad National Liberation Front (FROLINAT) with Libyan support; 1972, French prevented FROLINAT capture of the capital; 1973, end of the revolt; 1975, French-backed coup and Tombalbaye killed; 1979, Oueddai coalition; 1982, coup by Hissène Habré; continuing civil war with Christian South (US and French-backed) versus Muslim North (Libya-backed); Libyan forces reached capital; French military-supported South Army took most of the North; 1987, Southern Army and FROLINAT defeated Libyans (except for the Aozou Strip); !989, Chad-Libya treaty; 1990, General Idriss Déby coup; 1994, International Court of Justice restored the Aozou to Chad; 1996, Déby elected; 1990s, continued northern rebellion; 2001, Déby re-elected; 2003, peace with northern rebels; 2003 onwards, hundreds of thousands of refugees fled to Chad to escape genocidal militias in the Darfur region of Sudan.

2021 update: 2014, under Déby Chad cooperated with France and others in the French Operation Barkhane directed against Islamist rebels such as Boko Haram in the Sahel; 2019, Chad under Déby resumed diplomatic relations with serial war criminal, nuclear terrorist and genocidally anti-Arab anti-Semitic Apartheid Israel. 2020 onwards, Covid-19 pandemic with "Covid-19 deaths per million of population" of 9 as compared to 0.4 for Taiwan (March 2019). Subsistence and livestock farming. Drought threat from climate change and massive decrease in the area of shallow Lake Chad. Revised greenhouse gas (GHG) pollution 11.6 tonnes CO_2-e per person per year. Chad has not signed or ratified the TPNW. In 2020 the "under-5 infant mortality as a percentage of total population" (0.4841%) was 333.9 times greater than for Japan (0.00145%), but 2.0 times lower than that in 2003 (0.9700%).

Foreign occupation: France (pre-1950); France, Libya (post-1950); *post-1950 foreign military presence:* France, Libya; *1950-2005 excess mortality/2005 population* = 5.085m/9.117m = 55.8%; *1950-2005 under-5 infant mortality/2005 population* = 2.989m/9.117m = 32.8%; HIV positive (2003) 2.4%. Per capita GDP (nominal) $707.

Comoros: 5th century, Indonesian settlement; African and Madagascan settlement; 12th century, Muslim Arab settlement from the Persian Gulf; 1505, Portuguese arrival; 16th century,

Portuguese invasion; subsequently the Oman Sultanate expelled the Portuguese and took over the slave trade; 19th century, split from Arab Zanzibar; 1843, French occupation; 19th-20th century, French settlement; post-war anti-colonial struggle; 1974, plebiscite overwhelmingly supported independence; 1975, independence but French retained massive military presence on French colonial-dominated Mayotte; 1976, Mayotte population opposed independence; 1978, French mercenary coup; 1970s – present, repeated French, South African and Belgian foreign military interference; 1997, Anjouan and Moheli declared independence; the African Union subsequently brokered a resolution (2005).

2021 update: The major islands are Grande Comore (Ngazidja), Mohéli (Mwali), and Anjouan (Ndzuani). Comoros claims Mayotte (Maore), though Mayotte voted against independence from France in 1974, has never been administered by an independent Comoros government, and after a 2011 referendum was administered by France as an overseas department. France has vetoed UNSC Resolutions supporting Comorian sovereignty over Mayotte. Since independence Comoros has suffered 20 coups or attempted coups. 2020 onwards, Covid-19 pandemic with "Covid-19 deaths per million of population" of 165 as compared to 0.4 for Taiwan (March 2021). Comoros as a tropical Island Nation is acutely threatened by climate change. Revised greenhouse gas (GHG) pollution 1.6 tonnes CO_2-e per person per year. Comoros has signed and ratified the TPNW. The occupier of Mayotte, France, has 290 nuclear weapons, and rejects the TPNW. In 2020 the "under-5 infant mortality as a percentage of total population" (0.2062%) was 142.2 times greater than for Japan (0.00145%), but 1.3 times lower than that in 2003 (0.2700%).

Foreign occupation: Arabs, France (pre-1950); France (post-1950); *post-1950 foreign military presence:* France, (French, Belgian, South African mercenaries); *1950-2005 excess mortality/2005 population* = 0.204m/0.812m = 25.1%; *1950-2005 under-5 infant mortality/2005 population* = 0.149m/0.812m = 18.3%. Per capita GDP (nominal) $1,370.

Congo (Brazzaville), Congo Republic, Republic of the Congo:
500CE onwards, the original population of Mbuti Pygmies was
supplanted by Bantu settlement; 16th century, Kongo, Loango and
Teke Bantu kingdoms; 16th-19th century, British, Portuguese and
French slave trade; 1880, French invasion headed by de Brazza;
1880s-1930s, rule as part of French Equatorial Africa; genocide by
military violence and forced labour killed off about 70% of the
population; 1924-1934, Congo-Ocean Railway built with forced
labour; 1940-1943, Brazzaville the Free French capital; 1944,
Brazzaville Conference, liberalization and abolition of forced
labour; post-war, independence movement; 1960, neo-colonial
"independence" under Youlou; 1963, coup and French Army
forced to leave; 1963, provisional government leader Massamba-
Débat elected; 1968, Ngouabi military coup and declaration of a
"people's republic"; 1977, Ngouabi assassinated; 1979-1992,
Sassou Nguesso president leading the Congolese Party of Labour
(PCT); 1992, multi-party elections and victory to Pascal Lissouba;
defeated Sassou Nguesso opposition leader; 1997-1999, Second
Civil War, intervention by Angolan forces and installation of
Sassou Nguesso ; 2002, effectively one-party "elections" returned
Sassou Nguesso ; 2009 and 2016, Sassou Nguesso re-elected. 1960
to the present summary: independence, variously elected socialist
governments, several military coups and major oil exports.
2021 update: 2020 onwards, Covid-19 pandemic with "Covid-19
deaths per million of population" of 24 as compared to 0.4 for
Taiwan (March 2021). Logging and oil industries contribute to
revised greenhouse gas (GHG) pollution of 21.0 tonnes CO_2-e per
person per year. Congo (Brazzaville) has signed but not yet ratified
the TPNW. In 2020 the "under-5 infant mortality as a percentage of
total population" (0.1445%) was 99.7 times greater than for Japan
(0.00145%), but 3.3 times lower than that in 2003 (0.4800%).

Foreign occupation: France (pre-1950); France (post-1950); *post-
1950 foreign military presence:* France; *1950-2005 excess
mortality/2005 population* = 1.085m/3.921m = 27.7%; *1950-2005
under-5 infant mortality/2005 population* = 0.619m/3.921m =
15.8%; HIV positive (2003) 2.4%. Per capita GDP (nominal)
$2,304.

Congo (Kinshasa), Democratic Republic of the Congo, Zaire:
earliest inhabitants Mbuti Pygmies; 500CE onwards, Bantu
settlement; 700, Katanga copper mines; 1000, general settlement by
Bantus; 14th -19th century, Kongo Kingdom; major involvement in
the slave trade; 17th century, southern Kuba federation; 18th
century, Lunda kingdom; 1492, first Portuguese exploration; 19th
century, Arab, Swahili and Nyamwezi traders (ivory and slaves);
Portuguese Atlantic coast slave trade; 1874-1884, Stanley's
explorations and local treaties for the Belgians; 1884-1885, Berlin
Conference recognized Leopold II's claim; 1885, Leopold head of
the Congo Free State; 1890s, further Belgian conquest of mineral-
rich Katanga and eastern Congo; Belgian conquest; 1900s, reports
of Belgian atrocities from Casement and Morel; 10 million
Congolese butchered by the Force Publique (that notoriously cut
off limbs to enforce rubber collection quotas); 1908, Belgian
annexation under international outrage; 1921, prophet and healer
Kimbangu gaoled; 1920s, major mining commenced; 1960, Congo
independent under Lumumba; Katanga rebelled and became
independent under Tshombe (with Belgian and white mercenary
support); Belgian- and US-backed overthrow of the Lumumba
government; Lumumba murdered; 1961, UN forces intervened;
1965-1997, US-backed Mobutu dictatorship with gross human
rights abuses; 1990s, Rwandan Tutsi and thence Hutu refugees;
1994 onwards, civil war; 1996, Rwandan Hutu refugees joined with
Congolese Government forces against Congolese ethnic Tutsis;
1996-1997, Rwandan- and Uganda-backed rebel forces defeated
Mobutu and installed Laurent-Désiré Kabila as president of the
Congo (Zaire); 1997, Zaire renamed Democratic Republic of the
Congo; 1998-2003, war against Kabila-ruled Congo over Congo
government's expulsion of Rwandan and Ugandan military forces
from the country; 2002, Rwandan forces formally withdrawn from
the Congo but continued incursions seeking Hutu rebels; 2003,
peace deal with the Congo; 2001, Laurent-Désiré Kabila
assassinated and replaced by his son, General Joseph Kabila; 2006,
and 2011, Kabila elected president in successive elections.

2021 update: continuing wars in the eastern Congo with
Congolese rebels and rebels backed by Rwanda and Uganda; 2018,
elections in which Joseph Kabila did not stand; 2019, Joseph

Kabila replaced as president by the successful opposition candidate Félix Tshisekedi, leader of the Union for Democracy and Social Progress (UDPS), the DRC's oldest and largest party; this was the first peaceful, and democratic change in government since independence in 1960. The continuing civil war has killed several millions and HIV/AIDS has spread catastrophically (1950-1960 Belgian era excess mortality 2.8 million; 1960-1997 US-backed Mobutu era excess mortality 16.5 million; 1994-2005 civil war excess mortality 10.1 million). 2018, 12th Congo Ebola outbreak killed 2,300 people; 2021, continuing Ebola outbreak in Eastern Congo; 2020 onwards, Covid-19 pandemic with "Covid-19 deaths per million of population" of 8 as compared to 0.4 for Taiwan (March 2021). Major logging industry and deforestation. Revised greenhouse gas (GHG) pollution 29.3 tonnes CO_2-e per person per year. The Democratic Republic of the Congo has signed but not yet ratified the TPNW. In 2020 the "under-5 infant mortality as a percentage of total population" (0.3870%) was 266.9 times greater than for Japan (0.00145%), but 2.7 times lower than that in 2003 (1.0300%).

Foreign occupation: Belgium (pre-1950); Belgium, UN forces (post-1950); *post-1950 foreign military presence:* Belgium, UN peacekeepers (notably French); *1950-2005 excess mortality/2005 population* = 26.677m/56.079m = 47.6%; *1950-2005 under-5 infant mortality/2005 population* = 17.425m/56.079m = 31.1%; HIV positive (2003) 2.1%. Per capita GDP (nominal) $545.

Côte d'Ivoire (Ivory Coast): precolonial states including Gyaaman, the Kong Empire and Baoulé.; 15th-19th century, French, British and Portuguese slavery and ivory trade; 1842, Ashanti kingdom invaded by France; 1898, resistance by Touré finally overcome and the Côte d'Ivoire was incorporated into French West Africa (together with Burkina Faso, Chad, Guinea, Mali, Mauritania and Senegal); post-war independence movement; about 1920, final French conquest; 1940-1944, WW2, Vichy rule; 1946, Parti Démocratique de la Côte d'Ivoire (PCDI) formed by Félix Houphouet-Boigny; 1958, autonomy within the French Community; 1960, neo-colonial "independence" under Houphouet-Boigny after ferocious repression of the socialist independence movement by the French; 1990, opposition parties legalized; 1993, Houphouet-Boigny re-elected; 1993, Houphouet-Boigny died; replaced by Henri Konan Bédié; Ivory Coast experienced a coup d'état in 1999 and civil wars in 2002-2007 and in 2010–2011. 1999, candidacy disqualification of northern Muslim leader Alassane Ouattera; Christian versus Muslim dichotomy; 1999, Bédié ousted in a coup by General Robert Gueï; 2001, Laurent Gbagbo "elected" with Ouattera excluded; 2002, renewed rebellion; Gueï killed; 3 factions; French military intervention; 2004, UN peace-keeping force; anti-Muslim Apartheid Israel involvement in attack on French military; French destroyed the air force; anti-French riots in Abidjan; 2006, rebels rejected further term extension for Gbagbo; 2007 peace agreement between Gbagbo and the New Forces rebels with Guillaume Soro, leader of the New Forces, becoming prime minister; massive damage to water and sanitation infrastructure in the conflict.

2021 update: 2010 elections, Gbagbo retained power temporarily after disputed elections; 2010–2011 Ivorian crisis and the Second Ivorian Civil War with hundreds killed, other human rights violations and severe damage; 2010, Ouattara elected president but Gbagbo refused to go; 2011, French forces seized Gbagbo; 2016, Gbagbo acquitted by the International Criminal Court; 2015 and 2020 elections, Ouattara was re-elected president in successive elections. 21st century, formerly a very prosperous country; major cocoa producer (child slavery a major problem); continuing instability (1999-2005 excess mortality 1.5 million). 2020 onwards, Covid-19 pandemic with "Covid-19 deaths per million of population" of 9 as compared to 0.4 for Taiwan (March 2021). Massive legal and illegal logging and deforestation for agriculture, notably cocoa production (12 million hectares of forest in about 1960, less than 3 million in 2017). Revised greenhouse gas (GHG) pollution 29.1 tonnes CO_2-e per person per year. Côte d'Ivoire has signed but not yet ratified the TPNW. In 2020 the "under-5 infant mortality as a percentage of total population" (0.2896%) was 119.7 times greater than for Japan (0.00145%), but 2.4 times lower than that in 2003 (0.6900%).

Foreign occupation: France (pre-1950); France (post-1950); *post-1950 foreign military presence:* France, Apartheid Israel; *1950-2005 excess mortality/2005 population* = 6.953m/17.165m = 40.5%; *1950-2005 under-5 infant mortality/2005 population* = 4.196m/17.165m = 24.4%; HIV positive (2003) 3.5%. Per capita GDP (nominal) $2,276.

Djibouti: 1862, Tadjoura sold to French and adjoining areas subsequently subjugated as "Coast of Somalians" and thence as "Territory of the Afars and Issars"; 1946, territory within the French Union; post-war demands for independence; 1977, independence under Hassan Gouled Aptidon after an overwhelming referendum; 1979, formation of the Affar and Issar-Somali coalition People's Progress Assembly (RPP); 1981, RPP the sole political party; 1991, base for French participation in the Gulf War; 1991, Affar rebellion; 1992, new constitution allowing multi-party elections; 1993, Gouled re-elected in elections boycotted by the opposition; 1994, rebel accommodation with the Issar-dominated government; 1977-2005, major continuing Western military presence (US, UK and France) and tensions with Ethiopia, Eritrea and Somalia; 1990s, armed conflict involving the Front for the Restoration of Unity and Democracy (FRUD); 2001, final peace with rebels; 2002, US base agreement; 2003, government sought expulsion of 0.1 million Ethiopians and Somalis.

2021 update: Hassan Gouled's nephew Ismaïl Omar Guelleh increasingly assisting the elderly Hassan Gouled who indicated coming retirement in 1999; 1999, Guelleh elected president; 2016, Chinese People's Liberation Army Support Base in strategically placed Djibouti in relation to world trade and safety of shipping. 2020 onwards, Covid-19 pandemic with "Covid-19 deaths per million of population" of 66 as compared to 0.4 for Taiwan (March 2021). Climate change threat from drought. Revised greenhouse gas (GHG) pollution 2.4 tonnes CO_2-e per person per year. Djibouti has not signed or ratified the TPNW. In 2020 the "under-5 infant mortality as a percentage of total population" (0.0979%) was 67.5 times greater than for Japan (0.00145%), but 5.6 times lower than that in 2003 (0.5500%).

Foreign occupation: France (pre-1950); France (post-1950); *post-1950 foreign military presence:* France, UK, US, China; *1950-2005 excess mortality/2005 population* = 0.265m/0.721m = 36.8%; *1950-2005 under-5 infant mortality/2005 population* = 0.141m/0.721m = 19.6%; HIV positive (2003) 1.3%. Per capita GDP (nominal) $3,252.

Equatorial Guinea: 13th-17th century CE Bantu, Fang and Ndowe invaded, displacing the Pygmies; 1472, discovery by Portuguese de Po; 15th -19th century, slavery with Ndowe complicity involving the Spanish, Portuguese, Dutch and British; 1777-1778, Portugal ceded territory to Spain; 19th century, increasing British and French control; 1827-1843, British lease for anti-slavery activity; 1843-1858, Spanish resumed control; 1849, Cuban penal colony on the island of Bioko (formerly Fernando Po); 1894 Berlin Conference recognized Spanish ownership of coastal Rio Muni and the islands; 1900, treaty with France over borders; 1936, Spanish colonists supported Franco; 1959, overseas provinces of Spain; 1963, internal autonomy; 1968, independence under Francisco Macías Nguema; 1969, most Europeans fled after riots; 1970, one-party rule under the United National Party (PUN); 1972, Nguema president for life; severe repression; many fled the country (1970-1980 population decline about 130,000); 1979, military coup; Francisco Macías Nguema executed; Nguema's nephew Teodoro Obiang Nguema Mbsogo installed; 1992, theoretical multi-party constitution; 1993, 2002, "re-elections" of Mbsogo; 2004, coup involving South African mercenaries foiled; continuing repression and effective one-party rule; Equatorial Guinea is essentially a one-party state ruthlessly dominated by effective dictator Teodoro Obiang Nguema Mbsogo's Democratic Party of Equatorial Guinea (PDGE) (1968-2005 excess mortality 0.2 million).

2021 update: continuing repression, and human rights abuse, including human trafficking. 2020 onwards, Covid-19 pandemic with "Covid-19 deaths per million of population" of 71 as compared to 0.4 for Taiwan (March 2021). Major oil exploitation and deforestation contribute to the revised greenhouse gas (GHG) pollution of 47.5 tonnes CO_2-e per person per year. Equatorial

Guinea has not signed or ratified the TPNW. In 2020 the "under-5 infant mortality as a percentage of total population" (0.2846%) was 198.3 times greater than for Japan (0.00145%), but 2.2 times lower than that in 2003 (0.6300%).

Foreign occupation: Britain, France, Portugal, Spain (pre-1950); Spain (post-1950); *post-1950 foreign military presence:* Spain; *1950-2005 excess mortality/2005 population* = 0.305m/0.521m = 58.5 %; *1950-2005 under-5 infant mortality/2005 population* = 0.168m/0.521m = 32.2%. Per capita GDP (nominal) $8,130.

Eritrea: 2nd -7th century CE, part of northern Ethiopian Axum kingdom; mid-4 th century, adopted Christianity; 7th-16th century, Ethiopean rule or hegemony; 16th century, Ottoman Turkish control of coastal areas; 1869, Italian trading post established; 1885, Italians seized Aseb, Massawa and the surrounding region; 1889, Italian treaty with Menelik giving Italy rights in Eritrea; 1890, Italian colony of Eritrea; 1893-1897, Italian war with Ethiopia leading to Italian defeat but retention of Eritrea; 1935-1936, Eritrea the base for Italian invasion of Ethiopia; 1941, Italians defeated by the British; 1949, British administration as a UN trust territory; 1950, UN declaration of Eritrean federation with Ethiopia; 1952, formal federation with Ethiopia; 1962, Eritrean assembly voted for formal union with Ethiopia; Eritrean Muslim and Marxist groups led the revolt for independence; Eritrean Liberation front (ELF); 1972, Eritrean Popular Liberation Forces (EPLF) founded; 1974, Ethiopian Emperor Haile Selassie deposed; EPLF and ELF united for independence; 1976-1978, Eritrean control opposed by Ethiopia with Russian and Cuban help; 1978, Ethiopian victory; 1978-1993, continuing Eritrean struggle; 1991, Asmara captured by the Eritreans; 1993, UN-sponsored referendum and overwhelming support for independence; EPLF leader Isaias Afwerki president of independent Eritrea (200,000 killed in the war; 1962-1993 excess mortality 1.0 million); 1994, EPLF renamed itself the People's Front for Democracy and Justice (PFDJ); mid-1990s, Yemeni and Eritrean clashes over Red Sea islands; 1998, Yemen-Eritrea agreement; 1998-2001, border war with Ethiopia; Eritrea occupied disputed territory; Ethiopia invaded; 2001, cease-fire; 2002, Hague tribunal ruling over disputed territory; 1998-

2002, drought and famine; 21st century, drought, famine and political repression.

2021 update: 2020-2021, Tigray War initiated by attacks by the Tigray People's Liberation Front (TPLF) in Tigray part of Ethiopia; close cooperation between the Ethiopian National Defense Force (ENDF) and the Eritrean Defence Forces (EDF); refugee catastrophe, human rights abuses and war crimes; 2021, Eritrea is a one-party state and presidential elections have never been held. Isaias Afwerki has been president since 1994. 2020 onwards, Covid-19 pandemic with "Covid-19 deaths per million of population" of 3 as compared to 0.4 for Taiwan (March 2021). Revised greenhouse gas (GHG) pollution 5.3 tonnes CO_2-e per person per year. Eritrea has not signed or ratified the TPNW. In 2020 the "under-5 infant mortality as a percentage of total population" (0.1159%) was 79.9 times greater than for Japan (0.00145%), but 3.2 times lower than that in 2003 (0.3700%).

Foreign occupation: Italy, UK (pre-1950); Ethiopia (post-1950); *post-1950 foreign military presence:* Cuba, Ethiopia; *1950-2005 excess mortality/2005 population* = 1.757m/4.456m = 39.4%; *1950-2005 under-5 infant mortality/2005 population* = 1.036m/4.456m = 23.2%; HIV positive (2003) 1.5%. Per capita GDP (nominal) $567.

Eswatini (Swaziland): 19th century CE, Sobhuza I led various African groups in North East South Africa evading genocidal Boer and Zulu violence; 1839, Sobhuza I's son M'swazi the new leader; Zulu defeat by the Boers and increasing Boer threat; 1867, British Protectorate established; 1894, protectorate of the Transvaal; 1906, British High Commission Territory; 1961, South Africa cut British Commonwealth ties; continued British rule; 1963, local autonomy; 1967, constitutional monarchy; 1968, independence within the British Commonwealth under Sobhuza II but with close ties with South Africa; 1978, constitutional change entrenching royal power; 1986 onwards, absolute monarchy, ruled by King Mswati III; elections are held every five years to determine the House of Assembly and the Senate; 1980s, South African military incursions attacking ANC opponents; 1992, severe drought; 1990s-present,

pressure for democracy but continued royal power; HIV/AIDS
epidemic (highest incidence in the world).

2021 update: 2018, official re-naming to Eswatini ("land of the
Swazis"); 2018, 3-day strike organized by the Trade Union
Congress of Swaziland (TUCOSWA); 2020 onwards, Covid-19
pandemic with "Covid-19 deaths per million of population" of 570
as compared to 0.4 for Taiwan (March 2021). Revised greenhouse
gas (GHG) pollution 3.6 tonnes CO_2-e per person per year.
Eswatini has not signed or ratified the TPNW. In 2020 the "under-5
infant mortality as a percentage of total population" (0.1273%) was
87.8 times greater than for Japan (0.00145%), but 4.3 times lower
than that in 2003 (0.5500%).

Foreign occupation: Netherlands, Afrikaaner, Britain (pre-1950);
UK (post-1950); *post-1950 foreign military presence:* Afrikaaner
South African hegemony; *1950-2005 excess mortality/2005
population* = 0.471m/1.087m = 43.3%; *1950-2005 under-5 infant
mortality/2005 population* = 0.233m/1.087m = 21.4%; HIV
positive (2003) 20.6%. Per capita GDP (nominal) $4,002.

Ethiopia: 2nd millennium BCE, Cushitic people; Habashat to the
Egyptians; 10th century BCE, rule by Menelik I (by tradition the
son of King Solomon and the Queen of Sheba); from 500BCE,
Semitic trade and settlement on coastal areas; 2nd -7th century CE,
kingdom of Axum (northern Ethiopia); 4th century, ruling class
conversion to Christianity; 5th century, Christian Monophysitism
accepted; Jewish people ultimately became the Falashas; 7th
century, rise of Islam, loss of coastal areas and Ethiopian isolation
as their power retracted inland; 1530-1531, Muslim Somali
conquest; 16th-18th century, Gallas (Oromos) migrated from the
West with resultant conflict; civil wars between rival princes;
1755-1769, Galla emperor; 1855, united Ethiopia under Emperor
Tewodros II; 1868, British "revenge" expedition defeated the
Ethiopians and Tewodros suicided; 1869, opening of the Suez
Canal greatly increased the strategic importance of the Horn of
Africa; 1872, Emperor Yohannes IV; 1875-1876, Egyptian
incursion; 1880s, incursions from Sudan Mahdists; 1889, Yohannes
IV killed in battle with Mahdists; Menelik II took over with British

and Italian backing; treaty with the Italians; 1895, Italians invaded; 1896, Italians defeated at Adwa (with King David Biblical-style mass castration of Italian prisoners) with a settlement involving continued Italian occupation of Eritrea and Southern Somalia and Ethiopean independence backed by Britain and France; 1913, Iyasu Emperor; 1916, Iyasu (supported Germany) was deposed; Empress Zawditu with Ras Tafari as regent; 1930, Ras Tafari crowned as Emperor Haile Selassie I; 1935-1936, Italian re-invasion and occupation; use of poison gas; Ethiopia, Somalia and Eritrea ruled as Italian East Africa; 1941, Italians defeated by the British; 1948, British left and Haile Selassie returned as emperor; 1952, Eritrea federated with Ethiopia by the UN; 1962, Eritrea formally part of Ethiopia; 1956, commencement of conflict with the Eritreans (who initially had Cuban and Arab support) and Ogaden region conflicts with Somalians; 1973-1974, severe drought (1973-1974 excess mortality 1.0 million); 1974, Selassie overthrown by military coup, followed by further coups and rightist versus leftist violence; 1970s, under Colonel Mengistu Ethiopia continued war against the Eritreans and Ogaden Somali separatists with USSR support (US bases closed); 1978, Somalis and Eritreans defeated with Russian aid and Cuban forces; 1984-1987, huge drought and famine (1984-1987 excess mortality 2.1 million); 1987, Eritrean and Tigray rebel victories; 1988, peace with Somalia; 1989, attempted coup and Cuban troops left; 1990, Eritreans captured Massawa on the Red Sea and isolated Asmara; 1991, Tigrayan-led Ethiopian People's Revolutionary Democratic Front (EPRDF) defeated Mengistu who fled; Meles president; 1993, Eritrean independence; 1995, opposition boycotted elections; 1998-2002, border war with Eritrea; 2000-2003, drought and famine (2000-2003, excess mortality 2.9 million).

2021 update: 1995, first multiparty elections won by the EPRDF coalition, Meles Zenawi PM, Negasso Gidada president; 1995-2021, EDPRF rule with accommodation of Ethiopia's over 80 ethnic groups; 1998-2000, border dispute and expensive Eritrean–Ethiopian War; complex politics of multi-party elections; 2011-2012, worst drought in 60 years; 2015-2017, political turmoil, demonstrations, killing of demonstrators (75 killed in Oromia); 2016-2017, state of emergency; 2018, 6-month nationwide state of emergency following the resignation of PM Hailemariam Desalegn (the first modern Ethiopian leader to have voluntarily stepped down); 2018, Abiy Ahmed Ali from the Oromo region made PM; release of political prisoners; peace and accommodation with Eritrea; 2018, Ethiopia-Eritrea Summit; 2019, Abiy Ahmed awarded the Nobel Peace Prize; 2020-2021, Tigray War in the Tigray region of Ethiopia between the Debretsion Gebremichael-led Tigray Regional Government of the Tigray People's Liberation Front (TPLF), and the Ethiopian National Defense Forces (ENDF), with Eritrean forces supporting Ethiopia. Abiy Ahmed had merged the diverse parties of the ruling Ethiopian People's Revolutionary Democratic Front (EPRDF) which had governed Ethiopia for 27 years, into the new Prosperity Party. The influential and powerful TPLF refused to join and disputed electoral arrangements; destructive and deadly war, human rights abuses and refugee crisis. 2020 onwards, Covid-19 pandemic with "Covid-19 deaths per million of population" of 24 as compared to 0.4 for Taiwan (March 2021). Subsistence farming economy. Worsening impact of climate change and drought in the Sahel and East Africa. Serious dispute with Egypt over the damming of the Nile with the now-completed and filling Grand Ethiopian Renaissance Dam (GERD). Revised greenhouse gas (GHG) pollution 4.1 tonnes CO_2-e per person per year. Ethiopia has not signed or ratified the TPNW. In 2020 the "under-5 infant mortality as a percentage of total population" (0.1557%) was 107.4 times greater than for Japan (0.00145%), but 4.6 times lower than that in 2003 (0.7100%).

Foreign occupation: Italy, UK (pre-1950); none post-1950; *post-1950 foreign military presence:* Cuba, US; *1950-2005 excess mortality/2005 population* = 36.133m/74.189m = 48.7%; *1950-2005 under-5 infant mortality/2005 population* = 21.590m/74.189m = 29.1%; HIV positive (2003) 2.4%. Per capita GDP (nominal) $828.

Gabon: settled in the Paleolithic era; 16th century CE, Omiéné people on the coast; 18th century, Fang entry from the north; 16th-18th century, part of Loango Empire; late 15th century, Portuguese exploration; 15th -17th century, Portuguese, Dutch, English and French slave traders; 18th century, French control; 1815, Congress of Vienna outlawed the slave trade; 19th century, continuing slave trade; 1849, Libreville established for freed slaves; 1885, Berlin Conference recognized French "ownership"; 1911, Fang armed resistance ceased; 1913, Albert Schweitzer established a hospital at Lambaréné; 1958, self-governing part of the French Community; 1960, independent under Mba (a Fang); 1964, coup suppressed by French forces; 1967, Bongo established a one-party system; 1967-1970, Gabon assisted the Biafrans in the Nigerian civil war; 1989, riots suppressed by the army; 1990, multi-party elections permitted; 1993, multi-party elections were introduced but with continued return of Omar Bongo in 1998, 2001, 2005, 2007 and 2008 elections for a total of 6 terms.

2021 update: 2009, Bongo died; Omar Bongo's son, ruling PDG party leader Ali Bongo Ondimba, declared president by the Constitutional Court; violent protests in Port-Gentil, the country's second-largest city and anti-PDG; 2019, unsuccessful military attempted coup d'état against president Ali Bongo. 2020 onwards, Covid-19 pandemic with "Covid-19 deaths per million of population" of 48 as compared to 0.4 for Taiwan (March 2021). Major oil and logging industries contribute to the revised greenhouse gas (GHG) pollution of 23.1 tonnes CO_2-e per person per year. 92% tree cover. Gabon has not signed or ratified the TPNW. In 2020 the "under-5 infant mortality as a percentage of total population" (0.1354%) was 93.4 times greater than for Japan (0.00145%), but 2.1 times lower than that in 2003 (0.2800%).

Foreign occupation: France (pre-1950); France (post-1950); *post-1950 foreign military presence:* France; *1950-2005 excess mortality/2005 population* = 0.504m/1.375m = 36.7%; *1950-2005 under-5 infant mortality/2005 population* = 0.186m/1.375m = 13.5%; HIV positive (2003) 3.6%. Per capita GDP (nominal) $7,773.

Gambia, The Gambia: part of the Ghana and Songhai Empires; 9th –15th century CE, Arab trans-Saharan trade in slaves and ivory; 15th century, the Malinke and Wolof tribes were tributaries of the Mali Empire; 15th century, Portuguese exploration and commencement of Atlantic slave trade; 1588, British acquisition from Portugal; 1618, British royal charter for exploitation of the

Gambia; 1651-1661, Gambian colony by Poland-Lithuania; 17th century, British settlements around the Gambia River; 17th – 18th century, British and French conflict; 1783, British rights to the Gambia with French retention of the Albreda enclave (ceded to Britain in 1867); 1807, slave trading abolished (some 3 million slaves had been taken from the Gambia region); 1816, Bathurst (Banjul) founded; 19th century, variously administered from Sierra Leone; negotiations with the French (who ruled surrounding Senegal); 1889, crown colony; post-war, increased political activism; 1963, local autonomy; 1965, independence under Sir Dawda Kairaba Jawara (a Malinke) who was subsequently re-elected 5 times ; 1970, republic; late 1970s-early 1980s, drought; 1981, military coup suppressed by Senegal soldiers (the Gambia surrounds the lower reaches of the Gambia River and in turn is surrounded by Senegal); 800 people died; 1982-1989, Senegal-Gambia union (Senegambia); 1989, The Gambia permanently withdrew from the Senegambia confederation; 1994, the Armed Forces Provisional Ruling Council (AFPRC) deposed the Jawara government, banned opposition political activity and made Lieutenant Yahya A.J.J. Jammeh ruler; 2001-2002, Jammeh elected president and his Alliance for Patriotic Reorientation and Construction (APRC) dominated the national Assembly (the opposition United Democratic Party (UDP) boycotted the elections).

2021 update: 2013, The Gambia left the British Commonwealth citing rejection of neocolonialism; 2016, main opposition leader and human rights advocate Ousainou Darboe imprisoned and excluded from election; Adama Barrow elected president; Jammeh rejected the result; invasion by an Economic Community of West African States (ECOWAS) coalition; 2017 Jammeh stepped down; 2018, The Gambia re-joined the British Commonwealth 2020 onwards, Covid-19 pandemic with "Covid-19 deaths per million of population" of 65 as compared to 0.4 for Taiwan (March 2021). Climate change threat from drought. Revised greenhouse gas (GHG) pollution 3.0 tonnes CO_2-e per person per year. Gambia has signed and ratified the TPNW. In 2020 the "under-5 infant mortality as a percentage of total population" (0.2366%) was 163.2

times greater than for Japan (0.00145%), but 1.9 times lower than that in 2003 (0.4400%).

Foreign occupation: Britain (pre-1950); UK, Senegal (post-1950); *post-1950 foreign military presence:* UK, Senegal; *1950-2005 excess mortality/2005 population* = 0.606m/1.499m = 40.4%; *1950-2005 under-5 infant mortality/2005 population* = 0.363m/1.499m = 24.2%; HIV positive (2003) 0.5%. Per capita GDP (nominal) $776.

Ghana: pre-colonial coastal Fanti society, interior Ashanti dominance and Gonja and Dagomba societies in the North; 13th–19th century CE, Ashanti kingdom trading slaves and gold; 1482, Portuguese fort at Elmina; 15th- 19th century, coastal forts of the Portuguese, British, Danes and Dutch trading gold and slaves on the Gold Coast; 1807, slavery abolished in the British Empire; 1850, Danes withdrew; 1872, Dutch withdrew; 19th century, war against the Ashantis by the British in alliance with coastal Fantis; 1874, Ashanti defeated; 1896, British protectorate over northern regions; renewed fighting with the Ashantis; 1902, Ashanti territories annexed to Gold Coast; 1919, adjoining German Togoland placed under British League of Nations Mandate; post-war peaceful independence movement led by Kwame N'Krumah's Convention People's Party (CPP); 1951, N'Krumah elected while imprisoned by the British; 1952, N'Krumah PM of the Gold Coast; 1957, the Gold Coast, Ashanti, the Northern Territories and British Togoland were unified as Ghana; Ghana was the first black African country to gain independence; N'Krumah a major Third World, anti-colonial, pan-African and non-aligned leader; 1964, referendum for one-party rule and political parties banned; opposition outlawed; 1966, N'Krumah was overthrown by a military coup which was followed by successive flawed elections and coups; 1969, Busia elected; 1972, coup; 1978, coup; 1979 Rawlings coup; Limann civilian government; 1981, further coup by Flight Lieutenant Jerry John Rawlings of the Provisional National Defence Council (PNDC); 1992, Rawlings elected in a flawed process; 1994, 1,000 killed and 150,000 displaced in Northern inter-ethnic disturbances; 1996, Rawlings re-elected; 2000, opposition leader John Agyekum Kufuor elected; 2004, Kufuor re-elected.

2021 update: 2008, John Atta Mills of the National Democratic Congress (NDC) elected; 2012, Mills died and was succeeded by vice-president John Dramani Mahama; 2012 Mahama elected and installed in 2013; 2016, Nana Akufo-Addo (defeated in 2008 elections) elected and inaugurated as president in 2017 (evidence of re-established stable democracy). 2020 onwards, Covid-19 pandemic with "Covid-19 deaths per million of population" of 23 as compared to 0.4 for Taiwan (March 2021). Revised greenhouse gas (GHG) pollution 8.9 tonnes CO_2-e per person per year. Ghana has signed and but not yet ratified the TPNW. In 2020 the "under-5 infant mortality as a percentage of total population" (0.1438%) was 99.2 times greater than for Japan (0.00145%), but 2.2 times lower than that in 2003 (0.3100%).

Foreign occupation: Britain (pre-1950); UK (post-1950); *post-1950 foreign military presence:* UK; *1950-2005 excess mortality/2005 population* = 6.089m/21.833m = 27.9%; *1950-2005 under-5 infant mortality/2005 population* = 3.972m/21.833m = 18.2%; HIV positive (2003) 1.7%. Per capita GDP (nominal) $2,203.

Guinea: pre-colonial, Northern areas part of Ghana and of the Mali Empire; 16th–19th century CE, Fulah state; 15th century, Portuguese incursions; 15th-19th century, British, French and Portuguese slave trade; 1840-1898, Samori led state in Guinea region; 1849, French protectorate over the Boké region; 1886, French invasion; 1891, administratively separated from Senegal; 1895, part of French West Africa; 1898, Samori captured by French but resistance continued; pre-war, bauxite exploitation began; 1947, post-war independence movement led by Sekou Touré's Democratic Party of Guinea (PDG); 1958, Guinea rejected neo-colonial French Commonwealth membership and declared independence with consequent French retaliation; increased contact with the USSR; Sekou Touré a major non-aligned, pan-African and anti-colonial Third World leader; one-party Marxist rule; notional union with Ghana (1958) and Mali (1961); 1970, Portuguese mercenary invasion; 1978, rapprochement with France, aid and huge bauxite exploitation; 1984, death of Sekou Touré followed by military coup led by Colonel Lansana Conté who became president; 1990s, 0.4 million refugees from Sierra Leone and Liberia civil wars; overflow insurgencies; declining international aid; 1993, first multi-party elections won by Conté (opposition boycotts and campaign killings); 1996, army revolt suppressed; 1996, Conté re-elected; 1998, Conté re-elected in flawed elections; 2000, 2001, border conflict spilling over from adjoining civil wars; 2003, Conté re-elected in an election boycotted by the opposition.

2021 update: 2008, Conté died; coup led by Moussa Dadis Camara; violent protests and bloody military rampage; 2009 Camara wounded and went to Morocco for medical help; vice-president and defense minister Sékouba Konaté took over and pledged elections; 2010, Alpha Condé, leader of the opposition party Rally of the Guinean People (RGP) won elections; 2013, more violence over election legitimacy; inter-ethnic clashes between the Fula (opposition supporting) and Malinke (Condé supporting); Condé re-elected; 2014, Ebola outbreak in Guinea; Ebola virus disease (EVD) or Ebola hemorrhagic fever (EHF), is a viral hemorrhagic fever of humans and other primates caused by ebolaviruses; over 2,500 deaths by end of 2015; 2020, Condé re-elected for a 3rd term (a referendum in 2020 had permitted more than 2 terms); 2020 onwards, Covid-19 pandemic with "Covid-19 deaths per million of population" of 9 as compared to 0.4 for Taiwan (March 2021). 2021, recurrence of Ebola in Guinea and Congo. Increasing population, and deforestation through unregulated logging and slash-and-burn agriculture contributing to revised greenhouse gas (GHG) pollution of 12.5 tonnes CO_2-e per person per year. Guinea has not signed or ratified the TPNW. In 2020 the "under-5 infant mortality as a percentage of total population" (0.2688%) was 185.4 times greater than for Japan (0.00145%), but 2.4 times lower than that in 2003 (0.6500%).

Foreign occupation: France, Portugal (pre-1950); France (post-1950); *post-1950 foreign military presence:* France, Portugal (mercenaries); *1950-2005 excess mortality/2005 population =* 5.185m/8.788m = 59.0%; *1950-2005 under-5 infant mortality/2005*

population = 3.611m/8.788m = 41.1%; HIV positive (2003) 1.7%.
Per capita GDP (nominal) $967.

Guinea-Bissau: pre-European era Mali, Fulah and Mandingo
people; 1446-1447, first Portuguese incursions; 1500, Portuguese
invasion; 16th-19th century, slave trade and slave-based
plantations; 1879, administratively separated from Cape Verde
Islands; 1951, overseas province of Portugal; 1950s, Guinea-Bissau
and Cape Verde independence movement lead by Amilcar Cabral;
1956, African Party for the Independence of Guinea and Cape
Verde (PAIGC) founded by Cabral for independence of Portuguese
West African Portuguese colonies; 1959-1974, guerrilla war
against Portuguese; 1968, Portuguese confined to capital Bissau;
1973, unilateral declaration of independence but the leader,
Amilcar Cabral later assassinated by Portuguese agents; 1974,
Salazar regime overthrown in Portugal; 1974, independence under
Luis Cabral (brother of Amilcar Cabral) as president; killing of
Guinean soldiers who collaborated with Portuguese rule; 1980,
military coup by João Bernardo "Nino" Vieira ; 1984, unsuccessful
coup; 1991, sole party status of PAIGC removed; 1994, Vieira
elected in a multiparty presidential election; 1998-1999, army
mutiny and civil war; Senegal and Guinea intervened; 1999,
military coup installed Sanhá and Vieira exiled; 2000, leader of
opposition Party for Social Renewal (PRS), Kumba Ialá, elected
president; 2003, military coup and Ialá deposed; 2004, PRS leader
Junnior elected.

2021 update: 2005, presidential elections won by former president
João Bernardo Vieira who then defeated Malam Bacai Sanhá in a
run-off election (Sanhá initially refused to concede); 2008, PAIGC
won a strong parliamentary majority; Vieira's official residence was
attacked by members of the armed forces; 2009, Vieira was
assassinated; National Assembly Speaker Raimundo Pereira was
appointed as an interim president; 2009, election won by Malam
Bacai Sanhá of the PAIGC, against Kumba Ialá as the presidential
candidate of the PRS; 2102, Sanhá died of illness; Pereira again
appointed interim president; 2012, military coup d'état; General
Mamadu Ture Kuruma ruled; 2014-2019, Jose Mario Vaz elected
president and became the first elected president to complete his 5-

year term; 2019, Umaro Sissoco Embaló, elected president (the first non-PAIGC-backed president to be elected). 2020 onwards, Covid-19 pandemic with "Covid-19 deaths per million of population" of 30 as compared to 0.4 for Taiwan (March 2021). Guinea-Bisau vulnerable to global warming-induced drought, sea level change, and salinization. Loss of 77 percent of forests between 1975 and 2013 contributes to a revised greenhouse gas (GHG) pollution of 9.0 tonnes CO_2-e per person per year. Guinea-Bissau has signed but not yet ratified the TPNW. In 2020 the "under-5 infant mortality as a percentage of total population" (0.2639%) was 182.0 times greater than for Japan (0.00145%), but 3.9 times lower than that in 2003 (1.0300%).

Foreign occupation: Portugal (pre-1950); Portugal (post-1950); *post-1950 foreign military presence:* Portugal; *1950-2005 excess mortality/2005 population* = 0.945m/1.584m = 59.7%; *1950-2005 under-5 infant mortality/2005 population* = 0.611m/1.584m = 38.6%. Per capita GDP (nominal) $688.

Kenya: 2000BCE, agrarian settlers from Ethiopia; 500BCE-500CE, Bantu and Nilotic settlers from the Sudan; 10th century Arab foundation of coastal city Malindi; 100CE, trade with Arabia; 10th-16th century, major Muslim Arab-African trade; Malindi, Mombasa and Pate founded; 1498, Portuguese arrived; 16th century, Portuguese invasion; 1698, Portuguese withdrawal; 1729, Portuguese left Mombasa; 18th century, Mazrui Arab rule over Mombasa; Omani (Musquat) Busaidi coastal rule; 1832, Busaidi ruler took over Zanzibar; 1837, Busaidi conquest of Mombasa; 17th-19th century, Zanzibar-based Arab slave trade; 19th century Masai dominance ended by cattle disease epidemic; 1884, Berlin Conference gave Uganda, Kenya and Zanzibar to Britain and Tanzania to Germany; 1887, British group given a concession from the Sultan of Zanzibar; 1888, Imperial British East Africa Company; 1895, British East Africa Protectorate; 1895-1901, Mombasa-Lake Victoria Railway; 20th century, commencing in 1903 British settlement on most of the best land, with the Kikuyu and Masai people confined to the rest; 1920, interior Kenya colony and a coastal Protectorate of Kenya; 20th century, European settlement of the highlands, coffee plantations, Indian traders and mounting indigenous activism; 1944, Jomo Kenyatta started the independence movement; 1952-1960, Mau Mau Emergency, Kikuyu Mau Mau insurgency against the British, 0.3 million Kikuyu held in concentration camps, 1 million held in "enclosed villages", 0.1 million were either killed or otherwise died in custody, horrendous British atrocities, Kenyatta imprisoned (1952-1960 excess mortality 1.1 million); 1963, independence with Kenyatta as leader but the UK retained a military base in Mombasa; 1964, republic; many Europeans and Asians left; 1963-1968, Somalia-Kenya border clashes; 1969, leading politician Tom Mboya assassinated; 1970s, tensions with Uganda and Tanzania; 1978, Kenyatta died, replaced by Daniel arap Moi; opposition suppression; 1982, failed military coup; 1988, riots over political suppression; 1991, multi-party elections permitted; 1992, Moi re-elected in flawed, single-party elections in 1979, 1983 and 1988; 1980, Garissa Massacre of Somalis by Kenyan soldiers; 1982, unsuccessful air force-led coup; 1984, Wagalla Massacre of Somalis by Kenyan soldiers; 1988, voters had to queue behind favoured candidates instead of secret ballot; 1992, return to multi-party politics; Moi returned as president but with massive voter intimidation; Kenya African National Union (KANU) retained power but had big losses to the opposition; 1996, KANU government revised the constitution to allow Moi to remain president for another term; 1997, Moi elected for a 5th term; election criticised as fraudulent by his major opponents, Kibaki and Odinga; 1998, huge US embassy bombings in Nairobi and in Dar es Salaam (Tanzania); 2002, opposition leader Mwai Kibaki running for the opposition coalition National Rainbow Coalition (NARC), elected president; 2004, Masai calls for return of land held under British colonial leases; 2005, Kibaku re-elected but main opposition leader, Raila Odinga, disputed the elections; post-election violence killed 1,500 and displaced 600,000; Odinga agreed to be PM.

2021 update: 2010, referendum for a new constitution which limited presidential powers; 2011, Kenya began sending troops to US-occupied Somalia against indigenous Al-Shabaab; subsequent terrorism atrocities in Kenya; 2011-2012, worst drought in East Africa for 60 years; 2013, Uhuru Kenyatta elected president; 2017, Uhuru Kenyatta was re-elected as president but this was overturned by the Supreme Court after on Odinga protests; Uhuru Kenyatta was re-elected in an election boycotted by Odinga. 2020 onwards, Covid-19 pandemic with "Covid-19 deaths per million of population" of 38 as compared to 0.4 for Taiwan (March 2021). Revised greenhouse gas (GHG) pollution 7.1 tonnes CO_2-e per person per year. Kenya has not signed or ratified the TPNW. In 2020 the "under-5 infant mortality as a percentage of total population" (0.1225%) was 84.5 times greater than for Japan (0.00145%), but 3.3 times lower than that in 2003 (0.4100%).

Foreign occupation: Portugal, Arab, Britain (pre-1950); UK (post-1950); *post-1950 foreign military presence:* UK; *1950-2005 excess mortality/2005 population* = 10.015m/32.849m = 30.5%; *1950-2005 under-5 infant mortality/2005 population* = 5.358m/32.849m = 16.3%; HIV positive (2003) 3.8%. Per capita GDP (nominal) $1,817.

Lesotho: earliest settlement by San people (Bushmen); early 19th century, Sotho and other Bantu people fled from genocidal Zulu army of Chaka; 1839, war with Boers; 1858, 1865, wars with Boers; 1867, discovery of diamonds; 1868, British protectorate of Basutoland; 1871, under Cape Colony rule without Sotho agreement; 1884, direct British control; 1950s, Apartheid prevented British surrender of the country to racist South Africa; 1960, self-government; 1961, South Africa broke constitutional links with UK; 1965, constitution promulgated; 1966, Basotholand independence as a kingdom under the name Lesotho; 1970, Basutoland (later Basotho) Congress Party (BCP) under Mokhehle won elections; Jonathan coup; 1974, clashes with the BCP-linked Lesotho Liberation Army; 1978, Lesotho received ANC refugees; 1977, South Africa closed the border; 1982, airborne South African attack on the capital Maseru and subsequent Lesotho constraint of ANC activists; 1983, Lesotho-South African border incident; 1986, pro-South African Lekhanya coup after South African economic boycott; 1991, bloodless coup; 1993, BCP victory under Mokhehle in democratic elections; 1994, Mokhehle removed and then reinstated by the king; 1997, Mokhehle formed the Lesotho Congress for Democracy Party (LCD); 1998, Mokhehle died; LCD leader Mosisili elected; riots and South African and Botswana forces restored order; massive damage in Maseru and other towns; government and opposition rapprochement; 2002, LCD victory under Mosisili; 2004, drought; 21st century, HIV/AIDS scourge.

2021 update: 2009, armed men attacked Mosisili's residence; 2015, following elections Mosisili formed and lead a coalition government; 2017, electoral victory for Tom Thabane and his party, the ABC. 2020 onwards, Covid-19 pandemic with "Covid-19 deaths per million of population" of 146 as compared to 0.4 for Taiwan (March 2021). Revised greenhouse gas (GHG) pollution 5.7 tonnes CO_2-e per person per year. Lesotho has signed and ratified the TPNW. In 2020 the "under-5 infant mortality as a percentage of total population" (0.2050%) was 141.4 times greater than for Japan (0.00145%), but 1.2 times lower than that in 2003 (0.2400%).

Foreign occupation: Boer, Britain (pre-1950); UK (post-1950); *post-1950 foreign military presence:* UK, South Africa, Botswana; *1950-2005 excess mortality/2005 population* = 0.951m/1.797m = 52.9%; *1950-2005 under-5 infant mortality/2005 population* = 0.386m/1.797m = 21.5%; HIV positive (2003) 17.9%. Per capita GDP (nominal) $1,158.

Liberia: 15th century, first Portuguese arrival; 15th-19th century, slave trade abuses; 1821, Monrovia established by American Colonization Society on Sierra Leone land purchased from the British; 1822, first Afro-American settlers lead by Ashmun; 1847, independent republic; 1871, debt crisis and overthrow of the government; 19th-20th century, major US rubber holdings and minority American-Liberian economic dominance with US diplomatic backing; 1885, 1992 and 1919, loss of territory to the British and French; 1909, bankruptcy; 1926, Firestone company leased large rubber growing areas; 1930, League of Nations revealed forced labor export (i.e. slavery) scandal; King resigned; 1930-1944, Barclay president; 1944-1971, Tubman president; 1971-1979, William Tolbert president; increased cost of living and riots; 1979, Sergeant Samuel Doe (Krahn ethnicity) coup with Tolbert and many associates killed; continuing intimacy with the US and the IMF; 1985, Doe elected in fraudulent election; 1985, failed counter-coup; Doe troops executed members of the Gio and

Mano ethnic groups; 1980s, thousands fled repression to Guinea and Côte d'Ivoire; 1989, China broke relations over the issue of Taiwan; Taylor forces invaded from Côte d'Ivoire; US forces landed supposedly when Taylor forces threatened foreign hostage taking; 1990, Doe killed by Johnson rebel forces; Economic Community of West African States (ECOWAS) forces installed Sawyer; Taylor backed by Burkino-Faso and Libya; 1989-1997, guerrilla civil war, 400,000 refugees to neighboring countries, 150,000-200,000 killed, 700,000 displaced (1989-1967 excess mortality 3.4 million); 1995, peace deal; 1997, Taylor elected president; 1999, The Second Liberian Civil War began when Liberians United for Reconciliation and Democracy, a rebel group based in the northwest of the country, launched an armed insurrection against Taylor; 2000, UN embargo on blood diamond sales and illegal timber exports to fund the Revolutionary United Front backed by Taylor in the Sierra Leone Civil War; 2001, UN sanctions on Liberia; continued civil war; 2003, rebels held much of the country; 2003, a second rebel group, Movement for Democracy in Liberia, launched attacks against Taylor from the southeast. Peace talks between the factions began in Accra; Taylor was indicted by the Special Court for Sierra Leone for crimes against humanity; rebels attacked Monrovia; Taylor went into exile in Nigeria; replaced by Moses Blah; UN West African forces and off-shore US forces; Bryant president; 2004, massive disarmament of 100,000 soldiers; continued diamond embargo, corruption and insecurity; peace deal signed; United Nations Mission in Liberia arrived to monitor peace; 2005, economist Ellen Johnson Sirleaf elected president (2000-2005 excess mortality 0.3 million).

2021 update: 2006, Truth and Reconciliation Commission established; 2017, Liberian elections; 2018, great footballer George Weah sworn in as president; 2020 onwards, Covid-19 pandemic with "Covid-19 deaths per million of population" of 17 as compared to 0.4 for Taiwan (March 2021). Major logging industry. Revised greenhouse gas (GHG) pollution 55.0 tonnes CO_2-e per person per year. Liberia has not signed or ratified the TPNW. In 2020 the "under-5 infant mortality as a percentage of total population" (0.2236%) was 154.2 times greater than for Japan (0.00145%), but 5.3 times lower than that in 2003 (1.1800%).

Foreign occupation: Britain, US (pre-1950); none (post-1950); *post-1950 foreign military presence:* US; *1950-2005 excess mortality/2005 population* = 1.754m/3.603m = 48.7%; *1950-2005 under-5 infant mortality/2005 population* = 1.209m/3.603m = 33.6%; HIV positive (2003) 3.1%. Per capita GDP (nominal) $523.

Madagascar: 5th century–15th century CE, African and Indonesian settlement; 9th-14th century, Muslim Arab East African and Comoran traders, port establishment and Africanization; 1500, Portuguese contact; 1506-1507, Portuguese invaders destroyed port towns; 1600-1619, Portuguese attempts at conversion; 1642, small French intrusion commenced; 16th-19th century, various Malagasy kingdoms; 19th century, various attempts to stem European encroachment; 1787-1810, Andrianampoinimerina united Merina interior and defeated the Bétsiléo; 1810-1825, Radama I received British aid and stopped slavery; Merina culture dominant; Protestant missionary activity; 1821-1861, Queen Ranavalona, civil strife; 1835, Christianity outlawed; 1861-1863, Radama II; 1863-1868, Rasoherina; Christianity permitted; 1868-1883, Ranavalona II, became Christian; 1883-1896, Ranavalona III; 1883-1904, French invasion; 1885, French protectorate; 1890, British recognition of French control; 1896, Merina finally defeated and the monarchy abolished; 20th century, colonization, forest destruction and cotton, sugar and coffee plantations; 1942, British defeated Vichy French; post-war independence struggle; 1947-1948, French suppressed revolt with 11,000-80,000 deaths; 1958, autonomous part of French Community; 1960, independence under Tsiranana, but France retained military bases; coastal dominance over Merina interior; 1965, 1972, Tsiranana re-election; political repression; broke off with South Africa; 1972, General Ramanantsoa coup to disengage from French neo-colonialism; 1975, democratic election of Didier Ratsiraka; 1980s, coup attempts; 1989, Ratsiraka re-elected; 1991, strike and power-sharing coalition; about 400,000 people marched on the Presidential Palace; 1993, opposition Albert Zafy elected; 1996, Ratsiraka re-elected; 2001, opposition Marc Ravalomanana elected but Ratsiraka disputed the result; 2002, civil war; Ravalomanana controlled the capital, but Ratsiraka largely maintained control over the provinces; OAU and thence African Union involvement for democracy; Ravalomanana elected; Ratsiraka fled.

2021 update: 2009, effective coup d'état by Opposition leader Andry Rajoelina who was instated as president; 2010, new constitution; 2013, Hery Rajaonarimampianina elected president; 2018-2019, elections with Andry Rajoelina the ultimate winner. 2020 onwards, Covid-19 pandemic with "Covid-19 deaths per million of population" of 13 as compared to 0.4 for Taiwan (March 2021). Massive deforestation and drought. Madagascar is a biodiversity hotspot but deforestation threatens unique biodiversity. Slash and burn deforestation contributes to a revised greenhouse gas (GHG) pollution of 23.7 tonnes CO_2-e per person per year. Madagascar has signed but not yet ratified the TPNW. In 2020 the "under-5 infant mortality as a percentage of total population" (0.1236%) was 85.2 times greater than for Japan (0.00145%), but 4.4 times lower than that in 2003 (0.5400%).

Foreign occupation: Portugal, France, UK (pre-1950); France (post-1950); *post-1950 foreign military presence:* France; *1950-2005 excess mortality/2005 population* = 7.098m/18.409m = 38.6%; *1950-2005 under-5 infant mortality/2005 population* = 3.867m/18.409m = 21.0%; HIV positive (2003) 0.8%. Per capita GDP (nominal) $523.

Malawi: early San (Bushmen) people; 1st-4th century CE, early Bantu invasion; 14th century, later Bantu settlement; 15th-18th century, Maravi kingdom; 18th century, Maravi conquest of parts of Zimbabwe and Mozambique; Yao depredations and Yao slave trade of Malawians to Indian Ocean coast Arab and Swahili slavers; pre-colonial history related to that of the Zimbabwe civilization; 1835, extremely violent Zulu (Ngoni) expansion from the South impacted on internal conflicts; mid- to late-19th century, exploration, missionary activity and eventual British colonization; 1859, exploration by Dr Livingstone; 1873, British missionary presence; 1883, British consul; 1889, British Shire Highlands Protectorate; 1890, Portuguese East-West expansion blocked by the British who had North-South plans; Rhodes negotiated the British Central African Protectorate; 1890s, slave trade abolished; 1907, protectorate of Nyasaland; coffee plantations; 1915, revolt suppressed; 1944, Nyasaland African Congress formed; 1949, first African participation in legislative council; 1953, Federation of Rhodesia and Nyasaland, opposed Malawians; 1959-1960, Malawian opposition to British rule by the Malawi Congress Party (MCP) under Hastings Banda; state of emergency; 1963, Federation of Rhodesia and Nyasaland abolished; 1964, independence under Banda; 1966, republic; 1971, Banda declared president for life; retained European influence; controversially visited South Africa; cooperation with White Rhodesia, South Africa and the Portuguese; severe repression; 1965, Chipembere revolt crushed; 1967, Chisiza revolt crushed; 1970s, used as refuge by Mozambique rebels; 1980s, 1990s, 600,000 Mozambique civil war refugees; 1980, armed resistance to Banda; 1980s and 1990s, Malawi support for rightist rebels in Mozambique; 1992, drought; suspension of foreign aid over political repression; 1993, referendum for multi-party rule.

2021 update: Banda business empire eventually controlled 30% of the GDP; 1993, referendum supported multi-party democracy; 1994, elections in which Banda was defeated by Bakili Muluzi (former Secretary General of the MCP); 1999, Muluzi re-elected as president; 2004, Bingu wa Mutharika elected against a divided opposition; 2009, Mutharika re-elected; 2011, protests over poverty and cost of living; 18 demonstrators killed and 44 wounded; 2012, Mutharika died; Joyce Banda (no relation) appointed president; 2014, Peter Mutharika (brother of ex-president Mutharika) elected president; 2019, Peter Mutharika re-elected president in a result overturned by the Malawi Constitutional Court; 2020, Opposition leader Lazarus Chakwera elected president. 2020 onwards, Covid-19 pandemic with "Covid-19 deaths per million of population" of 57 as compared to 0.4 for Taiwan (March 2021). 11.5% tree cover. Deforestation and wood burning contribute to a revised greenhouse gas (GHG) pollution of 11.7 tonnes CO_2-e per person per year. Malawi has signed but not ratified the TPNW. In 2020 the "under-5 infant mortality as a percentage of total population" (0.1663%) was 114.7 times greater than for Japan (0.00145%), but 4.8 times lower than that in 2003 (0.7900%).

Foreign occupation: Portugal, Britain (pre-1950); UK (post-1950); *post-1950 foreign military presence:* UK; *1950-2005 excess mortality/2005 population* = 6.976m/12.572m = 55.5%; *1950-2005 under-5 infant mortality/2005 population* = 4.794m/12.572m = 38.1%; HIV positive (2003) 7.5%. Per capita GDP (nominal) $435.

Mali: early trade with the Mediterranean region; 4th-11th century CE, Ghana Empire; 7th century onwards, Muslim conversion; 14th century, Mali Empire; 1312-1337, Emperor Musa; wealth from gold; trade and high culture at Timbuktu and Jenne; 15th-16th century, Songhai Empire of Gao; 1590, defeated by Moroccans; 17th-18th century, smaller states; Touareg and Fulani incursions; 19th century, resistance to French invasion by Umar and Touré; 1850, French occupation with horrendous brutality; Mali grouped with Burkina Faso (Upper Volta), Benin and Senegal to form French Sudan and thence French West Africa; 1898, resistance largely destroyed; trade now directed to the Atlantic rather than to the North and East; postwar independence movements; 1958, self-rule as part of the French Community as the Sudanese Republic; 1959, joined with Senegal to form the Mali Federation; 1960, dissolution of the Mali Federation; 1960, independence of Mali under Modibo Keita; detached from the French Community; symbolic association with Guinea and Ghana; one-party socialist state; 1963, joined the Organization of African Unity (OAU); 1967, forced to rejoin the Franc Zone; 1968, repression led to military coup under Moussa Traoré; 1970s, severe drought in the Sahel; 1977, Keita died in prison (poisoned?); economic woes, civil unrest and repression; 1983, moved closer to France and the West; 1979, 1985, Traoré re-elected; armed conflict with Burkina Faso;1991, March Revolution; 300 demonstrators killed; coup by Lieutenant Colonel Amadou Toumani Touré; interim Touré government; 1992, Alpha Oumar Konaré won Mali's first democratic, multi-party presidential election; 1990s, Tuareg revolt in the North; 1995, peace with the Tuareg; return of refugees; 1997, Konaré re-elected but the opposition had boycotted the election; 2002, Touré elected president.

2021 update: 2012 Tuareg rebellion in Northern Mali led by the National Movement for the Liberation of Azawad (MNLA);

military officer Amadou Sanogo seized power in a coup d'état;
MNLA declared independence as Azawad; Islamists took over to
assert sharia law; 2013, French intervention; an Islamist-desecrated
Timbuktu recaptured; Ibrahim Boubacar Keïta elected president;
2015, conflict in central Mali between agricultural Dogon and the
Bambara peoples' militias, and the pastoral Fula (Fulani); 2018,
Ibrahim Boubacar Keïta re-elected president; 2019, massacre of
160 Fula villagers people; jihadi attacks on towns of Boulikessi and
Mondoro with 25 soldiers killed; 2020, military coup deposed
President Keïta. An estimated 200,000 slaves in Mali. 2020
onwards, Covid-19 pandemic with "Covid-19 deaths per million of
population" of 18 as compared to 0.4 for Taiwan (March 2019).
Cropping and livestock; seriously climate change-threatened
through drought in the Sahel. Revised greenhouse gas (GHG)
pollution 11.6 tonnes CO_2-e per person per year. Mali has not
signed or ratified the TPNW. In 2020 the "under-5 infant mortality
as a percentage of total population" (0.4004%) was 276.1 times
greater than for Japan (0.00145%), but 2.8 times lower than that in
2003 (1.1300%).

Foreign occupation: France (pre-1950); France (post-1950); *post-1950 foreign military presence:* France; *1950-2005 excess mortality/2005 population* = 6.808m/13.829m = 49.2%; *1950-2005 under-5 infant mortality/2005 population* = 6.438m/13.829m = 46.6%; HIV positive (2003) 1.1%. Per capita GDP (nominal) $887.

Mauritania: 1st millennium CE, Berber culture in the North and
black African society in the South; 8th-13th century, Hodh region
Ghana Empire (capital Kumbi-Saleh); 11th century, important
Berber Almovarid dynasty arose in Mauritania; 14th-15th century,
part of the Mali Empire; 1440s, Portuguese access to coastal areas;
17th century, Dutch, English and French trade in gum arabic; 1858,
French invasion to consolidate its territory from Senegal to the
Sudan; 1850s to 1930s, armed resistance to the French; 1903,
French protectorate; administered as part of Senegal; 1920, part of
French West Africa; 1930s, last resistance overcome; 1958,
Mauritania became part of the French Community; 1960, formal
independence under Daddah but French neo-colonial control; major
iron ore exploitation; 1961, Daddah elected; subsequent one-party

rule; bridge between Arab North Africa and Black Africa; 1973, Mauritania withdrew from the Franc Zone; 1974, iron ore mines nationalized; 1975-1979, allied with Morocco with French support to divide former Spanish Western Sahara; 1978, pro-Arabist and pro-peace Salek coup; 1979, Louly replaced Salek; peace with Polisario Front of Western Sahara; 1980, Heydalla coup; 1981, rift with Morocco over coup plot; 1984, Maaouya Ould Sid'Ahmed Taya coup; 1985, restored relations with Morocco; 1970s and 1980s, left-right and Arabization conflicts, French interference; 1989, conflict with Senegal over expulsion of 40,000 Senegalese; 1992, 1997, 2003, Taya elected in flawed elections; 1993, US hostility over maltreatment of black African Senegalese and pro-Iraq stance; 2004, locust ravages.

2021 update: 2005, a military coup led by Colonel Ely Ould Mohamed Vall ended Maaouya Ould Sid'Ahmed Taya's 21 years of rule. 2007, first fully democratic presidential elections; won by Sidi Ould Cheikh Abdallahi; 2008, coup by General Mohamed Ould Abdel Aziz 2008-2019, rule by Aziz; 2009, Union for the Republic (UPR) party founded by Aziz; Aziz elected in flawed elections; 2011, Arab Spring demonstrations; 2019, Mohamed Ould Ghazouani elected president 2020 onwards, Covid-19 pandemic with "Covid-19 deaths per million of population" of 94 as compared to 0.4 for Taiwan (March 2021). Climate change threat through drought. Revised greenhouse gas (GHG) pollution 19.7 tonnes CO_2-e per person per year. Mauritania has not signed or ratified the TPNW. In 2020 the "under-5 infant mortality as a percentage of total population" (0.2468%) was 170.2 times greater than for Japan (0.00145%), but 3.1 times lower than that in 2003 (0.7600%).

Foreign occupation: France (pre-1950); France (post-1950); *post-1950 foreign military presence:* France, Morocco; *1950-2005 excess mortality/2005 population* = 1.294m/3.069m = 42.2%; *1950-2005 under-5 infant mortality/2005 population* = 0.848m/3.069m = 27.6%; HIV positive (2003) 0.3%. Per capita GDP (nominal) $1,678.

Mauritius: 16th century, discovered by Portuguese; 1598-1710, Dutch occupation and naming; 1715-1810, French occupation; 1810-1968, British occupation; 19th century, indentured Indian labour for French plantations after abolition of slavery in 1835; 20th century, increasing Indian political activity; 1959, local elections; 1950s and 1960s, French and Afro-European creoles opposed independence fearing Indian domination; 1965, Chagos transferred to Britain, Diego Garcia a major naval base; 1968, independence with a neo-colonial pro-US-UK and pro-South African régime led by Ramgoolam; 1970, US-UK removal of all Diego Garcia inhabitants to Mauritius to permit huge US military expansion; 1982, elected socialist Mauritius Militant Movement (MMM) government under Anerood Jugnauth; objected to US, UK and French occupation of Mauritian islands; 1983, Jugnauth split the MMM and formed the Mauritius Socialist Movement (MSM); 1992, republic under president Uteem; 1995, son of Ramgoolam elected PM; 2000, Jugnauth re-elected PM to head a MMM-MSM coalition; 2002, Uteem resigned; Offmann elected president; 2003, Jugnauth resigned as PM and was replaced by Paul Bérenger; 2003, Jugnauth as president; 21st century, key sugar economy, excellent governance and wish for the return of the ethnically cleansed and UK-US militarized Chagos Islands.

2021 update: 2005-2014, Navin Ramgoolam PM; 2017, Anerood Jugnauth resigned, his son Pravind Jugnauth becoming PM; 2018, president Ameenah Gurib-Fakimr resigned over financial scandal; 2019 onwards, Prithvirajsing Roopun president; MSM general election victory and Pravind Kumar Jugnauth PM. 2020 onwards, Covid-19 pandemic with "Covid-19 deaths per million of population" of 8 as compared to 0.4 for Taiwan (March 2021). Tropical Island Nation Mauritius acutely threatened by climate change. Revised greenhouse gas (GHG) pollution 5.0 tonnes CO_2-e per person per year. Mauritius has not signed or ratified the TPNW. The nuclear-armed and genocidal Occupiers of the Chagos Islands, the UK, US and France have 215, 5,800 and 290 nuclear weapons, respectively, and reject the TPNW. In 2020 the "under-5 infant mortality as a percentage of total population" (0.0121%) was 8.3 times greater than for Japan (0.00145%), but 2.5 times lower than that in 2003 (0.0300%).

Foreign occupation: Netherlands, France, Britain (pre-1950); UK (post-1950); *post-1950 foreign military presence:* UK (and thence US, UK and French forces on militarized and seized Chagos islands); *1950-2005 excess mortality/2005 population =* 0.064m/1.244m = 5.1%; *1950-2005 under-5 infant mortality/2005 population* = 0.078m/1.244m = 6.3%. Per capita GDP (nominal) $11,169.

Mozambique: about 500CE, Bantu people settled Mozambique; 10th century, Sofala founded by Muslim Arab Shiraz and Swahili traders settled on the coast; trade between interior Zimbabwe and coastal Zandj Muslim culture; gold and ivory trade via Sofala and Kilwa (further North); 1498, Vasco da Gama visited; 16th century, Portuguese conquered the Indian Ocean coast; Swahili traders redirected trade further North; 1509-1512, Fernandes reached the gold-rich kingdom of Mwanamutapa; 1560-1561. Jesuit mission to Mwanamutapa; Portuguese attempts at conquest of the interior were defeated by disease and combat; 16th-17th century, increasing Portuguese estates; corn and cashews introduced; Arab Zanzibar-based slave trade; destruction of Mwanamutapa; 18th-mid-19th century, Portuguese slave trade to Brazil; 1820s, 1830s, invasion from the South by Nguni (Zulu-, Swazi- and Xhosa-related people); 19th century, Nguni Sgagana people dominated the South; Portuguese controlled the lower Zambezi; late 19th century Portuguese conquest and colonization of hinterland; Portuguese linkage with Angola blocked by British expansion into Rhodesia and Nyasaland (later Zambia, Zimbabwe and Malawi); 1891, British-Portuguese treaty on Southern African holdings; late-19th-20th century, Portuguese conquest; 1895-1897, the Shangana defeated; 1897-1900, the Nyanja defeated; 1912, Yao defeated; 1917, South conquered; 1926, post-revolution Portugal expanded settlement of Mozambique; ostensibly assimilatory African policies; post-war linked economically and militarily with White Rhodesia and South Africa; 1951, an overseas province of Portugal; 1960s, abolition of forced African labor; increasing Portuguese repression, Frelimo struggle; 1962, Mozambique Liberation Front (Frelimo) founded under Mondlane; 1964-1974, Frelimo-Portugal war; 1974, Salazar overthrown in Portugal; 1975, independence under Machel-led Frelimo (1964-1975 excess mortality 2.1 million); 1970s onwards, one-party, Marxist state; Mozambique support for African freedom fighters in South Africa (ANC) and Rhodesia (independence as Zimbabwe in 1980); 1979, White Rhodesian forces invaded; 1981, South Africa invaded, supported Portuguese colonist Renamo rebels with mercenaries; 1981-1992, war against Renamo terrorism; 1984, Mozambique-South Africa pact eventually collapsed; 1986 Machel killed (murdered?) in a plane crash; succeeded by Chissano; 1992, Renamo blocked drought-relief efforts; Frelimo-Renamo peace pact (1981-1992, excess mortality 2.5 million); 1994, UN overseen elections; Joaquim Chissano of Frelimo elected; Afonso Dhlakama of Renamo led the opposition; 1995, Mozambique joined the British Commonwealth (although never having been a British possession); by 1995 post-war return of 1.7 million refugees and 4 million internally-displaced persons (IDPs); 1999, Frelimo, Chissano electoral victory; 2000, devastating cyclone and huge Limpopo and Changane flooding, 1 million displaced; 2004, electoral victory to Frelimo and Guebuza.

2021 update: 2005, Armando Guebuza of Frelimo elected president and re-elected in 2010; 2015, Filipe Nyusi elected president and was re-elected in 2019; 2013-2019, Renamo violence in central and northern parts; 2014, Frelimo and Renamo peace deal but renewed hostilities and human rights abuses with 12,000 refugees fleeing to Malawi; 2015 onwards, jihadi terrorism in the north; 2020, Islamist insurgents captured Vamizi Island in the Indian Ocean; jihadi terrorism forced scores of thousands to flee in northern Mozambique ; 2021, determined attempt to suppress jihadi terrorists. 2020 onwards, Covid-19 pandemic with "Covid-19 deaths per million of population" of 24 as compared to 0.4 for Taiwan (March 2021). Revised greenhouse gas (GHG) pollution 5.8 tonnes CO_2-e per person per year. Mozambique has signed but not ratified the TPNW. In 2020 the "under-5 infant mortality as a percentage of total population" (0.2466%) was 170.1 times greater than for Japan (0.00145%), 3.2 times lower than that in 2003 (0.7900%).

Foreign occupation: Portugal (pre-1950); Portugal (post-1950); *post-1950 foreign military presence:* Portugal, South Africa, white

Rhodesians; *1950-2005 excess mortality/2005 population* = 12.462m/19.495m = 63.9%; *1950-2005 under-5 infant mortality/2005 population* = 7.200m/19.495m = 36.9%; HIV positive (2003) 7.0%. Per capita GDP (nominal) $504.

Namibia: Pre-colonial occupation of Kalahari desert and adjoining areas by San (Bushmen) (BCE), Nama (from 500CE), Herero (from 1600) and Ovambo people (from 1800); 15th century, Portuguese and Dutch contact; 18th century, British missionaries; 1840s, German missionaries; 1878, British took Walvis Bay; 1983, trading concession to the F.A.E. Lüderitz company from Bremen; 1884, German protectorate; 1880s, German invasion and settlement; 1903, Nama revolted; 1904-1907, Herero revolt and resultant Germany-imposed Namibian Genocide – the Herero population dropped from 80,000 to 15,000; populations were driven into the desert to die (a deadly tactic adopted by the Turks against the Armenians in 1915 onwards). 1908, diamonds discovered at Lüderitz; 1915, British invaded; 1918, League of Nations trust territory; 1921-1922, revolt by Bondelzwarts Nama people crushed (aeroplanes used); 1945, South Africa would not give up the Mandate; 1947, South African annexation opposed by UN; 1966, UN declared South African annexation illegal; South West Africa People's Organization (SWAPO) commenced armed resistance; 1975-1988, SWAPO increased resistance activity from Angola; 1970s and 1980s, US, UK and European mining (uranium and diamonds); 1988, South Africa, Angola, Cuba and US agreed on peace (1966-1988 excess mortality 0.2 million); 1989, SWAPO victory in democratic elections; 1990, independence as Namibia with Sam Nujomo as president: South Africa retained the port of Walvis Bay; 1994, Walvis Bay returned to Namibia; amnesty and reconciliation processes; 1994, 1999, Nujomo re-elected; 1998, Namibia Defence Force (NDF) troops were sent to the Democratic Republic of the Congo in a Southern African Development Community (SADC) contingent; 1999, secessionist attempt in the northeastern Caprivi Strip quashed; 2004, Hifikepunye Pohamba (SWAPO) elected and inaugurated as president in 2005; 21st century, huge HIV/AIDS problem.

2021 update: 2020 onwards, Covid-19 pandemic with "Covid-19 deaths per million of population" of 196 as compared to 0.4 for Taiwan (March 2021). Climate change threat from drought. Revised greenhouse gas (GHG) pollution 19.8 tonnes CO_2-e per person per year. Namibia has signed and ratified the TPNW. In 2020 the "under-5 infant mortality as a percentage of total population" (0.1118%) was 77.1 times greater than for Japan (0.00145%), but 1.9 times lower than that in 2003 (0.2100%).

Foreign occupation: Germany, Britain, South Africa (pre-1950); South Africa (post-1950); *post-1950 foreign military presence:* South Africa; *1950-2005 excess mortality/2005 population* = 0.672m/2.032m = 33.1%; *1950-2005 under-5 infant mortality/2005 population* = 0.281m/2.032m = 13.8%; HIV positive (2003) 10.7%. Per capita GDP (nominal) $4,957.

Niger: prehistory, Sahara grasslands were home to shepherd Berber, Tuareg, Fulah, Nilotic and Tibu people; 11th century CE, Tuareg movement South; 13th century, Arabs and Berbers brought Islam; 14th century, Tuareg states based on Agadez and Bilma involved in North Africa-Nigeria trade; 14th century, Hausa states in Southern Niger; 17th century, part of the Songhai Empire based on Gao on the Niger in Mali; 18th century, part of the Northern Nigerian Bornu state; 19th century, Fulani control of South Niger; 1985, Berlin Conference "awarded" Niger to France; 1890s, French invasion; 1900, French military territory; 1904, Agadez captured from Tuaregs; 20th century, introduction of cash crops such as cotton and peanuts; from 1922, part of French West Africa; 1946, part of the French Union; 1950s, pro-French Niger Progressive party (PPN) and the socialist Sawaba Party lead by Djibo; 1960, independence under neo-colonial PPN lead by Diori; Sawaba outlawed; 1960s, some rebel activity by Sawaba supporters; 1970s and 1980s, severe drought in the Sahel region; 1974, coup by Kountché; 1980s, uranium exports; 1983, attempted coup and Tuareg rebellion; 1984-1986, Nigeria closed border; 1987, General Seybou succeeded Kountché; 1991-1993, transitional civilian rule; 1993, Mahamane Ousmane elected; 1995, peace with Tuaregs; 1996, Mainassara coup; 1999, Mainassara killed in Wanké coup; suspension of French aid; Tandja Mamadou elected; 21st century, most people are agricultural but the human economy is compromised by low land tenure, deforestation and drought; traditional slavery still widespread.

2021 update: 1999 onwards, many economic and administrative reforms; 2004, Tandja Mamadou re-elected president; Hama Amadou was reappointed as PM; 1st Niger president to be elected twice without being deposed by military coup; 2007-2009, Tuareg rebellion in the north; 1999, constitutionality games and 3-year interim government with Tandja Mamadou as president; 2010, coup d'état led by Captain Salou Djibo over Tandja's attempted extension of his political term by modifying the constitution; 2012, Mahamadou Issoufou elected president; 2016, Issoufou re-elected; security issues from the Libyan Civil War, and Northern Mali war, Nigerian Boko Haram insurgency, a rise in attacks by Islamists, migrant transits to Libya, and French and US anti-Muslim forces of Operation Barkhane in the Sahel. 2020-2021, Issoufou announced retirement; Mohamed Bazoum of the ruling Parti Nigérien pour la Démocratie et le Socialisme (PNDS) finally elected, defeating a former president Mahamane Ousmane. 2020 onwards, Covid-19 pandemic with "Covid-19 deaths per million of population" of 7 as compared to 0.4 for Taiwan (March 2021). Part of the global warming-threatened and drought-ravaged Sahel. Shallow Lake Chad has shrunk 90% in area since the 1960s. Revised greenhouse gas (GHG) pollution 4.1 tonnes CO_2-e per person per year. Niger has signed but not yet ratified the TPNW. In 2020 the "under-5 infant mortality as a percentage of total population" (0.3552%) was 245.0 times greater than for Japan (0.00145%), but 4.0 times lower than that in 2003 (1.4300%).

Foreign occupation: France (pre-1950); France (post-1950); *post-1950 foreign military presence:* France; *1950-2005 excess mortality/2005 population* = 6.558m/12.873m = 50.9%; *1950-2005 under-5 infant mortality/2005 population* = 5.674m/12.873m = 44.1%; HIV positive (2003) 0.6%. Per capita GDP (nominal) $555.

Nigeria: 1st millennium BCE-200CE, iron-working Nok culture; 8th-19th century, Northern Kenem-Bornu state North and South of Lake Chad; pre-colonial Yoruba cities (South) and 11th -19th century, century, Muslim Hausa city states (North); sometime tributaries or foes of the Kenem-Bornu state; 16th century, Hausa cities part of the Songhai Empire; 14th-19th century, Oyo state in South West Nigeria ruled Dahomey and Yoruba people; 15th-17th century, sophisticated Benin state in South West Nigeria; 15th century, Portuguese arrival; 16th-19th century, Portuguese, British and French slave trade; Igbo and Ibibio city states based on slave procurement; 1804, Fodio, an Islamic Fulani leader, conquered Hausa cities; 1817, his son, Bello, consolidated the Fulani state based on Sokoto; Bornu remained independent until about 1880; 1807, British abolished slavery; 19th century, palm oil industry replaced slavery; civil war in the Oyo state; 1861, Britain took Lagos; 1880s, Goldie secured interests for Britain along the Niger; 1883, Britain invaded the Oyo state; 1886, Royal Niger Company dominated Niger trade; 1894-1895, Berlin Conference awarded Nigeria to Britain; 1897, Benin taken by the British; 1900, Royal Charter revoked for the Royal Niger Company; 1903, Lugard captured Sokoto; 1906, British Colony (Lagos), British Protectorates in the North and the South; 1914, British united these disparate areas administratively; British exploited indigenous leaders; major tropical cash crops exploited (palm oil, peanuts, cotton); 1947, constitution based on traditional rulers; 1950s, increasing democratization and self-government for major regions; 1960, independence under Ahmadu Bello (PM) and Nnamdi Azikiwe (governor-general); 1963, republic; Azikiwe president; dominant ethnic groups: the Hausa–Fulani ('Northerners'), Igbo ('Easterners') and Yoruba ('Westerners'); 1966, Igbo military coup under General Johnson Aguiyi-Ironsi; Abubakar Tafawa Balewa (first Nigerian PM) and Western and Northern PMs killed; Northern revolt, Hausa military coup, General Yakubu Gowon installed; Ironsi killed; massacres of Igbo (Ibo) people in the Hausa North; 1967, Lt. Colonel Emeka Ojukwu proclaimed independent Biafra in Eastern Nigeria; UK, USSR, Egypt and Zaire (Congo) backed the government, France and Apartheid Israel backed Biafra; 1970, Biafra defeated in the genocidal civil war (Nigerian 1967-1970 excess mortality, 2.5 million); 1960s, oil industry developed; 1971, joined OPEC; 1970s, Sahel drought; 1975, coup with General Murtala Mohammad installed; 1976, coup with General Olusegun Obasanjo installed; 1979, return to democracy; Alhaji Shehu Shagari of the National Party of Nigeria (NPN) was elected president; 1983 Shagari and the NPN were returned to power; 1983, coup and Major General Muhammadu Buhari installed; 1985, coup with General Ibrahim Babangida installed; 1993, Moshood Abiola of the Social Democratic Party (SDP) won elections, but Babangida annulled elections, imprisoned opponents, and installed an interim government led by Ernest Shonekan; coup d'état led by General Sani Abacha; 1995, outrage when activist Ken Saro-Wiwa was executed; Nigeria suspended from the British Commonwealth; 1996, Kudirat Abiola (activist for husband Moshood Abiola) murdered; 1998, corrupt and violent Abacha died and succeeded by General Abdulsalami Abubakar; Abiola died in custody, riots over Abiola's death; 1999, elections; General Olusegun Obasanjo president, this ending a period of 3 decades of mostly military rule (Nigerian military juntas ruled in 1966–1979 and 1983–1999); 21st century, Sharia Law-related violence in North; thousands were killed; 2002, Abacha's family agreed to return corruptly acquired billions; 2003, Ijaw violence against Itsekiri and oil installations; 2003, Obasanjo re-elected.

2021 update: Violence in the oil-producing Niger Delta region and insurgency in the North-East; 2007, Umaru Yar'Adua of the People's Democratic Party (PDP) won in flawed elections; 2010, Yar'Adua died; Goodluck Jonathan acting president of Nigeria until 2011; 2011, Goodluck Jonathan elected; 2015, PDP defeated by a coalition of opposition parties (the All Progressives Congress (APC)) and General Muhammadu Buhari elected; 2019, Buhari re-elected; continuing violent kidnappings in the north by Boko Haram terrorists. 2020 onwards, Covid-19 pandemic with "Covid-19 deaths per million of population" of 10 as compared to 0.4 for Taiwan (March 2021). Major oil industry and deforestation (11.4% tree cover in 2018) contribute to a revised greenhouse gas (GHG) pollution 11.7 tonnes CO_2-e per person per year. Nigeria has signed and ratified the TPNW. In 2020 the "under-5 infant mortality as a percentage of total population" (0.3557%) was 245.3 times greater than for Japan (0.00145%), but 1.7 times lower than that in 2003 (0.5900%).

Foreign occupation: Britain (pre-1950); UK (post-1950); *post-1950 foreign military presence:* UK, France; *1950-2005 excess mortality/2005 population* = 49.737m/130.236m = 38.2%; *1950-2005 under-5 infant mortality/2005 population* = 38.297m/130.236m = 29.4%; HIV positive (2003) 2.9%. Per capita GDP (nominal) $2,361.

Réunion: 1513, Portuguese found the island uninhabited; 1638, claimed for France by Cauche; 17th-19th century French settlement together with Chinese, Malay, African and Indian labor; 1869, opening of the Suez Canal greatly diminished its seaport importance; 1946, made an Overseas Department of France.

2021 update: 2005- 2006, epidemic of painful chikungunya disease, 255,000 infected, and consequent anti-mosquito campaign. 2020 onwards, Covid-19 pandemic with "Covid-19 deaths per million of population" of 113 as compared to 0.4 for Taiwan (March 2021). Climate change threatened as a tropical Island state. Revised greenhouse gas (GHG) pollution about 5 tonnes CO_2-e per person per year. Réunion is an overseas department and region of France and the Occupier, France, rejects the TPNW and has 290 nuclear weapons. In 2020 the "under-5 infant mortality as a percentage of total population" (0.0043%) was 3.0 times greater than for Japan (0.00145%), but 7.0 times lower than that in 2003 (0.0300%).

Foreign occupation: France (pre-1950); France (post-1950); *post-1950 foreign military presence:* France; *1950-2005 excess mortality/2005 population* = 0.047m/0.777m = 6.0%; *1950-2005 under-5 infant mortality/2005 population* = 0.041m/0.777m = 5.3%. Per capita GDP (nominal) $25,900.

Rwanda: early inhabitants Pygmies (Twa); 10th century CE, Hutu settlement; 15th century, Tutsi invasion from north; 19th century, major Tutsi kings Mutari II and Kigeri IV; 1890, Kigeri IV accepted German control as part of German East Africa; 1897, German colonization (together with Tanzania and Burundi); 1916, Belgian forces occupied Rwanda; 1918, after WW1 Rwanda and Burundi under Belgians and administered from the Congo; 1946, Ruanda-Urundi UN Trust Territory; 1959, majority Hutus demanded greater say; 1959, Hutu revolt, departure of Belgians and of 0.1 million Tutsis; 1961, UN-sponsored elections won by Hutus; 1962, independent Rwanda separate from Burundi; president Kayibanda; 1965, 1969, Kayibanda re-elected; 1963, Hutu-Tutsi civil war after Burundi Tutsi incursion; 20,000 dead, 160,000 Tutsis expelled; 1971-1972, tensions with Uganda's Idi Amin; 1973, renewed racial violence; 600 Tutsis fled to Uganda; General Habyarimana coup; 1978, new constitution; 1978, Habyarimana elected; 1982, Uganda expelled Tutsi refugees; 1983, 1988, Habyarimana successively re-elected; 50,000 Hutu refugees from Burundi; 1988, Uganda-Rwanda agreement on refugees; 1990, Rwandan Patriotic Front (RPF) composed of Tutsi refugees invaded from Uganda, initiating the Rwandan Civil War; 1993, peace agreement with power-sharing accommodation and UN mission established; 1994, Habyarimana and Burundi president killed in a plane crash; actively encouraged by the Rwandan Government, Hutu soldiers and gangs killed 0.5-1.0 million Tutsis and connected, politically moderate Hutus over 100 days (Rwanda Genocide); many minority Twa were also killed; Rwandan Patriotic Front (RPF) composed of Tutsi refugees responded and took over the country; 2 million Hutus fled; Hutu Pastor Bizimungu as president, Paul Kagame as Defence Minister; 0.1 million Hutus died of disease in Congo camps; 1995, commencement of genocide trials (1990-1995 pentade excess mortality 1.1 million); 1996, 1 million Hutu refugees returned; 1997, Rwandan army and Hutu rebels in conflict; 1996-1997, Rwandan- and Uganda-backed rebel forces defeated Mobutu and installed Kabila as president of the Congo (Zaire); 1998-2003, war against Kabila-ruled Congo over Congo government's expulsion of Rwandan and Ugandan military forces from the country; 2000, Bizimungu resigned; Paul Kagame president; 2002, Rwandan forces formally withdrawn from the Congo but continued incursions seeking Hutu rebels; 2003, peace deal with the Congo; 2003, Kagame elected in flawed elections; 2004, Bizimungu imprisoned.

2021 update: 2015, constitutional changes to permit continuing Kagame presidency. 2020 onwards, Covid-19 pandemic with "Covid-19 deaths per million of population" of 23 as compared to 0.4 for Taiwan (March 2021). Population pressures and massive deforestation but a rebound from 10% tree cover in 2009 to 20% in

2018. Revised greenhouse gas (GHG) pollution 6.1 tonnes CO_2-e per person per year. Rwanda has not signed or ratified the TPNW. In 2020 the "under-5 infant mortality as a percentage of total population" (0.1042%) was 71.9 times greater than for Japan (0.00145%), but 6.6 times lower than that in 2003 (0.6900%).

Foreign occupation: Germany, Belgium (pre-1950); Belgium (post-1950); *post-1950 foreign military presence:* Belgium; *1950-2005 excess mortality/2005 population* = 5.190m/8.607m = 60.3%; *1950-2005 under-5 infant mortality/2005 population* = 2.577m/8.607m = 29.9%; HIV positive (2003) 3.1%. Per capita GDP (nominal) $820.

Sao Tomé and Principe: 15th century, Portuguese slave trade base; Dutch, French, Spanish, British and Portuguese slavers used Sao Tomé; early slave rebellion put down but slave activism lived on in Brazil; 1869, cessation of slave trade but sugar, cocoa and coffee plantations run with indentured labor; 19th-mid-20th century, indentured labour system with "9-year slaves" from other Portuguese African colonies drew international protests; 1940s-1970s, severe repression under the Salazar Portuguese dictatorship; 1969, resistance organization Movement for the Liberation of Sao Tome and Principe (MLSTP) was founded; 1974, Portuguese dictator Salazar overthrown; 1975, independence with MLSTP Secretary General Manuel Pinto da Costa as president; departure of many Europeans disrupted cocoa production; plots for mercenary invasion from Gabon; 1991, first free elections; former PM Miguel Trovoada elected president; followed by frequent changes of government; 1995, 2003, coup attempts.

2021 update: 1996, Trovoada was re-elected; 2001, Democratic Action party candidate Fradique de Menezes elected; 2003, 1 week coup but Menezes restored; 2006, Fradique de Menezes re-elected; 2011, Manuel Pinto da Costa president; 2016, Evaristo Carvalho (Independent Democratic Action party (ADI)) president; 2018, Jorge Bom Jesus (leader of the Movimento de Libertação de São Tomé e Príncipe-Partido Social Democráta (MLSTP-PSD)) PM. 2020 onwards, Covid-19 pandemic with "Covid-19 deaths per million of population" of 153 as compared to 0.4 for Taiwan

(March 2021). Climate change threatened as a tropical Island Nation. Revised greenhouse gas (GHG) pollution 1.9 tonnes CO_2-e per person per year. Sao Tomé and Principe has signed but not ratified the TPNW. In 2020 the "under-5 infant mortality as a percentage of total population" (0.0930%) was 64.1 times greater than for Japan (0.00145%), but 4.2 times lower than that in 2003 (0.3900%).

Foreign occupation: Portugal (pre-1950); Portugal (post-1950); *post-1950 foreign military presence:* Portugal; *1950-2005 excess mortality/2005 population* = 0.039m/0.169m = 23.1%; *1950-2005 under-5 infant mortality/2005 population* = 0.033m/0.169m = 19.5%. Per capita GDP (nominal) $1,961.

Senegal: Pre-colonial Uolof, Fulani and Tukolor peoples; 9th-14th century CE, Tukolor settled the Senegal valley; dominant Tekrur state; 11th century, Muslim Almovarid Tukolors ruled in Morocco; 14th century, Mali Empire encompassed Senegal; Tekrur defeated; 15th-17th century, the Wolof people established the Joluf state; 1445-1446, Portuguese arrival; subsequent trading forts (notably on Gorée Island) ; 17th century, Dutch and French displaced the Portuguese; 1638, 1659, French posts near present-day Dakar; 1677, French captured Dutch Gorée; 1697-1720, Brüe headed Royal Senegal Company, extended French domain up-river (slaves, gum Arabic and ivory); 1756-1763, 7 Years War, Britain captured Senegal and formed Senegambia; 1775-1783, subsequent French recovery of possessions; 1815, Britain retained the immediate Senegal Valley (Gambia); 19th century, further French conquest; 1848, slavery abolished in France and thence cotton and peanut exports from Senegal; 1854-1885, war by the French; Walo defeated; Tukolor religious leader Umar constrained; 1895, Senegal a colony and part of French West Africa; 1902, Dakar HQ for French West Africa; 1930s and post-war, increasing pressure for independence; 1940-1942, Vichy rule; 1958, autonomous republic within the French Community; 1959, part of Senegal-French Sudan Mali Federation; 1960, independent within the French Community under Léopold Sédar Senghor; French domination of industry and cotton and peanut farming; political repression; 1981, Senghor resigned; Abdou Diouf president; Senegal intervened to suppress

Gambia coup; Senegambia Confederation (independent sovereignty but common defence and economic links); 1983-1985, major Sahel drought; 1988, Diouf socialist electoral victory in a flawed process, Senegal-Mauritanian tensions with civil violence and thousands of Senegalese refugees; 1989, Guinea-Bissau dispute; Senegal and Mauritania broke relations and Gambia-Senegal tensions; Senegambia was dissolved; 1993, Diouf re-elected president; 2000, opposition leader Abdoulaye Wade elected president; 21st century, continuing fighting with Casamance rebels south of the Gambia.

2021 update: 2012, Macky Sall elected president of Senegal; 2019, Macky Sall re-elected president 2020 onwards, Covid-19 pandemic with "Covid-19 deaths per million of population" of 60 as compared to 0.4 for Taiwan (March 2021). Climate change threatens Sahel with worsening drought, Revised greenhouse gas (GHG) pollution 7.0 tonnes CO_2-e per person per year. Senegal has not signed or ratified the TPNW. In 2020 the "under-5 infant mortality as a percentage of total population" (0.1355%) was 93.4 times greater than for Japan (0.00145%), but 3.7 times lower than that in 2003 (0.5000%).

Foreign occupation: France (pre-1950); France (post-1950); *post-1950 foreign military presence:* France; *1950-2005 excess mortality/2005 population* = 4.457m/9.393m = 47.5%; *1950-2005 under-5 infant mortality/2005 population* = 2.770m/9.393m = 29.5%; HIV positive (2003) 0.4%. Per capita GDP (nominal) $1,452.

Seychelles: 1502, Portuguese Vasco da Gama arrived; 1756, occupied by France; 18th century, French colonization with plantations and slaves from Mauritius; 1794, British conquered and ruled from Mauritius; 1814, formal British possession; 1903, Crown Colony; 1948, legislative council; 1960s, increasing Afro-Indian activism; 1974, legislative elections, anti-independence conservative leader James Mancham became interim president and gave key islands to UK; 1976, independence; 1977, Mancham deposed by socialist leader Albert René who demanded the return of Diego Garcia to Mauritius; 1979-1991, socialist one-party state; 1980s, coup attempts; 1981, South African mercenary coup attempt; 1984, René re-elected; 1986, further coup attempt defeated by requested Indian navy presence; 1993, multi-party democracy restored with new constitution; 1993, 1998, 2001, René re-elected president; 2004, René retired; replaced by his deputy James Michel, president 2004-2016.

2021 update: 2013, devastated by tropical cyclone Felleng; 2016-2020, Danny Faure president. 2020, Wavel Ramkalawan first opposition president to be elected. 2020 onwards, Covid-19 pandemic with "Covid-19 deaths per million of population" of 202 as compared to 0.4 for Taiwan (March 2021). Tourism industry contributes to a revised greenhouse gas (GHG) pollution of 7.0 tonnes CO_2-e per person per year. As a tropical Island Nation Seychelles is seriously threatened by climate change. Seychelles has signed but not yet ratified the TPNW. In 2020 the "under-5 infant mortality as a percentage of total population" (0.0214%) was 14.8 times greater than for Japan (0.00145%).

Foreign occupation: France, Britain (pre-1950); UK (post-1950); *post-1950 foreign military presence:* UK, South African mercenaries. Per capita GDP (nominal) $17,382.

Sierra Leone: pre-colonial coastal Temne people; 1460, Portuguese arrival; 15th century, Portuguese incursions; 16th century, Mande migration from Liberia; 16th-19th century, timber, ivory and slaves; 1787, 1792, attempts at free slave settlement at Freetown on land purchased from the Temne; 1807, British abolition of slavery; run-away slaves and the abolition of slavery in London led to Granville Sharp land purchase, colonization by Britain and takeover from the Sierra Leone company running Freetown; 19th century, 50,000 freed slaves settled; interior resistance to British rule; 1827, Fourah Bay College founded; 1896, British protectorate proclaimed over the interior; 1897, final British victory over indigenous resistance; post-war, palm oil, peanuts, diamonds and iron ore; 1960, autonomy with pro-British interim government; 1961, independence under conservative Mende Sir Milton Margai as PM and representing Creole, British and Syrian-Lebanese merchant interests; increasingly authoritarian measures against the opposition All People's Congress (APC); 1962, first general elections; 1964, Albert Margai succeeded his brother; 1967, elections won by Temne Stevens but overturned by coup; 1968, coup re-installed Stevens; 1971-1973, Guinean troops to support Stevens; 1978-1985 one-party rule; 1986, Saidu Momoh succeeded Stevens as president representing the APC; 1991, commencement of Liberian-backed Revolutionary United Front (RUF) rebel attacks; 1990s, rebel violence, coups, civil war and international intervention; 1992, military coup installed 1992-1996 junta headed by Captain Valentine Strasser; 1996, Brigadier Julius Maada Bio permitted elections; 1996, Ahmad Tejan Kabbah of the Sierra Leone People's Party (SLPP) elected president; cease-fire with rebels; 1997, Kabbah removed in a further coup; UN sanctions; Economic Community of West African states (ECOWAS) sent Nigerian-led forces; 1998, Kabbah restored and continued democratic rule to the present but with continued violence; 1999, peace accord with RUF leader Sankoh; continued violence; UN peace-keepers (eventually 13,000); 2000, UN forces held hostage by rebels; British forces critically involved in defeating the rebels; ban on rebel-funding diamond sales; 2001, sanctions on Liberia; rebel and pro-government militia disarmament (50,000 killed; hundreds of thousands of refugees; 1991-2001 excess mortality 1.1 million); 2002, elections; Kabbah re-elected; 2003, UN diamond ban lifted; 70,000 rebels and militias disarmed; 2004, 8,000 UN peacekeepers remained.

2021 update: 2005, UN peacekeeping forces pulled out of Sierra Leone; 2007, Ernest Bai Koroma (APC candidate) elected president; 2012, Koroma re-elected; 2018, SLPP candidate Julius Maada Bio elected president; 2014, Ebola virus epidemic in West Africa that killed 3,000 in Sierra Leone; 2016, WHO declared Sierra Leone free of Ebola. 2020 onwards, Covid-19 pandemic with "Covid-19 deaths per million of population" of 10 as compared to 0.4 for Taiwan (March 2019). Deforestation (57.8 % tree cover in 2018) contributes to revised greenhouse gas (GHG) pollution of 23.8 tonnes CO_2-e per person per year. Sierra Leone has not signed or ratified the TPNW. In 2020 the "under-5 infant mortality as a percentage of total population" (0.3337%) was 230.1 times greater than for Japan (0.00145%), but 4.2 times lower than that in 2003 (1.3900%).

Foreign occupation: Britain (pre-1950); Britain (post-1950); *post-1950 foreign military presence:* UK, Guinea, UN peacekeepers (Nigeria, UK); *1950-2005 excess mortality/2005 population* = 4.548m/5.340m = 85.2%; *1950-2005 under-5 infant mortality/2005 population* = 2.846m/5.340m = 53.3%. Per capita GDP (nominal) $528.

Somalia (Occupied Somalia): Early trade with Romans and Egyptians; Galla, Haussa and Yemeni settlements; 7th-10th century CE, Muslim Arab and Persian trading and settlements; 15th-16th century, Christian Ethiopian and Muslim Somali conflict; 1541, Portuguese destroyed major towns; 1698, Portuguese expelled; 18th–19th century, Ottoman Turkish control of north, Zanzibar Arab control of south; mid-19th century, the Suez Canal construction impelled territorial seizures by Italy (Eritrea), Britain (Berbera, Zelia) and France (Obuck, now Djibouti); 1870, partial Egyptian occupation; 1884, Egyptians withdrew; 1896, Italians defeated by Ethiopia; 1906, Italians took the South coast of Somalia; 1885-1920, Somali resistance to British crushed using air power; 1925, Jubaland conquered by the Italians; 1936, Italian-occupied Somalia incorporated with Ethiopia and Eritrea into Italian East Africa; 1941, British forces from Kenya defeated the Italians; 1950, Italian Somaliland a UN Trust Territory under Italian control; 1960, Italian and thence British Somalia independence; union as United Republic of Somalia; 1969, coup under Major General Mohamed Siad Barre; 1974, joined the Arab League; 1976-1988, war by US- and Saudi-backed Somalia against USSR-backed Ethiopia over the Ogaden region, 840,000 refugees fled to Somalia; 1980, US gained Berbera base; Somalia-Ethiopia peace accord (1976-1988 excess mortality 1.4 million); 1991, coup; North Somalia (formerly British) seceded; Mogadishu civil war between the General Mohamed Farah Aidid and Ali Mahdi Mohamed factions; 1992, famine due to drought exacerbated by civil war (0.3 million famine deaths); UN aid; 1993, Pakistan peacekeeper deaths; US forces entry; US left; 1995, last UN forces left; 1996, Aidid died of wounds; 1997, devastating floods; 1998, Northeast Puntland region and Jubaland (South Somalia) declared independence; 21st century, fragmented country (Northern Somaliland, Southwestern Somaliland, Northeast Puntland and

Mogadishu region); 2002, ceasefire covering most areas; continuing attempts at resolution with Kenyan facilitation (1991-2005, excess mortality 1.9 million).

2021 update: 2000, Transitional National Government (TNG) was established; 2000-2004, Transitional Federal Government (TFG); 2006-2007, Islamic Courts Union (ICU) administration; 2007, US-backed Ethiopian invasion, restoration of the TFG supported by African Union forces (African Union Mission in Somalia (AMISOM)), notably from Kenya; Islamic forces, notably Al-Shabaab, opposed foreign occupation of Somalia; 2007 onwards, US-led "antipiracy" and anti-wood exports in US Alliance naval operations; 2008 onwards, worsening drought in the Sahel. 2020 onwards, Covid-19 pandemic with "Covid-19 deaths per million of population" of 29 as compared to 0.4 for Taiwan (March 2021). Revised greenhouse gas (GHG) pollution not available. Somalia has not signed or ratified the TPNW. In 2020 the "under-5 infant mortality as a percentage of total population" (0.4554%) was 314.1 times greater than for Japan (0.00145%), but 2.6 times lower than that in 2003 (1.170%) for US Alliance-occupied Somalia - evidence of gross violation of the Fourth Geneva Convention by the US Alliance.

Foreign occupation: Turks, French, British, Italians (pre-1950); UK (post-1950); *post-1950 foreign military presence:* UK, US, UN (Pakistan peacekeepers), Ethiopia, Kenya; *1950-2005 excess mortality/2005 population* = 5.568m/10.742m = 51.8%; *1950-2005 under-5 infant mortality/2005 population* = 3.582m/10.742m = 33.3%. Per capita GDP (nominal) $105

South Africa: San (Bushmen) the earliest inhabitants; 1st century CE, Khoikhoi (Hottentot) people settled; 1488, Portuguese Dias arrived; 15th century onwards; Cape of Good Hope on route of Vasco da Gama and others to India; 1652, van Riebeeck, Dutch East Indian Company and first Dutch settlement; 1713, smallpox killed many Europeans and most of the Cape Khoikhoi; 17th-19th century, massive depopulation due to genocidal Zulu warfare under ruthless leaders Shaka and Dingane; Dutch Afrikaaner (Boer) expansion north; 17th-mid-20th century, wars against Africans ("kaffirs"), notably the Xhosa and Zulus; 1795, British occupation during the Napoleonic wars; 1814, formal British possession by the Congress of Vienna; 1834-1845, Great Trek of Boers inland; 1838, Boers defeated the Zulus; 1843, British annexation of Natal; 1852-1854, independence of Transvaal and Orange Free State; 19th century, Boers enslaved and exterminated native people; 1867, gold and diamonds discovered in Transvaal; 1860, first Indian indentured labour in Natal; late 19th century, major importation of Indian and Chinese indentured labour; 1895, Jameson's raid on Transvaal failed to precipitate a non-Boer (Uitlander) uprising; 1899-1902, British versus Afrikaaner Boer War, 50,000 dead, 28,000 (mainly women and children) died in British concentration camps; 1906, 11 September, Gandhi launches peaceful Satyagraha (force truth) movement at Johannesburg mass meeting protesting race-based ID; 1912, African National Congress (ANC) founded; WW2, leading Afrikaaner Nationalists imprisoned as Nazi sympathizers; 1948, Afrikaaner Nationalist victory and increasing racist Apartheid legislation legitimizing dispossession, confinement and control of the African, Asian and part-European majority; Dr Hendrik Verwoerd "architect of Apartheid" as Minister of Native Affairs (1950–1958) and as PM (1958–1966); 1960, Sharpeville Massacre of 69 African protesters (180 wounded) leading to increasing World opposition, sanctions and boycotts; 1961, South Africa cut British Commonwealth ties; 1960s-1980s, crucial covert UK, US and Apartheid Israeli support for South Africa; South African military attacks in the "front-line" neighbouring countries; 1990, Namibian independence; 1974, Mahlabatini Declaration of Faith, signed by Mangosuthu Buthelezi (Zulu tribal leader who founded what became the Inkatha Freedom Party (IFP)) and Harry Schwarz (a founding member of the Democratic Party and UN ambassador, 1991-1995); 1990, government lifted ban on the ANC and other political organizations; Nelson Mandela released from 27 years of imprisonment (18 years on Robben Island); 1993, Afrikaaner PM F.W. de Klerk opened bilateral discussions with Nelson Mandela; collapse of Apartheid and advent of majority rule under Nelson Mandela; surrender of nuclear weapons acquired with the assistance of Apartheid Israel; 1994, ANC victory in first universal suffrage elections (in power ever since); Mandela president; South Africa re-joined the British Commonwealth; Truth and Reconciliation Commission headed by Archbishop Desmond

Tutu; post-independence HIV/AIDS epidemic with 11.9% of the population infected (2003).

2021 update: 1999-2008, Thabo Mvuyelwa Mbeki president; absurd denial of science over HIV and ban of retroviral drugs in hospitals (300,000 died); soft attitude to Mugabe's Zimbabwe; South African life expectancy fell from a high point of 62.25 years in 1992 to a low of 52.57 in 2005; 2008-2009, Kgalema Petrus Motlanthe president; 2009-2018; Jacob Gedleyihlekisa Zuma president; massive corruption; 2019 onwards, Matamela Cyril Ramaphosa president. Continuing problems of HIV/AIDS, massive refugee influx (notably from Zimbabwe), poverty, inequity, violent crime, housing, and water shortages. Covid-19 pandemic with "Covid-19 deaths per million of population" of a bad 879 as compared to 0.4 for Taiwan (March 2021). Major coal exports, industry and wealthy minority lifestyle contribute to revised greenhouse gas (GHG) pollution of 19.4 tonnes CO_2-e per person per year. Climate change threats of drought and worsening urban water supply. South Africa has signed and ratified the TPNW. In 2020 the "under-5 infant mortality as a percentage of total population" (0.0655%) was 45.2 times greater than for Japan (0.00145%), but 2.4 times lower than that in 2003 (0.1600%).

Foreign occupation: Netherlands, Afrikaaner minority, Britain (pre-1950); Afrikaaner (post-1950); *post-1950 foreign military presence:* Afrikaaner, Apartheid Israel (nuclear weapons technology); *1950-2005 excess mortality/2005 population =* 13.534m/45.323m = 29.9%; *1950-2005 under-5 infant mortality/2005 population =* 4.623m/45.323m = 10.2%; HIV positive (2003) 11.9%. Per capita GDP (nominal) $6,001.

Tanzania: prehistoric Paleolithic cultures; 1st millennium CE, coastal trade with India, SW Asia and NE Africa eventually leading to trading settlements; trading contacts with present-day Indonesia; about 1000, Bantu settlers from the West and the South; about 1200, Kilwa traded with Sofala in Mozambique; 1498, Vasco da Gama arrived; 1505, Kilwa conquered by the Portuguese; 1587, Zimba people from the South massacred nearly half of Kilwa; 1698, Omani removal of the Portuguese; 17th-19th century, Omani commerce (slaves, gold, ivory and skins) was based on Zanzibar and Mombasa; 19th century, early European visits; Nyamwezi state in Central and Northern Tanzania; Tippu Tib controlled Zanzibar slave trade to Zambia and the East Congo; 1841, Omani Sayyid Said ruled from Zanzibar; 1886, Anglo-German agreement over areas of control; 1887, German East Africa company ruled Tanzania and Rwanda and Burundi (from 1890); indigenous resistance, plantations and missionaries; 1905-1907, Maji Maji revolt suppressed by the Germans with 75,000 Africans killed; 1916, WW1, British and Belgian occupation; 1919, Tanzania a British mandate; 1926, a legislative assembly was established; 1954, Tanganyika African National Union (TANU) founded by Nyerere; 1961, Tanzania became independent under Julius Nyerere; 1961-1995, effective one-party socialist rule; 1970-1975, China financed and helped build the 1,860-kilometre-long TAZARA Railway from Dar es Salaam to Zambia; 1978, Uganda invaded; 1979, Tanzania invaded Uganda and displaced dictator Idi Amin;1982, Tanzanian forces left Uganda (whereupon rebellion escalated); 1977-1983, tensions with Kenya resulting in the border closure; 1985, Nyerere resigned; Ali Hassan Mwinyi president; 1990s, 0.3 million refugees from war in Burundi; 1992, multi-party elections possible; 1995, multi-party elections; Benjamin Mkapa elected in flawed elections; 2000, Mkapa re-elected; 21st century, flawed democracy; HIV/AIDS epidemic.

2021 update: Every Tanzanian president has represented the ruling party Chama cha Mapinduzi (CCM), to whit Julius Nyerere (1962-1985), Ali Hassan Mwinyi (1985-1995), Benjamin Mkapa (1995-2005), Jakaya Kikwete (2005-2015), John Magufuli (2015-2021; died in office) and Samia Hassan Suluhu (2021 onwards; first female president). 2020 onwards, Covid-19 pandemic with "Covid-19 deaths per million of population" of 8 as compared to 0.4 for Taiwan (March 2021). Revised greenhouse gas (GHG) pollution 9.3 tonnes CO_2-e per person per year. Tanzania has not signed or ratified the TPNW. In 2020 the "under-5 infant mortality as a percentage of total population" (0.1872%) was 129.1 times greater than for Japan (0.00145%), but 3.5 times lower than that in 2003 (0.6500%).

Foreign occupation: Germany, Britain, Belgium (pre-1950); UK, Uganda (post-1950); *post-1950 foreign military presence:* UK, Uganda; *1950-2005 excess mortality/2005 population =* 14.682m/38.365m = 38.3%; *1950-2005 under-5 infant mortality/2005 population* = 8.991m/38.365m = 23.4%; HIV positive (2003) 4.4%. Per capita GDP (nominal) $1,084.

Togo: Pre-colonial Ewe people in the South, Volta people in the North; 16th-19th century, British, French, Portuguese, Spanish slavery in the "Slave Coast"; Ashanti participated in collecting slaves; 1840s, German missionaries and traders; 1884, German colony; 1897, treaty with France; 1904, treaty with Britain; 1914-1818, WW1; 1914, Anglo-French conquest and occupation; 1922, League of Nations mandate between France and Britain; 1946, UN Trust Territories; 1956, Western part to Ghana, Eastern part to France; major phosphate deposits; 1960, independence of French Togoland as Togo under Sylvanus Olympio; 1961, Olympio president; 1966, tensions with Ghana; 1963, military coup, Olympio killed and succeeded by his brother-in-law Nicolas Grunitzky; 1969, coup by General Gnassingbé Eyadéma who set up a one-party system; political repression; 1980s, refugees from Ghana and Burkina-Faso; 1985, Lomé Deal regulating EEC-Third World economic relations; 1986, attempted coup; 1979, 1986, 1993, 1998, 2003, Eyadéma "re-elected" in successive "elections" with a repressed opposition (multiparty elections since 1993); 21st century, poverty, repression and HIV epidemic.

2021 update: 2005, Gnassingbé Eyadéma died; his son Faure Gnassingbé was elected president and continues as president; 2020 onwards, Covid-19 pandemic with "Covid-19 deaths per million of population" of 13 as compared to 0.4 for Taiwan (March 2021). High deforestation of tropical rain forest contributes to a revised greenhouse gas (GHG) pollution of 10.9 tonnes CO_2-e per person per year. Togo has signed but not yet ratified the TPNW. In 2020 the "under-5 infant mortality as a percentage of total population" (0.2284%) was 157.5 times greater than for Japan (0.00145%), but 2.4 times lower than that in 2003 (0.5400%).

Foreign occupation: Germany, Britain, France (pre-1950); UK, France (post-1950); *post-1950 foreign military presence:* France (hegemony); *1950-2005 excess mortality/2005 population =* 1.950m/5.129m = 38.0%; *1950-2005 under-5 infant mortality/2005 population* = 1.186m/5.129m = 23.1%.; HIV positive (2003) 2.3%. Per capita GDP (nominal) $899.

Uganda: 500BCE, Bantu settlement; 13th century CE, shepherding Bacwezi people conquered northern Uganda; 14th Cwezi states; 15th century, Nilotic Luo people founded Buganda; 17th-18th century, rise of Eastern Buganda state; 16th-17th century, Bunyoro state in the South; 18th-19th century, extension of Buganda power; Ganda trade in slaves and ivory; 1869-mid-1880s, Bunyoro under Kabarega expanded using Western arms but was eventually defeated by Buganda; 1862, Speke explored the region; about 1875, US explorer Stanley and thence Christian missionaries in the region; late 19th century, increasing Muslim and Christian tensions; 1890, British-German treaty; 1894, British protectorate; 1904, beginning of cotton production; 20th century, British personal ownership-based "land reform" and cash crops distorted society; Indian immigration; disempowerment of Buganda; railway construction; 1903, Hungarian Zionist Theodor Herzl and "Uganda Plan" for Jewish settlement (the Zionists rejected it and the British took back their offer of 13,000 square kilometers of Kenya); 1953-1955, Mutesa II exiled; independence, Dr Milton Obote (a Lango) the first prime minister; 1966, constitution abolished Bugandan autonomy; 1971, coup installed General Idi Amin; cultivated the Ganda; split with US and Israel over destabilization; 1972, expulsion of Indians; severe repression (0.3-0.5 million killed); 1976, Apartheid Israeli Entebbe raid; 1978, Amin annexed part of Tanzania; Tanzania removed Amin; 1979, successive rule by Yusuf Kironde Lule and Godfrey Binaisa; 1980, democracy restored and Milton Obote victory; 1981, Tanzanian forces left; National Resistance Army (NRA) rebellion; 0.2 million refugees to Rwanda, Sudan and the Congo; 1985, Tito Lutwa Okello coup removed Obote; 1986, NRA Museveni took over; effective ban on political parties; Northern rebel activity by the Lord's Resistance Army (LRA) commenced involving former government soldiers; 1996, 2001, Yoweri Kaguta Museveni elected; 1997, forces helped install

Kabila in the Congo (Zaire); 1998, forces opposed Kabila; 1999, conflict with Rwandan forces in the Congo; 2000, religious mass murder-suicide event killed 778; 2003, final withdrawal of forces from the Congo; 21st century, continued LRA rebel activity in the North with atrocities against civilians; 21st century, persistent northern guerrilla war, crippled economy and HIV/AIDS epidemic.

2021 update: After constitutional amendments that removed term limits for the president, Museveni was able to stand repeatedly and was elected president in the 2011, 2016 and 2021 elections (in 2021 he defeated popstar-turned-politician Bobi Wine). 2020 onwards, Covid-19 pandemic with "Covid-19 deaths per million of population" of 7 as compared to 0.4 for Taiwan (March 2021). Revised greenhouse gas (GHG) pollution 5.1 tonnes CO_2-e per person per year. Uganda has not signed or ratified the TPNW. In 2020 the "under-5 infant mortality as a percentage of total population" (0.2132%) was 147.0 times greater than for Japan (0.00145%), but 3.3 times lower than that in 2003 (0.7000%).

Foreign occupation: Britain (pre-1950); UK (post-1950); *post-1950 foreign military presence:* Tanzania (Amin overthrow), Apartheid Israel (Entebbe airport hostage rescue); *post-1950 excess mortality/2005 population* = 11.121m/27.623m = 40.3%; *post-1950 under-5 infant mortality/2005 population* = 6.301m/27.623m = 22.8%; HIV infection (2003) 2.1%. Per capita GDP (nominal) $737.

Western Sahara: 4th century BCE, trade with Europe; 5th century CE, Tuareg, Berber (Moor) and Tubu people; 1434, Portuguese contact; 1884, Spanish protectorate asserted to protect the Canary Islands; 1886 Berlin Conference allocated Western Sahara territory to Spain and Morocco to France; 1904, border agreement between France and Spain; 20th century, French and Spanish war against indigenous resistance; 1934, Essemara captured by the Spanish; 1956, Morocco independent; 1957, Spanish ousted but restored with French help (1958); 1958, Spanish formed Spanish Sahara; 1950s onwards, phosphate deposit exploitation, increasing resistance; 1967, Polisario Front founded; 1970s, increased pro-independence activity (supported by Algeria) for the Sahrawi Arab

Democratic Republic; 1975, Morocco claim to Western Sahara (march of 300,000 Moroccans) was rejected; Spain ceded Spanish Sahara to Morocco (Northern 2/3) and Mauritania (Southern 1/3); 1976, Polisario Front war with Morocco and Mauritania; Polisario Front proclaimed the Sahrawi Arab Democratic Republic (SADR); 1979, Mauritania made peace with the Polisario Front; 1991, UN cease-fire, 2/3 ruled by Morocco, 1./3 ruled by Western Sahara; UN considers the Polisario Front to represent the Sahrawi people, and recognizes their right to self-determination; SADR recognized by 46 countries and a member of the African Union.

2021 update: 2017, Morocco readmitted to the African Union for ensuring peaceful resolution and cessation of building new walls (Morocco has built a 2,700 km long sand and stone "wall", the Moroccan Western Sahara Wall separating Moroccan and Polisario-ruled territory and the longest continuous minefield in the world); 2020, Trump US recognized Moroccan sovereignty over Western Sahara in exchange for Moroccan betrayal of the Arab and Muslim world by "normalization" of relations with an abnormal, nuclear terrorist, anti-Arab anti-Semitic and genocidally racist Apartheid Israel. 2020 onwards, Covid-19 pandemic with "Covid-19 deaths per million of population" of 2 as compared to 0.4 for Taiwan (March 2021). Climate change threat from exacerbated drought. Revised greenhouse gas (GHG) pollution not available. Western Sahara TPNW status not available. In 2020 the "under-5 infant mortality as a percentage of total population" (0.0632%) was 43.6 times greater than for Japan (0.00145%), but 7.9 times lower than that in 2003 (0.5000%).

Foreign occupation: France, Spain (pre-1950); Spain, Morocco, Mauritania (post-1950); *post-1950 foreign military presence:* Spain, Morocco, Mauritania; *1950-2005 excess mortality/2005 population* = 0.063m/0.324m= 19.4%; *1950-2005 under-5 infant mortality/2005 population* = 0.052m/0.324m = 16.0%. Per capita GDP (nominal) about $2,500.

Zambia: early San (Bushmen) people; 800CE, first Bantu settlement; 16th-18th century, Bantu people from Angola and Congo; 18th century, Lunda state; 18th -19th century, Portuguese and Arab slave trade from Mozambique; trade in copper and slaves; 1835, Ngoni (Zulu) invaded from the South; 1830s, Lozi Kingdom of Barotseland ruled by Kololo people from the South; 1851 onwards, British Dr Livingstone explored the Zambezi (in 1871, famously meeting American Henry Stanley of "Dr Livingstone I presume" fame); 1889, Cecil Rhodes' British South Africa Company given mining and trade monopolies by Lozi Kingdom and other groups; 1909, railway to Indian Ocean for copper and agricultural produce; increased European settlement; 1924, UK took direct control; late 1920s, copper exploitation began in the Copperbelt; 1930s, 1940s, 1950s, copper worker strikes; 1953, British Federation of Northern Rhodesia (future Zambia), Southern Rhodesia (Zimbabwe), and Nyasaland (Malawi); opposed by the Northern Rhodesia African Congress under Nkumbula; 1950s, African struggle for independence led by Kenneth Kaunda; 1958, European population about 70,000; 1959, Kaunda led the United African Independence Party (UNIP); 1964, Zambia independent under Kaunda but surrounded by racist states dominated by Europeans (US-Belgium-dominated Congo, White-ruled Namibia/Botswana/South Africa and Southern Rhodesia, and Portuguese-ruled Mozambique and Angola); 1965, joined sanctions against White-ruled Rhodesia; 1969, Dar-es-Salaam to Ndola oil pipeline; 1972, one-party state under Kenneth Kaunda's socialist United National Independence Party (UNIP); 1970-1975, China built the Great Uhuru Tanzania-Zambia (TAZARA) railway to avoid Portuguese Mozambique; 1965-1980, Zimbabwe struggle for majority rule; White Rhodesian military incursions and economic sabotage; 1980, Zimbabwe independence; 1986, South Africa invaded over Namibia guerrillas and ANC rebels; 1991, Frederick Chiluba's Multiparty Democracy Party (MDP) won the elections; 1993, emergency after coup plot; 1996, Chiluba re-election; 1997, coup attempt, emergency and repression; 2001, Levy Mwanawasa (MDP), Chiluba's chosen successor, elected in flawed elections; 1990s, 21st century, dire poverty and huge HIV/AIDS crisis.

2021 update: increasing Chinese investment in mining and agriculture; 2008, Levy Mwanawasa presided over Zambia from January 2002 until his death in 2008; Rupiah Banda acting president before being elected president; 2011 elections, Patriotic

Front party leader Michael Sata elected president; 2014, Sata died (the second Zambian president to die in office) and Guy Scott interim president; 2015, 2016, Edgar Lungu was elected as president. Covid-19 pandemic with "Covid-19 deaths per million of population" of 64 as compared to 0.4 for Taiwan (March 2019). Major legal and illegal logging. Revised greenhouse gas (GHG) pollution 97.5 tonnes CO_2-e per person per year. Zambia has signed but not yet ratified the TPNW. In 2020 the "under-5 infant mortality as a percentage of total population" (0.2011%) was 138.7 times greater than for Japan (0.00145%), but 4.3 times lower than that in 2003 (0.8700%).

Foreign occupation: Britain (pre-1950); UK (post-1950); *post-1950 foreign military presence:* UK, South Africa (invasion), White Rhodesia (invasion); *1950-2005 excess mortality/2005 population* = 5.463m/11.043m= 49.5%; *1950-2005 under-5 infant mortality/2005 population* = 2.848m/11.043m = 25.8%; HIV positive (2003) 8.6%. Per capita GDP (nominal) $1,292.

Zimbabwe: early Iron Age civilization; 5th century CE, Bantu settlement; 12th–15th century, Karanga (Shona) civilization with mining, trade and impressive fortifications (notably Zimbabwe); 16th century, Portuguese destruction of Indian Ocean Sofala disrupted Karanga trade via Mozambique; 1834, genocidal Zulu expansion forced Shona North; Zulu Ndebele branch settled in Southern Matabeleland; 1861, London Missionary Society; 1889, Rudd Concession from Ndbele opened up European invasion by Boers and British (Cecil Rhodes' British South Africa Company); 1890, Fort Salisbury founded by Jameson; 1893, Ndebele defeated and dispossessed of their land; 1896-1897, Ndebele and Shona revolts suppressed; 1914, Company charter renewed subject to future settler self-rule; 1923, self-governing White-ruled Rhodesia; 1953, Federation of Rhodesia and Nyasaland; 1960, the 5% European minority owned 70% of the land; 1960s, African National Congress (ANC) struggle for independence; 1963, Northern Rhodesia became independent Zambia; Nyasaland became independent Malawi; 1965, Ian Smith Unilateral Declaration of Independence (UDI); UK refused to suppress the rebellion; UN embargo violated by South Africa, Portugal and the

West (notably the UK and the US); 1970, Rhodesian republic; 1970s, guerrilla warfare by Mugabe's Zimbabwe African National Union (ZANU) (from Mozambique) and Nkomo's Zimbabwe African People's Union (ZAPU) (from Zambia); 1971, UK-Rhodesia accord for increased African role; 1975, Mozambique independence; Smith attacked Zambia and Mozambique; 1965-1980, war made 1 million homeless, huge mortality from violence, deprivation and disease; 1978, internal settlement; 1980, peace with interim formal UK control and supervised elections (1965-1980 excess mortality 0.7 million; 25,000 killed); Robert Mugabe (ZANU-PF or ZANU Patriotic Front) ruled as PM together with Joshua Nkomo's minority ZAPU; 1982-1987, repression of ZAPU stronghold Matabeleland; eventual rapprochement after widespread violence; 1988, ZAPU fusion with ZANU-PF and Nkomo return to government; 1987, 1992, 1996, 2002, Mugabe re-elected in flawed elections; 1992, Land Acquisition Act to restore land to Africans; 1990s, 21st century, UK hostility over land acquisition from Europeans, increasing repression, food shortages and poverty; 1997, one quarter of the population HIV positive; 2000, major electoral showing by the opposition Movement for Democratic Change under Morgan Changirai (Tsvangirai); followed by increased repression; 2002, forced removal of White farmers leaving 600 out of 4,500 pre-redistribution; 2005, deliberate rendering of nearly 1 million people jobless and homeless by the Mugabe government's politically-motivated "slum-clearance" program; huge HIV/AIDS problem.

2021 update: 2017, worsening economic situation with hyperinflation and mass unemployment; Mugabe placed under house arrest and shortly thereafter resigned; 2017 onwards, Emmerson Mnangagwa president. 2020 onwards, Covid-19 pandemic with "Covid-19 deaths per million of population" of 101 as compared to 0.4 for Taiwan (March 2021). Major legal and illegal logging. Revised greenhouse gas (GHG) pollution 23.3 tonnes CO_2-e per person per year. Zimbabwe has signed but not yet ratified the TPNW. In 2020 the "under-5 infant mortality as a percentage of total population" (0.1404%) was 96.8 times greater than for Japan (0.00145%), but 1.7 times lower than that in 2003 (0.2400%).

Foreign occupation: Britain (pre-1950); UK (post-1950); *post-1950 foreign military presence:* UK; *1950-2005 excess mortality/2005 population* = 4.653m/12.963m= 35.9%; *1950-2005 under-5 infant mortality/2005 population* = 1.800m/12.963m = 13.9%; HIV positive (2003) 14.1%. Per capita GDP (nominal) $1,464.

2020 statistical update for non-Arab Africa: Table 9.12 summarizes population, under-5 infant mortality (IM) and excess mortality (EM; avoidable mortality from deprivation) in non-Arab Africa in 2020 (pre-Covid-19 projection in 2019 for 2020 by the UN Population Division). Table 9.1 compares non-Arab Africa with other global regions. Presented in square brackets for each country and region is the "Relative EM Score" of EM/Pop (%) divided by that for the best-performing country, Japan (0.0020%), which accordingly has a "Relative EM Score" of 1.0.

In terms of "Relative EM Score" and "per capita GDP" the best performing countries are the Island Nations of Réunion (3.1 and $25,900) and Mauritius (8.5 and $11,169). The outcomes for the remaining countries range from Cape Verde (24.2 and $3,604) and South Africa (45.9 and $6,001) to Mali (280.3 and $887) and Chad (338.9 and $707). While the average "Relative EM Score" is 2.2 for Western Europe, and 54.5 for South Asia it is a shocking 176.6 for non-Arab Africa (Table 9.1).

The good news is that the global "under-5 infant mortality as a percentage of total population" in 2020 (0.0689%) had decreased from that in 2003 (0.1680%) by a factor of 2.4. Indeed for non-Arab African countries the decrease in "under-5 infant mortality as a percentage of total population" in this 17 year period ranged from 1.7-fold (Nigeria and Zimbabwe) to 7.9-fold (Western Sahara). The bad news is that in 2020 avoidable deaths from deprivation in non-Arab Africa (population 1,083 million) totalled a shocking 3.8 million, 51% of the total of 7.4 million avoidable deaths for the whole world (population 7,687 million).

7.3 Summary

Non-Arab Africa has in general the worst excess mortality, literacy, annual *per capita* income and HIV infection burden of all the major regions of the World. All of the countries of non-Arab Africa were still occupied by First World countries in the post-war era but eventually secured indigenous rule. The 5 century colonial period successively involved the European, African and Arab slave trade (15th-19th century, with slavery still continuing today in parts of the Sahel and coastal West Africa); resource-driven European conquest mainly in the 19th century and involving destruction of indigenous societies that had evolved to maximize nutrition and protection from disease (notably malaria); brutal exploitation (rubber, ivory, timber, minerals) variously involving terrorized populations (notably in the Belgian Congo), forced labour, indentured Asian labour (South Africa) and "economic slavery"; and extensive European colonization of African lands in Kenya and Southern Africa for European-style agriculture.

The period after colonial or minority White rule typically involved neo-colonial First World impositions that variously included continued dispossession from land, neo-colonial control, corrupt and incompetent rule by First World-installed client régimes (or successor governments dominated by the military and/or privileged élites), malignant interference by First World powers (notably the UK, the US, Portugal and France), economic exclusion, economic constraint, militarization, debt, civil war and international war. The horrendous HIV/AIDS epidemic in sub-Saharan Africa (and especially in the formerly British Empire countries of Southern Africa) reveals the dimensions of the appallingly incompetent governance in these countries. The spread of HIV was utterly preventable and the catastrophic, continuing further spread is *still* preventable with sensible governance. Continuing government incompetence, poverty, First World disregard and the general absence in these countries of life-saving pharmaceuticals for treatment of primary HIV infection and of consequent medical conditions all mean that this appalling avoidable mortality will continue.

CHAPTER 8: SYNTHESIS, CONCLUSIONS & SUGGESTIONS

"The ultimate privilege of the élite is not just their deluxe lifestyles, but deluxe lifestyles with a clear conscience."

Arundhati Roy in *The Chequebook and the Cruise Missile.*[1]

"You already know enough. So do I. It is not knowledge we lack. What is missing is the courage to understand what we know and to draw conclusions."

Sven Lindqvist in *Exterminate All the Brutes.* [2]

"You will do well to try to innoculate (sic) the Indians by means of blankets as well as to try every other method that can serve to extirpate this exorable race."

Sir Jeffrey Amherst, Commander-in-Chief, British forces in North America, 1765.[3]

"We don't do body counts."

General Tommy Franks, Iraq, 2003.[4]

"The corporate revolution will collapse if we refuse to buy what they are selling – their ideas, their version of history, their wars, their weapons, their notion of inevitability."

Arundhati Roy in *The Ordinary Person's Guide to Empire.*[5]

8.1 Finding causes and solutions

This book has been largely concerned with the horrendous post-1950 avoidable mortality in the world. This analysis has been possible because the relevant data have been quantitated by the United Nations[6], the administrative responsibility is explicit (especially in the case of foreign-occupied countries)[7] and the actual causes can be addressed. As stated in Chapter 1, the post-1950 era is also useful for such an analysis of mortality because in this era potentially *all* of humanity had access to adequate nutrition, clean water, soap, other antiseptics, sanitation, hygiene, antibiotics, pharmaceuticals, mosquito netting and other prophylactics, preventative medicine, major vaccinations, primary health care, literacy, public health education and preventive medicine.

It must be noted that *all* of these benefits protect Western bushwalkers (campers, treckers) when they leave "civilization" and go camping to recapture the connection to wilderness of our hunter-gatherer ancestors - and have done so for over half a century. Yet these life-preserving requisites are still not made available to billions of Third World people living under First World global hegemony, nor (in gross contravention of the Geneva Conventions) to the hundreds of million people living under threat of US Alliance violence, mainly in the Muslim World. [8]

Chapters 4-7 (including 2021 updates) have summarized pre-1950 and subsequent mass mortality events that were also potentially avoidable such as explicit genocide, dispossession, and the spread of epidemic diseases. Violent mass killing and deadly resource dispossession were clearly avoidable impositions. Further, the benefits of isolation and quarantining were known 3,000 years before bacteria and viruses and their animal vectors were discovered. Thus the Bible recommended isolation of the diseased [9]; plague victims were catapulted into besieged cities to spread infection [10]; people such as the young men and women of Giovanni Boccaccio's *Decameron* fled to the Italian countryside to escape urban plague epidemics [11]; and smallpox-contaminated sheets were used for genocidal infection of American Indians by European invaders. Religious mass gatherings during the Black Death contributed to infection [12]; the post-contact sickening of American Indians was known from the time of Columbus and certainly after the catastrophic epidemics after European invasion [13]; and mass mortality from introduced disease of the indigenous peoples of Australasia and the Pacific was thoroughly predictable and rapidly realized [14].

Sadly, man-made mass mortality continues apace in the 21st century despite the general lip-service to humanity and condemnation of *particular* past horrors such as the Jewish Holocaust. Three of the World's oldest democracies, namely the UK, the US and Australia (together with their generally prosperous allies) have been involved in the imposition on Iraq since 1990 of sanctions, war, invasion and occupation – the post-1990 avoidable mortality has totalled 2.9 million and the under-5 infant mortality 2.0 million. These deaths have been due to an apocalyptic quartet of violence, deprivation, disease and *lying*. Thus the Anglo-American-dominated mainstream media of the World indulges in deadly lying by omission and are still loath to report these UN-derived estimates of the *continuing* carnage imposed on Iraq by the US Alliance.

To dramatize the nature of this holocaust-ignoring that is tantamount to holocaust-denial, one can simply turn to the UNICEF web page. UNICEF data indicate that the annual under-5 infant deaths in the Occupied Iraqi and Afghan Territories total 0.5 million (2007 data) i.e. 1,300 daily or ONE PER MINUTE – and this is about 90% avoidable (2007 data) and largely due to gross Occupier violation of the Geneva Convention which unequivocally demands that Occupiers keep their Conquered Subjects ALIVE. The carnage and the culpability are kept from Western citizens by the lying by omission of politicians and mainstream media - yet the awful truth is only a few mouse clicks away.

The continuing "overseas" barbarity on the part of four of the world's oldest liberal democracies (the UK, the US, Canada and Australia) is paradoxical but can be rationalized in terms of the "benign racism" or "political correct racism" (PC racism) on the part of these Anglo-Celtic societies. Politically correct racism involves denying racism while simultaneously indulging in intrinsically racist abuses of humanity and ignoring the human consequences. In short, the UK, the US, Canada and Australia are internally decent, politically correct and deny racism but are involved in the violent, intrinsically *racist* violent occupation of foreign lands, and simply *ignore* the horrendous human consequences of their imperialist violence. War is the penultimate expression of racism, and genocide is the ultimate expression of racism, noting that Article 2 of the UN Genocide Convention defines genocide as "acts committed with intent to destroy, in whole or in part, a national, ethnic, racial or religious group".

A summary of the state of essentially all the countries of the World in relation to mortality, excess mortality, under-5 infant mortality and HIV/AIDS in 2003 is provided as an Appendix at the end of this Chapter (Tables 8.1-8.12). Tables 9.1-9.12 document the under-5 infant mortality and avoidable mortality from deprivation in 2020 (pre-Covid-19 projection) for all countries in the world.

This penultimate Chapter draws together major themes bearing on man-made global avoidable mass mortality, and concludes with sensible suggestions about how this continuing crime against humanity can be stopped, the horrendous consequences addressed and the World made safe for *everyone*.

8.2 Risk management

The industrial revolution and the development of novel high technologies has necessitated industrial safety approaches that are nevertheless applicable in principle to risk management in general. "World's Best Practice" risk management procedures (that are used in high risk areas such as the nuclear industry, defence and aviation) involve a successive three-fold approach of (a) untrammelled reportage; (b) honest, scientific analysis of the data (science involving the critical testing of potentially falsifiable hypotheses); and (c) systemic change to further minimize risk.[15]

These approaches have meant that the high risk nuclear industry, defence and aviation areas have good safety records. Society insists on such rational approaches to safety in these industries because of the potentially catastrophic consequences if nuclear plants malfunction, warships sink or planes crash. These areas are certainly not event-free (as we all know from periodically reported nuclear, military and aviation accidents) but rational risk management procedures mean that those involved in these areas learn from mistakes and implement systemic changes to minimize the likelihood of recurrence and to minimize harm when accidents inevitably happen.

Unfortunately, in most areas of human activity, risk management is affected by fear, self-interest and dishonesty. Thus (a) reportage is inhibited by censorship and self-censorship through fear of exposure, retribution or accusations of disloyalty; (b) analysis of the reportage that does occur is influenced by self-serving political considerations relating to economics, reputation, mutual loyalty and desire for unruffled calm (i.e. it involves anti-scientific "spin" involving the selective use of asserted facts to support a partisan position); and (c) when a matter has actually been reported and assessed, the typical responses involve blaming and shaming suitable culprits, "shooting the messenger" and avoidance of systemic change – thus leaving the system at even greater risk because of continuing inherent risks and fear of reportage when things inevitably go wrong.

This model can be applied to the subject of this dissertation, namely global avoidable mass mortality. We can readily see that World's Worst Practice describes the current global responses to avoidable mass mortality: (a) mass mortality is simply not reported properly by the mainstream media when it reflects poorly on their society (e.g. the continuing and extraordinary *non-reportage* of the British-complicit WW2 Bengal Famine (WW2 Bengali Holocaust, WW2 Indian Holocaust; 6-7 million victims), the post-1950 global avoidable mortality holocaust (1.5 billion victims) or the post-invasion excess mortality in UK- and US-occupied Iraq and Afghanistan (involving 3.4 million post-invasion avoidable deaths as of 2007); (b) analysis of any mass mortality events that get through the "media gate" in the "wall of silence" involves comprehensive white-washing of those in charge and hence responsible for the carnage; and (c) there is no systemic change and responses are largely confined to exposure and punitive action against some individuals ranging from suitable tyrants (e.g. Idi Amin and Milosevic) to minor war criminals (e.g. some Coalition murderers or torturers of prisoners in the Iraq War).

A rational, informed approach to the continuing Global Avoidable Mortality Holocaust would involve (a) honest, quantitative reportage as outlined in this book; (b) honest, scientific assessment of the causes; and (c) systemic changes to minimize the risk of recurrence. The remainder of this book attempts to apply such a rational, risk-minimization approach to global avoidable mass mortality. Chapter 9 updates this ongoing disaster for 2020 and critically deals with the existential threats from climate change and nuclear weapons.

8.3 Violent versus non-violent death

Whether an individual Iraqi child dies violently from a bomb or bullet or perishes from deprivation or potentially treatable and avoidable disease, the end result is the same – an avoidable death and a continuing tragedy for parents, family and friends.

Nevertheless, media reportage and consequent general public perception place a disproportionate weight on violent death. This selective reportage (racist and dishonest at worst, incompetent at best) has the convenient effect of hiding immense crimes involving major First World complicity such as the post-1950 avoidable mortality in the Muslim World (a Muslim Holocaust amounting to 0.6 billion people) or the post-1990 avoidable mortality of 2.9 million people in war- and sanctions-ravaged Iraq.

Iraq Body Count[16] keeps a tally of *violent* deaths in post-invasion Iraq – and in mid-2007 this totalled about 70,000 (although top US medical epidemiologists from the Bloomberg School of Public Health, Johns Hopkins University, estimated 0.6 million post-invasion violent deaths in Occupied Iraq at that time; by 2011 it had grown to 1.5 million). However from the latest UN data one can estimate that the post-1990 excess mortality in Iraq totalled about 2.9 million by 2011. By way of corroboration, the post-1990 under-5 infant mortality in Iraq has totalled 2.0 million (of which about 90% has been avoidable). From this we can estimate that most of the avoidable deaths in post-invasion Iraq have been *non-violent* – but, by definition, have been criminally *avoidable* due to deprivation of life-sustaining requisites such as proper nutrition, clean water, sanitation and primary health care. The Fourth Geneva Convention for the protection of civilians in time of war demands that the occupying country does everything within its power to preserve the health and life of the subject people.

The convenient exclusion of *non-violent* deaths from public perception has been the basis for spurious, right-wing, historical revision concerning the genocide of Indigenous Australians (referred to as Aborigines or Aboriginals in Australia). Thus it has been estimated that in 1788 there were 750,000 Australian Aborigines but by 1890 the Aboriginal population was only about 100,000. There is a wealth of historical documentation of massacres and other killings of Australian Aboriginals but even the scholarly proponents of the "violent genocide" version of Australian history (notably Aboriginal Professor Henry Reynolds) estimated violent deaths at only about 10,000 (however re-assessment taking the bloody Frontier Wars in Queensland into account could estimate about 0.1 million violent deaths). Most Australian Aboriginal people have died avoidably through dispossession, deprivation and disease i.e. passive genocide. Thus in contemporary Australia the passive genocide of Indigenous Australians is continuing – the "annual death rate" is 2.2% for Indigenous Australians, 2.4% (Indigenous Australians in the Northern Territory), 0.4% (what it should be for a demographically equivalent community), 0.7% (White Australians) and 2.5% (for sheep in paddocks on Australian sheep farms (2007). [17]

This non-violent avoidable mortality is dramatically exposed by the sad story of the genocide of the Tasmanian Aborigines. At the time of settlement in 1803 there were about 6,000 Tasmanian Aborigines but through killing, dispossession, deprivation and disease this shrank to zero "full blood" Aborigines with the death of the woman Truganini in 1876. Very detailed colonial records enable a good picture of what actually happened. Sensible non-revisionists have estimated that there were hundreds rather than thousands of violent Aboriginal deaths. Clearly deprivation and disease were largely responsible for the destruction of Tasmanian Aborigines. Thus after the cessation of the so-called Black Wars, there was an attempt to gather in and care for the remnant population. In 1830 there were several hundred "full blood" Tasmanian Aborigines but by 1876, none. Nevertheless, the revisionists are essentially arguing (quite incorrectly) that non-violent Aboriginal deaths consequent to European invasion simply do not "count" in a moral culpability sense. [18]

Notwithstanding detailed historical records and eye witness accounts, the genocide of the Aborigines remains controversial in present-day Australia, an intrinsically profoundly racist and extreme right wing country that prefers to look the other way, forget about the past and "dress things up" in an utterly dishonest guise of both genuine and disingenuous political correctness. My 2021 estimate of the human cost of the 2 century Aboriginal Genocide is about 2 million deaths from deprivation, disease and violence, with about 0.1 million violent deaths. The present extreme right wing Australian Coalition government (involved in passive genocide in Occupied Iraq and Afghanistan) refuses to say "sorry" for past wrongs to subject peoples – unlike the governments of Canada (over the Inuit), New Zealand (over the Maoris and the Samoans) and the UK (over the Irish Famine) – and totally ignores its current complicity in horrendous crimes.

The passive killing of Australian Aborigines continues. Despite 2 centuries of genocide and forcible removal of some 50,000 Aboriginal children from their mothers in the 20th century (the "Stolen Generations"; a process that is continuing at a record rate today for "social welfare" reasons), the current population of Aboriginal Australians (mostly part-European) is about 900,000. Even Tasmania has a population of about 5,000 part-European descendants of the Tasmanian Aborigines and of Mainland Aboriginal women captured by whalers and sealers. Many Australian Aborigines live in Third World conditions and male and female Aboriginal life expectancies are about 10 years lower than those of White Australians. As estimated in 2007, the difference in annual mortality rate between Australia as a whole (0.7%) and Australian Aborigines (2.2%) is about 15 deaths per 1,000 per year which translated (with an Indigenous population of 0.5 million) as about 7,500 per year i.e. the equivalent in terms of mortality of 2 World Trade Centres *every year* occurring in a population of 0.5 million rather than 300 million. This differential mortality translates into a life expectancy gap between Indigenous and non-Indigenous Australians of about 10 years.[19]

A further "denial" argument about horrendous non-European mass mortality is that such circumstances are somehow "normal" for such people. This kind of assertion is intrinsically racist and is demonstrated to be utterly false by the excellent mortality outcomes of "developing countries" such as Cuba, Costa Rica, the Gulf States, Mauritius, Malaysia, and Paraguay. A similarly unacceptably inhumane, racist and false argument is that European-style longevity in the non-European world would result in a catastrophic population explosion. However, this hypothesis ignores the reality in Europe and elsewhere of zero population growth (or indeed negative growth) associated with decent living conditions, high literacy and increased life expectancy.

Perhaps the most insidious argument used in the European "white-washing" of non-European mass mortality is that this is somehow "their own fault" and that European generosity through aid and helpful commercial dealings may address the problem. The previous 4 Chapters have exhaustively demonstrated the correlation between avoidable mortality and European violence and occupation. The following analysis reiterates the European *complicity* in the avoidable mortality in non-European countries.

8.4 The ruler is responsible for the ruled

A fundamental societal principle is that the rulers are responsible for the ruled. This rule is set out clearly through international agreement over the occupation of countries by foreign powers. The Fourth Geneva Conventions on the treatment of subject civilians (implemented in 1950) are quite explicit about the obligations of conquering occupiers to do everything in their power to preserve human life - thus Articles 55 and 56 state that *"to the fullest extent of the means available to it the Occupying Power has the duty of ensuring"* provision of food, medicine, public health, hygiene, prophylaxis and medical services.[20]

Of course "occupation" is not simply confined to explicit military occupation as in the examples of Nazi-occupied Europe, Soviet-occupied Eastern Europe or colonial era European-occupied Africa, Asia and South America. "Occupation" has variously continued in post-colonial countries due to a variety of "neo-colonial" impositions.

Major neo-colonial impositions have included: the installation of compatible post-colonial governments; retention of military bases by the colonial power; retention of colonial economic arrangements (e.g. European mines, farms and plantations); retention of colonial social disparity arrangements (e.g. impoverished masses dominated by European corporations and wealthy indigenous élites); economic constraint (lack of capital, expertise and market access); malignant interference and régime change; divide-and-rule post-colonial legacies of international conflict situations (e.g. US-backed Pakistan versus Russia-backed India); militarization to prop up pro-European regimes; active and pro-active military alliances (e.g. the Warsaw Pact, NATO, CENTO, SEATO, ANZUS and the US-led Coalition); post-colonial links to the colonial country (e.g. the British Commonwealth, the French Union, the OAS and the CIS); debt through militarization and client régime profligacy; explicit interference in civil wars (with many examples from Asia, Africa, Europe and South America); economic, political and military hegemony (as with the US in Latin America and the Caribbean); and re-invasion if necessary by the colonial powers or their European successors and agents (e.g. bloody French, British, Russian, US and Israeli military interventions in the post-war era).

Chapters 1-7 have already summarized a large number of examples of colonial and neo-colonial occupation – simple inspection reveals that post-1950 avoidable mortality clearly relates to First World colonial and post-colonial impositions, most notably militarization and violence. Rather than re-summarizing this sad litany, it is useful to consider some "boundary conditions" to see the impact of "low profile" occupations as compared to egregiously violent and explicit military occupations.

At the "soft" or benign end of the spectrum are the examples of Australia, the US and South Africa – countries with violent, racist histories but which are now ostensibly democratic and free with anti-racist legislation and the rule of law. The British invaded Australia in 1788 and within 1 century the indigenous population had dropped from about 0.75 million to 0.1 million through violence, dispossession, subjugation and introduced disease. However in 2021 about 0.9 million Australian Aborigines live in very poor conditions, many live in Third World conditions, female and male Aboriginal life expectancies are about 10 years lower than those of White Australia and the Aboriginal excess mortality is about 4,000 per year (numerically equivalent to over 1 World Trade Centre disaster per year).[21]

Slavery was ostensibly abolished in the US after the Civil War but *de facto* slavery continued in the South and reasonable *de facto* civil rights for Afro-Americans were only achieved in the 1970s. There is nevertheless a huge gulf between the Afro-American under-class and white America and for all that the US is the richest country in the world, over 10% of the American population (and 27% of the African American population) live below the poverty line, with many living in Third World conditions.[22] The recent Hurricane Katrina disaster in Louisiana has illustrated these disparities and attitudes – while the survival period without drinking water at 30^0C is only 3 days, large-scale systematic searches for the mostly Afro-American survivors only commenced a week after the catastrophic flooding of New Orleans.[23]

The appallingly violent and racist history of South Africa turned a corner in 1993 with the fall of the Apartheid régime and the beginning of majority rule. However the Anglo-American-dominated corporations and gross economic inequities of the Apartheid era remained, and criminally incompetent and ignorant governments permitted the explosion of HIV/AIDS to the point that about 12% of the population was infected, with such infection overwhelmingly affecting the African population (2007).[24] This avoidable mortality disaster is summarized by the following South Africa excess mortality statistics (in millions, m) for the 11 pentades (5 year periods) since 1950 (note the dramatic increase after 1995 and "freedom"; excess mortality rose sharply in the 1995-2005 decade):

1950-1955 (1.18m), 1955-1960 (1.16m), 1960-1965 (1.18m), 1965-1970 (1.15m), 1970-1975 (1.10m), 1975-1980 (1.04m), 1980-1985 (0.96m), 1985-1990 (0.80m), 1990-1995 (0.80m), 1995-2000 (1.27m), 2000-2005 (2.88m).

At the other end of the "occupation" spectrum we can usefully consider Iraq. This sophisticated and diverse country was the cradle of civilization and in the pre-Christian era was a major source of sophisticated agriculture, astronomy, writing, mathematics, architecture, medicine, commerce, ethics, law and philosophy. Between the 8th and 13th century Muslim Baghdad was a major commercial, cultural and scientific centre of the World. However Iraq was devastated by Mongol invasion in the 13th century and occupied as part of the Ottoman Turkish Empire since the 16th century. The British invaded in 1914 and finally secured Mesopotamia in 1918, the conquering general promising freedom for the Iraqis. Yet since then oil-rich Iraq has effectively remained under Western occupation, pro-Western puppetry or violent Western hegemony except for the period from 1958 (overthrow of the British-installed royal rule) until 1990 (commencement of Western-invigilated Sanctions with ultimate explicit military invasion and occupation in 2003) (Chapter 6).

The impact of egregious Western violence and hegemony for most of the last century has had a devastating impact on Iraqis as summarized by the following Iraqi excess mortality statistics (in millions, m) for the 11 pentades (5 year periods) since 1950 (note the dramatic increase after 1990 and the commencement of sanctions; excess mortality rose sharply in the 1990-2000 decade):

1950-1955 (0.50m), 1955-1960 (0.54m), 1960-1965 (0.55m), 1965-1970 (0.56m), 1970-1975 (0.54m), 1975-1980 (0.28m), 1980-1985 (0.29m), 1985-1990 (0.23m), 1990-1995 (0.57m), 1995-2000 (0.63m), 2000-2005 (0.60m).

It can be seen that in the post-1950 era the annual excess mortality remained roughly the same for the first 20 years despite a doubling of the population. The period of rule by the brutal Iraqi dictator Saddam Hussein rapidly saw a halving of annual excess mortality. However the return of Western forces with sanctions and war saw an immediate greater than doubling of excess mortality. These figures are at odds with UK-US media propaganda and represent an immense crime against humanity by these Western democracies (as well as a crime in gross violation of the Geneva Conventions).

These appalling figures are corroborated by independent estimations of under-5 infant mortality in Iraq which more than doubled after Western intervention in 1990:

1950-1955 (0.28m), 1955-1960 (0.27m), 1960-1965 (0.29m), 1965-1970 (0.29m), 1970-1975 (0.28m), 1975-1980 (0.23m), 1980-1985 (0.21m), 1985-1990 (0.19m), 1990-1995 (0.30m), 1995-2000 (0.53m), 2000-2005 (0.57m).

While the under-5 infant mortality rates in oil-rich Iraq and impoverished, partially-occupied Syria and were similar in 1990, after a dozen years of Western sanctions and war by 2003 the "annual under-5 infant death rate" was 2.74% in Occupied Iraq as compared to 0.54% in Syria.

8.5 Passive genocide in Occupied Iraq and Afghanistan

A distinction must be made between *complicity* (deriving from hegemony and interference) and *responsibility* (deriving from explicit occupation). As discussed above, the ruler is responsible for the ruled, a position codified explicitly by the Geneva Conventions for the protection of conquered civilians. The continuing carnage in Occupied Iraq and Afghanistan provides a macabre case study of the present-day consequences of economics-driven Western imperialism, violation of the Geneva Conventions, passive genocide, modern military technologies and strategies that maximize "enemy civilian"/"invading military" death ratios. The continuing tragedy in the US-devastated Occupied Iraqi and Afghan Territories illustrates the horrendous human consequences of the apocalyptic quartet of violence, deprivation, disease and *lying*.

Using the very latest UN and medical literature data it is possible to get even more up-to-date estimates of the post-1950 and post-invasion excess mortality and under-5 infant mortality in Occupied Iraq and Occupied Afghanistan as assessed as follows in the 2007 edition of "*Body Count: Global Avoidable Mortality Since 1950*".

The estimated Iraq excess mortality (in millions, m) is 5.386m (mid-1950-mid-2005), 5.480m (mid-1950-end-2005), 2.179m (mid-1990-end-2005), 1.661m (mid-1990-March 2003) and 0.518m (March 2003-end-2005), noting that sanctions began in mid-1990 and the final US-led invasion began in March 2003.

The estimated Iraq under-5 infant mortality is 3.630m (mid-1950-mid-2005), 3.690m (mid-1950-end-2005), 1.532m (mid-1990-end-2005), 1.204m (mid-1990-March 2003) and 0.328m (March 2003-end-2005).

The estimated Afghanistan excess mortality is 15.922m (mid-1950-mid-2005), 16.131m (mid-1950-end-2005), 8.101m (December 1979-end-2005) and 1.823m (October 2001-end-2005), noting that the Soviet invasion began in December 1970 and the US invasion commenced in October 2001.

The estimated Afghanistan under-5 infant mortality is 12.139m (mid-1950-mid-2005), 12.306m (mid-1950-end-2005), 6.443m (December 1979-end-2005) and 1.453m (October 2001-end-2005).

From these estimates we can see that the post-1950 Western-complicit excess mortality in Iraq and Afghanistan presently (beginning of 2006) total 5.5 million and 16.1 million, respectively, this being corroborated by under-5 infant mortalities totalling 3.7

and 12.3 million, respectively. The Iraqi and Afghan post-1950 avoidable mortality figures are commensurate, respectively, with the WW2 deaths associated with the Jewish Holocaust and the invasion of the Soviet Union.

The estimated excess mortality and under-5 infant mortality for Iraq by the end of 2005 have been 2.2 million and 1.5 million, respectively (since Western return with sanctions in 1990) and 0.5 million and 0.3 million, respectively (since the 2003 invasion). The estimated excess mortality and under-5 infant mortality for Afghanistan by the end of 2005 are 8.1 million and 6.4 million, respectively (since Soviet invasion and US-backed war in 1979) and 1.8 million and 1.5 million, respectively (since the 2001 invasion). These "killing fields" are entrenched as a war zone in the endless "War on Terror" espoused by UK-US "democratic imperialism" (or, rather, democratic tyranny or democratic Nazism).

The continuing evil of UK-US "democratic imperialism" is underscored by successive UNICEF reports. Thus the latest UNICEF report (2006) estimates that in 2004 the under-5 infant mortality in Occupied Iraq, Occupied Afghanistan and the occupying country Australia have been 122,000, 359,000 and 1,000, respectively (noting that in 2004 these countries had populations of 28, 29 and 20 million, respectively). From UN estimates of the proportion of under-5 year olds it can be calculated that about 90% of this horrendous infant mortality has been *avoidable*. The under-5 infant mortality in occupied Iraq and Afghanistan totals about 0.5 million annually, 1,300 daily and one (1) per minute.

From WHO and medical literature data it can be estimated that in 2004 the annual *per capita* medical expenditure in Iraq, Afghanistan, Australia and metropolitan USA was $37, $8, $3,100 and $7,000, respectively. The ruler is responsible for the ruled and the Fourth Geneva Conventions are explicit in demanding that the Occupier provide medical and other life-preserving requisites for the conquered population *"to the fullest extent of the means available to it"*. The horrendous excess mortality and under-5 infant mortality in US-occupied Iraq and Afghanistan are occurring in a continuing context of annual *per capita* medical expenditure of less than 1% of that in metropolitan USA. This avoidable mortality must be described as passive genocide in gross contravention of the Geneva Conventions.

An analogy of this horrendous Coalition "passive genocide" in Iraq can be found in the treatment of severely disabled new-born infants. Peter Singer, arguably the most influential living ethics philosopher, has controversially argued for the humane "active euthanasia" of extremely severely disabled infants. At present many experienced hospital doctors will administer pain relief but not sustenance to such infants by way of "passive euthanasia". According to Singer [25]:

"Doctors who deliberately leave a baby to die when they have the awareness, the ability, and the opportunity to save the baby's life, are just as morally responsible for the death as they would be if they had brought it about by a deliberate, positive action."

However, before analysing continuing Western "passive genocide" in greater detail it is useful to review explicit genocide over the last few thousand years.

8.6 Genocide

Through their very brevity, the "short histories" of Chapters 4 to 7 unintentionally gloss over the utter barbarity of human warfare. Nevertheless, humans have made some attempts to delineate acceptable victims of war. Thus there is a general bottom-line feeling that women, children, the elderly and indeed all non-combatants should be spared violence. Indeed the Fourth Geneva Conventions (implemented in 1950)[26] demand that war be confined to military combatants, that civilians not be targeted and that the conqueror is obliged to do everything within his means to preserve the lives of the conquered. Article 55 states: *"To the fullest extent of the means available to it, the Occupying Power has the duty of ensuring the food and medical supplies of the population ... "* and Article 56 states: *"To the fullest extent of the means available to it, the Occupying Power has the duty of ensuring and maintaining, with the cooperation of national and local authorities, the medical and hospital establishments and services, public health and hygiene in the occupied territory ... "*

However, even as these Geneva Conventions were being signed, the major European powers were entering into a Cold War premised on the threat of Mutually Assured Destruction of civilian populations and indeed of *all* human beings on the planet.

The Old Testament of the Holy Bible (that is used by many to justify horrendous crimes against international law and humanity in the Middle East) explicitly sets out and justifies the "divinely sanctioned" mass murder of the people of Jerusalem by Joshua and his followers (a crime to be repeated by the Crusaders) and the genocide of Canaanites by the kinsmen of Dinah - in effect describing the first Nazi-style war criminals of recorded history. Indeed King Saul was "divinely punished" because he did *not* commit total genocide as instructed. Nevertheless there are also examples of mercy – thus my namesake Gideon (the first person "in the literature" to have performed a controlled scientific experiment) gave the conquered Moabite women (and their camels) to his 300 victorious soldiers – while modestly keeping the Tyrrhian purple robes and gold trinkets for himself. A sit-down reading of the Bible nevertheless yields a wonderful experience as one leaves the merciless, genocidal darkness of the Old Testament and enters into the sunshine of love, kindness and humanity of the New. [27]

There is a huge literature on the appalling genocide of the WW2 Jewish Holocaust[28] and a solid body of scholarly analysis of other genocide in its various manifestations[29]. The most powerful accounts are those highly personal accounts by gifted diarists, novelists and film makers that convey humanity in the face of such evil.[30] One of the first genocides in more generally authenticated history was that of the Sparta-derived people of Melos by the Athenians in 416BCE. All the men were killed, the women and children sold into slavery and the island of Melos re-populated with Athenians. This acted as a salutary warning to other Aegean islands about the consequences of non-compliance with the will of Athens. The total destruction of the North African Phoenician city of Carthage by Rome in 146BCE was followed by enslavement of the survivors; an estimated 150,000 died out of 200,000, the site was forbidden to be re-settled and a 6 century civilization was thus totally destroyed (see Tunisia, Chapter 6).

It is likely that the 13th century Mongol Empire led by Genghis Khan deliberately struck terror into its opponents by a calculated policy of mass extermination practised in a bloody swathe from China, through Central Asia, the Middle East, Russia and Eastern Europe to the very gates of Vienna – 40-60 million people were killed. Mongolian return to Karakorum after the death of the great Khan Ogadei (1242) saved Vienna and Europe; successive storms in 1274 and 1292 saved Japan from a Mongolian naval invasion. However, on a much smaller scale, in the 13th century the Catholic French embarked on Crusades against the Cathar Albigensian heretics of Provence with the merciless massacres of the citizens of Béziers, general subjugation and introduction of the horrors of the Inquisition. Indeed the anti-Muslim Crusaders also indulged in mass murder, notably the sackings of Jerusalem (1099) and Constantinople (1204).

The 14th century Black Death killed 25 million in Europe and it took years for populations to recover in Western Europe. However ignorance and superstition compounded the problem (mass religious gatherings merely assisting the spread of the disease-carrying flea vectors) and fear led to scapegoats, notably the Jews in Western and Central Europe. The entrenchment of Church-sanctioned anti-Jewish anti-Semitism in Europe inevitably led to the expulsion of the Jews and Moors from Spain (1492), subsequent horrors of the Inquisition applied to alleged heretics and converted Christians who were allegedly secretly Muslim or Jewish, violent Prussian anti-Semitism (18th century), pogroms in Eastern Europe (notably in Galicia) (19th century), massive Jewish emigration from Russia and Eastern Europe (19th and 20th centuries), and ultimately the Jewish Holocaust of WW2 (5-6 million victims).

The Reformation and Counter reformation brought forth an immense catalogue of atrocities in the 16th-17th centuries involving Catholic-Protestant confrontations, Inquisition torture and burnings, bloody military conquests (notably the wars of the Spanish in the Netherlands, the Thirty Years War and horrendous atrocities in Ireland under Elizabeth I and Cromwell), and mass migrations from genocidal persecutions such as that of the Protestant Huguenots from France (after the 1572 Saint Batholomew's Day Massacre) and of Protestant Bohemians.

Western European also experienced the violent persecution of witches. While there was a major pre-Reformation distinction between white (healing) witches and black (malevolent) witches who were subjected to horrible medieval torture and execution, the deadly intolerance of the Reformation-Counter-reformation era spilled over into horrendous persecution of alleged witches in the 15th-18th centuries. About 100,000 people were tortured and killed (about 25% of the victims being male associates). The correlation between witchcraft hysteria and areas of cereal infection by the ergot fungus, suggests that many of the victims were simply tortured and murdered because of their mental derangement (interpreted as "Devil-possession") through ingestion of contaminated bread containing ergot-derived indole dopamine receptor agonists related to lysergic acid. However the basis of witchcraft hysteria is complex, noting that such persecution has occurred around the world.[31]

The European invasion of the New World caused an immense, 100 million deaths catastrophe due to the introduction of novel European diseases against which the Amerindians had little resistance. The population decline is variously estimated to have between 50-95%. The appalling morbidity and mortality associated with disease and the European possession of guns and horses enabled small numbers of invaders to conquer even numerous Amerindian civilizations such as those of the Mississippi, the Amazon, Mexico and Peru. In some instances (e.g. in New England) there was deliberate infection of Indians with smallpox. The devastation associated with invasion, disease and dispossession was compounded by brutal slavery and catastrophic depopulation to the extent that the European conquerors had to turn to Africa as a source of slaves.

The African slave trade began with the Portuguese in coastal Mauritania in the 15th century and then accelerated with the invasion of the New World, the peak years being 1750-1850. A total of about 15 million people were enslaved in Africa for "export" - with only about 9 million surviving the horrendous trans-Atlantic transit conditions to be sold in the Americas. Possibly another 15 million died in the African slave collection process. Ultimately, slavery became uneconomic because indigenous workers (whether workers in post-abolition Britain or Afro-Americans in the post-Civil War Deep South) could be forced to work without chains but in slavery conditions through simple economic necessity. Slavery was successively abolished in British colonies (1833), the South American republics, the USA (1865), and in Spanish Cuba and Brazil (1888). However the late 19th and 20th centuries saw the British and Australian introduction of indentured labour (e.g. 5 year slaves) from India and China into the West Indies, South Africa and the Pacific Islands. The British and Australians practised explicit slavery of Pacific Islander "kanakas" ("blackbirding") in the 19th century.[32] Slavery in various forms (explicit slavery, forced labour and indentured labour) continued in the late 19th century and the 20th century in Africa. Indeed slavery is still endemic in Niger and child slavery for cocoa production is a continuing West African scandal.

In a smaller scale version of the New World catastrophe, the British invasion of Australia (the 2 million deaths Aboriginal Genocide), Tasmania and New Zealand brought violence, dispossession and epidemic disease that devastated indigenous populations (Chapter 6). The "full-blood" Aboriginal population of Tasmania was about 6,000 at settlement (1803) but zero by 1876.[33] After discovery by European whalers of the peaceful democratic New Zealand Moriori islanders, a ship load of Mainland Maoris captured the island in 1835 and literally *ate* the thousands of inhabitants.[34] Mainly British and French missionaries, whalers, sealers, traders, sailors, soldiers and settlers brought epidemic disease to the Pacific in the 19th century resulting in catastrophic population decline. Thus introduction of measles from Australia wiped out 40,000 out of 150,000 Fijians in 1875 alone.[35] Further, in the 19th century disease was spread by Australian "blackbirders" enslaving Melanesian Kanaks for Australian sugar cane plantations.[36]

European colonial expansion into Asia, Africa and the Americas in the 19th and 20th century was associated with horrendous brutality. In the Americas the dispossession and extermination of indigenous peoples continued apace. From a pre-invasion population of about 5 million, the indigenous North American population shrank to 0.5 million by about 1800 and thence to about 250,000 by 1891. Disease, violence and dispossession were involved in the genocide of the American Indians. The expulsion of the Cherokee, Creek, Chickasee, Seminole, Choctaw and Shawnee Indians from East of the Mississippi in the first half of the 19th century was explicit, legislated US dispossession and "ethnic cleansing" of indigenous people. The West Coast Amerindians, the last to encounter Europeans, were decimated by disease in the 19th century.[37] In Argentina General Rosas was appointed to exterminate the indigenous Indians from the Pampas in the 1830s, a process of remorseless and comprehensive genocide that continued into the late 19th century. Similar violent genocide of millions of Indians took place in Paraguay and Uruguay.[38]

In Southern Africa the Dutch Boers and British collided with southward moving Zulus. The Zulus under Shaka (1818-1828) expanded through a process of ruthless conquest that involved virtually complete extermination of the women, infants and elderly of the conquered (some girls being spared and boys and young men being retained as future soldiers). A zone of death was created around the Zulu lands as people fled this remorseless killing machine. Some 40,000 perished in this genocidal period.[39] Northward moving Europeans subsequently brutally conquered and dispossessed Africans in a succession of Kaffir Wars and Zulu Wars and thence conquered what is now Zambia and Zimbabwe. The Hottentots of the Cape were decimated by smallpox. The Portuguese brutally suppressed resistance in Mozambique and Angola. The Germans seized territories corresponding to Tanzania, Burundi, Rwanda and Namibia. The conquest of the Boer territories by the British involved the incarceration of Boer women and children in the first concentration camps with some 25,000 perishing. The German invasion of South-West Africa displaced the Hereros from their lands. As in other such displacements, no land meant death and the Hereros revolted. The subsequent German genocide of the Hereros of South-West Africa was accomplished by outright killing and then driving the survivors into the desert to die. The Herero population was reduced from 80,000 in 1904 to 15,000 in 1911, this crime representing the first major genocide of the 20th century.[40]

The Belgian conquest and exploitation of the Congo in the late 19th century was accomplished with horrendous brutality. Africans were encouraged to supply ivory and rubber by extreme violence including atrocities such as the chopping off of hands. It is estimated that about 10 million Congolese died in this horrendous period. These atrocities were revealed to the world by Edward Morel and by Sir Robert Casement (who was subsequently hanged as an Irish patriot by the British in 1916). A glimpse of this kind of horror was provided by *Heart of Darkness* by Joseph Conrad, albeit with the author's evident sympathy for the perpetrators.[41]

In 19th and 20th centuries in the Sahel, West Africa, Central Africa, East Africa and Southern Africa the British, Belgians, Dutch, Italians, Germans, French, Portuguese and Spanish consolidated their territorial possession accompanied by brutal exploitation of the indigenous Africans. A horrendous episode was the 1898 Central African Expedition led by French psychopaths Paul Voulet and Charles Chanoine that left a trail of horrible massacres and burnt towns and villages through the Sahel from Burkina Faso through Niger to Chad. When an alerted French Assembly was apprised they sent out Lieutenant-Colonel Klobb from Timbuctoo in French Sudan to remove Voulet from his command. The honourable Klobb met up with Voulet on Bastille Day (July 14) but was shot in cold blood for his trouble. Huge African mortality was variously caused throughout the continent by massacre, dispossession, enslavement, brutal forced labour, cash crops instead of food crops and the smashing of exquisitely evolved indigenous economies that maximized nutrition and minimized disease such as malaria.[42]

The First World War saw the immense horrors of mass, industrial warfare on the Western Front, the Eastern Front, Northern Italy and at Gallipoli in the Turkish Dardanelles. The Allies essentially forced Turkey into this obscene war and then launched massive shelling in the Dardanelles as a prelude to the ultimately unsuccessful invasion and occupation of Gallipoli on 25 April 1915. Turkish xenophobia and the Allied invasion precipitated the horrendous Armenian Genocide that was initiated by the arrest and murder of Armenian professionals and community leaders on 24 April 1915. Massacres and forced deportations subsequently took the lives of 1.5 million Armenians and wiped out an ancient Christian civilization in Turkish-controlled Anatolia. Turkey has made assertion of this genocide effectively illegal (countered by the Belgians who recently made its denial illegal). The post-WW1 exchange of Greek and Turkish populations was accompanied by massacres and Kurdish Muslims and Syriac Christians suffered massacres at the hands of nationalist Turks.[43]

Immediately after WW1 with the global movement of millions of soldiers and civilians, the Spanish flu pandemic killed 50-100 million world-wide with some 17 million dying in India alone. Civil War and associated famine swept the Russian Empire. However, in the late 1920s Stalin commenced exporting grain from the Ukraine, collectivizing farms and deporting Ukrainians. The Ukrainian Famine (that had a wider regional impact) was man-made and contributed massively to a demographic deficit of 12 million Ukrainians in the period 1926-1939. The Ukrainian Famine was one major aspect of the horrendous rule of Josef Stalin that was associated with pre-war and post-war purges and deportations involving millions. Analysis of the 1959 Soviet census (total population 209 million) reveals an appalling sex ratio of about twice as many women as men in all 5-year span age groups older than 34. No doubt Soviet WW2 military losses (13.6 million) would have contributed to this female minus male post-34 year old disparity totalling about 17 million. Male gender-biased purging and deportations (gendercide) to the Gulag system would have contributed a minimum of about 3.4 million to the male deficit revealed in the 1959 census. The overall Soviet losses due to the Gulag have been estimated to be commensurate with the total Soviet losses in WW2 (about 20 million).[44]

The Japanese invasion and occupation of China (1937-1945) is estimated to have taken 35-40 million lives according the Chinese authorities and clearly constitutes massive and deliberate genocide. The Japanese knowingly invaded this poor and densely populated country well knowing what the consequences would be, and betrayed a deadly racism through horrendous mass rapes and massacres, most notably the Nanjing Massacre in which 0.3 million died.[45]

Between the two World Wars fascist militarism was exercised in the Spanish Civil War and in the Italian invasion of Ethiopia (that involved the use of poison gas against those resisting, a technology also used by the British against Iraqi "insurgents" in the 1920s). The conquest of Europe by the Nazis in WW2 (1939-1945) and of East and South-East Asia by the Japanese (1937-1945) took the lives of 84 million, the breakdown of casualties being 5.9 million Axis military, 18.6 million Allied military, 5.1 million Axis civilians and 54.4 million Allied civilians. Major mortality components include 35-40 million Chinese deaths, 24 million Soviet deaths, 13.6 million Soviet military casualties, 5-6 million Jews, 6 million Polish deaths (including 2.9 million Jews), 1 million Gypsies (Roma) and 6-7 million Hindu and Muslim victims of the man-made Bengal Famine in British-ruled India (an event that has been largely deleted from British history through entrenched British politically correct racism, lying by omission and "holocaust ignoring").[46]

As with other genocides and wars there was economic and political benefit to be gained from racist barbarity against the Jews of Europe in WW2. Thus Nazi anti-Jewish anti-Semitism garnered support within Germany and its subjects, especially those in Eastern Europe. Nevertheless, indigenous humanity dramatically saved all but 100 of Denmark's Jews from the Nazis, and similar humanity lead to *relatively* low and *delayed* Jewish mortality of

9,000/120,000 in the Fascist state of Italy, as compared to overwhelmingly high mass extermination in other countries of Nazi-occupied Europe, namely: 28,000/85,000 (Belgium), 65,000/300,000 (France), 180,000/250,000 (Germany), 60,000/70,000 (Austria), 60,000/81,000 (Czechoslovakia), 200,000/710,000 (Hungary), 58,000/70,000 (Yugoslavia), 60,000/67,000 (Greece), 40,000/48,000 (Bulgaria), 750,000/1,000,000 (Romania), 2,600.000/3,000,000 (Poland), 104,000/140,000 (Lithuania), 70,000/100,000 (Latvia) and 750,000/2,500,000 (German-occupied Soviet Union). [47]

Of course the Jewish Holocaust cannot be considered in isolation from centuries of egregious European racism culminating in the genocidal invasions, dispossessions and massacres in the non-European World. The incisive analysis *"Exterminate all the Brutes"* by Sven Lindqvist cogently makes this connection leading to the cross-over from "traditional" European anti-Jewish anti-Semitic pogroms to Nazi genocide: *"But the step from mass murder to genocide was not taken until the anti-Semitic tradition met the tradition of genocide arising during Europe's expansion into America, Australia, Africa, and Asia ... Auschwitz was the modern industrial application of a policy of extermination on which European world domination had long since rested"*. [48]

Setting aside numerous wars and associated atrocities, the post-war era saw successive racially- or religiously-dictated barbarities including Indian-Pakistan Partition [49], the mass rape and gendercide in Bangladesh by the West Pakistan Army (3 million mostly men and boys killed and 0.3 million women and girls raped),[50] the Cambodian genocide (1975-1980 excess mortality 1.2 million),[51] 4 decades of Indonesian military rule (1965-1999 excess mortality 33.3 million),[52] 4 decades of military dictatorship in Burma (1962-2005 excess mortality 15.5 million),[53] the Rwanda genocide aftermath (1990-1995 pentade excess mortality 1.1 million), tribally-influenced civil war on the Congo (1994-2005 civil war excess mortality 10.1 million), Indonesian genocide in East Timor (0.2 million killed or starved out of a population of about 0.6 million)[54] and the Sudan civil war and continuing Sudanese Arab atrocities against fellow Muslims in the Darfur region of Sudan (1955-2005 excess mortality 12.4 million). To this we should add intractable refugee injustices, notably those of the Israel-Palestine conflict[55] (7 million Palestinian refugees in the Middle East alone), 80 million refugees worldwide and the estimated 50 million "internal refugees" due to "big projects" in India.[56]

As already seen in this horrendous saga there are blurred boundaries between explicit, violent genocide and man-made mass mortality from epidemics through introduced disease; dispossession from land; total war; famine; passive genocide through non-provision of life-sustaining requisites by occupying powers; and hegemonic deliberate exclusion of huge swathes of humanity from basic "entitlement" to the minimal requirements for basic survival.

8.7 Famine

Famine is popularly perceived as happening when there is simply no food but the harsh reality is that major famines in the colonial and neo-colonial era have occurred because the subject victims do not have the money to purchase food ("entitlement" in the parlance of 1998 Economics Nobel Laureate Amartya Sen).[57] Famine has been used as a military weapon for millennia as in the clear cases of the besieging of fortresses and cities. However military supply lines are crucial for armies and food shortages clearly hampered major invasions such as the Napoleonic French and Nazi German invasions of Russia and the Japanese invasion of Burma. Wellington brilliantly used a "scorched earth policy" to defeat the Napoleonic French armies in the Iberian Peninsula. It has been speculated that the horrendous, man-made Bengal Famine (peaking in 1943-44) was part of a deliberate British policy to thwart Japanese invasion of British-ruled India.[58]

Some of the most catastrophic famines have been associated with racist European colonial excesses (e.g. the Great Bengal Famine of 1769-1770 that killed 10 million people, one third of the population of British-occupied Bengal). At a largely unreported level are the simple consequences of dispossession and the loss of the ability of conquered people to gather or grow enough food for themselves.

Dispossession, enslavement and taxation involved removal of people from the land, forcing them into cash crop production or allowing them insufficient land and resources for survival in bad times. These colonial abuses meant malnutrition, early death, enforced slavery or effective slavery that continues to this day in India and post-colonial countries of Africa.[59]

Dispossession of North American Indians simply meant starvation if there was no land for food acquisition and no ability to store food for access to in winter. The enclosures of Uruguay by cattle ranchers in the 19th century had a catastrophic impact on the indigenous Indians, and in neighbouring Paraguay 1 million Indians died associated with the 1865-1870 invasion by the British-backed Triple Alliance of Argentina, Brazil and Uruguay. The Argentinian Indians were cleared from the pampas by brutal genocide.

In the 18th century, enclosures forced a minority of English country folk into rural servitude and most into effective slave conditions in cities where the appalling death rate was equivalent to that of Indian subjects in British India. The clearances of Highland Scotland and associated famine dispossessed a people and forced them to emigrate to big cities, North America or to Australasia as alternatives to starvation.[60] Dispossession and exploitation of the Irish finally led to the catastrophic Potato Famine (1845-1850) in which 1 million died while grain was being exported from Ireland, and 1.5 million were forced to emigrate (with many dying in transit or on penniless arrival in new lands).[61]

Man-made famine was such a constant feature of British-ruled India that one is compelled to the suggestion that this was deliberate policy and enabled a relatively small British contingent to dominate a vastly greater number of people. A dozen years after the conquest of Bengal in 1757 and commencement of rapacious taxation, the Great Bengal Famine killed 10 million (one third of the population). Recurrent famines continued over the next 2 centuries, major famines including that in Northern India (1782-1784), the Deccan plateau (1876-1880), Bengal and Orissa (1873-1876), Northern India (around 1900) and recurrent famines in the famine-prone areas of Rajasthan and Sind (throughout the 19th century). In 1877 the death rate in labour camps in the Deccan Famine corresponded to an annual death rate of 94%.[62] The British had Famine Commissions to examine these events and suggest future responses. In 1942-1945, a huge man-made famine killed 6-7 million Indians in Bengal and the adjoining provinces of Assam, Bihar, and Orissa (Odisha) but the so-called Famine Codes were ignored. It has been suggested that the Bengal Famine was the result of a deliberate British strategy to present a starving province to any Japanese army invading India from Burma.[63] Independence in 1947, while not abolishing hunger and shortages, effectively ended the kinds of catastrophic famines experienced in the callous British-ruled period. The British kept the huge Indian population on the edge of survival. It can be estimated that the avoidable mortality in 2 centuries of British rule in India totalled 1.5 billion or1.8 billion including the native states.

Famines occurred in Africa under colonial rule (e.g. the Sahel famine in the 1930s) and have continued to recur in neo-colonial Africa, most notably in the French-dominated Sahel, and formerly British-ruled East Africa and Southern Africa. Neo-colonial realities (such as cash crops instead of food crops) continue to impose immense suffering upon the people of Africa that are compounded by war and the utterly avoidable scale of the HIV/AIDS epidemic.

In China massive famine was associated with the 19th century impositions of the British and other powers culminating in the Tai Ping rebellion (1850-1864; an estimated 20-100 million victims). Famine recurred in China in the 20th century. Not surprisingly, final post-war independence from foreign powers meant increased food security but hostility from both the USSR and the USA led to the seriously misdirected Great Leap Forward (1959-1961) in which some 30 million died of famine.[64] Not surprisingly, major Asian countries that did not experience First World hegemony or pre-war occupation, namely Japan and Thailand, have remained famine-free because of indigenous control and farming for food for indigenous consumption (rather than cash crops for colonialist profit).

Man-made food shortages associated with civil war and other social disruption have had a deadly effect in the 20th century. Thus famine in Russia in 1921 was a consequence of the Russian Civil War, and the subsequent Ukrainian famine (1928-1932) the result of ruthless socio-political policies of Stalin. Famine was rampant in war lord-wracked China (1928-1930). Famine was a major accompaniment of war in Nazi-occupied Europe. Thus of 5-6 million Jews killed by the Nazis, many died of malnutrition and accompanying disease. Starvation occurred in German concentration camps, Jewish ghettoes and in homeless refugee populations. In microcosm, a German platoon seizing the food supplies of a snow-bound Russian, Byelorussian, Lithuanian, Ukrainian or Polish village meant certain death by starvation for the villagers. The Netherlands suffered severe famine associated with the last months of German resistance against the advancing Allies in 1945.

Man-made famine still stalks a world dominated by a profligate and over-consuming First World. Thus food shortage affects about 2 billion people in the World of whom about 1 billion suffer severe food shortages. Conversely, type 2 diabetes (mature-age diabetes) affects about 5% of Westerners and is linked to obesity from excessive food consumption. Major post-war famines have been those of the West African Sahel, Ethiopia, Somalia, Southern Africa and the Sudan. More important than explicit starvation *per se* is lack of resistance to disease. Thus in British India malaria was described as a major famine disease. About 16 million people die avoidably each year, largely due to malnourishment- and deprivation-related causes (mainly disease) (2003 estimate; in 2020 global avoidable deaths from deprivation totalled 7.4 million) (Table 9.1). Food and clean water are among the cheapest of commodities and famine death is utterly avoidable.

8.8 Disease

Epidemic diseases are associated by definition with human populations large enough to sustain an infective pool of humans and/or disease vectors and consequent disease transmission. Many human diseases came from transmission of animal diseases or animal disease variants to humans, and arose from the development of agrarian communities, animal husbandry, close association of humans with animals (notably sheep, cattle, goats, ducks, hens and dogs), increased human population density and co-habitation with animals such as rodents, fleas, lice and carbon dioxide (CO_2)-attracted mosquito disease vectors. With continuing human invasion of tropical forests, more exotic zoonotic diseases (that can transmit between humans and animals) are likely as exampled by the present Covid-19 Pandemic that may have originated in bats. Summarized below are details of major diseases that have afflicted humanity.[65]

Plague is caused by the bacillus *Yersinia pestis* and is a disease of rodents, notably the rat (*Rattus*), and spread by blood-sucking fleas. Recent research shows that it was also spread by human-associated fleas and lice. Bubonic plague (associated with swellings of lymph nodes or buboes) is spread by fleas via rat populations and by fleas and lice by humans; deadly pneumonic plague attacks the lungs and the human victim is highly infective (death within 3-4 days); and the even deadlier septicaemic form involves the blood being infected (death within 1 day). *Yersinia* presence in rat populations is typically very low (enzootic) but high incidence (epizootic) infection can occur and hence threaten humans. Thus urban plague was associated with high density rat and human populations but rural (sylvanic or campestral) plague was associated with high populations of infected rats. Epidemics ascribed to bubonic plague devastated some early Christian era urban societies. The first Black Death pestilence in 14th century Europe killed about 2/3 to 3/4 of the affected populations and overall about 25 million died, or 1/4 of the whole population. The 14th century Black Death killed 75-200 million people in Europe, Asia and North Africa. A consequence was an increased empowerment of skilled workers in previously feudal societies dominated by the Church and a military nobility. Counterproductive responses included religious mass gatherings (that simply enhanced infection) and pogroms directed against Jews. The first order requiring quarantining against plague was promulgated in 1443. The Great Plague of London (1664-1665) killed 70,000 out of 460,000 inhabitants; London was finally cleansed by the Great Fire of London (1666). Plague remained endemic in the Turkish-occupied areas of Eastern Europe into the 19th century and was only eliminated from Egypt in the 19th century under the effective administration of Mohammed Ali. In 1894 plague killed 80,000-100,000 in Canton and Hong Kong in Southern China; subsequent British mercantile dissemination throughout the World killed an estimated 10 million over the next 2 decades (notably in British India). The horror of plague has been communicated in literature, most notably in *The Diary of Samuel Pepys from 1659 to 1669*, *The Plague* (*La Peste*) by Albert Camus (1957 Nobel Prize for Literature) and *Year of Wonders* by Geraldine Brooks.[66] Post-war outbreaks of plague were reported in India.

Epidemic typhus is caused by the bacterium *Ricketsia prowazeckii* and is spread by the body louse (*Pediculus humanus*) attached to human hair and skin. Typhus was reported as a major accompaniment of dirty crowding (as in armies) from the Middle Ages onwards. Major outbreaks were associated with the Napoleonic Wars (1794-1815) and the Irish Famine (1846-1850). Millions died from typhus in Eastern Europe (notably in Russia, Poland and Romania) at the close of WW1. WW2-connected typhus epidemics were associated with concentration camps, ghettoes and refugee camps. In the 20th century the spread of typhus could be controlled by delousing clothing and hair. In WW2 the insecticidal compound DDT was employed for delousing. DDT, a chlorinated aromatic compound, was first synthesized in 1874 but its insecticidal properties were discovered in 1939 by Swiss chemist Paul Müller (awarded the Nobel Prize for Medicine in 1948). DDT was subsequently important in killing insect vectors of major diseases including lice (typhus, plague), fleas (plague) and mosquitoes (malaria, dengue fever and yellow fever virus) as well as for control of important agricultural pests such as Colorado potato beetle. The accumulation of DDT in fatty tissue and adverse environmental effects through accumulation in animal food chains (notably exposed by Rachel Carson's *"Silent Spring"*)[67] led to progressive banning. However banning of DDT use in Sri Lanka ultimately led to resurgence of mosquitoes and thence of malaria.

Smallpox (variola) is a viral disease that was finally eradicated by 1979 (except for several laboratory stocks). Smallpox was reported in China (1122BCE) and had evidently infected the Egyptian Pharaoh Ramses V (who died in 1156BCE). There are no known animal carriers other than humans but the virus is long-lived and mildly affected people can act as infective carriers. Smallpox was common in Europe (natural selection favours non-lethality allowing for re-infection, and non-lethal exposure permitted immunological resistance). However smallpox was taken to the previously non-exposed New World by European invaders and (together with other introduced, exotic diseases) decimated indigenous peoples of the major civilizations of Mexico, Peru, the Mississippi, the Amazon and Eastern North America. The Hottentots of South Africa and the aboriginal people of Australia were decimated by smallpox brought by Europeans. Variolation (infection of healthy people with material from mildly affected smallpox victims) was practised in India, China and Africa but could prove fatal. English doctor Edward Jenner, realizing that those infected with cow-derived cowpox were protected from smallpox infection, inoculated a child with fresh cowpox lesion material from a dairymaid and produced protection against smallpox (1796). A major WHO vaccination campaign focussing on possible carriers of the disease finally completely eradicated the disease: there were 2 million deaths from smallpox in 1967 and the last normal case was in 1977 in Somalia (there were 2 accidental laboratory cases in the UK in 1978). Since nobody is vaccinated against smallpox anymore, a current fear is of a limited smallpox epidemic due to possible targeted, malevolent release from Russian or American stocks through state or non-state terrorism.

Cholera is caused by the water-borne bacterium *Vibrio cholerae*. A bacteriophage converts non-toxic bacteria to toxic bacteria. The *Vibrio* toxin enters small intestinal cells and induces the following biochemical events: chemical modification (specifically, ADP-ribosylation) of signal transduction G protein (type G_s) α subunit $\rightarrow$ inhibition of GTP hydrolysing (GTPase) activity $\rightarrow$ persistent G_s activation through a persisting α-GTP complex $\rightarrow$ persistent activation of adenylate cyclase $\rightarrow$ elevated cyclic AMP $\rightarrow$ PKA activation $\rightarrow$ protein phosphorylation $\rightarrow$ loss of cellular water and

sodium ions (Na^+) through the plasma membrane of intestinal cells-
> persistent diarrhoea (20 litres per day). Urgent saline treatment
with glucose restores water, sodium ions and energy. Cholera was
spread in British India through shipping (water ballast), railways
(water for steam) and Punjab canals; the 19th century death toll
from cholera in British India was about 25 million. In 1898-1907
(including a period of massive famine in India) there were 0.4
million cholera deaths. In London there were epidemics in 1831-
1832 (6,000 died), 1848-1849, 1854 and 1856. A total of 30,000
people died of cholera in the UK in the 19th century. In 1854 John
Snow demonstrated the water-based transmission of the disease
with consequent introduction of sanitation and clean drinking water
improvements. 19th century European authorities were resentful of
the spread of cholera by British shipping. In 1883 Robert Koch (of
Koch's Postulate fame) demonstrated the bacterial basis of cholera.
Children are particularly susceptible especially in famine
conditions and hence this has been a major cause of death in
famines in British Indian (especially in Bengal where cholera was
endemic) and in recent post-colonial African famines (notably
Ethiopia and the Sudan). The disease is prevented by sanitation and
clean drinking water – unfortunately still missing for several billion
people throughout the World, including many in Occupied Iraq
whose vital sanitation and water infrastructure was repeatedly
severely damaged by Coalition bombing. In West Bengal and
Bangladesh the avoidance of cholera-infected surface water by use
of pumped ground water has been complicated because such water
is widely contaminated with toxic and carcinogenic levels of
arsenate (recently shown to derive from the reductive action on
arsenate-containing minerals of anaerobic bacteria feeding on
surface-derived nutrients).[68]

Measles (rubeola) is caused by a virus and commonly infects
children, with death typically occurring from secondary bacterial
infection and bronchopneumonia. The disease was described in
detail (together with the plague and diphtheria) by French
physician Guillaume de Baillou (died 1616). Measles (introduced
by European invaders, traders and missionaries) killed millions in
vulnerable populations of the New World and the Pacific. Thus in
1874 Ratu Cakobau and his sons returned to Fiji from Sydney

where there was a measles epidemic; 40,000 Fijians died from measles in 1875 out of a total population of 150,000.[69] Mid-20th century discoveries of antibiotic drugs - notably the bacteriostatic sulphonamides and the key antibiotic penicillin (1945 Nobel Prize for Physiology and Medicine to Howard Florey, Ernst Chain and Alexander Fleming) – greatly decreased the danger from bacterial complications of measles infection. John Enders (1897-1985; Nobel Prize, Physiology and Medicine, 1954) developed the Enders-Weller-Robbins method for growing viruses in primate non-nervous tissue cultures that enabled the development of the Salk polio vaccine (1954) and the measles vaccine (1963) that were thence routinely given to Western infants.

Influenza (flu or grippe) is caused by orthomyxoviruses types A, B and C. Type A are the most common and have caused pandemics (e.g. type H2N2, the 1957 Asian flu and type H3N2, the 1968 Hong Kong flu). The pandemic flu viruses derived from avian viruses that infected humans involved in bird husbandry and thence mutated to permit human to human infection. Coughing and sneezing provides effective transmission and death can occur from bacterial bronchopneumonia complications, especially in the elderly. Vaccines involving attenuated viruses grown in hen eggs are required annually because of the rapid evolution of viral surface proteins. Mutation yielding altered surface proteins enables new strains to evade previously generated immune defences. However structurally relatively "constant" regions (epitopes) of the surface protein neurominidase have enabled synthesis of anti-infection agents. The 1918-1919 Spanish flu epidemic that originated in the US and was spread by travellers and soldiers, eventually killed 50-100 million worldwide, with some 17 million dying in crowded and impoverished India. Other flu pandemics were those of 1957 and 1968. A new avian flu strain (type H5N1) has recently emerged in South East Asia that can kill both birds and humans and there is fear that mutations permitting human-to-human transmission will generate a huge pandemic assisted by migrating birds and the speed and volume of First World international travel.

Malaria is caused by the protozoa *Plasmodium*, occurs in humans, some other primates and some other animals and is transmitted to humans by female *Anopheles* mosquitoes. CO_2-attracted female *Anopheles* mosquitoes ingest human blood containing *Plasmodium* –> sexual cycle –>zygote-> oocyst –>asexual sporozoites –> re-injected by feeding into the new human host –> invade erythrocytes (red blood cells) –> ring stage –> merozoite –> asexual division, feeding on haemoglobin –> release –> new red blood cells invaded –> new merozoites of which some differentiate into gametocytes –> ingested by female mosquito and the sexual phase begins again. Synchronous asexual division causes recurring fevers; adherence to capillaries can cause blockage and death from stroke. Sexual phase recombination allows rapid selection of new forms that are not recognized by human immune defences. Hippocrates described malaria in the 5th century BCE and Alexander the Great was a likely victim. Malaria impacted severely on the Roman Empire. The first epidemics occurred after 1492 in the New World. Malaria (and other tropical diseases) limited European settlement in tropical Africa, Asia, South East Asia and Melanesia. More humans have died from malaria than any other disease in history. 250 million cases of malaria and 2 million deaths occur each year. Most victims are located in tropical and semi-tropical regions and most deaths are due to *Plasmodium falciparum*. Evolved African settlement practices (avoidance of malarial swamps) minimized malaria but European colonization, exploitation economics, water-based transport, use of forced labour, destruction of indigenous societies and urbanization of Africans all promoted the spread of malaria. From the 19th century quinine from the *Cinchona* tree was used as an antimalarial. Synthetics such as chloroquine were developed in the mid-20th century but wide use (e.g. during US Asian wars) led to development of resistance. Derivatives of artemisinin from a Chinese herb[70] are also currently used and vaccines are being sought. The poverty of nearly all of the global victims has limited commercially-driven pharmacological research into anti-malarial remedies but the remarkable generosity of Bill and Melinda Gates has spurred research for anti-malaria vaccines.

HIV (Human immunodeficiency virus) is a retrovirus containing single-stranded RNA and is the causative agent of AIDS (Acquired Immunodeficiency Syndrome). HIV infects Helper T lymphocytes

(CD4+ cells, i.e. lymphocytes containing the protein CD4 on the surface of their cell membrane). The helper T cells produce cytokines, regulatory proteins that assist B lymphocytes (to produce antibodies), cytotoxic T lymphocytes (to kill cells), macrophages (to ingest detritus) and other cells involved in the immune responses. HIV infection and the killing of T helper lymphocytes thus causes immunosuppression. In the absence of vital medication, AIDS typically causes death through adventitious infection by agents such as *Pneumocystis carinii* (pneumonia), *Mycobacterium tuberculosis* (TB), *Mycobacterium avium*, herpes simplex virus, toxoplasma and cytomegalovirus. HIV-infected people are also susceptible to dementia and cancers such as Karposi's sarcoma and lymphomas. HIV binds to the host cell CD4 protein via HIV envelope protein gp120, this causing a subtle change in gp120 permitting it to bind to host chemokine receptors and enabling HIV gp41 protein to insert into the cell membrane and permit single-stranded HIV RNA entry. Inside the host cell, the HIV RNA is copied by the reverse transcriptase enzyme to form double-stranded DNA which can incorporate into the host DNA (the host genome). HIV replication inside the host cell occurs through transcription (generation of the viral RNA), translation of the viral RNAs (yielding viral protein), processing of the viral proteins by HIV protease (to yield gp120/gp41, integrase and reverse transcriptase) and then release of new infective HIV copies with gp120/gp41 complexes incorporated in a phospholipid bilayer membrane derived from the host cell membrane.

AIDS first appeared (notably in Western homosexual men) in 1981 and serological testing became available in 1985. As a result of a huge body of biochemical, molecular biological, medical and pharmacological research, anti-HIV drugs are now available. Combination therapy involving inhibitors of HIV protease and replication-inhibiting nucleosides (synthetic analogues structurally related to the nucleotide building blocks of RNA and DNA) is available to Westerners but effectively not to many of the 40 million infected world-wide. With antivirals and antibacterials and the best of modern medicine HIV infection is no longer a death sentence. However the consequent problem of antibiotic resistance coupled with readily available international travel has helped generate the looming problem of multi-drug resistant bacteria. Opposition by the US Religious Right Republicans (RRRs, R3s) and the pro-US and doctrinally-conservative Catholic Church to safe sex involving condom use coupled with *sheer incompetence* of Third World governments (typically dominated by post-colonial client élites) has contributed to an utterly avoidable and catastrophic spread of HIV/AIDS, especially in Africa. Thus USAID information (2007) gives the following sobering statistics: there are currently about 38 million HIV-positive people world-wide, 20 million have died from HIV/AIDS since and in 2003 4.8 million were newly infected and 2.9 million died.[71]

Tuberculosis (TB) in humans is caused mostly by the *Mycobacterium tuberculosis* (and to a much lesser extent by the bovine-infecting mycobacterium *M. bovis*). The TB mycobacteria were first discovered by Robert Koch (1882). "White death" was the stuff of writers as with the Puccini opera *La Bohème* and *The Magic Mountain* by Thomas Mann (1929 Nobel Prize for Literature). Scottish writer Robert Louis Stevenson died from TB in Samoa (1894).[72] Effective post-war drugs include isomiazid, rifampicin and streptomycin. The HIV/AIDS epidemic and immune suppression has led to an increased incidence of TB due to use of many antibacterial drugs on immuno-compromised people with inevitable selection for multi-drug resistant bacteria. A quarter of the world's 2 million annual deaths from TB occur in Africa.

Rotavirus diarrhoea causes the death of about 0.8 million worldwide (including about 0.5 million children) out of a total of about 2.1 million dying from diarrhoeal diseases. A commercial anti-rotavirus vaccine was released in 1998 but was withdrawn after intussusception (bowel obstruction) problems were found in 1 in 12,000 vaccinated children.

Viral hepatitis (hepatitis A, B, C, D and E) are caused by A, B, C, D and E type hepatitis viruses. Of about 360 million carriers of the dangerous Hepatitis B virus, nearly 80% are in Asia with China being a major repository. Hepatitis B causes hepatic scarring of the liver and later liver cancer. A hepatitis B vaccine is available. The hepatitis viruses are spread through contact with blood.

Further major diseases involved in suffering and mass mortality in the Third World include other respiratory diseases, other gastrointestinal diseases (in addition to those caused by cholera and rotaviruses), dengue fever (mosquito-borne viral disease) and yellow fever (mosquito-borne arbovirus disease). Adding to this burden are afflictions such as trachoma (unsanitary contact-, fly- and gnat-spread, avoidable, bacterial eye disease afflicting 400 million and leading to blindness); onchocerciasis (river blindness affecting millions in West Africa due to a parasite spread by black fly); leishmania (sandfly-spread, *Leishmania* protozoa disease variously affecting the liver and spleen or causing skin ulcers); filiaris (a tropical, mosquito-borne, parasitic worm disease, notably caused by *Wuchereria bancrofti*, affecting the lymphatic system and causing elephantiasis limb swelling); tapeworm diseases spread from herbivores by carnivores (e.g. *Taenia* spp infecting beef and pork; cysticercosis from infected pork; hydatid cysts from infection by *Echinococcus granulosum*, the hydatid tapeworm infecting sheep and dogs); trypanosomiasis or sleeping sickness (the tsetse fly-transmitted *Trypanosoma* protozoal disease threatening 60 million people in sub-Saharan Africa); schistosomiasis (bilharzia; a water snail-borne worm disease; agent *Schistoma* spp; 200 million affected world-wide); leprosy (a mycobacterial infection); new, animal-derived viral diseases (e.g. Ebola virus haemorrhagic disease; Marburg haemorrhagic disease; Hendra virus or equine morbillivirus that infects horses, bats, pigs and man); and long-term health risks deriving from unwise human activities such as smoking, excessive drinking and exposure to air pollutants.

2021 update re Covid-19: Covid-19 disease is caused by the highly infective SARS-Cov-2 coronavirus that kills by affecting the lungs. Since it took off in early 2020 it has so far infected 128 million worldwide and killed 2.8 million (March 2021). It has been substantially controlled in East Asia, Australia and New Zealand by border controls, hygiene measures (masks, hand sanitizer, social distancing), Lockdowns, PCR-based detection of infection cases and exhaustive contact tracing. A number of vaccines have been rapidly developed (most excitingly for future vaccines, novel mRNA-based vaccines). About 95% of deaths are those of people over 50, but rich countries of North America and Europe have violated intra-national human altruism and committed Gerocide (intentional killing of the old) by putting the economy before lives. Thus "Covid-19 deaths per million of population" - is 0.4 (Taiwan), 3 (China), 5 (New Zealand) and 35 (Australia) as compared to 1,687 (the US) and 1,857 (the UK), and total deaths have been 10 (Taiwan), 4,636 (China), 26 (New Zealand) and 909 (Australia) as compared to over 563,000 (the US) and over 127,000 (the UK).

Long-term health risks afflicting humanity include those from multi-drug resistant bacteria, smoking, drinking and exposure to carcinogens. Air pollution kills 9 million people each year. The mounting risk to the World from multidrug-resistant bacteria derives from Western multi-drug antibacterial therapy for HIV/AIDS victims and for bacterial infection patients in hospitals; anti-bacterial over-prescription by general practitioners; profligate Western agricultural use of important anti-bacterials in animal husbandry to increase meat yields; and inappropriate use of such drugs in the developing World – with transmission ensured by readily available international travel. Clear evidence of the lethal consequences of cigarette smoking became available in the 1950s but there are perhaps 2 billion cigarette smokers in the World and a smoking "epidemic" in China; the tobacco trade is dominated by the First World (notably by the UK and the US). There are about 5 million cigarette smoking-related deaths in the World each year – an utterly avoidable circumstance that will continue for many years (due to a 2 decade lead time) even if this highly-addictive habit and the Anglo-American-dominated trade are immediately banned worldwide.

The annual global death toll from tobacco, alcohol and illicit drugs is about 5 million, 1.8 million and 0.2 million, respectively (2007) – yet tobacco and alcohol are legal products. This is an utterly avoidable absurdity consonant with the other appalling realities exposed in this book – and dependent on entrenched societal unresponsiveness and lying by omission. Thus Anglo-American mainstream media will simply not report the palpable reality that after 9/11 (3,000 victims), the US-led invasion and occupation of Afghanistan resulted in the rapid restoration of the Taliban-destroyed Afghan opium industry from 6% of world market share in 2001 to 76% global market share and consequent US Coalition complicity in 0.5 million post-2001, opioid drug-related deaths worldwide (2007 estimate). Presently in 2021 illicit drugs kill 0.6 million each year, with most deaths due to opiates and opioids. The US Coalition-complicit, post-2001, opioid drug death toll includes many from the US Alliance countries, notably the US. One can understand why racism and embarrassment would prevent Western mainstream media from reporting the post-invasion avoidable mortality in the Occupied Palestinian, Iraqi and Afghan Territories that (September 2006) totaled 0.3, 0.5 and 2.0 million, respectively. But why won't Anglo-American media report the post-2001 drug deaths of tens of thousands of their *own kind* as a result of the US invasion and occupation of Afghanistan?[73]

8.9 Human cost of occupation

As outlined in the section on genocide, wars have involved mass murder of the following kinds (in rough ascending order of horror with some examples in parentheses): imprisonment or execution of the conquered leadership (common); effective extermination of prisoners (Germans by Russians and Russians by Germans in WW2); extermination of everybody but with retention of some women for sex and all the young men for soldiery (the Zulus under Shaka); extermination of all the men and boys (Milos, Carthage and Srebnica in Bosnia); attempted extermination of minorities (Nazi Germany, Rwanda); extensive random male gendercide (the Pakistan army in Bangladesh); random mass killing (the Nazis in Eastern Europe; Indo-Pakistan Partition); mass bombing of civilian targets (Germany bombing Britain; Allies bombing Germany in WW2); immense "collateral damage" due to war in heavily populated countries (Korea; Vietnam; Iraq; Afghanistan); near-total urban destruction (the US and Hiroshima, Nagasaki, Dresden, Tokyo and Hamburg; urban exterminations by the Mongols).

We can see that the liberal democracies are right up there with the 13th century Mongols at their worst in terms of the intensity of killing in particular zones of near-total death (Hiroshima, Dresden and Nagasaki). However the Western liberal democracies (notably the UK, the US and their allies) have vastly outdone anyone else in history by their excesses in the post-1950 era. Most of the carnage has arisen through non-violent deaths due to non-provision of life-sustaining requisites (water, food, sanitation, hygiene and primary health care). The data in Chapter 2 enabled upper limit estimates of what this carnage has been as set out in Chapter 3.

Thus the 1950-2005 excess mortality in occupied or partially-occupied countries has been summed for the various occupier countries (Chapter 3) and is re-presented here in *descending order* of absolute post-1950 excess mortality in which they have been complicit - we have the following order (in millions, m): UK (727.3m) > France (142.3m) > US (82.2m) > Netherlands (71.6m) > Pakistan (51.2m) > Russia (37.1m)> Belgium (36.0m) > Israel (23.9m) > Portugal (23.5m) > Spain (8.6m) (the Big League) followed by a Minor League of Australia (2.1m) > Ethiopia (1.8m) > Indonesia (0.7m) > South Africa (0.7m) > > > Iraq (0.09m) > Turkey (0.05m) > New Zealand (0.04m). However this list merely presents the horrendous outcome of a complex mixture of *opportunity* and *propensity*.

As discussed in Chapter 3, an estimate of moral propensity or moral disregard is obtained from "victim country"/ "occupier country" ratios of "1950-2005 excess mortality/2005 population ratios" (calculated for major post-war occupiers and their victims). With respect to this parameter we have the following descending order: Netherlands (63.4) > Israel (15.9) > Portugal (14.5) > Australia (11.4) > Spain (10.6) > US (8.6) > Belgium (6.9) > France (6.1) > New Zealand (5.9) > UK (4.4) > Indonesia (2.6) > Russia (1.7) > South Africa (1.1) = Pakistan (1.1) > Ethiopia (0.8) > Turkey (0.5) > Iraq (0.2) (noting that for the purposes of this calculation the "1950-2005 excess mortality/2005 population" ratio for the Netherlands was taken as about 1% i.e. the approximate value for the "best" Western European countries). This assessment gives a relative measure of *disregard* for the lives of victim people. However we cannot simply conclude that Americans *per se* are intrinsically 5 times more racist, disregarding or blood-thirsty than Russians. As amplified in the following section, US high technology war is "sanitized" by killing from afar (human beings don't normally like killing others face to face; close encounters are risky and traumatizing), and through media "ignoring" of the actual avoidable mortality associated with war and occupation (human beings don't care to know about the horrendous negative consequences of their actions).

8.10 High technology war, horrendous civilian/invader death ratios and PC racism

The "industrial war" strategy first applied massively in World War 2 involved overwhelming destruction directed against civilians to minimize politically-sensitive US casualties as illustrated by the conventional mass bombing of German and Japanese cities (most memorably Dresden and Tokyo) and ultimately the nuclear destruction of Hiroshima and Nagasaki in 1945. This same strategy, coupled with horrendous, ever bigger, "better" and "smarter" conventional weapons, better treatment of the wounded and progressively weaker and weakened opponents, saw a progressive *increase* of the "death ratio" of excess civilian deaths/US combat deaths.

The ratio of "enemy civilian deaths"/"US combat deaths" successively *increased* from 17 in World War 2 Europe to 24 in the Korean War and 277 in the Indo-China War. However the carnage has now become so great that Anglo-American mainstream media will simply not report it. Thus the "excess mortality" in Iraq since 1991 has been 2.3 million with US combat deaths totalling about 1,660, a ratio of 1,386 to 1 (2007 data). Compare this with the ratio of total casualties of World War 2 (80 million) to total Axis military deaths (5.9 million), a ratio of 13.5 to 1 – one hundred (100) times lower.[74]

In considering the immense numbers of civilian deaths in high technology war it is germane to consider the following comment by US General Curtis LeMay, commander of the 1945 Tokyo fire bombing operation, as quoted in *Rogue State: A Guide to the World's Only Superpower*, by William Blum: "*I suppose if I had lost the war, I would have been tried as a war criminal. Fortunately, we were on the winning side.*"[75]

423

The ratio of "enemy children deaths"/US combat deaths now dramatizes the obscenity of high technology war conducted typically against high density centres of civilian population as well as against minimally-armed, impoverished military opponents. It can be estimated that the under-5 infant deaths in Iraq since commencement of the US onslaught in 1990 (1.6 million) and in Afghanistan since the US invasion in 2001 (1.6 million) total 3.2 million and that US combat deaths have totalled about 3,000 giving an infant death/US combat death ratio of about 1,067 to 1 (2007 data). Compare this to the World War 2 ratio of 1.5 million Jewish children murdered to 3 million Nazi military deaths – a ratio of 0.5 children per Nazi military death.

Of course all of this highly profitable War Economy of the American Empire has had to be "dressed up" and justified in terms redolent of George Orwell's "*1984*"[76] - The War to End all Wars, Civilization versus Barbarism, Freedom versus Monolithic Communism and now the extraordinarily mis-named "War on Terror" (in terms of actual victims a War on Women and Children and a 32 million victim War on Muslims). Yet the US now talks about an "endless war", we are best buddies with all our former European enemies, Communist China is held up as a model of economic pluralism (2007 Anglosphere view) and every dozen days in Iraq alone more innocent children die avoidably in that war-ravaged country as did American civilians on 9/11 (2007 data).

In the domestically peaceful, prosperous, low-mortality Anglo-Celtic world the "intellectual" justification for US war mongering has been the notion of "democratic imperialism" i.e. that the democratic US has a duty to forcibly impose democracy on "uncivilized" countries. This view is rejected by both governments and people in Canada and New Zealand but is supported by the governments of Australia and the UK (but not necessarily by their people, who will nevertheless vote for their war-mongering governments on the basis of other "issues" such as "economic management" and "low home mortgage interest rates").

A corollary to the new kind of civilian-killing, high technology war is the need to "sanitize" both the conduct of war and its reportage.

Normal human beings have a natural revulsion against the killing of other creatures and particularly of human beings. Our extreme reluctance to kill others has presumably been selected evolutionarily as a sensible adaptation for a social existence. It is asserted that a substantial part of post-conflict trauma of soldiers comes from actual direct involvement in killing the enemy on the ground. Accordingly "good" military training (like video war games) involves desensitizing soldiers. However modern technology also "sanitizes" killing by permitting killing from a distance – from Cruise missile-launching ships hundreds of kilometres away or from high altitude bombers.[77]

As explored later in this chapter, the horrendous civilian casualties of modern war have to be minimized for a squeamish metropolitan public. In short, this is variously accomplished by media censorship, journalist and media self-censorship, "embedding" journalists within the military, military PR and non-counting of civilian casualties. When reportage of civilian casualties does occur it is confined to "violent deaths" – the non-violent, "collateral" deaths from war are almost invariably non-reported. Thus the post-invasion avoidable mortality in Iraq totaled about 1.2 million but the post-invasion violent deaths totaled about 1.5 million (2011). Only humane on-the-ground journalists can convey the appalling reality.[78] Arundhati Roy has stated the prevalent reality succinctly: *"The ultimate privilege of the élite is not just their deluxe lifestyles, but deluxe lifestyles with a clear conscience."*[79]

In relation to WW2, there is general acceptance that this was the one war that *had* to be fought because of the racist carnage of the Nazis in Europe against Slavs, Jews and the Roma (Gypsies). Nevertheless many people are extremely uncomfortable about the firebombing of German and Japanese cities and the nuclear destruction of Hiroshima and Nagasaki. The rationalization is that the UK and the US are decent, democratic societies but were forced into the horrors of total war in order to effectively defend human civilization. However this rationalization falls well short of defending the catastrophic annihilation of German and Japanese cities and their civilian populations.

Politically correct racism (PC racism) describes behaviour involving commission of intrinsically racist acts while simultaneously denying any racism and formally opposing racism. Unprovoked invasion and occupation of another country is clearly intrinsically racist. Invading and occupying another country while denying any racism and ignoring the horrendous human consequences to the racially distinct victims constitutes egregious politically correct racism (PC racism).

The US, UK and Australia are PC racist democratic countries that assert their political correctness and non-racism but have acted in a racist way in their unprovoked illegal invasion and occupation of the remote and impoverished country of Iraq. This racism is further evidenced by the comprehensive ignoring of the horrendous human consequences of their racist actions. Thus while denial of the actuality of the Jewish Holocaust is justifiably regarded with extreme disapprobation by Anglo-American and Australian media, academics and politicians, these same people are involved in comprehensive and continuing *ignoring* of the horrendous consequences of Coalition actions in Iraq and Afghanistan.[80] The post-invasion excess mortality in Iraq and Afghanistan in September 2006 totalled 2.5 million and the under-5 infant mortality totalled 2.0 million.

8.11 Killing by default – arms, debt, globalization and economic constraint

Decent people believe that the rich First World should address Third World poverty, disease and attendant low life expectancy by debt relief, helpful trading relations and aid. However before addressing any problem it is important to gather and organize the facts. The facts marshalled in this book make a strong case for First World complicity in and major responsibility for the appalling circumstances of the Third World. Increasing annual *per capita* income would obviously be helpful, but a key question remains: by how much? Inspection of the Tables in Chapter 2 reveals that very good, "European-like" post-1950 outcomes - with both 1950-2005 excess mortality/2005 population and 1950-2005 under-5 infant mortality/2005 population ratios less than 10% - have been achieved in the non-European world despite relatively low annual *per capita* incomes in the range $900-$2,400, namely in Sri Lanka ($930), Paraguay ($1,100), Cuba ($1,170), the Maldives ($2,300) and Fiji ($2,360) (2003 figures).

If we plot survivability versus annual *per capita* income we would expect a sigmoidal (S-shaped) function. Thus at zero income (in cash or kind) there is zero survivability and this continues until some threshold value for minimal survival is exceeded. Thus, at the risk of pedantry, we need about 2 litres of drinking water per day for survival (as well as minimal nutrition) and this has a market value that can be estimated. As income increases, so survivability increases in a quasi-linear fashion. However eventually, as income increases, survivability reaches a near-maximal plateau – thus the avoidable mortality outcome for Portugal (1950-2005 avoidable mortality/2005 population 4.3%, annual *per capita* income $12,130) is actually slightly worse than for Cuba (1950-2005 avoidable mortality/2005 population 4.1%, annual *per capita* income $1,100), even though Cuba's annual *per capita* income is 10 times lower (2005 data).

Inspection of the data in the Tables of Chapter 2 indicates that an annual *per capita* income of as little as $1,000 is necessary (together with other factors such as peace, good administration, preventive medicine, good primary health care and high literacy) for "reasonable" outcomes of the kind found in Eastern Europe countries and indeed in about half the countries of Latin America and the Caribbean. Using the data in Chapter 2, we can estimate how much "wealth" it would cost to achieve an annual *per capita* income of $1,000 for all countries who currently are poorer than this – the grand total is about $1,420 billion or 1.4 times the annual global military expenditure and about 2.6% of total global gross national product. The exact calculations (2007) are presented below.

In 2004 the sum of the gross national products (GNPs) of all countries in the world amounted to $55 trillion ($55 thousand billion) which yields an average *per capita* income for the whole World (population 6 billion) of about $9,200. Using the data tabulated in Chapter 2 we can calculate for every country the amount needed to be "injected" to bring the annual *per capita* income (PCI) up to $1,000. We can then add this up for every region and find the following totals (in billions, bn, of dollars): Eastern Europe ($8.511bn), Latin America and the Caribbean ($8.146bn), East Asia ($12.825bn), South East Asia ($185.620bn), Central Asia ($45.365bn), Arab North Africa and Middle East ($29.232bn), South Asia ($714.666bn), the Pacific ($3.122bn) and Non-Arab Africa ($409.984bn). The total of this notional sum for the World is $1,417.471 billion or 2.6% of globally summed GNPs.

These figures simply establish the magnitude of increased wealth required to lift all Third World countries up to the level of the club of Third World high performers with annual *per capita* incomes of about roughly $1,000 (Sri Lanka, Paraguay and Cuba) (2007). Clearly sustainability arguments indicate that this increased wealth should come from *increased indigenous productivity*. Further, there have been extraordinarily bad outcomes for many countries with annual *per capita* incomes greater than $1,000 (notably in the non-Arab African countries of Botswana, Cape Verde, Gabon, Namibia and South Africa and Swaziland), simply demonstrating that for good outcomes the available resources have to be spent sensibly and other things are also required (peace, high adult literacy, adequate sustenance, preventive medicine and good primary health care).

Nevertheless, in the context of current global annual expenditures of about $1,000 billion on military systems, $1,000 billion on cigarettes, $900 billion on alcohol, $800 billion on illicit drugs and $1 trillion on undesirably processed foods, there is certainly room in the "global economy" for a minimal global safety net, whether this is through aid or humanity-consistent prices for Third World commodities. Indeed these 5 areas of human activity are utterly undesirable, being associated with huge *annual* avoidable mortalities, specifically of 0.6 million (through the continuing war in Iraq and Afghanistan alone), 5 million (tobacco smoking-related causes), 1.8 million (alcohol), 0.2 million (illicit drugs), 0.1 million (opioid drugs, overwhelmingly opium-derived heroin) and millions annually through cardiovascular, diabetic and other complications associated with consumption of inappropriate processed foods (2007 data). A tragic combination of several of these 5 undesirable elements is illustrated by the post-9/11, US-led "War on Terror" as outlined below. [81]

In widely accepted interpretations of Islamic law, all mind-perturbing, addictive and death-dealing consumption, whether of tobacco, alcohol or illicit drugs, is forbidden. Thus alcohol was of course prohibited in Taliban-ruled Afghanistan. In 1997, the fundamentalist Taliban banned all cigarette smokers from Government and military employment. In 2000 the Taliban commenced destroying the lucrative Afghan opium poppy crop, notwithstanding the major contribution of opium to the Afghan economy. Afghan opium production fell from 4,600 tonnes (79% of world production) in 1999 to 200 tonnes (13% of world production) in 2001. However after 9/11 and the US invasion and conquest of Afghanistan, opium production rapidly expanded to 3,400 tonnes (76% of world production) by 2002 and thence to 4,200 tonnes (86% of world production) by 2004.[82] It can be estimated that the US Coalition-restoration of Afghan opium production is linked to 0.5 million global opioid-related deaths since 2001, this huge death toll including (from among countries allied to the US in Afghanistan) 1,200 Scots, 2,000 Australians, 3,000 Canadians, 3,200 Britons and 40,000-60,000 Americans (2007 data).[83]

In relation to a "global village" model involving responsibility for the weak and a notional annual 2.6% of globally summed GDPs to potentially "save" the Third World, it should be noted that health and welfare budgets of the OECD countries are of the order of 10% of GDP. An aid goal of 0.7% of GDP agreed to by 22 rich countries has already been achieved and exceeded by 5 decent countries, namely Norway, Luxembourg, Denmark, Sweden and the Netherlands. Notwithstanding its global hegemony and significant complicity in global avoidable mortality, the US is at the bottom of the list together with Italy, with aid as a percent of GDP being 0.16% and 0.15%, respectively (2007 data).

The tragedy of the global avoidable mortality holocaust is that the annual cost of preventing it is merely a few percent of the annual acquired wealth of the World. Big gains in agricultural food production can be achieved with modest investments in fertilizer, improved varieties, agricultural practices and infrastructure such as dams and roads. Huge gains in health can be achieved *at minimal cost* by comprehensive literacy (and notably female literacy), disease prevention education (notably in relation to hygiene, minimization of disease transmission, mosquito eradication and safe sex in the context of the disastrous HIV epidemics in Africa and Asia), sanitation, clean drinking water, mass vaccination programs, family planning, primary health care and minimally-trained community basic health care workers.

We have seen in Chapters 4-7 how the First World secured world resources through the *clever use of violence*. Latin American secured independence from metropolitan Iberian rule in the 19th century but then succumbed rapidly to continuing US hegemony with power typically exercised by US-linked military and capitalist élites but with explicit post-war occupation by US forces only in Panama and a few Caribbean islands. The avoidable mortality and under-5 infant mortality consequences in "free" Latin America and the Caribbean are generally worse than for Cuba but typically similar to the outcomes for the Soviet Empire countries. However the post-war colonial and post-colonial impacts in Third World Africa, the Pacific, and South, Central and South East Asia are tragically evident (with some notable exceptions such as Mauritius, Réunion, Thailand, the Philippines, Sri Lanka, the Maldives, Fiji and US- or France-linked Pacific island states) (2007 analysis).

The generally poor avoidable mortality outcomes of the Third World countries of Asia, Africa and Pacific Third World countries have been associated with occupation-related economic factors such as entrenched colonial cash crop economies (e.g. for produce such as palm oil, cocoa, coffee, tobacco, tea and lumber); failure of these economies to provide for basic biological need "products" such as adequate nutrition, clean water, sanitation, literacy and primary health care; massive debt run up by corrupt post-colonial military or civilian élite regimes (the 60 poorest countries still owe

about $520 billion from a debt of $540 billion and after payments
of $550 billion; Africa "owes" $300 billion) (2007 data); First
World "buyer's market" prices for Third World commodities
(notably except for OPEC-determined oil prices); regular
perturbation of the "global free market" philosophy by crude First
World invasion to secure resources or convenient resource access
(as with Iraq and Afghanistan); a major and expanding technology
gap between First and Third World countries and major, continuing
perturbation of the "free market" by major national or regional First
World restrictive and subsidy arrangements (e.g. US, EU and East
Asian agricultural subsidies and exclusive free trade agreements).
The minimum, "fair wage" arrangements insisted upon within
Western democracies just do not apply in Third World countries –
a situation of gross immorality and hypocrisy.

Thus a major economic factor involves imposition of draconian
"free market" demands on fragile Third World economies and an
extraordinary concomitant denial of history and of current First
World practices. Major First World economies historically arose
through violent colonialism (that only largely ceased formally in
the immediately post-war decades to be replaced by often violent
neo-colonialism), use of violently obtained capital to fund
industrialization (a process that is still continuing because of First
World global hegemony), and massive protection of metropolitan
industry and agriculture (that still involves subsidies ranging from
state universities to regional free trade arrangements). However
fragile Third World countries, burdened by debt, corruption and
First World-complicit violence, are expected to meet IMF, World
Bank and WTO demands for "level playing fields", and completely
de-regulated free market economies freely accessible by exclusive,
non-compliant and exploitative First World countries. The capital
sources, safety nets, industrial laws and subsidies of the First World
are forbidden to the 3 billion people of the World living on less
than about $2 per day – and as a consequence some 16 million such
people die annually from deprivation-linked causes (2003 data; 7.4
million in 2020).[84]

8.12 Excuses for war and the War on Terror

The most famous excuse for war was the adulterous elopement to
Troy by Helen with Paris (son of King Priam). Helen was the
reputed daughter of Zeus (from Leda or Nemesis), sister of the
Dioscuri, sister of Agamemnon's wife Clytemnestra and wife of
Menelaus, Agamemnon's brother. The Greeks invested Troy and
after Paris was slain Helen married his brother Deiphobus. After
the Trojan Horse deception, the Greeks destroyed Troy (recounted
in Homer's *Iliad* and *Odyssey* and Virgil's *Aeneid*). The actual
Troy in Asia Minor was destroyed by Greeks in about 1250BCE.
Menelaus returned to Sparta with Helen.[85]

A similar Biblical story is that of Dina who was seduced by a
Canaanite. The Hebrews accepted the Canaanites' desire for peace
through assimilatory circumcision. However on the third day, when
the pains were greatest, the Hebrews exterminated all the
Canaanites.[86] In the last analysis war occurs through philosophic
differences (notably state religion), xenophobia, and desire for
resources but a good story appealing to social mores helps
legitimize the appalling human consequences. Of course alleged
atrocities against innocent people has been a traditional winner, and
thus the Christian insistence (until recently) of Jewish
responsibility for the death of Jesus Christ (i.e. Deicide) has been a
core "excuse" for violent anti-Jewish anti-Semitism for 2 millennia.
Just as patriotism is the refuge of scoundrels, so racial bigotry
derives from pathetic, small-minded intolerance of difference or
individuality.[87] The Christian crusades were driven by religiosity
and hatred of the Muslim Saracens but had awful consequences
including the sacking of Christian as well as Muslim cities.[88]

The Black Hole of Calcutta story asserted that after the capture of
Fort William (Calcutta) in 1756, the Nawab of Bengal, Siraj-ud-
daulah, had imprisoned 185 British men and 1 Anglo-Indian
woman in a small room overnight and that only 23 (including the
woman) had survived by morning. The story was clearly highly
exaggerated and hid a contemporary British conspiracy but was
used for 2 centuries to demonize the conquered Indians. Actual,
horrendous and British-imposed "Black Hole" atrocities in India

during the Indian Mutiny (1857) and during troubles in the 1920s have been removed from general public perception in Britain.[89] British excuses for war (rather than negotiation and peace) included "avenging Indian atrocities" (the Indian Mutiny); "avenging the death of General Gordon" (the Sudan War), the asserted "bayoneting of Belgian babies" (WW1) and "stopping Communism" (Korea, Vietnam and Malaya).

The USA has a long record of using "good stories" to promote highly-advantageous wars including "British atrocities" (War of Independence; attempted conquest of Canada and resumption of the previously constrained land-grabbing march West); "Indians scalping prisoners" (genocidal wars against the Indians; conquest of Indian lands); "remember the Alamo" (imperialist wars against Mexico; seizure of Texas, SW North America and California); "the (probably accidental) blowing-up of the USS Maine in Havana harbour" (Spanish-American War; Latin American hegemony and seizure of the Philippines, Guam, Marianas, Puerto Rica and Cuba); "sinking of the Lusitania" that was provocatively loaded with weapons of war in violation of neutrality (US entry into WW1 and World Power emergence); and the "surprise Pearl Harbor attack" that was almost certainly pre-advised by UK and US intelligence and permitted by the US Administration (US entry into WW2 and subsequent world domination).[90]

Post-war "better dead than Red anti-Communism" was the basis for US involvements in the Korean War, Vietnam War, Asian, African and Latin American wars and Star Wars. These involvements led to immense growth of the US military-industrial complex. Specific "good stories" included: "(North) Korean invasion of (South) Korea" (remarkable prescience about which enabled huge US stock exchange profits in soybean futures)[91]; "the (fictitious) Gulf of Tonkin Incident" (2 Vietnamese patrol boats allegedly threatened the US Pacific fleet; the Vietnam War); "(CIA operative) Noriega involved in (CIA-promoted) drug dealing" (Panama Invasion; US re-occupation of the Canal Zone); "threats to some American students" (Grenada Invasion); "freedom, democracy etc" (invasions of Haiti, Panama, Dominican Republic, Grenada and Cuba; US-backed and University of the Americas-trained death squads, terrorists, repressive police, military coup participants and military regimes in Latin America); and "Soviet Communist imperialism" (US-backed mujaheddin and Al Qaeda forces in Afghanistan). [92]

The fall of Russian Communism in 1990 required replacement with new enemies - consult George Orwell's *1984* for a detailed account of why "enemies" are necessary for "freedom" (which is "slavery"), "peace" (= "war") and "strength" (= "ignorance"). The fall of the US-installed and backed Shah of Iran and the rise of Shi'ite fundamentalism provided a real threat to US interests (i.e. to the dollar, to the autocratically-ruled, US-backed Gulf sheikdoms and to the Saudi Arabian kingdom). The bloody Iran-Iraq war represented a major expansion of US military-industrial complex activity in the Middle East – on top of arming both the Israelis and Arabs – and was justified in terms of the "new enemy" of "fanatical Islamic fundamentalism". The anti-fundamentalist and secular dictator, US-backed Saddam Hussein, made an *apparent* error in accepting the US ambassador's declaration of US disinterest and invading Kuwait in 1990. The resultant Sanctions War (1990-2003) and Gulf War (1990-1991) had an immense human cost and was fought on the basis of the "Iraq invasion of Kuwait" (from a racial and cultural if not a legal perspective rather like "North Dakota invades South Dakota") and was decorated with an egregiously false and concocted story, namely "Iraqi soldiers hurled Kuwaiti babies out of humidi-cribs".[93]

The awkward discrepancy between the "fanatical Islamic fundamentalist" (Iranian) and "dangerous Arab dictator" (Iraqi) "threat stories" was finally resolved in the 21st century. Following the 9/11 atrocity in 2001, the US immediately launched the "War on Terror" – 9/11 was blamed on the Afghanistan-based Al Qaeda "fanatical Islamic fundamentalists" but a rapid escalation included Iraq with the utterly false complaint of complicity through (non-existent) Al Qaeda connections. The evidently pre-planned invasion of Afghanistan commenced rapidly with the justifying "story" of "Afghanistan failure to hand over (the formerly US funded) Osama bin Laden" (however sensible, peaceful negotiations would no doubt have secured this and indeed the Taliban agreed to hand him over to a third party). The manifest falsity of the "Iraq-Al Qaeda links" story meant that the US spent over a year advancing a plethora of other false "stories" based on the "dangerous Arab dictator" scenario, namely "Iraqi possession of weapons of mass destruction, mobile germ warfare laboratories, ability to strike the West in 45 minutes, uranium supplies from Niger etc etc". Three years (and 0.5 million avoidable deaths later) these "stories" were shown to be utterly false and the Iraqi reality is now one of a pro-Iranian fundamentalist Shi'ite Muslim political majority, secular Kurdish autonomy, secular Sunni disempowerment, hated US occupation and a combination of secular Ba'athist Sunni and "fundamentalist" Shi'ite, Sunni and Al-Qaeda-type insurgency ("terrorism").[94]

The "Star Wars" "story" of missiles, anti-missiles and anti-anti-missiles lost a lot of its plausibility when the Russians decided that they just couldn't afford to be players in this kind of *ostensible* lunacy. However the "War on Terror" has now been established as an ongoing, potentially "endless" war. After the comprehensive demonstration of the falsehood of US-Coalition pre-war lies about Iraq, the new "story" is one of "democratic imperialism"- the moral obligation of civilized, democratic countries like the US, the UK and their mostly democratic allies to impose democracy on the uncivilized Muslim World. The reality so far has been horrendous loss of life (excess mortality in Iraq and Afghanistan now totalling 2.9 million and 4.2 million, respectively), US backing of pro-US dictatorships, and acute US-Israeli threats to two of the very few Muslim "democracies", namely Lebanon and Iran. The anti-democratic theocratic veto over democracy in Iran demands comparison with "big money" corporate domination of US "democracy".

The ostensible basis for the US-led "War on Terror" was 9/11, an immense atrocity that shocked people around the world (who are nevertheless unmoved by the 44,000 global avoidable deaths that occurred *each day* (2007; 20,000 per day in 2020) (Tables 8.1 and 9.1). However there are reasonable *a priori* grounds for *suspicion* over the official US account of 9/11, namely the immense post-9/11 benefits to US imperialism (an extra $500 billion profits to the US military-industrial complex, global spread of US hegemony and substantial military occupation in the Middle East and Central Asia), and egregious lying by the US and Coalition Governments prior to the invasion of Iraq. Notwithstanding mainstream media hysteria and compliance with the lying Bush "official version of 9/11", alternative views have slowly gathered momentum with prominent, "mainstream" doubters including Dr Paul Craig Roberts and David Griffin. The alternative views (which have growing acceptance in disparate places in the West, including New York, Canada and France) range from criticism of the extraordinary US intelligence and air force failure to prevent the attacks to suggestions of active US complicity. Scholars for 9/11 truth (S9/11T) is an organization of US academics dedicated to rational, scholarly and scientific approaches to the actual truth of what happened on 9/11.[95]

The official story involved 2 planes being hijacked and hitting the Twin Towers which subsequently totally collapsed, as did the adjacent 40 storey WTC building 7; a 3rd plane crashing into the side of the Pentagon; and a 4th plane crashing in Pennsylvania. Major problems with the official "story" include hijacking with box-cutters; no survivors; extremely inexperienced hijacker pilots hitting the WTC buildings; important evidence consistent with planned demolition of the three WTC buildings (especially the 47 storey WTC7 building that had not been hit by a plane and did not have major fires); asserted mobile phone calls from high speed planes at high altitude; inexperienced light plane pilots flying a huge jet (with a core height of about 2 stories) just above the ground to hit the Pentagon exactly between the first and second floors; and the comprehensive failure of the air force to respond to *any* of the four off-course planes (notwithstanding decades of such rapid responses).[96]

These difficulties were compounded by evidence of stock market put options in WTC-9/11-related stocks; the notorious unconcern of Bush in the Florida kindergarten; the Saudi efflux from the USA while all other planes were grounded; the rapid implementation of the evidently pre-prepared, detailed civil rights-abusing and ostensibly "anti-terrorist" Patriot Act, and plans for invasion of Afghanistan; and plans for propagandizing enabling of the invasion of Iraq. Multiply bitten and multiply shy, the world is becoming increasingly critical of US "stories", informed by critical analyses from people such as Professor David Ray Griffin, Dr Paul Craig Roberts and others, including scientists such as Professor Steven Jones, Professor Niels Harrit and Dr Frank Legge.[97]

Indeed careful analysis has shown that the Bush Administration told 935 lies about Iraq between 9/11 and the invasion of Iraq. A similar accounting has shown that Donald Trump told 25,000 false statements during his administration.

An interesting statistical approach has been to assign a probability of 0.1 (10%) to each of a total of 22 somewhat unlikely contingent, successive parts of the extraordinary "official" story about 9/11 e.g. that a steel-reinforced building will completely mimic expert demolition after a limited fire or that a minimally light aircraft-trained pilot could fly a huge passenger jet into a spot between the first and second floors on the side of the Pentagon. The probability of the overall "official" story being correct then becomes an astronomically low 10^{-22} i.e. the "official" story is almost certainly *false*.[98]

2021 update: A team of scientists from the University of Copenhagen led by Professor Niels Harrit have demonstrated using the latest chemical physics techniques that all samples examined of the WTC dust to which these 3 huge buildings were "magically" reduced in about 10 seconds contain unexploded nanothermite high explosive particles. A recent detailed report by engineers from the University of Alaska, Fairbanks, found that Building WTC7 could not have been destroyed by fire as asserted by the US Government but must have been destroyed by precise and simultaneous explosive demolition.

A similar estimation can be made of the probability that *all* of the approximately 10 major US pre-war assertions about Iraq were merely "mistakes made in good faith" by the most all-seeing intelligence system in history, and assigning a probability of 0.1 to the "good faith" basis of each untruth e.g. Iraqi possession of weapons of mass destruction, poison gas supplies, bacteriological weapons, mobile germ warfare laboratories, Al Qaeda links, uranium supplies from Niger, ability to strike the West within 45 minutes, dire threat to the US, dire threat to the UK, and responsibility for 9/11. The probability that *all* of these assertions were simply "mistakes made in good faith" (rather than being egregious lies) is then a vanishingly small 10^{-10} i.e. the US and its allies were *lying*.

Another approach to assessing the hysterical lying and deception associated with the "War on Terror" is to actually quantitate the "empirical probability" expressed as "percentage annual mortality" for a variety of mortality events. Thus 5,000 Western civilians have been murdered by Muslim-origin terrorists or Arab insurgents over the last 20 years out of a total population of about 760 million Westerners, this corresponding to a "percentage annual mortality" of 0.00003%. It is instructive to compare the following "percentage annual mortality" statistics: 0.00003% (Western civilians at the hand of jihadists over the last 20 years); 0.00003% (shark attack); 0.0001% (Western civilians at the hand of jihadists over the last 4 years); 0.001% (death at the hands of family or acquaintances); 0.01% (Americans or Australians from car accidents); 0.1% (Americans or Australians from cigarette smoking-related causes); 0.7% (White Australians); 2.2% (Indigenous Australians); 2.4% (Indigenous Australians in the Northern Territory); 2.5% (sheep in paddocks of Australian sheep farms); 2.7% (Iraqi under-5 year old infants); 5.7% (Afghan under-5 year old infants); 10.4% (Australian prisoners of war under the Japanese in WW2; 8,000 died out of 22,000 over 3.5 years); and 94% (starving Indians in British labour camps in the Deccan Famine in British-ruled India in 1877).[99]

In 2005 Australia introduced draconian anti-terror laws with bipartisan support although only 3 Australians had died in 30 years from a terrorist incident within Australia (3 Australians died in the 1978 Sydney Hilton Hotel bombing but a policeman survivor has claimed that Australian Security were likely to have been responsible; a security guard was murdered by a right-to-life fanatic several years ago). However, some 2,000 Australians had died from opioid drug-related causes since 9/11, largely due to US

Coalition restoration of the Afghan opium industry that had been largely destroyed by the Taliban. A surprising feature of the bipartisan political and media Australian "terror hysteria" campaign that resulted in overwhelming public support for intrinsically racist and human rights-violating "anti-terror" legislation was the absence of any *quantitative assessment* of the (no doubt real) "terrorist threat". The approximate empirical annual probability of a person dying in Australia is about 1 in 1,000,000 (from a Muslim-origin terrorist attack), 1 in 100,000 (at the hand of a relative or acquaintance), 1 in 10,000 (from a car accident) and 1 in 1,000 (from smoking). These estimates were reported to a Senate Inquiry but failed to get through the "media gate" in the Wall of Silence – the Anglo-American mainstream media won't even report the US-linked avoidable deaths of their *own citizens* (2007 estimates).[100]

A major area of deception and double standards exists in relation to Israel. There are two histories of Israel – the truly heroic, romantic, David and Goliath history accepted by most ordinary Jews, Israelis, Westerners and Western-educated others[101] and another equally real and true history involving massive militarization, military nuclearization, racism, war, dispossession, colonial occupation, mass terror, disinformation and horrendous excess mortality and excessive subject Arab infant mortality.[102] Israel is now a key part of the US War economy and a major arms producer in its own right.

Just as the relatively ineffectual Muslim-origin "terrorism" directed against the US has led to a huge expansion of US power throughout the Muslim world, so Arab resistance to Israeli conquest has continually led to even greater Israeli abuses. Indeed the personal history of Ariel Sharon illustrates this point - notably his involvement in past Israeli military aggression, the Lebanon occupation, the Sabra and Shatila massacres in Israeli-occupied Beirut, the Al Aksa mosque violation, horrendous abuses in the Occupied Palestinian Territories and pro-active cooperation with genocidal, racist US policy in the Middle East. Remarkably ineffective Muslim-origin and Arab insurgent violence and terrorism has played into the hands of the vastly more violent and destructive Israeli, UK and US state terrorism – to the extent that it is now very reasonable to ask to what extent these Western powers have been responsible for *supporting* as well as *provoking* Muslim-origin terrorism. Indeed the jhadis are empirically the best US Alliance assets because every jihadi atrocity provides an "excuse" for US Alliance invasion and disproportionate violence.

Anglo-American-dominated global media have fervently drummed up hysteria about the conspicuously ineffectual Muslim-origin and Palestinian terrorists - while ignoring the immense benefits to the US military-industrial complex, to related military-commercial establishments in the UK and Israel, and to illegal and immoral extensions of US, UK and Israeli power. The benefits of Muslim-origin terrorism have been so huge that direct US, UK and Israeli complicity is a compelling proposition for which there is considerable evidence in the public domain. Thus, for example, Al Qaeda was supported by the West in Afghanistan for a decade. The Israeli Shin Bet (Internal Intelligence) supported the nascent Hamas as a fundamentalist counter to secular Palestinian resistance organizations. Anglo-American media steadfastly ignore the horrendous human cost of this egregious "war for profit"- and any dissenters risk labelling as anti-Semitic, sympathetic to "terrorism" or "enemies of freedom". Nevertheless peace *is* possible. Thus one "interim solution" for the Holy Land that could be implemented *immediately* could involve the following key elements - 2 formally independent states within defined borders; return to the 1967 borders and removal of all settlements; Palestinian disarmament and "total airport-level security" provided everywhere by Israel alone on an interim basis (as in 1967); internationally-guaranteed civil and human rights for all; reconciliation and abolition of racism and incitement; and unhindered access to essentially all parts of an extremely secure, peaceful and prosperous Holy Land for all of its inhabitants.[103]

2021 update: Apartheid Israel has now ethnically cleansed 90% of Palestine, thus rendering a "2-state solution", "interim" or otherwise, impossible. In 2018 I wrote: "The "two-state solution" has been a convenient fig-leaf for pro-Apartheid Western dishonesty and inaction over Palestine. The ethnic cleansing of

90% of Palestine has rendered the "two-state solution" dead but the continuing obscenity of a grossly human rights-abusing Apartheid Israel is intolerable to decent people around the world. However the racist Jewish Nation-State Law makes it abundantly clear that the racist Zionists running Apartheid Israel are resolutely committed to a neo-Nazi Apartheid State and endless, deadly subjugation of the Indigenous Palestinians with the ever-present threat of 100% ethnic cleansing of Palestine. The world must act over Apartheid Israel as it did over Apartheid South Africa. A clear, humane solution to the continuing human rights catastrophe in Palestine is a unitary state (a "one state solution") as in post-Apartheid South Africa that would involve return of all refugees, zero tolerance for racism, equal rights for all, all human rights for all, one-person-one-vote, justice, goodwill, reconciliation, airport-level security, nuclear weapons removal, internationally-guaranteed national security initially based on the present armed forces, and untrammelled access for all citizens to all of Palestine. It can and should happen tomorrow".

One measure of the human cost of Israel in this wider geo-political sense can be gauged from the post-1950 excess mortality and under-5 infant mortality in Israel's immediate neighbours, namely 24 million and 17 million, respectively. If we include more distant targets of Israeli armed aggression, e.g. Iraq, Libya, Tunisia, Sudan, Turkey, Uganda, and indeed the US, these figures expand to 43 million and 29 million, respectively. While Israel is clearly *complicit* in this carnage (and of course it takes 2 to tango), a clear estimate of direct Israeli *responsibility* derives from the post-1967 avoidable mortality and under-5 infant mortality in the Occupied Palestinian Territories that now total about 0.3 million and 0.2 million, respectively (2007 data). Thus the 1950-2005 excess mortality/2005 population ratio is 7.3% for Israel but 17.7% for the Occupied Palestinian Territories and the corresponding 1950-2005 under-5 infant mortality/2005 population ratios are 1.4% (for Israel) and 7.7% (for the Occupied Palestinian Territories). It has been estimated that the cost of Israel to the US has been $3 trillion.[104]

8.13 Feminist perspective - right to life, women and allo-mothering

Women typically represent a slight excess over males in any human population but this majority (normally sufficient to guarantee a clear victory in proper democracies) has not been generally reflected in political power. Male social dominance has derived from the evolution of the dominant male among highly social primates and the realities of might-means-right male physical superiority, male skills specialization in game acquisition and defence, and male group bonding in such activities. Of course Man has evolved socially not only through the selection of *genes* (DNA shuffled and transmitted through meiotic recombination in gametogenesis and sexual reproduction) but also through the transmission of socially-powerful *memes* - ideas or practices that are transmitted by example, words or symbolic records (art, music, pictograms, writing and ultimately the binary code and computer programs).[105]

Nevertheless, even in the most ostensibly repressive societies, women have their areas of prime responsibility. Further, matriarchy was not confined to the semi-mythological classical and South American Amazons. Thus there have been many female rulers and matriarchy is entrenched in Malay and Indonesian societies - thus the female-ruled Acinese were very impressed to learn from the first East India Company visitors in about 1602 that England was ruled by the unmarried Queen Elizabeth I. Female suffrage in democracies was first secured in Australia and the USA and (remarkably) was only secured in Switzerland in 1971. However one-man-one-vote even in long-term democracies is a patent fiction given the immense power of (male-dominated) corporations and the corporate mainstream media in particular (who have, of course, suppressed public perception of this palpable reality).

Thomas Jefferson had an Afro-American mistress-slave and generated "white" and "black" descendants (who are of course both very proud of their heritage). We should therefore amend the great Jeffersonian statement in the American Declaration of Independence to assert (my addition in italics) that all men *and women* are created equal and have the unalienable right to life, liberty and the pursuit of happiness. In the 21st century there is general lip-service acceptance of the UN Declaration of Human Rights and the equal rights of women. However as set out in this book about 100 million people have died avoidably so far this century (2007), about half have been female and about 60% have been helpless infants under the age of 5.[106]

One of the worst things that can happen to a woman (and indeed to anyone) is the death of a child. I know. Yet around the world about 29,000 infants under the age of 5 die *each day* and about 90% of this mortality is *avoidable* (2007 data). We live in a crowded world and are now used to virtually monthly mass human mortality events such as hurricanes and earthquakes involving hundreds to thousands of deaths and, on a roughly annual basis, even more horrendous events involving the death of tens of thousands. While the right to life of *unborn* infants is a major Catholic and US Religious Right political obsession, the continuing *daily* demise throughout the world of 35,000 infants and the grievous loss to 35,000 mothers and 70,000 parents is simply not reported (2007 data). This callous disregard of largely avoidable infant deaths reveals the extent of global hypocrisy about human rights, women's rights and the right to life of *born* infants. As briefly outlined below it also illustrates *de facto* departure from a fundamental human (and indeed primate) ethic of general care and regard for infants and mothers.

A fundamental behaviour exhibited by many primate species, including *Homo sapiens* (Man), is "allo-mothering" or care for others' infants. Among females allo-mothering is "aunt behaviour" - females without children (and indeed females in general) will care for the children of other females. The evolution of parental altruistic behaviour has been analysed in terms of enhanced survival of the progeny and hence increased probability of the parental genes being passed on to future generations. Parental altruism is most commonly observed with mothers but paternal altruism is often exhibited in longer-range activities e.g. the risky acquisition of protein-rich meat and defence of the family or the wider social group.[107] Allo-mothering would increase the survival of genetically-related children in a small primate band and would also increase survivability by "training" females through "hands-on" practice of child-rearing skills. Disregard by *women* of the global infant mortality holocaust involves an extraordinary general departure from a fundamental female ethos of care for the children of others.

Of course most women of the World are unaware of the magnitude of the global infant mortality holocaust and those that are aware are limited in what they can do because of the entrenched lying by omission and commission of corporate mainstream media. Nevertheless there are women (and men) who *can* get through the mainstream media "gate" as politicians, celebrities and journalists – and equal opportunity has greatly increased the proportion of women in such groups. Silence kills and silence is complicity. However some prominent female politicians and officials have gone well beyond mere complicity and have a major responsibility for mass infant mortality. As Peter Singer has stated *"We are responsible not only for what we do but for what we could have prevented".*[108]

In 1996 Madeleine Albright, a former US Secretary of State and US UN Ambassador during the child-killing Sanctions War against Iraq (1990-2003 Iraq under-5 infant mortality 1.2 million) was directly asked on "60 Minutes" by Leslie Stahl: "I understand that 500,000 Iraqi children have died due to our sanctions … was it worth it?" Albright notoriously replied: "The price was worth it". Condoleezza Rice, the former US Secretary of State, was a woman uniquely involved in the US invasions of Iraq and Afghanistan (total post-invasion under-5 infant mortality 2.0 million in 2007). These powerful women, by virtue of their positions and through action and inaction, are complicit in and variously responsible for the death of millions of infants and have accordingly departed from the fundamental *primate* ethos of allo-mothering. Their only excuse is that the silence of society - and of mainstream media in particular - has permitted their complicity in passive mass murder. In the British system, Her Majesty Elizabeth II as a constitutional figure-head is not responsible for the actions of her Ministers in the UK or in other countries of which she is the formal Head of State. Yet *half the voters are women* in Great Britain and the downside of the glorious New Elizabethan Age has been a total 1950-2005 excess mortality totalling 740 million and a total 1950-2005 under-5 infant mortality of about 0.5 billion in those countries occupied at any time by the UK as a major occupier in the post-war era (Chapter 3).

8.14 Academic, media, political and sectarian lying

Fundamental to any sensible, scientific approach to a problem is *truthfulness* as it applies both to the data itself and to honest analysis of the data. Lying about the data can be by omission (white-washing, rubbing out, deletion or non-reportage) or by commission (deliberate transmission of falsehoods). Lying by omission is clearly entrenched in corporate mainstream media and is deeply insidious. Thus lying by commission can be directly countered by the truth whereas comprehensive lying by omission largely pre-empts such debate.

The human cost of the continuing Coalition wars in Iraq and Afghanistan is surely a fundamentally important matter for public discussion. The UNICEF report (2006) estimates that 1,300 under-5 year old infants are dying in Occupied Iraq and Afghanistan every day (0.5 million per year) – and this is happening because of the non-provision by the Occupying Coalition of the life-preserving requisites demanded by the Geneva Conventions. Yet these publicly-available statistics are comprehensively non-reported by Anglo-American and Australia mainstream media, informed public debate is stifled and the carnage continues, 1,300 kids today, 1,300 kids tomorrow ...

Dishonest analysis in public life (notably over current, violent US foreign policies) typically involves many logic-abusing stratagems e.g. outright lies (WMDs); "slies" (spin-based untruths e.g. Iraq would like to have WMDs and therefore must have them in some form); *ad hominem* pejorative assertions, abuse and defamation (attacking persons rather than counter-arguments e.g. demonizing Iran, Saddam Hussein, peaceniks); *ad hominem* abuse of specific peacenik opponents via rhetorical questions (do you support dictatorships?); *ad hominem* abuse by demand (prove that you are not a racist, fascist etc); irrelevant appeals (to fear, greed, pity, conformism, tradition, religion, popular perception, hysteria, historical or racial origins and myth e.g. "defend our freedom from terrorists"); begging the question (circular arguments with prior assumption of the final conclusion e.g. there are actually no WMDs but the US will give Iraqis democracy); confusing cause and effect (confusing correlation and coincidence with causality e.g. Al Qaeda and some Iraqis are fundamentalist Muslims and therefore "anything goes"); assumption that what is true for a part is true for the whole (e.g. "Iraq did have war gases and therefore still has them"); false dilemmas (failing to present alternative options e.g. negotiations rather than war); equivocation (deceptive and incorrect use of language e.g. "War on Terror"); guilt by association (e.g. "some fundamentalist Muslims are terrorists and therefore all are"); non-sequiturs (assertions that do not actually follow from the argument or the evidence e.g. complicity in 9/11 adduced by false claims of Iraq-Al Qaeda links); red herrings (deceptive introduction of irrelevant matters e.g. alleged sexual violations by élite Iraqis); special pleading (double standards applying e.g. to Americans but not to others); straw man arguments (misleading and weakly relevant propositions e.g. Iraqis would like democracy and would therefore welcome invasion); assumed knowledge of interlocutors' or opponents' intentions ("the terrorists want to destroy our freedom"); and scientifically-unacceptable attempts to prove a negative (e.g. "there is no evidence that Iraq does not have weapons of mass destruction".

People who live in liberal Western democracies have great trouble dealing with the veritable mountain of deceit dished out to them each day. In contrast, many people living in explicitly repressive environments such as the former Soviet Union were supposedly well aware of the lies and "slies". The *tolerance* of deceit and lying by politicians and media has compounded the problem. Just as we talk of "compassion exhaustion" because of too many demands on our philanthropy, so we now are faced with "truth exhaustion" in dealing with the endless lying and deception. Indeed new words (neologisms) are needed to cope with the new kind of spin-based deception. As illustrated above, I have advanced the term "slying" (spin-based lying or untrue assertion) and hence "sliars slying by telling slies). A variant of this is required for the English Establishment habit of deception by blathering, namely "blying" (or blather-based lying or untrue assertion) and hence "bliars blying by telling blies".[109]

Lying by omission and commission are frequently dismissed cynically by statements such as "the victor writes history" and "the papers publish what their bosses want" but there is a deadly serious side to lying when it relates to mass mortality. The sheer evil, remorselessness, racial-specific and all-encompassing horror of the Jewish Holocaust has set an important standard for moral responsiveness largely because of the determination of the survivors and other Jews that this horrendous atrocity should never be forgotten and should never happen again. It is illegal to deny the Jewish Holocaust in a range of countries (Austria, France, Germany, Israel and Switzerland) and "Holocaust denial" is regarded as utterly repugnant. However there is a moral generality arising from the Jewish Holocaust that is summarized by the acronym CAAAA (C4A), namely the need for Cessation of the mass murder and post-holocaust Acknowledgement, Apology, Amends and Assertion of non-repetition by those complicit. Germany has met *all* these C4A requirements in relation to its responsibility for the Jewish Holocaust - but for *other* contemporary holocausts the World has not got to the first stage of Cessation let alone Acknowledgement.[110] Indeed in Turkey it recently became *illegal* to admit to the actuality of the horrendous 1915-1923 Armenian Genocide (1.5 million victims) or to demand Turkish military withdrawal from Cyprus. In contrast, Belgium legislated in 2005 to make *denial* of the Armenian Genocide illegal.[111]

As outlined in Chapter 1, the man-made Bengal Famine in British-ruled India killed 6-7 million people and involved the famine-enforced sexual violation of possibly hundreds of thousands of women and girls.[112] It has been suggested that this man-made catastrophe may have been part of a scorched earth policy to defend India from the Japanese.[113] Yet this appalling cataclysm has become a "forgotten holocaust" that has been generally deleted from British history and from general public perception – an immense academic and political scandal that continues to be kept well under wraps by the entrenched dishonesty of the presstitutes of British academia, media and politics. None of the As of C4A have yet been met by the British over this immense WW2 atrocity. Thus Churchill's lengthy, 6-volume and authoritative *The Second World War* (which helped win him the 1953 Nobel Prize for Literature) contains no mention of the disaster he helped to create; indeed the following excerpt implicitly denies the actuality of the 2.4 million Indians who served in the Allied forces in WW2 and actually states the categorical reverse of the horrendous famine reality: "*No great portion of the world population was so effectively protected from the horrors and perils of the World War as were the people of Hindustan. They were carried through the struggle on the shoulders of our small island.*"[114]

For all that Bengal suffered horrendously at the hands of the British over 2 centuries and provided a significant dollop of the cash that drove the British Industrial Revolution, it is on the other side of the World and inhabited by non-English-speaking, non-Christian, non-Europeans. However Ireland is a mere 10 kilometres from the Mull of Kintyre in Western Scotland and it is instructive to see how British atrocities in Ireland have been minimized and indeed deleted. Ruin of the Irish potato crop by the fungal potato blight (*Phytophthora infestans*) precipitated the Irish Potato famine of 1845-1850 which killed 1 million, forced 1.5 million to emigrate (many dying in transit or on penniless arrival in hostile lands) and was associated with an 1841-1851 Irish demographic deficit of 3 million. The public servant who supervised this disaster was one Charles Edward Trevelyan who scorned both his own Celtic Cornish origins and the Irish. The Irish starved to death while grain was being exported from Ireland by their English masters. [115]

Trevelyan's comment on the Irish population and the effects of the famine are chilling: "*This being altogether beyond the power of man, the cure has been applied by the direct stroke of an all-wise Providence in a manner as unexpected and as unthought of as it is likely to be effectual*".[116] However Trevelyan's grandson, G.M. Trevelyan, Master of Trinity College and Regius Professor of History at Cambridge University, in his classic *History of England* allowed himself the following few words on the Irish famine as something *avoided* by English decency, in utter perversion of historical reality: *"and partly because of the potato-blight in Ireland in 1845-6 left him* [Prime Minister Peel] *no other choice than either to suspend the Corn Laws or to allow the Irish to die by tens of thousands."*[117] In 1997 British Prime Minister Tony Blair (perhaps prompted by his Irish Catholic-origin wife) Acknowledged and Apologized for the Irish famine. However the other elements of C4A have not been met – the UK is complicit in a world order that avoidably kills 44,000 people each day around the First World-dominated world, and is part of the US-led Coalition responsible for 1,200 avoidable under-5 year old infant deaths daily in Occupied Iraq and Afghanistan (2007 data).

Numerous other examples can be given of evil holocaust-denial. However the most appalling examples in a quantitative sense derive from the 21st century. Arguably one of the *worst lies* in history was the pre-invasion lie of Iraqi possession of weapons of mass destruction. This and a related set of lies were used by the US and its Coalition partners to justify the illegal invasion of Iraq that has (2007) been associated with 0.5 million avoidable deaths and 0.3 million under-5 infant deaths. On the other hand, surely the *greatest crime* in human history has been the post-1950 global avoidable mortality that totals 1.3 billion people and includes an avoidable under-5 infant mortality component of about 0.8 billion (2007). Yet how have these events been reported by mainstream English-language media? One way of approaching this is to do a Google search for relevant terms. Thus a search for the phrase "weapons of mass destruction" coupled with "Iraq" yields 11 million URLs. On the other hand, "under-5 infant mortality" is a key parameter used by UNICEF to assess and compare the health of the countries of the World. A Google search for "under-5 infant mortality" yields a mere 500 URLs (2007). Thus an immensely destructive *lie* has received saturation coverage from media whereas the greatest avoidable catastrophe in human history has been overwhelmingly *ignored*.[118]

Resorting to the *standard* of the Jewish Holocaust, it is readily seen that denial of this event would constitute egregious and racist holocaust-denial. The continuing denial of avoidable mortality that is quantitatively 100 times greater than the Jewish Holocaust is clearly repugnant and racist. The extraordinary collective amnesia currently afflicting academia, politicians, public figures and media over avoidable mortality in Iraq and Afghanistan is permitting continuation of immense passive genocide that constitutes a major war crime. Unfortunately we must draw the conclusion that racist lying by omission is entrenched in the great Anglo-Celtic democracies – it is the *rule* rather than the *exception* and simply demonstrates the politically correct racism (PC racism) of these societies. This denial is the subject of analysis in Whiteness Studies now taught at a number of major US universities.

A final example of Anglo-American media lying by omission is even more astonishing than the foregoing because while one can understand the ignoring of the deaths of foreigners (especially if your own kind are responsible), it is very hard to believe that editors and journalists would utterly ignore the fate of their *own* people. Thus while the British media and historians and politicians overwhelmingly ignore the WW2 man-made famine in British-ruled Bengal (6-7 million victims), Jewish people have quite rightly made absolutely certain that nobody would forget the WW2 Jewish Holocaust (5-6 million victims). The 0.5 million global 2001-2007 opioid drug deaths occurred largely because of the US Coalition invasion of Afghanistan and the subsequent restoration of the world-dominating Afghan opium industry that had been almost wiped out by the Taliban. Yet mainstream Anglo-American media, while repeatedly apprised, have resolutely refused to report the 2001-2007 opioid drug-related deaths of 1,200 Scots, 2,000 Australians, 3,000 Canadians, 3,200 Britons and 50,000 Americans.[119]

Numerous examples of resolute academic lying by omission can be given of which one of the more serious is racist holocaust denial over the WW2 Bengal Famine in numerous British historical works. Media lying by omission appears to be *de rigeur* in relation to major mortality events that detract from national good name (e.g. the 6-7 million deaths of the WW2 Bengal Famine and the 2.5 million post-invasion avoidable deaths in the Occupied Iraqi and

Afghan Territories) (2007 estimate). This deliberately-induced collective amnesia simply over-rides any sensible public analysis of major mortality events, and simply ensures their repetition. Reference to the example of the Jewish Holocaust clearly establishes the evil and racism implicit in such holocaust-denying lying by omission.

Chalk and Jonassohn in *"The History and Sociology of Genocide"* conclude: *"Our review of history of genocide and its neglect has led us to the conclusion that until very recently scholars participated in a process of pervasive and self-imposed denial. Many factors entered into this process of collective denial. Throughout most of recorded time, it was the victors who wrote the history of their conquests, and even the victims of mass exterminations accepted their fate as a natural outcome of defeat."* [120]

Comprehensive denial in a society is a fearful circumstance that permits continuing abuses of human rights by simply resolutely ignoring them. Silence kills and silence is complicity - as illustrated by the tardiness of the world to recognize the actuality of the Jewish Holocaust. Polish hero Jan Karski went to the West with harrowing accounts of the Warsaw Ghetto and concentration camps and tried to tell an unbelieving world. It was not until 17 December 1942, a mere 30 months before the end of the war in Europe, that the Allied Governments finally formally admitted the reality of the systematic extermination of the Jews in a statement read to the British House of Commons by Anthony Eden in response to a question put by Sidney Silverman, M.P. and reporting these Allied Governments' intelligence of: *"numerous reports from Europe that the German authorities, not content with denying to persons of Jewish race in all the territories over which their barbarous rule has been extended the most elementary rights, are now carrying into effect Hitler's oft-repeated intention to exterminate the Jewish people in Europe ... None of those taken away are ever heard of again. The able-bodied are slowly worked to death in labour camps. The infirm are left to die of exposure and starvation or are deliberately massacred in mass executions. The number of victims of these bloody cruelties is reckoned in many hundreds of thousands of entirely innocent men, women and children*".[121]

It is difficult to assess how many Jews would have been saved if the World had been more responsive to all the evidence at hand from the time of accession to power of the Nazis in 1933 and particularly from the start of mass murder of Jews from 1941 onwards. Laqueur has carefully addressed this question in his carefully researched and damning testament *"The Terrible Secret. Suppression of the Truth about Hitler's "Final Solution"* - but he also comments that *"The ideal time to stop Hitler was not when he was at the height of his strength"*.[122] Fundamentally, *ignoring* racism, racist threats and racist murder inexorably permitted the Jewish Holocaust to happen. Silence kills and silence is complicity. It can be reasonably asserted as a generality that it pays to be extremely alert and alarmed at the first sign of trouble.

A personal family story about *rational risk assessment* may assist here. My paternal great-grandfather Jakab Pollák was born of Mózes and Janka (née Diamant) Pollák in the small Hungarian town of Békésszentandrás as one of 10 children. It seems likely that he had uncles and aunts with large families. Jakab was a lawyer and economist and made a sensible decision - based on economic necessity and observation of Eastern European nationalism and anti-Jewish anti-Semitism - to Hungarify his name in 1882 from the Jewish-indicating Pollák (meaning "from Poland") to the similar-sounding Hungarian Pólya (a swaddling cloth).[123] By 1939 one can estimate that there would have been about 100 relatives of my father's generation in this line from Jakab Pollák and his siblings – and perhaps another 100 deriving from the other related Pólláks from Békésszentandrás. In 1939 my father and 2 other siblings fled Hungary (a remaining sibling hid successfully from the Nazis with her mother). By 1945 there were only 6 survivors out of this estimated 100 in my father's generation, namely my father, his siblings and 2 cousins. Because Pólya is a very rare (if famous) name, in 2004 we discovered that 2 other Pólyas in my father's generation had also fled Hungary just before the war – they had a tradition of being related to "us" (indeed my famous surgeon grandfather had performed a "Pólya gastrectomy" on their father in about 1920), they had changed their name from Pollák to Pólya in the early 1920s and are accordingly likely to be survivors of the "other" related Polláks of Békésszentandrás. It appears that as a result of *informed risk assessment*, 2 vigorous and talented Pollák/Pólya lines have survived - albeit scattered across the world - despite the horrendous extermination of a very large and energetic family.

Not only millions of Jews died avoidably because of resolute *ignoring* of the evidence to hand. C.P. Snow's classic *"Science and Government"* relates the scientifically flawed war-time decision-making that led to the diversion of Allied air war efforts from the protection of Atlantic shipping to the bombing of German population centres. This decision involved Churchill taking the advice of his "pet" scientist Dr Lindeman (later Lord Cherwell) to the exclusion of numerous eminent physicists and almost cost the Allies the war in the Atlantic (fortunately for the war effort his pre-war advice *against* the development of radar was *not* taken). Personalities aside, this saga illustrates the continuing problem of non-scientist politicians simply not understanding the fundamentals of the scientific process.[124] As explained by Karl Popper, science is about testing potentially falsifiable hypotheses. However, as well illustrated by the post-9/11 conduct of the UK and US Administrations over "Iraqi weapons of mass destruction" and other untruths, typical politicians incompetently seek expert advice and evidence that support their causes and ignore testimony opposing or even invalidating their positions. (Thus in the 21st century, the late Dr Kelly tried to tell the UK Government about non-existence of Iraqi biological WMDs; Captain Andrew Wilkie resigned and went public just before the outbreak of the Iraq War over Australian Government "spin" ignoring intelligence of no evidence for WMDs; and Dr John Gee tried in vain to tell the Australian Government post-invasion that he and his colleagues had not been able to find evidence of Iraqi WMDs). However the Churchill/Lindeman bombing decision also had catastrophic consequences for distant Bengal. In the words of historian A.J.P.Taylor: *"A million and a half Indians died of starvation for the sake of a white man's quarrel in North Africa."* [125]

The consequences of the Churchill/Lindeman bombing position can be conveniently summarized by the following "causal pathway": ignoring of alternative scientific advice –> massive bombing of German cities –> deficient air protection for Atlantic shipping –> huge shortage of Allied shipping –> massive reduction by Churchill of Indian Ocean Allied shipping (Casablanca, 1943) –> further decrease in grain imports to India–> contribution to grain price inflation –> major contribution (with other factors including *sangfroid* military strategic policy) to the Bengal Famine –> 6-7 million Hindu and Muslim deaths –> overwhelming deletion of the Bengal Famine from British history and hence from general public perception –> informational and moral vacuum –> Bengal under threat from further man-made disasters (notably inundation from global warming, sea level rise, super-hurricanes and storm surges –> much of Bangladesh inundated by excessive monsoon run-off in recent years.[126] After the worst hurricane season ever in the Gulf of Mexico and the New Orleans Hurricane Katrina tragedy, the generally practical Americans are already showing much greater preparedness to discard neo-conservative denial about global warming.

8.15 Conclusions and suggestions – how to save the world

This book has documented and analysed potentially avoidable mass mortality over the last 70 years and over the last few centuries. The 1950-2005 excess mortality has been 1.3 billion for the World, 1.2 billion for the non-European World and 0.6 billion for the Muslim World - a Muslim Holocaust 100 times greater than the Jewish Holocaust (5-6 million victims) or the "forgotten" Bengal Famine (6-7 million victims). By way of corroboration, the 1950-2005 under-5 infant mortality has been 0.88 billion for the World, 0.85 billion for the non-European World and 0.4 billion for the Muslim World – and about 90% of the under-5 infant mortality in the non-European world has been avoidable. The First World (principally the UK, the US, France, Portugal and Russia) have had major complicity in post-1950 excess mortality, this variously involving colonial occupation, neo-colonial hegemony, corrupt client régimes, economic constraint, economic exclusion, militarization, debt, malignant interference, international war and civil war. Non-reportage by media, academics and politicians of the horrendous extent of global excess mortality and infant mortality ensures a continuing *status quo* and a continuing carnage of about 44,000 avoidable deaths every day (2007; 20,000 avoidable deaths each day in 2020).

What can be done to stop this continuing global avoidable mortality holocaust? I have succinctly set down a series of suggested courses of action to address this continuing disaster and have listed the suggestions in rough order of *decreasing* perceived importance (informed readers may well have a different order of priorities and indeed other priorities). This list also represents a summary of important humanitarian arguments presented already in this work.

1. Equality, the right to life and global community. The great Jeffersonian principles of the equality of all men and women and the right of all to life, liberty and the pursuit of happiness is fundamental to a global consensus for a decent life for *everyone*. Such consensus involves the idea of a global community with mutual obligations that are willingly met, especially in relation to life and death matters. Given universal peace and reasonable governance, a global annual "tax" of a few percent of global wealth coupled with fair trading régimes and abolition of the *circa* $0.5 trillion debt of the poorest 5 dozen Third World countries (2007) would ensure rapid achievement of this fundamental goal that could then be sustained by the rescued and activated recipients. Of course crucial to saving lives will be how such morally-demanded global health and welfare budgets would be spent.

Perhaps a mere 10% of this annual health and welfare "tax" and amounting to only about $100-200 billion per year would have a dramatic effect on Third World "self-help" through food production, industry, commerce, education, preventative medicine and primary health care – *provided* it is directed to *fundamental needs* such as basic infrastructure (roads, dams and communications), agricultural improvement (advice, fertilizers and pesticides), education (potentially rapidly achievable universal literacy), preventative medicine (immunization, public health education, insecticide-impregnated mosquito netting), primary health care (affordable drugs, basic medical requisites, basic medical services and access to centralized specialist services), sensible arrangements for industry and commerce (seed funding, low cost banking, business nurture, advice, communications and education) and security (law and order, respect for legal institutions and security services dedicated to domestic peace and preparedness for natural disasters).[127]

2. Reason, free speech and human rights. Rational approaches to analysis of data relating to any problem lead to sensible models of reality, perceptions of the dimensions of the problem and hence to practical courses of action. Of course rational, dialectical discourse involves general *de facto* and *de jure* acceptance of the right of free speech and other human rights as set out in the 30 Articles of the Universal Declaration of Human Rights. Big Money buys truth, public perception of reality and hence votes in ostensible democracies. Corporate and government control over mass media currently severely limits *effective* free speech. Untrammelled Internet access and usage partly addresses this major deficiency.[128]

3. Universal literacy. Proper global democratic participation and basic access to preventative medicine and agricultural, industrial and public health advice all require universal literacy. Attainment of universal literacy fundamentally involves simple, universal political will since even in the poorest countries a *circa* 1 in 2 literacy provides a huge pool for *pro bono publico* literacy instruction. Implicit in this requirement is empowerment of women and tremendous advantages for health, agriculture, industry, commerce and population control.

4. Humanitarian consensus and true global democracy. The world has generally agreed to the UN, its agencies such as the FAO, WHO and UNICEF and protocols such as the UN Charter, the Universal Declaration of Human Rights, the Geneva Conventions and the International Criminal Court. The "might is right" unilateralism of Anglo-American democratic imperialism threatens many countries and has weakened these important installations. Global democracy needs to be strengthened by proper representation on the UN Security Council (notably of India, representing about 1/6 of the world's population), democratic representation on world bodies such as the International Monetary Fund, and proportional representation in a World Parliament. [129]

5. Information and intolerance of lying. Correct information is crucial to any sensible scientific approach to solving any problem. It follows that lying by commission, lying by omission, spin, hysteria and bigotry by politicians, academics, public servants and media are utterly counterproductive and can be extraordinarily dangerous. In a crowded planet (Spaceship Earth) with diminishing renewable resources we cannot afford the catastrophic consequences of lying, ignoring and deception. We must be as intolerant of public lying and constraint of free speech as we are of ordinary criminality within decent, ordered societies. Satisfaction of this requirement would lead to the global avoidable mortality holocaust going *immediately* from almost zero coverage in mainstream media to the top of the global agenda. In a wider sense, life-preserving technical information and temporary patent rights-abrogation for life-saving medical products are required in life-threatening circumstances (e.g. of HIV and virulent influenza epidemics). Global warming is an acutely threatening reality which is nevertheless still denied and obfuscated for partisan and commercial reasons. Hundreds of millions may die if the dire predictions of mainstream scientists are realized (most notably those of Dr James Lovelock FRS in his latest book, *"The Revenge of Gaia"* in which he asserts that the fundamental global homeostatic processes are close to essentially irreversible damage).

6. Science. Scientific approaches involve using the avoidable data to generate experimentally testable, potentially falsifiable hypotheses about reality, with subsequent critical experimental testing and thence better models of reality. Rational regional and global risk assessment involving reportage, scientific analysis and intelligent systemic change is required to minimize the enormous risk to life in the Third World (the annual avoidable mortality rate for the bottom 2 billion is about 1%) (2003). Removed from this approach would be the common political processes involving proposition of invalid, non-testable hypotheses and selective, spin-based choice of supportive evidence. General acceptance of truth, reason, free communication and critical assessment of scientific, potentially falsifiable hypotheses would eliminate malignant, politicized disruption of sensible decision making. [130]

7. Eliminating war and occupation. Invasion and occupation of other countries is forbidden by the UN Charter without special UN sanction. Yet we see the continuing, illegal involvement of Western armies in the Occupied Palestinian, Iraqi and Afghan Territories that has so far been associated with post-invasion avoidable mortalities of 0.3, 0.5 and 2.0 million, respectively, and post-invasion under-5 infant mortalities of 0.2, 0.4 and 1.6 million, respectively (as of September 2006). Clearly there is need for resolute opposition to illegal war and occupation, notwithstanding US vetoes applied to Security Council sanctions. An important part of such humanitarian opposition to violent conduct will involve *informing* others of the human consequences of such criminal behaviour and will consequently require untrammelled vehicles for effective free speech. The bottom-line of this book is that Occupation is associated with immense avoidable mortality.

8. Population control and resource allocation. The world currently has a population of about 7.7 billion and this is set to rise to about 9 billion by about 2050. There is already a major depletion of renewable resources such as potable water, irrigation water, aquifers, agricultural land, forests, fisheries and oil. There is competition for dwindling resources and the competition for actual land (exemplified by the 18th and 19th century colonizations of North America, Southern Africa, Central Asia and Australia) has given way to the brutal realities of globalization and First World domination of global resources (including Anglo-American control over Middle Eastern oil resources through horrendous military violence). Global democracy will yield better resource allocation. However population control (advanced by literacy and modest economic security enhanced to annual *per capita* incomes of $1,000- $2,000) will also be required for sustainable use of scarce resources. [131]

9. Biological sustainability and rewards for compliance. Notwithstanding better resource allocation, there is a need for fundamental biological sustainability. This is dramatized by considering the global impact if everyone in the growth economies of China and India (over 1/3 of the world population when combined) had an American standard of living and consumption. Greenhouse gas emissions and global warming may well provide the impetus for a general movement to more modest and efficient use of resources. The excellent health outcomes of countries such as Cuba, Fiji, the Maldives, Paraguay, Tunisia, Sri Lanka and Syria with annual *per capita* incomes of about $1,000-$2,400 (2003 figures) instruct that very modest wealth is compatible with excellent low mortality outcomes. Implementation of Greenhouse Gas Credits will encourage energy efficiency and industrial responsibility and hopefully enable control of global warming before it is too late.[132] Similarly, economically highly efficient countries (e.g. Bangladesh with an annual *per capita* income of only $400 as compared to nearly $40,000 for the US) should be rewarded by "economic efficiency credits" that, sensibly applied, will enable the humane health, welfare, population control and mortality outcomes discussed elsewhere in parts 1 and 8. As discussed in Chapter 9, there is a crucial need to apply a properly accounted Carbon Price to all human activities.

10. Preservation of wild nature. The total annual wealth generation of the world is valued at about $85 trillion (2020) and it has been estimated that the annual value of nature's services is about $38 trillion. Accordingly it is vital to conserve wild nature. In many systems that have been carefully studied, sustainable use of wild nature is much more profitable than destructive exploitation. It has been estimated that the annual cost of preserving what is left of wild nature on land and sea would be about $45 billion and that the net economic benefit from doing so (i.e. after subtracting the benefits from destructive conversion) would be about $4,800 billion. Since these estimates of benefits are conservative (e.g. they ignore the increased value of commodities with diminished supply) it has been considered that the annual economic benefits of preserving wild nature will exceed the annual cost of doing so by a factor of over 100 to 1. Third World economies typically involve smallholder agricultural operations intimate with nature, and accordingly this important directive must be urgently observed in the Third World countries, notwithstanding exploitative, First World-driven globalization demands.[133]

Final conclusion

The continuing, horrendous global avoidable mortality holocaust is fundamentally due to violence, deprivation, disease and *lying*. We are one species confined to one planet and we revel in the richness of nature and human cultural diversity. The peace and cooperative community we commonly experience at the level of village, town, city and nation should apply internationally throughout Spaceship Earth. *Intolerance* of dishonesty, bigotry and violence, *respect* for human rights, international law and our common environment, and *commitment* to truth, reason and a modestly decent life for *everyone* will end the global avoidable mortality holocaust and ensure that it will never be repeated.

8.16 APPENDIX – State of the World (2003) in relation to mortality, excess mortality, under-5 infant mortality and HIV/AIDS.

Table 8.1 Global mortality, excess mortality and under-5 infant mortality (2003)

REGION	2003 MORT (m)	2003 EM (m)	2003 <5IM (m)	2003 Pop (m)	2003 MORT/ Pop (%)	2003 EM/ Pop (%)	2003 <5IM/ Pop (%)	2003 <5IPOP (m)	2003 <5IPOP/ Pop (%)	2003 <5IM/ <5IPOP (%)
Overseas Europe	2.9086	0	0.0390	357.713	0.81	0	0.011	24.3370	6.8	0.16
Western Europe	3.9593	0.1782	0.0239	392.442	1.01	0.05	0.006	20.812	5.3	0.12
Eastern Europe	4.4622	1.0717	0.0571	342.510	1.30	0.31	0.017	16.438	4.8	0.38
Latin America & Caribbean	3.4166	0.1759	0.3720	535.281	0.63	0.03	0.069	56.483	10.6	0.66
East Asia	10.8653	0.1231	0.7707	1528.963	0.71	0.01	0.050	102.642	6.7	0.75
Central Asia, Iran & Turkey	1.7464	0.5904	0.5033	228.919	0.76	0.26	0.220	24.766	10.8	2.03
Arab North Africa & Middle East	1.9046	0.7393	0.4990	289.956	0.67	0.25	0.172	37.379	12.9	1.33
South East Asia	3.8645	1.4158	0.5659	539.255	0.72	0.26	0.105	54.634	10.1	1.04
Pacific	0.0667	0.0320	0.0180	8.184	0.82	0.39	0.220	1.135	13.9	1.59
South Asia	12.0343	5.3275	3.2570	1400.532	0.86	0.38	0.233	163.949	11.7	1.99
Non-Arab Africa	11.5099	6.3866	4.4590	659.995	1.74	0.97	0.676	114.385	17.3	3.90
EUROPE	11.3301	1.2499	0.1200	1092.665	1.04	0.11	0.011	61.587	5.6	0.19
NON-EUROPE	45.4083	14.7906	10.4449	5191.085	0.87	0.28	0.201	555.373	10.7	1.88
TOTAL	56.2044	16.0405	10.5649	6283.750	0.89	0.26	0.168	616.960	9.8	1.71

Abbreviations: MORT, 2003 mortality; EM, 2003 excess mortality; <5IM, 2003 under-5 infant mortality; Pop, 2003 population; <5IPOP, 2003 under-5 infant population; m, million.

Notes. Overseas Europe includes Australia, Canada, Israel, New Zealand, Puerto Rico, USA and US Virgin Islands. Armenia and Georgia as Christian countries of the former Soviet Union are included conveniently in the Eastern Europe. Population and mortality data have been conveniently rounded-off in Tables 8.1-8.12.

Table 8.2 Mortality, excess mortality and under-5 infant mortality in Overseas Europe (2003)

Country	2003 MORT (m)	2003 EM (m)	2003 <5IM (m)	2003 Pop (m)	2003 MORT/ Pop (%)	2003 EM/ Pop (%)	2003 <5IM/ Pop (%)	2003 <5IPOP (m)	2003 <5IPOP/ Pop (%)	2003 <5IM/ <5IPOP (%)	2003 HIV+ (%)
Australia	0.1452	0	0.00145	19.623	0.74	0	0.007	1.2725	6.5	0.11	0.071
Canada	0.2352	0	0.00226	31.371	0.75	0	0.007	1.7295	5.5	0.13	0.179
Israel	0.0382	0	0.00076	6.364	0.60	0	0.012	0.6440	10.1	0.12	0.047
New Zealand	0.0293	0	0.00030	3.858	0.76	0	0.008	0.2775	7.2	0.11	0.036
Puerto Rico	0.0321	0	0.00046	3.866	0.83	0	0.012	0.2860	7.4	0.16	-
USA	2.4280	0	0.03400	292.521	0.83	0	0.012	20.1190	6.9	0.17	0.325
US Virgin Islands	0.0006	0	0.00001	0.110	0.57	0	0.012	0.0085	7.7	0.15	-
TOTAL	2.9086	0	0.03900	357.713	0.81	0	0.011	24.3370	6.8	0.16	

Notes. Other abbreviations are as for Table 8.1. HIV+ (%), % of population HIV positive (2003). Notwithstanding substantial non-European populations, Israel is conveniently grouped here and the US Virgin Islands and Puerto Rico are similarly conveniently included here with metropolitan USA.

Table 8.3 Mortality, excess mortality and under-5 infant mortality in Western Europe (2003)

Country	MORT 2003 (m)	EM 2003 (m)	<5IM 2003 (m)	Pop 2003 (m)	MORT/ Pop 2003 (%)	EM/ Pop 2003 (%)	<5IM/ Pop 2003 (%)	<5IPOP 2003 (m)	<5IPOP/ Pop 2003 (%)	<5IM/ <5IPOP 2003 (%)	HIV+ 2003 (%)
Austria	0.0803	0.0000	0.0003	8.110	0.99	0.00	0.003	0.396	4.9	0.071	0.123
Belgium	0.1030	0.0000	0.0007	10.305	1.00	0.00	0.007	0.568	5.5	0.123	0.097
Cyprus	0.0060	0.0000	0.0001	0.798	0.75	0.00	0.007	0.051	6.3	0.104	-
Denmark	0.0606	0.0348	0.0002	5.354	1.13	0.65	0.004	0.333	6.2	0.057	0.097
Finland	0.0510	0.0000	0.0003	5.201	0.98	0.00	0.005	0.287	5.5	0.098	0.029
France	0.5580	0.0000	0.0038	60.004	0.93	0.00	0.006	3.687	6.2	0.104	0.200
Germany	0.8700	0.0494	0.0047	82.421	1.060	0.06	0.006	3.763	4.6	0.125	0.052
Greece	0.1148	0.0055	0.0004	10.941	1.049	0.05	0.004	0.519	4.7	0.077	0.083
Iceland	0.0020	0.0000	0.0000	0.288	0.69	0.00	0.006	0.021	7.3	0.076	<0.174
Ireland	0.0326	0.0000	0.0003	3.930	0.83	0.00	0.009	0.285	7.2	0.119	0.071
Italy	0.6256	0.0516	0.0030	57.395	1.090	0.09	0.005	2.656	4.6	0.114	0.244
Luxembourg	0.0037	0.0000	0.0000	0.450	0.82	0.00	0.006	0.029	6.4	0.098	<0.111
Malta	0.0031	0.0000	0.0000	0.393	0.79	0.00	0.007	0.022	5.5	0.127	<0.127
Netherlands	0.1432	0.0000	0.0012	16.099	0.89	0.00	0.007	0.972	6.1	0.120	0.118
Norway	0.0448	0.0000	0.0002	4.552	0.99	0.00	0.005	0.292	6.4	0.074	0.046
Portugal	0.1086	0.0080	0.0007	10.048	1.08	0.08	0.007	0.559	5.4	0.118	0.318
Spain	0.3728	0.0000	0.0023	40.968	0.91	0.00	0.006	2.066	4.9	0.110	0.342
Sweden	0.0940	0.0053	0.0003	8.876	1.06	0.06	0.003	0.475	5.3	0.058	0.041
Switzerland	0.0702	0.0000	0.0004	7.165	0.98	0.00	0.005	0.375	5.2	0.100	0.181
United Kingdom	0.6150	0.0236	0.0050	59.144	1.04	0.04	0.009	3.456	5.8	0.145	0.086
TOTAL	3.9593	0.1782	0.0239	392.442	1.01	0.05	0.006	20.812	5.3	0.115	

Notes. Abbreviations are as for Table 8.2. Andorra, Lichtenstein and Monaco are not included.

Table 8.4 Mortality, excess mortality and under-5 infant mortality in Eastern Europe (2003)

Country	MORT 2003 (m)	EM 2003 (m)	<5IM 2003 (m)	Pop 2003 (m)	MORT/Pop 2003 (%)	EM/Pop 2003 (%)	<5IM/Pop 2003 (%)	<5IPOP 2003 (m)	<5IPOP/Pop 2003 (%)	<5IM/<5IPOP 2003 (%)	HIV+ 2003 (%)
Albania	0.0171	0.0000	0.0016	3.167	0.54	0.00	0.049	0.268	8.7	0.58	-
Armenia	0.0237	0.0000	0.0009	3.078	0.77	0.00	0.030	0.180	5.9	0.51	0.084
Belarus	0.1310	0.0317	0.0017	9.922	1.32	0.32	0.017	0.446	4.5	0.37	-
Bosnia & Herzegovina	0.0332	0.0000	0.0007	4.093	0.81	0.00	0.018	0.206	5.3	0.35	0.022
Bulgaria	0.1198	0.0404	0.0010	7.931	1.50	0.51	0.013	0.331	4.2	0.30	<0.006
Croatia	0.0522	0.0080	0.0004	4.426	1.18	0.18	0.009	0.221	4.9	0.18	<0.005
Czech Republic	0.1106	0.0082	0.0005	10.243	1.08	0.08	0.004	0.452	4.4	0.10	0.024
Estonia	0.0181	0.0048	0.0001	1.331	1.81	0.36	0.009	0.063	4.6	0.19	0.586
Georgia	0.0510	0.0000	0.0016	5.144	0.99	0.00	0.030	0.256	5.6	0.61	0.058
Hungary	0.1334	0.0346	0.0008	9.898	1.35	0.35	0.008	0.491	4.8	0.16	0.058
Latvia	0.0315	0.0083	0.0004	2.319	1.36	0.36	0.016	0.099	4.3	0.38	0.328
Lithuania	0.0400	0.0055	0.0003	3.451	1.16	0.16	0.009	0.168	4.9	0.18	0.038
Macedonia	0.0172	0.0000	0.0008	2.050	0.84	0.00	0.038	0.124	6.2	0.63	<0.010
Moldova	0.0456	0.0030	0.0016	4.271	1.07	0.01	0.037	0.228	5.4	0.69	0.124
Poland	0.3860	0.0000	0.0030	38.594	1.00	0.00	0.008	1.916	5.0	0.15	0.036
Romania	0.2794	0.0558	0.0046	22.354	1.25	0.25	0.021	1.080	5.0	0.43	0.029
Russia	2.0964	0.6604	0.0260	143.583	1.46	0.46	0.018	6.910	4.8	0.38	0.599
Serbia & Montenegro	0.1116	0.0064	0.0023	10.534	1.06	0.06	0.022	0.620	5.9	0.38	0.095
Slovakia	0.0530	0.0000	0.0005	5.401	0.98	0.00	0.092	0.272	5.1	0.18	<0.004
Slovenia	0.0194	0.0000	0.0001	1.985	0.98	0.00	0.004	0.088	4.5	0.09	<0.025
Ukraine	0.6920	0.2046	0.0082	48.735	1.42	0.42	0.017	2.019	4.2	0.41	0.739
TOTAL	4.4622	1.0717	0.0571	342.510	1.30	0.31	0.017	16.438	4.8	0.38	-

Notes. Abbreviations are as for Table 8.2. For convenience and consistency, Armenia and Georgia are included with the other Christian countries of the former Soviet Union and Soviet Empire.

Table 8.5 Mortality, excess mortality and under-5 infant mortality in Latin America and the Caribbean (2003)

COUNTRY	MORT 2003 (m)	EM 2003 (m)	<5IM 2003 (m)	Pop 2003 (m)	MORT/Pop 2003 (%)	EM/Pop 2003 (%)	<5IM/Pop 2003 (%)	<5IPOP 2003 (m)	<5IPOP/Pop 2003 (%)	<5IM/<5IPOP 2003 (%)	HIV+ 2003 (%)
Argentina	0.2902	0.0000	0.0123	38.193	0.76	0.00	0.032	3.399	9.0	0.36	0.34
Bahamas	0.0026	0.0000	0.0001	0.312	0.82	0.00	0.029	0.030	9.8	0.30	1.80
Barbados	0.0021	0.0000	0.0000	0.269	0.78	0.00	0.017	0.017	6.2	0.28	0.93
Belize	0.0001	0.0000	0.0003	0.253	0.05	0.00	0.106	0.034	13.2	0.80	1.42
Bolivia	0.0706	0.0358	0.0182	8.728	0.81	0.41	0.208	1.215	13.9	1.49	0.06
Brazil	1.2588	0.0000	0.1188	177.297	0.71	0.00	0.067	17.718	9.9	0.67	0.37
Chile	0.0880	0.0000	0.0034	15.705	0.56	0.00	0.022	1.283	8.1	0.27	0.17
Colombia	0.2368	0.0000	0.204	43.860	0.54	0.00	0.047	4.742	10.9	0.43	0.43
Costa Rica	0.0161	0.0000	0.0007	4.128	0.39	0.00	0.017	0.395	9.6	0.18	0.29
Cuba	0.0812	0.0000	0.0012	11.278	0.72	0.00	0.010	0.697	6.3	0.17	0.03
Dominican Republic	0.0608	0.0000	0.0087	8.676	0.70	0.00	0.100	0.988	11.6	0.88	1.01
Ecuador	0.0748	0.0000	0.0083	12.900	0.58	0.00	0.064	1.452	11.4	0.57	0.16
El Salvador	0.0381	0.0000	0.0060	6.459	0.59	0.00	0.093	0.801	12.2	0.75	0.45
French Guiana	0.0007	0.0000	0.0001	0.176	0.37	0.00	0.049	0.022	12.4	0.39	-
Guadeloupe	0.0027	0.0000	0.0001	0.437	0.62	0.00	0.032	0.037	8.4	0.39	-
Guatemala	0.0817	0.0330	0.0225	12.667	0.65	0.26	0.178	1.936	16.3	1.16	0.62
Guyana	0.0069	0.0000	0.0012	0.764	0.90	0.00	0.151	0.078	10.4	1.49	1.44
Haiti	0.1208	0.0878	0.0301	8.277	1.46	1.06	0.364	1.123	13.6	2.68	3.38

COUNTRY	2003 MORT (m)	2003 EM (m)	2003 <5IM (m)	2003 Pop (m)	2003 MORT/Pop (%)	2003 EM/Pop (%)	2003 <5IM/Pop (%)	2003 <5IPOP (m)	2003 <5IPOP/Pop (%)	2003 <5IM/<5IPOP (%)	2003 HIV+ (%)
Honduras	0.0391	0.0000	0.0076	6.857	0.57	0.00	0.111	0.971	14.3	0.78	0.92
Jamaica	0.0151	0.0008	0.0011	2.641	0.57	0.03	0.041	0.271	10.4	0.40	0.83
Martinique	0.0027	0.0000	0.0001	0.392	0.69	0.00	0.027	0.028	7.1	0.39	-
Mexico	0.5184	0.0000	0.0627	102.659	0.51	0.00	0.061	11.061	10.7	0.57	0.16
Netherlands Antilles	0.0014	0.0000	0.0001	0.220	0.62	0.00	0.030	0.013	7.3	0.51	-
Nicaragua	0.0275	0.0060	0.0072	5.400	0.51	0.11	0.133	0.731	13.8	0.98	0.12
Panama	0.0155	0.0000	0.0017	3.093	0.50	0.00	0.055	0.337	10.9	0.10	0.52
Paraguay	0.0297	0.0064	0.0052	5.815	0.51	0.11	0.089	0.798	13.8	0.51	0.26
Peru	0.1644	0.0054	0.0207	26.960	0.61	0.02	0.077	3.040	11.3	0.14	0.30
Saint Lucia	0.0088	0.0000	0.0001	0.149	0.59	0.00	0.041	0.014	9.1	0.44	-
Saint Vincent & Grenadines	0.0007	0.0000	0.0000	0.120	0.58	0.00	0.040	0.012	9.8	0.08	-
Suriname	0.0026	0.0000	0.0003	0.434	0.59	0.01	0.070	0.047	10.7	1.28	1.20
Trinidad & Tobago	0.0095	0.0000	0.0004	1.300	0.73	0.00	0.029	0.089	6.9	0.08	2.23
Uruguay	0.0310	0.0007	0.0008	3.403	0.91	0.02	0.024	0.285	8.3	0.06	0.18
Venezuela	0.1172	0.0000	0.0116	25.459	0.46	0.00	0.046	2.819	11.1	0.08	0.43
TOTAL	3.4166	0.1759	0.3720	535.281	0.63	0.03	0.069	56.483	10.6	0.66	

Notes. Abbreviations are as for Table 8.2. The Falkland Islands (Malvinas) are not included.

466

Table 8.6 Mortality, excess mortality and under-5 infant mortality in East Asia (2003)

Country	2003 MORT (m)	2003 EM (m)	2003 <5IM (m)	2003 Pop (m)	2003 MORT/ Pop (%)	2003 EM/ Pop (%)	2003 <5IM/ Pop (%)	2003 <5IPOP (m)	2003 <5IPOP/ Pop (%)	2003 <5IM/ <5IPOP (%)	2003 HIV+ (%)
China	9.0913	0.0000	0.7344	1298.760	0.70	0.00	0.057	89.996	7.0	0.82	0.065
Hong Kong	0.0413	0.0000	0.0002	6.995	0.59	0.00	0.003	0.310	4.6	0.08	0.037
Macao	0.0022	0.0000	0.0000	0.461	0.47	0.00	0.004	0.205	4.5	0.09	-
Japan	1.0454	0.0000	0.0047	127.480	0.82	0.00	0.004	5.963	4.7	0.08	0.009
North Korea	0.2483	0.1174	0.0202	22.572	1.10	0.520	0.090	1.821	8.3	1.12	-
South Korea	0.2803	0.0000	0.0023	47.508	0.59	0.00	0.005	2.744	5.8	0.08	0.017
Mongolia	0.0186	0.0057	0.0053	2.584	0.72	0.22	0.204	0.269	10.5	1.96	<0.019
Taiwan	0.1379	0.0000	0.0036	22.603	0.61	0.00	0.016	1.334	5.9	0.27	-
TOTAL	10.8653	0.1231	0.7707	1528.963	0.71	0.01	0.050	102.642	6.7	0.75	

Notes. Abbreviations are as for Table 8.2.

Table 8.7 Mortality, excess mortality and under-5 infant mortality in Central Asia, Turkey and Iran (2003)

Country	2003 MORT (m)	2003 EM (m)	2003 <5IM (m)	2003 Pop (m)	2003 MORT/ Pop (%)	2003 EM/ Pop (%)	2003 <5IM/ Pop (%)	2003 <5IPOP (m)	2003 <5IPOP/ Pop (%)	2003 <5IM/ <5IPOP (%)	2003 HIV+ (%)
Afghanistan	0.5092	0.4140	0.2885	23.681	2.15	1.75	1.218	5.048	18.9	5.72	-
Azerbaijan	0.0467	0.0000	0.0156	8.342	0.56	0.00	0.187	0.646	7.9	2.41	0.017
Iran	0.3634	0.0892	0.0542	68.559	0.53	0.13	0.079	6.009	8.9	0.90	0.045
Kazakhstan	0.1472	0.0000	0.0193	15.502	0.95	0.00	0.125	1.107	7.5	1.75	0.106
Kyrgyzstan	0.0362	0.0160	0.0067	5.100	0.71	0.31	0.131	0.540	10.6	1.24	0.076
Tajikistan	0.0373	0.0125	0.0110	6.223	0.60	0.20	0.176	0.853	13.5	1.29	<0.003
Turkey	0.4248	0.0000	0.0592	70.792	0.60	0.00	0.084	7.250	10.3	0.82	-
Turkmen-istan	0.0314	0.0121	0.0106	4.829	0.65	0.25	0.220	0.487	10.5	2.18	<0.003
Uzbekistan	0.1502	0.0466	0.0382	25.891	0.58	0.18	0.148	2.826	11.1	1.35	0.042
TOTAL	1.7464	0.5904	0.5033	228.919	0.76	0.26	0.220	24.766	10.8	2.03	

Notes. Abbreviations are as for Table 8.2. Mongolia is conveniently included with East Asia (Table 17).

Table 8.8 Mortality, excess mortality and under-5 infant mortality in Arab North Africa and Middle East (2003)

Country	MORT 2003 (m)	EM 2003 (m)	<5IM 2003 (m)	Pop 2003 (m)	MORT/ Pop 2003 (%)	EM/ Pop 2003 (%)	<5IM/ Pop 2003 (%)	<5IPOP 2003 (m)	<5IPOP/ Pop 2003 (%)	<5IM/ <5IPOP 2003 (%)	HIV+ 2003 (%)
Algeria	0.1736	0.0360	0.0360	31.561	0.55	0.15	0.114	3.086	9.8	1.17	0.029
Bahrain	0.0022	0.0000	0.0002	0.716	0.31	0.00	0.032	0.066	9.4	0.35	<0.084
Egypt	0.4423	0.1570	0.0646	71.331	0.62	0.22	0.091	8.568	12.2	0.75	0.017
Iraq	0.2190	0.1194	0.1144	24.890	0.88	0.48	0.460	4.172	15.5	2.74	<0.002
Jordan	0.0232	0.0016	0.0048	5.393	0.43	0.03	0.090	0.734	13.8	0.66	0.011
Kuwait	0.0047	0.0000	0.0005	2.459	0.19	0.00	0.020	0.226	9.2	0.22	-
Lebanon	0.0195	0.0000	0.0021	3.620	0.54	0.00	0.059	0.339	9.7	0.63	0.077
Libya	0.0231	0.0000	0.0017	5.503	0.42	0.00	0.030	0.606	10.9	0.27	0.182
Morocco	0.1820	0.0606	0.0289	30.336	0.60	0.20	0.095	3.300	10.9	0.88	0.049
Occupied Palestinian Territories	0.0151	0.0010	0.0031	3.503	0.43	0.03	0.089	0.617	18.1	0.51	-
Oman	0.0093	0.0003	0.0022	2.815	0.33	0.01	0.079	0.310	12.4	0.72	0.049
Qatar	0.0022	0.0000	0.0002	0.605	0.37	0.00	0.026	0.063	9.0	0.25	-
Saudi Arabia	0.0884	0.0048	0.0196	23.887	0.37	0.02	0.082	3.149	13.7	0.62	-
Sudan	0.3888	0.2560	0.1020	33.239	1.17	0.77	0.307	5.109	14.8	2.00	1.208
Syria	0.0687	0.0000	0.0132	17.605	0.39	0.00	0.075	2.430	13.6	0.54	<0.003
Tunisia	0.0538	0.0000	0.0047	9.781	0.55	0.00	0.048	0.822	8.4	0.57	0.010
United Arab Emirates	0.0071	0.0000	0.0004	2.963	0.24	0.00	0.015	0.304	7.9	0.15	-
Yemen	0.1816	0.1026	0.1004	19.749	0.92	0.52	0.508	3.478	17.9	2.89	0.061
TOTAL	1.9046	0.7393	0.4990	289.956	0.67	0.25	0.172	37.379	12.9	1.33	0.061

Notes. Abbreviations are as for Table 8.2. Notwithstanding a substantial Arab population and a substantial Jewish population deriving from Arab countries, Israel has been conveniently included with "Overseas" Europe in Table 8.2.

Table 8.9 Mortality, excess mortality and under-5 infant mortality in South East Asia (2003)

Country	2003 MORT (m)	2003 EM (m)	2003 <5IM (m)	2003 Pop (m)	2003 MORT/Pop (%)	2003 EM/Pop (%)	2003 <5IM/Pop (%)	2003 <5IPOP (m)	2003 <5IPOP/Pop (%)	2003 <5IM/<5IPOP (%)	2003 HIV+ (%)
Brunei	0.0010	0.0000	0.0001	0.354	0.28	0.00	0.014	0.039	11.0	0.13	0.056
Cambodia	0.1399	0.0840	0.0678	13.986	1.00	0.60	0.485	1.773	13.2	3.83	1.216
Indonesia	1.5946	0.7208	0.1900	218.436	0.73	0.33	0.087	21.243	9.9	0.89	0.050
Laos	0.0705	0.0482	0.0195	5.599	1.26	0.86	0.349	0.866	15.5	2.26	0.030
Malaysia	0.1112	0.0000	0.0038	24.163	0.46	0.00	0.016	2.735	11.4	0.14	0.215
Myanmar	0.5500	0.3536	0.1256	49.120	1.12	0.72	0.256	4.822	9.8	2.61	0.672
Philippines	0.4040	0.0080	0.0722	79.260	0.51	0.01	0.091	9.852	12.5	0.73	0.011
Singapore	0.0218	0.0000	0.0002	4.194	0.52	0.00	0.004	0.246	5.9	0.07	0.098
Thailand	0.4438	0.0000	0.0292	62.503	0.71	0.00	0.047	5.027	8.0	0.58	0.912
Timor-Leste	0.0103	0.0072	0.0020	0.780	1.32	0.92	0.259	0.140	16.4	1.45	-
Vietnam	0.5174	0.1940	0.0556	80.860	0.64	0.24	0.069	7.891	9.7	0.71	0.272
TOTAL	3.8645	1.4158	0.5659	539.255	0.72	0.26	0.105	54.634	10.1	1.04	

Notes. Abbreviations are as for Table 8.2.

Table 8.10 Mortality, excess mortality and under-5 infant mortality in the Pacific (2003)

Notes. Abbreviations are as for Table 8.2. The tiny Pacific states of Tuvalu, Kiribati, Palau, American Samoa, Pitcairn Island, the Marshall Islands and Nauru are not included.

Country	MORT 2003 (m)	EM 2003 (m)	<5IM 2003 (m)	Pop 2003 (m)	MORT/ Pop 2003 (%)	EM/ Pop 2003 (%)	<5IM/ Pop 2003 (%)	<5IPOP 2003 (m)	<5IPOP/ Pop 2003 (%)	<5IM/ <5IPOP 2003 (%)	HIV+ 2003 (%)
Federated States of Micronesia	0.0006	0.0002	0.0001	0.109	0.59	0.19	0.056	0.016	14.2	0.39	-
Fiji	0.0046	0.0000	0.0004	0.834	0.55	0.00	0.047	0.094	11.3	0.42	0.072
French Polynesia	0.0016	0.0000	0.0001	0.243	0.48	0.00	0.022	0.024	9.7	0.22	-
Guam	0.0008	0.0000	0.0001	0.162	0.49	0.00	0.041	0.018	10.9	0.38	-
New Caledonia	0.0011	0.0000	0.0000	0.226	0.49	0.00	0.021	0.022	9.7	0.22	-
Papua New Guinea	0.0530	0.0306	0.0166	5.647	0.94	0.54	0.294	0.821	14.7	2.02	0.283
Samoa	0.0010	0.0003	0.0001	0.178	0.55	0.15	0.069	0.027	14.7	0.46	-
Solomon Islands	0.0022	0.0003	0.0004	0.471	0.46	0.06	0.080	0.070	15.5	0.54	-
Tonga	0.0007	0.0003	0.0001	0.104	0.72	0.32	0.053	0.013	12.4	0.44	-
Vanuatu	0.0011	0.0003	0.0002	0.210	0.54	0.14	0.119	0.030	14.7	0.84	-
TOTAL	0.0667	0.0320	0.0180	8.184	0.82	0.39	0.220	1.135	13.9	1.59	-

Table 8.11 Mortality, excess mortality and under-5 infant mortality in South Asia (2003)

Country	2003 MORT (m)	2003 EM (m)	2003 <5IM (m)	2003 Pop (m)	2003 MORT/Pop (%)	2003 EM/Pop (%)	2003 <5IM/Pop (%)	2003 <5IPOP (m)	2003 <5IPOP/Pop (%)	2003 <5IM/<5IPOP (%)	HIV+ (%)
Bangladesh	1.2058	0.6246	0.3065	145.273	0.83	0.43	0.211	17.126	11.9	1.79	-
Bhutan	0.0192	0.0102	0.0071	2.228	0.86	0.46	0.317	0.285	12.8	2.48	-
India	8.9838	3.7000	2.3142	1056.928	0.85	0.35	0.219	120.424	11.4	1.92	0.483
Maldives	0.0004	0.0001	0.0002	0.315	0.12	0.04	0.054	0.046	14.6	0.37	-
Nepal	0.2416	0.1420	0.0451	24.904	0.97	0.57	0.181	3.641	9.1	1.24	0.245
Pakistan	1.4582	0.8506	0.5780	151.903	0.96	0.56	0.381	20.789	13.7	2.78	0.049
Sri Lanka	0.1253	0.0000	0.0059	18.981	0.66	0.00	0.031	1.638	8.6	0.36	0.018
TOTAL	12.0343	5.3275	3.2570	1400.532	0.86	0.38	0.233	163.949	11.7	1.99	

Notes. Abbreviations are as for Table 8.2.

Table 8.12 Mortality, excess mortality and under-5 infant mortality in non-Arab Africa (2003)

Country	2003 MORT (m)	2003 EM (m)	2003 <5IM (m)	2003 Pop (m)	2003 MORT/ Pop (%)	2003 EM/ Pop (%)	2003 <5IM/ Pop (%)	2003 <5IPOP (m)	2003 <5IPOP/ Pop (%)	2003 <5IM/ <5IPOP (%)	2003 HIV+ (%)
Angola	0.3176	0.2638	0.1830	13.460	2.36	1.96	1.36	2.774	18.7	6.60	1.8
Benin	0.0952	0.0686	0.0429	6.663	1.43	1.03	0.64	1.359	17.4	3.15	1.0
Botswana	0.0377	0.0307	0.0064	1.763	2.14	1.74	0.37	0.226	12.9	2.85	19.9
Burkina Faso	0.2236	0.1720	0.1230	12.852	1.74	1.34	0.96	2.307	18.9	5.33	2.3
Burundi	0.1399	0.1128	0.0570	6.793	2.06	1.66	0.84	1.239	17.7	4.61	3.7
Cameroon	0.2677	0.2044	0.0959	15.841	1.69	1.29	0.61	2.393	15.4	4.00	3.5
Cape Verde	0.0025	0.0006	0.0005	0.459	0.54	0.14	0.11	0.069	14.3	0.76	12.7
Central African Republic	0.0848	0.0702	0.0260	3.839	2.21	1.83	0.68	0.630	16.1	4.13	6.8
Chad	0.1656	0.1316	0.0822	8.489	1.95	1.55	0.97	1.715	19.1	4.79	2.4
Comoros	0.0064	0.0033	0.0020	0.759	0.84	0.44	0.27	0.121	16.2	1.68	18.3
Congo (Brazzaville)	0.0567	0.0420	0.0176	3.684	1.54	1.14	0.48	0.695	18.7	2.53	2.4
Congo (Zaire)	1.1198	0.9100	0.5384	52.325	2.14	1.74	1.03	10.372	19.3	5.19	2.1
Côte d'Ivoire	0.3300	0.2640	0.1142	16.496	2.00	1.60	0.69	2.714	15.6	2.00	3.5
Djibouti	0.0123	0.0095	0.0038	0.694	1.77	1.37	0.55	0.118	15.7	3.20	1.3
Equatorial Guinea	0.0082	0.0062	0.0031	0.489	1.67	1.27	0.63	0.083	17.5	3.73	-
Eritrea	0.0486	0.0322	0.0151	4.084	1.19	0.79	0.37	0.690	17.4	2.19	1.5
Ethiopia	1.2370	0.9574	0.4960	69.890	1.77	1.37	0.71	12.580	17.3	3.94	2.4
Gabon	0.0151	0.0099	0.0037	1.317	1.15	0.75	0.28	0.192	14.5	1.95	3.6
Gambia	0.0179	0.0122	0.0061	1.406	1.27	0.87	0.44	0.221	15.6	2.78	0.5
Ghana	0.2070	0.1243	0.0648	20.713	1.00	0.60	0.31	3.011	14.4	2.15	1.7
Guinea	0.1360	0.1022	0.0551	8.453	1.61	1.21	0.65	1.520	17.1	3.63	1.7
Guinea-Bissau	0.0289	0.0230	0.0152	1.476	1.96	1.56	1.03	0.288	19.5	5.27	-
Kenya	0.5294	0.4026	0.1308	31.699	1.67	1.27	0.41	5.343	16.4	2.45	3.8
Lesotho	0.0460	0.0389	0.0042	1.791	2.57	2.17	0.24	0.234	13.1	1.81	17.9
Liberia	0.0704	0.0573	0.0385	3.273	2.15	1.75	1.18	0.605	19.1	6.36	3.1

Country	2003 MORT (m)	2003 EM (m)	2003 <5IM (m)	2003 Pop (m)	2003 MORT/ Pop (%)	2003 EM/ Pop (%)	2003 <5IM/ Pop (%)	2003 <5IPOP (m)	2003 <5IPOP/ Pop (%)	2003 <5IM/ <5IPOP (%)	2003 HIV+ (%)
Liberia	0.0704	0.0573	0.0385	3.273	2.15	1.75	1.18	0.605	19.1	6.36	3.1
Madagascar	0.2269	0.1581	0.0930	17.190	1.32	0.92	0.54	2.992	17.3	3.11	0.8
Malawi	0.2886	0.2406	0.0940	11.971	2.41	2.01	0.79	2.271	18.7	4.14	7.5
Mali	0.2084	0.1570	0.1457	12.867	1.62	1.22	1.13	2.451	19.5	5.94	1.1
Mauritania	0.0406	0.0292	0.0219	2.857	1.42	1.02	0.76	0.492	17.2	4.44	0.3
Mauritius	0.0081	0.0000	0.0004	1.215	0.67	0.00	0.03	0.099	8.2	0.36	6.3
Mozambique	0.4390	0.3642	0.1470	18.678	2.35	1.95	0.79	3.186	16.9	4.60	7.0
Namibia	0.0351	0.0273	0.0041	1.963	1.79	1.39	0.21	0.280	14.3	1.48	10.7
Niger	0.2256	0.1783	0.1688	11.808	1.91	1.51	1.43	2.654	20.6	6.36	0.6
Nigeria	1.6782	1.1882	0.7184	122.491	1.37	0.97	0.59	21.423	17.2	3.35	2.9
Reunion	0.0041	0.0000	0.0003	0.750	0.55	0.00	0.03	0.072	9.5	0.35	5.3
Rwanda	0.1780	0.1453	0.0564	8.166	2.18	1.78	0.69	1.431	16.8	3.94	3.1
Sao Tome & Principe	0.0009	0.0003	0.0006	0.159	0.58	0.18	0.39	0.022	14.8	2.83	-
Senegal	0.1218	0.0819	0.0504	9.990	1.22	0.82	0.50	1.781	16.2	2.83	0.4
Sierra Leone	0.1430	0.1234	0.0680	4.878	2.93	2.53	1.39	0.868	17.3	7.83	-
Somalia	0.1722	0.1333	0.1141	9.731	1.77	1.37	1.17	1.387	18.2	8.23	-
South Africa	0.7548	0.5761	0.0727	44.662	1.69	1.29	0.16	5.241	11.3	1.39	11.9
Swaziland	0.0271	0.0228	0.0059	1.066	2.54	2.13	0.55	0.142	13.8	4.14	20.6
Tanzania	0.6624	0.5161	0.2388	36.601	1.81	1.41	0.65	5.890	16.2	4.05	4.4
Togo	0.0712	0.0508	0.0261	4.846	1.47	1.05	0.54	0.964	16.8	2.71	2.3
Uganda	0.4268	0.3245	0.1801	25.555	1.67	1.27	0.70	5.472	20.6	3.29	2.1
Western Sahara	0.0024	0.0012	0.0015	0.305	0.79	0.39	0.50	0.041	12.7	3.79	-
Zambia	0.3005	0.2575	0.0937	10.731	2.80	2.40	0.87	1.951	17.5	4.80	8.6
Zimbabwe	0.3458	0.2946	0.0312	12.807	2.70	2.30	0.24	1.776	13.9	1.76	14.1
TOTAL	11.5099	6.3866	4.4590	659.995	1.74	0.97	0.68	114.385	17.3	3.90	-

Notes. Abbreviations are as for Table 8.2.

CHAPTER 9: PROGRESS BY 2020 BUT URGENT ACTION NEEDED ON GLOBAL AVOIDABLE MORTALITY AND KEY EXISTENTIAL THREATS

9.1 Insufficient action on the existential threats from climate change and nuclear weapons

When I published the first edition of "Body Count. Global avoidable mortality since 1950" in 2007, it had been apparent to fellow scientists for 20 years (if not to the general public) that man-made global warming from greenhouse gas (GHG) pollution was a worsening threat to Humanity. Notwithstanding continuing denial and effective climate change denial through climate inaction from industry lobbyists, politicians and neoliberal Mainstream media, in 2021 most ordinary citizens are aware of the problem as a result of increasing temperatures, deadly urban temperatures, more high intensity storms, sea level rise, storm surges, droughts and catastrophic forest fires. However, as with addressing the continuing Global Avoidable Mortality Holocaust, the basic problem is unwillingness to act. The 2021 edition addresses this inaction problem in the circa 200 national "short histories", the 2021 updates and the updated pre-Covid-19 2020 avoidable mortality data as summarized below (Tables 9.1-9.12).

Humanity and indeed the Biosphere are presently at a pivotal, tipping point position and facing massive losses in the coming century. The species extinction rate in the present Anthropocene Era is 1,000 times greater than normal, this posing a huge threat to the survival of Humanity which crucially depends upon Nature, from pollinators to carbon-sequestering forests.[1] Humanity and the Biosphere are existentially threatened by (a) man-made climate change (unless requisite action is taken 10 billion people will die in a worsening Climate Genocide en route to a sustainable human population in 2100 of only1 billion),[2] and (b) by nuclear weapons (a post-nuclear exchange nuclear winter threatens to decimate Humanity and the Biosphere).[3] One of Humanity's greatest minds, Stephen Hawking, has concluded "We see great peril if governments and societies do not take action now to render nuclear weapons obsolete and to prevent further climate change."[4]

In 2021 I published a huge 846 page book entitled "Climate Crisis, Climate Genocide & Solutions" that set out the details of the worsening Climate Crisis and offered about 40 partial solutions, of which the most fundamental is adoption of a fully costed Carbon Price. However with fossil fuel use steadily increasing (except possibly for coal) and atmospheric carbon dioxide (CO_2) and methane (CH_4) steadily increasing, it is increasingly apparent that the Paris Agreement target of a 1.5 degree Centigrade (1.5C) of warming will be exceeded in the coming decade, and that a catastrophic plus 2C is now unavoidable. I concluded: "Nevertheless we are inescapably obliged to do everything we can to make the future "less bad" for our children, our grandchildren and future generations". [5]

It is apparent from the 2021 updates of the circa 200 national "short histories" in this book that rich and very low avoidable mortality countries are substantially locked into profligate consumption and continuing exploitation of fossil fuels, methanogenic livestock, cement and Nature as reflected in high values for "annual per capita greenhouse gas pollution". However many poor, high avoidable mortality countries also have high values for "annual per capita greenhouse gas pollution" because of land-clearing for agriculture, forestry and fossil fuel exploitation.

And as for the world banning nuclear weapons (moving to "render nuclear weapons obsolete" in the words of Stephen Hawking), inspection of the 2021 updates of the circa 200 national "short histories" in this book (Chapters 4-7) reveals that only a quarter of the world's nations (and overwhelmingly non-European nations) have so far ratified the 2021 UN Treaty on the Prohibition of Nuclear Weapons (TPNW) that came into force for States Parties on 22 January 2021 and prohibits States Parties from possession of nuclear weapons or assisting such possession "in any way". [6]

9.2 Carbon Price, Carbon Debt, and costing air pollution deaths and avoidable deaths

Generating greenhouse gas (GHGs), notably carbon dioxide (CO_2) and methane (CH_4), is associated with environmental damage. Climate economist Dr Chris Hope (Cambridge University) and climate scientist Professor James Hansen (NASA and Columbia

University) have independently estimated a damage-related Carbon Price of about \$200 per tonne CO_2-equivalent.[7]

The International Monetary Fund (IMF) has concluded that application of a properly costed Carbon Price would be an effective way of tackling man-made climate change. In short, dirty processes would have to stop not just because they are bad for the Planet but primarily because they would be un-economic. The IMF estimated that the present global average Carbon Price is presently only \$2 per tonne CO_2, a tiny fraction of what is needed for keeping below the 2°C target. Importantly, the IMF determined that with implementation there would be "725,000 fewer premature deaths in 2030 for a \$75 a ton tax for G20 countries alone". This estimate corresponds to 4 million avoidable deaths in the period 2020-2030 i.e. refusal of the world to implement this modest change now would kill 4 million people over the next decade.[8]

This massive corporate and political deceit in ignoring the gigantic economic "externality" measured by a damage-related Carbon Price has created a huge, inescapable and assiduously ignored Carbon Debt for future generations of \$200-250 trillion that is increasing each year by 63.8 Gt CO_2-e per year x \$200 /t CO_2-e = \$13 trillion annually. While conventional financial debt can be voided by default, bankruptcy or printing money (quantitative easing), Carbon Debt is inescapable – thus, for example, unless sea walls are built, cities, towns and arable land will be inundated by rising sea levels.[9]

Polya's 3 Laws of Economics are modelled on the 3 Laws of Thermodynamics of chemistry and physics, to whit (1) the energy of a closed system is constant, (2) entropy (S, disorder, chaos, lack of information content) strives to a maximum, and (3) zero mobility at absolute zero (0 degrees Kelvin or minus 273.15 degrees Centigrade). Polya's analogous 3 Laws of Economics are (1) Profit = Price – Cost of Production (COP), (2) deceit about COP strives to a maximum, and (3) zero jobs on a dead planet. The success of the greed-driven denialists and effective climate change denialists in ignoring the cost of carbon pollution is a deadly and disastrous example of Polya's Second Law of Economics, i.e. deception about the Cost of Production strives to a maximum.[10] In stark contrast to the lobbyist, media and politician anti-science denialists, science-trained Pope Francis has stated: "Yet only when the economic and social costs of using up shared environmental resources are recognized with transparency and fully borne by those who incur them, not by other peoples or future generations, can those actions be considered ethical."[11]

Eminent UK economist Lord Nicholas Stern has described this massive deceit over these economic "externalities" thus: "The problem of climate change involves a fundamental failure of markets: those who damage others by emitting greenhouse gases generally do not pay. Climate change is a result of the greatest market failure the world has seen. The evidence on the seriousness of the risks from inaction or delayed action is now overwhelming. We risk damages on a scale larger than the two world wars of the last century. The problem is global and the response must be a collaboration on a global scale."[12]

Air pollution kills 9 million people each year, with about half due to indoor pollution (notably for cooking in poor countries) and half due to carbon pollution from transport and fossil fuel burning for power. It is estimated that full implementation of the proposed Adani coal mine in Australia for coal export to India would on combustion eventually kill 1.4 million Indians over the life time of the mine.[13]

These 9 million annual air pollution deaths are the Human Cost or unpaid Human Debt associated with current global economic arrangements that overwhelmingly ignore the damage-related cost of carbon pollution in a global Carbon Economy. At a risk avoidance-based Value of a Statistical Life (VSL) of $1 million per person (it is $7 million per person for Americans) these 9 million annual deaths from air pollution correspond to $9 trillion. Similarly the 7.4 million annual avoidable deaths from deprivation correspond to an annual Human-related Cost of $7.4 trillion. They are all "collateral costs" or "externalities" that are resolutely ignored by the One Percenters running the world.

9.3 Infant mortality has halved in 17 years but 96% of avoidable mortality occurs in non-European countries

Table 9.1 summarizes population, under-5 infant mortality (IM) and excess mortality (EM; avoidable mortality from deprivation) for the whole world in 2020 (pre-Covid-19 projection in 2019 for 2020 by the UN Population Division). Presented in square brackets for each country is the "Relative EM Score" of EM/Pop (%) divided by that for the best-performing country, Japan (0.0020%), which accordingly has a "Relative EM Score" of 1.0.

In terms of "Relative EM Score" and "per capita GDP" the best performing countries are Japan (1.0 and $40,063) and Singapore (1.2 and $64,103) and the worst are Mali (280.3 and $887) and Chad (338.9 and $707). While the average "Relative EM Score" is 4.4 for European countries it is a shocking 54.4 for non-European countries (Table 9.1).

The good news is that the global "under-5 infant mortality as a percentage of total population" in 2020 (0.0689%) had decreased from that in 2003 (0.1680%) by a factor of 2.4 (Tables 8.1 and 9.1).

The bad news is that in 2020 avoidable deaths from deprivation in non-European countries (population 6,625 million) totalled a shocking 7.357 million, 95.7% of the total of 7.450 million for the whole world (population 7,687 million). Black and brown lives matter.

9.4 Poverty kills as revealed by comparing regional wealth and avoidable mortality

It is useful to compare the "Relative EM Score" in relation to Japan (1.0) and available "per capita GDP (nominal)" data for different regions. (UN, 2019). [14]

(i). At the top of the pile we have Europe with "Relative EM Scores" of 2.2 (Western Europe), 5.4 (Overseas Europe, pushed up by America) and 6.7 (less prosperous Eastern Europe) with an average "per capita GDP" for EU countries of $28,896. [14].

(ii). The rich East Asian countries have "Relative EM Score" and "per capita GDP" combinations ranging from 1.0 and $40,063 (Japan) to 2.7 and $26,910 (Taiwan). China scores 8.7 and $10,004.

(iii). The rich Gulf States have good "Relative EM Scores" of 4.3-9.3 and average "per capita GDP" values of about $15,000-$43,000.

(iv). Latin America and the Caribbean has a "Relative EM Score"of 19.9 and an average "per capita GDP"of about $8,400.[14] However there are some relatively rich Caribbean Island entities with good outcomes and Cuba is a standout (3.7 and $9,296)

(v). South East Asia has an average "Relative EM Score" of 27.4 and an average "per capita GDP"of $2,187. The best performers are Singapore (1,2 and $64,000), Thailand (1.2 and $7,785), Malaysia (7.4 and $11,414) and Brunei (9.4 and $31,086). The other countries have been variously ravaged by war (or civil war in the case of the Philippines) with "Relative EM Scores" in the range of 22.4 (Vietnam) to 87.7 (Timor-Leste).

(vi). In the Pacific good outcomes are obtained with rich countries, namely French Polynesia (6.3 and $21,567), Guam (10.7 and $30,550) and New Caledonia (12.0 and $34,942) and a standout is Samoa (3.9 and $4,285). The rest have outcomes in the range 24.8-90.6 and $1,657-$$6,185).

(vii). The Arab states have relatively poor outcomes except for the rich Gulf States (see (iii) above) and standout democracies Lebanon (12.3 and $7,784) and Tunisia (13.9 and $3,398). Sudan (133.7 and $815), South Sudan (226.9 and $448) and Yemen (110.8 and $855) show the impact of extreme poverty and war. The remaining countries range from Jordan (23.9 and $4,405) to Iraq (52.3 and $5,730).

Occupied Palestine (37.7 and $3,424) is in stark contrast to its war criminal and Fourth Geneva Convention-violating ruler, Apartheid Israel (4.1 and $46,376). The 14.4 million Subjects of Apartheid Israel include 6.8 million Jewish Israelis, 2.0 million Palestinian Israelis, 0.4 million non-Jewish and non-Arab Israelis, and 5.2 million Occupied Palestinians. The Jewish Israelis that rule all of Palestine plus part of Syria represent a 47% minority of the Subjects of Apartheid Israel. Indigenous Palestinians represent 50% of the Subjects of Apartheid Israel but 72% of them, the Occupied Palestinians, have zero human rights, live under Israeli guns and cannot vote for the government ruling them.

(viii). Kazakhstan (11.2 and $9,793), Turkey (13.1 and $9,127) and Iran (16.8 and $7,282) are the better performers for Turkey, Iran and Central Asia. US-occupied Afghanistan is disastrous (118.5 and $470), evidence of egregious US Alliance war crimes in gross violation of the Fourth Geneva Convention. The outcomes for the remaining ex-Soviet Union Central Asian nations range from Azerbaijan (26.0 and $4,782) to Turkmenistan (76.9 and $8,124).

(ix). In South Asia the 2 standout good cases are the Island Nations of the Maldives (6.4 and $10,626) and Sri Lanka (5.0 and $3,940). The remaining bad cases are Bhutan (31.0 and $3,361), Bangladesh (35.1 and $1,846), Nepal (40.9 and $1,074), India (43.3 and $2,116), and Pakistan (134.3 and $1,187).

(x). In non-Arab Africa the standout good cases are the Island Nations of Réunion (3.0 and $25,900) and Mauritius (8.3 and $11,169). The rest range from the Island Nations of the Seychelles (14.8 and $17,382) and Cape Verde (23.8 and $3,604) to Mali (276.1 and $887) and Chad (333.9 and $707).

The above comparisons demonstrate that poverty is deadly. In the most extreme comparison the UN reports a 2019 average wealth of "Europe" as $28,896 and of "Africa" as $1,884[14] and Table 9.1 reports "Relative EM Scores" of 2.2 (Western Europe), 5.4 (Overseas Europe) and 6.7 (Eastern Europe) versus a shocking 176.6 (non-Arab Africa). Nevertheless there are exceptional cases – notably Cuba (3.7 and $9,296) in the Americas, and China (8.7 and

$10,004) in East Asia – that show that relatively poor countries can achieve outcomes comparable to those of European countries with peace, good governance, good health care and good education.

9.5 Entitlement of everyone in the World to a modest survival in a decent life

Nobel Prize-winning economist Amartya Sen defined "entitlement" as "The set of alternative commodity bundles that a person can command in a society using the totality of rights and opportunities that he or she faces". He argued that famines occur not because of an absolute food deficit but because of denial of the "entitlement" of people to acquisition of life-sustaining food.[15] Thus in the "forgotten" WW2 Bengali Holocaust (1942-1945 Bengal Famine, WW2 Indian Holocaust; 6-7 million deaths) the price of the staple rice rose up to 4-fold for a variety of reasons but those who could not afford to buy rice (notably fishermen denied their boats by the British, and landless and unemployed rural workers) simply starved to death. In the "forgotten" WW2 Bengal Famine 6-7 million Indians were deliberately starved to death for strategic reasons by the British with Australian complicity in Bengal and the adjoining provinces of Assam, Bihar and Orissa. Food was of course available for the massive industrial war effort in the Bengali capital Calcutta. [16]

The famous French aphorism "Plus ça change, plus c'est la même chose" ("the more it changes the more it remains the same") is extremely pertinent to the continuing Global Avoidable Mortality Holocaust in which presently each year 7.4 million people die avoidably from deprivation on Spaceship Earth with the One Percenter-controlled First World in charge of the flight deck.

The Human Genome has been sequenced, individual human genomes can be readily determined, there are astonishing advances in molecular biology, physics and cosmology, quantum computing is in reach within decades, there is the immediate prospect of rapidly evolving Artificial Intelligence to possible self-awareness (i.e. creation of evolving, self-repairing, self-replicating and sentient life), detection of life elsewhere in the Universe is imminent, colonization of the Moon and Mars are realistically envisaged this century... (subscribe free of charge to Nature Briefing and be endlessly amazed each week). And yet technologically straightforward satisfaction of this basic "entitlement" to a modestly decent life is denied to much of Humanity.

Indeed while this Global Avoidable Mortality Holocaust has halved in magnitude over the last 17 years (Tables 8.1-8.12 and Tables 9.1-9.12), neoliberal greed is determining that things are set to be much worse and indeed near-terminal this century. Unless requisite action is taken Humanity is facing a worsening Climate Genocide involving the avoidable death of 10 billion people en route to a sustainable population in 2100 of only 1 billion i.e. an average annual avoidable death rate of 100 million people per year this century. [17]

Nevertheless the examples of Cuba (providing peace, a modestly decent life, good governance, good health and good education notwithstanding egregious American sanctions) and China (a burgeoning economic miracle and bringing 800 million people out of poverty) inspire confidence that the Global Avoidable Mortality Holocaust can be stopped in the ever-diminishing small window left to Humanity for such action.

9.6 Solutions – sustainable social humanism (eco-socialism) not neoliberalism, global annual wealth tax, aid, debt relief, and a one-person-one-vote World Parliament

The 2007 first edition of "*Body Count. Global avoidable mortality since 1950*" concluded with the following general observations that merit repetition: "The continuing, horrendous global avoidable mortality holocaust is fundamentally due to violence, deprivation, disease and *lying*. We are one species confined to one planet and we revel in the richness of nature and human cultural diversity. The peace and cooperative community we commonly experience at the level of village, town, city and nation should apply internationally throughout Spaceship Earth. *Intolerance* of dishonesty, bigotry and violence, *respect* for human rights, international law and our common environment, and *commitment* to truth, reason and a modestly decent life for *everyone* will end the global avoidable mortality holocaust and ensure that it will never be repeated" (see Chapter 8). However in this concluding chapter of this 2021 second edition I offer some concrete Solutions to this predicament that is presently set to worsen this century notwithstanding significant improvement in the last 17 years.

(a). Sustainable social humanism (eco-socialism) and not neoliberalism.

The 17th century onwards Enlightenment replaced superstition, dogma, subjugation and subservience with science, reason, freedom and human rights, and has led to huge improvements in the human condition. However that expansion of human freedom was accompanied by expansion of capitalism, colonialism, slavery, imperialism and the appalling high technology and genocidal wars outlined in the circa 200 "short histories" of Chapters 4-7. Greed-driven neoliberalism is presently the globally dominant ideology, and a New Enlightenment is urgently needed to reverse the impacts of rampant neoliberalism and to save Humanity from deadly inequity and excessive exploitation of resources. Neoliberalism involves maximizing the freedom of the smart and advantaged to exploit human and natural resources for private profit – as opposed to social humanism (socialism, eco-socialism, communalism, human rights-cognizant communism, "Greenism", the welfare state, Universal Basic Income) that seeks to sustainably maximize human happiness, opportunity and dignity for everyone through evolving, culturally cognizant, intra-national and international social contracts.[18] Neoliberalism has brought Humanity to the edge of the precipice and must be urgently replaced with sustainable social humanism (eco-socialism).

(b). Annual Wealth Tax, aid and debt relief to greatly reduce egregious, deadly and anti-democratic inequity.

French economist Thomas Piketty has argued cogently against the enormous and growing wealth inequity in the world. Thus the One Percenters own about 50% of the world's wealth. Professor Piketty argues that massive inequity is bad for the economy (the poor cannot afford to buy the goods and services they produce) and bad for democracy (Big Money buys public perception of reality and hence votes). Piketty has proposed international wealth transparency and a progressive annual wealth tax ranging up to 10% for the richest. It should be noted that France already has a graded annual wealth tax of up to 1%, and for 1,400 years Islam has had a 2.5% annual wealth tax (zakat).[19] In 2014 I estimated that an annual global wealth tax of about 4% would yield US$16 trillion annually and enable raising all countries to annual per capita incomes equivalent to the then $6,000 per person per year of China and Cuba, countries for which annual avoidable mortality was then estimated to be zero (0).[20] A conceptually related approach has long been to increase aid from the rich North to the poor South to 1% of GDP, a goal so far only achieved by Norway, Sweden and Luxembourg.

A further morally as well as technically well-justified proposal would be to reduce Developing Country Debt to rich Developed Countries, and in particular to take the huge Historical Carbon Debt of rich, highly polluting industrialized Developed Countries into account. Thus, for example, in 2015 the pro-One Percenter Eurozone and IMF were demanding timely repayment of Greece's huge Government Debt but ignored the huge Carbon Debt of major industrialized countries like Germany that measures huge and deadly global environmental damage. The per capita Government Debt plus Carbon Debt is much greater for Germany than for Greece, which accordingly should insist with indebted Developing Countries that Carbon Debt is also put on the debt repayment and global action discussion table.[22]

(c). A one-person-one-vote, gender-equality World Parliament empowered in relation to environmental sustainability and economics.

In addition to the one-nation-one-vote UN General Assembly and the world power-dominated UN Security Council, there is an urgent need for a third new World Government element, to whit a World Parliament that is elected on a one-person-one-vote basis and is devoted to equitable economics and environmental sustainability in a world that is badly running out of time to act and of sustainably exploitable resources.[23]

Since about half the world's population are female, and in view of continuing damaging misogyny and patriarchy (that came about with the Agrarian Revolution 10,000 years ago), 50% of the MPs from each country would have to be women (e.g. with MPs. elected by all adults, with all voting for both a Female List and a Male List in a compulsory, preferential voting system, and with free, untrammelled, and UN-supervised elections and solely UN-funded candidate electioneering).

This one-person-one-vote World Parliament would be dominated by the non-European world (2020 "Relative EM Score" 54.4, population 6,625 million) and not by the European world ("Relative EM Score" 4.4, population 1,062 million). The 2 major national groups in the World Parliament would be China ("Relative EM Score" 8.7 and 1,439 million population) and India ("Relative EM Score" 44.0 and 1,380 million population). The presently disastrously impoverished non-Arab Africa bloc ("Relative EM Score" 176.6 and 1,083 million population) (Tables 9.1-9.12) would at last have a major say in the affairs of a world that is presently dominated by the neoliberal, Western One Percenters, and heading for disaster in the coming century.

(d). The World most face up to hard realities, stop lying by omission, exercise altruism and save the Planet – here is no Planet B.
As recognized nearly 50 years ago by the "Limits to Growth" report to the Club of Rome,[24] there are limits to human resource exploitation. Thus Professor Dabo Guan has estimated that "For everyone in the world to have an American lifestyle, we would need seven planets, and three to live as Europeans."[25]
Unfortunately, we are presently exploiting resources on a 2-Planet basis.

Similarly, one would hope that violent serial invaders like the Establishments of the US, the UK and their European allies would at least exercise altruism towards their own people in their internally peaceful nations. However as recorded in 2021 updates of the succinct "short histories" of this book, "Covid-19 death per million of population" in NATO countries range from 120 (Norway) to 1,962 (Belgium) with the UK and US scoring 1,855 and 1,684, respectively (March 2021). In contrast, Taiwan achieved 0.4, 300-4,900 times better than NATO countries. Even Overseas Europe Australia and New Zealand achieved 35 and 5, respectively. The Establishments of the rich and technologically sophisticated NATO countries failed horribly in altruism towards their own citizens and in particular the elderly, putting economic gain before the lives of their own people.[26]

For a safe and sustainable planet for all peoples and all species there must be (1) negative carbon pollution (atmospheric CO_2 draw-down to the pre-Industrial Revolution level of about 300 parts per million CO_2) (300 ppm CO_2), (2) negative population growth (population decline by about 50% (the world's coral started dying when the atmospheric CO_2 reached 320 parts per million at which time the earth's human population was 3.3 billion, or roughly half of today's), and (3) corresponding negative economic growth (de-growth) by about 50% to halt and reverse this worsening disaster (with most of the burden being borne by the rich countries to permit the Developing World to improve their circumstances).[27] Peace is the only way but silence kills and silence is complicity. The world has to collectively stop ignoring the horrendous realities, stop lying by omission, and urgently embark on what has to be done before it too late. Every Article of the Universal Declaration of Human Rights must apply to every person on the Planet, most notably Article 3: "Everyone has the right to life, liberty and security of person".[28] As quoted on the first page of this book, "We hold these truths to be self-evident, that all men are created equal, that they are endowed by their Creator with certain unalienable Rights, that among these are Life, Liberty, and the pursuit of Happiness."[29] Put most simply and powerfully by the wonderful humanitarian Jesus: "Love thy neighbour as thyself".

9.7 APPENDIX – State of the World (2020 pre-Covid-19 projection) in relation to population, under-5 infant mortality and excess mortality.

Table 9.1 Global mortality, excess mortality and under-5 infant mortality (2020)

REGION	Pop (m)	<5IM	EM	<5IM/Pop (%)	EM/Pop (%)
Western Europe [2.2]	425.584	13,576	18,332	0.0032	0.0044
Overseas Europe [5.4]	410.689	31.755	44,480	0.0077	0.0108
Eastern Europe [6.7]	225.074	22,142	30,109	0.0098	0.0134
East Asia [7.9]	1,678.089	189,253	264,850	0.0113	0.0158
Latin America & Caribbean [19.9]	650.118	186,287	258,306	0.0287	0.0397
South East Asia [27.4]	668.620	265,524	370,341	0.0397	0.0554
Central Asia, Iran & Turkey [36.6]	291.738	152,429	213,438	0.0522	0.0732
Arab North Africa & Middle East [50.5]	423.173	304,807	426,919	0.0720	0.1009
South Asia [54.5]	1,817.448	1,403,524	1,978,917	0.0772	0.1089
Pacific [76.4]	12.110	13,215	18,500	0.1091	0.1528
Non-Arab Africa [176.6]	1,083.491	2,714,272	3,825,507	0.2505	0.3531
EUROPE [4.4]	1,061.975	66,495	92,942	0.0063	0.0088
NON-EUROPE [54.4]	6,624.787	5,229,311	7,356,778	0.0789	0.1110
TOTAL [47.5]	7,686.762	5,295,806	7,449,720	0.0689	0.0969

Abbreviations and notes: EM, excess mortality; EM/Pop (%), EM as a percentage of population; <5IM, under-5 infant mortality; <5IM/Pop (%), under-5 mortality as a percentage of population; Pop, population; m, million. EM has been calculated as 1.4 times the <5IM, this being the case for non-European countries in 2003 as determined from independent assessment of EM in the first edition of "Body Count" (see Table 8.1).

In square brackets after each country, sub-group and TOTAL is the "Relative EM Score" from EM/Pop(%) divided by that for the best-performing country, Japan (0.0020%), which accordingly has a "Relative EM Score" of 1.0. Because EM has been simply estimated as 1.4 times the <5IM for each country, the "Relative EM Score" is the same as a "Relative <5IM score" from <5IM/Pop(%) divided by that for the best performing country, Japan (0.0015%). Country groupings in Tables 9.1-9.12 (2020 data) are as for Tables 8.1-8.12 (2003 data) to permit ready comparison.

Overseas Europe includes Australia, Canada, Israel, New Zealand, Puerto Rico, the USA and the US Virgin Islands. Armenia and Georgia as Christian countries of the former Soviet Union are included conveniently in Eastern Europe. Population and mortality data have been conveniently rounded-off in Tables 9.1- 9.12. All calculations are based on pre-Covid-19 pandemic demographic data from the 2019 Revision of World Population Prospects of the United Nations Department of Economic and Social Affairs, Population Dynamics. This data thus represents a key global benchmark before the impact of the Covid-19 pandemic.

Table 9.2 Mortality, excess mortality and under-5 infant mortality in Overseas Europe (pre-Covid-19 projection for 2020).

COUNTRY	Pop (m)	<5IM	EM	<5IM/Pop (%)	EM/Pop (%)
Australia [3.1]	25.500	1,116	1,564	0.0044	0.0061
Canada [3.6]	37.742	1,944	2,721	0.0052	0.0072
Israel [4.2]	8.656	512	716	0.0059	0.0083
New Zealand [4.0]	4.822	271	380	0.0056	0.0079
Puerto Rico [2.7]	2.861	94	154	0.0038	0.0054
USA [5.9]	331.003	27,804	38,926	0.0084	0.0118
US Virgin Islands [9.3]	0.105	14	19	0.0133	0.0185
TOTAL [5.4]	410.689	31,755	44,480	0.0077	0.0108

Notes. Abbreviations and other details are as for Table 9.1. This Overseas Europe grouping includes former British colonies, Israel and several US colonial possessions. Other abbreviations are as for Table 9.1. Notwithstanding substantial non-European populations, Israel is conveniently grouped here and the US Virgin Islands and Puerto Rico are similarly conveniently included here with metropolitan USA.

Table 9.3 Mortality, excess mortality and under-5 infant mortality in Western Europe (pre-Covid-19 projection for 2020).

COUNTRY	Pop (m)	<5IM	EM	<5IM/Pop (%)	EM/Pop (%)
Austria [2.4]	9.006	312	436	0.0035	0.0048
Belgium [2.3]	11.590	374	524	0.0032	0.0045
Cyprus [2.8]	1.207	48	68	0.0040	0.0056
Denmark [2.7]	5.792	221	310	0.0038	0.0053
Finland [1.3]	5.541	100	140	0.0018	0.0025
France [2.7]	65.274	2,524	3,357	0.0039	0.0054
Germany [2.3]	83.794	2,756	3,859	0.0033	0.0046
Greece [1.6]	10.423	230	321	0.0022	0.0031
Iceland [1.7]	0.341	8	11	0.0024	0.0033
Ireland [2.2]	4.938	150	210	0.0030	0.0043
Italy [1.6]	60.462	1,324	1,854	0.0022	0.0031
Luxembourg [2.6]	0.626	23	32	0.0037	0.0051
Malta [3.8]	0.442	24	33	0.0054	0.0075
Netherlands [2.2]	17.135	522	732	0.0031	0.0043
Norway [1.6]	5.421	121	169	0.0022	0.0031
Portugal [1.7]	10.197	237	333	0.0023	0.0033
Spain [1.5]	46.755	959	1,342	0.0021	0.0029
Sweden [1.7]	10.099	238	334	0.0024	0.0033
Switzerland [2.5]	8.655	309	433	0.0036	0.0050
United Kingdom [3.2]	67.886	3,096	4,334	0.0046	0.0064
TOTAL [2.2]	425,584	13,576	18,832	0.0032	0.0044

Notes. Abbreviations and other details are as for Table 9.1. Infant mortality data for Andorra, Lichtenstein and Monaco were not available.

Table 9.4 Mortality, excess mortality and under-5 infant mortality in Eastern Europe (pre-Covid-19 projection for 2020).

COUNTRY	Pop (m)	<5IM	EM	<5IM/Pop (%)	EM/Pop (%)
Albania [8.4]	2.878	345	482	0.0120	0.0168
Armenia [11.2]	2.963	471	660	0.0159	0.0223
Belarus [2.8]	9.449	375	525	0.0040	0.0056
Bosnia & Herzegovina [3.7]	3.281	167	234	0.0051	0.0071
Bulgaria [4.1]	6.948	400	559	0.0058	0.0081
Croatia [2.7]	4.105	159	222	0.0039	0.0054
Czechia [1.8]	10.709	270	376	0.0025	0.0035
Estonia [1.8]	1.327	34	47	0.0025	0.0036
Georgia [8.6]	3.989	489	684	0.0123	0.0172
Hungary [3.6]	9.660	409	695	0.0042	0.0072
Latvia [3.6]	1.886	97	136	0.0052	0.0072
Lithuania [3.2]	2.722	123	172	0.0045	0.0063
Macedonia, North [8.0]	2.083	239	335	0.0115	0.0161
Moldova [8.9]	4.034	514	720	0.0127	0.0178
Montenegro [2.5]	0.628	22	31	0.0035	0.0049
Poland [2.4]	37.847	1,265	1,770	0.0034	0.0047
Romania [5.0]	19.238	1,378	1,928	0.0072	0.0100
Russia [5.5]	145.934	11,430	15,997	0.0078	0.0110
Serbia [3.6]	8.737	449	629	0.0051	0.0072
Slovakia [3.9]	5.460	305	427	0.0056	0.0078
Slovenia [1.3]	2.079	39	54	0.0019	0.0026
Ukraine [5.1]	43.734	3,184	4,457	0.0073	0.0102
TOTAL [6.7]	225.702	22,164	30,140	0.0098	0.0134

Notes. Abbreviations and other details are as for Table 9.1. Armenia and Georgia as Christian countries of the former Soviet Union are included conveniently in Eastern Europe.

Table 9.5 Mortality, excess mortality and under-5 infant mortality in Latin America and the Caribbean (pre-Covid-19 projection for 2020).

COUNTRY	Pop (m)	<5IM	EM	<5IM/Pop (%)	EM/Pop (%)
Argentina [12.8]	45.196	8,278	11,585	0.0183	0.0256
Bahamas [6.3]	0.393	35	49	0.0084	0.0125
Barbados [8.6]	0.287	35	49	0.0123	0.0172
Belize [19.9]	0.398	113	158	0.0284	0.0397
Bolivia [67.7]	11.673	11,286	15,801	0.0967	0.1354
Brazil [13.2]	212.559	40,025	56,035	0.0188	0.0264
Chile [6.4]	19.116	1,735	2,430	0.0091	0.0127
Colombia [14.1]	50.883	10,258	14,361	0.0202	0.0282
Costa Rica [8.0]	5.094	580	812	0.0114	0.0159
Cuba [3.8]	11.327	611	854	0.0054	0.0075
Dominican Republic [36.1]	10.848	5,623	7,873	0.0518	0.0726
Ecuador [20.2]	17.643	5,081	7,113	0.0288	0.0403
El Salvador [19.3]	6.486	1,789	2,494	0.0276	0.0386
French Guiana [16.4]	0.299	70	98	0.0234	0.0328
Guadeloupe [3.7]	0.400	21	29	0.0052	0.0073
Guatemala [40.2]	17.916	10,277	14,387	0.0574	0.0803
Guyana [44.1]	0.787	475	693	0.0603	0.0881
Haiti [126.4]	11.403	20,587	20,822	0.1805	0.2528
Honduras [29.5]	9.905	4,170	5,838	0.0421	0.0589
Jamaica [15.9]	2.961	672	940	0.0227	0.0318
Martinique [4.1]	0.375	22	31	0.0059	0.0082

Mexico [17,9]	128.933	32,878	46,029	0.0255	0.0357
Nicaragua [25.4]	6.625	2,427	3,367	0.0366	0.0508
Panama [23.3]	4.315	1,437	2,012	0.0333	0.0466
Paraguay [28.8]	7.133	2,932	4,104	0.0411	0.0575
Peru [15.7]	32.972	8,655	10,340	0.0262	0.0314
Saint Lucia [12.6]	0.184	33	46	0.0180	0.0252
Saint Vincent & Grenadines [14.7]	0.111	23	33	0.0209	0.0293
Suriname [23,5]	0.587	197	275	0.0335	0.0469
Trinidad & Tobago [21.1]	1.399	422	590	0.0301	0.0422
Uruguay [9.1]	3.474	449	628	0.0129	0.0181
Venezuela [37.2]	28,436	15,091	28,430	0.0531	0.0743
TOTAL [19.9]	650.118	186,287	258,306	0.0287	0.0397

Notes. Abbreviations and other details are as for Table 9.1.

Table 9.6 Mortality, excess mortality and under-5 infant mortality in East Asia (pre-Covid-19 projection for 2020).

COUNTRY	Pop (m)	<5IM	EM	<5IM/Pop (%)	EM/Pop (%)
China [8.7]	1,439.324	178,116	249,262	0.0124	0.0173
Hong Kong [1.6]	7.497	164	232	0.0022	0.0031
Macao [2.6]	0.649	24	34	0.0037	0.0052
Japan [1.0]	126.476	1,834	2,567	0.0015	0.0020
North Korea [15.8]	25.779	5,827	8,156	0.0226	0.0316
South Korea [1.3]	51.269	910	1,270	0.0018	0.0025
Mongolia [31.6]	3.278	1,478	2,069	0.0451	0.0631
Taiwan [2.7]	23.817	900	1,260	0.0038	0.0053
TOTAL [7.9]	1,678.089	189,253	264,850	0.0113	0.0158

Notes. Abbreviations and other details are as for Table 9.1.

Table 9.7 Mortality, excess mortality and under-5 infant mortality in Central Asia, Turkey and Iran (2003) (pre-Covid-19 projection for 2020).

COUNTRY	Pop (m)	<5IM	EM	<5IM/Pop (%)	EM/Pop (%)
Afghanistan (Occupied) [118.5]	38.928	75,913	106,273	0.1950	0.2730
Azerbaijan [26.0]	10.139	3,772	5,280	0.0372	0.0520
Iran [16.8]	83.993	20,070	28,104	0.0239	0.0335
Kazakhstan [11.2]	18.777	2,991	4,180	0.0159	0.0223
Kyrgyzstan [27.6]	6.524	2,573	3,599	0.0394	0.0552
Tajikistan [60.1]	9.538	8,188	11,457	0.0858	0.1201
Turkey [13.1]	84.339	15,738	22,080	0.0187	0.0262
Turkmenistan [76.9]	6.031	6,620	9,271	0.1098	0.1537
Uzbekistan [34.7]	33.469	16,564	23,194	0.0495	0.0693
TOTAL [36.6]	291.738	152,429	213,438	0.0522	0.0732

Notes. Abbreviations and other details are as for Table 9.1.

Table 9.8 Mortality, excess mortality and under-5 infant mortality in Arab North Africa and Middle East (pre-Covid-19 projection for 2020).

COUNTRY	Pop (m)	<5IM	EM	<5IM/Pop (%)	EM/Pop (%)
Algeria [36.4]	43.851	22,794	31,911	0.0520	0.0728
Bahrain [7.0]	1.702	170	239	0.0100	0.0140
Egypt [32.4]	102.334	47,424	66,333	0.0463	0.0648
Iraq (Occupied) [52.3]	40.223	30,059	42,065	0.0747	0.1046
Jordan [23.9]	10.203	3,485	4,879	0.0342	0.0478
Kuwait [6.8]	4.271	412	576	0.0096	0.0135
Lebanon [12.6]	6.825	1,222	1,711	0.0179	0.0251
Libya (Occupied) [16.9]	6.871	1,472	2,320	0.0214	0.0338
Morocco [26.7]	36.911	14,069	19,699	0.0381	0.0534
Palestine (Occupied) [37.7]	5.101	2,743	3,839	0.0538	0.0753
Oman [9.3]	5.107	678	949	0.0133	0.0186
Qatar [4.9]	2.881	200	280	0.0069	0.0097
Saudi Arabia [7.7]	34.814	3,813	5,337	0.0110	0.0153
South Sudan [226.9]	11.194	36,284	50,792	0.3241	0.4537
Sudan [133.7]	43.849	83,698	117,191	0.1909	0.2673
Syria (Occupied) [24.6]	15.501	6,144	8,602	0.0351	0.0491
Tunisia [13.9]	11.819	2,347	3,286	0.0199	0.0278
United Arab Emirates [4.3]	9.890	602	843	0.0061	0.0085
Yemen (Occupied) [110.8]	29.826	47,191	66,067	0.1582	0.2215
TOTAL [50.5]	423.173	304,807	426,919	0.0720	0.1009

Notes. Abbreviations and other details are as for Table 9.1. South Sudan is included here for comparison with Sudan.

Table 9.9 Mortality, excess mortality and under-5 infant mortality in South East Asia (pre-Covid-19 projection for 2020).

COUNTRY	Pop (m)	<5IM	EM	<5IM/Pop (%)	EM/Pop (%)
Brunei Darussalam [9.4]	0.437	59	82	0.0134	0.0188
Cambodia [37.7]	16.719	9,007	12,609	0.0539	0.0754
Indonesia [28.2]	273.524	110,093	154,130	0.0403	0.0564
Laos [69.6]	7.276	7,235	10,129	0.0994	0.1392
Malaysia [7.4]	32.366	3,440	4,817	0.0106	0.0148
Myanmar [53.5]	54.410	42,236	59,144	0.0776	0.1087
Philippines [37.3]	109.581	58,368	81,708	0.0533	0.0746
Singapore [1.2]	5.850	100	141	0.0017	0.0024
Thailand [1.2]	69,800	1,187	1,661	0.0017	0.0024
Timor-Leste [87.7]	1.318	1,651	2,312	0.1253	0.1754
Vietnam [22.4]	97.339	31,148	43,608	0.0320	0.0448
TOTAL [27.4]	668.620	265,524	370,341	0.0397	0.0554

Notes. Abbreviations and other details are as for Table 9.1.

Table 9.10 Mortality, excess mortality and under-5 infant mortality in the Pacific (pre-Covid-19 projection for 2020).

COUNTRY	Pop (m)	<5IM	EM	<5IM/Pop (%)	EM/Pop (%)
Micronesia [48.25]	0.115	79	111	0.0689	0.0965
Fiji [33.9]	0.896	434	607	0.0484	0.0678
French Polynesia [6.5]	0.281	26	36	0.0092	0.0129
Guam [10.9]	0.169	26	37	0.0155	0.0217
Kiribati [95.3]	0.119	162	227	0.1361	0.1906
New Caledonia [12.2]	0.285	50	69	0.0174	0.0243
Papua New Guinea [92]	8.947	11,758	16,461	0.1314	0.1840
Samoa [4.0]	0.198	11	16	0.0056	0.0079
Solomon Islands [41.8]	0.687	410	574	0.0597	0.0835
Tonga [25.1]	0.106	38	53	0.0359	0.0502
Vanuatu [50.4]	0.307	221	309	0.0720	0.1008
TOTAL [76.4]	12.110	13,215	18,500	0.1091	0.1528

Notes. Abbreviations and other details are as for Table 9.1. Infant mortality data was not available from the UN Population Division World Population Prospects 2019 Revision source for other smaller Pacific island states, namely American Samoa, Cook Islands, Marshall Islands, Nauru, Niue, North Mariana Islands, Palau, Tokelau, Tuvalu, and the Wallis & Futuna Islands.

Table 9.11 Mortality, excess mortality and under-5 infant mortality in South Asia (pre-Covid-19 projection for 2020).

COUNTRY	Pop (m)	<5IM	EM	<5IM/Pop (%)	EM/Pop (%)
Bangladesh [35.7]	164.689	83,818	117,357	0.0509	0.0713
Bhutan [31.5]	0.772	347	486	0.0450	0.0630
India [44.0]	1,380.004	866,919	1,213,300	0.0628	0.0879
Maldives [6.5]	0.541	50	70	0.0093	0.0130
Nepal [41.7]	29.137	17,342	24,279	0.0593	0.0833
Pakistan [139.7]	220.892	430,380	616,890	0.1948	0.2793
Sri Lanka [15.3]	21.413	4,668	6,535	0.0218	0.0305
TOTAL [54.5]	1,817.448	1,403,524	1,978,917	0.0772	0.1089

Notes. Abbreviations and other details are as for Table 9.1.

Table 9.12 Mortality, excess mortality and under-5 infant mortality in non-Arab Africa (pre-Covid-19 projection for 2020).

COUNTRY	Pop (m)	<5IM	EM	<5IM/Pop (%)	EM/Pop (%)
Angola [210.9]	32.866	99,007	138,589	0.3012	0.4217
Benin [224.9]	12.123	38,948	54,532	0.3213	0.4498
Botswana [59.7]	2.352	2,007	2,809	0.0853	0.1194
Burkina Faso [199.7]	20.903	59,643	83,491	0.2853	0.3994
Burundi [154.8]	11.891	26,295	36,807	0.2211	0.3095
Cameroon [200.5]	26.546	76,014	106,439	0.2864	0.4010
Cape Verde [24.2]	0.556	192	269	0.0345	0.0483
Central African Republic [280.2]	4.830	19,329	27,061	0.4002	0.5603
Chad [338.9]	16.426	79,518	111,326	0.4841	0.6777
Comoro [144.4]	0.870	1,794	2,512	0.2062	0.2887
Congo (Brazzaville) [101.4]	5.518	7,971	11,191	0.1445	0.2028
Congo (Zaire) [270.9]	89.561	346,570	485,241	0.3870	0.5418
Cote D'Ivoire [202.7]	26.378	76,384	106,938	0.2896	0.4054
Djibouti [68.6]	0.988	967	1,354	0.0979	0.1371
Equatorial Guinea [210.3]	1.403	4,035	5,649	0.2876	0.4026
Eritrea [81.2]	3.546	4,111	5,754	0.1159	0.1623
Eswatini (Swaziland) [89.1]	1.160	1,476	2,067	0.1273	0.1782
Ethiopia [109.0]	114.964	178,973	250,599	0.1557	0.2180
Gabon [94.8]	2.226	3,015	4,220	0.1354	0.1896
Ganbia [165.6]	2.417	5,718	8,006	0.2366	0.3312
Ghana [100.7]	31.073	44,684	62,550	0.1438	0.2013
Guinea [188.2]	13.133	32,299	49,418	0.2688	0.3763
Guinea-Bissau [184.7]	1.968	5,193	7,271	0.2639	0.3694

COUNTRY	Pop (m)	<5IM	EM	<5IM/Pop (%)	EM/Pop (%)
Kenya [85.7]	53.771	65,844	92,180	0.1225	0.1714
Lesotho [143.5]	2.142	4,391	6,148	0.2050	0.2870
Liberia [156.5]	5.058	11,308	15,832	0.2236	0.3130
Madagascar [86.5]	27.691	34,222	47,909	0.1236	0.1730
Malawi [116.4]	19.130	31,817	44,544	0.1663	0.2328
Mali [280.3]	20.251	81,085	113,519	0.4004	0.5606
Mauritania [172.8]	4.650	11,474	16,063	0.2468	0.3455
Mauritius [8.5]	1.272	153	214	0.0121	0.0169
Mozambique [172.6]	31.255	77,062	107,887	0.2466	0.3452
Namibia [78.3]	2.541	2,840	3,976	0.1118	0.1565
Niger [248.7]	24.207	85,986	120,380	0.3552	0.4973
Nigeria [249.0]	206.140	733,199	1,026,478	0.3557	0.4980
Reunion [3.1]	0.895	39	54	0.0043	0.0061
Rwanda [73.0]	12.952	13,497	18,896	0.1042	0.1459
Sao Tome & Principe [65.1]	0.219	204	285	0.0930	0.1302
Senegal [94.9]	16.744	22,684	31,756	0.1355	0.1897
Seychelles [15.0]	0.098	21	29	0.0214	0.0300
Sierra Leone [233.6]	7.977	26,621	37,269	0.3337	0.4672
Somalia (Occupied) [318.8]	15.893	72,376	101,327	0.4554	0.6376
South Africa [45.9]	59.309	38,850	54,395	0.0655	0.0917
Tanzania [131.1]	59.734	111,825	156,551	0.1872	0.2621
Togo [159.9]	8.279	18,911	26,475	0.2284	0.3198
Uganda [149.2]	45.741	97,497	136,496	0.2132	0.2984
Western Sahara [44.3]	0.597	377	528	0.0632	0.0885
Zambia [140.8]	18.384	36,978	51,769	0.2011	0.2816
Zimbabwe [98.3]	14.863	20,868	29,215	0.1404	0.1966
TOTAL [176.6]	1,083.491	2,714,272	3,825,507	0.2505	0.3531

Notes. Abbreviations and other details are as for Table 9.1.

10. Notes

Full bibliographic details are provided in Section 11.

Preamble

1. Camus (1946).
2. United Nations Office of the High Commissioner for Human Rights (2005).
3. Congress (1776).
4. Austen (1818), *Northanger Abbey*, Chapter 24, pp201-202.
5. Rabindranath Tagore quoted in Henry Miller (1992), *Moloch or, this Gentile World*, p257.
6. Polya (2007).
7. Polya (2021b, c), Polya, editor (2021m)
8. Hawking (2018), Polya (2020c), Polya, editor (2021c, 2021i, 2021n).
9. Hawking (2018).
10. Polya (2016a, 2016b, 2021b).
11. ICAN (2021).
12. Wikipedia (2020).
13. Worldometer (2021).
14. Polya (2020d).

Chapter 1

1. Lem (1967), *The Cyberiad*, Tale of the Three Story-telling Machines of King Genius, p148.
2. McCullers (1943), p136.
3. Hansard of the House of Commons, Winston Churchill speech, Hansard, vol. 302, cols. 1920-21, 1935; quoted by Jog (1944), p195.
4. Wasserstein (1979), p357.
5. Molière (1664); see Oxford University Press (1981), p171.
6. Popper (1976).
7. Kuhn (1970).
8. Koestler (1964).
9. Santayana (1953), "Those who cannot remember the past are condemned to repeat it".
10. Chatterjee (1944, 1984); Das (1949); Drèze & Sen (1989); Drèze, Sen & Hussain (1995); Ghosh (1944); Greenough (1982); Greenough (1988); Jog (1944); Mason (2000); Polya (1995, 1998a,b, 1999a,b,c, 2001a,b, 2005); Ray (1973); Sen (1945); Sen (1981a,b); Uppal (1984); Villager (1945).
11. Mason (2000), pp177-178.
12. Carter & Mears (1962).
13. Greenough (1982); Jog (1944); Polya (1998); Sen (1945).
14. Hitchens (2001).
15. UN Population Division (2004); UN Population Division (2005).
16. Laqueur (1980); Wasserstein (1979).
17. Wasserstein (1979), p357; Holy Bible, *Luke*, 10:30-35.

Chapter 2

1. Marsden (1988), p23.
2. Singer (2000), ppxv-xvi.
3. Holy Bible, *Exodus*, 20:13.
4. UN (1948), UN Universal Declaration of Human Rights, Article 3.
5. American Declaration of Independence, Congress, July 1776; see Orwell (1949) p236.

Chapter 3

1. Shakespeare, *Julius Caesar*, III, I, line 273.
2. Davidoff (1942), p425.
3. Goldsmith, The Deserted Village, lines 51-52; Eastman et al. (1970), p500.
4. Schopenhauer (1860), Essays, On Books and Reading; Davidoff (1942), p148.
5. Hemingway (1932), Ch1.

Chapter 4

1. Suetonius, *Divus Julius*, 37.2.
2. Marsden (1988), p42.
3. Knightley (1975).
4. Orwell (1946); Orwell & Angus (1968).
5. Widely attributed to Albert Einstein.
6. Bradfield (1996); Flannery (1994); Gilmore (1934, 1935); Macintyre (1999); Macintyre & Clark (2003); Manne (2003); McQueen (1971); Reynolds (1990); Polya, editor (2021a)
7. Gilbert (1969), p88; Gilbert (1982).
8. Polya (2006a); Treurniet *et al.* (2004); see Funder (2002), Chapter 19 & Uhlig (2001) *re* Stasi radiological tagging of East German dissidents; differential mortality of Roma may contribute to excess mortality in Hungary in particular.
9. Koestler (1976); Elhaik (2016, 2018); Polya (2021a), Richards et al (2013), Sand (2009).
10. Korsgaard et al (2020), Polya (1998a, 2008, 2011a, 2011b, 2020a, 2020b, Polya, editor (2021b).
11. Polya (2020a), Polya, editor (2021a).
12. Agee (1975), Blum (1995, 2000, 2003), Polya (2015a, 2020a, 2020b, Korsgaard et al 2020), Polya (2020), Polya, editor (2021c, d, e, f, g, h, i, j, k, l), UN (1948).
13. Polya (2021b, c), Polya, editor (2021m).
14. Hawking (2018); ICAN (2021), Polya (2020c), Polya, editor (2021n); United Nations Treaty on Prohibition of Nuclear Weapons (2020);

Chapter 5

1. Todorov (1982), p134; Chalk & Jonassohn (1990), p178.
2. Todorov (1982), pp137-138; Chalk & Jonassohn (1990), p178.
3. Darwin (1839), Ch.5; quoted by Lindqvist (1992), p116.

4. Lindqvist (1992), p116; Scobie (1964), Ch.1.
5. Butler (1933) speech, quoted by Ali (2002), p260; see also Butler (1935) and Butler & Palfrey (2003).
6. Chalk & Jonassohn (1990); Darlington (1969); Diamond (1997).
7. Bissio (1990).
8. Polya (2016a, 2016b, 2021b).
9. ICAN (2021).
10. Wikipedia (2021a).
11. Worldometer (2021).

Chapter 6

1. Mason (2000), pp177-178.
2. Ali (2002), p264.
3. Eisenhower (1961); Ali (2002), p266.
4. Arnett (2001).
5. 1966 *60 Minutes* interview of UN Ambassador Madeleine Albright with Lesley Stahl
6. Bissio (1990).
7. Diamond (1997).
8. Mao Tse-Tung (1965)
9. Indian Child (2000); Mason (2000); Monbiot (2005); Polya (1998a); Schama (2002); Singh *et al.* (1997); Singh & Singh (1997); US Library of Congress (1998), Country Studies/Area Handbook Series: India; Polya (2011b).
10. Polya (2011a, b).

Chapter 7

1. Conrad (1899).
2. Sven Lindqvist (1992), *"Exterminate All the Brutes"*, an analysis of European racism and colonialism.
3. Chalk & Jonassohn (1990), p241.
4. Chalk & Jonassohn (1990), p243.
5. Lindqvist (1992), p160.
6. Mandela (1994), p386.
7. Bissio (1990); Blum (1995, 2003).
8. UNAIDS (2005).
9. Bissio (1990); Blum (1995, 2003); Diamond (1997); Lindqvist (1992); Schama (2002).
10. Polya (2016a, 2016b, 2021b).
11. ICAN (2021).
12. Wikipedia (2020a).
13. Worldometer (2021).

Chapter 8

1. Roy (2004a).
2. Lindqvist (1992), p 2.

Watts, S. (1997), *Epidemics and History. Disease, Power and Imperialism* (Yale University Press, New Haven).

Weissberg, A. (1958), *Advocate for the Dead. The Story of Joel Brand*, transl. C. Fitzgibbon & A. R. Foster-Melliar (Andre Deutsch, London).

Wells, H.G. (1930), *The Outline of History* (revised edition, Cassell, London, 1956).

WHO (2006) [see: http://www.who.int/en/].

Wikipedia (2005) [see: http://en.wikipedia.org].

Wikipedia (2020a) "List of countries by GDP (nominal) per capita": https://en.wikipedia.org/wiki/List_of_countries_by_GDP_(nominal) per_capita.

Wikipedia (2021b), "List of countries by population", Wikipedia: http://en.wikipedia.org/wiki/List_of_countries_by_population.

Wikipedia (2021c). "List of development aid country donors": https://en.wikipedia.org/wiki/List_of_development_aid_country_donors.

Windschuttle, K. (2002), *The Fabrication of Aboriginal History* (Macleay Press, Sydney).

Worldometer (2021), "Covid-19 coronavirus pandemic", Worldometer, 2021: https://www.worldometers.info/coronavirus/.

Zinsser, H. (1934), *Rats, Lice and History* (Bantam, New York).

Printed in the USA
CPSIA information can be obtained
at www.ICGtesting.com
LVHW071939200923
758858LV00024B/89